SOCIAL INTELLIGENCE
for
AMERICA'S FUTURE

EXPLORATIONS IN
SOCIETAL PROBLEMS

BERTRAM M. GROSS
Editor

Allyn and Bacon, Inc., Boston

To Nora

Library of Congress Catalog Card Number: 69-16333

Printed in the United States of America

PREFACE

WHO KNOWS WHERE WE'RE GOING?

Bertram M. Gross and Michael Springer

American society is experiencing some very rapid and, to some, threatening upheavals. The social order appears to be coming apart at the seams. Established institutions are being judged inadequate. Old value patterns have lost their force. A new physical environment is being created. The roots of these changes are quite complex and only dimly understood by even our finest minds. For many, it appears that our society is like a ship —its masts sheared off and its rudder torn away—which is being broken up by an uncharted and violent whirlpool.

Many aspects of our social transformation are tragic; there are significant increases in disorder and violence, a rise of local demagogues to national political prominence and massive alienation of large sectors of our society.

These developments reflect only a small portion of the changes taking place in our society. The responses of some of our more visible political leaders to this narrow range of problems are not always encouraging. Far too often they are found leading public prayers for the return of order and stability, and their cants for "law and order" appear to be fatuous exercises in religious mysticism, making no serious demands on men to bring about a placid and orderly kingdom of God. Almost as futile is their invocation of part-time oracles to which they refer by latter day euphemisms such as "task forces", "committees" or, if sufficiently august, "commissions." Created after the nation or a locality has experienced the violent shock of riot, or a sharp increase in "official" crime rate, these oracles are asked to come up with expeditious remedies for our social ills. At best, the oracles dispense wisdom that mirrors the depth of our social problems. Such oracles usually are quietly ignored;[1] most commonly, they affirm the basic soundness of the established order.

While many of our political leaders smugly celebrate the virtues of the *status quo*, large numbers of young people and intellectuals view our social order as so tainted, immoral and corrupt that it can be redeemed only by the cleansing action of revolution. The activists of this self-proclaimed "New Left" provide a moral critique of American society that is as full of insight as it is searing. But they have yet to risk the emotional security of their passionate alienation by developing plans for purposeful action—revolutionary or otherwise.

America is in deep trouble, but hokum, hypocrisy and demagoguery are not going to transform our present social nightmares into the American dream. There are formidable social problems to be met and equally formidable opportunities for social progress. Our society is caught up in dynamic processes of rapid social change. These processes cannot be stopped. Black Americans have broken the bondage of psychic slavery and will not be placid. The concrete and steel of urban America cannot be turned into rural villages. Town-meeting democracy is of antiquitarian interest only when social organization rests on massive bureaucratized collectivities.

Although we face no grand apocalyptical choices, each public decision opens or forecloses alternatives. The cumulative consequences of these decisions will determine our societal future. We can move toward a future in which black citizens will be ignored or exterminated, or in which they will have become ful-fledged members of society. The macro-structures of our collective activities will be managed by technocratic elites or new mechanisms of democratic expression will be developed. Cities will be built solely on the logic of real estate transaction and the physical demands of automobiles, or they will somehow be designed for civilized habitation. Social institutions will be allowed further to fragment and dehumanize social life or they will be geared to the development of man's creativity and sense of worth. We face these and other broad alternatives. Social consequences can come about through inaction and

---

[1] Such ritualism is not something particularly new. It could be easily argued that the invocation of "oracles" is a well established institution for diverting attention and energies from the solution of our most pressing social problems. For example, after the series of race riots throughout the mid-west that culminated in the Chicago Riot of 1919, a "blue-ribbon" commission was established to investigate the causes of these disturbances. The commission's report sharply outlines situations in income, jobs, housing, education, public opinion and police inefficiency and brutality that form the basis of social problems today as well as then. See, The Chicago Commission on Race Relations, *The Negro in Chicago: A Study In Race Relations and Race Riot* (Chicago: University of Chicago Press, 1922).

ignorance or they can be achieved through a series of conscious choices made with some knowledge of outcomes of our actions.

There are, of course, many Americans in and out of positions of power, who have not become immobilized by our present social upheavals. They refuse to assume that American society is so corrupt that it is doomed, or that some fictitious "good old days" will reappear. They are aware that dynamic social processes have been set in motion, but are audacious enough to believe that these processes can be channeled so that they serve human needs rather than assault man's body and destroy his spirit. These are the vast numbers of Americans who have learned to live with social change and appreciate the opportunities it presents. Among them are the countless natural and social scientists who have undertaken the task of charting the contours of our changing social environment and the tentative mapping of possible social futures. Their efforts in turn have been supported and are keenly followed by large numbers of individuals whose efforts require timely and accurate social intelligence. Among this group are public officials, politicians, community activists, school administrators, social workers, urban planners and corporate executives who have come to realize that their decisions require detailed information that touches on many elements of our changing social system.

These groups of intelligence users and producers represent the vanguard of a political movement that is introducing new symbols into American politics and is altering the basis for public policy formulation. Economic and sociological jargon is rapidly supplanting "the flag," "patriotism" and "God" in the public announcements of many political figures. More importantly, solid social analysis has been introduced into Congressional debates, White House staff meetings, and occasionally crops up in city halls and state houses. The mass media are being slowly converted to this approach to public policy. Television, magazines and, to a lesser degree, newspapers are drawing from serious social research for their analysis of current problems.

Thus, if we look beyond the sanctimonious pleas for "law and order" and the ever so proper commissions on the demise of the Dodo bird, we can find an emerging politics of relevance. It entails a political style that eschews rhetoric and traditional ideology. It rests on a basic commitment to confront our social ills and is buttressed with candor, flexibility, and empiricism. The new politics demands public leaders who will admit their confusion, uncertainty and mistakes. Such politicians can be found in both political parties and at all levels of government. They can also be found operating outside the party structure and holding non-governmental posts. While they tend to be younger than their colleagues, one sometimes may find among them men in their 50's, 60's and 70's. What binds them together is their commitment to a rather unique practice of politics which is distinguished by the following characteristics:

1. It takes an open and experimental approach to the formulation of public policy and rejects any traditional *Weltanschauung* which links social goals with particular administrative mechanisms.

2. It emphasizes probabilities rather than possibilities. Offering no grandiose dreams, it calculates incremental improvements on existing conditions.

3. Its chief instruments of political persuasion are well-ordered information and careful analysis. Its appeal is explicitly cerebral rather than visceral.

It is thus a politics whose major strength and most significant weakness is its general lack of passion. It lacks the passion that allows men to conceive and to accomplish that which reason suggests is impossible. It also lacks the passion that allows men to commit monstrous crimes in the name of just causes. While the practitioners of this new politics have a strong sense of social mission, their deeper feelings are carefully held in check. These liberal, secure and well-disciplined men are often unable to strike that emotional chord that elicits widely based and enthusiastic public support. Such men find it difficult to create popular political pipe-dreams that in the long run tend to erode public trust and lead to political apathy. Perhaps given the fear, hate and bitterness that appears to be enveloping our society, a politics without passion is what is sorely needed.

Possibly, the singularly passionate and exciting element in this new politics is its concern with the future—where our society is heading and what it can become.[2] In both the academic world and government there has been a growing interest in what the next 15, 30 and 40 years holds in store and how in choosing among a set of alternative social futures we can channel societal processes. Presently, much intellectual energy and a good deal of grant money is being spent in projecting these alternative futures. Some of this effort has been quite productive, but the art—perhaps the science—of projecting futures is in its formative stages and suffers from a variety of deficiencies. There has been too much willingness to speculate about what America will be like in the year 2000 without first de-

---

[2] For some indication of how this futurist orientation is being introduced into American politics see the very provocative proposals put forth by Stewart Udall in his *1976. Agenda for Tomorrow* (New York: Harcourt, Brace and World, 1968).

veloping a firm grasp of present conditions.[3] Further, many analysts readily posit alternative patterns of societal development, but have been loathe to examine the political requirements of particular choices. It is critical that these weaknesses are overcome because the ultimate success of this new politics rests on a highly developed capability to lay bare America's future.

This volume demonstrates the style, substance, and promise—and also the weaknesses—of this new politics which we believe may come to dominate the American public arena in the 1970's and 80's. The volume will also provide a wide ranging estimate of its most potent political asset—the quality of its social intelligence. From this perspective it will dispel the simplistic notion that there exist super social engineers who can sort out our social problems as easily as an industrial engineer plans a production line in an automobile plant. It will also dispel the equally simplistic notion that our present social intelligence is of little practical value.

The genesis of this volume is quite revealing in these respects. The volume was initially motivated by an over-generous evaluation of human ability to achieve high-quality social intelligence. As a finished product, it presents a more sober yet hopeful estimate of the quality of our social information.

The inception of this volume can be traced back to the President's message on Health and Education of March, 1966. In that message, President Lyndon B. Johnson instructed John Gardner, then Secretary of the Department of Health, Education, and Welfare, to undertake an interdepartmental mission to collect and develop a set of social statistics and indicators that would be required for a Presidential Social Report. This projected report would synthesize this mass of social information and somehow come up with a cogent appraisal of our social problems and progress. In style and approach the Social Report would be analogous to, but go well beyond, the scope of our present Economic Reports.[4]

This effort led to publication in the final hours of the Johnson administration of what may become an historic document. On the morning of

---

[3] One effort that does not suffer from this handicap is the wide-ranging "monitoring of social change" project directed by Eleanor B. Sheldon and Wilbert E. Moore of the Russell Sage Foundation. The first publication of this project is *Indicators of Social Change* (New York: Russell Sage Foundation, 1968). This collection of studies edited by Sheldon and Moore addresses itself to the critical elements of structural changes taking place in American society. Five or six subsequent publications will focus on social-psychological change, theories of social change, statistics of change and key problems brought about by social change.

[4] The background and implications of social reporting at the presidential level are being explored by Michael Springer in "Social Scientists and Politics: The First Social Report of the President," a doctoral dissertation in progress.

January 20, 1969, *Toward a Social Report* was made public by Wilbur Cohen, outgoing Secretary of HEW. Cohen stated that it represented a first step toward a system of social reporting and that the first of what should become annual Social Reports could be produced in two years. The Inauguration Day editorial of the *New York Times* urged President Nixon to continue the effort, but argued that Social Reports should be issued every four years.

About the time President Johnson explored the possibility of a Social Report, Dr. Thorsten Sellin, editor of *The Annals* of the American Academy of Political and Social Science, asked the editor of this volume to prepare a special issue of *The Annals* as a trial-run Social Report. The request was accepted and with a small grant from the Stern Family Fund, the project was begun. The project was intellectually taxing yet richly rewarding. To those associated with it, it provided sharp insights into the quality of our social intelligence, and into the profound difficulties of making rigorous academic information relevant to broad areas of public policy formulation.

It was quickly realized that a trial-run Social Report could not be put together in a short period of time with only limited resources available. In many areas information was weak or non-existent, and in other areas rich information existed but it would take much effort to make it relevant to policy formulation. As a result *The Annals* volume was viewed as a series of rough soundings for a Social Report rather than a trial-run report.

Even with this less ambitious goal, the authors of *The Annals* volume were faced with profound difficulties. They were not asked to prepare the typically neat and often irrelevant academic exercises nor where they expected to prepare glib pronouncements about a particular policy area. They had to confront the far more difficult tasks of grappling with broad policy areas such as crime, health, education, the arts, etc., and of distilling a vast array of information in such a way that it would bear directly upon significant social goals and vital questions of public policy. This effort required that areas of uncertainty be pointed out, paradoxes explained and dilemmas honestly stated. This was no mean task. Some people dropped out of the project and those who remained put far more into their chapters than they originally had intended. The one small issue of *The Annals* grew into two large ones which were published in May and September of 1967.

While the scope of the project turned out to be more modest than originally intended, the impact of the project exceeded even the most optimistic expectations. Several of the articles set off heated debates in the academic world. The volumes were used in the preparation of *Toward a Social Report*. They found their way into government agencies in Washington and elsewhere and have been quoted in Congress. Suggestions made in the volumes have been taken up by major research organizations. The volumes have been used in courses in social planning in schools of architecture, education and social work and in "social problems" courses conducted by departments of sociology.

As a result, the limited supply of these volumes was quickly exhausted. In order to fulfill the existing demand and to attempt to reach a wider audience, arrangements were made to produce this volume which contains *The Annals* material in reorganized and slightly revised form. We hope that with this publication these materials will be made available to groups and individuals who generally are not reached by the rather limited circulation of an academic journal. In particular, we believe that this volume will be of considerable interest to lawyers, trade union officials, corporate planners, journalists and local community activists—in short, anyone who is wrestling with, and is concerned about our social problems.

The above review of this volume's genesis should forewarn the reader that its purposes are not entirely academic. It is intended to present a particular political point of view. Implicit in most of its chapters is the message that the old political slogans and symbols—be they of the left or of the right—are of little relevance to our rapidly changing society. The volume does not, however, suggest specific solutions to pressing problems or neat models for the future. It rather demonstrates a method by which we can develop an understanding of our current social problems and explore social possibilities. This method is rooted neither in a politics of joy and happiness nor of a politics of woe and despair, but in a politics of relevance, candor and hope.

We hope that this volume will stimulate the introduction and development of this method in local, state and regional arenas of political action. Much of our existing social intelligence (including all of this volume except the Moynihan and Gottehrer chapters) has been cast in terms of broad national aggregates. Such approaches will remain useful, but as we begin seriously to confront our society's problems we will require *locally based systems of social intelligence*. An annual Social Report for the United States as a whole may very well become a highly useful political instrument, but equally important will be the development of systems of social intelligence for every urban area in the nation. If we are successfully to confront our present social problems and creatively meet the future, our social intelligence must be able to account for the complexity and diversity that exists throughout our society.

BERTRAM M. GROSS
MICHAEL SPRINGER

CONTENTS

Four— Social Problems

Five— Environments

ABOUT THE AUTHORS

RAYMOND A. BAUER, Ph.D., Cambridge, Massachusetts, is Professor of Administration, Harvard University, where he has taught, mainly, since 1946, in addition to teaching or research for Massachusetts Institute of Technology (1953-1957) and the Center for Advanced Study in the Behavorial Sciences, Stanford, California (1955-1956). He is a member of various professional organizations and the author of numerous books and articles on business, the most recent of which is *Advertising in America* (1967). In 1966, he edited *Social Indicators*. He is a member of the Panel on Social Indicators, Department of Health, Education, and Welfare, and is Chairman of the National Academy of Science/National Research Council Committee on Social and Behavioral Research.

WILBUR J. COHEN, Washington, D.C., is the Secretary of Health, Education, and Welfare. He was Undersecretary from 1965 to 1968 and Assistant Secretary (for Legislation) from 1961 to 1965. Mr. Cohen is on leave from his position as Professor of Public Welfare Administration, University of Michigan, where he taught from 1956 to 1961. In 1960, President Kennedy appointed him Chairman of the Task Force on Health and Social Security, which recommended Medicare and other significant health and social security proposals. In 1934, 1935, Mr. Cohen served as research assistant to the Executive Director of President Roosevelt's Cabinet Committee on Economic Security, which drafted the original Social Security Act. He is the author of several books and many articles in the social security, health, and welfare fields.

OTIS DUDLEY DUNCAN, Ph.D., Ann Arbor, Michigan, is Professor of Sociology and Director of the Population Studies Center at the University of Michigan. He serves as a member of the Census Advisory Committee on Population Statistics and of the Panel of Consultants on Social Measurements, Department of Health, Education, and Welfare. He is coauthor, with Peter M. Blau, of *The American Occupational Structure* (1967), coauthor, with Beverly Duncan, of *The Negro Population of Chicago* (1957), and author of monographs and articles on human ecology and social stratification.

AMITAI ETZIONI, Ph.D., New York City, is Professor of Sociology at Columbia University. He is the author of *The Active Society* (1968), *Studies in Social Change* (1966), *Political Unification* (1965), and *A Comparative Analysis of Complex Organizations* (1961), among others.

JOSEPH L. FISHER, Ph.D., Arlington, Virginia, has been, since 1959, President of Resources for the Future, Inc., where he was Associate Director from 1953 to 1959. From 1939 to 1943, he was Planning Technician, U.S. Natural Resources Planning Board and (1943) Economist, U.S. Department of State. From 1947 to 1953, he was Economist and Executive Officer, U.S. Council of Economic Advisers. He has taught at Harvard University, Allegheny College, and the University of Colorado and is a member of the American Economic Association, the American Society of Public Administration, and other professional organizations. He is the author (with others) of *Resources in America's Future* (1963) and of articles in various scholarly journals.

ANDRÉ FONTAINE, Syracuse, New York, spent more than thirty years as writer and editor for both newspapers and magazines before becoming Associate Professor of Journalism at the Newhouse Communications Center, Syracuse University. He was Sunday Editor of the *Long Island Press,* City Editor of *Newsday,* Associate Editor of *Collier's,* Editor of *Bluebook,* Senior Editor of *Redbook.* He has contributed articles to *Reader's Digest, Saturday Evening Post, Look, McCall's, Good Housekeeping, Ladies' Home Journal,* and virtually all the other mass magazines. He has won three national awards for magazine writing.

DANIEL GLASER, Ph.D., Urbana, Illinois, is Professor, Department of Sociology, Rutgers University, and Associate Commissioner in Charge of Research, New York State Narcotic Addiction Control Commission. He is the author of *The Effectiveness of a Prison and Parole System* (1964), of "Criminology," in the *Encyclopedia Britannica,* and of articles on crime and corrections in various scholarly journals.

NATHAN GOLDMAN, Ph.D., (Sociology), M.A. (psychology), is Professor and Chairman of the Department of Sociology at University of California,

Berkeley, and has served as clinical psychologist in mental hospitals and correctional institutions. He has published two major studies: *The Differential Selection of Juvenile Offenders for Court Appearance* (1963) and *A Socio-Psychological Study of School Vandalism* (1959), as well as articles in various journals. He is actively involved in local governmental and community agencies which deal with the problems of alcoholism, juvenile delinquency, and rehabilitation.

BARRY GOTTEHRER, M.S., New York City, is an assistant to Mayor John V. Lindsay of New York, Chairman of the Urban Action Task Force, specializing in the areas of race relations, neighborhood problems, the poverty program, and recreation. Before joining the Lindsay administration, he worked as press editor of *Newsday,* as columnist for the *New York Herald Tribune,* and as editor and chief writer of the *Herald Tribune's* "New York in Crisis" series. He is the author of five books and more than a hundred free-lance magazine articles and has won several awards for the "New York City in Crisis" series.

BERTRAM M. GROSS, Detroit, Michigan, is Professor of Political Science and Director of the Center for Urban Studies, Wayne State University. He also serves as Chairman, Executive Committee, International Group for Studies in National Planning (INTERPLAN) and is the editor of the National Planning Series, Syracuse University Press. Mr. Gross has formerly been visiting professor at Harvard Business School, University of California (Berkeley), and the Hebrew University. From 1961 to 1962, he was a Fellow of the Center for Advanced Study in the Behavioral Sciences. Other former activities include: Executive Secretary of the President's Council of Economic Advisers, member of Arlington County Planning Commission, Northern Virginia Regional Planning Commission, and First Chairman of the National Capital Regional Planning Council. He is editor of *A Great Society?* (1968) and *Action Under Planning* (1966), author of *The State of the Nation: Social Systems Accounting* (1966), *The Managing of Organization* (2 Vols., 1964), *The Legislative Struggle: A Study in Social Combat* (1953), and "Political Process," *International Encyclopedia of the Social Sciences* (1968).

LEON H. KEYSERLING, A.B., L.L.B., Dr. Bus. Sc. (honorary), Washington, D.C., former Chairman of the Council of Economic Advisors, is now a consulting economist and attorney, President of the Conference on Economic Progress, and a frequent lecturer on economics and related problems. During 36 years in Washington to date, Mr. Keyserling served as legislative assistant to Senator Robert F. Wagner; participated in drafting and developing the economic basis for such legislation as the National Industrial Recovery Act, various public works and relief acts, the original Social Security Act, the National Labor Relations Act, the U.S. Housing Act and the General Housing Act of 1949, and the Employment Act of 1946; served at various times as consultant to members of Congress and to congressional committees; and for nine years occupied various posts in housing agencies. Mr. Keyserling is the principal author of *A "Freedom Budget" for All Americans* (1966). The most recent of his published studies of book length include *Goals for Teachers' Salaries in Our Public Schools* (1967), *The Role of Wages in a Great Society* (1966), *Agriculture and the Public Interest* (1965), and *Progress or Poverty* (1964).

MILTON R. KONVITZ, J.D., Ph.D., Ithaca, New York, is Professor of Industrial and Labor Relations and Professor of Law, Cornell University. He is also Director (since 1952) of the Liberian Codification Project. He was a member of the Institute for Advanced Study and Fellow of the Center for Advanced Study in the Behavioral Sciences, and a Fellow of the Ford Foundation, Guggenheim Foundation, and Fund for the Republic. He is the author of *Expanding Liberties: Freedom's Gains in Postwar America* (1966), *Bill of Rights Reader* (1965), *Fundamental Liberties of a Free People* (1957), and *Constitution and Civil Rights* (1947).

PHILIP R. LEE, M.D., M.S., Washington, D.C., is Assistant Secretary for Health and Scientific Affairs in the Department of Health, Education, and Welfare (DHEW). In his present position he is particularly concerned with health policies, legislation, and the coordination of the many health programs in DHEW. His concerns range from family planning to Medicare, from the training of physicians' assistants to child health, from federal support for basic biomedical research to the cost of drugs. He is a former practicing physician, associated with the Palo Alto Medical Clinic. He was a member of the clinical faculty of Stanford University School of Medicine. He is a graduate of Stanford University (A.B., 1945; M.D., 1948) and the University of Minnesota Graduate School (M.S., 1956).

EDWARD W. LEHMAN, Ph.D., New York City, is an Assistant Professor of Sociology at New York University. For the past several years, he has been engaged in research on social and psychological factors in coronary heart disease within a large industrial organization.

JOHN MCHALE, Carbondale, Illinois, is presently Research Associate/ Executive Director, World Resources Inventory, Southern Illinois University, engaged in long-range studies of the utilization of man's resources on the global scale. Artist, writer, and sociologist, he is a Fellow of The World Academy of Art and Science and of the Royal Society of Arts (England). In 1966, he was awarded the Medaille d'Honneur en Vermeil, Société d'Encouragement au Progrès (France), and he has published extensively, in Europe and the United States, on the impact of technology on culture, mass communication, and the future.

S. M. MILLER, Ph.D., New York City, is Professor of Education and Sociology, New York University, and Program Advisor in Social Development, Ford Foundation. His publications include *Social Class and Social Policy, Comparative Social Mobility* (1960), and *The Dynamics of the American Economy* (1956).

DANIEL P. MOYNIHAN, Ph.D., Cambridge, Massachusetts, is Director, M.I.T.—Harvard Joint Center for Urban Studies, Cambridge, Massachusetts. From 1955 to 1958 held, successively, the positions of Assistant to the Secretary, Assistant Secretary, and Acting Secretary to Governor W. Averell Harriman of New York. From 1959 to 1961, he was Director, New York State Government Research Project, Syracuse University, and from 1961 to 1965, he was successively, Assistant to the Secretary of Labor and Assistant U.S. Secretary of Labor for Policy Planning and Research. He is coauthor of *Beyond the Melting Pot* (1963) and author of articles in various journals.

MARTIN REIN, Ph.D., Bryn Mawr, Pennsylvania, is Professor of Social Work and Social Research, Bryn Mawr College. He is coauthor of *Dilemmas of Social Reform,* N.Y. Atherton Press (1966), and the author of *Social Policy,* N.Y. Random House.

PAMELA ROBY, New York City, is Research Assistant to S. M. Miller, Instructor of Educational Sociology, New York University, and Research Assistant, Russell Sage Foundation.

RICHARD M. SCAMMON, Chevy Chase, Maryland, has been director, Elections Research Center, Governmental Affairs Institute, Washington, D.C., since 1955. From 1961 to 1965, he was on leave as Director of the United States Bureau of the Census. From 1948 to 1955, he was Chief, Division of Research for Western Europe, United States Department of State. He served as a member of the OAS Electoral Mission to the Dominican Republic, 1966; Chairman of the President's Commission on Registration and Voting Participation, 1963; and Chairman of the United States Delegation to Observe Elections in the U.S.S.R., 1958. He is the editor of *America at the Polls* (1965) and of *America Votes, Volumes 1 through 6* (1956-1964).

MICHAEL SPRINGER, Detroit, Michigan, is a Research Associate at the Center for Urban Studies, Wayne State University. He is presently engaged in a study of the role of social information in the formulation of public policy.

ALVIN TOFFLER, New York City, is a professional writer and author of *The Culture Consumers* (1964). A former associate editor of *Fortune,* he has contributed to most major American magazines, including *Saturday Review, New Republic, Horizon,* and the *New York Times Book Review,* and to numerous anthologies, including *Politics, U.S.A., Changing Concepts of Productive Living,* and *A View of the Nation.* He teaches at the New School for Social Research, and is a member of the Board of Directors and the Policy Planning Committee of the Salzburg Seminar in American Studies, and the advisory board of the American Foundation for Continuing Education.

ROBIN M. WILLIAMS, JR., Ph.D., Ithaca, New York, is Henry Scarborough Professor of Social Science at Cornell University. He was with the Research Branch, United States War Department, 1942-1946, and served in the European Theater of Operations, 1943-1945. He has been a member of the Scientific Advisory Board, United States Air Force, and of the National Advisory Mental Health Council. He is currently a member of the Advisory Committee for Social Sciences of the National Science Foundation. He is author of *Strangers Next Door* (1964), co-author of *What College Students Think* (1960), co-editor of *Schools in Transition* (1954), author of *American Society* (1951, 1960), co-author of the first and second volumes of *The American Soldier* (1949), and author of *The Reduction of Intergroup Tensions* (1947).

SIDNEY VERBA, Ph.D., Chicago, Illinois, is currently Professor of Political Science at the University of Chicago. He has been a Fellow of the Center for Advanced Study in the Behavioral Sciences and is a member of the Social Science Research Council's Committee on Comparative Politics. He taught at Stanford University where he directed the Berkeley-Stanford Cross-National Program on Political and Social Change, a comparative study of political participation and political change. Professor Verba is coeditor and coauthor of *Political Culture and Political Development* (1965); coauthor of *The Civic Culture: Political Attitudes and Democracy in Five Nations* (1963); coeditor and coauthor of *The International System: Theoretical Essays* (1961); and author of *Small Groups and Political Behavior* (1961).

SYNOPSES of CHAPTERS

ONE— SOME BASIC ISSUES

1. Developing Social Intelligence
Bertram M. Gross and Michael Springer

In this period of confusing social change a domestic "intelligence gap" impedes rational consideration of both public and private choices. Efforts to develop the social intelligence required to close this gap has been given impetus by: (1) the growing awareness of the contributions and limitations of economic information; (2) the implementation of the Planning-Programming-Budgeting System within the federal government; and (3) specific proposals for increased utilization of social information, such as the Technology Commission's call for social accounting, action toward annual Social Reports of the President, and the initiation of Congressional act on the "Full Opportunity and Social Accounting Act." Normative concerns require that our "data system" remain "unsystematic," with promotion of both multiple sources and dissonance. The development and use of social information should not be thought of solely in executive agency terms—there is a creative role for Congress in this area. An intelligent strategy for developing our social intelligence requires action on many fronts. One of these is to remedy the "concept lag" produced by the comparability-relevance conflict and difficulty of recognizing social changes. As indicated by the table "Indicator Suggestions," this is the main task assumed by most of the authors in both volumes. Instead of discussing statistical computation, they have concentrated on conceptual innovations that make it possible to upgrade obsolescent data and obtain new forms of social information, both quantitative and qualitative.

2.   Some Dangers in "Valid" Social Measurement
Amitai Etzioni and Edward W. Lehman

This paper is a preliminary statement on the dysfunctions that social measurement may have for societal planning. Three problem areas associated with questions of internal validity are examined. The most general one is the area of fractional measurement, which concerns dysfunctions stemming from lack of coincidence between a social concept and its operational definition. Also examined are problems of indirect measurement and problems of formalistic-aggregative measurement of collective attributes. The area of indirect measurement concerns potential negative consequences of using data collected originally for other purposes as measures of social concepts. The area of formalistic-aggregative measurement concerns dysfunctions flowing from imprecise measurement of the states of social systems. The broad classes of dysfunctions in these three areas are identified: (1) arriving at invalid conclusions which become the bases for erroneous policy decisions and (2) ignoring those dimensions and indicators of a concept that are most susceptible to social manipulation.

3.   Societal Feedback
Raymond A. Bauer

This essay examines the nature of a potential societal information system. If we take the modern management-control system as a prototype, the societal system would be broader based, multifunctional, and more open-ended. The general functions of any information system are detection, evaluation, diagnosis, and guidance to action. The exercise of these functions is easier, to the extent that the problems dealt with are of a relatively narrow range and a relatively repetitive nature. The problems toward which a societal information is directed are not only widely varied but also complex and unique. Given the breadth, complexity, and uniqueness of the problems, the number of actors and evaluators whose information needs must be met, and the lack of consensus on any model of our society, one cannot devise a set of social indicators closely tailored to more than a few of the potential uses to which they are to be put. In the selection of the indicators themselves, one must to a large extent rely on consensus that certain aspects of the society are "important" regardless of the societal model one holds. A system such as this is highly reliant on rapid feedback because it is weak on providing anticipations of the full range of consequences of one's actions. Furthermore, the casual relations between one's actions and changes measured by a broad societal information system are indirect and diffused. A good deal of *ad hoc,* analytic research is required to bridge the gaps of inference in such a system.

TWO— THE POLITY

4. Electoral Participation
Richard C. Scammon

The report of the Kennedy Commission on Registration and Voter Participation, the 1964 *Current Population Survey* of the Census Bureau, and other data indicate a number of facts about United States voter participation. People tend to "overstate" their participation in elections. Men vote more than women, the middle-aged more than the young and the elderly, whites more than Negroes. The curve of voter turnout parallels those of education and income. Turnout is lower in the South than in other areas and also varies by urban, suburban, and rural areas. Turnout is generally greater in elections for higher government levels and greater in general than in primary elections. One group of nonvoters is deterred by such major legal-administrative obstacles as citizenship, registration, and absentee voting requirements, racial and religious disabilities, and administrative regulations for voting times and locations. A second group of nonvoters are those who meet legal-administrative requirements but exhibit "lack of involvement." Age, sex, and social-economic status affect lack of involvement. So do importance and closeness of elections and competitiveness of the political atmosphere. Total voter participation in elections is a dubious goal. Perhaps the goal should rather be to increase *access* to the polls by eliminating or altering legal and administrative barriers to voluntary voting.

5. Civil Liberties
Milton R. Konvitz

Our political institutions are based on certain moral principles. Some are stated in the Constitution; others, unmentioned, are necessary to give "breathing space" to those enumerated. The freedoms expressly stated may be interpreted as expressions of even more fundamental values. And the Constitution also protects the traditions and collective conscience of our people. However, it is not enough for a nation to profess to be a democracy. Totalitarian states have made the same profession. A nation must look at the facts to estimate the degree to which it lives by its ideals. We have, on the one hand, our values, and, on the other, a considerable amount of data which show how inadequately the values are fulfilled. There is an unconscionable lag of time between proof of malfunction and its cure. The problem is, then, to get the guardians of our goals to read the indicators. There are enough instances of honest governmental reporting to warrant the calculated risks of relying on it. We also have private watchdog organizations interested in civil liberties, and their efficacy is shown in their record. Watchdogs—like the presidential veto—are built into our political system, and independent observers of our national scene also contribute to raising our sights. However, there still remains a need for a privately financed organization for research into civil liberties.

6. Democratic Participation
Sidney Verba

Democratic participation refers to acts that are intended to influence the behavior of those empowered to make decisions. In a society where participation is a value, inability to participate represents a severe deprivation. This essay focuses on participation *vis-à-vis* governmental decision-makers, though the term refers to nongovernmental decisions as well. The variety of participatory acts is discussed, as are the conditions for effective participation. There is need to consider a wide range of participatory acts, including participation in relation to administrative decisions. In addition, one must study not only why citizens participate, but why decision-makers are responsive. Several problems of participation are discussed, including the problems of scale, of technical complexity, and of inequalities in participation.

THREE— THE CULTURAL CONTEXT

7. Individual and Group Values
Robin M. Williams, Jr.

Because values, defined as generalized criteria of desirability, are deeply involved in all of the specialized areas treated in this volume, much of the needed analysis is implicit in other articles. There remains a need to render explicit the first-order tasks for making data on values a viable part of societal self-awareness and self-direction, in an age of Great Societies. Values are important causal components in individual conduct and in the functioning of social systems. To develop adequate indicators for the needed analysis will require major efforts and much ingenuity. Yet practicable methods already are available for the systematic empirical study of values. Because of the lack in the past of standardized measures and comprehensive reporting, the existing data are scanty, fragmentary, and diffuse. Yet cautious and imaginative use of existing information has added to our knowledge of distinctive value patterns in the United States, and some illuminating comparisons have been made with other societies. Better data and more explicit analysis of value problems will enhance effectiveness of goal-achievement, widen the scope of awareness in decision-making, and provide enhanced capacities for sensing limits and hazards in current societal trends and policies. That new problems thereby will be created is inevitable, and not undesirable.

8. Education and Learning
Wilbur Cohen

The American people have set important social goals to improve the quality of American life. Although there is some evidence of progress toward these goals, there are few accurate indicators of the changes actually taking place and the problems encountered along the road to attainment. The development of statistics and other pertinent information is essential because of the rapid and reverberating changes that are taking place. Significant changes are being generated in the American educational system in terms of people, expenditures, activities, and innovations. The educational indicators that are developed must take into account the variety of goals, as well as the changes in definitions and emphases of the goals. There is a need for both quantitative and qualitative data. Although some quantitative indicators exist, the data disclose little about the quality of the educational system or its products. New indicators, relating to educational opportunities, the quality of education, fundamental human behavior, and political and economic behavior are needed. The responsibility for developing these indicators must be shared by public and private interests—government, business, educators, labor unions, and civic and community groups.

9.   Science, Technology, and Change
John McHale

Science and technology are major change agencies now operating on a global scale. The narrowing interval between scientific discovery, technological implementation, and social use has increased the general rate of change. Our monitoring and accounting procedures for the differential rates of such changes in various sectors of society, and for their short- and long-term consequences, are presently inadequate. The available indicators in these areas tend to be quantitative rather than qualitative. To provide more positive measures of social progress, and earlier warning of the social and environmental effects of new scientific-technical developments, we need to redesign our present indicator procedures. Such extended and qualitative indicators will further require integration, and interpretation, within a comprehensive system of social accounting.

10.   The Mass Media: A Need for Greatness
André Fontaine

United States mass media are probably the world's greatest, and in excellent health, more mature and more responsible today than fifty years ago. But they are not good enough because: (1) People do not believe what they read; (2) the media do not have enough or the right kind of information; (3) editors need more power; and (4) there are large gaps in knowledge of the impact that the media have on the audiences. Once these shortcomings have been remedied, the media can face the really difficult questions of the times: (1) To what extent has newsmen's reportage only of the dramatic distorted readers' concepts of reality? (2) To what extent has media's exploitation of violence made violence prevalent? (3) To what extent have media contributed to increase in promiscuity and the cheapening of sex? (4) To what extent have the media contributed to the popularity of extremism and the devil theory of international relations?

11. The Art of Measuring the Arts
Alvin Toffler

The transition to postindustrialism is marked by increasing political concern for the quality of life. The arts, an important determinant of the quality of life, are affected by this transition in the following ways: growth of mass participation in cultural activities; elaboration of the institutional framework of the arts; formation of a "culture lobby"; and politicalization. Decision-makers in government, business, research, and education must begin to take into account, as one entry in their cost-benefit ledgers, the cultural consequences of their actions. A cultural data system is needed to provide information for rational policy-making in the cultural field and to assist those outside the field in understanding their impact on it. A tentative model is constructed to facilitate the monitoring of qualitative, as well as quantitative, changes in the arts in contemporary society. Fifteen variables are suggested, which, taken together, comprise an index of the state of health of a nation's culture. Ways are proposed by which changes in these variables can be statistically measured.

FOUR— SOCIAL PROBLEMS

12. Poverty, Inequality, and Conflict
S. M. Miller, Martin Rein,
Pamela Roby, and Bertram M. Gross

Groping concern with poverty has ushered in the much more controversial issue of inequalities within the affluent society. In America, relative deprivation is a more important aspect of "poverty" than poor physical conditions. Income alone is an inadequate indicator of level of living. This paper proposes six dimensions for the measurement of well-being: income, assets, basic services, social mobility and education, political position, and status and satisfaction. Questions of "who does and should get what" within each of these dimensions are issues arousing acrimonious debate. Social indicators are suggested which would create greater awareness of the extent of inequalities and make discussions of inequalities more useful. These indicators will not tell us what choices to make in inequality-reduction, but they can prevent us from complacently ignoring the fact that choices *are* being made.

13. Employment Goals and the "New Economics"
Leon H. Keyserling

The main focus of national economic and related social policies should be upon federally guaranteed full employment and a federally initiated nationwide system of guaranteed income for those who cannot be brought within the employment stream. Progress toward these objectives will add more to personal development and national achievement than a further proliferation of marginal programs called "new." Full-time unemployment should be reduced to about 2 per cent of the civilian labor force, and the true level of unemployment to about 3 to 3.5 per cent. Full employment, optimum economic growth, and optimum allocation of resources, in line with the great social priorities of national needs, are inseparable objectives and do not involve much programmatic differentiation. The prevalent view that these objectives involve excessive or even enlarged inflationary pressures is not justified by empirical observation. The aggregate and structural approaches to full employment need a new synthesis. We need, particularly under the aegis of the Employment Act of 1946, a ten-year budget of our needs and resources. All national public policies importantly affecting resource-allocation, including the federal budget, should be made an integral part of this long-range budget.

14. Discrimination Against Negroes
Otis Dudley Duncan

The functions of indicators to measure fullness of participation of minorities in American society can best be understood by relating them to strategic junctures in the socioeconomic life cycle. Data for Negroes, in particular, reveal the operation of two types of handicaps—those common to all members of the society subject to disadvantages of background or misfortune, and those specific to minority status. To distinguish between them, and thus to measure progress in reducing discrimination, requires not only comprehensive time series but also methods and models suited to the analysis of causal sequences. Despite the growing fund of valuable indicators of the status of "nonwhite" Americans, a number of statistical hazards must be circumvented before reliable inferences and realistic recommendations become possible. In reaching interpretations in this field, social science should operate as a "third force," complementing the work of policymakers and program-administrators, on the one hand, and civic action groups on the other. Present knowledge is inadequate to the task of formulating specific proposals for redirecting trends. It could rapidly become more nearly adequate with the availability of sufficient resources for research, full cooperation of official statistical agencies, freedom to investigate so-called sensitive problems, and concerted attempts to improve analytical and interpretive models. For the moment, we can only be sure that formidable obstacles remain in the way of achieving freedom from discrimination.

15. Social Breakdown
Nathan Goldman

Although problems of family breakdown, drug and alcohol addiction, mental disorder, suicide, and sexual deviation appear to be increasing, the available data are either so deficient or so incomplete that accurate appraisal of the situation is impossible. However, some of these problems seem to be more or less socially sanctioned adjustments to strains in the social system rather than maladjustments in themselves. To achieve our goal of maximizing the social health of American society, we must consider these problems as indicators of strain, and focus our national resources on the reduction of these strains. We need to improve the collection of data on these indicators, and to devise new ones, in order to identify and locate those situations which interfere with the ideal functioning of our social system. A significant aspect of social breakdown is seen in the inability of the society to mobilize for an attack on situations which it has defined as undesirable. Our concern should be with the identification of these processes as well as the underlying social strains of which social problems are overt indicators. We must establish standard definitions or criteria of social problems and increase the scope and accuracy of our data-collection. Information-gathering on the local or state level would need to be coordinated on a nationwide basis to provide a useful set of indicators of the social state of the nation.

16.   Crime and Delinquency
Daniel Glaser

Optimum procedures for measuring the prevalence of crime vary tremendously by type of offense, because these procedures depend on whether the crime creates a death, a complaining victim, a satisfied customer, an annoyed audience, or a dangerous condition. Assessing the effectiveness of criminal correction requires long-term data on criminal careers, to compare the subsequent criminality of similar offenders who receive different kinds of correctional action. The formulation of crime reduction goals must take into account the instability of crime definitions, and the social costs of crime control actions, in addition to the dimensions of crime. Because of the multiplicity of data sources and the breadth of perspective required for this diversity of measurement, it should be the primary responsibility of a single national agency, to be assisted by the many other agencies now oriented to segments of this task.

17. Health and Well-Being
Philip Lee

Health is discussed as both a generalized and a very relative concept, defined to include not only freedom from physical disease and pain, but also social well-being. The importance of environmental factors is stressed. Measuring health status in the past has been largely dependent on the negative aspects of health—death rate and morbidity. Although still important, they no longer yield enough information on which to establish goals and determine policy. Increasing emphasis has been placed on disability, costs, and the social and emotional consequences of disease. During the past thirty years, the federal government has been increasingly involved in a number of health-care programs designed to: (1) advance research; (2) meet manpower, facility, and other resource requirements; (3) stimulate local, regional, and state initiative and improved co-operation with the federal government; (4) remove financial barriers; (5) improve quality and availability of services; and (6) protect the consumer and improve the quality of our environment.

FIVE— ENVIRONMENTS

18. The Natural Environment
Joseph L. Fisher

In the United States, the problem of sheer quantity of raw materials has given way in importance to the qualitative problem of environmental pollution. On the quantitative side, physical and economic indicators and goals are available, but on the qualitative side, such goals and indicators are more difficult to conceive and work with because the more subjective problems of individual and social welfare must be taken into account. As exemplified by the water-quality studies of the Delaware Estuary, probably the basic indicator for social welfare would be the net social benefits (minus costs or losses in some sense) that would result from various selected measures to deal with a specific problem. Where estimates of benefits seem impossible, a second-best objective would be minimizing the social costs of selected measures. In view of the interrelatedness of environmental pollution problems, the concept of the "environmental problem shed" has been suggested—taking into account the various interrelated physical and social problems and indicators within a given area. Research is also needed on the processes by which environmental quality standards and programs are reached, the direction and rates of change for which statistical indicators are necessary, and to create and improve the indicators of trends in environmental pollution and its effects on people.

19. The Urban Environment: New York City
Barry Gottehrer

Many people believe that the future direction of modern cities will be considerably determined by the success or failure of New York City's present experimentations. When Mayor Lindsay's administration took office (1966), the city's fiscal affairs were in serious disorder, and the governmental structure was chaotic and wasteful. For years, foundations and special committees had been issuing reports calling for reform of the proliferation and duplication of agencies. Mayor Lindsay's administration has initiated fiscal reform and a sweeping governmental reorganization. Integrated with these programs is the Mayor's new program-planning-budget system which defines governmental programs actively in terms of evaluating alternative ways to reach program objectives. Fiscal experts agree that New York must receive substantially increased federal and state aid, and Mayor Lindsay is joining with other city mayors to press for additional federal funds. The Mayor is also advocating greater regional ties for solving regional problems; increased home-rule powers; and Neighborhood Mayors' Offices throughout the city. Improving the quality of and co-operation between the cities' agencies and setting up task forces independent of the bureaucracy will also be major goals. In the long run, however, the success of these reforms will depend on the judgment of the man at the top.

20. The Urban Environment: General
Daniel P. Moynihan

Solving United States urban problems is an increasingly important concern of the public and of government officials. Social science can make an important contribution to solutions by providing urban social indicators.

Three general propositions concerning this process are: (1) Social scientists must be prepared for accusations of betrayal from proponents of causes which they have previously supported, if data conflict with objectives of such causes. (2) How indicators are developed will influence at what level problems are resolved. (3) Social indicators will be developed by professors and government executives whose judgments will be based on a value-background different from that of the urban masses being measured. In the light of these propositions, four guidelines for social indicators are suggested: (1) They should be in the realm of disaggregation and correlation. (2) As they cannot be apolitical, they must be pan-political. (3) They should be concerned with the future as well as the present. (4) They should provide comparisons of local, national, and "best practice" data. The indicators should report urban conditions in three categories: (1) people as individuals—numbers, distribution, density, mobility, employment, income, behavior, health, and participation rates; (2) families—unemployment and welfare statistics' correlations and "poverty neighborhood" studies; and (3) institutions—public service and voluntary organizations, business, mass media, education, and urban ecology.

ACKNOWLEDGMENTS

This volume was originally intended as a private effort that would provide some of the intellectual spade-work for a possible Social Report of the President. This project was conceived by Dr. Thorsten Sellin, editor of THE ANNALS of the American Academy of Political and Social Science. Dr. Sellin commissioned me to produce a special volume of THE ANNALS, "Social Goals and Indicators for American Society." This one volume was expanded to two, which were published in May and September 1967. Throughout our efforts Dr. Sellin provided encouragement and advice.

I would also like to acknowledge the Stern Family Fund for having helped me in producing this volume. Their assistance facilitated the convening of a series of exploration and review sessions which focused on many of the substantive areas in this volume and on the broader problems of social intelligence. Their financial support provided for research and editorial assistance. Continuous encouragement was provided by Dean Stephen K. Bailey and Associate Dean Irving Swerdlow of the Maxwell School of Citizenship and Public Affairs, Syracuse University. At a time when university administrators often look to active scholars for conspicuous performance as snaggers of fat foundation grants or large government contracts, they steadily supported an austere activity that covered no overhead.

Acknowledgment must also be made for the ideas, encouragement and stimulus provided by the participants in these exploration-and-review sessions: Milton Babbitt, Composer, The Electronic Music Center of Columbia and Princeton Universities; Louis H. Bean, Election Analysis, Ltd., Washington, D.C.; Albert D. Biderman, Bureau of Social Science Research; Alfred Blumstein, Institute for Defense Analyses; Ann Carter, Economics Research Program, Harvard University; Michel Chevalier, Executive Officer, Institute of Environmental Studies, University of Pennsylvania; Albert K. Cohen, Professor of Sociology, University of Connecticut; Donald Cook, Applied Education Division, Xerox Corporation, New York City; Michel Crozier, Department of Social Relations, Harvard University (on leave from Centre de Sociologie des Organizations, Paris); John Dixon, Basic Systems, Xerox Corp.; Julius C. C. Edelstein, Director of Urban Studies Center, C.U.N.Y.; William Ehling, Professor of Journalism, Syracuse University; Marilyn Etchinson, Office of the Secretary, Department of Health, Education and Welfare; Hy Faine, National Executive Secretary, American Guild of Musical Artists, New York City; William C. Fleming, Chairman, Department of Fine Arts, Syracuse University; Fred M. Frohock, Assistant Professor of Political Science, Syracuse University; Robert W. Gregg, Chairman, Department of Political Science, Syracuse University; William G. Grigsby, Dean of Graduate School of Fine Arts, University of Pennsylvania; David Gross, Society of Fellows and Department of Physics, Harvard University; Larry Gross, Lehman Fellow, Department of Social Psychology, Columbia University; Michael Harrington, League for Industrial Democracy; Jack B. Haskins, Professor of Journalism, Syracuse University; Tom Hayden, Community Union Project, Newark, New Jersey; Howard Houseman, William Morris Agency, New York City; Moyomo Ise, Crusade for Opportunity, Syracuse, N.Y.; Esther M. Jackson, Professor of Fine Arts, Shaw University; Joe Kappel, Office of the Secretary, Department of Health, Education and Welfare; Gerald J. Karaska, Associate Professor of Geography, Syracuse University; Andrew Kopkind, Associate Editor, *New Republic;* Stanford Lackoff, Professor of Political Science, S.U.N.Y. at Stony Brook; Peter Lejins, Professor of Sociology, University of Maryland; Isador Lateiner, Concert Violinist; William F. Lipman, Federal Office, California Legislature; Kenneth Mabuchi, Vice-President, Central Economic Development Organization, Washington, D.C.; Michael Marien, Graduate Student (Doctorate in Social Science Program), Syracuse University; Charles C. Mark, Director, State and Community Operations, National Foundation on the Arts and Humanities; Walter McCann, Legislative Assistant to United States Representative John Brademas (Indiana); Francis Mechner, President, Institute of Behavior Research; Donald Meiklejohn, Director, Public Affairs and Citizenship Program, Syracuse University; S. M. Miller, Professor of Sociology, New York University (on leave to Ford Foundation); Howard E. Mitchell, Director, Human Resources Program, Institute for Environmental Studies, University of Pennsylvania; Robert B. Mitchell, Chairman, Department of City and Regional Planning, University of Pennsylvania; Pearl Peerboon, Program Analysis Officer, Office of the Secretary, Department of Health, Education and Welfare; G. Holmes Perkins, Chairman of Council, Institute for Environmental Studies, University of Pennsylvania; I. E.

Peterson, *New York Times,* Washington Bureau; Douglas W. Rae, Assistant Professor of Political Science, Yale University; Stuart Rice, Surveys and Research Corporation, Washington, D.C.; John Rider, Associate Professor of TV/Radio, Syracuse University; Pamela Roby, Graduate Student in Sociology, New York University; James K. Rocks, Director, Office of Plans and Programs, National Center for Educational Studies, Health, Education and Welfare Department; Bruce M. Russett, Professor of Political Science, Yale University; Seymour Sacks, Professor of Economics, Syracuse University; Edward Schneider, Associate Professor of Political Science, Princeton University; Jay Schulman, Associate Professor of Sociology, New York State School of Industrial and Labor Relations, Cornell University; Marshall H. Segall, Professor of Psychology, Syracuse University; Faith Seidenberg, Attorney at Law, Syracuse, N.Y.; William Shands, Congressional Fellow, Office of Senator Mondale; Eleanor B. Sheldon, Russell Sage Foundation; William H. T. Smith, Chief of Police, Syracuse, N.Y.; Howard Taubman, Critic, *New York Times;* Irene Taviss, Research Associate, Program of Technology and Society, Harvard University; Stanton Wheeler, Russell Sage Foundation; Oliver P. Williams, Professor of Economics, University of Pennsylvania; Preston Wilcox, Columbia University; Marvin E. Wolfgang, Professor of Sociology, University of Pennsylvania; Robert Wolfson, Professor of Economics, Syracuse University; and, Roland E. Wolseley, Professor of Journalism, Syracuse University.

Finally, acknowledgment must be made to Michael Springer for his devoted work in helping to set up the exploration-and-review sessions, organizing this volume, editing many of the chapters, and co-authoring the first chapter in this volume. In part of this work he obtained help from Lambert Wenner, general editorial assistant in the National Planning Studies Program (and doctoral candidate in the Doctorate in Social Science Program), and Stanley Moses, graduate assistant in political science. With sustained, pertinent and impertinent skepticism, Mr. Springer helped make some of the authors of this volume aware of the wide generation gap between themselves and those who have not yet "made it" in the 1960's. He has helped raise some of the formidable questions that will confront his generation when, in the 1970's and 1980's, they are confronted by new intelligence gaps and perhaps, still more formidable challengers.

BERTRAM M. GROSS
Director
Center for Urban Studies
Wayne State University
Detroit, Michigan

ONE

SOME BASIC ISSUES

Measure what is measurable and make measurable what is not measurable.

GALILEO GALILEI

Any measure of a social science concept that relies on a single indicator should be viewed as dubious.

AMITAI ETZIONI

An information system does not tell what courses of action are conceivable. Man himself must conceive them.

RAYMOND A. BAUER

Designers of statistics are indeed philosophers, however unwilling to claim the name, and are fully aware that different aspects of reality can be lit up if alternative sets of concepts are used.

BERTRAND DE JOUVENEL

1

DEVELOPING
SOCIAL INTELLIGENCE

BERTRAM M. GROSS
and
MICHAEL SPRINGER

In the middle third of the twentieth century, the United States made historic advances in developing regular, well-ordered, and increasingly reliable economic data. These advances were of some help to private and public decision-making in meeting the challenges of the Great Depression and World War II. They have been of increasingly greater help, it is widely acknowledged, since 1946.

As Americans enter the last third of the century, a subtle but profoundly significant shift is beginning to take place in the informational premises of decision-making throughout the country: *more explicit attention to transeconomic goals and data.* This shift is associated with a variety of efforts to map out and plot courses into our society's future. These maps attempt to outline almost every aspect of our political, social and economic life. The social intelligence required to secure accurate details for these maps may prove to be the most challenging and important tasks facing both the political and academic communities. This volume is intended to introduce the scope of this mapping operation and frankly identify some of its profound difficulties.

These efforts at societal mapping raise many new problems for the structure of American government, the relations between private and public agencies, and the place of the individual is an increasingly organized society. This chapter will focus on some more prosaic issues which must be understood before one can begin to face these larger questions. Specifically, it will attempt to introduce these issues by touching upon:

3

—the domestic intelligence gap,
—the information explosion in social indicators,
—our unsystematic national data system,
—social change and concept obsolescence, and
—some steps toward conceptual advance.

Our approach is somewhat discursive. We hope to develop a wide range of issues rather than deal exhaustively with a few.

THE DOMESTIC INTELLIGENCE GAP

At a time when America and the world are in the throes of confusing revolutionary change, it is increasingly difficult for anyone to know where we have been and where we are, let alone where we may want to go.

Our intelligence machinery tends to creak along in bureaucratic conformance with routines set up in a previous era. Our "conservative" defenders of the *status quo* rarely see much of the *state at which* we are. Our "radical" attackers of the present "system," "power structure," or "establishment" are usually blind to the radical changes already taking place as we move from advanced industrialism into the first stages of a new postindustrial society. Executive officials and members of Congress alike are misled by *inadequate interpretation* of *bad information* based on *obsolete concepts* and *inadequate research* and collected by *underfed and overlobbied statistical agencies.*

When people talk about a "credibility gap," it is assumed that various officials are misleading the public by withholding *good* information. An "intelligence gap," however, is rooted in *one-sided, missing, distorted, misinterpreted, or unused information.* The initial impact of the intelligence gap is that national policy-makers *themselves* are misled—or, to put it more mildly, are led into *oversimplified, partial, and out-dated views of major policy problems.*

Each chapter in this volume isolates certain of the dimensions of this intelligence gap. The two other chapters in Part One explore some of the more fundamental reasons for this gap. The substantive chapters of the following parts of this volume note some of the more glaring defects in our social information. Part Two, *The Policy,* pinpoints some of the deficiencies in the *status quo* of domestic intelligence in the critical fields of electoral participation, civil liberties, and democratic participation. Part Three, *The Cultural Context,* provides sharp analyses of the critical weaknesses in our information on individual and group values, education and learning, science and technology, the mass media and the arts. Part Four,

Social Problems, enumerates a plethora of weaknesses in existing data on poverty, employment, discrimination, social breakdown, crime and delinquency, and health and well-being. Our inability to secure adequate information on our natural and urban environments is examined in Part Five, *Environments.*

But the basic thrust of the entire discussion is more positive than negative; informational deficiencies are analysed in order to provide the hard-nosed intelligence estimates required to make strategic advances over difficult terrain. Our table, "Indicator Suggestions" illustrates the scope and variety of the intelligence required for the social mapping of the 1970's and 1980's. We have freely adapted the suggestions of the authors of this volume for improved information and have made some of our own.

In the area of United States government statistical series, there are proposals both for new data and for better use of existing data. The "Other" column includes proposals for the studies needed to provide both better interpretation of available data and the conceptual framework for more effective data collection and interpretation. These proposals more than reflect the authors' ideas for improved social indicators. They also reflect the types of demands that are now being made upon both public and private data gathering agencies.

TABLE—Indicator Suggestions

Area	United States Government Statistical Series		Other
	New Data	Better Use of Existing Data	
Electoral participation (Chpt. 4)	Bureau of Census: bi-yearly estimates by states of numbers of citizens of voting age eligible under state law to vote.	More detail in statistical abstract on Negro voter registration. Compilation of state and local registration and voting statistics.	Research on: (1) factors affecting turnout and registration; (2) characteristics of those who run for office; and (3) influence of turnout on parties and local government.

TABLE—Indicator Suggestions (cont'd)

Area	United States Government Statistical Series		Other
	New Data	Better Use of Existing Data	
Civil Liberties (Chpt. 5)	Continued utilization of presidential and congressional commissions to explore the most pressing problems in the area of civil liberties.		Research on: (1) effectiveness of fair housing, employment, and education acts; (2) the exercise of academic freedom; and (3) the effects of pornography. Development of tools to evaluate such complex questions as the relationship between non-violent demonstrations and respect for law. More research by such institutions as Columbia's Center for Research and Education in American Liberties.

TABLE—Indicator Suggestions (cont'd)

| Area | United States Government Statistical Series | | Other |
	New Data	Better Use of Existing Data	
Democratic Participation (Chpt. 6)	Data on size of professional and paraprofessional groups and on community organizations by locality. Collection and analysis of electoral participation data for local and state elections.	New section in *Statistical Abstract of the United States* on role of women and minority groups in political, social, and economic institutions. Better assembly of international comparative data on major forms of participation.	Research on: (1) extent of participatory democracy in schools, business firms, government agencies, community groups, and the like; (2) "participation of the poor"; (3) sensitivity of officials to the demands upon them; (4) expectations that are associated with various forms of participation; (5) how many Americans feel a loss of sense of belonging; (6) examination of international rate of participation in terms of resources, constraints, capabilities, and cultural ideals.

TABLE—Indicator Suggestions (cont'd)

| Area | United States Government Statistical Series | | Other |
	New Data	Better Use of Existing Data	
Individual and Group Values (Chpt. 7)		Compilation of non-government attitude surveys.	Research on: (1) intensity of commitment to particular values and beliefs; (2) relation between apparent reduction of ethnocentrism and growth of more intellectual evaluations; (3) extent of concern over leisure; (4) extent of loss of belongingness, loss of norms, uprootedness, etc.; and (5) relationship between overt acts and expressed values.
Learning and Education (Chpt. 8)	Collection of educational expenditure data for the "nonestablish-ment" sectors of education, so that total educational expenditures can be computed. Implementation of new Carnegie plan for assessment of educational performance.	Improved estimates on "learning force" as a whole, particularly those enrolled in "nonestablish-ment" educational programs.	Research on: (1) educational administration at all levels; (2) costs and benefits of alternative training methods for the same job; (3) impact of education (longitudinal studies); and (4) student culture and social system of schools (in situ studies).

TABLE—Indicator Suggestions (cont'd)

| Area | United States Government Statistical Series | | Other |
	New Data	Better Use of Existing Data	
Science and Technology (Chpt. 9)	Substantive content classification of scientific and technological research (in output-program budget terms).	More sustained and comprehensive presentation and analysis of basic series on scientific personnel, organizations, expenditures, publications, and the like. Link reports on substantive content of scientific activities with information-retrieval facilities.	Research on: (1) time lags between basic science findings and technological implementation by the industrial sector; (2) extent of technological spillover from space and military Research & Development (R&D) programs; (3) role of scientific organizations; (4) evaluation of the quality of scientific output; and (5) how to estimate the social impacts of technological innovations.
The Mass Media (Chpt. 10)	Federal Communications Commission to publish national and local time series on the proportion of advertising and news time by the networks and broadcasters, the size of listening audiences, and the types of programs.		Professional appraisals of extent of depth reporting systems and editorial professionalism. Research into the effect of mass media on values and behavior, where people get information, and functions of newspapers.

TABLE—Indicator Suggestions (cont'd)

| Area | United States Government Statistical Series | | Other |
	New Data	Better Use of Existing Data	
Art and culture (Chpt. 11)	Annual data on audience size for performing arts, including semiprofessional, by areas. Recurring Census of the Arts to include economic and institutional data covering not only the high arts but also the amateur movement and popular entertainment.	Compilation of federal, state, and local expenditures on the arts. Art and Culture section in *Statistical Abstract of the United States.*	Research on: (1) the type of musical education provided in primary and secondary schools; (2) the costs of the tools and media used by artists; (3) the administration of artistic enterprises; (4) the recruitment and training of professional artists; (5) the decline in recitals; and (6) the scope of the "amateur movement."
Poverty and Inequality (Chpt. 12)	Regular publication of Gini index for both wealth and income distribution.	Serial data in *Statistical Abstract of the United States* on the extent of population below minimum standards of income, assets (liquid and fixed), and unpaid-for services (public and private).	Developments of new statistical profiles of wealth and income, for example, top-bottom ratios. Research on the psychological and sociological dimensions of the self-image of the poor.

TABLE—Indicator Suggestions (cont'd)

| Area | United States Government Statistical Series | | Other |
	New Data	Better Use of Existing Data	
Employment Goals and the "New Economics" (Chpt. 13)	Periodic reports on location of job openings in the fifty largest Standard Metropolitan Statistical Areas (SMSA's).	Regular and improved reporting on subemployment in low-income areas. This includes not only regular application of traditional unemployment measures, but also: estimates of those (1) working part-time and looking for full-time work; (2) earning sub-standard wages; (3) labor force dropouts because of lack of openings; and (4) not ordinarily counted.	Research on: (1) changes taking place in length the work week; (2) recruitment into skilled and semiskilled trades; (3) relationships between education and occupational mobility; (4) relationship between productivity gains and employment rates; and (5) future employment trends.

TABLE—Indicator Suggestions (cont'd)

Area	United States Government Statistical Series		Other
	New Data	Better Use of Existing Data	
Discrimination against Negroes (Chpt. 14)	Bureau of Census and other agencies		More extensive analysis of existing ecological data.
	Separate orientals from "nonwhite" category. Statistics of intermarriage. Publication of Equal Opportunity Commission data on Negro employment by sectors of industry and by job category.	Publication of key indicators on conditions of Negroes (i.e., employment, income, housing, education, voter registration, etc.) School segregation status for all regions (not just the South). More extensive group	Repeated standardized field observation studies of Negro communities and problem areas (for race relations).

TABLE—Indicator Suggestions (cont'd)

| Area | United States Government Statistical Series | | Other |
	New Data	Better Use of Existing Data	
Social Breakdown (Chpt. 15)	Divorce Registration Area to be representative of entire country with data on divorce, separation, and remarriage (including time interval between divorce and remarriage). Incorporation into official series of suicide data from insurance companies. More systematic methods for estimates of users of illegal drugs including "week-end" user, regular user, and seller.	Relate divorce and separation data to existing information on extended duration of marriages (with increased life expectancy).	Studies on better classification of alcoholics by state agencies. Research on: (1) number of those arrested for public intoxication who are chronic alcoholics; (2) various forms of violence; (3) physiological and psychological effects of marijuana use; (4) changes in premarital sex practices; and (5) *in situ* studies of deviant behavior. All states to require doctors to report cases of "battered children."

TABLE—Indicator Suggestions (cont'd)

Area	United States Government Statistical Series		Other
	New Data	Better Use of Existing Data	
Crime and Delinquency (Chpt. 16)	Survey to determine whether offenses are reported to police and, if so, with what consequences. Surveys of corporations, government agencies, etc., to determine extent of white-collar crime. Surveys of women to determine incidence of rape.	Periodic reports on separate categories of crime to include thorough analysis of data. Revision of FBI *Uniform Crime Reports* to include: (1) comparison of police and survey data on particular offenses and (2) adequate assessment of crime rates for similar offenders who received diverse judicial and correctional treatment.	Assessment of alternative crime control measures, including their unintended consequences, such as other kinds of crimes.
Health and Well-Being (Chpt. 17)	More refined surveys of mortality and life expectancy by income groups and by localities— including major slum areas.	Readjustment of "Cause of Death" data, with improved interpretation.	More research on the development of positive measures of health and vitality.

TABLE—Indicator Suggestions (cont'd)

| Area | United States Government Statistical Series | | Other |
	New Data	Better Use of Existing Data	
The Natural Environment (Chpt. 18)	Data on physical characteristics and contaminants in streams, estuaries, lakes, air above metropolitan areas, solid wastes, etc. Estimates of costs and benefits (social as well as economic) and other measures to achieve specified standards of quality.	Combining of existing series relating to water and air conditions; placing them on a common basis of concepts, definitions, and methods of measurement. Further efforts to standardize underlying assumptions and procedures for estimating costs and benefits associated with environmental projects and programs.	Development of statistical information on environmental quality for more effective pollution-abatement programs.

TABLE—Indicator Suggestions (cont'd)

Area	United States Government Statistical Series		Other
	New Data	Better Use of Existing Data	
Urban conditions (Chpts. 19 & 20)	More detailed information on intercity migration. Employment data that can be disaggregated to areas within a city. Information on location of jobs within the Standard Metropolitan Statistical Area (SMSA). Segregation data for private as well as public schools. Local components of other indicator suggestions.	Census data further organized according to political jurisdictions. Taeuber indices for every SMSA in the country. Urban area data books for the nontechnical reader. Further efforts to indicate the limitations and inaccuracies of existing data.	Research on: (1) participation in all aspects of community life; (2) use of cultural facilities; (3) changing social and economic structure of low-income areas; (4) effects of urban density; and (5) patterns of educational quality within SMSA's. More extensive support of *in situ* studies of urban neighborhoods. Local components of other indicator suggestions.

No attempt will be made in this volume to identify—let alone analyze —the myriad interrelationships among these subjects. While the reader will be given an opportunity to learn about a number of trees, we shall not help him see the forest. Our major purpose is to indicate the scope and limitations of some available social indicators. Implicit in this effort, also, is a demonstration of the futility of simple-minded holistic views of social life. This may reflect the probability that the growth of science and self-awareness can lead to confusion and ambiguity as well as surety.

This paradox of a poverty of perspective in the midst of a growing abundance of data is a central problem for both the social scientist and those who attempt to guide our society toward a full realization of its potentials. To begin to cope with both the intellectual and the policy problems presented by this bewildering array of information, we must attempt to develop more adequate overviews of society and social change. These must be of a different order than the *Verstehen* theories bequeathed to us by such social philosophers as Spencer, Marx, and Weber. Our new overviews must confront the social problems of today and tomorrow, and not those of the turn of the past century. They must be open-ended rather than deterministic. They must be rich in concepts and at the same time deal directly with our growing array of empirical information. Here lies the ultimate challenge of the intelligence gap.

THE INFORMATION EXPLOSION IN
SOCIAL INDICATORS

The chapters in this volume are like the small above-water tip of the proverbial iceberg. Underlying them are many less obvious (but rapidly expanding and widely dispersed) efforts to obtain more and better social data.

Among the historical sources of these efforts are such factors as the following:

—the increasing maturation of the social sciences during the first two-thirds of this century, with ever greater attention to quantitative methods;

—the emergence of corporation executives with fact-based styles of management and broader social perspectives;

—the entry into public policy positions of a broadening array of intellectuals, professionals, modern-style managers, technologists, and natural and social scientists;

—the acceptance of the "new economics" by both conservatives and liberals, with increasing attention by both to social as well as economic objectives (as illustrated by political slogans referring to a "great," "free," "creative," or "just" *society*); and

—continuing efforts to provide more rational bases for political decision-making.

With such factors in mind, let us look at some key points in the current expansion of social indicator activity.

IF ECONOMIC INDICATORS, WHY
NOT SOCIAL INDICATORS?

Many years ago, when the final version of the Employment Act of 1946 was being drafted in the Senate-House Conference Committee, the

Act's provisions for the President's annual Economic Report were a "sleeper." Most observers paid exclusive attention to disputes over symbols such as "full" versus "maximum" employment. Indeed, many participants in the legislative debate seemed to think of government influence over the economy exclusively in terms of spending and controls. Few people realized the subtle power of highly credible quantitative information on which public attention is focused through presidential messages and joint committee hearings.

Since then, it has become clear that the public reporting provisions were of strategic significance. The President's annual Economic Report, along with the accompanying reports of the President's Council of Economic Advisers, have become an important institution. In addition, the Council's monthly *Economic Indicators,* published by the Joint Economic Committee of Congress, provides a carefully organized set of economic charts and tables. This wealth of factual information on economic trends and potentials provides major premises for private and public decision-making even by those who may disagree with specific presidential proposals.

"If we have highly organized *economic* indicators, why can't we set up a system of social indicators as well?" In the Spring of 1962, Raymond A. Bauer of the Harvard Business School posed this question to an informal group of scholars. The same question was in the minds of the President's Science Advisory Committee when, at about the same time, it called for "the systematic collection of basic behavioral data for the United States . . . data that are comparable, systematic and periodically gathered."[1] Under this stimulus, with sponsorship by the American Academy of Arts and Sciences, Bauer and a few others, including the senior author of this paper, went to work on the various sections of *Social Indicators.*[2]

In the course of preparing *The State of the Nation: Social System Accounting,*[3] the senior author of this paper became increasingly convinced of the possibility of using the precedent of the Employment Act. He discussed this matter with high government officials and advisors in 1964 and early 1965 and was encouraged to prepare a series of specific proposals. In November 1965, believing that subjects of this importance should be

---

[1] Life Sciences Panel. *Strengthening the Behavioral Sciences: Statement By the Behavioral Sciences Subpanel,* President's Science Advisory Committee, Washington, D.C., April 20, 1962. It is quite conceivable that the new Behavioral Science Division of the National Academy of Science will play an important role in fostering the systematic collection of social information.

[2] Raymond M. Bauer (ed.), *Social Indicators* (Cambridge, Mass.: M.I.T. Press, 1966). This work was supported by a grant from the National Aeronautics and Space Administration to the American Academy of Arts and Sciences' Committee on Space.

[3] Also published separately in London by Tavistock Publications, 1966.

publicly discussed, he broached the theme in one of the new journals specializing in general social science topics.

> The very success of the President's Economic Reports is—from a broader view—a serious shortcoming. In raising the level of economic awareness and sophistication among American elites, they have at the same time contributed to the "new Philistinism" that expresses national goals and performance in dollar-sign figures. The remedy, obviously, is not to eliminate the Economic Reports. Indeed, even in strictly economic terms, they need extension and deepening. The remedy is to counter-balance the monetary data with non-monetary data, the economic information with non-economic information, the quantitative with the qualitative.
>
> But this cannot be done effectively unless the President himself provides leadership by centering public attention on such "countervailing information." Carloads of economic data had been regularly published in the United States before the Employment Act of 1946. Yet it took the President's annual Economic Reports to make the country economics-conscious. Nothing less than an annual Social Report of the President is needed to make America more conscious of the factors involved in enriching the "quality of life" and moving toward something that might be termed a "great society."[4]

In addition to awakening interest in government circles not yet aware of the proposal, the article also led Thorsten Sellin, editor of THE ANNALS of the American Academy of Political and Social Science, to suggest that an issue of THE ANNALS be devoted to the subject of social indicators.

During this same period Eleanor B. Sheldon and Gilbert E. Moore of the Russell Sage Foundation prepared a major paper for the American Statistical Association on quantitative measures of "large-scale structural transformation." This was part of the foundation's "Monitoring Social Change" Project. It led to the commissioning of thirteen papers by different specialists, "each focusing on one aspect of social change and covering a review of the past, current, and prospective state of trend knowledge for the particular topic under inspection."[5]

Also in the Fall of 1965, *The Commission on the Year 2000* (under the auspices of the American Academy of Arts and Sciences and the chairmanship of Daniel Bell) started to work on a broad, imaginative probe of the future. Its two aims were (1) to identify problems that will be coming

---

[4] Bertram M. Gross, "The Social State of the Union," *Trans-Action* November-December 1965.

[5] The subjects of these papers are as follows: population magnitudes and distribution; the polity; social stratification and mobility; labor force and occupations; welfare and its measurement; recreational and expressive activities; cultural homogeneity and diversity; family and kinship; and religion.

to a head around 2000 A.D. and to propose appropriate strategies or new institutions to cope with them, and (2) to identify major structural changes in the society and related shifts in values and to specify some of the possible consequences of these changes. The Commission has circulated privately four volumes of working papers and transcripts, and a selection of these appeared as a special issue of *Daedalus* (Summer 1967). A group of eight working parties has been set up for more detailed consideration of particular problems. The Commission's work is very similar to the *Futuribles* project of Bertrand de Jouvenel in Paris, and various long-range forecasting exercises at the Rand Corporation, Hudson Institute, and Syracuse University's new Educational Policy Center.

THE NEW PLANNING-PROGRAMMING-BUDGETING SYSTEM

Moreover, in the Fall of 1965, the Bureau of the Budget launched its new Planning-Programming-Budgeting System (known widely as PPBS). Potentially the most significant management improvement in the history of American government, PPBS has already involved hundreds of government officials, with widely varying understanding and skill, in sustained efforts to obtain more useful data on current and projected government activities. Whereas previous federal budgeting was mainly based in the listing of inputs, these modern efforts, if carried out to their full potential, would provide appraisals of

1. the network of outcomes or impacts (benefits and disbenefits direct or indirect, aggregated or disaggregated) likely to result from . . .
2. certain types, quantities, and qualities of end-product outputs (often intangible services) made possible by . . .
3. the use of inputs whose total costs are realistically estimated.[6]

These complex variables are employed in making long-term projections and comparing alternative programs.

PPBS may very well be a significant innovation in the policy-making process, but its full implementation must confront a paucity of adequate social indicators. In this regard, it soon became clear that among the weakest links in these benefit-output-cost analyses was the lack of (in the previously quoted works of the President's Science Advisory Committee) social "data that are comparable, systematic and periodically gathered."

---

[6] We should like to express our gratitude to Mr. Itzhak Galnoor, a graduate student at Syracuse University, who assisted us in developing this formulation.

No conscientious budget-examiner could rely uncritically on the data presented on education, mental illness, crime, delinquency, transportation, and urban problems by scores of competing bureaus anxious to justify budget proposals by magnifying their past record or their future contributions to the "public interest." Thus, the logic of the new budget system originating in the pioneering work of cost-benefit economists pointed unmistakably toward an enlarged role for transeconomic information, particularly information bearing on the "quality of life."

THE TECHNOLOGY COMMISSION'S
CALL FOR SOCIAL ACCOUNTING

In January 1966, major support for new ways of dealing with social information came from the National Commission on Technology, Automation, and Economic Progress. Despite disagreements on other subjects, the Commission was unanimous in stating that our ability to measure social change has lagged behind our ability to measure strictly economic change.[7]

The Commission called for some system of social accounts to assess the utilization of human resources in four areas:

1. The measurement of social costs and net returns of innovation.
2. The measurement of social ills (for example, crime and family disruption).
3. The creation of "performance budgets" in areas of defined social needs (for example, housing, education, and welfare).
4. Indicators of economic opportunity and social mobility.

Action along these lines, it was stated, could help put economic accounting into a broader framework.

THE HEALTH, EDUCATION, AND
WELFARE DEPARTMENT'S
TRANSDEPARTMENTAL MISSION

In March 1966, President Johnson formally assigned the following mission to John Gardner, then Secretary of the Department of Health, Education, and Welfare (HEW):

---

[7] *Report of National Commission on Technology, Automation and Economic Progress* (Washington, D.C.: U.S. Government Printing Office, 1966).

Through the programs entrusted to its care, the Department of Health, Education and Welfare exercises continuing concern for the social well-being of all our people. Already, as I have indicated in this message, it has become possible to set ambitious goals for the future. . . .

To improve our ability to chart our progress, I have asked the Secretary to establish within his office the resources to develop the necessary social statistics and indicators to supplement those prepared by the Bureau of Labor Statistics and the Council of Economic Advisers. With these yardsticks, we can better measure the distance we have come and plan for the way ahead.[8]

HEW was given this transdepartmental mission for several reasons. Under the effective leadership of former Secretary John Gardner, and the present Secretary Wilbur J. Cohen, the department has been able to develop a broad base of political support and respect within government and the academic community. This has allowed HEW to assume a job that not only could have significant effects on every department in the federal establishment, but also requires the wholehearted co-operation of a good number of "free intellectuals" from in and out of government. Furthermore, since Secretary Arthur Fleming under the Eisenhower Administration, HEW had taken the lead in organizing available social data and developing new programs of data collection. Under the active sponsorship of Wilbur J. Cohen, now Secretary, the HEW's Office of Program Analysis continuously improved its monthly *HEW Indicators* (with charts and tables modeled on the Council of Economic Advisers' *Economic Indicators*) and its annual supplement, *HEW Trends*.[9] To the surprise of HEW, a White House review of the situation showed no comparable transeconomic work by any other department. Moreover, even within its own area, the Department's key officials, with many new, enormous programs to administer, were deeply dissatisfied with the statistical status quo. They wanted the better information required for effective handling of their new managerial burdens.

Within HEW, major responsibility for the new mission was assigned to William Gorham, Assistant Secretary for Program Co-ordination. An economist and "systems analyst" from the Rand Corporation and Secretary McNamara's office in the Department of Defense, Mr. Gorham is also in charge of the new PPBS activity in HEW. He has organized a Social Indicators Panel composed of about two dozen scholars and experts from

---

[8] President Lyndon B. Johnson, *Message to the Congress on Domestic Health and Education,* March 1, 1966.

[9] *HEW Indicators* (monthly) has been recently discontinued while the annual *HEW Trends* (under the editorship of Pearl Peerboon) has been substantially enlarged.

universities and other non-governmental research institutions and has asked Daniel Bell to serve with him as the Panel's cochairman.[10] An economist, Mancur Olsen, Jr., has been appointed Deputy Assistant Secretary for Social Indicators. It is his responsibility to coordinate and direct the drafting of a trial-run of a first Social Report.

Under the guidance of Gorham, Bell and Olsen, the experts on the panel have been encouraged to consult widely with their colleagues and to seek help from the best minds available. They have worked in collaboration with an ever widening panel of data experts from many other government agencies. This activity has proceeded in an open and nonsecretive manner, with increasing coverage in the press.

THE POSSIBLE SOCIAL REPORTS
OF THE PRESIDENT

By early 1967 it became widely known that work was under way to prepare professional materials that could be used in proposing a first Social Report of the President. The rationale for developing such a proposal was expressed in a working memorandum by the two cochairmen as follows:

> No society in history has, as yet, made a coherent and unified effort to assess those elements in the society which facilitate and which bar each individual from realizing to the fullest extent possible his talents and abilities, in order to allow him to find a job, or establish a career commensurate with his talents, to live a full and healthy life equal to his biological potential, to establish the conditions for an adequate standard of living which allows him to live in a civilized fashion, and which provides a physical and social environment which enhances his sense of life. We believe that these are aims implicit in the American purpose. We believe that the means of realizing these are possible. If it is agreed that this is an appropriate and adequate focus, the function of the Social Report

---

[10] The consultants to the Social Indicators panel are: Daniel Bell, Chairman, University of Chicago; Raymond A. Bauer, Harvard Graduate School of Business; William G. Bowen, Princeton University; Ewan Clague, Consultant to Secretary of Labor; Otis Dudley Duncan, University of Michigan; G. Franklin Edwards, Howard University; Solomon Fabricant, The National Bureau of Economic Research; Joseph Fisher, Resources for the Future, Inc.; Howard E. Freeman, University of Wisconsin; Bertram Gross, Syracuse University; Philip Hauser, University of Chicago; Carl Kaysen, The Institute for Advanced Study; C. V. Martin, Carson, Pirie Scott & Co.; *Daniel P. Moynihan, Harvard University; Selma Mushkin, State and Local Finances; Harvey Perloff, Resources for the Future, Inc.; Stuart Rice, Surveys and Research Corporation; T. W. Schultz, University of Chicago; Eleanor Sheldon, Russell Sage Foundation; Anne R. Somers, Princeton University; Sydney Stein, Stein Roe and Farnham; and Ralph Tyler, Center for Advanced Studies.

would be to provide a continuing assessment of our abilities to realize these aims.

At this present stage of social science development, deficiencies in both data and theory impose serious constraints. First, the analysts must "make do" with existing data. Second, they must also get along without the kind of "overview framework" provided for economic information by national economic accounting. The first difficulty is eased by the assumption that the social reports themselves would promote action to fill the most critical "social data gaps." As for the second difficulty, some fear that this is inherent in the nature of the information explosion in social indicators. Others hope that with the resulting loss of perspective there will be increasing interest in serious efforts to develop operating models for systematizing social data.

An awareness of these constraints on the part of external observers has even led to calls for quicker action. Thus, the columnist Joseph Kraft summarized a discussion of the subject as follows:

> To be sure, an annual social report is not going to end congested streets, air pollutions, and the shortchanging of the consumer interest. But it can create a climate of continuous self-correction; a barrier against irrevocable mistakes, not to say disasters, such as the loss of a Negro generation. And that, it seems to me, is perhaps the most important domestic business now before the Nation.[11]

In February 1967, Senator Walter G. Mondale (Minn.) and his group of ten other senators called for a legislative structure for annual social reporting by the President, professional assistance, and congressional participation.[12] Their proposed "Full Opportunity and Social Accounting Act" (S 843) parallels in many ways the Employment Act of 1946. Its major sections provide for:

> 1. the annual transmission to the Congress of a President's Social Report that can bring together, in terms meaningful for the Congress and the public as a whole, the work of countless specialized experts on all major aspects of the "quality of life."
> 2. the creation of a small social intelligence staff to help prepare this continuing synthesis and improve the quality and relevance of

---

[11] *Washington Post,* January 4, 1967.

[12] Senators Clark (Pa.), Hart (Mich.), Harris (Ind.), Inouye (Hawaii), Kennedy (Mass.), McCarthy (Minn.), McGee (Wyo.), Muskie (Maine), Nelson (Wis.), and Proxmire (Wis.). Senator Proxmire, it may be noted, is Chairman of the Joint Economic Committee of Congress.

social information. It still remains to be seen whether or not the "Council of Social Advisors," as precisely proposed in Section 4 of S.843, is the most practical and desirable of all possible instrumentalities.

3. the creation of a Congressional Joint Committee on the Social Report.

OUR UNSYSTEMATIC

NATIONAL DATA SYSTEM

"The Johnson Administration," the *Wall Street Journal* has reported, "is considering a major centralization of its sprawling statistical empire— hopefully without giving it a 'police-state' image."[13]

The idea of national "data centers" (or, if one may use a popular but misleading metaphor, "data banks") has developed as a natural result of the increasing need for "administrative statistics," the rising capacity of each generation of electronic computers to store, process, retrieve and deliver such data, and the mounting aspirations of computer designers, producers, and users. The social indicator explosion has contributed to interest in this idea.

In the short compass of this chapter, we can merely identify a few of the "data system" issues made more acute by the social indicator explosion. We cannot directly discuss the broader problems of "information management," the so-called "credibility gap," or the "dossier problem" (which might become more acute when there are more life-cycle and longitudinal studies along the lines suggested by Otis Dudley Duncan and Daniel Glaser in chapters 14 and 16 respectively.[14] Our remarks will be limited to suggesting three normative principles for dealing with three basic questions:

Who should collect social indicators?

What should be done about conflicting data and interpretation?

What should be the role of the Congress?

---

[13] Article by Richard F. Janssen, *Wall Street Journal*, November 11, 1966. The possible difference between image and reality was not mentioned.

[14] At the Russell Sage Foundation, Stanton Wheeler is exploring this problem by examining a series of case studies. The subject is also being studied by the Budget Bureau's panel on a national data center, although without the participation of lawyers such as Milton Konvitz who have specialized on civil liberty problems.

THE PRINCIPLE OF
MULTIPLE SOURCES

Even the strongest proponents of a national data center recognize the need for some types of decentralized collection, analysis, and dissemination of data. Thus, within the federal government, we have recently seen the creation in HEW of a National Center for Education Statistics and the National Health Survey. There is widespread support for a national bureau of criminological research, as proposed by Daniel Glaser in Chapter 16. The National Science Foundation is developing new sources of information on the volume and type of scientific activities. New government programs often involve specialized agencies in the collection of the social data required under their legislation—as with the Negro employment data collected by the new Equal Employment Opportunity Commission. True, the Bureau of the Census provides remarkably expert facilities for conducting surveys for other agencies or processing the information they collect. But the impact of the Bureau's work has been less to replace decentralized data collection than to provide the central services needed to facilitate it. The next few years will see the growth of perhaps dozens of specialized data centers run or financed by the federal government—mostly in areas beyond the traditional boundaries of economics.

This proliferation of data calls for the Census Bureau to increase its efforts in developing more useful compendia of "processed" data such as the *Statistical Abstract* and the *Historical Statistics of the United States*. Given the scope of presently available information, these documents could easily include separate sections on civil liberties and discrimination against Negroes. In the near future they could include a section on the arts and greatly expanded sections on health, crime, and other areas about which more reliable information is being developed. Furthermore, the Bureau should seriously consider producing more special-purpose compendia of easily understood summaries of information, such as the urban area data books suggested by Daniel P. Moynihan in Chapter 20. Such efforts will make information available to a vast number of citizens—some of whom may very well be congressmen, government officials, and political activists —who do not have the machines, money, or skills to make meaningful numbers from computer tapes.

Both the Census Bureau and other federal agencies must probably limit themselves to the collection and analysis of what Daniel P. Moynihan labels "pan-political" data. This notion refers to the simple fact that no piece of information is apolitical, but that the type of information collected by federal agencies has been and will in the future be designed to service the widest possible spectrum of political interests. This, of course, places certain constraints upon the statistical services within the federal government, and there are certain questions they cannot examine. For this and a number of other reasons, the "multiple source" principle extends beyond the federal government to at least four other areas: local and state governments; public action associations; private research institutions; and the press. Cities, regional planning agencies, and state governments are collecting social data that is far more sophisticated than is possible on a nationwide basis. In so doing, of course, they usually start off with Census data and other federally provided information. Chambers of Commerce and other business organizations are increasingly engaged in surveys bearing on the widening interests of business enterprise. It may be presumed that their example will be followed by labor unions, Community Chests, and other civic action groups on the brink of entering the twentieth century.

One of the most strategic of all roles is played by private research institutions, whether or not university-based. In the 1920's, the National Bureau of Economic Research patiently laid the basis for the national income work taken over by the Department of Commerce in the 1930's. Maintaining the initiative, it then mobilized the intellectual resources needed to guide the continuous improvement and extension of this work by government. Although there is (as yet) no comparable institution in the field of social indicators, there are many research institutions with rapidly expanding capacities and scope. Some specialize in sample surveys on almost any conceivable subject. Some concentrate on specific subject-matter areas. A few of the smaller foundations—particularly the Twentieth Century Fund and the Russell Sage Foundation—have conducted pathbreaking studies involving the collection and analysis of social data.

It seems both likely and desirable that the present multiplicity of sources will become still "more multiple." Technically, specialization demands it. The dynamics of both political action and scientific research suggest that more and better production of social indicators by the federal government (like public expenditures in the Keynesian model) might have a "multiplier effect" on nonfederal collection, analysis, and interpretation.

THE PRINCIPLE OF
"SYSTEMIC DISSONANCE"

There is a delightful (albeit somewhat terrifying) ambiguity behind pending proposals for a national data center. Among advanced students of "information theory," this should be no cause for surprise. Information engineers may be relied upon, in their recurring bursts of artistic enthusiasm, to contribute to misinformation about their work. "Their skill in the precise language of mathematics has not been matched by an ability to cope with the greater ambiguities of the word-language in which mathematics is embedded."[15]

One view of a national data system is rooted in the "informational retrieval" problem. From this point of view, we face an information crisis that may be defined as "the overproduction of information relative to the capacity for the storage, analysis, and distribution to point of need."[16] Under a glutted "market place of ideas," to use the phrase of Oliver Wendell Holmes, information cannot flow freely, an immobility probably far more serious than constraints on the mobility of capital and labor. The exploitation of advancing technology for storing, processing, and distributing information opens up new potentialities for "assembling scientific and technical information and disseminating it to those who need it, whenever and wherever they need it." The more naïve model-builders think these potentialities can be developed through formal structure modeled in accordance with the hierarchical pyramids of Weberian or so-called "classical" organization theory. More realistic organizers think in terms of a two-directional "grid" or network of interconnected organizations. Here the emphasis must be placed on the creation of both (1) a multiplicity of decentralized stations and (2) facilities for the rapid intercommunication of information at a level of sophistication that recognizes data differences.

Another view emphasizes co-ordination through standardized definitions and strongly enforced priorities. If limited to certain kinds of standardized economic data, this could unquestionably lead to cheaper and quicker services. It might also lead to two critical data pathologies: "hardening of the categories," and the monopolization of information.

In the field of transeconomic indicators, the co-ordination approach is particularly dangerous. While more standardization is needed in statistical series, there is an equally serious need for sustained and sophisticated

---

15 Bertram M. Gross, "Information Theorists," *The Managing of Organizations* (New York: Free Press, 1964), Vol. 1, pp. 210–213. Reference is here made to Bar Hillel's "An Examination of Information Theory," *Philosophy of Science* (1955): "We see again and again that, in spite of the official disavowal of the interpretation of 'information' as 'what is conveyed by a signal sequence,' 'amount of information,' officially meant to be a measure of the rarity of the kinds of transmissions of signal sequences, acquires also and sometimes predominantly, the connotation of a measure . . . of the kinds of facts . . . designated by these signal sequences" (p. 94). Shannon and Weaver themselves contribute to this ambiguity by stating that their use of the word "communication" involves "not only written and oral speech, but also music, the pictorial arts, the theatre, ballet, and in fact all human behavior" (Claude Shannon and Warren Weaver, *The Mathematical Theory of Communication* [Urbana: University of Illinois Press, 1949], p. 95). Norbert Wiener has done his share by equating the engineer's kind of "information" with meaning (*The Human Use of Human Beings* [Boston: Houghton-Mifflin, 1950], p. 7–8).

16 Bertram M. Gross, "Operation Basic: The Retrieval of Wasted Knowledge," *The Journal of Communications* (June 1962), pp. 67–83.

challenge of standardized definitions and methods of interpretation. A splendid example is the constructive criticism that Daniel Glaser and Albert D. Biderman[17] have been leveling for years against the Federal Bureau of Investigation (FBI) Crime Index. Although sociologists regard the index as a statistical monstrosity, we should bear in mind that the FBI under J. Edgar Hoover has merely been carefully following the best advice obtainable from the sociologists of a now-defunct era. Is there not a danger that—with large federal grants and contracts "guiding" the work of dispersed data centers and research institutions—this experience may be repeated on a larger scale?

It has been pointed out that "official data will always be too 'official,' reflecting the bias of collection agencies or the institutional rigidities of major interpreters. The categories themselves will never be automatically adjusted."[18] Hardening of the categories is hardly curable without continual challenges and debates that might lead to recurring reconstruction of categories.[19] Within the federal government, both the Bureau of Labor Statistics and the Census Bureau have often been sensitive to these debates. Other agencies with a political stake in outmoded concepts and inaccurate statistics turn a deaf ear to all calls for innovation.

Here the media of communication could play strategic roles. As Fontaine points out in Chapter 10, radio, the press, and magazines have a long way to go in communicating significant information. Indeed, their record in keeping up with the advances in the social sciences will have to improve considerably before achieving mediocrity. But there is also the role of *challenge* and *exposé*—as played by the long line of "muckrakers" and crusading journalists. These free-wheeling challengers may bring to public attention official data that has been suppressed. They may find flaws or inconsistencies in officially released data. At times, they even collect information on their own and prepare the way for the official data of the next generation. Insofar as the mass media are concerned, these roles are played by only the small handful of first-class newspapers in the country: the *Washington Post*, the *New York Times*, the *Wall Street Journal*, and perhaps four or five others. Fortunately, a healthy yeast is provided by small circulation publications. Most of these—like the *New Republic*, the *Nation*, *Ramparts*, the *Reporter*, the *I. F. Stone Weekly*, and *Dissent*—are on the "Left." Fortunately, with the emergence of a know-something "Right,"

---

[17] See section entitled "A Case Example: Crime Rates," in his "Social Indicators and Goals," Bauer (ed.), *Social Indicators, op. cit.*, pp. 111–129.

[18] "The State of the Nation," in Bauer (ed.), *op. cit.*, p. 260.

[19] The National Bureau of Economic Research is presently preparing major extensions of national income accounting. It will be of considerable interest to see how quickly their proposals are introduced into the "official" accounts.

some slow progress is being made along these lines by William Buckley's *National Review.*

With the increasing utilization of social indicators in the political process, hardening of the categories could have a profound impact on public policy. We now must begin to ask whether, as we develop better information retrieval facilities, they should not ease the flow of *dissonant—* as well as coordinated—information and whether, if major parts of our national data system (such as the census, for example) are to be made more systematic, to tolerate, preserve, or perhaps even promote the dissonance of those who challenge the relevance, accuracy, or credibility of official data. Should we not recognize an important role for "systemic dissonance?"

With the increasing utilization of sophisticated information in the policy-making process, the old aphorism "knowledge is power" has a particularly contemporary ring. With government playing a greater role in the production of this information, there is an obvious danger of government monopolization of information. This could manifest itself in two ways: (1) narrow specification of information produced and (2) tight control of access to it. We suspect that many city planning and urban renewal agencies often sit on data lest "progress" be impaired by those who would learn they must suffer "short-run" hardships. While much of this condition is the result of bread-and-butter political expediency, it often stems from a misguided determination that the maintenance of ignorance is a beneficial form of social control.

A more subtle and possibly more significant problem is that much of our information is being produced for and by a few groups in our society. In this regard Andrew Kopkind, an informed but skeptical observer of the growth and utilization of specialized information within government has warned:

> There is no general agreement on "human values." But the people who frame the questions about society and plan the future can easily, and unconsciously, inject their own values into the answers they receive. . . . The danger is that government and corporate elites will monopolize the business of question-asking, and so manipulate the attitudes of the society they are pretending to serve as disinterested technicians.[20]

In a similar vein, conservatives may argue, with a certain amount of justification, that most empirical data generated by contemporary social science has been motivated by and supports a liberal critique of American society.

---

[20] "The Future-Planners," *New Republic,* February 25, 1967.

Both liberal and conservative discussions will be illuminated by Amitai Etzioni's perceptive warnings, in Chapter 2, against the dangers or "dysfunctions" in internally valid indicators. Both will be aided by Raymond A. Bauer's profound observations, in Chapter 3, on the inevitability of error and the indispensibility of human judgment.

There are no simple solutions to these problems, which will become more acute as social indicators are further introduced into the political process. It is hoped that our discussion of multiple sources and "systemic dissonance" will suggest some possible solutions. The success of these solutions will in large measure be determined by whether Congress assumes a creative and critical role in the future development of social indicators.

THE PRINCIPLE OF LEGISLATIVE RESPONSIBILITY

The Founding Fathers of the United States, true children of the Enlightenment, clearly recognized the informational functions of government. In Article 1, Section 2, they provided for a decennial census (the first ever called for by a national constitution). In Article II, Section 3, they recognized the importance of making information available to Congress instead of having it carefully guarded by executive officials: "The President shall from time to time give to the Congress Information of the State of the Union." In the Bill of Rights they provided safeguards for the freedom of speech and the press, as well as personal privacy. But their greatest contribution was the "systemic dissonance" built into its provisions for the separate authority of the Congress, the President, the Supreme Court, and the states.

This is not the place to review the circumstances under which this "separation of powers" may lead to deadlock and breakdown or those under which it may lead to unified and concerted action, nor is there space to discuss the role of the Supreme Court (touched upon by Professor Konvitz in Chapter 5) or that of the states and localities (briefly referred to above) with respect to social data.

But since the provision of more and better social indicators is usually discussed by technicians whose natural orientation is toward the agencies in the executive branch of government, we find it essential to conclude this discussion with a few words on the responsibility of the Congress.

This responsibility takes two forms: (1) the airing of new ideas (including those that may be "born before their time"); and (2) the criticism of, and debate on, executive information and proposals. The former is essential to bring hidden issues into the open and rescue creative ideas that may get knifed in the dark. The latter provides opportunities for almost any organized group in the country, no matter how weak, to have its views expressed indirectly in committee hearings or represented by some member of Congress.

We would be less than frank if we did not concede that the great majority of technicians concerned with the development of social indicators are rarely aware of the constructive role played by Congress in laying the groundwork for major innovations in public policy. Similarly, in the development of the Employment Act of 1946, many of the most ardent proponents of full (or maximum) employment thought almost exclusively in executive agency terms. Some of them regarded the Act's provisions for a Joint Economic Committee of Congress as merely a sop to congressional critics.

Twenty-one years after the Act's passage, the Joint Economic Committee has, in the words of one observer, become "the nom de plume of the world's largest class in economics, in which astute and overworked Congressmen and Senators take turns in being pupils and instructors to most of the Nation's economists."[21] It has investigated data gaps and challenged one-sided or defective executive interpretations. In the sphere of economic data, the Joint Economic Committee has probably been the most significant source of healthy and invigorating "systemic dissonance."

At present, various members of Congress have offered a wealth of important proposals bearing upon our knowledge of social conditions, problems, and change. Among these are measures to set up a National Social Science Foundation (proposed by Senator Harris of Oklahoma), for contracts with nongovernmental agencies for the application of "systems analysis" to social problems (proposed by Senator Nelson of Wisconsin), to provide for a mid-decade census (proposed by Senator Ribicoff of Connecticut), and to set up an "office of legislative evaluation" in the General Accounting Office (proposed by Senator Ribicoff of Connecticut). The first three of these, let it be noted, provide for executive activities alone, and the fourth for activities by a so-called "autonomous agency" to help the legislature.

Like the Employment Act of 1948, the "Full Opportunity and Social Accounting Act" sponsored by Senator Mondale and his group deals directly with *both* the executive and legislative branches. Obviously, if there is to be an annual Social Report of the President, the President will need sustained, professional work of a transdepartmental nature and on a full-time basis. The legislative proposal for a Council of Social Advisers focuses attention on this organizational problem. But it would be unfor-

---

[21] Stanley Lebergott, *Men Without Work* (New York: Prentice-Hall, 1965), p. 174.

tunate if this proposal should detract attention from the equally significant idea of a Joint Committee on the Social Report.

As indicated at the beginning of this chapter, it is possible that the President may soon initiate a series of annual Social Reports to Congress. This could be done without new legislative authority. But what will happen to such reports? Will they receive serious and sustained attention and review in Congress? Outside of Congress, will they be accepted as more authoritative than they could possibly be?

At this point let us be perfectly clear that the analogy with economic indicators and goals should not be carried too far. In the noneconomic aspects of social measurement and social policy, we have lagged far behind the progress made in measuring economic change and ordering economic information. With broader social measures, the complexities are still greater and the dangers of oversimplification still more threatening. Here, even more than in the economic field, we need legislative responsibility in encouraging a variety of approaches, promoting multiple sources, and nourishing "systemic dissonance." Thus far, the only proposal in this important area is that of Senator Mondale and his ten colleagues (including the Chairman of the Joint Economic Committee) for a Joint Congressional Committee on the Social Report. If this is to be the "nom de plume" for the world's largest classroom in social information and social policy, its teachers and students—be they social scientists or legislators—must be willing to face intellectual and moral problems of monumental dimensions.

An important set of Senate hearings on the Mondale Bill was conducted in the summer of 1967 by the Senate Subcommittee on Research under the chairmanship of one of the measure's sponsors, Senator Fred Harris (Okla.). The hearings began with an unusual "Senate Seminar" presided over by Senators and participated in by many academics. A week or so later, they were interrupted by the urban disorders that had been predicted by many of the participants. The Harris-Mondale initiatives in focussing upon these problems during the hearings and in proposing government action led to the creation of the National Advisory Commission on Civil Disorders and the appointment of Senator Harris as a commission member.

SOCIAL CHANGE AND CONCEPT–
OBSOLESCENCE

Westerners are quick to point out that in the "transitional" societies of Africa, Asia, the Middle East, and Latin America, rapid technological change is usually accompanied by institutional, cultural, and conceptional rigidities. Our social scientists can easily see that people who grew up in agricultural peasant societies have difficulty in understanding—let alone keeping statistical track of—the confusions of the industrialization process.

We are somewhat less eager to see the motes in our own eyes. Although living in societies undergoing changes at least equally—and probably much more—confusing, we have not distinguished ourselves by an awareness of our own rigidities. Many of us cling to old concepts as tightly as some people in other societies may cling to caste lines, taboos, astrology, and witch-doctor cures. Our faithfulness to the past may, indeed, be reinforced by the modern magic overtones provided by an elaborate statistical series and electronic computers. The case to which Professor Etzioni refers in the first article is no exception. Information on *residence* provided more or less definitive reports on land congestion a century or so ago, when many more of man's activities took place near his home. Today, although only multidimensional population measures can cope with the greater complexities of people-land relations, many people—even some urban planners—rely on residence information alone. Similarly, some proposals for large-scale "data banks" tend to remind one of the man who tried to build his fortune by collecting the world's biggest stockpile of calendars from previous years. The bank metaphor (used repeatedly by those whose enthusiasm for data-processing machinery exceeds their concern for what is processed) obscures the fact that information, in our era of information explosion, may depreciate as rapidly as money in the wildest of currency inflations.

We hope that, during the coming years, increasing attention will be given to the processes of obsolescence at work on the concepts and the definitions underlying our social information. Obviously, custom and habit are important factors. Basic theory and research in the halls of academe tend to lag behind the mad rush of events. As Albert D. Biderman has graphically illustrated, strong interest and pressure groups usually mobilize to defend existing statistical series and to resist basic conceptual and definitional changes.[22] Any such changes are apt to have political implications at some time in the future. These implications may be particularly anxiety-producing for people more fearful of "rocking the boat" than of sticking an ostrich-like head in the sand. A single, misleading measure—such as the "absolute income line" discussed in the article "Poverty, Inequality, and Conflict"—may serve the "administrative convenience" of an embattled government agency.

---

[22] "Social Indicators and Goals," in Raymond A. Bauer (ed.), *Social Indicators* (Cambridge, Mass.: M.I.T. Press, 1966), pp. 68–153.

We urge special attention to the *technical imperative of data-comparability*. The time series is the hard core of our national information system. The essence of a good time series—on unemployment, burglary, students, scientists, or anything else—is that the figure on 1967 be based on *exactly the same definitions as were used in 1957*. Otherwise, the figures on change will reflect changes in *both* situations and definitions. Accordingly, all data-collection establishments are very wary about definitional changes. Knowing that they cannot change the conceptual rules every year, they tend to postpone all suggested improvements until consensus may be reached on the most significant ones. This calculated "hardening of the categories" may last a decade or more. When changes are made, it is sometimes possible to recalculate the old series in accordance with the revised definition or at least to develop some useful estimates. This is a costly and time-consuming enterprise. In other cases, there is no choice but to start afresh, signaling the use of new definitions and calling attention to the lack of comparability with the past.

This comparability-relevance conflict may be technically by-passed whenever the conceptual innovation leads not to the revision of an old statistical definition but to the addition of new statistical dimensions. Yet these new dimensions—apart from their policy implications—can easily disturb the neat orderliness of old-fashioned data. It is always safer to be precisely irrelevant or wrong rather than vaguely relevant or right.

SOME STEPS TOWARD
CONCEPTUAL ADVANCE

In looking through the various chapters of this volume, the reader will notice there is little discussion of statistical techniques or methods of numerical analysis. Indeed, where authors address themselves most directly to various statistical series—as with Miller, Cohen, Glaser and Goldman, for example—their purpose is to suggest new *concepts* and *definitions* that precede the tasks of collection, computation, or recomputation. In the broadest sense, most of the authors are attempting to create new definitions of the situations with which they deal. From his own perspective (a combination of both personal background and institutional role), each author shows how a variety of new frames of reference could be best employed in policy analysis.

Let us now briefly summarize the efforts toward conceptual advance illustrated by these chapters.

STRESSING THE UTILITY OF
SOME TRADITIONAL MEASURES

Two powerful personalities, Richard C. Scammon and Leon H. Key-serling, focus on concepts that are solidly imbedded in our political rhetoric but the significance of which is often ignored or not fully understood. In "Electoral Participation," Scammon, a former Director of the Bureau of the Census and one of the most respected election analysts in the country, examines the simple act of voting. In a straightforward and lucid fashion, he sketches out the basic "facts" of voter participation in the United States. Implicit in the presentation of "facts" is that during a period when there is great stress on expanding democratic participation beyond the annual trip to the polling booth, there remains much to be done to make these excursions more available to more Americans.

In "Employment and the 'New Economics,'" Leon H. Keyserling criticizes present unemployment statistics as seriously understating the extent to which manpower resources are wasted. Pointing out how the present concept of unemployment contributes to inadequate policy-formu-lation, he urges the modernization of the unemployment definitions, used by the Bureau of Labor Statistics and of the employment goals set forth by the Council of Economic Advisers.

As a member (and finally Chairman) of the Council of Economic Advisers throughout the Truman administration, Keyserling was one of the leaders in establishing sustained economic growth as a major objective of public policy. Since then his role has been that of a "Prophet in the Wings," relentlessly criticizing deviations from this goal and continuously proposing policies for using economic resources to meet basic social needs.

REDEFINING KEY PROBLEM AREAS

"Poverty" and "Crime" are the labels that are applied to what many Americans believe are most pressing social problems. How these labels are officially defined has a profound impact on policies in these areas. S. M. Miller *et al* in "Poverty, Inequally and Conflict" and Daniel Glaser in "Crime and Delinquency" suggest fully developed conceptual schemes that go well beyond currently employed official definitions. Both can serve as the basis of a critique of existing policies and for developing new, and hopefully, more effective programs.

In "Crime and Delinquency" Daniel Glaser presents a frame of refer-ence with which we can view the variety of types of crime and how they relate to various agencies attempting to reduce their occurrence. The clarity of Glaser's presentation could be deceiving to some because he has been able to approach a complex and emotion-charged subject without visceral appeals or prolix prose. His approach is straightforward and clear; this most probably reflects the many years he has spent in educating public officials as well as students. Furthermore, as a man with long experience in improving correctional practices, his conceptual scheme is geared to the goals of police and correctional officials rather than to the development of some abstract notions about criminality.

In "Poverty, Inequality, and Conflict," S. M. Miller sharply attacks the present "income line" definition of poverty. First, he shows the need for using "comparative income" as well as absolute income and for dealing with income security as well as income level. Secondly, he demonstrates the desirability of a three-dimensional economic approach that includes assets and basic services along with income. Thirdly, he sets forth the social dimensions of poverty—in terms of deficiencies in self-respect, status, and opportunities for participation in decision-making. He thereby develops—with the help of his collaborators—a sophisticated conceptual formulation capable of dealing with, rather than dodging, emerging issues of justice and injustice in American society.

Miller's formulation is written from an unusual perspective. Trained first as an economist and then as a sociologist who has made major contributions in the area of social mobility, he does not bother about artificial distinctions between economic and social factors. It is thus not surprising that he brings mobility-analysis into the framework of poverty policy. Further, Miller keeps his feet in several political camps. An advisor to a number of community and militant action groups, he also serves as an official of the Ford Foundation and as a consultant to several government agencies. In this light, one could interpret his piece as an attempt to approach "the Establishment" with the social critique of the civil rights movement and elements in "New Left" thought, thereby demonstrating to the militants the terms of discourse and the type of analysis with which to approach policy-makers.

REEXAMINING POLICY PARAMETERS

The chapters written by Wilbur Cohen and Philip Lee deal with difficult policy areas with candor and intellectual sophistication. Their efforts are particularly remarkable because both men are high government officials and the semi-official pronouncements of men in such positions are generally exercises in polished banality. These men, however, confront us with conceptual explorations of great insight and probity.

In "Learning and Education," Wilbur Cohen first delineates the major structural changes taking place in American education. He shows where our concepts have been outdated and demonstrates that we must not limit or take the narrow view that education is something that takes place during a person's youth and only within the traditional educational institutions. The new concept of "the learning force" indicates that education can be a life-long process and need not be limited to the traditional educational establishment.

Cohen's outline of a wide-ranging research program is a sharp departure from the traditional "educationist" approach. Coming from an "action intellectual" who is a principal architect of Great Society measures (as well as the Health, Education, and Welfare Under Secretary), his views provide "White Paper" intimations of the future direction of national policy.

In "Health and Well-Being," Philip R. Lee presents a definition of health that encompasses far more than the typical clinician's view based on the incidence of disease. Lee views mortality, morbidity, and disability in the context not only of physiological but also of social and economic factors. Looking beyond our present definitions of health, Lee points to the day when research presently underway may lead to positive measures of well-being.

Dr. Lee is a practicing physician now serving as Assistant Secretary of Health, Education, and Welfare for Health and Scientific Affairs. Without the pretensions that often characterize academics and government officials, he presents a broad vision of what constitutes the parameters of health. Like Cohen's paper, Lee's has the character of a non-official "White Paper" in the area of health and well-being.

GRAPPLING WITH COMPLEX
MULTIDIMENSIONAL INDICATORS

The chapters by Joseph Fisher, Daniel Moynihan and Robin Williams present careful analyses of the variety of measures within a broadly defined area. Each essentially asks what sort of data is relevant to a given area and what does it mean. Furthermore, each man addresses himself to some vast and complex landscape—Fisher, the natural environment; Moynihan, the urban environment, and Williams, our society's values.

In "The Urban Environment: General," Daniel P. Moynihan, a man with one foot in government and the other in the academic world, asks what sort of information social scientists can provide to urban policy-makers. This linkage between social science and public policy has been a long-time concern of Moynihan. As an Assistant Secretary in the Department of Labor, he authored the now famous (and to some infamous) "Report on the Negro Family," which brought together a wealth of information about the family structure of low income people.[23] Reaction to this report helped celebrate (if not terminate) Moynihan's last stint in government service.

Now, out of government and presently the Director of the M.I.T.-Harvard Joint Center for Urban Studies, Moynihan has not abandoned his role of providing linkages between Academia and the world of politics. His chapter is addressed to two audiences—social scientists and public officials. For social scientists he indicates the utility of a "social systems" model in dealing with urban areas as contrasted with the traditional "City of Things" model used by city planners. In so doing he indicates to local officials the kinds of relevant information that can be provided by social scientists.

Similar linkage-functions are performed by Joseph C. Fisher in his chapter, "The Natural Environment." An economist with long and varied background in government, Mr. Fisher is now President of Resources for the Future, a private research organization which specializes in the study of natural resources. His chapter is an attempt to develop understandable indicators of our natural environment from a base of information which is both technically complex and incomplete. Fisher has made great strides in this painstaking effort, but his major finding is that greater efforts will be required in the future.

Robin M. Williams, Jr. focuses more on academic and humanistic issues in his chapter, "Individual and Group Values." A sociologist who has made major contributions in survey research and social theory, Williams pulls off a brilliant *tour de force* by developing a conceptual framework which he uses to describe and analyze vast amounts of social science information about value. The scope, insight and clarity of this exercise is directed primarily at an academic audience, but his piece is of vital interest to anyone seriously considering the condition of our society. For his colleagues, Williams outlines a good deal of their unfinished business and for the general reader he explains what social science has to offer about the subtle question of the nature of American values.

IMPROVING INFORMATION IN
"BACKWARD AREAS"

In some areas there is very little available information or the existing data is grossly misunderstood. Here the problem is to perform the intellec-

---

[23] *Report on the Negro Family* (Washington, D.C.: U.S. Department of Labor, 1966).

tual spade-work to prepare the ground for the collection and interpretation of relevant data. The chapters of the arts, science and technology, democratic participation, and social breakdown are efforts directed to this end.

In "The Art of Measuring the Arts," Alvin Toffler attempts to initiate both quantitative and qualitative definitions of a situation just beginning to become a concern of national policy-makers. In addition to calling for the systematic collection of information in all the arts, he suggests a series of quite specific criteria for the qualitative evaluation of artistic activities.

As a professional journalist, Mr. Toffler is free from that intellectual timidity which is endemic to Academia. He has been sufficiently uninhibited to give us a wide-ranging framework which could serve as a baseline for debates over future government perspectives toward the arts. Broad and provocative statements are very much in Toffler's style. His book *The Culture Consumers* opened up recent debates over the extent and characteristics of what is referred to as the "culture explosion."[24]

"Science, Technology and Change" is a wide-ranging piece in which John McHale explores the inadequacy of present indicators on the substantive content and organizational setting of scientific activities. In calling for new conceptual frameworks, McHale underscores the superficiality of the use of purely quantitative surrogates and calls for direct consideration of the quality of scientific efforts.

One would expect such broad and bold proposals from a colleague and collaborator of Buckminster Fuller, that remarkably creative engineer-architect-inventor. Quite on his own, McHale addresses himself to his subject from a rich and varied background that includes previous careers as both an artist and a medical technician.

Sidney Verba's "Democratic Participation" gives us a definition of democracy that goes far beyond the ballot box and relates all forms of political participation to the resources, motivations, and institutions that make it possible. He raises vital questions concerning the successfulness of participation and the decision-makers' willingness to accede to greater participation. He raises a series of major paradoxes that demand attention both in improving and in interpreting all data in this field.

While Verba is well known in academic circles, he is one of the West Coast intellectuals geographically removed from the Boston-New York-Washington consultation network. As a political outsider with strong convictions, he opts for broader official interest in democratic participation. A first-rate scholar, Verba presents a careful and reasoned critique that could greatly expand traditional perspectives toward democracy.

In "Social Breakdown," while not directly outlining new concepts, Nathan Goldman begins to lay bare some widely held notions about social

---

[24] Alvin Toffler, *The Culture Consumers* (New York: St. Martin's Press, 1964).

disorganization—or in more popular terms, "a breakdown in morality." In examining available data on family breakdown, addiction, personal breakdown, and sexual deviation, he casts series doubts on the reliability of the conventional evidence of social breakdown. More significantly, he suggests that such things as divorce and even addiction may not be signs of social breakdown, but may, in fact, be factors in social organization and stability.

The nature of Goldman's piece can, in good part, be understood by two factors. First, while Goldman has had considerable clinical experience in the problems he discusses, he has been somewhat distant from national policy-making processes and thus does not have to pay homage to the conventional wisdom. Secondly, like many University-of-Chicago-trained sociologists, he questions the meaning of "accepted morality," which, if taken at face value, will stand in the way of creative social analysis.

THREE MEN AND THEIR PASSIONS

The chapters by Barry Gottehrer, Milton R. Konvitz, and Andre Fontaine differ markedly from the other chapters in this volume. The primary focus of these chapters is not on either the development of better indicators or on how social information can be best employed in the formulation of public policy. All three men make valiant efforts to be "objective" and "scientific", but their overwhelming concerns—civil liberties for Konvitz, New York City for Gottehrer, and newspapers for Fontaine—lead them away from a discussion of indicators *per se* and toward more normative presentations. The emphasis of these chapters is instructive. It reminds us that the observation of society must ultimately be rooted in human passions and values. To ignore these concerns can make one's claim to being human dubious and one's analysis somewhat fatuous.

In "The Urban Environment: New York City," Barry Gottehrer presents a testament to both the administration of Mayor John Lindsay and the ability of the citizens of New York City to confront their massive problems. This testament reflects Gottehrer's passionate commitment to New York City—its people and their difficulties. As a journalist he was the chief writer of the award-winning "New York in Crisis" series in the *Herald Tribune*. Now in a more active role as assistant to the Mayor, he is Lindsay's "Man in the Slums"—attempting to control over-zealous policemen during draft protests, developing communication between neighborhood groups and the Mayor's offices—any place where the cutting edge of government confronts the citizens of New York City.

A different sort of passionate commitment comes through in Milton R. Konvitz' "Civil Liberties." Konvitz is a man of deep moral commitment and a long-time activist in securing both civil liberties and rights for all citizens. From this perspective he argues that one does not have to count how many books are banned or how many men are deprived of their right to vote before one can act. Implicit in this is that our civil liberties are best protected by men steeped in the prophetic, rather than the sociological tradition.

André Fontaine in "The Mass Media: A Need for Greatness," gives evidence of his love-hate relationship with the American newspapers and magazines. This relationship was developed during his long career as a journalist. Now an inspired teacher of the craft of journalism, on one hand he asserts that American newspapers and magazines are the best in the world and on the other he presents a catalogue of their defects. The qualitative nature of these defects has not and possibly cannot be subjected to "objective" measurement. For Fontaine their cure, and not their measurement, is the first order of business.

EXPLORING INFORMATION METHODOLOGY

Methodology—the changing body of rules and principles that govern inquiry—poses very difficult problems to all who attempt to develop more useful social indicators. These problems are intellectually challenging and little understood outside Academia. But how they are resolved can have a significant impact on the quality of information provided to policy-makers. It is fortunate that this volume provides three cogent and provocative examinations of methodological issues. Chapter 14 by Otis Dudley Duncan, Chapter 2 co-authored by Amitai Etzioni and Edward W. Lehman, and Chapter 3 by Raymond A. Bauer provide the general reader with a useful introduction to methodological concerns.

In "Discrimination Against Negroes," Otis Dudley Duncan uses his substantive question as a vehicle to explain how one goes about ecological and life-cycle analyses. From this exercise we learn a good deal about the condition of black people in the United States. But we learn even more about the intellectual strategies involved in measuring discrimination. The carefulness and clarity of this effort is typical of Duncan, who has the well-deserved reputation of being one of the most competent ecologists in American sociology. Duncan does not limit himself to a discussion of the craft of analysis, but uses his more narrow and technical presentation to raise larger methodological questions, such as what are social indicators, what do they indicate, and what sort of data is required to produce them?

Etzioni and Lehman in "Some Dangers in 'Valid' Social Measurement," examine two related questions, one methodological and the other political. They first explore the problem of internal validity: the relationship between our concepts and their measures. They then go on to examine how the quest for more "valid" measures can produce a store of information that is dysfunctional in decision-making. These concerns synthesize Etzioni's diverse interests. His interest in validity quite obviously stems from his extensive work in organization theory. How more "valid" measures influence political action is an issue related to his activities in liberal political action groups and to his somewhat more academic interest in societal guidance.

In "Societal Feedback" Bauer presents an overview of how an information system can best service the needs of government decision-makers in coming to grips with the future. Bauer is well equipped to deal with such a vast question. Trained as a psychologist, he has made major contributions to political science, Soviet studies, sociology, and business administration. This varied and intense academic background, coupled with consultation experience at the higher levels of government and business, has prepared him to begin to develop a series of guidelines for the vast information system that will be required in the last third of the century. These guidelines reflect Bauer's intimate awareness of the social sciences' potential and limitations in providing information that is timely and relevant to policy decisions.

In conclusion, we feel that we can speak for all the authors in this volume in predicting that the development of new theories, concepts and information to meet the critical needs of our changing society will be a slow and painful process. This volume amply demonstrates the inadequacy of many of our present concepts. It also demonstrates the tremendous potential for improved social information, indicating some of the roads that must be traversed in order to achieve this potential.

There is, however, a good deal of nonsense written about this quest for better social intelligence. One is often confronted with a vision of the year 2000, when lab-coated social scientists will scurry about some vast computer facility and announce at regular intervals the latest increment to the Index of Social Progress (or Gross Social Product). It would be well, in conclusion, to point out the fantastic nonsense that lies behind such visions.

Effective social intelligence will require human information systems designed to meet human needs. Such systems must be able to produce a variety of up-to-date information on a wide range of questions and also must be sufficiently flexible, so that they can respond rapidly to requests for new sorts of data. Such information systems cannot rely solely on rigorous quantitative data. More often than not, significant policy questions precede the existence of relevant quantitative data and must be answered well before such data can be produced. The vital dimensions of many policy questions can only be established with phenomenological research methods such as interviewing and participant observation.

Moreover, effective information systems need not necessarily require trained social scientists. One of the authors of this volume, Barry Gottehrer, has helped develop in New York City a system that feeds into the mayor's office a rich array of information about thirteen neighborhoods in New York City. This information system can rapidly answer such questions as: how well are the police trusted in neighborhood X, or how many jobs are needed for drop-outs in neighborhood Y? It is staffed by bartenders, housewives, cab drivers, neighborhood leaders—ordinary human beings who are sensitive to what is going on around them.[25]

Finally, there is something more to the "quality of life" than can ever be fully expressed in quantitative measures. The moral and aesthetic goals which many of us seek can be only partly comprehended by the hard indicators which we use to bring them to fruition.

This matter has been vigorously raised by Corinne Gilb:

> Human needs for myths, festivals, dignity, love, belongingness, and self-realization cannot be adequately assessed solely by social science methods. . . . As you know, the economic, scientific, military, and governmental systems in the United States are increasingly interdependent. They in turn influence—directly or indirectly —every other aspect of American life. We need deeper knowledge of what these interconnections are. Questions and research methods are needed which cut through and transcend the methods of approaches now being used by particular segments of the total system or by particular disciplines such as economics or sociology.[26]

Elsewhere, the same author has suggested that "for scholars the ultimate goal should be not the kind of artificial scientific reductionism whose logical endpoint is the Brave New World, but rather a multi-dimensional set of values, theories, concepts, and methods which converge at that high point where science and art are—in a sense—the same."[27]

Professor Gilb has thus defined the paradox underlying our goals for social information. To cope with the intelligence gap intelligently, we must develop conceptual innovations that help us not only to obtain and use improved quantitative data, but also to appreciate the importance—in Galileo's words—of "what is not yet measurable," and may, indeed, never be.

---

[25] For a report on this effort, see Barry Gottehrer, *Summer in Our City: Report to Mayor John V. Lindsay,* mimeographed, Feb. 1, 1968.

[26] Testimony before Senate Subcommittee on Research, Senate Committee on Government Operations, on S. 843, July 20, 1967.

[27] Corinne Lathrop Gilb, "Time and Change in Twentieth-Century Thought," *Journal of World History,* Vol. IX, No. 4 (1966), pp. 867–880.

2

SOME DANGERS IN "VALID" SOCIAL MEASUREMENT

AMITAI ETZIONI
and
EDWARD W. LEHMAN

R arely have social analysts been as forthright about the pitfalls and limitations of their programs as the proponents of the systematic measurement and accounting of society's present and changing states.[1] While most
of the other chapters in this book have focused on the problems of
measurement in specific substantive areas, this chapter represents a preliminary effort at a general statement of some of the potential dysfunctions[2]

[1] Basic to the field is Bertram M. Gross, *The State of the Nation: Social Systems
Accounting* (London: Tavistock, 1966). See also his "The Social State of the
Union," *Trans-Action,* Vol. 3 (1965), pp. 5–11. For various relevant essays, see
Raymond A. Bauer (ed.), *Social Indicators* (Cambridge, Mass.: M.I.T. Press, 1966)
and Wilbert E. Moore and Eleanor Bernert Sheldon, "Monitoring Social Change: A
Conceptual and Programmatic Statement," *Proceedings of the Social Statistics Sec-
tion, 1965* (Washington, D.C.: American Statistical Association, 1966), pp. 144–149.

[2] For the nonsociologists in our audience, it may be worth-while to explain that
the notion of "dysfunction" refers to the negative consequences of a particular social
item for specified part(s) of a specified social system. It is a useful concept for the
analysis of the "dangers" of social measurement because it makes clear that the
referent of the potential negative consequences we are considering is some social
collectivity and not a single individual or congeries of random individuals. For the
most part, the collectivity discussed in our examples is society or one or more of its
major subsystems. For a systematic treatment of the concept of dysfunction and for
an analysis of its location in the "paradigm of structural-functional analysis," see
Robert K. Merton, "Manifest and Latent Functions," in *Social Theory and Social
Structure* (rev. ed.; Glencoe, Ill.: Free Press, 1957), pp. 19–84.

involved in the use of social measurements. We are not suggesting that social accounting cannot or ought not to be carried forward; on the contrary, we hope that pointing to some of the possible negative consequences will allow reducing if not eliminating these side-effects, and thus enhance the effectiveness of the program as a whole.

Our treatment is entirely preliminary. As yet, we are unable to present anything approaching a full paradigm of potential dysfunctions of social measurement and of mechanisms for avoiding them. We here focus on one segment of such a paradigm: the dysfunctions which flow from problems of *internal validity*, since it seems to us that several pitfalls of social measurement relate in one way or another to this problem. Internal validity refers to the extent of correspondence between a social science concept and its operational definition. We are eschewing consideration of the negative consequences that derive from: (1) the extent to which the procedures described in an operational definition produce unambiguous data (that is, reliability), and (2) the "truth" of hypotheses that relate operationally defined categories to one another (that is, external validity).

The basic premise of this paper is that the dangers of what Bertram Gross has labeled the "New Philistinism" are neither unique to economic measurement nor merely passing phenomena in the history of societal analysis[3]; rather, they point to abiding dilemmas in most social measurements. In the pursuit of greater and greater accuracy, there often develops a disparity between a societal concept as theoretically formulated and the operational definition by which it is empirically measured. *Fractional measurement* appears to be a permanent problem for social research, since it is difficult to construct an operational definition that covers a concept in all its ramifications and dimensions.

In addition to the difficulties of fractional measurement, social accounting gives rise to two related problems. First, there is the question of *indirect measurement*. Social analysts frequently find it expedient to measure societal concepts by using data originally collected for other purposes. Although such measurements have distinct advantages, they tend to intensify —we shall see—some of the problems that flow from fractional measurements. The second problem arises from *formalistic-aggregative measurement* of collective attributes. In characterizing social systems, there is a tendency to confuse real social units with formal social units and to focus on system qualities which stem from the members' qualities at the expense of system attributes not deriving from the characteristics of individual members. These problems are theoretically subsumable under the general rubric of fractional measurement. However, since the states of social

---

[3] See Gross, *The State of the Nation, op. cit.*, especially pp. 17–19.

systems *per se* are of particular interest in social accounting, the limitations of these measurements deserve separate consideration.

FRACTIONAL MEASUREMENT

SINGLE VERSUS MULTIDIMENSIONAL MEASUREMENTS

The adequate measurement of a social science concept frequently requires the use of more than one indicator. The concept of mental health implies more than the avoidance of psychiatric hospitalization; the quality of a society's educational system cannot be gauged solely by the number of Ph.D.'s it produces; and a man's satisfaction with his job involves more than satisfaction with his income. To build an adequate measurement for such a concept, the various dimensions which underlie it must be specified, and one or more indicators must be found for each dimension. If the research situation required a unified scoring system, these indicators may then be combined into an over-all index. Index-construction demands that at least two decisions about weighting be made: (1) decisions on the relative importance of the various dimensions and indicators; and (2) decisions on the statistical procedures are to be applied to represent the relative value of the various dimensions and indicators.[4]

Erroneous accounting, and hence misbased strategies in societal planning, becomes likely when it is assumed that a concept is measured in its entirety though, in fact, only a fraction of it is measured. For instance, the statistics on discharge rates from mental hospitals and the average length of hospitalization for mental illness might lead to the conclusion that mental illness is becoming less of a problem for our society and that hence the number of beds needed for psychiatric patients can be dropped. At the same time, however, *re*admissions have increased at an even greater pace.[5] As Freeman and Simmons have put it: "fewer beds may be needed, but the patients keep them warm for each other."[6]

---

[4] For a comprehensive treatment of operationalization in the social sciences, see Paul F. Lazarsfeld and Morris Rosenberg (eds.), *The Language of Social Research* (Glencoe, Ill.: Free Press, 1955), Section I, pp. 19–108.

[5] See: The Joint Commission on Mental Illness and Health, *Action for Mental Health* (New York: Basic Books, 1961), esp. pp. 5–23.

[6] Howard E. Freeman and Ozzie G. Simmons, *The Mental Patient Comes Home* (New York: John Wiley and Sons, 1963), p. 3.

Moreover, even among those patients who succeed in remaining in the community, there are, as a number of studies show,[7] considerable differences in the levels of their performances in the familial, occupational, recreational, and associational realms. Many patients are functioning at very marginal levels, and some have "turned their homes into small private hospitals catering to one patient."[8]

It should by now be clear that the advances which have reduced the number and lengths of psychiatric hospitalizations do not imply either that mental illness is declining in the United States or that funds can now be diverted to other action programs. Rather, these statistics should lead to the realization that mental illness has multidimensional ramifications, and that with the decline of the in-hospital population, there seems to be an increase in the out-of-hospital population. Before we can tell what the state of the mental health of the nation is—if resources can be cut and the like— our measurements need to cover *both* populations.

We suggest that, as a general rule, *any measurement of a social science concept that relies on a single indicator should be viewed as dubious.* While simply adding more indicators is of little value if they measure the same dimension, drawing on two or more indicators of *different dimensions* provides at least partial insurance against fractional coverage and its dysfunctions.

In many cases, combining several indicators to form an index yielding a single score may be as misleading as failing to uncover sufficient numbers of dimensions and indicators. The chief danger here is that in the pursuit of a single score, the internal variation among the dimensions that are covered by the index will be ignored. Thus, in his contribution to this symposium, Glaser, after praising the Federal Bureau of Investigation (FBI)'s Index of Crime as a considerable improvement over previous crime indices, notes that "all seven offenses used in this Index are given equal weight, so that a theft of $50 counts as much as murder in the total Index."[9] To return to our earlier example, if only an over-all index is

---

[7] For example, see Leta M. Adler, "Patients of a State Mental Hospital: The Outcome of Their Hospitalization," in Arnold Rose (ed.), *Mental Health and Mental Disorder* (New York: W. W. Norton, 1955), pp. 501–523; Eva Deykin, "The Reintegration of the Chronic Schizophrenic Patient Discharged to His Family and Community as Perceived by the Family," *Mental Hygiene,* Vol. 45 (1961), pp. 235–246; Simon Dinitz, Shirley Angrist, Mark Lefton, and Benjamin Pasamanick, "The Posthospital Psychological Functioning of Former Mental Patients," *Mental Hygiene,* Vol. 45 (1961), pp. 579–588; Freeman and Simmons, *op. cit.;* Thala Weiss and Betty Glasser, "Social Adjustment of Adolescents Discharged from a Mental Hospital," *Mental Hygiene,* Vol. 49 (1965), pp. 378–384.

[8] Weiss and Glasser, *op. cit.,* p. 384.

[9] Daniel Glaser, "National Goals and Indicators for the Reduction of Crime and Delinquency," THE ANNALS of the American Academy of Political and Social Sciences, Vol. 371 (May 1967), pp. 104–126. While this problem may be solved by weighting and still producing one index score, it may often require *also* distinct subindices to assess more adequately the variation within the area covered.

provided for mental health, it may record "no change" over a period of time, while actually there was considerable decline in the in-hospital population and a parallel increase in the out-of-hospital one. Both subindices and over-all ones are hence needed, with the subindices each covering one dimension of the concept being measured.

QUANTITATIVE VERSUS QUALITATIVE DIMENSIONS

Dimensions of a qualitative nature are ignored more frequently than quantitative dimensions, as both Biderman and Gross have noted.[10] For example, Gross and others have shown that national investment has been calculated entirely in terms of quantities of hard goods, to the exclusion of "hidden investments" in improvements in health, education, research and development, training methods,[11] and the qualities of the hard goods themselves. While the distinction between qualitative and quantitative is a relative one, in that the qualitative can be, in principle, converted into quantitative ones, the fact is that number of objects—which is a "natural" quantitative aspect—tends often to be included, while other aspects of the objects, those aspects which cannot be readily counted, are neglected.

The tendency to give preference to the quantitative dimensions of a concept over the qualitative becomes particularly pronounced, the greater the pressure from a sponsor of a project or a program for "immediate, tangible" results. In such situations, quantitative dimensions are focused on, since they are frequently more "visible"[12] and lend themselves more easily to direct and rapid measurement. Such a procedure is often less costly in terms of time, effort, and resources but may be more costly in its broader implications, notably in its misleading effects on policy.

Examples of the excessive reliance on "natural" quantitative dimensions abound in the history of Soviet economic planning. The abuses that occurred during periods when economic quotas were set largely in quantitative terms are highlighted by the story about a Soviet railroad manager,

---

[10] See Albert A. Biderman, "Social Indicators and Goals," in Bauer (ed.), *op. cit.,* pp. 80–82, and Gross, *op. cit.,* pp. 236–238.

[11] For Gross' discussion, see *ibid.,* p. 21. See also: John Kendrick, *Productivity in the United States* (Princeton, N.J.: Princeton University Press, 1961), pp. 104–110; Theodore Schultz, "Investment in Human Capital," *American Economic Review,* Vol. 51 (1961), pp. 1–17; and Theodore Schultz, "Capital Formation by Education," *Journal of Political Economy,* Vol. 68 (1960), pp. 571–583.

[12] "Visibility" refers to the extent to which a social item is capable of being observed by an individual because of his occupancy of a social status. See Merton, *op. cit.,* pp. 219–222.

charged with having to deliver X wagons, but, having nothing to deliver, sending his wagons back and forth—empty. Undue emphasis on quantity over quality was important in Soviet economic statistics even into the post-Stalin era. Nor were the subterfuges of such a system confined to the *sub rosa,* deviant behavior of plant and regional managers. In some instances, they, at least initially, affected governmental policy. For example, under Stalin and until 1958, Soviet agricultural statistics measured output in the form of "biological yield" rather than "barn yield"—that is, *in terms of everything harvested as opposed to the usable harvest.* Whatever the propaganda value of such measurement procedures, this undue stress on quantity (as Khrushchev himself admitted in 1958) made effective governmental agricultural planning very difficult.[13]

As a partial antidote for overreliance on quantitative dimensions, index-builders dealing with societal concepts should ask themselves *as a matter of routine* whether or not their concept has any qualitative dimensions. This would provide the realm of social accounting with mechanisms analogous to the quality-control units that exist in some industries. Automobile manufacturers, for instance, have found that the danger of producing numerous defective cars is reduced by placing a special unit engaged in quality or precision control at the end of the assembly line. The effectiveness of a plant is, thus, judged not only by the amount and cost of production but also by the number of cars sent back for readjustment. In measuring societal aspects, there ought to be a routine procedure for "sending back" newly constructed indices in which qualitative considerations have been omitted. The nearest approximation of such a situation probably occurs in the computation of the cost-of-living index, in which constituent items are periodically re-evaluated.

MEANS VERSUS GOALS

The means used by social units to attain their goals are often more easily measured than the goals themselves. This seems to be the case because means are more inherently quantifiable than goals. The measurement of means involves the measurement of the human and nonhuman resources which are applied to goal-attainment as well as some measurement of the human activities geared to the acquisition and allocation of

---

[13] See: Abram Bergson, "Reliability and Usability of Soviet Statistics: A Summary Appraisal," *The American Statistician,* Vol. 7 (June–July 1953), pp. 19–23, and Robert W. Campbell, "Problems of United States–Soviet Economic Comparisons," in *Comparisons of the United States and Soviet Economics,* Part I (Washington, D.C.: Subcommittee on Economic Statistics, Joint Economic Committee, Congress of the United States, 1959), pp. 13–30.

these resources. Goals, in contrast, are more "intangible" because they are "symbolic" items and not part of social structure; that is, as we see it, the goals of any social unit are desired states of affairs which the unit attempts to realize. Goals are thus *intended outputs*. (We deal here with real goals and not those announced for public relations, or "stated goals.") The goals, of course, are those subject to study and not necessarily those of the observer or analyst.

The temptation to substitute the measurement of means for the measurement of goals increases, the more "intangible" the goals are themselves. For instance, the goals of religious organizations are inherently more "intangible" than those of comercial or industrial enterprises. Churches are in the business of "salvation," but it is easier to measure church attendance, the participation in parish clubs, or contributions to fund-raising campaigns than to measure the intensity of religious experience or authentic religious commitment. Many studies in the sociology of religion treat religious behavior as if it were much the same as automobile traffic—for example, only in terms of how many are inbound and how many are out-bound.[14]

While goals like "salvation" are difficult if not impossible to measure, an analyst ought to focus on activities that are as proximate as possible to "salvation" on a means-ends chain of religious actions. Thus, activities such as regular prayer, having "religious experiences," and participating in social action programs motivated by theological considerations appear to be means which are more immediately linked to religious goals, while attending church on Sunday and membership in the parish men's club are more remote.

The problems of finding and including goal-measurements are much like those related to qualitative measurements. If anything, the measurement of goals is more difficult, since they are *future states of affairs* while most other qualitative dimensions refer to present states *of* or *in* existing systems. The dysfunctions stemming from the exclusion of goal-measures are also much like those stemming from the omission of qualitative measurements. Excluding measures of quality leads to dilution of services to the real goal; excluding the measurement of goals or goal-linked activities may lead to "ritualization"—that is, to viewing the means as ends-in-themselves, to the neglect of the actual goals.[15] Thus, pastors become administrators, and their effectiveness is judged not in terms of transcendental ideals but in terms of whether or not they fulfilled their quota in the latest fund-

---

[14] For a recent effort to see "religious commitment" in multidimensional terms and to construct an index to measure it, see Charles Y. Glock and Rodney Stark, *Religion and Society in Tension* (Chicago: Rand-McNally, 1965).

[15] See Merton, *op. cit.*, pp. 184–187, 199–200.

raising drive or were able to build a new wing on the parish community center.[16]

THE MEASUREMENT OF SUCCESS: A GOAL-MODEL VERSUS A SYSTEM-MODEL

The foregoing discussion suggests some of the problems that may be encountered if a social analyst is not sufficiently concerned with a unit's goals. But taking goals into account can itself have dysfunctional consequences if it leads to omission of other systemic considerations. Especially important are the pitfalls which emerge if an analyst evaluates a social unit's performance solely in terms of how well it reaches its real goals (or "output goals"). This distortion is probably most common in assessments of complex organizations, since these units are established for the purpose of producing specified and limited outputs. However, in theory, the comments which follow seem also to apply to other kinds of social systems, from a dyadic friendship relationship to a nation-state.

It has been common for a social analyst to evaluate an organization's success in terms of its goals. The question frequently asked is: How close does the unit come to achieving its assignments? However, this *goal-model* approach tends to define success solely as a full or at least substantial realization of what the organization sets out to do. Since most organizations, most of the time, do not attain their goals, in any final sense, many monographs are frequently detoured into lengthy discussions about lack of success, to the exclusion of more penetrating types of analyses.

This perspective is not the only way to evaluate organizational success. Growing interest in the comparative analysis of organizations has given rise to an alternative approach which may be referred to as the *system-model*.[17] This approach involves the analysis of relationships which must exist for organizations to operate at various levels of effectiveness. It asks

---

[16] For example, Fichter reports: "Many a priest has been dismayed by the inroads which the business role has made on the spiritually more important priestly roles. Not only is it time-consuming but it is worrisome and, worst of all, it obtrudes on the spiritual values. . . . As one priest remarked, " 'Matthew may be the businessman's saint, but he became a saint only after he stopped collecting money.' " See Joseph H. Fichter, *Social Relations in the Urban Parish* (Chicago: University of Chicago Press, 1954), p. 34 ff. See also Samuel Blizzard, "The Minister's Dilemma," *Christian Century,* Vol. 73 (1965), pp. 508–510.

[17] For a discussion of this viewpoint as well as the alternative approach, see Amitai Etzioni, "Two Approaches to Organizational Analysis: A Critique and A Suggestion," *Administrative Science Quarterly,* Vol. 5 (1960), pp. 257–278.

what is the balance among the various component-parts which will make for higher achievements as compared to other combinations. Using a *system-model*, we are able to see a basic distortion that is not visible or explicable from a *goal-model* perspective. The latter approach expects organizational effectiveness to increase with the assignment of more and more means to the organization's goals. The *system-model* leads to the conclusion that just as there may be too little allocation of resources to meet the goals of the organization, so there may also be an overallocation of these resources to goal-activities. For the *system-model* explicitly recognizes that the organization needs to solve certain recurrent problems other than those directly related to the achievement of the goals, and that excessive concern with the latter may result in insufficient attention to other *necessary* activities and in a lack of articulation between the inflated goal-activities and the de-emphasized nongoal-activities.

Once again, Soviet economic planning under Stalin provides us with a particularly graphic example. David Granick reports that:

> . . . in April and May, 1936 many metallurgical plants experienced an absolute drop in production. One director explained this failure in his plant by the fact that he and his management had in the previous months neglected repair for the pursuit of monthly production records. Other directors have organized their plants so as to make one-day records, and immediately afterwards suffered reduced production because proper routine had been destroyed. Some management concentrated on giving individual workers conditions in which they could establish national records although the mass of workers paid for this in poorer working conditions, and thus the production of the plant as a whole suffered. In all these cases, the management concerned evidently felt that their success would be measured more by making records than by their total production results.[18]

Past neglect of the *system-model* approach has not always been due to purely theoretical concerns; providing measurements for a *system-model* is more exacting and expensive than for a goal-model. The *goal-model* requires that the researcher determine the goals the organization is pursuing—and little more. The *system-model* requires as a first step that the analyst specify what he considers to be a highly effective allocation of resources. This often requires considerable knowledge about the way the particular organization functions. While acquiring such knowledge is often quite demanding, the efforts in obtaining the added indicators required for a *system-model* are not wasted, since the information collected in the

[18] David Granick, *Management of the Industrial Firm in the USSR* (New York: Columbia University Press, 1954), p. 155.

process of developing a *system-model* index will be of much value for the study of most organizational problems.

CONCEPT-REDUCTION

A perfect coincidence between a social concept and its operational definition is unlikely. An abiding temptation in seeking a solution for the problem of fractional measurement is the positivistic tactic of defining the social concept as only that which is measured by the operational definition. This procedure seems to remove the problem of fractional measurement once and for all. Unfortunately, the solution is more apparent than real. Concepts have an established content, institutionalized either in common parlance or in technical, theoretical formulations—and occasionally in both. To act as if an operational definition were automatically the same as the underlying concept is a questionable procedure, and it is also likely to have important negative consequences in the realm of policy-making.

For example, when intelligence tests were first widely used, they were often assumed to measure "native" intelligence. However, as data have accumulated, it has become apparent that such factors as cultural background, social class, past learning experiences, and the like, influence performance on these tests. At best, intelligence tests measure present ability to perform rather than innate intellectual capacity.[19] To state, then, that intellectual capacity is whatever Intelligence Quotient (IQ) tests measure, is highly misleading for two main reasons: first, because people told that they have a low IQ will continue to interpret this statement more or less in the original and established sense of the term; second, because there is a significant residue in the concept which needs measurement. While this is not provided by existing IQ tests, to deny its intellectual importance is to block the road to better IQ tests and more encompassing (or "covering") measurements. The recognition of the gap, the tension, between the concept and its measurement is essential for progress in social accounting.

At least two general rules for avoiding concept-reduction can be suggested. First, as we have stressed previously, operational definitions should adequately cover as many different dimensions of a concept as possible. Second, if fractional measurement is inevitable, the reader or client should be apprised of the extent of incongruity between the concept and the operational definition. This rule points to a potentially important role for outside

---

[19] See Anne Anastasi, *Psychological Testing* (2nd ed.; New York: The Macmillan Company, 1961), pp. 187–334; and R. M. Dreger and K. S. Miller, "Comparative Psychological Studies of Negroes and Whites in the United States," *Psychological Bulletin*, Vol. 57 (1960), pp. 361–402.

critics, since researchers cannot be relied upon in all cases to interpret objectively the deficiencies in their own measurements. The critics can make a valuable contribution by focusing attention on those dimensions of a concept that have been systematically ignored as well as by questioning the relevance or completeness of the dimensions that generally have been accepted. Institutionalization of such criticism is useful. Thus, if the government is to devise social indicators, some nongovernmental bodies, independently financed, should have access to the data and critically examine the measurements. Much of the work in the essays collected here and in others cited illustrates this mechanism.

INDIRECT MEASUREMENTS

Many social science concepts currently in use are measured by secondary analysis; that is, they draw on data originally collected or measurement computed for purposes other than the study at hand. Indeed, the analysis of societal structures and processes would be severely hampered if analysts were unable to use such data as national census reports and United Nations' handbooks.[20] Nevertheless, severe pitfalls are inherent in such an approach. Oskar Morgenstern, for example, has argued that indirect measurement is a major stumbling block for truly accurate economic analysis. He says:

> In general, economic statistics are merely by-products or results of business and government activities. . . . Therefore, they often measure, describe or simply record something that is not exactly the phenomenon in which the economist would be interested.[21]

We feel that this dilemma is present in most areas of societal analysis, and not localized to economics. In this section we touch on two hazards of indirect measurement which seem to be particularly prevalent.

---

[20] Bruce M. Russett *et al, World Handbook of Political and Social Indicators* (New Haven, Conn.: Yale University Press, 1964).

[21] Oskar Morgenstern, *The Accuracy of Economic Observations* (rev. ed.; Princeton, N.J.; Princeton University Press, 1963), p. 14.

The inadequacies of indirect measurement provide one of the bases for Morgenstern's critique of the accuracy of national income data. National and international policymakers, he feels, impute far greater precision to these statistics than the facts actually warrant. Morgenstern notes that frequently "the existing data are not collected in a form directly suitable for use in estimating gross national product or one of its component parts" (*ibid., p. 251*).

INDIRECT MEASUREMENT AS A SOURCE
OF FRACTIONAL COVERAGE

The various problems, outlined above, which haunt fractional measurements appear with special power when the measurements are also indirect. Not only is the full range of dimensions ordinarily not covered in this way, but often even those that are covered are only fractionally measured. The basic dilemma here is that the data available frequently do not permit adequate coverage of *any one* of the esssential dimensions of the concept.

For instance, the type of demographic data that is most accessible may distort an analyst's view of the nature of urban problems. One author (who is by no means unsympathetic to the problems of our cities) seeks to minimize complaints about urban congestion by pointing out that the population of New York City has barely increased over the past twenty-five years.[22] This does not take into account the fact that although the number of people sleeping in the five boroughs has not risen, there are apparently many more people working, shopping, and recreating there than ever before. However, systematic data about these latter phenomena are more difficult to find. Thus, one tends to rely on census residential data collected and frequently used by federal agencies.

From data made available to us by the New York State Department of Labor's Division of Employment, on those covered by state unemployment insurance, we have some evidence that the number of people working in New York City increased markedly over the past quarter-century. The number of people with state unemployment benefits increased by 31.3 per cent between 1940 and 1965. Even when one adjusts for the expanded coverage of the program, the figure is still 24.5 per cent.[23] Further, from data furnished by the Visitors Information Bureau of the City of New York, we calculated that the annual number of visitors to the city increased by about 26.0 per cent between 1955, and 1965.[24] These scattered facts lend

---

[22] Irving Kristol, "It's Not a Bad Crisis to Live In," *The New York Times Magazine,* January 22, 1967, p. 23.

[23] In a private communication, the New York State Department of Labor's Division of Employment informed us that the number of people covered by state unemployment insurance increased from 2,172,000 in 1940 to 2,851,000 in 1965. Approximately 150,000 of those included in the 1965 figure were in jobs not covered by benefits in 1940. (We were required to use these fractional measures as our indicator of change in the city working population because reliable figures on all persons employed in the five boroughs are not available for the period before 1950.)

[24] The Visitors Bureau of the City of New York estimated to us in a private communication that there were 12,500,000 visitors in the city in 1955 and that the figure rose to 15,750,000 in 1965. The Visitors Bureau bases their statistics on a survey of hotels, motels, and the like, within the city.

support to our assertion that New York is indeed becoming more and more crowded. To rely upon the available census measurements, thus, seems to "mask" certain problems and may lead us to underestimate the pressing reforms needed in our transportation system, in our housing programs, and the like.

Even when several indicators are available, it may be difficult to combine them into a single index because, frequently, various measures are not comparable. A useful strategy is suggested in Lipset's study of the relationship of economic development to the likelihood of stable democratic governments. Since there is no one single satisfactory measure of a society's economic development, Lipset first specifies four basic dimensions of this phenomenon (wealth, industrialization, education, and urbanization). He then introduces three or four indicators for each and relates each indicator to the likelihood of stable democracy. Only because every tabulation produces the *same* basic result does he conclude that there is a relationship between greater economic development and the emergence of stable, democratic societies.[25] By using several indicators, he safeguards himself, to a degree, against the distortions that indirect measurement may introduce. Note, however, that often the source of error may run through all indirect data available. A direct measurement, even of only a much smaller sample, is often unavailable if validity is to be checked, though of course the cost of this added accuracy must be weighed against those of direct measurement. On other occasions—for example, United States studies of Tibet—only indirect ones are feasible.

RITUALISTIC SCIENTISM

Elaborate statistical procedures are all too often applied to essentially unreliable data. The array of correlations, significance tests, simultaneous equations, and factor analyses often leaves the unwitting impression of precision and reliability. In actuality, the basic figures on which these operations have been performed are often highly inaccurate, and they have been collected with some systematic bias. For instance, in a statistically elaborate analysis of arms races, the renowned British mathematician L. Richardson reached several conclusions about ways to avoid wars. How-

---

[25] Seymour M. Lipset, *Political Man* (Garden City, N.Y.: Doubleday, 1959), chap. ii, pp. 45–76. For a discussion of the general problem of the interchangeability of indicators, see Paul F. Lazarsfeld, "Problems in Methodology," in Robert K. Merton, Leonard Broom, and Leonard S. Cottrell (eds.), *Sociology Today* (New York: Basic Books, 1959), pp. 47–67.

ever, at the very beginning of his inquiry, he admitted that "information that is uncertain by 20 per cent must be accepted as good enough."[26] If one reviews his subsequent operations, it becomes clear that the data are not accurate enough to validate his claim that an *arch* is more appropriate than a *straight line* on his scattergrams, which casts serious doubt on his basic findings.

If the data on which indirect indicators are based are of questionable quality, it may be useful to introduce some safeguards employed by the more conscientious survey analysts. For instance, many survey analysts do not present percentages derived from base figures which fall below some minimal number (for example, five, ten or fifteen cases); instead, they place an asterisk in the relevant cells of their table. Of more significance is the fact that survey analysts frequently present their data in categories such as "high, medium, and low" when the margin of error does not justify the ues of more refined statistical operations. Clearly, although such reservations are useful, additional safeguards are needed.

A special case of ritualistic adherence to the forms of scientific analysis is the interpretation of trend data without consideration of the changing quality of the measures employed. A familiar example of this practice is the purported dramatic rise in crime rates in the United States reported by the FBI and other crime control agencies. These reports have been greeted at home with alarm about "moral decay" and abroad with unfavorable comments about the nature of contemporary life in America. Moreover, "crime on the streets" has become a domestic political issue of considerable importance. In fact, this "rise" probably can be explained, at least in part, by improved methods of data-collection and changes in the procedures of classification and reporting.[27] When confronted with the societal liabilities of mismeasurement, one sometimes wonders if those publishing and interpreting societal data ought not to be licensed, and whether those found projecting questionable trends from faulty figures ought not to have these licenses revoked.[28]

---

[26] Lewis F. Richardson, *Arms and Insecurity*, ed. Nicholas Rashevsky and Ernesto Trucco (Pittsburgh: Boxwood Press, 1960), p. 4.

[27] Ours is not intended to be a comprehensive discussion of the shortcomings of crime indices. Both Biderman and Glaser have made rather extensive critiques of these measures. Their analyses make it clear that such indices are deficient for reasons in addition to those we have mentioned. See Biderman, *op. cit.*, pp. 111–129; and Glaser, *op. cit.*, pp. 115–117. In addition, see *The New York Times* for March 22 and 23, 1965 for a survey of the dispute between law enforcement agencies, particularly the FBI, and social scientists over the validity of the agencies' statistics.

[28] Controls on the uses of social statistics have been urged in a more serious vein by A. J. Wickens. See his "Statistics and the Public Interest," *The Journal of the American Statistical Association*, Vol. 48 (1953), pp. 1–14.

THE MEASUREMENT OF
COLLECTIVE ATTRIBUTES

A social science concept may refer to the attributes of individuals, of interrelationship, of individuals, or of collectivities.[29] For those concerned with social accounting of the states of society, the measurement of collective attributes takes on considerable importance. Two prime kinds of the pitfalls inherent in such measurement are (1) when the measurement of formal units is substituted for the measurement of real ones, and (2) when aggregated data are used to measure a collective property for which a global measure would be more appropriate.

FORMAL SOCIAL UNITS INSTEAD
OF REAL SOCIAL UNITS

There is a tendency in some sociological research to treat formal administrative units, such as countries, church parishes, and school classes, as if they were automatically meaningful social units. Actually, the formal units may cut across or be smaller or larger than the real units. The methodological pitfalls of this approach are commonly associated with the "ecological fallacy,"[30] but the confusion between formal and real social units is not confined to ecological analysis. Nor is the uncritical use of ecological procedures confined to purely sociological research. For instance, there are three well-known studies of the relationship between social class and coronary heart disease that rely wholly or in part on such procedures. Lilienfeld measures social class by using the median rental in census tracts in Baltimore, and relates this to the rates of coronary deaths within these tracts.[31] Kent and his associates rank 83 health areas in Manhattan on the

---

[29] See Paul F. Lazarsfeld and Herbert Menzel, "On the Relation between Individual and Collective Properties," in Amitai Etzioni (ed.), *Complete Organizations* (New York: Holt, Rinehart & Winston, 1961), pp. 422–440.

[30] This procedure can result in misleading statistics, as pointed out by W. S. Robinson in "Ecological Correlations and the Behavior of Individuals," *American Sociological Review*, Vol. 15 (1950), pp. 351–357. Sounder methods for inferring individual correlations from ecological data are proposed by Leo A. Goodman, "Ecological Regressions and Behavior of Individuals," *American Sociological Review*, Vol. 18 (1953), pp. 663–664, and by Otis Dudley Duncan and Beverly Davis, "An Alternative to Ecological Correlations," *ibid.*, pp. 665–666.

[31] A. M. Lilienfeld, "Variation in Mortality from Heart Disease," *Public Health Reports*, Vol. 71 (1956), pp. 545–553.

basis of median income and death rates from arteriosclerotic heart disease.[32] Stamler relates median family income in census tracts in Chicago to coronary death rates within these tracts.[33] Each of the studies finds some positive relationship between lower-class status and coronary heart disease.

However, the studies have not measured differing heart disease rates among different classes but only among different administrative units assumed to represent these classes. Of the three studies we have cited, only Lilienfeld considers this distinction. He states:

> Because the method is based on average characteristics of an area rather than actual characteristics of an individual, nonwhites, for example, may be classified in a socioeconomic group higher than their socioeconomic circumstances warrant when they are located in a census tract that is predominately white. The same difficulty is present with regard to the white population but probably to a lesser extent.[34]

Nevertheless, he ends by concluding that the median monthly rental of a census tract is a valid measure of socioeconomic status and that it "provides an inexpensive and readily available method for studying the socioeconomic distribution of mortality from arteriosclerotic disease."[35] It is unwarranted to state that lower-class persons are more prone to heart disease because administrative units made up largely of lower-class individuals have higher coronary death rates. It is quite possible that a disproportionate number of the coronaries may occur in the minority of non-lower-class persons in the area (as no area is "pure"—that is, absolutely homogeneous). Also, other studies of class and coronary heart disease have not all reached the same conclusions.[36] Whenever possible, the units "real" to the problem should be used as the basis of constructing a measurement.

---

[32] A. P. Kent, J. R. McCarroll, M. D. Schneitzer, and H. N. Willard, "A Comparison of Coronary Artery Disease (Arteriosclerotic Heart Disease) Deaths in Health Areas of Manhattan," *American Journal of Public Health,* Vol. 48 (1958), pp. 200–207.

[33] J. Stamler, "The Epidemiology of Arteriosclerotic Coronary Heart Disease," *Postgraduate Medicine,* Vol. 25 (1959), pp. 610–622, 685–701.

[34] Lilienfeld, *op. cit.,* p. 546.

[35] *ibid.*

[36] For example, see: L. Breslow and P. Buell, "Mortality from Coronary Heart Disease and Physical Activity of Work in California," *Journal of Chronic Diseases,* Vol. 11 (1960), pp. 421–444; and Walter I. Wardwell, M. Hyman, and Claus Bahnson, "Stress and Coronary Heart Disease in Three Field Studies," *Journal of Chronic Diseases,* Vol. 17 (1964), pp. 73–84. For a discussion of the general problem of measuring the relationship between social class and coronary heart disease, see Edward W. Lehman, "Social Class and Coronary Heart Disease: A Sociological Assessment of the Medical Literature," *Journal of Chronic Diseases* (forthcoming).

AGGREGATED VERSUS
GLOBAL MEASURES

There is a strong tendency in the measurement of collective attributes to use aggregated data (data based on the statistical manipulation of attributes of the members or of attributes of their relationships) rather than global measures (data characterizing the collectivity itself, apart from its members).[37] Thus, a nation's educational system is more likely to be assessed in terms of the number of teachers with postgraduate degrees or the number of B.A.'s. M.A.'s, and Ph.D.'s it produces than in terms of whether its organization is centralized or decentralized or how many universities of international renown it has.

Global dimensions are more frequently mentioned when collectivities are described, but when actual data-analysis begins, researches tend to rely on aggregated data. This is because global dimensions tend to be inherently more qualitative and, thus, lend themselves less directly to statistical manipulation. As a consequence, the problems of quantitative versus qualitative dimensions, discussed earlier, tend also to apply here.

We are not suggesting that global attributes are inherently unquantifiable. The number of political parties in a country is as "hard" an empirical datum as the percentage of voters who vote for each of these parties. The first of these two data is a global characteristic of a political system, since it does not depend on the attributes of the individual members. The latter example is an illustration of an individual attribute that can be aggregated to characterize a political system—for example, to measure the degree of "radicalness" of the electorate. Nevertheless, aggregated collective attributes are inevitably quantitative in nature, but this need not be the case for global properties. For instance, societies may be classified by whether they use money as a medium of exchange, by whether they have an establishd state religion, by whether they have recently become independent, or by a host of other qualitative dimensions.

Aside from the fact that they are more likely to be qualitative, global dimensions may be overlooked for at least two other reasons. First, because the basic referents of aggregated data (often individuals) are more concrete, the meaning of such data seems more immediately evident. The other reason lies with the type of social theory subscribed to by the researcher, either implicitly or explicitly. Often these theories are reductionist; that is,

---

[37] Cf. Lazarsfeld and Menzel, *op. cit.,* pp. 426–429. "Aggregation as a means of measuring the collective property in sociological analysis has somewhat more restricted meaning than the same term has in economics. For a clearer understanding of how "aggregation" is used in economic analysis, see Morgenstern, *op. cit.,* pp. 36–84; 101; 132; 163; 243; 266; 278; and 283.

they are based on the belief that higher social properties can be reduced to either psychological or microsociological categories. Such a position leads the researcher to conceptualize and measure collective attributes solely in aggregated terms.[38]

The dysfunctions which flow from the slighting of global dimensions are like those we dealt with under fractional measurement. However, global dimensions warrant special attention because of their implications for policy-making. Global factors on certain occasions might be precisely the ones most amenable to manipulation for instituting a desired social change. If such change is perceived as always having to involve modification of attributes of the members of the collectivity, some key opportunities may be missed. The president of Webster College, a Roman Catholic institution, may have been aware of this point when she recently sought to upgrade her school. She did this not through the usual devices of increasing the proportion of Ph.D.'s on the faculty or raising the average scores of incoming freshmen on the college boards, but by changing the status of her college from church-controlled to secular.[39]

In summary, since all social measurements face the problem of internal validity, persons who use these measurements, either for research or for policy-making, ought to be alert to dysfunctions which may emerge. The more obvious kinds of dysfunction arising from the measurement problems that we have discussed occur when policy is instituted from weak findings based on uncritical measurements. Another kind we pointed to is, however, of equal if not greater interest. Dysfunctions in this instance occur not because of dubious facts but because fractional measurement has left the social planner unaware of critical dimensions of the phenomenon in which he is interested. Increased investment, intellectual as well as financial, no doubt can go a long way to increase the efficacy of social measurements and to reduce much of the likelihood of dysfunctions. But, in the final analysis, these problems can never be eliminated entirely. Hence, the client of systematic measurement and accounting should be alerted to the limitations of social indicators, both to make his use of them more sophisticated and to prevent him from ultimately rejecting the idea of social accounting when he encounters its limitations.

---

[38] For additional discussion, see Etzioni, *The Active Society, op. cit.*, chap. iv.

[39] See *The New York Times,* January 12, 1967. For similar practices at other Roman Catholic institutions, see *The New York Times,* January 22, 1967 and January 24, 1967.

3

SOCIETAL FEEDBACK

RAYMOND A. BAUER

The concern over measurement of social phenomena reflected in this book must be viewed as part of a larger concern with the planning and control of society which has developed in the United States in the past decade, a matter in which we have lagged somewhat behind other Western countries. The shift in the American attitude toward planning might be traced to very many sources. Probably the key factor was our success in our management of the economy in the period since World War II. But perhaps almost as important are our changes in affluence and in the nature of the society itself.

FEEDBACK AND PLANNING

Planning demands a reasonably long time perspective. Without that time perspective, there is no point to planning. Similarly, planning demands that the planner have reasonable confidence in his ability to control his own fate or, at least, that planning and relatively deliberate control will improve his prospects enough to be worth the cost. Finally, planning demands that one have the resources to bring to bear to implement one's plans. These necessary conditions are meet in modern American society, despite such notable failures or stalemates as the Vietnam war and the race problem.

Stimulants to planning and control, beyond the necessary conditions cited, are the rapidity of change and the increasing interrelatedness of our society. Perhaps the most concrete manifestation of the pressure for planning and control arising from the interrelatedness of our society is pollution of various forms. What one man does to the air, water, and sound in his environment affects other men, and the volume of such effects has risen to the point where they can no longer be ignored.

But the nature of planning and control has also changed. For decades, the Soviet Union was the established model of a planned and controlled society. What distinguished the Soviet model was the assumption that a blueprint for a desired future state could be drawn up, together with the necessary steps to the achievement of that state, and that one could then proceed literally to "carry out the plan" in full and reach that state. The Soviet experiment demonstrated that a limited amount of social action can be carried out according to this model, but that it is a costly way of proceeding. All social action produces unintended consequences, some of which may be regarded as incidental cost, some of which may be unexpected benefits, and others of which represent substantial inversions of the original purpose. To the extent that one can avoid adverse unintended consequences, one operates more efficiently.

A modern version of planning and control places a much higher premium on early detection of the consequences of one's actions, with a consequent adjustment of one's plan. Detection of these consequences may cause one to take different steps toward the goal, and to alter that goal or goals. To a large extent, this view of planning and control is influenced by the cybernetic model of electrical engineering, which stresses the importance of feedback to correct errors resulting from one's actions. While the cybernetic model has undoubtedly had a strong impact on our view of planning and control, it does not *per se* provide for the reassessment of one's goals—namely, for the correction of one's course toward an established goal. Probably the most profound contribution of cybernetics to our thinking is the establishment of error as a systematic inevitable feature of all action.

The notion of adjustment of goals comes from an approach to planning and control that stresses the plurality of future possible states and consequences of one's actions. Probably the best known proponent of this view is Bertrand de Jouvenel, director of the French *Futuribles* project.[1] The version presented here is a more familiar one, which was developed in connection with our book *Social Indicators*.[2] To my knowledge it may differ from that of de Jouvenel only in some slight preferences in terminology.

The term "prediction," commonly associated with planning, is misleading in that it connotes the identification of a single most probable state of affairs and an implication that the probability of this state of affairs may

---

[1] Cf. Bertrand de Jouvenel, *The Art of Conjecture* (New York: Basic Books, 1967).

[2] Raymond A. Bauer (ed.), *Social Indicators* (Cambridge, Mass.: M.I.T. Press, 1966).

approach certainty. While it may be argued that a "prediction" need not and should not be treated as though it were made with certainty, in practice it seems that concentration on a single most probable future state deflects proper attention away from alternate possible states. For planning purposes, it is preferable to employ the concept of "anticipation" (de Jouvenel uses "conjecture"). One uses whatever information and stimulants to one's imagination that are available to anticipate that range of future states of reasonable possibility and importance that might flow from one's actions. (De Jouvenel calls these "conjectured" future states *futuribles.*) One then decides which of these future states one wants to make most probable. (A highly desirable state may appear difficult to attain, and therefore a less desired state may be aimd at.) Having chosen such a target future state, one then devises and inaugurates a course of action aimed at increasing the probability of its occurrence. Having inaugurated that course of action, one takes readings of the consequences of those actions, reassessing the probable future states and the probability of their being attained, and making the adjustments of action and goals referred to above.

Clearly, in this version of how one should plan and act, a high premium is placed on accurate and rapid information about the existing state of the system on which one is acting and on one's ability to relate those states of the system to actions already completed. It could be contended both that no model of planning and control ever devalued information and that the model, as sketched, is one which is seldom if ever used. To the extent that this model is approximated, feedback becomes a more crucial element.

> Several authors state that the aim of control is to assure that the results of operations conform as closely as possible to plans. . . . To the extent that middle management can make decisions that are better than those implied in the plans, top management wishes to do so. . . . Since no one can foretell that future precisely—that is, since people are not clairvoyant—it follows that in some respects actual events will differ from the assumed events that the plans are designed to meet. . . . Therefore top management does *not* necessarily want operations to conform to plans. . . . Furthermore, since people are not omniscient, their plans do not necessarily show the best course of action; they merely show what was thought of as best when the plans was made.[3]

Views such as these are obviously, philosophically and practically, radically at variance with early stereotyped notions such as a Five-Year

---

[3] Robert N. Anthony, *Planning and Control Systems* (Boston: Division of Research, Harvard University Graduate School of Business Administration, 1965), pp. 28, 29.

Plan which it was expected would be adhered to rigidly and which was changed only grudgingly. Error is considered inherent in planning and action; change of plan and action is a central part of the process; and, of course, feedback is vital.

FORMAL INFORMATION SYSTEMS

In recent years, "information systems" have come into considerable vogue as a management tool in business. But, in practice, at the time this is being written, the number of sophisticated information systems in operation is apparently very small. Despite this, the logic of their use is so persuasive that this use is bound to spread. An information system is no more than a formal set of procedures for gathering, storing, retrieving, and reporting data relevant to the decisions and actions that must be taken in an organization. In their prototypic fashion, information systems may actually take over some of the decisions and actions ordinarily done by people, by feeding the relevant data directly into a machine or other mechanism for action. Thus, sales or shipping records may be fed into an inventory system which will automatically order additional production to fill the inventory or order shipments to retail outlets to replace items which have been sold.

Such systems for the control of routine operations have been in existence for more than a decade. They have applied, however, *only* to such situations in which decisions and actions can be routinized and generally where optimum courses of action can be calculated. Of more interest to us, and of more recent origins, are information systems which are designed to serve those situations in which human judgment is essential. This latter class of situations is a large one. And while many of the decisions and actions in which human judgment is presently involved may become routinized in the future, there will always be some irreducible number of situations for which this is neither possible nor desirable. These are situations in which th decision is unstructured, which is to say that the problem with which one is confronted demands the invention of new courses of action and/or demands tradeoffs of values. A structured decision is one in which, for all practical purposes, the full range of actions is known; the consequences of the actions are known with substantial accuracy; and there is agreement on the value to be maximized.

Quite obviously, there are very few important issues in the public arena which involve structured decisions of this sort. At a minimum, there is no clear agreement on the weight to put on the various values involved or on whose interests are to be preferred over others, and usually there is the need for the invention of some unique course of action that will reconcile a sufficient coalition of interests. The logic of what a formal information system does for a person in such a situation is not new. It is substantially what the military have done for centuries in presenting generals with up-to-date position statements, displaying, in as appropriate a fashion as possible, information on his own and his enemy's situation. Furthermore, war games and simulated war games, such as chess, gave him a basis for anticipating the probable consequences of the various courses of action open to him.

What a modern computer-based information system does is to make available more information, more rapidly, and in many forms. In its most developed form it includes (1) ongoing data series such as the "social indicators" that are the subject of this book; (2) stored data that an executive may want to use, for example, the demographic characteristics of the population a hospital serves, past records of illness in various segments of the population, and the results of experiments which have been carried out; and (3) a simulation model of the system on which the executive wishes to act. This model might, for example, be a model of the market for toothpaste, which will tell him the probable reactions of consumers and of competitors if he does something such as change the price of his product or the amount of his advertising.

We have, of course, precedents for such models in the public arena. The economic models used for control of the economy in the past two decades actually predated the computer-based simulation models used in business. The economists have, of course, updated their own models as the state of the art advanced.

Granting that there are earlier precedents or approximations for each of its components, the image of a modern, sophisticated information system *suggests* the posibility of planning and control of a sort that would have been impossible in the past. I have not mentioned yet, for example, the notion of a "real time" system which, for practical purposes, presents a man with a picture of the state of the world in which he is interested, with no time lag. Thus, sales of a company's products from wholesale houses, or potentially even from retail outlets, can be recorded directly in a computer as they are made so that a sales manager could know within a matter of minutes the precise state of sales of his product on a company-wide basis, by region, by city, or in any combination he chose. He could also know the state of his own organization, if he wanted to: the rate of production of various products, cash available, or, if he cares, the health of the labor force or the existence of unusual skills. Whether this is a good thing or not can be discussed separately.

The image referred to above is, then, that of a man with virtually instantaneous feedback of many of the consequences of his actions or, at least, instantaneous feedback of those things which he has chosen to measure. (There will be an organizational lag between his own actions and the impact of the organization's actions on the environment; for example, it may take many months for a program of inoculation to be organized and executed, and to have its effect on incidence of a disease.) In any event, he has a very up-to-date and complete picture of the world in which he operates and of the state of his own organization. Furthermore, his ability to anticipate the consequences of his possible future actions is improved by trial runs on a simulation model.

An information system of this sort is the logical tool for the type of planning and control which are described above. It in no way changes the rationale. The use of a simulation model to make trial runs is no more than a refinement of the process of "anticipation," but does not reduce the need for feedback. Since simulation models are based on historical data and are, of necessity, simplifications of the real world, they can only reduce, but never eliminate, the errors which will inevitably result from any course of action.

Systems of this sort have, of course, their own difficulties. For example, a person whose feedback system is "perfect" may react too rapidly to changes in reactions to his actions and cause great damage. The tendency of executives to overreact to information is a real and serious one. Also simulation models must, of necessity, make assumptions to bridge our gaps in information and in our understanding of the state of the world, and some of these assumptions turn out to produce seriously erroneous answers at time. And, of course, the information system does not tell one what courses of action are conceivable. Man himself must conceive them.[4]

Whatever its limitations, a formal, computer-based information system is a good prototype of the sort of system one might want for planning and control. It is also a good point of departure for consideration of the limitations of a societal informational system for planning and control in the public arena.

We may now move from this idealized world to the real one.

---

[4] Here, as at other places in this essay, the knowledgeable reader will be searching for qualifications. It is not true that an information system cannot be built that will generate possible courses of action. However, this development will generally have to wait until our understanding of human thought processes is better developed. Work on programming computers to play chess has shown that if one were to use the computers' tremendous calculational capacities to have it consider all logical possibilities, it would play an untenably long chess game. Its human opponents would have died of old age. Chess masters have heuristic devices—decision rules which simplify such enormous complexity.

LIMITATIONS OF

FORMAL INFORMATION SYSTEMS

This section is devoted, in part, to an explication of the inherent limitations of formal information systems and, in part, to the extent to which a societal information system cannot, at this point in time, achieve the degree of sophistication that seems possible for the informational systems of single-purpose institutions such as the military, health systems, or business firms.

The primary limitation of any information system is that it is finite. But on the other hand, if it were not finite, it would be impossible to use, even if cost and effort were no consideration. The goodness of an information system is dependent on the extent to which it is efficient in serving the informational needs of specifiable individuals in an organization. Ordinarily, the development of an effective information system begins with an analysis of the decisions made by various persons in the organization, their preferences in the use of information, and the like. The purpose of this analysis is, in the first instance, to make sure that these individuals will get the information they need and want; but, in the second instance and equally important, that they will not get information that they do not need or want. The need to sort out unrequired information not only produces inefficiency but may even have the worse result of tempting a person to meddle in organizational affairs which are "none of his business." For example, the chief executive of a business firm who gets daily reports on sales in specific cities may begin interfering in tactical maneuvers that are properly the affair of the regional marketing director.

We may begin to differentiate a societal information system from that designed to serve a single institution by noting the multiplicity of users of the societal system. Not only must a vastly larger number of *actors* be served, but a societal system must also serve as a vast array of *evaluators*: the public, the Congress, the press, and future historians, for example. It must be aimed at comparability over a very long time span. Hence, its data series cannot be closely designed to serve one clientele.

The most efficient informations systems must, of course, contain some surplus information. If the flow of information to a man were restricted to only that which he was *certain* to need, it would inevitably miss information which probably would be useful to him. The amount of potentially surplus information to include is a difficult matter to decide, but the proper answer lies somewhere between "everything" and the certainly useful. This decision obviously can be made more sensibly for repetitive types of problems. The immediate corollary of this is that formal information systems are less useful for broad strategic problems than for routine ones.

Strategic or policy decisions are, by definition, responses to major opportunities or threats which could not entirely be anticipated. The first sign that a major threat or opportunity exists *may* manifest itself in some sharp discontinuity in regular data gathered for routine purposes, or in some shift in the relationship of two or more data series. One of the standard features of formal systems is "exception-reporting," which notifies the relevant person that some one indicator has deviated beyond some pre-established limit. Generally speaking, however, such changes of pattern will indicate merely that "something is happening," and thereby serve as a stimulus to search for pertinent data. It is just as likely that the signal for a strategic or policy decision will come from some source entirely outside the formal information system—a newspaper story, a conversation with an informed person, or some other. This matter of how strategic information is sought out will be dealt with in more detail later. At this point, it should be established that formal information systems are, by their nature, better suited to servicing relatively narrow repetitive problems than broad, unique ones. They can indeed be very valuable for servicing broad, unique policy problems, but such problems demand additional activities which will be discussed below.

We can get additional perspective on the limitations of a societal information system if we review the broad functions for which one would expect an information system to be useful. (Note that the word "serve" was not used. This was to avoid the implication that an information system could, even under ideal circumstances, be expected to do the entire job.) These broad functions are: (1) detection of the state of affairs, (2) evaluation, (3) diagnosis, and (4) guide to action.

Social indicators, like any other series of trend data, are *per se* means for detecting the state of affairs.

For some matters, the job of evaluation may be virtually automatic in that there is a strong consensus that some states of affairs (for example, health) are "good," and others are "bad" (for example, sickness). However, in the majority of instances, evaluation depends on the system model one holds, whether that model be explicit or implicit. For example, a setback in educational opportunity for Negroes might be viewed favorably if one thought that revelation of the situation would create such a feeling of indignation that it would create unprecedented support for increasing opportunities for Negroes. If the reader thinks that this type of reasoning is far-fetched, it rests on logically the same type of process as that behind the frequently used argument that the pace of Negro progress should be contained for fear that the white backlash would more than offset the gains.

What is important, however, is that, in many instances, evaluation is not self-evident. And the difficulties of evaluation do not rest soley on personal differences in taste or values, but on empirical questions as to what will be the eventual consequences of the state of affairs that has been detected. It is here that the adequacy of the model one has, and consensus on a model among parties, becomes most relevant. It is gratuitous to say that, whatever difficulties one may have in developing a model of a market for a business firm, the difficulties of developing one for the United States social system, or even that of a metropolitan area, are infinitely greater.

The absence of consensus on a model, of course, poses problems at the very point of selection of what indicators to measure. What one has to look to is consensus on the indicators independently of consensus on a model of the society. For example, most of the relevant parties can agree that unemployment is something that we want to have information on, even though they do not agree as to what conclusions they will draw from the data.

The steps from detection, to evaluation, to diagnosis—let alone to prescription for action—are usually taken too blithely. Few, if any, of the social indicators proposed in these volumes will tell us *automatically* what caused a given state of affairs. Accurate data may, however, spoil one of our favorite sports of invoking preferred explanations of dubiously existent phenomena, for example, blaming an "increasing" crime rate on the collapse of our moral fiber. Actual causal relations must be inferred, with the gaps of inference being narrowed by *ad hoc* research designed to establish the linkage. We may infer, for example, that the white backlash has been caused by some combination of the advances of the Negro community, anxiety over threats to their own position on the part of whites, moral indignation, guilt, or what have you. Research directed to this issue can, with varying adequacy, sort out the plausible causes.

Any information system requires provision for *ad hoc* research directed toward two ends: (1) diagnosis, for example, exploration of the casual origin of trends reflected in regular social indicators or of any other observable important social changes, and (2) measurement of the impact of discrete events whose impact may be expected to be reflected in regular data series only partially, indirectly, or with some delay.[5] Included in the latter category is the study of unexpected events such as a presidential assassination but, perhaps more importantly, as a regular matter, program evaluation. The evaluation of public programs demands rapid feedback, and it also demands measures of phenomena that one would not ordinarily think of including in regular indicator series. We may take as an example Project Headstart of the current poverty program. If it achieves its goal of

---

[5] Cf. Albert D. Biderman, "Anticipatory Studies and Stand-by Research Capabilities," in Bauer (ed.), *op. cit.*

increasing the opportunities of underpriviledged children, this ultimate objective will be detectable only some years from now in the educational and occupational performances of such groups as Negroes. The immediate traceable impact may be found in such things as the degree of enthusiasm for the program on the part of parents and children (this at least will ensure their continued participation) and some improvement in the motivation and social skills of the children, which may be the preface to an improvement in learning ability and in learning itself and *subsequently* to improved educational and occupational performance.

While such measures are necessary in any information system, they play an increased role in a broad-gauged, multi-purpose system of social indicators. Or to put the matter in reverse, the more closely a system is tailored to a limited set of objectives, the higher the proportion of relevant effects which will be included in regular data series and the fewer will be the steps of inference required to establish causation. This is probably a tautology, but it underscores the general need for such *ad hoc* research in a societal information system.

Finally, any presently constructed societal information system will suffer from the *relative* lack of models with which to test out the consequences of possible courses of action. This lack is, of course, relative. Economists can test out the probable consequences of economic policies. One can also predict that a frontal attack on infectious diseases will almost certainly result in an increase in such diseases as heart trouble and cancer. On the whole, however, we lack dynamic models of most of the areas of our society which will help us to "anticipate" the consequences of programs we might introduce. This circumstance dictates the relative importance of feedback, of being able to detect these consequences as rapidly as possible after their occurrence.

In sum, formal information systems, like all of man's creations, have inherent limitations, and these inherent limitations get accentuated in anything we might contemplate in the way of a societal information system. Information systems are most adequate for handling repetitive, routinized problems and to the extent that the system is tailored closely to the needs of a limited range of problems. While societal information systems are useful for routine operating purposes, they are most pertinent for the handling of broader policy problems of an unprogrammed nature. Furthermore, a societal information system applies not only to a wide range of problems, but also to a variety of interests. It is not merely a tool for action for those who must devise and carry out actions (as in a business firm or health system), but also for those people who evaluate such actions. And a societal information system must be designed with a relatively poor model of the society.

The result of all these conditions is that the parameters to be measured must be selected only on the basis of a general agreement that they are "important," even though their importance cannot be justified *via* reference to an agreed-upon model. Furthermore, measures of such parameters must be, in general, oriented toward multiple usage. On the whole, this means, in turn, that the problems of evaluation and of diagnosis and of drawing inferences for action are based on complex inferences. Such a system will be relatively unusually dependent on the quality of the inferences drawn, on *ad hoc* research to establish casual connections and evaluate the effects of discrete events such as public programs, and on feedback to detect the consequences of actions which can only inadequately be anticipated.

SCANNING FOR
STRATEGIC INFORMATION

Formal information systems become increasingly less adequate as we are concerned with policy or strategic problems, as contrasted to repetitive operational problems. It is clear that the writers of all the chapters in this volume are primarily concerned with broad problems of evaluating trends in the society, of the impact of broad programs, and of the need for revising programs or adopting new ones. We are concerned with the national welfare, but, in this context, not with the day-to-day problems of operating a local welfare office.

The difficulty in saying anything systematic about the procurement of strategic policy information is simply that it is an amorphous, complex topic about which little of a systematic nature has been said.[6]

One thing that is certain is that strategic policy problems must involve persons in high positions who are simultaneously concerned with operating problems which tend to saturate their attention.

> We noted how routine, immediate, familiar, and programmed considerations tend to crowd out strategic, long-range, unfamiliar, and unprogrammed considerations.[7]

---

[6] For recent exceptions to this generalization, see Francis Joseph Aguilar, *Scanning the Business Environment* (New York: The Macmillan Company, 1967); and Warren J. Keegan, *Scanning the International Business Environment: A Study of the Information Acquisition Process* (A thesis submitted in partial requirement of the degree of Doctor of Business Administration, Harvard Graduate School of Business Administration, 1967). See also Raymond A. Bauer, Ithiel de Sola Pool, and Lewis Anthony Dexter, *American Business and Public Policy* (New York: Atherton Press, 1963), *passim*.

[7] Aguilar, *op. cit.*, p. 187.

This, of course, is recognized in most organizational arrangements by the provision of specific staff functions. On the national level, it is the function of the Council of Economic Advisors to review the evidence bearing on policy questions and to report the evidence and ˉrecommendations for action. The proposal of Senator Mondale for a Council of Social Advisors[8] reflects a realization that establishing a staff function to review evidence beyond the strictly economic will ensure greater attentiveness to non-economic social matters.

The provision of a staff function for reviewing a wider range of information is one thing. The process of this viewing is another. Scanning the environment for strategic information can, to some extent, be systematic, to the degree that it involves the monitoring of regular data series for evidence of discontinuity or changes of pattern. Thus, one might find, on the one hand, a sharp jump or a sharp drop in unemployment or, on the other hand, a shift in balance of the aspirations and achievements of Negro youth. Either of these circumstances might signal the existence of an imminent new threat or opportunity.

However, there is a large random element in scanning for strategic information. Unprogrammed problems manifest themselves in unexpected places and unexpected forms. The work of Keegan[9] suggests two further generalizations that may be cited.

The first of these is that one can better decide *where* to look for strategic information rather than *what* to look for. The executives he studied were much more likely to report that they had found strategic information by monitoring a source known in general to be useful rather than by deliberate investigation or by research.

The second is that a high proportion of strategic information is transmitted by personal, usually face-to-face communications. Various sources of evidence suggests to me that this may be due to the fact that matters of broad policy importance are, to some extent, only vaguely sensed in their early stages. The person who senses that "something is in the air," who "makes a connection," has difficulty in coding his perceptions into words which he knows will be relevant to his potential audience. He may also be reluctant to put into writing or into print that which may make him look foolish. However, when he meets a potential user of his, still only partially formulated, "information" he can explore, in a transactional fashion, what it may mean, with someone equipped to assess its meaning.

The last of these generalizations obviously implies a fairly well-accepted generalization, namely, the usefulness of personal contacts.

---

[8] S. 843, 90th Congress, 1st Session, February 6, 1967; introduced by Senator Mondale.

[9] Keegan, *op. cit.*

Out of all of this, can any specific suggestions be made? Two seem straightforward and have been implied above. Provision should be made for an explicit function of scanning the environment for evidence that policy changes might be in order. And there must be sufficient organizational slack to provide for a certain amount of directed random behavior —monitoring of selected channels of information in which strategic information may occur and the maintenance of a network of interpersonal contacts.

Less straightforward, but also implied in preceding pages, is the importance of the social system model which one has. The richer that model, the greater the likelihood that the potential implications of a given item of information will be seen.

HOW TO USE INFORMATION

The question of what data to gather and how to use it is one which has been addressed in detail in each of the papers in these volumes. Most of the decisions which have to be made are matters of judgment, and judgment must be specific to the situation in which it is applied. Granting this, some general comments may offer some guidance to the application of the necessary judgment.

The weight of the testimony of the chapters in this volume is that the United States is not suffering from a glut of information of adequate quality in the various areas of concern. We may expect the expansion and refinement of existing data series. This expansion and refinement will unquestionably take place as a function, not only of the need for such series but of the bargaining power of those who propose them and of the technical resources that they can bring to bear.[10]

Some centralization of decision-making on statistical series can be helpful in assuring that criteria of relevance play as much a role as possible. The Bureau of the Budget has, to some extent, played such a mediating role. The existent Social Indicators Panel of the Health, Education, and Welfare Department will have some *ad hoc* impact. A Council of Social Advisors, such as that proposed by Senator Mondale, would unquestionably play such a role. Such a centralized group must weigh the relative priority of general, over-all social needs for information against the urgency of the needs of particular parties, especially those who require information for

---

[10] For a discussion of the practical problems in introducing or refining statistical series, see Albert D. Biderman, "Social Indicators and Goals," in Bauer (ed.), *op. cit.,* pp. 95–105.

direct operational purposes. This balancing off of immediate, specific needs against broader long-term needs is a matter on which one cannot prescribe at a distance, except to point out that staff persons (such as those who are likely to be setting such priorities) are likely to be biased in favor of the broader, long-range problems while line operators will have a selective preference for the most specific, short-range data. In business organizations, the line operator tends to control the organization and is generally able to have his way. In the government, the line operators are likely to have the ear and sympathy of the Congress which appropriates funds. These circumstances are relevant.

However, decisions as to what measures to take are not simply a matter of priorities. The decision to observe a phenomenon implies a decision to be responsible for it, if such responsibility is within one's power. On the one hand, the decision to observe can be used constructively and positively as a way of commanding attention. This is obviously one of the intentions of Senator Mondale's proposals. But whether one intends to assume responsibility or not, the knowledge that phenomena are being observed will create the expectation that such responsibilities will be assumed. For example, measurement of the aspirations of Negro youth seems to offer a valuable contribution to our understanding of the movement of Negroes into the mainstream of American life. However, the making and publication of such measurements will undoubtedly call attention to the disparity between the expectations we have created and our ability to meet those expectations. Similarly, a health information system that discloses that some segments of the population do not receive certain medical services will generate the expectation that these services be supplied.

It is wisdom, not cynicism, to urge caution in extending diagnostic measures of social phenomena beyond the system's capacity to respond to the problems which are unveiled. While it is necessary to illuminate problems for planning purposes and to stimulate the requisite actions, such illumination can also produce trouble and disillusionment. ("Why did they ask me what I wanted, if they aren't going to do anything about it?")

Another issue that must be faced is that of the level of aggregation of data. It is the ideal of a good information system that the data stored in it be disaggregated, that is, stored in the units in which it was gathered, so that it may be combined in whatever forms are desired. However, many of the newer statistical series, for example, the monthly Health Survey, and to some extent the Survey of Employment, are gathered on a sample survey basis and can provide us with estimates only for the population of the United States or, at most, for broad regions. For certain purposes, the estimates are adequate. Persons with operational responsibility for smaller units—states, towns, cities, and portions of cities—have complained of the inadequacy of such data for the tasks with which they are confronted. This is an established problem, well recognized. Less well recognized, however, is the extent to which aggregation can produce misdiagnosis. For example, if one paid attention only to over-all employment figures, one would miss the extraordinary concentration of this unemployment among young Negro males. Happily, this particular fact has been realized, and appropriate measures among Negro youth are being taken.

As long as data are available only on some level of aggregation, one cannot, of course, not know with certainty that no such anomalies are hidden behind the aggregation. Yet completely disaggregated data for the United States population on all of the data series presented in this volume are impossible. The essentiality of using sample surveys must be accompanied by acute awareness of the problem of aggregation and by *ad hoc* diagnostic studies when there is reason to suspect that the aggregation hides some phenomena of interest.

In some instances the problem of aggregation may suggest that one retain administratively gathered statistics available on a disaggregated basis even though the measure may be somewhat inferior to that which might otherwise be made. In other situations, such administratively gathered series might be monitored for clues to problems that might be hidden by aggregation; for example, hospital records might reveal the clustering of health problems that the sample survey does not reflect.

Finally, one must consider the organizational problems of using the information that a societal information system offers.[11] Any information on the society in which an institution exists presents potential opportunities or threats. This information will have varying values on a number of dimensions: its clear relevance for a given institution, the degree of effort involved in responding to a threat or opportunity, the organization's capacity to respond effectively (regardless of level of effort), and the extent to which it will favor one element in the organization over another.

This latter problem of organizing to use information is one of sufficient complexity that in this brief essay it can only be touched on; the interested reader is advised to consult some more extensive treatment such as that of Anthony or of Weiss and Rosenthal, cited above.

---

[11] For an extended discussion of this issue see Robert A. Rosenthal and Robert S. Weiss, "Problems of Organizational Feedback Processes," in Bauer (ed.), *op. cit.*, pp. 302–340.

TWO

THE POLITY

4

ELECTORAL PARTICIPATION

RICHARD M. SCAMMON

Four years ago the late President Kennedy, believing that "popular participation in Government through elections is essential to a democratic form of Government," appointed a special Commission to "study the reasons for the failure of many citizens to register to vote." The work of the Commission and the studies of many others prior to and following its efforts have underlined the facts of participation and nonparticipation well enough. The "indicators" of our voting activity are spelled out in the following tables in this chapter. What do these tables and the research behind them tell us?

THE INDICATORS

Foremost, they indicate that Americans simply do not participate in national elections as much as do the citizens of many other democratic states. The figures are not as low as they seem, due to the inclusion in the American base of such groups as aliens, "movers," and the like,[1] but even if the statistical low sixties for voter participation be actually in the low seventies, the United States would not rank very high on an international voter turnout chart. To cite just one example, the French presidential vote in 1965 has a turnout of 85 per cent.

---

[1] Percentages of those voting in the United States are habitually calculated from a base of total population, total civilian population, total resident population, or the like. Whatever base is used, it includes large numbers of persons who are actually not legally entitled to vote. For two excellent treatments of this whole problem, see William G. Andrews, "American Voting Participation," in *The Western Political Quarterly* (December 1966) and Meyer Zitter and Arnold Starsinic, "Estimates of 'Eligible' Voters in Small Areas," in *Proceedings of the Social Statistics Section* (Washington, D.C.: American Statistical Association, 1966).

TABLE 1—Voter Participation, Elections for President and
House of Representatives, 1920-1964

Election Year	Voters as a Percent of Voting Age Civilian Population	
	For President	For Representatives
1964	63.0	58.7
1962		46.7
1960	64.0	59.6
1958		43.4
1956	60.1	56.6
1954		42.4
1952	62.6	58.6
1950		41.6
1948	51.3	48.4
1946		37.4
1944	52.9ᵃ	49.8
1942		33.9
1940	59.2	55.7
1938		44.1
1936	57.0	53.6
1934		41.4
1932	52.5	49.8
1930		33.7
1928	51.9	47.8
1926		29.8
1924	43.9	40.6
1922		32.1
1920	43.5	40.8

ᵃ Total voting-age population, including Armed Forces abroad.
Source: U.S., Bureau of the Census, *Statistical Abstract of the United States*
(Washington, D.C.: U.S. Government Printing Office, 1966).

monumental effort made in 1964 by the Bureau of the Census has estab-
Second, they show that our voter turnout record varies greatly as
measured by social class, geographic area, sex, age, and other criteria. The
lished useful benchmarks for us in the matter of variant voter turnout. That

TABLE 2—Voter Participation, Presidential Election, 1964, by State

| State | Estimated Civilian Resident Population of Voting Age | | | State | Estimated Civilian Resident Population of Voting Age | | |
	Population (in thousands	Vote for President (in thousands)	Percent Voting		Population (in thousands	Vote for President (in thousands)	Percent Voting
Ala.	1,905	690	36.2	Mont.	388	279	71.9
Alaska	106	67	63.3	Nebr.	855	584	68.4
Ariz.	846	481	56.8	Nev.	243	135	55.8
Ark.	1,111	560	50.4	N.H.	392	288	72.9
Calif.	10,665	7,058	66.2	N.J.	4,092	2,848	69.6
Colo.	1,090	777	71.3	N. Mex.	500	329	65.6
Conn.	1,697	1,219	71.8	N.Y.	11,247	7,166	63.7
Del.	279	201	72.1	N.C.	2,678	1,425	53.2
D.C.	494	199	40.2	N. Dak.	352	258	73.4
Fla.	3,404	1,854	54.5	Ohio	5,962	3,969	66.6
Ga.	2,537	1,139	44.9	Okla.	1,458	932	64.0
Hawaii	338	207	61.3	Oreg.	1,129	786	69.7
Idaho	378	292	77.5	Pa.	7,071	4,823	68.2
Ill.	6,344	4,703	74.1	R.I.	532	390	73.4
Ind.	2,825	2,092	74.0	S.C.	1,310	525	40.1
Iowa	1,635	1,185	74.9	S. Dak.	389	293	75.4
Kans.	1,294	858	66.3	Tenn.	2,212	1,144	51.7
Ky.	1,932	1,046	54.1	Tex.	5,780	2,627	45.4
La.	1,873	896	47.9	Utah	506	401	79.2
Maine	565	381	67.4	Vt.	232	163	70.4
Md.	1,959	1,116	57.0	Va.	2,416	1,042	43.1
Mass.	3,237	2,345	72.4	Wash.	1,704	1,258	73.8
Mich.	4,655	3,203	68.8	W. Va.	1,064	792	74.5
Minn.	2,017	1,554	77.1	Wis.	2,386	1,692	70.9
Miss.	1,214	409	33.7	Wyo.	188	143	76.1
Mo.	2,703	1,818	67.2	U.S.	112,184	70,645	63.0

Sources: U.S., Bureau of the Census, *Pocket-Data Book USA, 1967* (Washington, D.C.: U.S. Government Printing Office, 1967); and Richard M. Scammon, *America Votes 6* (Pittsburgh: University of Pittsburgh Press, 1966).

TABLE 3—Voter Participation by States, Presidential Elections, 1920–1960

State	Vote as a Percent of Voting-Age Civilian Population										
	1960	1956	1952	1948	1944	1940	1936	1932	1928	1924	1920
Ala.	31.1	28.3	24.6	12.7	16.4	18.9	18.4	17.6	18.8	13.6	20.8
Alaska	45.5	—	—	—	—	—	—	—	—	—	—
Ariz.	54.5	50.8	54.4	44.0	43.4	52.0	45.6	46.6	38.8	34.9	35.4
Ark.	41.1	39.9	37.6	22.8	22.0	18.2	17.1	22.5	20.9	15.4	21.2
Calif.	67.4	63.8	68.0	58.9	62.9	66.9	59.6	55.9	49.7	41.9	40.7
Colo.	71.4	67.6	75.1	64.4	76.2	76.9	73.3	71.5	64.6	56.5	51.7
Conn.	76.8	76.6	79.6	63.7	70.2	67.4	63.8	58.3	57.7	44.8	43.6
Del.	73.6	72.1	79.8	66.9	68.9	76.8	77.3	72.8	73.5	67.8	69.5
Fla.	50.0	45.9	50.3	34.5	36.3	39.8	31.8	30.2	30.5	16.7	36.0
Ga.	30.4	29.7	30.1	20.4	18.2	17.6	17.7	16.4	15.6	11.5	10.4
Hawaii	51.3	—	—	—	—	—	—	—	—	—	—
Idaho	80.7	77.6	82.2	65.3	76.3	75.1	71.3	73.4	62.7	63.1	57.9
Ill.	75.7	73.2	76.0	68.1	79.4	78.4	76.3	68.6	65.5	55.8	53.1
Ind.	76.9	71.8	74.4	65.3	76.2	79.8	76.5	76.4	72.3	68.1	71.0
Iowa	76.5	73.2	75.7	62.8	72.0	74.1	72.3	67.8	68.3	67.9	62.7
Kans.	70.3	67.2	72.0	64.1	68.3	74.0	73.4	68.9	65.0	63.0	55.7
Ky.	59.2	58.8	59.2	49.8	59.7	59.3	60.2	67.4	68.1	60.6	71.2
La.	44.8	36.4	39.9	27.1	26.3	27.1	25.4	22.5	19.7	12.1	13.6
Maine	72.6	62.8	62.5	47.6	60.5	60.2	58.8	60.2	54.1	40.1	41.6
Md.	57.2	54.5	58.8	40.7	47.5	55.7	56.2	49.1	54.2	39.2	49.7
Mass.	76.1	75.7	77.8	65.9	73.0	69.5	63.1	58.0	59.7	44.3	41.2
Mich.	72.4	68.1	67.0	52.4	63.7	61.8	58.5	56.6	48.8	46.0	47.3
Minn.	77.0	67.7	72.3	65.5	70.2	69.6	66.5	62.7	63.3	56.1	53.3
Miss.	25.5	21.7	24.1	16.7	16.8	14.7	14.4	13.8	15.2	12.1	9.4
Mo.	71.8	67.8	72.2	61.2	68.9	73.3	75.4	68.7	67.6	61.7	65.4
Mont.	71.4	71.0	72.6	65.4	70.8	69.6	68.0	67.4	61.0	55.7	55.8
Nebr.	71.4	67.1	73.4	59.6	75.9	73.6	72.9	69.1	68.6	60.9	51.8
Nev.	61.2	62.8	71.5	59.2	62.3	70.6	63.5	63.7	54.9	48.1	52.1
N.H.	79.4	75.2	78.9	67.3	78.1	72.4	70.1	68.5	66.9	57.4	56.6
N.J.	71.8	69.0	71.1	59.2	70.9	69.6	67.4	62.3	63.6	50.4	48.0
N. Mex.	62.1	59.6	61.0	57.1	59.0	64.4	65.2	66.2	55.9	57.3	56.9
N.Y.	67.0	66.0	68.3	60.8	74.1	67.4	61.7	56.0	60.2	47.2	44.5
N.C.	53.5	48.2	52.8	36.7	43.1	42.6	47.3	43.7	43.0	36.1	44.5
N. Dak.	78.5	70.6	75.2	64.0	71.0	75.2	74.8	71.4	69.7	61.4	63.7
Ohio	71.3	65.0	70.0	55.8	69.5	72.4	67.7	61.3	61.6	52.1	56.8
Okla.	63.8	63.6	71.8	56.2	62.0	60.3	55.6	53.7	50.1	47.4	47.6
Oreg.	72.3	68.2	67.5	55.9	59.7	64.3	59.9	57.5	53.1	51.5	48.2
Pa.	70.5	65.7	66.3	54.6	64.1	64.2	68.3	48.8	55.3	39.7	36.7
R.I.	75.1	73.7	81.6	62.3	65.3	67.4	70.1	62.9	58.9	52.0	47.3
S.C.	30.5	25.2	29.4	13.4	11.0	10.1	12.4	12.1	8.5	6.5	8.6
S. Dak.	78.3	73.5	75.1	66.7	70.8	79.5	75.6	73.4	69.5	55.9	52.8
Tenn.	50.3	46.3	44.8	28.5	31.0	30.6	29.9	26.1	25.9	23.0	35.3
Tex.	41.8	37.9	42.3	24.7	30.5	27.0	23.4	25.8	23.0	23.9	19.8
Utah	80.1	75.2	81.4	74.7	76.2	80.3	75.2	75.1	68.2	64.3	63.8

TABLE 3—Voter Participation by States, Presidential Elections,
1920–1960 (cont'd)

| State | Vote as a Percent of Voting-Age Civilian Population | | | | | | | | | | |
	1960	1956	1952	1948	1944	1940	1936	1932	1928	1924	1920
Vt.	72.5	67.4	66.2	54.1	63.6	62.7	64.1	62.0	62.0	47.6	41.4
Va.	33.4	33.5	31.7	22.1	23.9	22.0	22.3	21.7	23.6	17.7	19.1
Wash.	72.3	70.8	71.9	61.4	65.6	66.5	63.3	59.9	50.4	45.4	46.5
W. Va.	77.3	75.2	75.9	67.5	74.1	81.4	81.2	78.5	73.5	72.4	67.8
Wis.	73.4	67.4	73.3	59.2	71.2	69.6	65.3	60.7	58.6	50.9	45.9
Wyo.	74.0	67.8	75.1	62.2	75.6	72.2	71.3	71.3	65.5	63.4	45.4

Source: U.S., *Report of the President's Commission on Registration and Voting Participation,* 1963.

survey,[2] taken with other relevant data, indicates the following.

(1) MEN VOTE MORE THAN WOMEN. Though there are now some millions more women than men in the adult citizen population, the higher turnout of males has meant that more men have actually cast ballots in most American elections than have women. As the participation of women rises, and it has risen in the generation and a half since women were fully enfranchised after World War I, the "overage" of adult women will likely soon result in women actually casting a majority of votes in American elections. Within the generally larger turnout of men, the predominance of male voters is most notable among older voters, those with lower educational attainment, and in the South.

---

[2] In November, 1964, the Bureau of the Census for the first time included voting questions in its Current Population Survey. The survey was made about two weeks after the national election and represents a sample comprised of some 33,000 households with 65,000 persons of voting age—by far the most comprehensive survey research into voting participation ever made in the United States. In the course of this survey it was discovered that some respondents had undoubtedly "overstated" their voting behavior, since the percentage of those indicating that they had voted was some percentage points higher than actual calculations based on votes cast. Some of this no doubt was due to the "gap" between the valid vote for president and the total number of persons physically going to the polls, but more was due simply to over-reporting. As the Census Bureau noted in its report on this work— *Voter Participation in the National Election, November 1964*—this phenomenon has long been known to survey research people. Indeed, it has been noted again in the advance statistical material published by the Bureau, dealing with its enquiry into turnout in the November 1966 congressional elections.

TABLE 4—Voter Participation, by Selected Classes, November 1964

Classification	Voters as a Percent of Voting-Age Civilian Noninstitutional Population		
	Total	Male	Female
United States	69.3	71.9	67.0
Age 18–20 years	39.2	(a)	33.5
Age 21–24 years	51.3	51.7	51.0
Age 25–34 years	64.7	65.2	64.2
Age 35–44 years	72.8	74.2	71.5
Age 45–54 years	76.1	78.3	74.1
Age 55–64 years	75.6	78.7	72.7
Age 65–74 years	71.4	77.4	66.4
Age 75 plus	56.7	66.4	49.4
White	70.7	73.4	68.2
Negro	58.5	59.1	58.0
Northeast	74.4	76.7	72.4
North Central	76.2	77.8	74.8
South	56.7	61.4	52.6
West	71.9	72.4	71.4
Metropolitan in Central Cities	69.5	71.9	67.4
Metropolitan outside Central Cities	72.2	74.2	70.4
Nonmetropolitan	66.5	69.8	63.5
Elementary School (b)	59.0	64.4	53.7
High School	72.3	74.1	71.0
College	84.8	84.5	85.1
Employed	73.0	73.5	71.9
Unemployed	58.0	56.9	59.2
Family income (b)			
Under $2,000	49.6	53.6	46.4
$ 2,000–$2,999	57.6	60.5	55.2
$ 3,000–$4,999	62.7	65.6	60.1
$ 5,000–$7,499	72.4	75.3	69.6
$ 7,500–$9,999	78.3	79.9	76.7
$10,000 and over	84.9	86.1	83.6

Source: U.S., Bureau of the Census, *Voter Participation in the National Election, November 1964.* For the age group–male 18–20, (a) indicates inadequate base. For schooling and family income, (b) indicates figures exclude the small number of voters under 21 years of age in the four states permitting such persons to vote. Income data includes only those persons actually in primary families. The school categories include respondents with *any* educational experience in the group indicated.

(2) YOUNGER PEOPLE VOTE LESS THAN THE MIDDLE-AGED, AND THE YOUNGEST VOTERS BALLOT EVEN LESS THAN THOSE OVER 75. It has long been remarked that voter turnout follows a definite age pattern, in other countries as well as in the United States. The youngest voters have the least interest in politics and public affairs; many are still in school, others in military service, still others moving about getting started on careers and families. The participation curve rises sharply in the early thirties, then reaches its peak in the 45–65 group. In later years it drops off, as interest may decrease and physical and mental capacity lessen.

(3) NEGRO CITIZENS VOTE LESS FREQUENTLY THAN WHITE. While in the past the facts of disfranchisement have contributed significantly to this variant, this is less so today, and, hopefully, will be less so in the future. Even allowing for this factor, however, Negro voter turnout has been less than white, quite possibly since so many of the socio-economic factors marking low turnout are found in such larger concentration in the Negro areas of our large metropolitan communities.

(4) THE CURVE OF VOTER TURNOUT PARALLELS THAT OF EDUCATIONAL ATTAINMENT. Men and women of no educational experience, or of educational attainment limited to the elementary school, vote least often. As the educational curve rises through high school and on to college, the voter turnout rises with it—and the differentiation between male and female voters declines.

(5) THE CURVE OF VOTER TURNOUT PARALLELS THAT OF INCOME. The more affluent the citizen, the more likely he and his family are to be voters. Voter participation rises on a direct curve with income, the man or woman below the poverty level being far less likely to vote than the elector with an income of over $10,000 per year. With this income variant, as might be expected, the unemployed are substantially less likely to vote than the employed.

(6) VOTER TURNOUT IN THE SOUTH IS APPRECIABLY LESS THAN ON OTHER PARTS OF THE UNITED STATES. Though participation is rising rapidly in the Southern states, voting, both white and Negro, is markedly lower than in other sections of the country. Partly due to exclusion of the Negro from the franchise, partly as a result of the long dominance of one-party politics in the South, voting in general elections in this part of the country has been low. In recent years, however, as the effective right to vote has broadened and as two-party competition in the South has developed, the voter participation rate has risen sharply.

While these findings are borne out in almost all voter participation research, there are areas in which the indicators are not so clear-cut. For example, turnout in central cities is almost always lower than in adjacent suburbs, but rural area voter participation is much more variable. An examination of Table 2 will show that the higher-participation states include Idaho and South Dakota as well as Illinois and Massachusetts. While the lower range of participation state includes several with high rural populations, factors relative to the South are probably more important in this rank order than are the figures for nonurban populations.[3]

Religious persuasion and voter participation is another area in which the available data indicate some differences between religious groups, but differences less marked than those of, say, income and education. Jewish citizens tend to vote slightly more than Catholic, and Catholic slightly more than Protestant. But, again, as with the urban-rural turnout rates, this may well be due to a whole series of characteristics in these religious groups rather than to the effect on voting of religious feeling itself.

Note should be taken of the very real difference in voting participation on electing officers for the various levels of government. Table 1 indicates the general drop-off in voting in the "off-year" elections for state officers, senators, and representatives. Habitually, the vote for representatives is less than that for president even in presidential election years, and it drops off markedly from that figure two years later. In Minnesota, for example, a state in which voter participation has normally been fairly high, the "off-year" vote for governor in recent years has been some two to three hundred thousand below that cast for president two years earlier.

Moreover, local election participation tends to be even lower than that at these "off-year" national elections. Many an editorial writer has commented woefully on the lack of interest of the voters in contests for mayor and other local officials. As an example, the city of Minneapolis cast over 200,000 votes for president in 1964, dropped to under 100,000 for mayor in 1965, and rose again to 160,000 for governor in 1966. In some cities municipal elections will not see so dramatic a drop-off, and some actually have a fairly high participation, but the rule is that presidential, "off-year," and municipal voting operate on a diminishing elector turnout. Lowest of all would be noncontroversial local bond-issue elections, in some of which the number of election judges may exceed the total voters.

---

[3] For some further considerations of the data on urban-rural voter participation, see the author's "The Electoral Process," *Law and Contemporary Problems* (Spring 1962). The Current Population Survey report of the Bureau of the Census in November 1964 also contains helpful sampling data on this question, and the new report of the Bureau on similar studies of the 1966 voting patterns will provide additional materials.

Finally, voter participation in primary elections is normally less than in general elections. Examples of this pattern exist in any number, and the rule of low primary interest and turnout is general save in some of the Southern states. There, by reason of the long dominance of the Democratic party in state and local affairs, voter participation in the Democratic primary has often exceeded the turnout in November. However, much of the differentiation was due to the decisive character of the primary vote; as Republican general election candidates make *that* election the decisive one rather than the preliminary balloting in a Democratic primary, it may be assumed, the Southern pattern will come more in line with that of other states.

These variations in participation rates around the nation indicate the interrelation of many of the aspects of voter turnout in the United States. It may be correct to say that the highest voter participation may be in a presidential election and by a wealthy, white, middle-aged, college-educated, executive male living in a suburb. It may also be correct to say that the lowest rate may be found in a local county bond-issue vote and by a young, low-education, low-income, Negro farm girl in the South. But to say this alone is not enough.

THE WHYS

Why these rates are what they are involves two basic kinds of analysis. The first of these deals with the administrative and legal obstacles to voting, the second with the variety of reasons why those otherwise entitled to vote do not actually do so. It is not possible to determine exactly what share of the 37 per cent who did not vote for president in 1964 were hindered by legal obstacles and what share simply were those eligible to vote who did not do so. Since the noneligible share would be relatively constant, the apathetic group within the nonvoters would rise as the curve of nonvoting rises in "off-year" and local elections.

The legal barriers to voting are significantly less today than they were fifty years ago, due to the general enfranchisement of women following World War I and the recent abolition of the poll tax, but many still operate to keep people from the polls. Here are the major obstacles in current American electoral legislation.

(1) CITIZENSHIP. Since citizenship is a basic requisite to vote in all our states, alien status is a total bar to electoral participation. In earlier days noncitizens, especially those with "first papers," were permitted to vote, and in the more casual procedures of a century ago, it may be pre-

sumed that many an alien did help to swell the total votes cast. But today upwards of 3,000,000 alien adults are kept from the polls by the requirement of citizenship.

(2)   REGISTRATION. The need in most jurisdictions to preregister personally is doubtless the greatest single block to a larger voter turnout in America today. In the majority of other nations the act of registering the citizenry for voting is undertaken as a state function. Registers of voters are made up by local officials in a variety of ways; appeals and reviews are provided with respect to these registers; and a final, official listing of those eligible to vote is prepared. The responsibility—and the work—of registration is thus borne by the community, not by the individual. Though some people are doubtless missed, and indeed whole streets are sometimes inadvertently omitted from the voting lists, the resultant registers of voters contain a far greater percentage of those eligible than do voters' lists in this country, made up as they normally are by the voluntary, personal action of individual citizens.

It should be noted that there are areas of the United States in which no registration whatever is required for elections—the prospective elector simply goes to the polling place and votes. While registration is primarily designed to protect the electoral system against fraud, it is no absolute guarantee against abuse. Fraud can exist—and has been alleged—in areas with very sophisticated registration systems. Equally, North Dakota— which has no requirement for registration—has rarely had charges of fraud in its elections.

(2)   DIFFICULTY OF REGISTRATION. While the act of personal registration is in itself a block to voter participation not common to many other countries, the day-to-day administration of registration procedures often acts as an additional barrier to maximum turnout. In some jurisdictions, registration places are open only during normal business hours and often are limited to a single office in a given city or county. In others, special registration arrangements are made for certain days and places, but these must be discovered by those seeking registration so that they may enroll as voters.

(4)   RESIDENCE REQUIREMENTS FOR REGISTRATION. Since one-fifth of all Americans move in any given year, requirements of a period of residence prior to election day as a condition of registration also prevent a substantial number of citizens from voting. Limited residence is no doubt required both to protect against fraud and to ensure that the elector knows something of the conditions, issues, and candidates on which he is passing

judgement on election day. However, long residence is no guarantee that the voters' judgments will be improved, and would seem unnecessary to prevent fraud. In recent years a movement has developed to permit voters moving from one state to another to vote at least for presidential and vice-presidential electors, on the theory that the voter's views of national affairs have little relation to the place from which he has come or to which he has gone.

(5) EARLY CLOSING OF REGISTRATION BOOKS. In some juris-dictions the registration work is stopped and the lists of voters closed many weeks—even months—before election day. Naturally, the interest of the voting public tends to develop in any election as voting day approaches. Closing off the possibility of registration long before that interest has heightened—in some instances even before it has begun to develop—acts as an administrative block to maximum voter turnout.

(6) FREQUENT PURGING OF LISTS. In order to keep voting lists current and up-to-date, and as a protection against fraudulent voting in the name of absent or deceased registrants, many election authorities "purge" their voting lists at stated intervals. Failure to do this leads to the anomalous situation of more names on the voting list than the total number of adults in the community and invites criticism, if not open fraud. How-ever, "purging" every two years instead of quadrennially has led to a special kind of inhibition on voting by those who habitually vote only in presidential election years. In effect, they are required to reregister for each presidential contest, and an additional burden is imposed upon them by reason of their evaluation of the importance of the "off-year" elections.

(7) LITERACY TESTS FOR REGISTRATION. In some states it is required that a prospective voter be able to read and write. Often this requirement must be met only via the use of English; sometimes it can be satisfied in any language. Even though illiteracy is limited to a small per-centage of citizens, there are groups of potential voters denied the ballot by this barrier. The largest number of such citizens will be found among the old, the poor, and the rural Americans, with a special representation of those speaking another language (say Spanish) in states admitting only English as a qualifying language.

(8) CIVIL DISABILITIES. The states have a variety of disqualifi-cations from the franchise resulting from mental incapacity, felony convic-tion (if unpardoned), pauperism, and the like. In addition, the right to vote is usually denied to persons living on federal property, since the

majority of states hold that such residence does not establish "residence" for voting purposes. Thus, military personnel living on an Army post are not normally deemed "residents" of the state in which the post is located. Equally, citizens living in the District of Columbia are ineligible to vote for governmental offices other than in a quadrennial ballot for presidential electors.

(9)   VOTING BY PERSONS AWAY FROM HOME IS OFTEN DIFFICULT. Registration as a voter by a person away from home is often not permitted by state law, and the casting of an absentee ballot is not always easy. Persons living abroad are especially handicapped by requirements of personal registration and by complexities in the application for, and voting of, absentee ballots.

(10)   RACIAL AND RELIGIOUS DISABILITIES. For many years there was a disgraceful denial of the ballot to many of our Negro citizens living in the South. The methods used to achieve this denial were legion. Some were "legal" disqualifications, situations in which a Negro lawyer or teacher might be denied registration because he could not "interpret the Constitution." Some methods were those of social and economic pressure —jobs were lost; credit was denied at the local grocery store; teacher contracts were not renewed. Still other situations involved simple violence —the mob, the shotgun, the bomb. In many parts of the South these methods worked; no Negro citizens—or at best only a token minimum— were permitted to vote.

Happily, this situation has changed. Partly because of federal intervention, but certainly as much because of a change of viewpoint in the South itself, these barriers to registration and voting are melting away. Some—especially the nonlegal ones—still exist, but great progress has been made in the past few years in this area, and there is reason to believe that the near future will see the elimination of all but small pockets of this sort of un-American denial of the right to vote.

Of religious disabilities there remain none in American law. Total negation of the act of voting or denial of voting on a certain day or at a certain time of day may act as a barrier to citizens of certain religious views, but there are no general religious barriers in the electoral law of any American states.

(11)   ELECTORAL ADMINISTRATION. In the day-to day administration of registration, there are real barriers to the citizen, as indicated above. There may also be barriers in the administration of voting itself. Often, comparisons have been made between the relatively low turnout of

voters in this country, with voting on a working day, and the turnout in those nations which vote on Sunday. In certain localities, the closing of the polls as early as five or six o'clock in the afternoon may be an effective inhibition to voting by some registrants, though provisions for "time off" to vote theoretically provide a solution to this problem. So arranging the polling places in terms of voter load that the man or woman seeking to vote must stand hour after hour in line is not a formal, legal barrier to voting, but it certainly becomes an effective administrative discouragement to voter participation. The same may be said of locating polling booths in distant, inaccessible places, or setting them up in unsavory areas to which citizens may be unwilling to go to vote.

There are others, too, in the listing of the legal and administrative obstacle course for the hopeful registrant and voter, though those cited here are the main barriers. But these *are* in the law, or in the administration of the law. Even if all were by some fell swoop to be altered, the necessary with the unnecessary, it certainly would not guarantee total voter participation, even if that were itself desirable. In no democratic society, even in those in which voting is legally compulsory, is there the virtually total turnout as in a dictatorship. Nor would we wish such a torrent at the polls —neither via a law of compulsion nor by the "unofficial" pressures of a totalitarian regime.

The fact is that apathy, or acceptance, or resignation, or disinterest, or alienation, or whatever it may be called, will keep a number of otherwise qualified citizens from the polls. It does so now; with present legal barriers to voting lessened, there would still be a number of Americans who simply would not vote.

This is the second group of nonvoters with which we are concerned— not those to whom registration and the vote are denied by reason of some legal or administrative obstacle to their participation, but those citizens, otherwise eligible to vote, who just do not bother to do so.

Some of the characteristics of this group have been cited above in the listing of indicators, but the basic reason for most voluntary nonvoting may be summarized in the phrase "lack of involvement."[4] Thus, the women of America vote less than the men; insofar as this abstention is voluntary, women are "less involved" in elections than men. Young people vote less than the middle-aged. Here, too, insofar as this lack of voting is by volition

4 The general area of political participation as a matter of involvement has been most usefully outlined by Lester W. Milbrath in his *Political Participation* (Chicago: Rand, McNally, 1965). For an international consideration of these same problems, see Stein Rokkan (ed.), *Approaches to the Study of Political Participation* (Bergen: Chr. Michelsen Institute, 1962). In the September 1967 issue of THE ANNALS, study material in this field will also be found in the "Democratic Participation" commentary by Professor Sidney Verba.

rather than through, say, inability to meet a residence requirement, there is "less involvement" than that of older citizens. The same factor is present with another major group in the population having lower levels of voter participation—that of citizens substantially less advantaged in income and education than the national average.

Reasons for the greater sense of involvement in higher turnout groups are not difficult to determine. By and large, men are measurably more concerned with public affairs than women; men hold the great preponderance of public offices. As Milbrath has pointed out: "The traditional division of labor which assigns the political role to men rather than women has not vanished." Naturally enough, those who do the job are more concerned with it than those who do not.

On the age differentials, as suggested in the list of indicators, younger prospective voters are much more likely to be involved in attendance at school, military service, and the beginnings of careers and families than are those in the middle-age brackets. Moreover, physical movement, for these reasons among others, is more likely to prevent the young citizen from acquiring local knowledge and forming local attachments. Moreover, the younger citizens may have political views less developed and less firmly held than those of people in the middle years, and therefore have less commitment and involvement than their fathers and mothers.

Certainly, one of the strongest elements in determining voluntary nonvoting is that of social and economic status as measured by income, education, and, to some extent, occupation. If there be no differentiation whatever in a community with respect to legal barriers to registration and voting, it is almost axiomatic that the higher-income, better-educated suburban areas will vote in considerably larger proportions than do low-income, low-education slum and semi-slum sections of a central city. In rare situations, the figures may approach equality; in even rarer ones, the central city area may have a higher voter turnout, but the normal rule is that the rich vote more than the poor, the higher educated more than the lower educated.

The knowledge of issues, the involvement in public affairs, the commitment to public affairs, the commitment to public purposes, the discussion of public matters—all of these appear to involve the high-income, high-education citizen more than they do the low-income, lower-education voter. In almost every way in which we can measure attitudes and opinions, the high-income group ought to be more involved and more committed—and they are, as electoral statistics and sample surveys demonstrate again and again.

Involvement is not only a measure of voter turnout in these various groups: it is also a measure of the more active forms of political participation. If the act of registration is the minimal electoral act of citizenship and that of voting the next step, there is an ascending scale of political life and work beyond just registering and voting. Wearing a compaign button (or its automotive equivalent—putting a bumper sticker on the family car) is perhaps the next, then attendance at a campaign rally, next active campaigning itself, perhaps then managing a campaign, and lastly running for office—all these involve larger and larger involvement, and these greater commitments most usually vary by groups of our citizens as do voter participation.

But it should not be presumed that these various differences in involvement, and thus in voluntary nonvoting, are constant and never-changing. While it is correct that the sense of efficacy, the sense of accomplishment, the sense of a capacity to "change things" is doubtless higher in the groups with the heavier voter participation, even these will change and alter from election to election. For example, there is a general improvement in turnout when any given election is felt to be "important." This underlies the continuing higher voter turnout in presidential election years. The voter perceives the choice of a president to be more meaningful to him than that of, say, a local alderman—and indeed he may be right in that perception.

Alternatively, heavily contested local elections, with a vigorous— even bitterly contested—local issue or personality at stake may also bring out a heavy vote. In both cases it is the sense of involvement of the elector which is responsible. If the prospective voter sees meaning in the vote for president, and none in that for alderman, he will vote in the one election, not in the other. If he sees meaning in the local contest, he will usually find the time and make the effort to get to the polls. This sense of meaning underlies turnout in most elections, but not in all. The presidential vote in 1964, for example, saw a campaign which most observers agreed was a clearer definition and delineation of issues than any in a generation. Yet the participation figure was lower in 1964 than in 1960, very likely because few voters felt the election to be close.

This factor of the closeness of the vote, the marginality of the contest, plays an important role in the turnout picture. In most elections in which one candidate is clearly ahead of the other, the vote curve tends to drop off as the less involved and less committed voters see less purpose in their trip to the polls. In 1964 the meaningfulness of the Johnson-Goldwater contest was evidently sidetracked by the evidence of an easy Johnson victory.

General competitiveness remains as a final aspect of voting and nonvoting in our American electoral process. Purely apart from a clear lead for a candidate in any specific election, the overall competitive—or noncompetitive—atmosphere of politics and public affairs has an important bearing on how many voters actually vote on election day. If competition in the political system is strong, if elections tend to be contested by two vigorous candidates or parties, more and more voters tend, in turn, to get involved, to get committed to the choice-making process. Under such conditions many of the other factors tending to produce a low vote—a (temporary) lack of meaningful issues, the prospect of a (relatively) easy victory in a particular election—have less effect than were these same factors to be at work in party situations of minimal competition.

THE GOALS

Voter participation is often considered a goal in itself—a good goal by some, a dubious one by others. Actually, a democratic system could function with minimal citizen interest and participation—and it could fail with interest and participation at maximum levels. Perhaps the real goal of our American democracy should be *access* to the polls rather than just maximization of the number of bodies present and accounted for on election day.

It was in this thought that President Kennedy's Commission on Registration and Voting Participation made its report in 1963,[5] and it is in this thought that useful goals for our democracy are suggested here, goals which would make the ballot box more readily accessible to more Americans, without trying to drag our total population kicking and screaming to the polling place.

Efforts to bring our voting system closer to our people could easily concentrate on our registration systems. These are today the major blocks to access to the polling place. Consideration might well be given to the adoption in our country of that kind of official system of listing of voters which is so common in other countries—a system in which the first respon-

_____

[5] The President's Commission of Registration and Voter Participation was appointed by President Kennedy in March 1963, and presented its report to President Johnson in December 1963. The work of the Commission touched on many of the aspects of political participation discussed here in the three segments of this article and included a set of twenty-one "standards" which were recommended to the states for action. The Commission's *Report on Registration and Voting Participation* was published in 1963 by the U. S. Government Printing Office, Washington, D.C.

sibility for registration is placed, not on the citizen, but rather on the community.

There are other adjustments which could help in increasing accessibility: shorter residence requirements, closing of registration books closer to election day, purging of voter lists on a four-year rather than a two-year basis, absentee registration, more polling places, ending of literacy tests, and polling places open later in the evening—perhaps open even for a full

24 hours. But more important than any of these would be the acceptance by government of the primary responsibility in the compilation of registration lists of voters.

There is no guarantee that this change, or indeed all these changes, would ensure that all our eligible electors appear at the polls, nor is there any reason to believe that they should do so. Democracy does not require total voter participation, and totalitarian "'elections" with their 99.9 per cent voter turnouts are mere exercises in contempt of the democratic idea. But democracy *does* require that the voter have not only the right to vote, but also an administratively easy way to put that right to use. It has been nearly fifty years since women were fully enfranchised in America, and the Negro is still in progress of winning the right to vote in all parts of the nation. Perhaps the next step may be so to arrange our management of the registration and voting process that a new goal in making the ballot box accessible will have been reached—that of total registration of all eligible American voters.

5

CIVIL LIBERTIES

MILTON R. KONVITZ

In his recent study of the Hebrew Scriptures, Erich Fromm describes one of the functions of the prophets as follows:

> They do not think in terms of individual salvation only, but believe that individual salvation is bound up with the salvation of society. Their concern is with the establishment of a society governed by love, justice and truth. They insist that politics must be judged by moral values, and that the function of political life is the realization of these values.[1]

OUR FUNDAMENTAL VALUES,
GOALS OR PRESUPPOSITIONS

Today it is doubtful if, in the light of our experience of states, governments, and nations, we can accept, without serious qualifications, the prophetic belief "that politics must be judged by moral values, and that the function of political life is the realization of these [moral] values." We would be much more inclined to agree with Reinhold Niebuhr, whose political realism clearly recognizes and accommodates itself to the limits of morality in political life and accepts the fact that

> political realities are power realities and that power must be countered by power; that self-interest is the primary datum in the actions of all groups and nations.[2]

---

[1] Erich Fromm, *You Shall Be as Gods: A Radical Interpretation of the Old Testament and Its Tradition* (New York: Holt, Rinehart and Winston, 1966), pp. 117–118.

[2] Gordon Harland, *The Thought of Reinhold Niebuhr* (New York: Oxford University Press, 1960), p. 180.

But this extreme statement also needs qualifications. For politics and morals are not altogether separate. There is room for the moral judgment of political action, provided that the moral principles are not kept and used as pure abstractions; provided that our judgment takes into account the indescribable complexities of social life; provided that our thinking is far removed from utopian commitments and fanatic claims; provided, in a word, that our judgment proceeds from humility in the face of the complexity of forces, recognition of the small role left for creative action, and obligation to try to accommodate and harmonize competing values.

These considerations make the moral judgment harder than was apparent to the prophets of the Hebrew Scriptures, or to Jesus when he preached the Beatitudes; but when hedged in these ways, the moral judgment is inseparable from political action that is more than naked tribalism or a front for the narrowest form of selfishness.[3] With these qualifications, the moral judgment may even be said to be basic in the sense that it is the indispensable condition for the social life of man—who is, we assume, in his social character more than a social insect.[4]

In one of his many attempts to translate biblical insights and ideas into modern conceptions. Niebuhr has said that the first problem, in the creation of community and the establishment of justice, is the recognition of the following three presuppositions:

1. Recognition must be given to the dignity of man which assures that in the ultimate instance he is regarded as an end in himself and not merely as an instrument in a social or political process. . . .

2. The law of love must be presupposed as the law of human existence.

3. At the same time the perennial force of self-love and self-interest must be taken for granted.[5]

These "presuppositions" are not essentially different from the prophetic ideas of love, justice, and truth. Indeed, Niebuhr's first presupposition—the dignity of man—may be said to encompass the ideals of love, justice, and truth; or love may be thought to entail human dignity, justice, and truth. No matter; for what is important for us it that, once we recognize, with the prophets, that "politics must be judged by moral values," it becomes necessary for a community to assume that its existence pre-

---

[3] Cf. Reinhold Niebuhr "Moralists and Politics," in Neibuhr's *Essays in Applied Christianity*, ed. D. B. Robertson (New York: Meridian Books, 1959), p. 78.

[4] Sidney Hook, *Political Power and Personal Freedom* (New York: S. G. Phillips, 1959), p. 94.

[5] Reinhold Niebuhr, "The Cultural Crisis of Our Age," *Harvard Business Review* (January-February 1954), p. 33, p. 36.

supposes certain broad and basic moral values or ideals; for "nations do become the bearers of values which transcend their national interests."[6] These values may comprise the vision which keeps a people from perishing. In a case decided in 1967, Justice Fortas said:

> There are great and important values in our society, none of which is greater than those reflected in the First Amendment, but which are also fundamental and entitled to this Court's careful respect and protection.[7]

Although this was said in a dissenting opinion, and while there may be differences among the Justices of the Supreme Court as to the implied "preferred" position accorded the First Amendment,[8] it is dubious if any member of the Court would question the proposition that "there are great and important values in our society."

There are, obviously, different ways of stating what these great and important values are, where to find them, and their order. Even so conservative a jurist as Justice Sutherland spoke of those "fundamental principles of liberty and justice which lie at the base of all our civil and political institutions."[9] This would imply that our civil and political institutions are not the only values; for there are values that transcend them and which serve as their foundation, and these values can be summarized in the concepts "liberty" and "justice."

While "justice" and "liberty" are terms used in the Preamble to the Constitution of the United States, and "liberty" is used in the Fifth and Fourteenth Amendments, "justice" is not used anywhere in the body of the Constitution. Yet it is often referred to as one of our great and fundamental values.

Justices of the Supreme Court have not restricted their catalogue of American ideals to those expressly enumerated in the Constitution. The Declaration of Independence speaks prominently of the "pursuit of happiness." Yet "happiness" is not a word that one will find in the Constitution. This, however, was no obstacle to constitutional interpretation as practiced by Justice Brandeis, as evidenced by, for example, the fol-

---

6 Reinhold Niebuhr, *op. cit., supra,* note 2, p. 181.

7 *Time, Inc.* v. *Hill,* 87 S. Ct. 534 (1967), p. 554, dissenting opinion, in which

7 *Time, Inc.* v. *Hill,* 87 S. Ct. 534 (1967), p. 554, dissenting opinion, in which

8 Justice Rutledge in *Thomas* v. *Collins,* 323 U.S. 516 (1945); Justice Stone in *U.S.* v. *Carolene Products Company,* 304 U.S. 144 (1938), footnote 4, pp. 152–153. *Contra:* Justice Frankfurter in *Kovacs* v. *Cooper,* 336 U.S. 77 (1949), and in *Ullmann* v. *U.S.,* 350 U.S. 422 (1956).

9 *Powell* v. *Alabama,* 287, U.S. 45, 67 (1932), quoting from *Hebert* v. *Louisiana,* 272 U.S. 312, 316 (1926).

lowing passage from his important opinion in *Olmstead* v. *United States,* in which he argued for the constitutional right of privacy:

> The makers of our Constitution undertook to secure conditions favorable to the pursuit of happiness. They recognized the significance of man's spiritual nature, of his feelings and of his intellect. They knew that only a part of the pain, pleasure and satisfaction of life are to be found in material things. They sought to protect Americans in their beliefs, their thoughts, their emotions and their sensations. They conferred, as against the government, the right to be let alone—the most comprehensive of rights and the right most valued by civilized man.[10]

But in *Whitney* v. *California,* a case involving the constitutionality of a criminal syndicalism statute, Justice Brandeis made happiness a part of liberty:

> Those who won our independence believed that the final end of the State was to make men free to develop their faculties. . . . They valued liberty both as an end and as a means. They believed liberty to be the secret of happiness. . . .[11]

These passages are quoted to point up the fact that the words of the Constitution—what Justice Cardozo spoke of as the "great generalities of the Constitution"[12]—as important as they are, cannot be taken as an exhaustive compendium of constitutional rights and liberties. "It is," said Justice Frankfurter,

> an inadmissibly narrow conception of American constitutional law to confine it to the words of the Constitution. . . .[13]

In a number of recent cases, the Supreme Court recognized and protected liberties which, the Court itself acknowledged, are not to be found in the words of the Constitution, for, said the Court, liberties expressly mentioned in the Constitution need "breathing space to survive."[14]

---

[10] *Olmstead* v. *United States,* 277 U.S. 438, 478 (1928), dissenting opinion.

[11] *Whitney* v. *California,* 274 U.S. 357, 275 (1927) concurring opinion.

[12] Benjamin Cardozo, *Nature of the Judicial Process* (New Haven, Conn.: Yale University Press, 1921), p. 17.

[13] *Youngstown Sheet & Tube Company* v. *Sawyer,* 343 U.S. 579, 610 (1952), concurring opinion.

[14] *N.A.A.C.P.* v. *Button,* 371 U.S. 415, 430 (1963), opinion by Justice Brennan. The reference was specifically to the First Amendment freedoms, but nothing was said that would necessarily limit the principle to these freedoms. See also *New York Times Co.* v. *Sullivan,* 376 U.S. 254, 272 (1964), opinion also by Justice Brennan.

In the Court's opinion by Justice Douglas in *Griswold* v. *Connecticut*,[15] the Court re-interpreted certain constitutional guarantees as "emanations," "penumbras," "zones," or "facets" of "privacy." Thus, the First Amendment freedoms are derivative from "privacy," the more ultimate or fundamental conception or ideal. So, too, said the Court, other constitutional liberties flow out of "privacy," are "emanations" from "privacy," such as the prohibition in the Third Amendment against the quartering of soldiers in any house in time of peace without the owner's consent; the affirmation in the Fourth Amendment of the "right of the people to be secure in their persons, houses, papers, and effects, against unreasonable searches and seizures"; and the guarantee against self-incrimination in the Fifth Amendment.

But just as express constitutional liberties flow out of the more fundamental but unwritten right of privacy, so the express constitutional liberties themselves generate other unwritten liberties. Thus, the First Amendment freedoms have a "penumbra" in which "freedom to associate" and "privacy in one's associations" are to be found. So, too, the First Amendment freedoms generate the right to educate one's children as one chooses; the right to study foreign languages in a private school; the right to distribute publications, to receive publications, to read, to teach, to pursue inquiry. So, too, the constitutional amendments generate protection of the intimate aspects of the marital relation and of the relation of husband and wife and their physician—these fall into a "zone of privacy created by several fundamental constitutional guarantees." The Constitution does not mention these zones of privacy, but the express provisions "create zones of privacy."

Thus, privacy is the mother of express constitutional guarantees, which in turn become the mother of other zones of privacy.

One is tempted to question the logic of these circular generative processes, but no one should undertake to criticize the logic unless he can produce a more appealing or convincing conceptual scheme. Adapting a passage from Justice Holmes in the Gompers case, I would say that the provisions of the Constitution cannot be read as abstractly as one reads a mathematical formula; they are organic, living institutions; their significance is not formal but vital.[16] We constantly need to be careful not to mistake "the form in which an idea was cast for the substance of the idea."[17]

We have noted that Justice Brandeis found happiness to be a part of liberty. So, too, Justice Douglas found property to be a part of liberty. For in the Heart of Atlanta Motel case, the Court had to meet the challenge that

---

[15] *Griswold* v. *Connecticut*, 381 U.S. 479 (1965).

[16] *Gompers* v. *U.S.*, 233 U.S. 604, 610 (1914).

[17] Chief Justice Vinson in *American Communications Association, CIO* v. *Douds*, 339 U.S. 382 (1950).

the Civil Rights Act of 1964, by forbidding racial discrimination or segregation by a motel, deprived the owner of his liberty and property without due process of law. Justice Douglas, concurring in the Court's decision upholding the constitutionality of the act as a proper exercise of the commerce power, added that Congress also had the power to enact the legislation under the Fourteenth Amendment; and in part resolved the conflict between property and liberty—both of which receive equal mention and dignity in the Due Process Clause—by maintaining that property is an instrumental value serving liberty. It is a means to an end. He quoted appprovingly the following passage from the Senate Committee report on the act:

> But there are stronger and more persuasive reasons [than the commerce power] for not allowing concepts of private property to defeat public accommodations legislation. The institution of private property exists for the purpose of enhancing the individual freedom and liberty of human beings. . . .
> Is this time-honored means to freedom and liberty [i.e., property] now to be twisted so as to defeat individual freedom and liberty [by allowing segregation]?[18]

Thus, one might say, in the clash between liberty and property under the Due Process Clause, liberty won out, not because it is "preferred," but because property is only a means to liberty, which is the end.

Justice Goldberg, concurring in the decision, chose to use a concept of even greater reach than liberty, though it is not a term to be found in the Constitution. The primary purpose of the Civil Rights Act of 1964, he said, is "the vindication of human dignity and not mere economics [the regulation of commerce]."[19]

The most candid admission that the Court may look for constitutional liberties outside the Constitution itself came from Justice Goldberg. In his concurring opinion in Griswold, he argued that

> The "liberty" protected by the Fifth and Fourteenth Amendments . . . is not restricted to rights specifically mentioned in the first eight amendments. . . . There are fundamental personal rights . . . which are protected from abridgment by the Government thought not specifically mentioned in the Constitution.[20]

We have seen that political institutions and values are not ultimate but are subject to moral criticism and moral judgment. As Sidney Hook

---

[18] *Heart of Atlanta Motel* v. *U.S.,* 379 U.S. 241, 285 (1964).

[19] *ibid,* p. 291.

[20] Case cited *supra,* note 15, pp. 493, 496. Justice Goldberg contended that the Ninth Amendment "lends strong support" to his view, p. 493.

has said, "The moral question is primary and it cuts across all categories."[21] Our civil and political institutions presuppose or are based on certain fundamental moral principles, ideals, or values. Some of them are specifically stated in the Constitution especially in the First Amendment. But the statement of the principles in the Constitution does not exhaust their meaning or reach. These principles need "breathing space"; thus, for example, there is freedom of association, though it is not mentioned in the Constitution, for without it the freedoms specifically enumerated in the First Amendment could not be fully enjoyed. In turn, freedom of association also needs "breathing space"—without the assurance of "privacy in one's associations," one would not be secure in one's "freedom to associate."

Then, too, the freedoms expressly stated in the Constitution may be interpreted as exemplifications or expressions of even more fundamental values. Thus, privacy is more fundamental than the First Amendment freedoms. The latter may, then, be read as "emanations" of privacy. The First Amendment may then be read as guaranteeing the fundamental right of privacy. But, then, the First Amendment and the other provisions of the Constitution will be read as exemplifying and as implementing some "facets" or "emanations" of this right; however, they do not exhaust the meaning, reach, or power of what the Constitution will protect as the right of privacy.

But even privacy may not be the ultimate value. It may be only an "emanation" or "facet" of a value found to be more fundamental, more encompassing, and more generative, just as happiness may be only a "facet" of liberty, and property only an aspect of liberty.

Finally, as our discussion has demonstrated, there are values, goals, ideals, that our Constitution protects which are not specifically mentioned in the Constitution. They are such as may be found in the "traditions and [collective] conscience of our people."[22]

The words of the Constitution are a "form." The "substance" of the ideas often transcends the form. The relationship of the form to the substance, as Plato discovered, can be described only allegorically: the terms of the Constitution are only "shadows," which the fire that is the substance throws on the opposite wall of the cave.[23] Just as "astronomy compels the soul to look upwards and leads us from this world to another," [24] so constitutional interpretation forces us to read the text but to look beyond it and to see further.

It is this process of transcendence that keeps the Constitution, and especially the Bill of Rights, from being "merely a literary composition"

---

[21] See note 4, *supra.*

[22] Case cited *supra,* note 15, p. 493, quoted by Justice Goldberg.

[23] Plato, *The Republic,* Book VII.

[24] *ibid.*

instead of "an organism."[25] It is this process that has made it possible for the Constitution to survive. This principle frees the Constitution from the paralysis of literalism and the disabling effect of narrow historicism.[26] The ideals of the Constitution, as important as they are, point beyond themselves to ever richer, greater goals, which become our national values and our constitutional presuppositions. The law, even the law of the Bill of Rights, points to a "higher" law.

THE INTERACTION OF
GOALS AND FACTS

We started with the proposition that there is room for the moral judgment or the higher law in the social-political realm, provided that the moral principles are not kept as mere abstractions and not used as if they provide simple answers to complex questions. Abstractionist and simplistic reasoning are often the trouble of sermonizing and moralizing. Yet sometimes goals or ideals need to be affirmed and vindicated *as if* the facts could make no difference: facts must then accommodate themselves to the values, and the latter will not give an inch. We sometimes say: "Let justice be done though the heavens fall."

We cannot always be concerned with consequences. Aristotle noted the fact that good things at times have harmful consequences. Wealth is a good thing, but some people have been ruined by it. Courage is a virtue, but in some cases courage has cost men their lives. Now, if wealth always meant ruin of the rich man's life or character, if courage always meant death, we would not think of these values as virtues or goods. We must, therefore, be content if, in dealing with premises that are uncertain, we succeed in only "a broad outline of the truth: when our subjects and our premises are more generalities, it is enough if we arrive at generally valid conclusions."[27]

Thus, for example, in the recent library sit-in case, it was not proper for Justice Black to be

> deeply troubled with the fear that powerful, private groups throughout the nation will read the Court's action . . . as granting them a license to invade the tranquility and beauty of our libraries

---

[25] Justice Frankfurter in *Burstyn* v. *Wilson*, 343 U.S. 495, 518 (1952).

[26] Justice Black is perhaps the only member of the Court who would attack this proposition. It is not relevant to our purpose to discuss Justice Black's position.

[27] Aristotle, *Nicomachean Ethics*, I, iii.

whenever they have quarrel with some state policy which may or may not exist.[28]

For, certainly, good things may have harmful consequences; but this is no argument against freedom of speech or any of the other freedoms guaranteed by the First Amendment. Freedom of religion is, we believe, a good thing even if it means the creation or spread of religions that may do more harm than good. Freedom of the press is, we believe, a good thing even if we may also believe, with Luther, that "the multitude of books is a great evil," that some books are downright wicked—for example, Hitler's Mein Kampf—and that most books are mere scribble and a waste of precious time and substance. A Negro family has a right to move into the house they have purchased even if their white neighbors may become a lawless mob which would try to keep them out. James H. Meredith had a right to be admitted into the University of Mississippi even if the enforcement of his right took 5,000 soldiers and National Guardsmen to accomplish.

From this standpoint, it probably would have been better if the Supreme Court in *Brown v. Board of Education*[29] had left out the controversial footnote 11, in which the Court referred to certain psychological and sociological studies; for the constitutional question was not whether racial segregation in the schools was in 1954—or in 1896, when *Plessy v. Ferguson*[30] was decided—good or bad for all the people, or for the white race, or for the Negro race.[31] What scientific studies were available in 1865 to prove that slavery was bad for Negroes or for the Nation, so that it should be outlawed by a constitutional amendment? When, in 1920, we adopted the Nineteenth Amendment, outlawing discrimination in voting rights on account of sex, how much did we know about women that had not been known to the previous generations of Americans? Many things certainly were different in the United States of 1920 from the United States of 1820, but it is doubtful if among the differences we could cite a greater amount of knowledge about the nature of women. Is it their superior knowledge of women that is the basis of women's suffrage in Uganda, as contrasted with the ignorance of the Swiss, who deny to their women the right to vote?[32]

---

28 *Brown* v. *Louisiana,* 383 U.S. 131, 167 (1966).

29 *Brown* v. *Board of Education,* 347 U.S. 438 (1954).

30 *Plessy* v. *Ferguson,* 163 U.S. 537 (1896).

31 See M. R. Konvitz, "The Use of the Intelligence in Advancement of Civil Rights," *Aspects of Liberty,* ed. M. R. Konvitz and Clinton Rossiter (New York: Johnson Reprints, 1958), p. 79.

32 In Switzerland, women vote in three (out of twenty-two) cantons. A (male) referendum in 1954 rejected women's suffrage for the federal republic.

In recent years there have been published monographs and tracts on the "costs of discrimination."[33] It would be interesting to find out, if one could, how many people have been persuaded by the argument on "costs" to come over to the side of civil rights. I suspect that those who were committed to racial segregation—in the United States, in South Africa, in Rhodesia—would say, with righteous indignation, that segregation was a matter of "principle," a question of a way of life, so what does "cost" matter? Is it an argument on behalf of Protestantism that it "costs" more to be a Roman Catholic?

All that I have said is not intended as an argument against empirical studies of problems connected with civil liberties or civil rights. I mean, however, to point up several considerations:

(1) It should by no means be assumed that we know in advance that empirical data should or will influence the ultimate value judgment. Facts and values may each be on their own street, and the streets may or may not intersect.

An individual or a nation may place such stress on an ideal that everything else in relation to it becomes incommensurable. "For what does it profit a man to gain the whole world and lose his soul?"[34] Facts were of no avail against Socrates or Thomas More in prison, to persuade either to change his mind. "I can do no other," said Luther at the Diet of Worms— *Ich kann nicht anders.* Many martyrs and heroes, and many peoples, have said the same; and they have all, in their various ways, followed the counsel of Emerson:

> Give all to love:
> Obey thy heart.
> Friends, kindred, days,
> Estate, good fame,
> Plans, credit, and the Muse,
> Nothing refuse. . . .
> Follow it utterly. . . .

Hume stressed the distance between values and facts, between the *is* and the *ought.* It is not, he said, "contrary to reason to prefer the destruction of the whole world to the scratching of my finger. . . . 'Tis as little contrary to reason to prefer my own acknowledg'd lesser good to my greater, and have a more ardent affection for the former than the latter."[35]

---

[33] For example, Bucklin Moon, *The High Cost of Prejudice* (New York: Julian Messner, 1947).

[34] Mark 8:36.

[35] David Hume, *A Treatise of Human Nature* (1734–1740), Book II, Part III, Sec. III.

(2) But Hume went perhaps too far in keeping values and facts separate and apart. He concluded from their differences and separation that values, which he significantly called "passions," cannot be ruled by reason. "Nothing," he said, "can oppose or retard the impulse of passion, but a contrary impulse." A passion can be replaced by another—similar or contrary—passion, but not by an argument, not by a chain of reasoning. "Abstract or demonstrative reasoning, therefore, never influences any of our actions, but only as it directs our judgment concerning causes and effects." Passions provide us with our goals; reason and considerations of fact may help us in our choice of means—"Reason is, and ought only to be the slave of the passions, and can never pretend to any other office than to serve and obey them."[36]

Empirical studies, for example, may show that it is probable that poverty breeds disease and crime. If men want to reduce or eliminate disease and crime, then they may be influenced by these studies to fight against poverty as a means to their goal. But the demonstration of a probable causal relationship between means and end will not itself produce a commitment to seek to achieve that end. If we are interested in the end, then we may be interested in finding the best means; but if we are not really interested in the end, discussion of means is a waste of time.

But Hume perhaps went too far to keep facts and values—or "reason" and "passion"—separate and apart. *They may cross and interact.* The mind and character of man are complex, and their ways are indescribably subtle.

Suppose, for example, empirical studies were to show that the poor have diseases that are relatively peculiar to poverty and that the rich also have diseases, such as are peculiar to their ways of life, and that on balance there was not much to choose between them: that in the end, both the rich and the poor end up in the doctor's office and in the hospital. Support, too, it could be shown that while the poor contribute a major proportion of criminals who committed certain types of crime, the same could be shown of the rich with respect to other types, so that, on balance, again there was not much to choose between them. Without the benefit of empirical investigations, Swedenborg was able to observe that

> Poverty seduces and withdraws men from Heaven as much as wealth. Great numbers among the poor are as ready as the wicked among the rich to defraud others, and to live in sordid pleasures when they have the opportunity.[37]

Concern with such empirical investigations and with the problem of means and ends may, however, lead to the conclusion that our real con-

---

36 *ibid.*
37 Emanuel Swedenborg, *Heaven and Hell* (1758).

cern with poverty is not that it may be the cause of certain tangible, even measurable, evils, such as disease or crime, but that, regardless of such considerations, it is in itself—like disease or crime—an evil which society should seek to mitigate or end. After years of study and the work of many projects has been completed, we may reach the common-sense conclusion of Dr. Johnson:

> All the arguments which are brought to represent poverty as no evil show it to be evidently a great evil. You never find people laboring to convince you that you may live very happily with a plentiful furtune.[38]

Separate consideration of means and ends may help to clarify our understanding of what our ends *really* are, and empirical investigations may contribute to an exposure of our misconceptions. When we get all through with our research, we may suddenly discover that we are not really seeking what we purported to be seeking. The illumination might have come without the great expenditure of time, resources, thought and effort, but our common experience is that often it comes the hard way.

Some abolitionists probably thought that they could demonstrate the evil of slavery by showing, with empirical data, that slavery breeds sickness and criminality. Suppose, however, that their investigations disclosed that slaves enjoyed longer life than their masters, and that they were relatively healthier men and women (after all, slaves were valuable property, which deserved concern and care) and that, when judged by the standards of the criminal law, slaves were better behaved than their masters (after all, they had less exposure to temptation to commit embezzlement, fraud, adultery, arson for profit, and many other offenses; besides, the risk to them, if caught, was much greater). After reviewing their findings, it might come to the investigators to cry out to themselves: "Can it be that we really, at one time, thought that slavery was a great evil *because* we could consider it a cause of sickness and crime? Did we want to abolish slavery *because* we thought that it breeds these evils? How foolish could we be?"

Hume, therefore, exaggerated when he claimed that

> Reason is wholly inactive and can never be the source of so active a principle as conscience, or a sense of morals.[39]

Empirical investigations of questions of fact may help explicate and may illumine values and value judgments; and such investigations, even when

---

[38] James Boswell, *The Life of Samuel Johnson* (1791), entry recorded for July 20, 1763.

[39] Hume, *op. cit., supra,* note 35, Book III, Part I, Sec. I.

based on hypotheses which prove to be misconceived, have value in compelling deeper criticism of the ends to which they may be related.

(3) Hume performed a great service for philosophy, law, politics, and science when he sharply differentiated ideal and fact, "passion" and "reason." But a bridge had to be built to connect them, and that connection may be described in words adapted from Kant—who was awakened out of his dogmatic slumbers by Hume: *Ideals without facts are empty, and facts without ideals are blind.*

Thus, for example, the ideal of equality before the law could be only a pious fraud unless we made the effort to find out the disparity between rich and poor defendants in the availability of defense counsel, transcripts of records for appeal, bail, and related rights.

As far back as 1865, Massachusetts placed on its books a civil rights law that banned discrimination on account of color or race in places of public accommodation. This pioneering law introduced an "activist" principle into our legal order, for the law presupposed the principle that a state has a *positive* role to play in race relations, to protect one race against the stronger, dominating will of the other; to prevent the development of a caste system based on race or color; to make the suffering of a public indignity on account of race or color an offense against the public order. By 1964, when Congress enacted the Civil Rights Act, there were thirty additional states with laws forbidding racial discrimination in places of public accommodation.[40] But how much have we ever known about the effectiveness of our state civil rights acts? Those who were concerned with such questions knew, in a general way, that the promise of these laws far outran the performance,[41] but there were no broad studies, no empirical data to inform the judgment. The ideals on which the laws were based remained, to a degree no one can say authoritatively, abstract from the facts of life.

(4) There is a large area where values need to be asserted, where moral positions need to be taken, with the realization, however, that the inexpressibly complex situations make it practically impossible to prove or disprove cause-effect relations between values and facts, between the *ought* and the *is*. Let me cite a number of such situations:

(a) When George C. Wallace was barred by the constitution of the State of Alabama from running for another term as governor, he placed his wife in the Alabama Democratic gubernatorial primary, which she won with 52 per cent of the vote. In the election on November 8, 1966, Mrs.

---

[40] See M. R. Konvitz, *Expanding Liberties: Freedom's Gains in Postwar America* (New York: Viking Press, 1965), pp. 255–256; M. R. Konvitz and Theodore Leskes, *A Century of Civil Rights* (New York: Columbia University Press, 1961), chap. 6.

[41] See Konvitz and Leskes, *op. cit., supra,* note 40, pp. 159–168; M. R. Konvitz, *The Constitution and Civil Rights* (New York: Columbia University Press, 1947), pp. 121–123.

Wallace received 512,970 votes, while her Republican opponent received less than half that number. As a candidate Mrs. Wallace admitted that, if she won the general election, she would turn over all power to her segregationist husband. At her inauguration of January 16, 1967, twenty-one bands played "Dixie" as they marched by the Wallaces on the inauguration stand; the area where the inauguration took place was decorated with Confederate flags; Mrs. Wallace took the oath of office on the spot where Jefferson Davis had taken his oath as President of the Confederacy. In her inaugural address, the governer charged that federal judges were undermining the Constitution, and that a federal agency was telling the people of Alabama with whom their children "shall associate." This, she said, was "an effort to gain control of the hearts and minds of our children. I resent it. As your Governor and as a mother, I shall resist it."[42]

Now, one is tempted to ask what effect these events may have on the hearts and minds of the same children in Alabama for which Mrs. Wallace expressed so much concern. What could children—and their parents and grandparents as well—have been thinking of the meaning of "constitutionalism," "democracy," "the rule of law," "a government of laws, and not of men," as they saw through the hypocrisy, the cant, of the heads of their government and of the hundreds of thousands of voters who supported them?

The people of Alabama who chose to violate—flagrantly and dramatically—the spirit of the constitution of their own state are, no doubt, great believers in "states' rights," in the "sovereignty" of their state, and in the superiority of the state over the federal Constitution. Having learned that it is all right to ignore, if one can, the federal Constitution, why cannot one treat the state constitution in the same way?

When the first Governor Wallace was informed that the federal district court—the court later attacked by his wife in her inaugural address—had ordered the admission of Vivian Malone and James Hood, Negro citizens of Alabama, to the University of Alabama, he said: "I am the embodiment of the sovereignty of this state and I will be present to bar the entrance of any Negro who attempts to enroll at the University of Alabama." This was said *nine* years after the Supreme Court's decision in the school desegregation cases. What effect did the spectacle have on millions of people who saw on their television screen Governor Wallace as he stood in front of the auditorium door to bar the two Negroes from registering?[43] How could one find out?

Some thirty-five years before these events, Justice Brandeis wrote:

---

[42] *New York Times,* January 17, 1967.

[43] Anthony Lewis, *Portrait of a Decade* (New York: Random House, 1964), chap. 11.

> In a government of laws, existence of the government will be imperiled if it fails to observe the law scrupulously. Our government is the potent, the omnipresent teacher. For good or for ill, it teaches the whole people by its example. . . . If the Government becomes a lawbreaker, it breeds contempt for law, it invites every man to become a law unto himself; it invites anarchy.[44]

This sounds plausible. But how much do we really know about the connection between the government as teacher—for good or ill—and the citizens as pupils? Indeed, with the example of the Wallaces in mind, could one not say that it may be equally true—or plausible—that the government learns from the citizens? that George C. Wallace told the people of Alabama what they wanted to hear, and that his actions were in part determined by the role expected of him by his constituents?

We know very little about such matters, and we know, perhaps, even less about ways to get at the facts.

(b) Many persons—including Dwight D. Eisenhower, Harry S. Truman, and J. Edgar Hoover—have said harsh things about nonviolent civil disobedience and Dr. Martin Luther King, Jr., as subversive forces which contribute to general disrespect for law and order, and to a moral and psychological atmosphere that induces or tolerates criminality. But nonviolent civil disobedience was, in fact, first proclaimed and undertaken by at least six Southern states when they adopted the theory of interposition, according to which states need not obey "unconstitutional" decisions of the United States Supreme Court. Following the decision in *Brown v. Board of Education* in 1954, the Southern states, declaring that they are the final judges of unconstitutionality, took the position that they would not desegregate their schools and would use every possible device to defeat the "unconstitutional" decision. Southern attacks on the Supreme Court and the states' obstinate refusal to recognize the validity of the Court's mandates preceded by some five or six years the civil disobedience movement led by Dr. King.

Now, if there has been a slackening of respect for law and order, how much is due to the civil disobedience movement, how much to the actions of Southern states since 1954, and how much to other "causes"? Who can tell? How could one find out? How can one measure the slack in respect for law and order? What time span should one use—months, a year, a decade? What section of the country or the population should be the guinea pigs?

When, in January 1965, the Supreme Court reversed the conviction of a civil rights leader for leading a demonstration near a courthouse in Louisiana, Justice Black dissented and used the occasion to say:

---

[44] Case cited *supra,* note 10, at p. 470.

Those who encourage minority groups to believe that the United States Constitution and federal laws give them a right to patrol and picket in the streets whenever they choose, in order to advance what they think to be a just and noble end, do no service to those minority groups, their cause, or their country.[45]

This is a sweeping condemnation of the civil disobedience movement. If true, it should remove all respectability and legal protection from the demonstrations. *But is it true? Can* the truth—or falsity—of so broad a judgment be established?

In February 1966, in a case involving a peaceful demonstration in a segregated library in Louisiana, Justice Black again dissented from a decision which reversed the conviction of the five young Negro demonstrators, and said:

. . . But I say once more that the crowd moved by noble ideals today can become the mob ruled by hate and passion and greed and violence tomorrow. If we ever doubted that, we know it now. . . . The holding in this case today makes it more necessary than ever that we stop and look more close at where we are going.[46]

How could the Supreme Court find out *where it is going,* where a decision on a set of facts may take the Court or the country or a segment of the civil rights movement? How could Justice Black be sure how the majority decision will be read and applied or be misread and misapplied? How do we know that the crowd of today will become the mob of tomorrow, or that those ruled by noble ideals will be replaced by men ruled by hate, passion, greed, and violence? "If we ever doubted that," said Justice Black, "we know it now." *But what is it that we know?* Do we *know* that the summer riots of Watts, Harlem, and Rochester would not have happened but for the peaceful demonstrations which preceded them? Do we *know* that if the Supreme Court majority had *upheld* the convictions in the peaceful demonstration cases in which Justice Black had dissented, there would have been no mobs, no riots? His first dissent in a demonstration case came June 22, 1964;[47] the seven riots in the summer of 1964 came between the middle of July and Labor Day.[48] But can anyone establish a causal relationship between the decisions of the Supreme Court, which involved peaceful sit-in

---

[45] *Cox* v. *Louisiana,* 379 U.S. 559, 584 (1965).

[46] Case cited *supra,* note 28, p. 168.

[47] Justice Black started his dissents in the civil rights trespass cases with *Bell* v. *Maryland,* 378 U.S. 226 (1964); *Bouie* v. *Columbia,* 378 U.S. 347 (1964); *Griffin* v. *Maryland,* 378 U.S. 130 (1964); *Barr* v. *Columbia,* 378 U.S. 146 (1964). All the cases were decided June 22, 1946.

[48] See M. R. Konvitz, *Expanding Liberties, op. cit., supra,* note 40, pp. 297–298.

demonstrations, and the riots in Rochester, Jersey City, Philadelphia, and several other cities? Did the rioters know of the decisions of the Supreme Court? What happened during the intervening month—was it a "heating-up" period?

(c) In the recent case involving the conflict between privacy and freedom of the press, Justice Harlan, concurring in part and dissenting in part, contended

> that a State should be free to hold the press to a duty of making a reasonable investigation of the underlying facts and limiting itself to "fair comment" on the material so gathered.

This statement of principle was followed by two sentences which bristle with empirical questions:

> Theoretically, of course, such a rule might slightly limit press discussion of matters touching individuals. . . . But, from a pragmatic standpoint, until now the press, at least in New York, labored under the more exacting handicap of the existing New York privacy law and has certainly remained robust.[49]

How much of a limit on the press is only a "slight" limit? How does one judge a press to be "robust"? How can one tell how much of its "robustness" has been sacrificed by the press in New York on account of the statute on privacy? How could one make a reliable study of the instances in which newspapers refrained from publishing reports because of the existence of the statute on privacy?

Justice Harlan concluded his attack on the principle formulated by the majority with the prediction that the principle would prove to be "ultimately harmful to the permanent good health of the press itself." How can he possibly know this? What qualities of the press, specifically attributable to the Court's ruling, could be identified as "harmful" to the press? How long a time is required to measure the "harmful" effects of a legal ruling on the "permanent good health" of the press?

The questions we have asked are mainly rhetorical, put without expectation of hearing answers. For not only are answers lacking, but also lacking is the knowledge sufficient to put the questions intelligibly.

We have, however, seen men of great responsibility, including Presidents of the United States and Justices of the Supreme Court, state propositions that touch the heart of vital rights and liberties, which neither they nor anyone else could prove to be true by facts or by arguments based on facts and experience. If challenged, their appeal would be, I assume, to

---

[49] Case cited *supra*, note 7, p. 553.

common sense. They could also point to the apology offered by Aristotle for the imprecision with which he undertook his investigation of politics. His treatment of this subject, he said

> will be adequate, if it achieves *that amount of precision which belongs to its subject matter.* The same exactness must not be expected in all departments of philosophy alike, any more than in all the products of the arts and crafts . . . ; for it is the mark of an educated mind to expect *that amount of exactness in each kind which the nature of the particular subject admits.* It is equally unreasonable to accept merely probable conclusions from a mathematician and to demand strict demonstration from an orator.[50]

With respect to some broad, complex questions, we shall need to be satisfied—at least for the foreseeable future—with only the "probable conclusions" which Aristotle allowed the orator. Thus, we are not to expect anyone to demonstrate that the nonviolent civil disobedience demonstrations in the civil rights movement had the effect of increasing or decreasing respect for law, legal process, and authority; or that they prevented race riots by serving as safety valves; or, on the contrary, that they acted to stimulate race riots by accustoming young people to take their demands to the streets and other public places. We must be reconciled to the possession of only fragmentary knowledge, or perhaps almost total ignorance, with respect to some highly significant issues involving relations between values and facts.

(5) There is, however, the danger that many questions of fact will not be investigated simply on the exaggerated assumption that the facts and their relations make such a "big, blooming, buzzing confusion" that the mind cannot penetrate them or reduce them to an intelligible order; and so there will be no commerce between the realm of *is* and the realm of *ought.* Each will flourish in its own impenetrable kingdom. This would give up more than may be warranted.

Consider how little we really know about academic freedom. In the case decided by the Supreme Court in 1967 in which the Court, by 5-to-4, struck down three antisubversion laws of New York, including the Feinberg Law, Justice Brennan, for the majority, said:

> It would be a bold teacher who would not stay as far as possible from utterance or acts which might jeopardize his living by enmeshing him in this intricate [statutory and administrative] machinery. . . . The result must be to stifle "that free play of the spirit which all teachers ought especially to cultivate and practice."[51]

---

[50] Aristotle, *op. cit., supra,* note 27.
[51] *Keyishian* v. *Board of Regents,* 87 S. Ct. 675 (1967).

"The result must be . . .," said the Court, but Justice Brennan did not stop to document this proposition. Later in the opinion, the Court said:

The stifling effect on the academic mind from curtailing freedom of association in such measure [as is accomplished by the Feinberg Law] is manifest, and has been documented in recent studies.

And here the Court cited a half-dozen studies, most of them of a general nature and several—perhaps no more than two—that may pass as empirical studies.

Admittedly, it is difficult to find out what effects teacher loyalty oaths and regulations may have on the teachers and their work. We know that in the school and college system of New York City, some four hundred teachers and other employees have been dismissed or have terminated their services as a result of inquiries under the Feinberg Law. Most were dismissed for refusal to answer questions about themselves.[52] There are those, however, who contend that "a bold teacher" is always bold; that bold teachers were not silenced or curtailed in their freedom even in the McCarthy period; that timid teachers are timid even in an atmosphere of freedom. We should try to find out more about such matters than we have done in the past. We may not be able to establish much, but we have not thus far really tried to establish anything. What shall be the indicators of academic freedom? Surely the absence of loyalty oath and similar laws and regulations must signify something or there would not be so much emotion generated by their existence; but we have here a matter to which we have not tried to give "that amount of precision which belongs to its subject matter."

A similar point may be made about the law of obscenity. We know that the Supreme Court has avoided saying that obscene publications may be prohibited *because* they have evil affects on those who read them, or on the youth, or on some other special group—that such publications may be prohibited because they create a "clear and present danger" to certain "substantive evils" which a state may have a right to prevent.[53] The Court has, however, said that obscene publications are outside the protection of the First Amendment because they are "utterly without redeeming social importance."[54] Suppose that reliable studies were to show that such publications "often" achieve "beneficial" effects and only "seldom" achieve "evil" effects. It may then well be that the Court, the legislatures, and the informed public generally would change their attitude. In 1963 the [London] *Times Literary Supplement* called upon the Home Secretary to

---

[52] Article by Mary Hornaday in *Christian Science Monitor*, January 26, 1967.

[53] See Konvitz, *Expanding Liberties, op. cit., supra,* note 48, pp. 117, 168–242.

[54] *ibid.,* p. 185.

institute a thorough study of the effects which different types of supposedly pernicious literature . . . can have on more or less susceptible readers. For the first essential is that we should all stop simply speculating one way or another on this head. At present the whole question is based on guess work.[55]

There have been some factual studies of the problem, but they barely scratch the surface.[56] One should not, of course, underestimate the difficulties involved in setting up and pursuing such empirical, and even experimental, inquiries, but more difficult tasks have been accomplished.

It should be added that the value of empirical studies in such an area would be considerably lessened if they were not set up on a continuing basis; for we live in a time in which moral standards are rapidly shifting. The reactions of a generation to whom *Fanny Hill, Tropic of Cancer,* and *Playboy* magazine are readily available and who assume such publications as a matter of course must be different from a generation to whom they were as unthinkable as they were unseeable. The changes are rapid and deep; for example, the National Catholic Office for Motion Pictures, formerly the National Legion of Decency, made its 1966 awards to *Georgy Girl* as one of the two best pictures of the year, and the Broadcasting and Film Commission of the National Council of Churches made one of its awards to *Who's Afraid of Virginia Woolf?*[57] The time dimension would need to fit prominently in any investigations; this will make general conclusions more hazardous; still, considerable room may be left for significant empirical analysis, which may interact with our relevant constitutional or other principles.

(6) The recent case of *Kent* v. *United States*[58] poignantly calls attention to another aspect of the problem of connection between goals and indicators. The case involved the waiver of jurisdiction over a juvenile delinquent by a juvenile court without a hearing and without stated reasons for the waiver, thereby subjecting the child to the possibility of a death sentence instead of treatment for a maximum of five years. In unanimously reversing and remanding the case, the Supreme Court, in an opinion by Justice Fortas, said that studies and critiques in recent years raised serious questions as to whether the actual performance of juvenile courts

> measures well enough against the critical purpose to make tolerable the immunity of the [juvenile court] process from the reach of constitutional guarantees applicable to adults. There is much evi-

---

[55] *ibid.,* p. 229.
[56] See some of the literature cited *ibid.,* p. 405, note 4.
[57] *New York Times,* February 3, 1967.
[58] *Kent* v. *U.S.,* 58 S. Ct. 1045 (1966).

dence that some juvenile courts . . . lack the personnel, facilities and techniques to perform adequately as representatives of the State in a *parens patriae* capacity, at least with respect to children charged with law violation. There is evidence, in fact, that there may be grounds for concern that the child receives the worst of both worlds: that he gets neither the protections accorded to adults nor the solicitous care and regenerative treatment postulated for children.[59]

This indictment of our juvenile courts—an institution of which most Americans could naturally assume we could be justly proud as evidence of our great concern over the welfare of children—underscores the fact that some of our institutions are praiseworthy only if we judge them by their façade. When we open them for inspection, we get quite a different picture, and even a different smell. In recent years we have become aware of the low quality of education provided for millions of our children in the public and the parochial schools; hardly a day passes when we are not reminded of the shabbiness of the performance inside our attractive-looking hospitals. What Florence Nightingale is reported to have said of hospitals may, unfortunately, be said of many of our institutions of which we are—sometimes insufferably—proud: "The least you can expect of a hospital," she said, "is that it should not spread disease!"

For years, the evidence was available that the way legislative apportionment worked, our much-vaunted democracy was only the barest approximation of the democratic ideal; yet hardly anyone stirred before the Supreme Court, in 1962,[60] opened the door for judicial review of apportionment and made relief possible. For years, the evidence was available that the "separate but equal" principle was a cheat and a fraud; yet hardly anyone cared before the Court exploded the fiction in the face of the American people in the 1954 decision.[61]

Surely, for years, it was no secret that in criminal cases, defendants who were too poor to engage legal counsel often failed to receive a fair trial; yet Americans went about their work and business and undoubtedly often remarked that in totalitarian countries, like the Soviet Union, men could not be sure that they would, when in trouble, receive a fair trial. The Irish proverb that "the hills look green that are far away" must often be reversed: the hills look green that are near. Again, we waited for the Supreme Court, in 1963, to correct our vision. "That government hires lawyers to prosecute and defendants who have the money hire lawyers to defend are," said the Court,

---

[59] *ibid.*, p. 1054.

[60] *Baker* v. *Carr*, 369 U.S. 186 (1962).

[61] Case cited *supra*, note 29.

the strongest indications of the widespread belief that lawyers in criminal courts are necessities, not luxuries. The right of one charged with crime to counsel may not be deemed fundamental and essential for fair trials in some countries, but it is in ours. . . . This noble ideal [of fair trials before impartial tribunals in which every defendant stands equal before the law] cannot be realized if the poor man charged with crime has to face his accusers without a lawyer to assist him.[62]

These are only a few instances of shocking discrepancies between our noble ideals and our practices, where for years the practices have been known to exist, and yet the American people were, on the whole, indifferent and pretended innocence. We tend to sweep under the rug our inconsistencies and failures. As the civil rights demonstrations dramatically showed, we are as a people prone to believe that once we have approved an ideal, nothing further remains to be done: the ideal is assumed to be self-fulfilling; yet there is hardly an aspect of our ideals of which we can truthfully say that it has been fully, or even substantially, achieved.

SUMMARY

It is not enough for a nation to profess to be a democracy. East Germany calls itself the German *Democratic* Republic, and North Vietnam calls itself the *Democratic* Republic of Vietnam. Nor is it enough for a nation to have a constitution and a bill of rights. Stalin gave the Soviet Union in 1936 a constitution with provision for universal, direct suffrage, with secret ballot, and with a bill of rights that professes to guarantee freedom of conscience, freedom of speech, the press, assembly, mass meetings, street processions and demonstrations, and the inviolability of homes and privacy of correspondence.[63] The statement and affirmance of ideals are important: for while nations—like St. Paul[64]—follow the worse, their bills of rights are admissions against interest, admissions that they see the better; they are the tribute that vice pays to virtue. And as our own case has shown, there is no telling when—sometimes even after the passage of a century or more—a provision of a bill of rights gets called in like a promissory note, and we are told by a court, or by a group of college and

---

[62] *Gideon* v. *Wainwright,* 372 U.S. 335, 344 (1963); opinion of Justice Black for the Court.

[63] United Nations, *Yearbook on Human Rights for 1946* (New York: United Nations, 1947), pp. 315–316.

[64] Romans 7:19.

high school students in a demonstration, that we either put up or shut up.

For a nation honestly to estimate the degree to which it lives by its vision and its self-image, it must look at the facts. If the facts are not apparent, it must set up machinery to get at the facts, for ideals without facts, consistent with the ideals, are empty.

In looking for the facts, it is necessary to keep in mind different situations. We have dealt, in the second part of this chapter, with only six different situations. There are many others, but these should suffice to point up the complex question of the relation between goals and indicators as the question touches fundamental rights and liberties. The different situations touched on were the following:

(1) There are values that seem to demand vindication without regard to the proofs of what they may produce; for example, starting in 1954, our federal courts have been ordering and compelling desegregation of universities and schools and will not listen to arguments about hardships, unrest, and violent resistance.[65]

(2) Investigations of fact, even when directed toward hypotheses which prove to have been misconceived, may have value in throwing light upon values which may have been misunderstood, disregarded, or falsely estimated. For example, I think that many of the attempts to establish that poverty is a source of this evil or that are not likely to prove success-ful; yet the attention focused on poverty is itself justified as possibly con-tributing to an intensified sensitivity to poverty as in itself an evil: an evil not because it leads to other evils, but simply because the state of poverty is by itself an evil. Empirical investigations may contribute to a refine-ment of our sense of values and may be a process out of which new values may emerge.

(3) We lack the knowledge of how our ideals are effective, or even if they are at all effective in life; for example, many states had civil rights acts, fair employment practice acts, fair housing acts, fair educational practices acts, but we seemed satisfied that we have done our duty fully when we enacted these laws and provided some enforcement agencies. These steps may, as a matter of fact, have had the bad effect of soothing our consciences—prematurely. We made almost no effort to find out how effective—or ineffective—these statutes and agencies in fact were.

(4) Some questions seem to be too large and too complex for fruitful empirical inquiry; for example: Have the civil rights nonviolent demon-strations contributed to a greater respect for law and the rule of law, or to an increase in criminality, a proneness to rioting, and a general disrespect for authority? Has the privacy statute of New York State had good or bad

---

[65] *Cooper* v. *Aaron,* 358 U.S. 1 (1958).

effects on the ideal of freedom of the press? Questions of such complexity —at least in the present state of the tools and methods of social science— had better be left unexplored as likely to be fruitless or impossible. But eventually the tools may be sharpened, and the methods may become more sophisticated. In any case, we can look only for "that amount of precision which belongs to its subject matter" and make no exaggerated claims.

(5) There are vast stretches of unexplored regions; for example, we have little reliable knowledge of the effects of obscenity or pornography. We know little about the extent to which teachers and professors use the academic freedom that they are supposed to have, and the extent to which laws, regulations, practices, or traditions impinge upon or curtail their freedom.

(6) We have, on the one hand, values, more or less clearly defined, and, on the other hand, a considerable amount of data which show how inadequately these values are fulfilled in our society; for example, studies of legislative malapportionment were available for years before *Baker* v. *Carr*. There is in our society and in our governmental system often an unconscionable lag of time between proof of the existence of an institutional disease or malfunction and the cure: the values seem to exist in compartments which are effectively insulated from the facts of life. The problem is how to get those who can do something about an evil to recognize its existence "with all deliberate speed"—to get the guardians of our goals to read the indicators.

QUIS CUSTODIET IPSOS CUSTODES?

There is the danger that the government of the United States—or of any nation—will naturally pretend that its goals are the purest and most noble and that its conduct has been most virtuous. Politics tend to corrupt the highest values—generally not by direct attack but by pretending that the government or the administration or the party is better than it is. "The devil is always an angel who pretends to be God. Therefore, while egoism is the driving force of sin, dishonesty is its final expression." [66] We may grant, and continue to assume, that a nation or government "is not as virtuous as it pretends to be; and also less virtuous than it might be if it made fewer pretensions." [67]

There are, however, enough instances of honest governmental reporting to warrant our feeling that the risks are calculated risks which pru-

---

[66] Reinhold Niebuhr, *An Interpretation of Christian Ethics* (New York: Meridian Books, 1935), p. 83.

[67] *ibid.,* p. 85.

dently may be taken. A number of examples in support of this feeling may be cited:

(1) Soon after Congress enacted the Immigration and Nationality Act of 1952 (the McCarran-Walter Act) over President Truman's veto, the President appointed the President's Commission on Immigration and Naturalization to study and evaluate the immigration and naturalization policies and to make recommendations. The Commission's report, *Whom We Shall Welcome,*[68] is a model of candor, sincerity, and truth. No outside, even foreign, group could have made a more honest report. It is free of any taint of cant, hypocrisy, or sugar-coating. This report had to wait some twelve years for its full vindication; but it was vindicated when President Johnson signed, on October 3, 1965, the act of Congress that provided for the elimination of the national-origins system of quotas.

(2) In the spring of 1946, after the last of the relocation centers had been closed, the War Relocation Authority (WRA) issued ten reports on the tragedy that hit the Japanese-American people immediately following the attack on Pearl Harbor. The integrity of this official study, published by the United States Department of the Interior, may be measured by this passage from the final—tenth—volume:

> But perhaps the most disturbing results are the least tangible ones—the pattern we have established for undemocratic behavior, the stain on our national record in the eyes of freedom-loving peoples throughout the world, and the physical discomfort and mental anguish we have brought upon thousands of sincere, well disciplined and patriotic people. If we had learned to judge people by their individual worth instead of by the pigmentation of their skin and the slant of their eyes, these things would not have happened and we would be a prouder, more widely respected Nation today.[69]

(3) The historic report of 1947 by President Truman's Committee on Civil Rights cannot be praised too highly. Had it been prepared by a tribunal of foreigners, with Bertrand Russell at their head, it could not have been more critical. The stance and tenor of this report—*To Secure These Rights*—may be sensed from the following general recommendation of the Committee:

---

[68] U.S., President's Commission on Immigration and Naturalization, *Whom We Shall Welcome.* The report was submitted to President Truman on January 1, 1953, just before he left office. Philip B. Perlman, one-time Solicitor General of the United States, was chairman; Harry N. Rosenfield was executive director.

[69] *WRA: A Story of Human Conservation* (1946), p. 190. J. A. Krug was Secretary of the Interior. D. S. Myer was Director of the War Relocation Authority.

In general: The elimination of segregation, based on race, color, creed, or national origin, from American life. The separate but equal doctrine has failed in three important respects. First, it is inconsistent with the fundamental equalitarianism of the American way of life in that it marks groups with the brand of inferior status. Secondly, where it has been followed, the results have been separate but unequal facilities for minority peoples. Finally, it has kept people apart despite incontrovertible evidence that an environment favorable to civil rights is fostered whenever groups are permitted to live and work together. There is no adequate defense of segregation.[70]

It should be underscored that this was said seven years before the Supreme Court overruled its "separate but equal" rule and ten years before Congress enacted the first civil rights act in eighty-two years.[71] On the whole, the reports of the United States Commission on Civil Rights, starting with the report published in 1959, have been up to the standard set by the 1947 report.

Indeed, one may venture to suggest that by now the United States enjoys something of a "tradition" of honest and courageous governmental reporting. A significant older document that is evidence of this "tradition" is the famous report on the Chicago strike of 1894, made by a commission appointed by President Cleveland to examine into the causes of the Pullman strike. The commission looked at the facts without fear or favor, and its most important recommendations had to wait for some thirty to forty years for adoption by Congress.[72] I think that when a historian investigates the history of governmental reporting, he will find many reports that he will want to list in his honor roll.[73]

Our society is not, however, completely dependent on governmental agencies for periodic examination and reporting of national goals. Private watchdog organizations are indispensable for the progress of civil liberties and civil rights. We could not sleep or be awake securely without private organizations that neither slumber nor sleep—such as the American Civil Liberties Union, the National Association for the Advancement of Colored People, the American Jewish Congress, the American Jewish Committee, the B'nai B'rith Anti-Defamation League, and the Association on American Indian Affairs. Such organizations are important as long as they are led by persons who are totally dedicated to the pursuit of their organizations'

---

[70] U.S., President's Committee on Civil Rights, *To Secure These Rights* (1947), p. 166. Charles E. Wilson was chairman. Robert K. Carr was executive director.

[71] Civil Rights Act of 1957, 71 Stat. 634 (1957).

[72] Railway Labor Act of 1926 and National Labor Relations Act of 1935.

[73] He would, I think, make special mention of the reports of the National Resources Planning Board, created in 1939, and abolished in 1943.

goals and programs, maintain their organizations in complete independence of government, administration, and party, and are not afraid of antagonizing public opinion and even a large segment of their own membership. I would submit that the record of these organizations bears out the judgment that they have been loyal to their purposes with exemplary dedication and courage.

Fortunately, too, watchdogs are built into our system of government. There are many notable veto messages by the President which have the prophetic quality. They remind the Congress and the nation of the permanent ideals which threaten to be weakened or destroyed. President Truman's veto of the Internal Security Act of 1950 (the McCarran Act)[74] is an instance of this important Presidential power. There are numerous opinions of the United States Supreme Court—opinions for the Court, as in the School Desegregation Cases of 1954; dissenting opinions, as that of Justice Stone in the first Flag-salute case;[75] sometimes even a footnote[76]— that serve to raise our sights.

There are examples, too, of solitary, unofficial voices crying out and being heard. One thinks readily of the article on privacy by Warren and Brandeis,[77] John Steinbeck's *The Grapes of Wrath* (1939), and the more recent *The Other America: Poverty in the United States* (1962) by Michael Harrington. Who can estimate the great influence of the writings by the late Zechariah Chafee, Jr.? We live in an age of noise and mass media; but the power of the still small voice, before or after the fire, is not to be belittled.

There is a crying need, however, for a privately financed, independent agency for research in civil liberties. Perhaps the recently established Center for Research and Education in American Liberties, at Columbia University,[78] will achieve the financial resources and the moral support to become the great institution in this area that other institutions have become for research in the biological sciences, mathematics, aeronautics, and almost all other aspects of our technological civilization.

We would stress, as a caveat, the importance of the precaution that private research in civil liberties be conducted only by agencies which are

---

[74] U.S., 81st Congress, 2nd Session, House Doc. No. 708, September 22, 1950.

[75] *Minersville School District* v. *Gobitis*, 310 U.S. 586 (1940). Cf. *W. Virginia State Board of Education* v. *Barnette*, 319 U.S. 624 (1943).

[76] For example, the footnote in *U.S.* v. *Carolene Products Co.*, 304 U.S. 144, 152, note 4 (1938), which has played an important role in the discussion over the "preferred position" of certain constitutional freedoms.

[77] "The Right to Privacy," 4 *Harvard Law Review* 193 (1890).

[78] The Center was established in January 1965. It is under the direction of Professor Alan F. Westin.

exclusively or primarily committed to these liberties. If the agency is interested, for example, in judicial administration generally, or in the sociology of law, it may be tempted to study the jury by the use of concealed microphones in the jury room.[79] As in other fields of human interest and concern, so also in civil liberties: the frontiers of our knowledge can best be attained by an exclusive—perhaps even obsessive—dedication of the mind to one end. American liberties are far too important for research in them to be entrusted to anyone other than civil libertarians.

[79] See F. L. Strodtbeck, "Social Process, the Law, and Jury Functioning," *Law and Sociology,* ed. Wm. M. Evan (New York: Free Press, 1962), p. 151, note 8.

6

DEMOCRATIC PARTICIPATION

SIDNEY VERBA

This chapter will deal with some of the problems and dilemmas of democratic participation. Loosely defined, democratic participation refers to the processes by which citizens influence or control those who make major decisions affecting them.[1] Any social inventory for a democratic society would have to pay attention to measures of democratic participation, since this is so crucial a value. And the topic is particularly important now when we may be said to be going through a crisis in participation. The civil strife in American cities during the summer of 1967 has many sources, but one important source of the massive violence is the perception on the part of many Negro slum dwellers that they are powerless to control those who make decisions affecting them.

"Participatory democracy" is not an all-or-nothing thing; every society allows some means of participation for some citizens, and no society is run on the basis of equal participation by all citizens.[2] The United States is one of the happy few nations of the world which have passed many of the traditional crises of participation—for example, the incorporation of most of the working class, through the spread of the franchise and the growth of mass political parties, and the incorporation of a multiplicity of ethnic

---

[1] We shall consider this definition more closely below and try to justify using one that is so inclusive.

[2] See Gabriel Almond and Sidney Verba, *The Civic Culture* (Princeton, N.J.: Princeton University Press, 1963) for some comparative data on participation in the United States and elsewhere. See also Deane E. Neubauer, "On the Theory of Polyarchy: An Empirical Study of Democracy in Ten Countries" (unpublished Ph.D. dissertation, Department of Political Science, Yale University, 1966) for data that ranks the United States somewhat lower. These comparisons will be discussed more fully below.

groups into democratic politics.[3] But the problems of participation are
The issues of participation are, to paraphrase Harold Lasswell: *Who*
participates, about *what* and *how*? There is an acute crisis of participation
in the contemporary United States because all three issues are being raised
at once: new people want to participate, in relation to new issues, and in
new ways. The question of who ought to participate has been raised most
strikingly by Southern Negroes; but, in colleges, students want to participate and, in welfare agencies, clients want some voice. At the same time,
participation is demanded in relation to a wider range of issues or governmental activities: the subjects of administrative programs demand chances
to participate within such programs; parents demand more voice in school
planning; and students demand more voice in deciding what they are
taught. In the field of foreign policy—an area in which democratic control is particularly difficult—the war in Vietnam has triggered widespread
public attempts to have some voice. Indeed, in relation to almost every
substantive area of political controversy in contemporary America there
is a parallel controversy over who participates in decisions relevant to that
area.[4] And, lastly, new modes of participation have become current: sit-ins
and demonstrations are but two examples of a wide expansion in the use
of direct action.

In no single respect are we dealing with a new phenomenon. The
franchise has expanded many times in the past to incorporate new groups;
participation has spread to new issues; and new modes of participation
have been devised before. But the cumulation of these three types of
expansion—and in relation to issues that are of burning importance to
the potential participants—makes it appropriate to talk of a crisis of
participation.

There are many reasons for the crisis. The sources lie in many changes
of a social, economic, and ideological nature, a fact that illustrates the
close linkage between problems of participation and the other topics discussed in this volume. An economy that is expanding and changing rapidly,
but in ways that benefit some but not others; a social structure with great

---

[3] Robert A. Dahl, "The American Oppositions," in Dahl (ed.), *Political Oppo-
sition in Western Democracies* (New Haven: Yale University Press, 1966), chap. ii;
Stein Rokkan, "The Comparative Study of Political Participation: Notes toward a
Perspective on Current Research," in Austin Ranney (ed.), *Essays on the Behavioral
Study of Politics* (Urbana: University of Illinois Press, 1962); and Seymour M.
Lipset, *The First New Nation* (New York: Basic Books, 1963).
never solved once and for all. As societies change and new problems arise,
issues of participation come to the fore again, as they do in the current
racial crisis.

[4] If the New Left movement has a philosophy, it seems to revolve around the
notions of participatory democracy.

mobility opportunities through education for some, but not others; and a broad set of emerging values that reject traditional means of social control —all form the background of the crisis. Furthermore, the expansion of governmental intervention in the economic and social life of the nation increases the stakes of participation: the government does more, and, therefore, more is to be gained by having a voice over what it does. A full consideration of the source of the participation crisis lies well beyond the scope of this paper. But, whatever its source, the crisis raises some fundamental issues and dilemmas about the nature of our democracy.

In the following sections, we shall attempt to lay out the problem of participation by (1) defining it, (2) discussing some of the reasons that it is an important goal in a democratic society, (3) discussing some dimensions and components of participation, (4) discussing some of the conditions for effective participation from the point of view of both the participant and the decision-maker, and (5) discussing more fully some of the particular problems and dilemmas associated with the current crisis in participation. Only then will we consider (6) the social indicators on which information would be useful.

PARTICIPATION DEFINED

As a rough beginning, we may define participation as referring to acts by those not formally empowered to make decisions—the acts being intended to influence the behavior of those who have such decisional power. And successful participation refers to those acts that have (at least in part) the intended effects.[5]

Several further comments on the definition are needed.

(1) The definition stresses *intention* to influence decision-makers.[6] The definition thus excludes those situations where government officials act independently to make policy on the basis of their own beliefs and values and not in response to some communication or demand from the citizenry.

(2) The definition does not include what can be called "ceremonial" or "support" participation, where citizens "take part" by expressing support for the government, marching in parades, working hard in community

---

[5] The definition is "rough," but this is not too much of a problem. The purpose of the definition is to delimit the area of concern rather than to provide a clear set of operations to distinguish between participatory acts and other acts.

[6] The "intentionality" of an act is a complicated notion. For the present moment, we can ignore how precise or stable the intentions are. The act is intentional so long as those who are participating want the political leaders to "get the message," even if the message has no more precise content than an expression of general discontent.

projects, participating in youth groups organized by the government, or voting in ceremonial elections.

(3) Participation is not confined to the electoral process nor is it limited to any particular type of political act such as voting, letter-writing, picketing, or political-party activities. The question is left open as to whether the standard modes of participation, such as voting, represent the most effective modes.

(4) Participation is not limited to any particular government level. As long as the official has some discretion in the handling of a situation, he is a potential target. And most officials, high and low, have some discretion in most situations—even if it is limited to the all-important choice of whether or not to treat the citizen with courtesy.

(5) Participatory acts refer to interactions between citizens and decision-makers. This means that to understand participation and its effects, one must study both the participants and the decision-makers.

(6) Participation is not necessarily successful participation. The distinction between successful and unsuccessful participation attempts is crucial and will be returned to later.

(7) Participation has been defined in terms of acts aimed at those empowered to make decisions. This essay will continue to deal with participation in relation to government decisions. But a focus on democratic participation requires that one look beyond the relations between citizen and government to the relations between individuals and authorities in the families, schools, organizations, and other nongovernmental institutions to which individuals belong. Participation involves having a voice in decisions that affect us, and it is clear that decisions of this sort are made in a variety of nongovernmental settings.

The distinction between governmental decisions and nongovernmental decisions is far from clear, and nongovernmental decisions partake of some of the characteristics of governmental ones. For one thing, decisions—in schools, on the job, in private organizations—are binding on those in the organizations. And membership is often far from voluntary. The university administrator who replies to students' claims for a greater voice in university decisions by indicating that their attendance at the university is voluntary may miss the point that university attendance has almost become a necessity for full access to the social and economic benefits in contemporary America. In addition, a variety of private organizations monopolize access to specific careers and to various social services. In this sense, they make decisions that are binding on the entire society.

There are, furthermore, reasons why participation in nongovernmental decisional units is relevant even if one's major concern is with participation vis-à-vis government. For one thing, participation in nongovernmental settings may be a training ground for participation in relation to the government. If, in the crucial social institutions with which the individual first has contact—the family and the school—he comes to consider it normal to have his fate decided by unresponsive and authoritarian decision-makers, he may be more likely to expect and accept such decision-making in the political sphere as well. But if he has learned to participate in these institutions, he may be likelier to be a participant in other areas.[7] And, secondly, many nongovernmental organizations are prime actors in the political process. Unless the members of these organizations have some opportunity to participate in them, the degree of effective participation *vis-à-vis* the government would decline substantially.

WHY IS PARTICIPATION IMPORTANT?

An argument can be made that other social goals—employment, schooling, peace, and the like—are more important than democratic participation and deserve more substantive consideration. Indeed, this is an argument current in many of the newer nations of the world and is not irrelevant in the American context. But participation deserves a special place for reasons that should be explicated.

(1) For one thing, participation represents a general value in our society; we expect individuals to have some autonomy and control over their own fate.

(2) Though participation is often thought of as a means to some other end—we vote to install political leaders to our liking; we write a letter to a congressman to induce him to act in some way we prefer—it is also an end in and of itself. If all decisions are made for us—in circumstances where there are accepted democratic norms—our self-esteem may decline. The individual who has no chance to participate is, in some sense, not a full member or citizen.[8]

---

[7] There are some data on this subject—though hardly conclusive—in Almond and Verba, *op. cit.*, chap. xii. It is also the justification often given for more democratic techniques within the school.

[8] One of the major historical justifications for barring individuals and groups from the franchise was that they were not "members" of the society. Thus, slaves were barred in Athens and the United States, and Negroes have not been considered full members in many sections of the United States. And aliens are barred from participation on similar grounds. See Herbert McClosky, "Political Participation," article prepared for the *Encyclopedia of the Social Sciences;* and Robert E. Lane, *Political Life: Why People Get Involved in Politics* (Glencoe, Ill.: Free Press, 1959), chaps. ii and iii, on the arguments about the franchise. I am turning the argument over and saying that lack of access to means of participation is a measure of lack of full membership.

(3) Participation represents a goal *per se,* but it also has a particularly important role as a means to other ends. It is a way in which goals can be set for a society. Such an approach avoids the presumptions involved in the setting of goals by one group for other groups.[9]

(4) The matter is not that simple, however. Participation may have costs as well. Policies that arise out of a process of political participation will be less satisfying to those with less political access. Furthermore, the relationship between participation in the making of decisions and the effectiveness of those decisions is also ambiguous. The argument is made that widespread participation in the making of decisions increases the likelihood that decisions will be effectively carried out. The reason is that participation gives the decision-makers two vital resources: information and support. If grievance mechanisms are blocked and if individuals and groups do not attempt to influence the government to correct what they feel to be wrongs, the decision-makers must plan in ignorance of the needs of the populace and of the effects of their previous activities. Similarly, participation is alleged to provide support for decisions: those who take part in decisions are more likely to support those decisions.[10]

But participation may not work that easily. From a different perspective, participatory democracy appears inefficient. Programs have to be compromised to suit the needs of multiple participants, and they lose the coherence and consistency possible in centrally designed plans. Technical questions are not easily dealt with, since the needed skills are lacking on the part of the participants; programs get diverted; decisions are delayed.

(5) One last reason why participation is highly relevant in connection with other social goals: the more the government does in relation to the life of a society, the higher the stakes of political participation. And in recent years, more of the life of the populace as a whole is affected by governmental activities; their opportunities for bettering their income, for preserving their health, for educating their children are mediated by governmental activity. This makes control over major decisions in these spheres of greater importance than it would be in a society where most of such aspects of life are regulated by the private sector. Secondly, the variety of types of activities entered into by the government means that a number of specific groups will find the stakes of political participation particularly high in relation to particular programs. Thus, more special groups with

---

[9] As the old saying goes, "Do not do unto others as you would have them do unto you. Their tastes may be different."

[10] For some indirect political evidence, see Almond and Verba, *op. cit.,* pp. 239–253. Evidence for the proposition comes largely from the literature of small groups and organizations. See Sidney Verba, *Small Groups and Political Behavior* (Princeton, N.J.: Princeton University Press, 1961) chaps. ix and x.

interests in particular governmental programs are likely to become involved in attempts to influence those programs.

This latter phenomenon has an impact not only on the amount of political participation found in a society, but upon the type of participation as well. As the government moves into more and more precise involvements in the life of society, the decisions over these governmental activities, of necessity, move into highly specialized technical agencies. These specialized agencies control the expertise and information necessary for decision-making in relation to a particular program. Participation *vis-à-vis* these agencies may require a new perspective; it may require new kinds of activities and new means of public control. Thus, the very fact that the government acts in new ways requires new modes of participation.

VARIATIONS IN PARTICIPATION

The definition of participation is broad. This is done deliberately so that many types of activities relevant to a wide range of issues and governmental structures can be considered. But this broad and abstract beginning means that one must go several steps farther before one can begin to look for specific indicators of participation. In this section, we would like to deal with the question of the different types of participation in which individuals engage; for it is only in relation to specific types of participation that one can assess the degree of effective participation open to particular groups.

We know the standard acts of participation—voting, letter-writing, campaign activity, and the like—but there are many more, and some not yet invented. Ten years ago, who would have listed the sit-in as a technique of participation? And the catalogue of political participatory acts is complicated by the fact that the same act may have different meanings in different contexts. Not all votes represent equally effective means of political participation; much depends on the characteristics of the voting system. To circumvent this problem, we will look at variations in means of participation in a somewhat more analytical way and ask about some of the general dimensions along which concrete acts of participation might vary.

THE PRIME DISTINCTION: IS THE PARTICIPATORY ACT SUCCESSFUL?

As was pointed out above, our definition of participation involves the intention of the actor to influence a political decision-maker; it does not imply the success of that act in changing the behavior of the decision-maker in the direction that the participant desires. Consistently successful acts of participation would indicate membership in what might be called a "ruling elite" group—that is, a group which can introduce a measure that is subsequently enacted by the government, or which can veto a measure introduced elsewhere.[11] For reasons that will be more fully explored below, such acts are rare in any large-scale social institution. It is, therefore, more useful to think of successful and unsuccessful acts as representing the two ends of a continuum: successful acts involve the initiation or veto of government decision; unsuccessful acts are those that have no measurable effects on the officials.[12]

In between the two ends of the continuum lie many acts of inter-mediary effectiveness. Policies are rarely initiated or vetoed by participants, but they can be modified or delayed. More marginally, participation may lead to second thoughts and unease among decision-makers that affect future policies.

To ascertain if a participatory act had any degree of success world, ideally, require nothing less than an experimental design, and such social experiments are barred to us in real life. Futhermore, this major dimension of participation makes clear why one crucial set of indicators of the effectiveness of participation would involve measures of the behavior of decision-makers. We only know half the story—and perhaps not the crucial half—when we look at the participants. The methodological problem involved is not easily solved. All we may achieve are weak, approximate measures of elite responsiveness—if we achieve that. But the problem must be kept in mind if the attempt to measure participation is to have any meaning.

The success, or lack of success, of a participatory act is further com-plicated because we may talk of the success of the act of an individual or the success of the acts of an aggregate of individuals. There are situations where the individual's own activities can have measurable effects. When he writes a letter to a congressman asking for some specific help, one can observe whether or not he receives a reply and what kind of reply. On the other hand, certain activities, such as voting or marching in protest demon-strations—especially when the demonstrations are large—mean that the

---

[11] See Robert A. Dahl, "A Critique of the Ruling Elite Model," *American Political Science Review*, LII (June 1958), pp. 459–463.

[12] The scale might be extended farther in the negative direction to encompass acts of participation that have a boomerang effect: that have an effect on decision-makers but in the opposite direction from that which the participants intended. "Just because you asked for it (or demanded it), you are not going to get it" is a not-unknown attitude among parents and school administrators; or even some major political figures. "We will not yield to pressure" is the more usual political phrasing.

individual's own contribution to the effects of the collective activity will not be noticeable.

In addition to the prime successful-unsuccessful distinction, we can distinguish three broad aspects of participation: the goals of the acts; the social structures within which they take place; and the distributional patterns of such acts. Once we have explicated these analytical dimensions, it will be easier to ask questions concerning the meaning of any particular act of participation.

THE GOALS OF THE PARTICIPATORY ACT

Participation, as we define it, involves an intention to have some effect on decision-makers. The content of those intentions becomes important in understanding participation.

1. The level of the goal: This distinction refers to the extent to which an individual or group is interested in general goals that affect the entire society, in more specific goals that affect only a few within the society, or perhaps in goals that affect only the participant. More specifically, we can distinguish the following:

> a. Desired governmental activities or decisions that would affect only the individual participant.
>
> b. Decisions that affect a large number of citizens or groups—in most cases, a number larger than the number actually engaging in the participatory acts—but not the entire society.
>
> c. Decisions that affect the entire society. These include policies that affect all, such as foreign policies and major economic policies, as well as changes in the ruling personnel of the society, as in elections.

Distinguishing among a, b, and c is something like the traditional distinction between rule-making (legislation) and rule-application (administration): the former involving general rules and the latter, the application of rules to specific cases. However, that distinction is a murky one, and the simple distinction of how many people are affected seems more useful. Of course, even this distinction is complicated. Individuals or narrow groups seeking some benefit for themselves will often couch their demands in universalistic terms, as a way of gaining allies and legitimating their claims. Or, conversely, a decision that in form affects one individual or a small group of individuals may be a precedent for general social policy. The level of the goal of the participation is closely related to the distinction between successful participation on an individual basis and successful participation by an aggregate. It is clear that successful participation of either sort in relation to goals for the society as a whole is likely to be rare in any large-scale social unit. But participation in relation to a goal at that level is almost impossible on an individual basis.

2. The amount of information carried by the act of participation: Acts of participation are intended to influence decision-makers in ways desired by the participants, but not all acts convey enough information so that the decision-maker can know what the intentions of the participant are. The vote as an act of participation may—for any individual—contain little information as to policy preference,[13] and even in terms of the aggregate of voters, it is hard to say what policy preference is conveyed by an election (except, of course, the preference for one candidate over another). At the other extreme, a visit by an individual to his congressman's office asking for aid in obtaining an immigration visa for a relative is quite precise in the outcome desired. In the visa case, one can tell if the congressman does something or not, but it is more difficult to tell whether an elected official is complying with the preferences expressed in the vote.

The notion of intentionality is central to my concept of participation, but it is a complicated one. Individuals do not always know what they want. Acts of participation often express a more diffuse discontent. Or through the act of participation itself, the goals of the participation are set or changed. The response to a diffuse expression of discontent may be an offer of a relatively specific ameliorative policy which then becomes the goal of the participants; or the participants may start with a specific goal but switch to another during the bargaining process.

This suggests that one has to look at the informational content from the points of view of both the sender of the participatory message and the recipient. Government officials, being more policy-oriented, may see more specific content than was originally put into the participatory act. Indeed, one measure of their effectiveness as decision-makers might be their ability to do this.

3. Protective versus innovative goals: In some cases, individuals and groups participate in order to protect themselves from some encroachment on their present position: they protest some planned or executed government action that would damage them. Other participatory acts have goals that are more innovative: they are not in reaction to some governmental initiative. Rather, the initiative comes from the participants.

---

[13] See Angus Campbell, et al., The American Voter (New York: John Wiley & Sons, 1960), chap. x.

THE SOCIAL STRUCTURES WITHIN
WHICH PARTICIPATION
TAKES PLACE

Here again, we can distinguish three subaspects: the degree of organization of the participation, the target of the participation, and the degree
to which it carries sanctions.

1. The organization of the participatory act: Individuals may act as
individuals; they may act individually but as part of an aggregate of individuals engaging in a participatory act (voting is the best example); they
may act as members of either informal or formally organized groups. The
difference between acting as a member of an aggregate of individuals (voting the same way as other members of one's ethnic group) and acting
through an organized group (pressure applied by an ethnically based
organization) is that, in the latter case, there is some structure whereby an
organized group—through its leaders—speaks for the members. Of particular relevance here may be the extent to which individuals are capable
of forming groups when there is some political need. Informal groups of
friends, *ad hoc* committees to protest some government action, and newly
created organizations to deal with a particular problem are some of the
prime actors in politics, especially on the local scene. And they may represent a particularly powerful means to enhance the power of the individual.[14]

2. The target of the participatory act: The act of participation may be
directed at any one of a number of targets: the President, congressmen,
party leaders, bureaucrats. We have deliberately included officials of all
levels in our scope.

One major distinction among targets is the extent to which they are
centralized or dispersed. Is there one central place where relevant decisions
are made, or are there many such places? This will have a major effect on
the kind of participation and the likelihood of success. Attempts to influence foreign policy all ultimately have to be aimed at a few central figures
and offices in Washington. Attempts to influence civil rights measures can
be aimed at innumerable national and local targets.

3. Does the participatory act carry sanctions or the threat of sanctions? Some acts of participation merely inform governmental officials of a
point of view or perhaps request some compliance. Other acts of participation carry more explicit sanctions or threats of sanction. The borderline
between the two types of participation is not clear. Messages that merely
seem to convey information also may imply possible sanctions—a letter to
a congressman may imply (or, at least, he may infer) a threat of with-

---

14 See Almond and Verba, *op. cit.*, chap. vii.

drawal of a vote or of campaign support. In addition, if approval by his constituents is positively valued by a decision-maker, any statement of preference implies at least a weak sanction. But the distinction between sanctioned and unsanctioned participation remains important—especially when one is dealing with formal governmental institutions that foster participation. Free-speech laws open the way for the expression of preference; elections provide more direct sanctions for noncompliance on the part of governmental officials. Paternalism is replaced by democracy when government leaders have no choice but to respond to public demands because of sanctions for noncompliance.

THE DISTRIBUTION OF
PARTICIPATORY ACTS

Thus far, we have been characterizing *acts* of participation, but in order to understand how effective these are likely to be, we must look at the set of participatory acts going on at any moment of time. How many people are trying to influence the government? And in what direction?

(1) For any particular type of participation, we can ask how many take part (in absolute numbers or as a proportion of the population). And, more important, we can ask about the equality with which such acts of participation are distributed among the population.

(2) In addition, however, one must take into account the direction of the participation. Are all attempting to influence the government in the same way, or are the intentions of some opposite to those of others? Obviously, the likelihood of success is affected by this.

The above delineation of the dimensions of participation was compiled for several reasons. It makes it easier to understand the relative importance of any concrete act of participation—voting, letter-writing, and the like—by asking where that act would fall on the dimensions listed above. We have some standard for the importance of various acts. And this is possible because the various subdimensions mentioned above are related to the prime dimension—the extent to which the act of participation is effective. The next step would be to combine these various subsidiary dimensions and relate them, on the one hand, to specific acts of participation and, on the other, to the likelihood of the success of these particular acts.

But before doing that, we beg the reader's indulgence for one other excursion through a forest of dimensions. We would like to list some possible *conditions* for effective participation—that is, what makes it likely that an individual or group will participate effectively?

THE CONDITIONS FOR EFFECTIVE
POLITICAL PARTICIPATION

The likelihood that any individual will participate in politics is related to the resources he possesses, his motivation to participate, and the conduciveness of the social structure and the culture in which he lives. These four broad sources of participation are related but can be independent. Individuals who have resources may lack motivation. Or those who are motivated may not have available to them the social structures through which they can participate. Or, conversely, the availability of social structures for participation (the existence of periodic elections or complaint offices in government agencies) may not lead to much participation if individuals are neither motivated nor have the resources to take advantage of these structures.

The structure of the following section is based on the assumption that individuals ordinarily will not take part in politics. We then ask: What is likely to make them take part? This is a not unreasonable assumption, though it turns upside down the usual assumption that people ordinarily take part in politics and the usual question: What obstacles stop them? The difference in perspective, however, is not that important.

Let us look more closely at these conditions.

RESOURCES

1. INTELLECTUAL RESOURCES: There are a number of intellectual resources that increase the likelihood that an individual will attempt some participatory act and that it will be successful. These include: (a) information about politics, issues, channels of communications, and the rules of political participation and (b) skills in manipulating these channels of access. Skills in written and oral expression, in reasoning, and in manipulating others are important.[15]

2. MATERIAL RESOURCES: These include all those material possessions that can be used to increase one's political effectiveness: money, control over jobs, land, or other resources.[16] Note that all of these must be considered from two points of view: the availability of the resource to the individual and its usability for political purposes.

---

[15] See the studies cited in Lester W. Milbrath, *Political Participation* (Chicago: Rand, McNally, 1965), pp. 64–72.

[16] See the studies in *ibid.,* pp. 114–128.

3. SOCIAL RESOURCES: These include the people or organizations that one can manipulate and can get to support one in a political act. People who have friends, who belong to organizations, or who work in places where it is possible to organize one's fellows (which may depend on the size of the place and the organization of the work) are more likely to participate and to participate successfully.[71]

4. SOME GENERAL COMMENTS ON RESOURCES: A major distinction to be kept in mind is the extent to which various resources are cumulative or dispersed. If the individuals who possess one resource are likely to possess all the others, and those who are missing one are likely to have none of the others, the distribution of participation in a society is likely to be badly skewed. As Dahl has pointed out, there is a wider distribution of political power if resources are dispersed. In New Haven (and in many other cities), those who control wealth may not be those who control votes, The former do not possess a social resource—ethnic identity —that makes it possible for them to mobilize a bloc of voters.[18]

COSTS OF PARTICIPATION

The notion that resources will be useful for political participation implies the opposite side of the coin: that participation will cost something in the way of resources. Participation takes time, money, and effort.[19]

In relation to certain kinds of issues, the costs of participation may be more relevant than the resources available. If the chances of success are slim and, particularly, if the individual's own contribution to the outcome is hard to measure or very small, costs may be a major deterrent. Where the costs of voting are high—through restrictive laws which mean that one has to invest more time or money into registering or voting—the rate of voting goes down. And it particularly goes down for those least motivated and involved in the election.[20]

MOTIVATIONS TO PARTICIPATE

Whether or not an individual will attempt to participate depends not only on the resources he possesses, but on his motivation to do so. The

---

[17] Almond and Verba, op. cit., chap. xi; Milbrath, op. cit., pp. 130–133.

[18] Robert A. Dahl, Who Governs? Democracy and Power in an American City (New Haven: Yale University Press, 1961), pp. 85–86.

[19] See Stanley Kelley, Jr., Richard E. Ayres, and William G. Bowen, "Registration and Voting: Putting First Things First," American Political Science Review, LXI (June 1967), for a discussion of the costs of registration as a deterrent to voting.

[20] Angus Campbell, et al., op. cit., chap. xi.

following represent a few ways of looking at the motivational aspects of participation.

1. DOES THE INDIVIDUAL BELIEVE IN THE EFFECTIVENESS OF POLITICAL PARTICIPATION? Those who have had no experience of successful participation—either in relation to politics or elsewhere—are likely not to believe in the efficacy of their acts. This makes clear the extent to which political participation depends upon a learning process—both in relation to politics and in relation to other social situations.[21]

2. DOES THE INDIVIDUAL HAVE SPECIFIC INTERESTS FOR WHICH HE CONSIDERS GOVERNMENTAL ACTIVITY RELEVANT? Everyone has a wide range of subjectively defined needs, but not all are perceived as having anything to do with decision-makers. The more an individual perceives governmental activity as relevant to his own needs, the more likely he is to attempt political participation. How issues become politicized in this way is not clear, though one major process involved in this is simply the expansion of the range of governmental activities. As the government becomes active in a particular field—culture or health, for example—it makes it more likely that individuals will define problems within that realm as having some political content and as needing governmental action.

3. IS POLITICAL PARTICIPATION DIRECTLY SATISFYING? Participation is conceptualized as goal-directed activity, but this does not rule out the possibility that participation may represent a satisfaction in and of itself. Through participation in political activities the individual can meet other people and satisfy social needs. Political rallies can be fun, and the very act of participating can be satisfying, even if the consequences are uncertain. Indeed, the direct pleasures of participation may need more emphasis than they have received in the past; they help explain why so much participation takes place. If one is convinced that a single vote will not affect an election (and, indeed, it does not), and if one gets the benefit of the "right" candidate's election even if one did not vote, one can argue that it is not economical to bear any voting costs but one should let others

---

[21] See the studies cited in Milbrath, *op. cit.,* pp. 56–62, and Almond and Verba, *op. cit.,* chap. ix.

go and do the voting.[22] In fact, however, people do vote under these circumstances—which suggests that the motivation for voting is only in part the desire to influence the outcome. Voting is a satisfying act *per se*.[23]

STRUCTURAL CONDUCIVENESS

Thus far, we have considered attributes of individuals or groups that would be related to their likelihood to participate, in particular the resources they possess and their motivation. But the likelihood that an individual or group will participate depends upon the degree to which there are available channels for such participation. If the structures of politics are not conducive to participation, it will take place less frequently.

1. The formal participatory structures: The most important set of structures that are relevant are the formal and legal structures within which participation takes place. Most such legal rules are permissive as far as the individual participant is concerned; they allow him to participate, but he must do so voluntarily. Free speech and other civil liberties allow individuals to speak their minds about politics; they do not require them to do so. Though some nations have laws requiring voting, the United States permits it without requiring it.[24]

The fact that the structures are permissive rather than prescriptive is important. Historical evidence indicates, for instance, that there may be a great time gap between the institution of universal suffrage and widespread use of the vote.[25] The same may be true for opportunities for free speech, for government offices set up to receive citizen's grievances, and for court review procedures of governmental activities.[26] That such institutions are available does not imply that they are used. The problem can be seen as one of the relationship among the broad conditions for political participa-

[22] This is the argument of Mancur Olson's *Logic of Collective Action* (Cambridge, Mass.: Harvard University Press, 1965).

[23] Almond and Verba found that 71 per cent of the respondents they interviewed in the United States reported that they got a "feeling of satisfaction" out of going to the polls to vote (*op. cit.,* p. 143). Another reason for voting not connected with the goals of voting would be social pressures.

[24] The laws are not permissive from the point of view of the government, however. It has no choice but to hold periodic elections and allow free speech—though, of course, there are ways around this as well.

[25] Stein Rokkan, "Mass Suffrage, Secret Voting, and Political Participation," *European Journal of Sociology,* II, No. 1, pp. 132–152, and "The Comparative Study of Political Participation: Notes toward a Perspective on Current Research," in Austin Ranney (ed.), *Essays on the Behavioral Study of Politics, op. cit.,* pp. 47–90.

[26] See Walter Gellhorn, *When Americans Complain* (Cambridge, Mass.: Harvard University Press, 1966), esp. pp. 142–145.

tion which I have been outlining. The existence of social structures that allow participation will not lead to greater participation unless people are motivated to use them and have the resources necessary. Unless individuals have the knowledge needed to use the structures of participation, unless they have the material resources needed, and unless they believe that these are likely to be effective means of participation, they are unlikely to use the opportunities available.[27]

2. Nongovernmental organization: Much participation is through nongovernmental organizations: voluntary associations, unions, and the like. These organizations may be both direct providers of benefits for citizens and means to attain further benefits for them from the government. In general, the unorganized in any society will be more likely to be exploited and less likely to participate effectively. Since the density of organizational membership varies from social group to social group, this channel of participation will vary in its availability to different groups.[28]

3. Are there regularized procedures for participation? This distinction cross-cuts the two listed above on the availability of governmental and nongovernmental channels of participation. Some participatory acts go through channels set up for such acts. A letter is written to a congressman: this is both a recognized and accepted channel, and congressmen have staffs that do nothing but answer the mail. An even more formal regular procedure would be some office like that of the Ombudsman to process citizen complaints.[29] On the other hand, there may be cases where no channel exists and an *ad hoc* one has to be created.

4. Are there procedures for eliciting participation? One further distinction may be made about different types of social structures through which participation may take place. Most of these structures involve voluntary participation—that is, individuals use them who are motivated to use them. But we can distinguish between structures of participation which are used only when individuals or groups are spontaneously motivated to use them and structures that present special occasions for eliciting participatory acts. An example of the latter is the periodic election, which presents special opportunities for citizens to participate. Another example would be relatively formal consultative committees for government agencies, where interested parties are invited in to take part in decision-making. In a sense,

---

[27] On this general subject—particularly the need for education and other social benefits as a means of making political rights useful—see T. H. Marshall, *Class, Citizenship, and Social Development* (Garden City, N.Y.: Doubleday, 1964), chap. iv.

[28] See Table 1 below and Almond and Verba, *op. cit.*, chap. xi.

[29] See Walter Gellhorn, *Ombudsmen and Others* (Cambridge, Mass.: Harvard University Press, 1966).

public opinion polls or congressional polls represent examples of "elicited" participation—individuals do not come forth with their views, rather they are sought out and asked.

These modes of eliciting participation often bring into the participatory process groups that ordinarily would not get involved—the group for whom the issue at stake is of marginal importance and that has little motivation to take part. Get-out-the-vote campaigns may get out the least interested voters (the others would have voted anyway); public opinion polls may get many opinions from people totally uninvolved in the subject of the poll. One can argue as to whether this is good or bad. It must, in any case, be kept in mind in relation to other participatory techniques.

CULTURAL CONDUCIVENESS

Just as the structural setting within which an individual finds himself would affect his likelihood to participate, so will the cultural setting. If the general beliefs of the culture—or of his own relevant subculture—are such as to foster participation, the individual is more likely to take part. There are many such general beliefs that are relevant and on which one finds variations from group to group. These include general beliefs in the manipulability of the environment, the responsiveness and trustworthiness of government, the trustworthiness of one's fellow citizens (insofar as one wants to collaborate with them), and the legitimacy of political activism.

CONDITIONS FOR EFFECTIVE
PARTICIPATION FROM THE POINT
OF VIEW OF THE DECISION-MAKERS

As pointed out at the beginning of this essay, participation involves a relationship between participants and decision-makers: messages are sent, but they may or may not be received and acted upon. Much depends on the people to whom the messages are sent. We assumed that the citizen does not ordinarily take part in politics, and then asked what conditions are likely to make him an effective participant. As for the decision-maker, we can assume that he will act autonomously if he can—without paying attention to or complying with citizen demands. We then ask what conditions affect the degree to which the decision-maker gives up some autonomy to become more responsive.[30]

The problem of the responsiveness of the decision-maker can be looked at in terms of the conditions listed for the participation of citizens— resources, motivation, structural conducivenes, and cultural conduciveness.

1. RESOURCES: The more autonomous are the resources of the decision-maker, the more likely is he to be autonomous rather than respon-sive. If the decision-maker is not dependent on the participants for his job (he is a permanent civil servant rather than an elected official) ; is not dependent on the participants for resources (he receives funds for his pro-grams from higher governmental levels and not from locally voted taxes or bond issues) ; and is not dependent on the participants for information or skills (he works in a technical field in which he monopolizes the relevant skills and for which he can gather his own information), he is likely to be less amenable to influence.

In those cases where the decision-makers are not dependent upon a citizen clientele for needed information, they will be less amenable to influ-ence from below. But if citizens control some vital information, they will have greater influence.[31]

2. MOTIVATION: Just as the beliefs and values of the citizens affect the likelihood that they will participate, the beliefs and values of the citizens affect the likelihood that they will participate, the beliefs and values of the decision-maker affect the likelihood that he will comply. If he believes citizens are potent and that he will suffer some loss if he is not

---

[30] The choice of words to use here is difficult, but reflects the real dilemma involved. The decision-maker who acts without considering the participatory mes-sages he is receiving can be described as "autonomous" or "independent," if one likes that, or as "authoritarian" and "unrepresentative," if one does not. Conversely, the decision-maker who does respond can be considered "responsive" or "demo-cratic" (good) or "weak" and "dominated by the public" (bad). The dilemma is that the two interpretations of governmental roles are both current. Some decision-makers are expected to be autonomous and some responsive; autonomy is expected on some issues and not on others. But often the borders are not clear, and the role adopted by the decision-maker will depend upon the particular situation in which he finds himself and upon the pressures he receives.

I use the words "autonomous" and "responsive" since both are positive words and do not, I hope, load the case.

On the dilemma as seen in the role of the legislator, see Heinz Eulau, *et al.,* "The Role of the Representative: Some Empirical Observations on the Theory of Edmund Burke," *American Political Science Review,* 53 (September 1959), pp. 742– 756; and Warren E. Miller and Donald E. Stokes, "Constituency Influence in Con-gress," *ibid.,* 57 (March 1963), pp. 45–56.

[31] This, it has been suggested, is one resource which interest groups have that makes them valuable to decision-makers and at the same time gives such groups greater influence.

responsive, he will be more likely to comply. Similarly, if he believes that such participation is right and proper, he will also be more likely to comply. In fact, a decision-maker may have dual views because of the ambiguity of the "autonomy-responsiveness" delimma or he may have one view in connection with one issue, and another in connection with another issue. Or he may believe that the participation of one group is legitimate, but not that of another.

3. STRUCTURAL CONDUCIVENESS: The relevant legal rules are important here. As was pointed out above, many of these are permissive from the point of view of the citizen but prescriptive from the point of view of the decision-maker. Individuals *may* vote, *may* work in a campaign; government officials *must* conduct elections, must count the ballots, and the like. In general, the rules of democracy permit citizens to participate and require officials to let them participate.

However, there can be great variation on this. Election laws and the administration of these laws vary in the extent to which they enforce certain electoral procedures on officials. And in the area of relations with administrative officials, the legal structures that enforce responsiveness are varied, vague, and sometimes nonexistent.[32]

4. CULTURAL CONDUCIVENESS: Government decision-makers both share the general culture of the United States and are members of particular subcultures. Insofar as public participation is legitimate within the society as a whole, they are likely to share that belief. Evidence suggests, in fact, that they may be more likely to support the general norms of democracy than is the ordinary citizen.[33] There are, however, probably great variations among types of officials in the extent to which public participation is acceptable, and this probably varies from issue area to issue area, and from one governmental level to another.

SOME PROBLEMS AND DILEMMAS IN
PARTICIPATION

Thus far, I have laid out an elaborate scheme for looking at modes of political participation and the conditions for it. With these conceptual

---

[32] See Gellhorn, *When Americans Complain, op. cit.*

[33] See Herbert McClosky, "Consensus and Ideology in American Politics," *American Political Science Review,* LVIII (June 1964), pp. 361–382; James W. Prothro and Charles M. Grigg, "Fundamental Principles of Democracy: Bases of Agreement and Disagreement," *Journal of Politics,* XXII (May 1960), pp. 276–294; and Samuel Stouffer, *Communism, Conformity, and Civil Liberties* (Garden City, N.Y.: Doubleday, 1958).

tools, we can now look at some of the problems associated with participation. These are by no means the only such problems one could look at, but they suggest the kinds of questions for which one would want data on participation.

HOW MUCH POLITICAL
PARTICIPATION IS THERE
IN THE UNITED STATES?

This is the obvious first question that must be asked, but before it can be answered, we must consider two problems: What kind of participation? And compared with what?

On the issue of "what kind of participation?" it is clear that the question is most answerable in terms of electoral participation. There is a large amount of data on voting participation and the correlates of it.[34] These data, however, are usually on the national level. Participation in state and local elections may be equally important, but the data have not been compiled as yet.

There is less available evidence on other means of participation, particularly on participation between elections: on the numbers who write letters to congressmen or newspapers; who make use of appeals procedures or governmental decisions; who engage in protest movements; or who become involved in local political affairs in relation to a particular issue. Many of the most important acts of participation are diffused and hidden in local communities and are on local issues. The decision-makers are zoning boards, school boards, and other local agencies. The channels include Parent-Teacher's Associations, or local service clubs, or informal groups of irate parents or citizens. Survey studies have provided a small amount of information on these modes of participation. And we have some data on participation in voluntary groups (on membership in such groups as well as on participation within them) and on participation in other nongovernmental institutions.[35]

In the *Civic Culture* study, Almond and I gathered data on political participation from the United States and four other nations. Some of these

---

[34] See, for instance, Richard M. Scammon, "Electoral Participation," *Social Goals and Indicators for American Society*, Vol. 1, THE ANNALS, Vol. 371 (May 1967), pp. 59–71.

[35] See Milbrath, *op. cit.*, and the literature cited there.

data are reported in Table 1. In general, they show that participation is more frequent in the United States than elsewhere.[36]

TABLE 1—Some Comparisons of Political Participations:
Percentages that Reported Participating in Various Ways in the United States,
Great Britain, Germany, Italy and Mexico[a]

Mode of Participation	Country				
	U.S.	Britain	Germany	Italy	Mexico
Attempted to influence the local government	28%	16%	14%	8%	6%
Attempted to influence national legislature	16	6	3	2	3
Follow accounts of political affairs	80	68	72	36	55
Pay attention to campaigns	87	72	68	42	53
Sometimes discuss politics	76	70	60	32	38
Belong to voluntary associations	57	47	44	29	25
Belong to voluntary association involved in politics	25	19	18	6	11
Number of cases	970	963	955	955	1,007

[a] For further details on these data, see Gabriel A. Almond and Sidney Verba, *The Civic Culture* (Princeton, N.J.: Princeton University Press, 1963), especially pp. 89, 116, 188, 302, and 306.

These data from other nations give us some benchmark for comparison, but ought not to be a source of complacency. Comparisons of this sort involve a number of complexities[37] and must be made with caution. On other indicators—voting participation, equality of apportionment, and access to

---

[36] For further discussion of these comparisons, see Almond and Verba, *op. cit.* For other comparisons, see Philip Converse and George Dupeux, "Politicalization of the Electorate in France and the United States," *Public Opinion Quarterly,* XXVI (Spring 1962), pp. 1–24. Also, Stein Rokkan and Angus Campbell, "Norway and the United States of America," in *Citizens Participation in Political Life,* an issue of the *International Social Science Journal,* XII, No. 1, pp. 69–99. See also W. D. Burnham, "The Changing Shape of the American Political Universe," *American Political Science Review,* 59 (March 1965) 7, for data on one other type of comparison—present participation rates in the United States compared with those in the past.

[37] On some of the issues involved in making comparisons of such aspects of politics as rates of participation over time or across countries, see Sidney Verba, "The Uses of Survey Research in the Study of Comparative Politics: Issues and Strategies," in Stein Rokkan, Sidney Verba, Jean Viet and Elina Almasy, *Comparative Survey Analysis: A Trend Report and Bibliography.*

a range of opinions in the mass media—the United States was found to rank fairly low in a group of ten democracies.[38] In addition, the comparative participation data must be evaluated in terms of the available resource base. It may be that the United States would rank below the other nations if one took into account the higher performance expectations that could be derived from the greater availability of those material resources which we have suggested are important conditions for effective participation.[39] Lastly —and most important of all—the data must be considered with caution because they represent average figures for the entire nation. Thought these figures may be high, the important comparisons that have to be made are comparisons within the United States when we ask how equally distributed is this participation.

TABLE 2—Participation among Negroes and Whites

	Percentages Who Report Participating in Various Ways[a]							
Race	Influence Local Government	Influence National Government	Follow Politics	Pay Attention to Campaigns	Discuss Politics	Belong to Voluntary Association	Belong to Voluntary Association and Active in Politics	Number of Cases
Negro	29%	17%	82%	89%	77%	57%	26%	865
White	13%	5%	68%	85%	66%	59%	25%	100

[a] See Table 1 and the references there for more detail.

---

[38] See Neubauer, *op. cit.* Neubauer attempted to rank ten democratic nations in terms of their degree of "polyarchy"—the extent to which they afforded equal access to effective means of participation in competitive politics. The key dimensions were electoral equality, effectiveness of the elections, and the freedom of political opposition. He used five indicators of electoral equality, five of effectiveness of control, and two of freedom of opposition. The procedures are involved, and the reader can consult Neubauer's study, which is soon to be published. His summary conclusion, using all dimensions of "polyarchy," was that the United States ranked eighth. His rankings were: Sweden, Great Britain, Japan, West Germany, France, Italy, Chile, United States, India, and Mexico.

[39] See Adam Przeworski and Henry Teune, "Equivalence in Cross-National Research," *Public Opinion Quarterly*, XXX, 1966–1967, pp. 551–569, for some analysis of the *Civic Culture* data that suggest this.

INEQUALITIES IN PARTICIPATION

If further data on participation were to reveal anything of value in terms of the making of social policy, they would probably reveal great-inequalities in participation. There is much evidence for this in terms of voting turnout, though there is much less information on between-elections participation acts.[40] The picture of participation in the United States compared with other nations, as seen on Table 1, is less bright if one looks at the data of Table 2, which compare Negroes and whites in America on these measures. The dispatities are striking in connection with actual influence attempts on the local and national levels; less so in terms of interest in politics; and nonexistent in connection with voluntary association membership. This suggests that the Negro population in quite "ready" for participation in terms of interest and organization but does not yet participate as much as the while population—a situation of obvious tension.

The difference among groups represent a very old fact of politics. The source of the differences probably lies in the distribution of the conditions for effective participation: all societies are characterized by inequalities in intellectual, material, and social resources; in motivation; and in the availability of social structures through which one can participate. In this way, the study of the "state of the nation" in terms of political participation ties in closely with the state of the nation in other respects—in the distribution of economic or educational benefits, for instance.

But, though the conditions for participation may differ for different groups in the society, several aspects of these conditions would deserve careful study if data were made available.

1. The criteria of access and democratic norms: One major distinction is whether the resources for participation and access to participatory structures are determined at birth or can be attained by the individual's own efforts. If access to the vote is limited on the basis of race, there is no chance for those who are not of the proper race to obtain opportunities to participate without changing the nature of the structures. Or if the major resource needed to participate is ownership of land, and if land is owned only by a particular class that passes it from generation to generation, participation is permanently closed to other groups. On the other hand, if education or motivation is the key to participation (and if there is a school system not completely closed to social groups, or enough information around so that individuals and groups can change their motivations), there are possibilities for individuals and groups to increase their amount of

---

[40] See Richard M. Scammon, *op. cit.*, and Milbrath, *op. cit.*

participation, even without changing the social structures of their society. In the United States, most of the conditions for effective participation are not ascribed at birth, but rather can be achieved by the efforts of groups and individuals. In part, this is due to the existence of democratic norms that run against ascribed criteria either for those conditions that affect participation—such as the possession of various resources—as well as against ascribed criteria for participation itself. These democratic norms may not be firmly held; indeed, the commitment to them is rather weak, especially when one gets beyond the level of glittering generalities.[41] The norms are, therefore, not self-enforcing; many violations of the norms will go unnoticed by most. But the norms do exist as a "court of appeals": if some group is motivated to challenge the existing distribution of participation opportunities, it has a set of values to which to appeal. And, in the connection, the fact that those more involved in politics—political and nonpolitical leaders—are more likely to express adherence to these norms is important. [42] It means that such appeals may fall on sympathetic ears.

On the other hand, if the criteria of participation are ascribed at birth, more radical change in the structure of participation or in the social structures will be needed to expand participation.

2. The degree of inequality: Whether we are looking at the conditions for effective participation or at the acts of participation themselves, we can ask a variety of questions as to the degree to which they are unequally distributed. The conditions—material possessions, education, and the like—may be concentrated in a few hands or widely spread out. And the same is true of acts of participation.[43]

3. How cumulative are the inequalities? As Professor Dahl has pointed out, the resources available for effective political activity may be dispersed or cumulative.[44] Insofar as there is a multiplicity of resources that makes participation feasible and insofar as different individuals or groups possess different resources, the distribution of participation will be more equal. One group possesses monetary resources and another the social resource of ethnic identity that allows it to mobilize voters. But if the possession of one resource implies the possession of others, there will be a

---

[41] McClosky, op. cit., Prothro and Grigg, op. cit., and Stouffer, op. cit.

[42] McClosky, op. cit., Prothro and Grigg, op. cit., and Stouffer, op. cit.

[43] See Haywood Alker and Bruce Russett, "Indices for Comparing Inequality," in Richard Merritt and Stein Rokkan, Comparing Nations (New Haven: Yale University Press, 1966), pp. 349–372, for considerations of various ways to measure inequality.

[44] Dahl, Who Governs? Democracy and Power in an American City, op. cit., pp. 85–86.

tendency for participation to cluster around those few who monopolize these resources. These are complicated areas. Dahl argues that for New Haven, at least, resources are dispersed—those who control highest social status, do not control the major wealth, nor do they have the social resource of ethnic identity that allows them to control votes. For the United States as a whole, we do not know how cumulative is the distribution of resources. It is clear that there is quite a bit of cumulation, but some dispersion as well. This is an important question that would have to be asked of data on this subject.

The degree to which resources for participation relate cumulatively to motivation also would affect the equality of participation. The "stake in society" argument would suggest that those with more resources would be more motivated to participate, since they have more to lose if they do not take adequate part. On the other hand, the "human need" argument would suggest high motivation on the part of those with fewer resources because their needs are greater. In general, those with resources are more likely to be motivated, but not perhaps for reasons suggested in the "stake in society" argument. Motivation does not depend only upon the existence of interests that can be satisfied via political participation, but, as suggested above, upon beliefs that one can adequately influence governmental activity. And there is evidence that, for a variety of reasons, this motivation is somewhat weaker among those of lower social or economic status.[45] On the other hand, it is clear that motivation may be independent of resource position—especially if aspirations increase via media exposure or exposure to leaders who suggest or demonstrate to nonparticipants that there is a stake in participation.

4. How unequal and how cumulative unequal are the different types of participation? Thus far, we have discussed inequality in terms of the conditions for participation. But the same set of questions can be asked about the acts of participation themselves—how unequally are they distributed; which kind of act is more unequally distributed than others; and how cumulative are the inequalities? Because the data on nonelectoral modes of participation are somewhat weaker than those on voting, it is hard to compare across modes of participation. But in the light of the discussion of resources, we can hypothesize that inequalities will be greater for those acts that require greater resources, or—to put it another way—for which the costs are high.

And to estimate this, one would have to take into account all kinds of costs. Thus, voting may be relatively inexpensive in terms of time, or effort,

---

[45] See Almond and Verba, *op. cit.*, chaps. vi, vii, and xiii; Seymour M. Lipset, *Political Man* (Garden City, N.Y.: Doubleday, 1960), chap. v; and Milbrath, *op. cit.*, chap. iii.

or information needed (except where there are strong legal or extralegal pressures against voting). But more specific and individually oriented acts, such as protesting an administrative decision, may be more costly in terms of time and effort, and particularly in terms of skill and information needed. Participation of the latter sort often requires (or at least could benefit from) technical advice and assistance from a lawyer or accountant or other specialized person. Since access to these auxiliary personnel may be very unequally distributed, many of these more precise and highly relevant participatory acts may be badly distributed indeed.[46] In the absence of more precise data on the various modes of participation, this remains speculation.

PRECISE VERSUS BLUNT MODES
OF PARTICIPATION

The difference in the distributional patterns of such activities as voting, on the one hand, and complaining in the government office, on the other, is important because these modes of participation have quite different consequences and represent different means of relating to the government.

The vote, in the aggregate, a powerful means of participation but one that conveys little information. It is a powerful but blunt weapon that does not closely guide the behavior of decision-makers, largely because the relation of the election outcome to any specific policy is usually quite ambiguous.[47] And, as an individual act, the vote is both blunt and weak. The individual voter qua individual has relatively little effect on the election outcome and cannot really evaluate the effectiveness of his vote in terms of the extent to which it moves decision-makers in directions he would have preferred.

On the other hand, the type of participation where the goal is not some general policy, but the attainment of some benefit for a limited group or for an individual, is not as powerful as elections in the aggregate sense (it has little effect on general policy or on who runs the country). But from the point of view of the idividual, it may be much more powerful and convey much more information. He expresses a particular interest or asks for the redress of a specific grievance. Because the information as to his preferences is so specific, he can estimate the extent of his success. If he is skillful and has the right set of resources, he may be successful. In the broader-based and more blunt acts, such as voting, the estimate of success is more diffi-

---

46 Gellhorn, *When Americans Complain, op. cit.,* pp. 142–145.

47 For an example of the ambiguity of the relationship between voting preferences and foreign policy, see Sidney Verba, *et al.,* "Public Opinion and the War in Vietnam," *American Political Science Review,* LXI (June 1967).

cult, as the demand is usually diffuse and the likelihood of success much lower.

Voting and elections are "blunt" instruments for several specific reasons that also enhance the importance of the more precise between-elections modes of participation. Elections cannot reflect well the intensity of preferences of the participants; all have one vote.[48] The more precise modes of participation that involve expression of a specific interest reflect intensity because only those deeply concerned will take part. Secondly, elections are periodic and, for the reasons just mentioned, often settle little. The other forms of participation between the elections fill this gap. And, in this last sense, they are particularly relevant for those who lose the election. Why, one may ask, should supporters of parties that are in a relatively permanent minority position (as was the Republican party *vis-à-vis* the presidency from 1932 to 1952, and as are many state and local parties) continue to give allegiance to and feel themselves participants in the political system? The election gives them little influence over decisions. The answer is, in part, that there are many other participation opportunities between elections that relieve what could otherwise be a quite frustrating situation.[49]

THE PROBLEM OF SCALE

The above discussion is closely related to the problem of scale and political participation. Insofar as one is dealing with a large-scale social system, the likelihood that any individual or group will have an effect on policy is slim. If large numbers have an effect on the outcome—as in elections—the contribution of any single individual is likely to be very limited. Under such circumstances, the payoff for any individual to participate is small. He can accomplish little by himself, and the effects of his participation on the outcome are not noticeable.[50] The chances of successful participation are limited further by the fact that decisions that cover the entire society are likely to involve competing interests. This immediately limits the numbers who can successfully participate, for if one group is successful, the other is not; or if both groups are satisfied, it can only be partial satisfaction and partial success. Scale, therefore, puts severe limits on the amount of successful participation.

---

48 Though, of course, intensity can be reflected in other activity in election campaigns.

49 See Stein Rokkan, "Norway: Numerical Democracy and Corporate Pluralism," in Robert A. Dahl (ed.), *Political Oppositions in Western Democracies* (New Haven: Yale University Press, 1966), chap. iii, for discussion of this problem in relation to Norway, which had a socialist government over an extended period of time.

50 See the argument above on why this situation causes problems in terms of the motivation to participate.

But if the scale of the decisional unit is smaller, there is much greater opportunity for participation that is high in informational content and high in its likelihood of success. In a sense, the more precise between-elections type of participation is effective because the scale of the decision is limited and decision-making is highly decentralized. This suggests that the student of participation must look carefully at the question of decentralization. The more decision centers, the more opportunities for successful participation—and, furthermore, the more rapid and effective is the feedback of information to the decision-makers as to the effects of their decisions.

But several qualifications must be made. In the first place, not every decision can be decentralized. Insofar as there is an inevitable centralization, the problems of scale are inevitable. Compare, for instance, protest movements in relation to school desegregation and in relation to the war in Vietnam. The former problem can be pursued in Washington through certain central offices, but it also can be pursued in a myriad of local communities and before a large number of school boards that have the power to respond. The demands can be made fairly specific and related to the local situation, and the participants are in good position to observe if the demands have been fulfilled—a criterion for high-information participation. The Vietnam protestors, on the other hand, must focus attention on a single decisional center and can find few decentralized targets for anything but symbolic protests.

Secondly, it must be kept in mind that the decentralization of decision-making may have contrary effects on opportunities to participate. In some cases, it may mean that decisions are turned over to local units whose decision-makers have narrower views on the legitimacy of participation than do the central decision-makers. Many civil rights decisions that have increased participatory opportunities have been made in Washington because the local decision-makers—though closer to the potential participants—were closed to influences from Negro citizens.

THE PROBLEM OF TECHNICAL
COMPLEXITY

As the government becomes more and more involved in programs affecting American life—from space to urban development to education—the needs for specialized agencies and technical expertise increase. The essays in this volume reflect this tendency. They represent a major attempt to use some of the techniques of social science to gather the expert knowledge needed for effective planning and administration of government programs. But this has serious implications for participation. As the decisions come more and more to be made by experts who possess a monopoly of the relevant information and skills (and who are often quite jealous of the special position this monopoly gives), what kind of citizen-influence will be possible?

Some opportunities for participation may be enhanced. This will be the case where the relevant technical information and skill is held by those outside of the government or is at least shared by those outside. Consultations, bargaining, and other close relations are likely to be the order of the day. But in cases where those affected by government policies do not possess the requisite skills, opportunities for participation are weaker. In these circumstances, the effectiveness of participation may depend upon the availability to participants of auxiliary skill and informational resources. Earlier, the example was used of the need for expert advice from lawyers or accountants, and it was suggested that the availability of these technical aids was likely to be highly skewed. And, in general, effective participation may depend on the availability of independent sources of technical skills and information for participants. Technical complexity is related to the decentralization of decision-making. It may create more opportunities to participate as decisions disperse into specialized agencies. But the increased opportunities may be opportunities missed unless auxiliary resources are available that foster use of these specialized channels.

PARTICIPATION AND THE
EFFICIENT ATTAINMENT OF OTHER
SOCIAL GOALS

This is perhaps the greatest dilemma in the area of participation—so great that it can only be touched on here. It really must be dealt with in terms of the problems found in each specific situation. Effective governmental programs may require slow and careful planning, technical control, and a willingness to defer gratification. Programs based on widespread participation are likely to represent greater compromise and less careful planning and technical control, and to be aimed at relatively rapid gratification. The best calculated plans of urban developers are shattered in clashes with the residents whom the development displaces; the calculations of educators for curriculum-reform are often thrown off by complaints from parents' groups. The problem is real and is indeed no less a problem than that of the efficiency and effectiveness of democracy.[51] And all one can say here is that

---

[51] On this general subject in relation to developing countries, see Samuel P. Huntington, "Political Development and Political Decay," *World Politics,* 17 (April 1965), pp. 386–430; and Samuel P. Huntington, "Political Modernization: America vs. Europe," *World Politics,* 18 (April 1966), pp. 378–415.

no easy generalizations are possible. It will not do to ignore the "irrationalities" introduced into planning that come from widespread participation: the intrusion of uninformed opinions, the need to satisfy a widespread clientele which dilutes the major purpose of programs, and so forth. On the other hand, the word "irrationalities" must be kept in quotation marks because participation can make planning *more* efficient in some respects by providing planners and decision-makers with information available only to the participants. Only the slum dweller really knows what the impact of urban renewal is on his community. And, in any case, efficiency is but one possible goal. Widespread participation may lead into something resembling chaos, but it is chaotic because there are many different values operating at the same time and there are many different people involved with many different goals. Under such circumstances, clear-cut policies are difficult to achieve. But such are the circumstances of democracy.

THE PROBLEM OF RECEPTIVE
DECISION-MAKERS

As has been suggested over and over again in this paper, the problem of participation concerns both the participants and the decision-makers. It is as important that decision-makers respond as it is that the participants participate. But what makes a decision-maker—and remember we are talking not only of congressmen or mayors or other elected officials, but of government employees of all sorts from postmen to policemen to planners who can make decisions affecting individuals or groups—listen to participants and modify his behavior to suit them? Several answers can be suggested in the light of our earlier discussion of resources.

(1) Just as motivation—beliefs and values—are important for participants, they may be crucial for decision-makers. Their attitude as to the propriety and value of public participation may be crucial.

(2) Motivation does not all come from internalized values and norms. It is possible to structure the situation so that decision-makers benefit from allowing participation and lose from blocking it. One way in which the situation can be so structured is by the provision of specific legal mechanisms for enforcing responsiveness on the part of the decision-maker.

(3) Another way in which motivation to allow participation can be externally generated is by the structuring of the decisional or planning situation so that a decision-maker perceives that the participation of others is needed to achieve his own goals. This will be the case if there are likely to be nongovernmental groups or other decision-makers who are opposed to a particular decision-maker. In cases of this sort, the decision-maker may

foster participation of others in order to mobilize support for his own position. This is, of course, what happens in competitive elections, but it can happen in other situations if the decision-maker perceives that he needs allies.

Participation is a challenge to government leadership and to particular governmental personnel whose jobs are impinged on by it. The powerful and effective leader is often thought of as the one who goes his own way and pushes through the programs he wants. Power, in Karl Deutsch's definition, is the ability to act without taking into account information or feedback.[52] But perhaps we have to consider another type of effective leader: one who can take into account many views, who can respond flexibly to new ideas and new pressures, and for whom the sharing of decisional power with a large number of others is not seen as representing a challenge to his own authority.

TOWARD INDICATORS OF
PARTICIPATION

The search for social indicators is complicated by the multiplicity of forms of participation and the complexity of our goals. We do not know what a "participatory utopia" would look like; and this for several reasons. There are many different ways in which people can participate, and no single set of indicators will enable us to evaluate performance. Furthermore, it is hard to set standards as to *how much* participation represents adequate performance. One cannot say unambiguously, "the more the better." Participation has its benefits for the policy-maker, but it also has its costs; under some circumstances, governmental effectiveness may go down. And for the participant it has costs, as well; the time and effort spent on participating in political life cannot be spent elsewhere. One important social right may be the right not to participate.

If we try to use a comparative standard to arrive at an optimum amount of participation, we have problems as well. The experience of other nations is interesting from a scholarly point of view, but the level of participation elsewhere may not be that relevant in setting goals for the United States. Nor is the "American ideal" an adequate standard of comparison as it provides only the vaguest of guidelines. Perhaps the best comparative standard is one that is internal to the United States; it is a standard that sets no absolute level of participation as optimum but focuses on inequalities

---

[52] Karl Deutsch, *The Nerves of Government* (New York: Free Press, 1963), p. 111.

among groups within the nation. We do not know how active people should, on the average, be, but there ought not to be gross disparities in activity. More important, there ought not to be gross disparities in *opportunities* to be active. It is less important that there be equality in actual participation than that there be equality in access to participation. The citizen may still choose passivity. But the term "opportunity" must be interpreted broadly in the light of the previous discussion. It must include not only the legal opportunities—the existence of structures through which individuals can participate—but the equal availability of the auxiliary resources, such as information and technical assistance. And we may even have to talk of equal access to motivation as being part of the equal opportunity to participate. If some group—because of past experience or a special pattern of socialization—is less self-confident of its ability to influence decision-makers, it does not, in a real sense, have equal opportunity to participate.

To sum up the implications of this essay for the selection of indicators of participation:

(1)   All indicators of participation will have to be gathered in such a way as to allow comparisons among the various subgroups in the United States.

(2)   We will need broad measures of participation in the electoral process. This means continuing to gather data on voting turnout, and increasing data on state and local elections, but also stressing data on other forms of electoral participation. What kinds of people are party workers, or are active in trying to convince others during a campaign? These data already exist in a variety of survey studies and could be used for these purposes. More important, perhaps, we want to know how many and who take part in decisions made about the nomination of candidates. And who are the candidates? What kinds of people, representing what groups, enter political careers?

(3)   We will have to go beyond electoral participation to those activities whereby individuals attempt to influence governmental decisions between elections. These include activities aimed at influencing one's representative, such as writing letters to congressmen, as well as activities aimed at administrative officials. How many have appealed adverse decisions, and what kind of person is most likely to do so? How many—and who—are active in community action groups? How many—and who—become involved in various protest movements? In a sense, we need an inventory of the ways in which the government impinges on the lives of individuals, and, particularly, of those areas where there is some decisional discretion. Thus, Congress has discretion in writing tax legislation, and we can ask how many and what kinds of people actively participate in trying to influence such legislation.

But tax auditors have some discretion in applying these laws, and we can ask how many and what kinds of people appeal tax decisions.

We have not stressed memberships in nongovernmental associations in this essay. But it is an important mode of participation, and data on the distribution of this would be important. Participation goes on in many places—we must study it where it occurs.

(4) In gathering data on this broad range of participatory activities, it will be necessary to look at the following aspects:

a. Are there channels available for various kinds of participation, and does availability differ from section of country to section of country, or from group to group? This means study of electoral laws and the way in which they structure participatory opportunities, but also a study of the availability of appeals and review boards of various kinds in various parts of the nation.

b. How many and who use these channels?

c. What are the auxiliary resources needed for effective use of these channels? How much information about these channels is needed, and who has this information? To what extent is independent technical advice needed to use a particular channel effectively, and to whom is this advice available? How useful is the advice of an accountant in a tax-appeal procedure, and what is the distribution of access to accountants?

d. How receptive are decision-makers to the participation of particular groups? To participation using particular techniques? To participation on particular issues? In a sense, we must know how decision-makers chart the domain of legitimate participation to understand where there may be important blockages to effective participation.

(5) Since the above requirements are broad and complicated, and since the modes of participation and the relevant decision-makers may differ from issue area to issue area, it may be necessary to have such data gathered in relation to specific policy areas. Thus, one might take major policy areas—education, taxes, health, and so forth—and chart the patterns of participation in relation to them.

All of this means that the data on participation is part of and closely related to the data on other aspects of society.

We will not go into more specific measures and more specific techniques. In many cases, we have a lot of data which can be reorganized for the purposes outlined; in other cases, additional studies would have to be made. The above points are but the most general of guidelines. But they do suggest that we must take a broad perspective when we consider participation and must study access to it in many ways and at many places.

THREE

THE CULTURAL CONTEXT

7

INDIVIDUAL
AND GROUP VALUES

ROBIN M. WILLIAMS, JR.

It is striking that the social diagnoses of our times that have attracted the widest popular attention and acclaim are interpretations only loosely connected with any systematic analysis of "hard" data. Are Americans today more "other-directed" than in the 1890's? Where is the unequivocal evidence? Is our society being deadened by overconformity—or is it disintegrating through lack of consensus and commitment? Is the Organization Man of the 1960's more stereotyped than the businessmen of the 1920's? Are the urban middle classes today more preoccupied with "status-seeking" than the newly rich of the Gilded Age or the respectable small-town citizens of the age of Babbitt? Have the contemporary American people lost humane sensitivity in an urban world hurrying on under the awareness of genocide, hydrogen bombs, and technologically advanced surveillance and brutality in a thousand forms? Where is the evidence? Yet confident assertions abound.

Many observers of the national society suggest that the intensity of commitment to particular values and beliefs has diminished. It is said that exposure to a vast variety of experiences reduces exclusive beliefs, and absolute commitments.[1] Is there systematic evidence of changes in commitment? If change in this respect has taken place, does it really mean an important change in such behavior as paying taxes, answering the call of

---

[1] Cf. this statement: "It is becoming rare to value any belief more than life. To be willing to die for a belief means to be unable to conceive of an acceptable life outside the framework of that belief. The pluralistic and heterogeneous quality of present-day experience undermines such exclusive beliefs" (Allen Wheelis, "The Quest for Identity," in Bernard Rosenberg [ed.], *Analyses of Contemporary Society* [New York: Thomas Y. Crowell Company, 1966], p. 21).

the military draft, abiding by marriage and familial norms, defending political principles, and so on? In our view, the presently available data on the alleged value changes are very far from satisfactory—yet the allegations in question bear on the very foundations of societal survival.

"Ethnocentric" values are not all of one piece, and it is essential to make distinctions concerning both content and "formal" properties (intensity, rigidity, differentiation, explicitness). If successive studies, using a large battery of comparable indicators, show a reduction in conventionalized, simple, rigid, dogmatic evaluations and streotypes of racial, ethnic, and religious groupings, it will be important to know the extent to which the apparent reduction in "prejudice" is paralleled by growth in more complex and intellectualized invidious evaluations.[2]

Knowledge, beliefs, and values evolved out of psychiatric and social science research and experience have been influential to an appreciable degree in a limited shift away from punishment and custody toward treatment and rehabilitation.[3] Periodic sample studies of values relevant to this area would be highly useful in evaluating national and state and local policies and practices.

Currently it is difficult to gauge the extent to which an "apprehensive concern" with leisure[4] extends outside a few limited circles of intellectuals and publicists. Certainly, however, the complex and changing evaluations of work and leisure in different strata and segments of the nation will be highly relevant to many future policies.

Great debate has centered upon alleged changes in expressive or aesthetic values supposed to have occurred with the extension of literacy and the rise of "mass" media.[5] The criticisms against "popular culture" are sufficiently repetitive to bear the appearance of "an established ideology or critique." The critique asserts that popular taste is low and is being further lowered by commercialized popular culture—a process which in turn debases high culture, adversely affects values and emotional processes of consumers, and corrodes the social structure.[6] What are the value facts?

---

[2] Melville Jacobs, *Pattern in Cultural Anthropology* (Homewood, Ill.: Dorsey Press, 1964), p. 293.

[3] There is evidence that in some organizations the belief-value systems influence both individual conduct and the main patterns of behavior of whole organizations. Cf. David Street, Robert D. Vinter, and Charles Perrow, *Organization for Treatment: A Comparative Study of Institutions for Deliquents* (New York: Fress Press, 1966), p. vi.

[4] Paul Hollander, "Leisure as an American and Soviet Value," *Social Problems*, Vol. 14 (Fall 1966), pp. 179–188.

[5] Herbert J. Gans, "Popular Culture in America: Social Problem in a Mass Society or Social Asset in a Pluralist Society," in Howard S. Becker (ed.), *Social Problems: A Modern Approach* (New York: John Wiley & Sons, 1966), pp. 549–620.

[6] *ibid.*, p. 552.

Does anyone know? If not, why not?

Many critics of American society today seem to concentrate upon two alleged characteristics—*shapelessness* and *meaninglessness*. Under the first, we find recitals of loss of sense of belonging, absence of standards, loss of norms, uprootedness, destruction of traditions, disintegration of multi-bonded groups and "organic" communities, loss of cultural continuity and sense of history, and blurring of qualitative distinctions in experience. Under the second indictment we encounter references to "existential nausea," emptiness, loss of interest in work, alienation, diffusion of identity, total relativism, "failure of nerve." Are these foreboding diagnoses incorrect? If there is serious truth in them, where and how and to whom do they apply?

The listing of "needed" information on values easily could be extended. We are under no illusions, however, that anything like "full coverage" is to be expected. The suggestions here advanced are intended only to illustrate a range of promising possibilities.

In any case, we do believe that—whatever else is done or not done in this field—we should work toward a comprehensive system of social data-reporting and analysis in which information concerning values would contribute to a diagnosis of the main emphases of the national societal system. In the past, heavy emphasis in American policy has been upon the *goal-attainment* sector, with secondary effort toward maintaining and strengthening generalized *adaptative* capacities (capital formation, some technological development, some—instrumental—education). Conspicuously neglected have been the other two main functional aspects of social systems—the *integration* of components and *pattern-maintenance*. In our national drive to "get things done," we have generated vast internal social cleavages and frictions—dislocations and disintegrations that represent enormous societal "overhead costs" of a peculiarly serious kind. Similarly, the intense concentration upon political, military, technological, and economic attainments probably has severely strained the maintenance of some parts of the central systems of beliefs and value criteria; this might be thought of as a kind of depletion of cultural capital. It would be conceivable that inadequate sensitivity to such, largely unintended, consequences could set off such sequences of maldistribution of the flow of societal energies as to eventually interfere in a major way with the system's generalized capacities to survive in its environment, for example, through poisoning and pollution of the biosphere, through disabling internal social conflicts, or through excessive dissipation of human and material resources in exhausting national-political enterprises.

If the needs for systematic data on values are as great as we have just suggested, how may we begin the necessary work?

DEFINITIONS

In this field, where vague discourse is no stranger, we must first establish the meanings here given to such key terms as belief, norm, value, ideology, and institution. To speak of values is to imply that a line can be drawn between values and other phenomena that are not values. Values are manifest in human behavior, but not all behavior shows forth values: physiological activities are not values, nor are sheer reflex acts. On the other hand, a disinterested moral judgment of a governmental policy is clearly an evaluative act. Between such widely separated cases lie numerous activities of appraisal, preference, and selection: interests, aversions, attractions, desires, wants, needs, choices, likes, affections, pleasures, duties, moral obligations, and many others. To consider all selective behavior as "valuing" is to broaden the term beyond any analytical usefulness. To narrow the meaning of value to "moral value" is to constrict its scope so narrowly as to necessitate numerous *ad hoc* extensions for dealing with matters which we are forced to recognize as value-laden.

In view of these considerations, we here define values as those *conceptions of desirable states of affairs* that are utilized in selective conduct as *criteria* for preference or choice or as *justifications* for proposed or actual behavior. Values are closely related, conceptually and empirically, to social norms, but norms are the more specific, concrete, situation-bound specifications; values are the criteria by which norms themselves may be and are judged. Values are not the same as needs, desires, or motives—for everyone at some time has desires that he judges negatively, and one may evaluate highly, for others, a condition he himself does not desire to attain or experience. There would be no human values were men not energetic organisms, but "energy" alone cannot generate the standards we call values. The remarkable thing is, rather, that values can "steer" or "canalize" or actually "define" powerful needs and gratifications in ways far removed from primary biological promptings.[7]

The term value often is used interchangeably in two senses that must be kept separate here. In one meaning, the reference is to the specific *evaluation* of any object, for example, "the best inheritance is a good education," or "peace at any price," or "no other sculpture approaches its beauty," or "the worth of his work is extraordinary." Here we are told how an object is rated or otherwise appraised, but not what standards are used to make the judgments. The second meaning of value refers to the *criteria* or standards in terms of which evaluations are made, for example, "education is good because it increases economic efficiency," or "racial segregation

---

[7] The present formulations are adapted from the article "Values" by the author for the forthcoming *International Encyclopedia of the Social Sciences*.

threatens personal integrity." Value-as-criterion is usually the more important usage for social analysis.

For purposes of anchoring and clarifying discussion, then, we are using a descriptive definition, which is continually being tested for adequacy by confrontation with the values actually experienced or observed *via* behavior. Thus, the description must be empirically verified or it must be changed. The value facts are implicit in evaluative acts; therefore, explicit definitions of value are always potentially open to reformation in the face of new evaluative acts.[8]

Values and beliefs are related but not identical. Beliefs have primarily an existential reference: they concern what the believer takes as reality— the properties of and relationships among entities and processes. Beliefs are true or false, valid or invalid, or not testable. There is in beliefs *as such* no criterion of good or bad—only "is" or "is not" (in some sense and in some degree). The standards involved are cognitive. Valid cognitive beliefs constitute knowledge. Knowledge, error, and untestable beliefs comprise the storehouse of cognitive culture.

Concretely, beliefs usually involve a normative (evaluative) aspect in addition to the evaluation of them as valid or invalid, that is, the belief itself is either desirable or undesirable on grounds other than its cognitive correctness, or it refers to a state of affairs that is thus desirable or undesirable.

Evaluative beliefs concerning desirable social states represent applications of cognitive, cathectic, and evaluative standards to real or imagined social relationships, units, and processes. When such beliefs fall together into relatively coherent and relatively stable clusterings, such organized aggregates of beliefs and values may be termed *ideologies*. A "justifying" ideology says, "Here is an existing set of desirable social arrangements." A "radical" or "utopian" ideology says, "Here is a good future state of affairs which should replace the present one." Ideologies have been highly salient, to say the least, in this century of continuous revolution.

Institutions are organized sets of widely accepted and strongly supported obligatory norms. Obligatory norms tend to be clustered into statuses, and interrelated sets of statuses are organized around main foci of values and interests in recurrent situation, for example, birth of children, allocation of scarce means, and use of power. These organized networks of statuses constitute the main structures of kinship, social stratification, economy, polity, education, religion, and recreation.

Obviously, a description of any total society must deal with beliefs,

---

[8] Cf. Stephen C. Pepper, *The Sources of Value* (Berkeley and Los Angeles: University of California Press, 1958), p. 300.

ideologies, norms, and institutions, as well as the values that are here the main focus of attention.

SOURCES OF VALUES

Values emerge "in experience"; indeed, where else? There is already at least an incipient value criterion in the child's first experience with hot objects. All value at some point developed as generalizations from some experiences with certain kinds of action and their consequences. Once generalizations were established, they could then be taught and learned without the necessity of passing through the full experience of alternative consequences. So, the sources of values are no more mysterious—and no less mysterious—than the sources of any other component of human behavior.

Values, then, do not suddenly emerge from nowhere as mysterious, self-generating, uncaused causes in human life, but rather have sources and contexts. First, some "natural norms" are built into the organism—knees cannot properly bend backwards, salt concentration in tissue cells must rather precisely follow a species-rule—or else. Then, the physical environment meets the human animal with severe restrictions and imperious claims. In short, the ultimate *conditions* of biological survival and functioning are influential in the genesis of values. It is always possible for men to choose, or to inadvertently select values that are incompatible with survival—but the conditions of survival are not irrelevant to the existence of the values. Similarly, some values are inherently connected with the development and maintenance of personalities as more or less integrated systems, and other evaluative criteria develop directly out of the intrinsic requirements of social collectivities. Men are inevitably social, if they are men at all: this is insured by the prolonged dependence, symbolic behavior, and affective capacities of the species. Being social, they cannot *in general* dispense with standards in terms of which they judge their relationships with their fellows.

Furthermore, once given a culture and within it a set of value standards, additional value standards develop as questions emerge concerning (1) congruity and priority among values, (2) the desirability of various means and mechanisms that maintain or work toward change of values, (3) the metavalues of the ultimate desirability of culture itself, and, correspondingly, of human life as a meaningful, worth-while enterprise.

Value-analysis and analysis of non-value conditions are not *opposed* to one another; in a reasonable world of scientific discourse, at least, they would be supplementary and complementary. Thus, there is no doubt that *given* technologies and social conditions may affect values. For example, it may be hypothesized that, across societies, the higher the average per capita daily intake of calories the less will be the social evaluation of purely contemplative or mediative, noninstrumental use of time, and the higher the social evaluation of active leisure. Basic conditions of goal-attainment likewise are highly relevant to values, for example, if a given technology requires for effectiveness co-operative rather than individualistic action, over time, the relevant value criteria are likely to change accordingly, placing a premium on collective goals and conformity to group norms.

CONSEQUENCES OF VALUES

Values have consequences. This statement would be made true only by definition if one said, "Values are criteria of desirability that affect selections among alternative modes of behavior." We intend the assertion, however, as an empirical claim: given the existence or nonexistence of a value standard as ascertained by specified observational operations at Time$_1$, we predict a different outcome at Time$_2$ under otherwise identical conditions, depending upon the presence or absence of the value in question. If our problem is to predict from an external stimulus to subsequent behavior, we may treat values as intervening variables, inside the black box of the social actor. If the stimulus field is constant and our problem is to predict to subsequent behavior, we can treat values as independent variables. So conceived, the question as to whether values "cause" behavior is the same kind of question as whether hormones or food deprivations cause behavior; the answer is an empirical one of extent and degree of effect upon defined variables under specified conditions.

In the long debate over the place of values in the *explanation* of behavior, much of the discussion has been both inconclusive and confused. At one pole, values are simply dismissed as either epiphenomenal or else as unknowable by scientifically acceptable operations.[9] Behavior then becomes the result of "conditions"—physical, biological, or (nonvalue) social elements. At the other pole, behavior would be interpreted as a sheer emanation or expression of values (although this position seems empty of tenants among present-day social scientists). Intermediate positions either take conditions as independent and primary and values as intervening or of minor causal importance, or reverse this formulation. A more complex explanatory

---

[9] For a skeptical treatment of the concept—tending to discount values as either predictive constructs or causal variables—see Judith Blake and Kindsley Davis, "Norms, Values, and Sanctions," chap. 13, in Robert E. L. Faris (ed.), *Handbook of Modern Sociology* (Chicago: Rand-McNally, 1964), p. 456–484.

model is the one implicit in the present treatment. We conceive of values as initially emerging out of physical, biological, and social conditions, but, once formed, as exerting direct influence upon behavior. Behavior, in turn, reacts back upon both values and conditions, and so on indefinitely. The empirical weights of the many specific variables to be found under these several rubrics are, of course, not deducible from the concepts but must be ascertained by direct investigation in particular contexts.

Lest there be misunderstanding, two other main reservations must be clearly stated. First, we do not assume that values have to be taken directly into account to explain *every* major social process or product. Many very important processes do not appear to be *directly* linked to values. For example, a certain kind of social stratification can be generated by purely random events; a minimum level of unemployment will always be present solely as a consequent of "friction" in mobility and training; many characteristics of direct social interaction arise directly from ecological factors; delays in the courts partly result from random "queueing" in the arrival of cases.[10]

An interest in values does not force us to renounce the rule of parsimony; where values are not needed for prediction or explanation or control, there we may dispense with values.

Second, the empirical importance of values as controlling variables differs greatly in different realms of behavior and under differing conditions. As the horse responds to the delicate signals of a skillful rider only if properly trained, so human social behavior is shaped by values only when the values are actually implanted in the individual's control-system and then only when not counteracted by other values. Value determinants give maximal predictions for highly socialized persons who are embedded in and dependent upon groups of high consensus. Under conditions of great cultural heterogeneity, rapid change, and low social interdependence, behaviors may show no clearly consistent patterning in terms of generalized values. Also, the prime importance of values often is not in their direct role as internalized guides to an individual's own need-gratifications, but rather in eliciting his reactions as a third party to the conduct of others, for example, as a judge. Thus, relatively low-energy inputs of information steer the high-energy activities of men in society. Present-day American society invests a substantial percentage of its energy into development and transmission of the cultural system, through research, development, and education.

Among the society's store of cultural resources, values constitute especially economical sets of high-level guidance signals. Their economy lies in

---

[10] Cf. Harrison White, "Uses of Mathematics in Sociology," in James C. Charlesworth (ed.), *Mathematics and the Social Sciences* (Philadelphia: American Academy of Political and Social Science, 1963), pp. 87–90.

their generality. To give someone *full* instructions for behavior in each particular situation, for example, *exactly* how to tie the shoelace, is enormously difficult and costly of time and energy. If rules of behavior, covering many recurring situations, can be learned, a great reduction in subsequent costs of control is achieved. Still further economy is attained if generalized standards of desirability can be encoded, so that the actor has instantly available criteria for selection of behavioral alternatives that are applicable to thousands of concrete circumstances—as when a generalized evaluative conception of "personal honesty" does service for an indefinitely large potential set of specific injunctions and prohibitions.

In the world of social preferences and choices, then, values occupy a distinctive place as the selective standards by reference to which judgments of desirability may be made and justified or defended, nor are values merely carried diffusely by the general population—as it were "in solution"; special agencies are devoted to them. Along with high specialization in the division of labor, our society has developed organized bodies that have as a major part of their concern the codification and synthesis of values—for example, courts, the Supreme Court,[11] law schools, seminaries and theological institutes, and universities.

MODES OF ORGANIZATION
AMONG VALUES

To discuss values in the context of societal planning and action, it is advisable to note just "where" values enter into the processes of governance. Although values enter into every social action, the *primary* location of values at the macroscopic level of social structure is as one of the sources of goals and criteria for policy formation. Schematically,

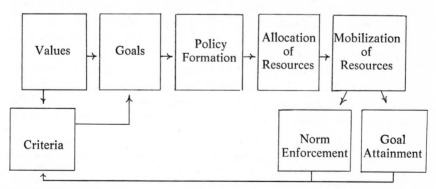

---

11 For examples, see Milton R. Konvitz, *Expanding Liberties: Freedom's Gains in Postwar America* (New York: Viking, 1966).

The inventory of values held by a particular person or shared within a population are not jumbled together in a completely random assortment. Rather, they are assembled into organized sets or systems, to an important extent. Although compartmentalization of subsets does occur, as well as disconnectedness of unit values, the total evidence of patterned aggregation is quite convincing. Further, many different individuals hold the same values, and this sharedness also exhibits orderliness, for example, high intercorrelations of certain values and subsets of them. Therefore, societies may be characterized by value distributions, and by the arrangements of subsystems of values in different portions of the social structure.

Like all other human behavior, the conduct of political and administrative affairs is partly guided by values. ("Partly" because a great variety of other causally important "reality conditions" also exert influence.) This is true whether or not the actors make their selective criteria explicit, and it remains true even if those who make the political and administrative decisions are not aware of their own evaluative standards. Values, we repeat, are inherently consequential.

Societal decisions that are made in ignorance of the values of the populations affected by the decisions frequently have unexpected results. This nonsurprising fact is often ignored in practice. Disregard of values in this way might be reduced by providing reliable and valid data concerning the most important values operative in relevant populations. Although such data obviously would not be completely determinative in political decisions, they would hold out the possibility of improved capacities for prediction of proximate consequences.[12]

In a highly differentiated large-scale society, values governing collective policies necessarily become *generalized* across many varieties of situations. By that very fact, the values upon which consensual decision can be made and legitimated do not provide detailed guidance for specific actions; it follows that *respecification*[13] in the form of particular norms always will be required before national policies can be executed through the numerous social units that typically will be involved.

Whatever the level of social structure, however, values always gain their "hands and feet" when shared in definite social groupings which follow and enforce particular norms that are in some sense "consistent with" the values. It is entailment in social action that makes evaluative standards

---

12 A general brief for the usefulness of comparative value-analysis has been illustrated by Seymour Martin Lipset, "The Value Patterns of Democracy: A Case Study in Comparative Analysis, *American Sociological Review*, Vol. 28 (August 1963), pp. 515–531.

13 Cf. Charles Ackerman and Talcott Parsons, "The Concept of 'Social System' as a Theoretical Device," in Gordon J. Direnzo (ed.), *Concepts, Theory, and Explanation in the Behavioral Sciences* (New York: Random House, 1966), pp. 37 ff.

more than empty verbalisms or mere formalistic rationalizations. But if values are kept alive in the processes of social interaction, that very involvement means that they *must* be organized. Only in limiting cases will any one value criterion have exclusive jurisdiction over a full sequence of social interaction; multiple value referents are typical, and hence value priorities and interrelations are almost omnipresent. Furthermore, values are not added or subtracted as discrete bricklike units; rather, they fuse, overlap, reinforce, catalyze, hybridize, interpenetrate, and combine in numerous complex ways. Now, the full exposition of the intricacy of subtle value-analysis is no more feasible at the level of national social accounts than would be all the conceptual and computational work behind national economic accounts. Nevertheless, because of the profound hazards of treating human values *only* aggregatively and in terms of abstracted general tendencies, any gross inventory should be supplemented by detailed, in-depth study of strategic examples of the fusions, separations, and other *processes of interrelation* among values. A new combination of value standards may produce evaluative modes not obviously to be anticipated—an emphasis on rationality joined with the value of individual personality may emerge in the form of a high evaluation of psychological self-knowledge and an injunction to direct one's conduct in terms of this self-knowledge. These new evaluative products may, in turn, be "captured" by prior commitment to instrumental achievement values—eventuating in a "cult of self-improvment" in the service of occupational activity rather than in a dedication to contemplative modes of life.

MODES OF CHANGE IN VALUES AND BELIEFS[14]

Among the ways in which values and beliefs can change, the following are noteworthy:

1. *Creation:* a new evaluative criterion or belief is developed out of new experience and becomes effective, at some level, in regulating behavior.

2. *Relatively sudden destruction:* Although extremely rare, there are some instances in which there is a quick extinction of a previously accepted value.

3. *Attenuation:* Slow diminution of the intensity of affect and commitment; decrease in interest and attention, as fewer and fewer persons promote, support, teach, or defend the belief or value orientation.

---

[14] This section is adapted from the author's "Changing Value Orientations and Beliefs on the American Scene," *Illinois in Transition* (Urbana: Co-operative Extension Service, University of Illinois, 1966), pp. 119–122.

4. *Extension:* Application to objects and events in addition to those included in the original sphere of relevance.

5. *Elaboration:* The value of belief is progressively rationalized, symbolized, dramatized, documented and otherwise made more complex or more embedded in its sociocultural context.[15]

6. *Specification:* A generalized orientation increasingly is defined in terms of a variety of particular contexts, resulting in modifications and restrictions. In the United States it seems that "freedom" is not now felt to be violated by compulsory vaccination, compulsory school attendance, or peacetime military conscription.

7. *Limitation:* It would be a limiting case if any given value—in confronting other values—were not altered at all; generally there is some change even if only in the direction of absolutism. A frequent outcome, however, is that a particular value comes to be bounded or limited by the recognized claims of other values. Thus, in American democratic creeds and practices, it has always been necessary to accommodate a persisting strain between *freedom* and *equality:* each is necessary for the democratic position, but neither can be pushed to extremes without negating the other.

8. *Explication:* In the form of folk virtues, values are typically implicit—indeed, often altogether inaccessible to explicit formulation by their bearers. At the opposite extreme, highly systematic explications of values are formulated in creedal or philosophical systems. In American society there is a vast accumulation of explicit value statements. Scattered evidence suggests increasingly expilict affirmation of major values. Such explication seems to be favored by rapid changes in specific social conditions and norms as well as by direct challenges to the standards themselves, for example, the attacks of totalitarian political movements.

9. *Consistency:* A concern with consistency itself represents a distinctive value position. Greater systematic explicitness at the level of national political assertions and mass-media creeds almost certainly increase a sense of "contradiction," "inconsistency," and "hypocrisy" when viewed against some of the daily realities of behavior.[16]

10. *Intensity (absolutism, centrality):* A value initially accepted as one among many standards may become so intensely held and promoted as to become the center of life. A value formerly the focus of many other criteria may lose its central intellectual and emotional *raison d'être,* become relativized, and recede into the ranks of the ordinary criteria of daily life.

---

15 See Richard E. Du Wors, "Persistence and Change in Local Values of Two New England Communities," *Rural Sociology,* Vol. 17 (September 1952), pp. 207–217.

16 Awareness of inconsistencies between traditional beliefs and values and new knowledge may lead to change. Cf. Herbert H. Hyman and Paul B. Sheatsley, "Attitudes toward Desegregation," *Scientific American,* Vol. 211 (July 1964), pp. 16–23.

A society in which the store of knowledge concerning the consequences of action is large and is rapidly increasing is a society in which received norms and their "justifying" values will be increasingly subjected to questioning and reformulation. As our knowledge concerning the consequences of racial segregation has exposed effects upon education, employment, income, family life, crime, and intergroup hostility and conflict, value conflicts have been revealed, and some appear to have been sharpened. As we learn more about the consequences of different kinds of childhood discipline upon personality development, pressures are generated to re-evaluate punitive measures, permissiveness, and so on.

It is likely that in the United States over the last three decades there has developed an increase in the positive evaluation of *cognitive* criteria for judging both individual conduct and collective policy and practice. As levels of formal education rise—both on the average and in terms of the proportion of persons mastering really high levels of knowledge and conceptual skills—and as societal processes inexorably call attention to interdependence of consequences of social actions, the disregard of facts and causal reasoning is likely to be increasingly regarded as a *moral* fault. This tentative prediction is not intended to be an expression of wish-fulfillment. Rather we believe that the indicated direction of value movement already is objectively present, as suggested by the increased part played in legislative, administrative, and even judicial decisions by relatively systematic attention to cognitive considerations as to both "the facts of the case" and to "causes and consequences"—with regard to military strategy and tactics, welfare policies, penal and correctional practices (rehabilitation, the death penalty), effectiveness of educational and therapeutic practices, economic policies, transportation, urban development, environmental pollution, and many other areas. Obviously, this is not to say that "rationality" (however conceived) is necessarily increasing, nor that attempted solutions to problems are necessarily increasingly "adequate," whatever that might mean. It is only to suggest as worthy of further definition and study the proposition that a "knowledgeable society"[17] will increasingly give a positive evaluation of knowledge—up to some limit not yet closely approached.

MEASURES AND INDICATORS

Values must not be truistic inferences—constructed by the observer by noting regularities present in a sample of behavior and then improperly used to "explain" that same behavior. Rather the predictive usefulness of

---

[17] Robert E. Lane, "The Decline of Politics and Ideology in a Knowledgeable Society," *American Sociological Review*, Vol. 31 (October 1966), pp. 649–662.

values can be shown by formulating values from one set of data, and then using the formulations to predict to a *different* sample of behavior, under specified conditions. The proportion of variations in behavior that can be accounted for by differences in values will vary greatly from situation to situation and from one type of behavior to another, for example, certain generalized values might be highly predictive of political oratory, much less indicative of detailed administrative decisions in technically complex operations. In general, values may be expected to play a prominent part in the initiation of policy and in the rationale for policy.[18]

For specific societal diagnosis it is essential to know how value positions are distributed in the social structure. Particularly significant are likely to be the values of various elite strata—political leaders, government administrators, high military officials, business and union executives, religious leaders, scientists, educators, writers, artists, and outstanding figures in the mass media. And particularly significant also are likely to be the values, beliefs, and aspirations of deprived, frustrated, and alienated elements of the population—those blocked from legitimate upward mobility and social dignity, doomed and defeated strata, anomic youths, and others predisposed to dissatisfaction with the existing state of affairs.

What is a feasible strategy of data collection and analysis that is likely, when consistently followed, to generate the most useful information? It seems reasonable to begin by applying the existing interpretations of main value patterns to already available records[19] of behavior and opinions, for example, legislative materials and court decisions concerning racial discrimination and segregation in education, housing, employment, political rights, and access to facilities and services. Patterns and trends thus indicated would then be checked and further revealed on a sampling basis by content analysis of public records (hearings, briefs, editorials, and the like) and by interviews and experiments. The detailed studies always will show complex combinations of values being used as bases for evaluative judgments. Identification of the components and development of measures of their interrelations will then supply empirical guides for interpreting data series for the nation as a whole.

Intensive "spot studies," therefore, appear to be indispensable for valid interpretation and the avoidance of major errors in societal value-appraisals. Such appraisals can help to guard against the dangers of over-aggregation by providing samplings from all the main social strata, ethnic

---

18 Cf. Wilbert E. Moore, *Social Change* (Englewood Cliffs, N.J.: Prentice-Hall, 1963), pp. 93–94.

19 See the reference to existing collections of data in Raymond A. Bauer (ed.), *Social Indicators* (Cambridge, Massachusetts and London, England: M.I.T. Press, 1966.)

and religious categories, and other obviously important social formations.

One obvious and accessible source of data for a national inventory of value patterns is the output of the mass media. Relatively sophisticated methods of content analysis are available, and computer programming is rapidly opening up new possibilities. Masses of data, published and unpublished, are available for analysis that can show in detail how these media permeate different portions of the social system. The total coverage is, alone, suggestive of an unprecedented exposure to translocal information, education, and propaganda.[20] As of 1961, each 100 households had 107 television sets and 322 radio sets, sent 10 persons per week to see motion pictures, and received 117 daily newspapers—in short, the average household was suffused with an incessant flow of external communication.

Observational and experimental data may be used to cross-check changes that appear in expressive cultural products and in opinions, for example, observations of group competition versus individual competition among school children; experiments on yielding or conformity behavior; studies of choices of future versus present rewards. Such sweeping questions as, "Are Americans becoming more other-directed?" can in this way be subdivided and studied so that meaningful specific answers are possible.

Among the other sources of evidence to be considered are: time-budgets, expenditures for goods and services, content of expressive culture (art, recreation, popular heroes, and the like), public opinion surveys, educational and occupational choices, and studies of social conflicts and disorders and of deviant behavior. The possibilities may be briefly illustrated.

Significant systematic evidence permitting inferences concerning political values can be obtained not only from analysis of electoral voting, legislative voting, and judicial decisions, but also from surveys of opinions and attitudes.[21] Single-opinion items on topical issues (Korean war, Taft-Hartley Act, nuclear test ban, medicare) change rapidly and are difficult to interpret as evidence of values. Much more useful for ascertaining values and changes in them are multi-item opinion scales (especially those that can be repeated from time to time), which index more generic orientations such as humanitarianism, individual personality,[22] or commitment to freedom.

Popular fiction serves as one source of evidence for value themes.

---

20 Melvin L. De Fleur, *Theories of Mass Communication* (New York: David McKay Company, 1966), pp. 156–157.

21 Samuel A. Stouffer, *Communism, Conformity, and Civil Liberties* (Garden City, N.Y.: Doubleday, 1955.)

22 For example see the "faith-in-human-nature" scale reported in Rose K. Goldsen *et al.*, *What College Students Think* (Princeton, N.J.: D. Van Nostrand, 1960), pp. 133–139, 150–152, 187–195, 221.

Albrecht has shown that stories in wide-circulation magazines stress a central pattern of marital and familial values.[23] "Racist" and "group-superiority" themes have been traced in magazine short stories for 1937 and 1943.[24] Changes in religious beliefs and values have been indicated by analysis of religious best sellers from 1875 to 1955.[25] Studies of fictional heroes have drawn inferences concerning underlying value criteria.[26] Similarly, successful use has been made of content analysis of popular long-run plays in New York and Berlin.[27] Although the relationships of art to social reality are exceedingly complex, some reasonable inferences concerning changes in values can be drawn from changes in expressive arts.[28]

Thus, Melville Jacobs has pointed to the unique self-conscious intensity of Euro-American attitudes concerning "art": "a striking ideological theme and value-ideal . . . to select and respond with a required intensity of appreciation to a small percent of expressive products as 'works of art.' "[29]

Again, changes in beliefs and values associated with organized religious bodies have been documented by descriptions not only of official creeds, sermons, and the like, but also by opinion surveys[30] and detailed local studies. Indicators of public attention have been used.[31]

As a final illustration, note that already we have had estimates of national time-use budgets (for 1900, 1950, and projections for 2000 A.D.).[32] More accurate and detailed data could be obtained fairly readily from sample surveys, permitting, for example, a periodic appraisal of the

---

[23] Milton C. Albrecht, "Does Literature Reflect Common Values," *American Sociological Review*, Vol. 21 (December 18, 1956), pp. 722–729.

[24] Bernard Berelson and Patricia J. Salter, "Majority and Minority Americans: An Analysis of Magazine Fiction," *Public Opinion Quarterly*, Vol. 10 (Summer 1946), pp. 168–197.

[25] Louis Schneider and Sanford H. Dornbusch, *Popular Religion: Inspirational Books in America* (Chicago: University of Chicago Press, 1958.)

[26] Patrick Johns-Heine and Hans H. Gerth, "Values in Mass Periodical Fiction, 1921–1940," *Public Opinion Quarterly*, Vol. 13 (Spring 1949), pp. 105–113.

[27] Donald V. McGranahan and Ivor Wayne, "German and American Traits Reflected in Popular Dramas," *Human Relations*, Vol. I (August 1948), pp. 429–455.

[28] Vytautas Kavolis, "Art Content and Social Involvement," *Social Forces*, Vol. 42 (May 1964), pp. 467–472.

[29] Melville Jacobs, *Pattern in Cultural Anthropology*, op. cit., p. 296.

[30] Charles Y. Glock and Rodney Stark, "Is There an American Protestantism?" *Transaction*, Vol. 3 (November/December 1965), pp. 8–13, 48–49.

[31] Hornell Hart, "Changing Social Attitudes and Interests," chap. 8 in *Recent Social Trends* (New York: McGraw-Hill, 1933.)

[32] Mary A. Holman, "A National Time-Budget for the Year 2000," *Sociology and Social Research*, Vol. 46 (October 1961).

main uses of leisure time ("leisure" was 27 per cent of total time in 1900; 34 per cent in 1950).

Inventories of values can never be complete; it is a property of valuing that the process is never closed. This characteristic must be built into comprehensive description and analysis in the form of explicit categories of "change," "omitted areas," "likely and unlikely next developments," and some equivalent of, "what else is there that we cannot possibly imagine at this time?" (The fact that the last category will necessarily be empty is the most important reason for making sure it is there.)

PRESENT KNOWLEDGE OF VALUES IN AMERICAN SOCIETY

It is not possible here, of course, to present the massive materials required to support synthesizing descriptions of values in the total social system of the United States. On the basis of an earlier extended analysis we have distinguished some fifteen major value-belief clusterings that are salient in American culture, as follows:

(1) activity and work;
(2) achievement and success;
(3) moral orientation;
(4) humanitarianism;
(5) efficiency and practicality;
(6) science and secular rationality;
(7) material comfort;
(8) progress;
(9) equality;
(10) freedom;
(11) democracy;
(12) external conformity;
(13) nationalism and patriotism;
(14) individual personality;
(15) racism and related group superiority.

Running through these complex orientations, as still more highly generalized themes, is an emphasis on the worth of active mastery rather than passive acceptance of events; an external rather than an inward view of the world; an outlook that perceives society and history as open-ended, not static; an inclination to prefer or put trust in rationalism as opposed to traditionalism; an interest in orderliness; a universalistic rather than a particularistic social ethic; horizontal or equalitarian rather than hierarchical social relationships; and a high evaluation of individual personality rather than collective identity and responsibility.[33]

A highly useful synthesis of data on public opinion by V. O. Key, Jr., has added specificity to several of the above characterizations and contains important analyses of the structures and processes that intervene between the orientations of the populace and the decisions and actions of legislators and administrators and executives. One of the clearest findings is that political and governmental decisions in the short-run often are not closely connected with the diffusely held values of the unorganized electorate.[34]

The most important evidence on values comes from records of actual behavior in all areas of American life. Supplemental data from research on records of expressive culture have only recently begun to accumulate. The following examples may suggest how this type of new information is being generated.

That the possibilities of value-analysis through studies of mass-readership fiction goes beyond any simple "counting" procedure is illustrated by an ingenious and fine-grained study of magazine fiction.[35] Comparing 1890, 1925, and 1955, the analysis shows that major characters in more recent times have been depicted more often in terms of "fun morality" (rather than "puritanism"), technological progress (rather than technological conservatism), and lessened familism. Positive orientations to sexual freedom and rejection of marriage reached a peak in 1925, declining somewhat by the mid-1950's. For most of the values studied, the magazine fiction seems to have appealed to an urban and well-educated readership that was considerably more "liberal" than the general population. Thus, the fictional accounts did not simply "reflect reality" in some average or total way, but showed quite specific kinds of transformation directed toward the readership population. Allowing for this selectivity, the stories seem to reveal important directions of change in values. Major omissions of certain ideological values, for example, concerning religion, divorce, sexual promiscuity, capitalism, or overtly political issues, suggests

---

33 Adapted from Robin M. Williams, Jr., *American Society* (2nd ed.; New York: Alfred A. Knopf, 1960), chap. xi.

34 *Public Opinion and American Democracy* (New York: Alfred A. Knopf, 1961), especially chaps. 16 and 19.

35 Martin U. Martel and George J. McCall, "Reality-Orientation and the Pleasure Principle: A Study of American Mass-Periodical Fiction (1890–1955)," in Lewis A. Dexter and David M. White (eds.), *People, Society, and Mass Communications* (New York: Free Press of Glencoe, 1964), pp. 283–334.

"veto" or "censoring" mechanisms intervening between prevailing values and published content.

A number of works have relied heavily upon a variety of historical documents and commentaries; although many of the conclusions thus derived are necessarily impressionistic, they do provide usual points of departure for establishing base lines of change.[36]

Increasingly, the assertions of such studies are being tested by more detailed and systematic approaches. Thus, the general impression that recent decades have witnessed a decline in achievement values has been examined by several specific analyses of cultural products. For instance, classification of a random sample of editorials in the *National 4-H Club News* from 1924 to 1958 showed a significant decline in emphasis on the value of achievement (and no significant change in *affiliation* or *co-operation* values).[37] Similar results were found in an analysis of advertising in the *Ladies' Home Journal* from 1890 to 1956.[38] Magazine fiction and mass heroes (for example, entertainers) also show indications of lessened stress on excellence of achievement and more on the "rewards" of being successful. McClellan shows that frequency of achievement imagery in stories in widely used children's readers rose to a peak about 1890 and then declined to a point in 1950 at about the level of 1850. (An index of innovation patents issued per million population rose also to a peak in 1890 and then declined.[39]) Several other studies have pointed in the same direction.[40] Our own impression from the assorted available information is that "achievement" has indeed receded in salience and intensity in relation to "success,"

---

[36] Clyde Kluckhohn, "Have There Been Discernible Shifts in American Values During the Past Generation?" in Elting E. Morison (ed.), *The American Style* (New York: Harper, 1958), p. 204; Seymour Martin Lipset, *The First New Nation* (New York: Basic Books, 1963), chap. 3; Michael McGiffert (ed.), *The Character of Americans* (Homewood, Ill.: Dorsey Press, 1964), Part VI; Talcott Parsons, "The Point of View of the Author," in Max Black (ed.), *The Social Theories of Talcott Parsons* (Englewood Cliffs, N.J.: Prentice-Hall, 1961), pp. 346–347; David Riesman, *The Lonely Crowd* (New Haven: Yale University Press, 1950); William H. Whyte, *The Organization Man* (Garden City, N.Y.: Doubleday, 1956).

[37] Murray A. Straus and Lawrence J. Houghton, "Achievement, Affiliation, and Co-operation Values as Clues to Trends in American Rural Society, 1924–1958," *Rural Sociology*, Vol. 25 (December 1960), pp. 394–403.

[38] S. M. Dornbusch and L. C. Hickman, "Other-Directedness in Consumer-Goods Advertising: A Test of Riesman's Historical Theory," *Social Forces*, Vol. 38, No. 2 (December 1959), pp. 99–102.

[39] David C. McClellan, *The Achieving Society* (Princeton, N.J.: D. Van Nostrand Company, 1961), p. 150.

[40] An investigation of the content of children's readers from 1800 to 1950 showed a decline during the decades since 1880 in the frequency of "achievement imagery" (Richard de Charms and Gerald H. Moeller, "Values Expressed in American Children's Readers: 1800–1950," *Journal of Abnormal and Social Psychology*, Vol. 64 [February 1962], pp. 136–142).

but that the change is a shift in emphasis rather than a reversal of values and that achievement remains an outstanding value orientation.

In an ingenious study, Greenstein was able to fit together a number of studies of children's heroes and exemplars ("What person you would most like to resemble?"), dating from the 1890's down to very recent years.[41] The data indicated declining interest in "serious" as over against "popular" entertainers, consistent with Lowenthal's finding concerning magazine biographies.[42] But there is no clear evidence of any trend in identification or

Value-Belief Complexes	Direction of Change—Period (Approximate)	
	1900–1945	1945–1966
Activity	Indeterminate	−a
Work	−	−
Achievement	−	+ (post-Sputnik I)
Success	+	+
Material Comfort	+	+
Humanitarianism (Domestic)	+	+
Humanitarianism (War)	+	−
"Absolute" Moral Orientation	−	Indeterminate
Practicality	+	−
Efficiency	+	−
Sciences and Secular Rationality	+	+
Progress	+	−
Freedom	Indeterminate	−
Equality	+	+
Democracy	+	Indeterminate
Conformity (to Social Pressure)	+	+
Individual Personality	+	Indeterminate
Nationalism	+	− to +
Racism—Group Superiority	−	−
Totals		
Increase	13	8
No Change or Indeterminate	2	3
Decrease	4	8

a(−) is decrease; (+) is increase.

[41] Fred I. Greenstein, "New Light on Changing American Values: A Forgotten Body of Survey Data," Social Forces, Vol. 42 (May 1964), pp. 441–450.

[42] Leo Lowenthal, "Biographies in Popular Magazines," in Paul F. Lazarsfeld and Frank N. Stanton (eds.), Radio Research, 1942–43 (New York: Duell, Sloan and Pearce, 1944), pp. 507–548.

aspiration with regard to business and political leaders—such figures always have been chosen as objects of avowed emulation by only a very small percentage of the children studied at any particular period. We suggest the hypothesis that *achievement* values will be stressed in a society that has both a strong consensus on moral standards and relatively good objective opportunity for goal-achievement. On the other hand, *affective* values, stressing "enjoyment," tend to come to the forefront in two different types of situations: (a) in prosperous and secure societies, or (b) in societies in which rewards for sustained achievement are low and risks high. *Collective-integrative* values, yet again, will be stressed in societies severely and persistently threatened by other societies. War and the threat of war are major stimuli to collectivism, both as a condition and as a value orientation.

Space forbids similar documentation of change and continuity for the other fourteen themes in our list. In another place the writer has tried to summarize tentative impressions of change, based on a fuller review of existing studies, in the following tabular form:[43]

In terms of these broad estimates, during the period from around 1900 up to the end of World War II, the major thrust was in the direction of further positive development of the themes analyzed. Since 1945, however, there is a suggestion of lessened emphasis on activity and achievement, some disillusionment concerning "progress," and some loss in humanitarianism under the exigencies of war. The available information is highly imprecise, and these changes should not be overemphasized; on net balance, during the last half-century the conclusion probably has to be "the same main values—only more so." The changes that have occurred are clearly important, but for the most part they grow directly out of elements already present at the beginning of the period of review.

LIMITATIONS AND CAUTIONS

From the basic conceptions of value and value problems here reviewed, it follows as a normal expectation that societal value-reporting and value-analyses will not be without their potential hazards and possible disutilities. It is conceivable that action predicted upon well-defined data concerning explicit values could create unanticipated imbalances, deficiencies, and conflicts because the very existence of convincing data led to ignoring or underestimating the importance of subtle, diffuse, or implicit values that are difficult to index. Continuous inputs of information on current changes might encourage overemphasis in policy decisions upon short-run considera-

---

[43] "Changing Value Orientations and Beliefs on the American Scene," *op. cit.*, p. 131.

tions, leading to overly rapid and excessive oscillations in the societal guidance system. Proliferation of information and of requirements for analysis could overload channels of research, develop overly expensive monitoring arrangements, and saturate channels of dissemination and reception—all of which, in turn, might excessively delay decisions and increase problems of coordination. It is not impossible that a continuously high level of explication of values would increase rigidity of commitments to overgeneralized guidelines and reduce adaptive flexibility. On the other hand, recognition of this possibility might further encourage centralized efforts to manipulate values held by the general public or selected segments of it.

We have just tried to make the hazards stand out as sharply as possible. But all the possibly undesired side-effects suggested are likewise conceivable in *any* kind of expansion of social knowledge. Did we not believe that the advantages far outweigh any imaginable disadvantages, we would not be presenting this article. In any case, the appropriate recommendation would seem to be that research be undertaken on such problems of possible effects of value-analysis, concurrently with efforts to improve the basic data.

It is to be expected that the proposal to develop and utilize data on values as part of systemic national self-appraisal will be without attraction to many Americans and strongly resisted by some. Indeed, the author in early attempts to explain this approach has encountered such reactions from supposedly sophisticated academic audiences. Some individuals fear that the data will be misleading, either because of unwise selectivity or unreliability or lack of validity of indicators. Others fear that the proposed efforts will be all too successful in generating valid information—which, they fear, will be used to increase centralized power, public deception, and mass manipulation. Some will argue, whether seriously or not, that it is better that decision-makers be ignorant of the values held by the population at large; they claim to put full trust in the intuitive wisdom and moral strength of a few experienced leaders. Our view, of course, is that the systematic explication and analysis of values as causes and consequences of social action is an essential part of the urgent task of purposive, objective diagnosis of societal functioning.[44]

Finally, we must emphasize, it would be neither realistic nor desirable to seek for a "complete" assembly and analysis on data concerning values as such. As in all other areas of knowledge, there are limitations of opportunity-costs relative to other types of knowledge as well as to all other

---

[44] Compare the observations of Bertram M. Gross, "The State of the Nation: Social Systems Accounting," in Raymond A. Bauer (ed.), *Social Indicators* (Cambridge, Massachusetts, and London, England: M.I.T. Press, 1966), p. 260: "In very human fashion they will prefer . . . bewailing the loss of human values as against enlisting in a positive effort to restore human values to a central position in man's thought and action."

potentially competing uses of resources. It has been no part of our intention here to present an "imperialistic" case by arguing for an exclusive or dominant emphasis in societal accounting upon value phenomena. The appropriate relative magnitude of the effort to be expended in this particular area will have to be gradually determined through successive experiences. Here we have hoped only to establish the general usefulness and feasibility of bringing systematic knowledge of operative value standards directly into major societal diagnoses and planning.

8

EDUCATION AND LEARNING

WILBUR J. COHEN

A Nation's greatness is measured by its concern for the health and welfare of its people. Throughout the history of our democracy, this commitment has grown and deepened.

LYNDON B. JOHNSON

The American people from their beginnings as a nation have set ambitious social and economic goals to improve the quality of life. The evidence of history shows that the nation has made remarkable progress. And further advancement toward these goals continues. But few accurate indicators are available to gauge the rate of progress or to measure the changes in American society that are currently under way and the obstacles that impede attainment of the goals.

PROBLEMS OF ESTABLISHING
INDICATORS OF
NATIONAL ACHIEVEMENT

The task of enunciating meaningful and relevant national goals is an essential first step for achieving them. Pertinent statistics and other facts are necessary to develop effective programs and plans, to evaluate progress, and to assess resources needed for accomplishing the nation's aims.

Setting up relevant indicators is not an easy undertaking. Not only must they be applicable to complex ideas and concepts, they also are concerned with vital and challenginsg issues. But the urgency of the task is

186

great. There has already been widespread public discussion of the social changes which are occurring with a rapidity unequaled in history and of the problems concerned with vastly increasing population and mass migration to urban-suburban areas; with substandard education, substandard housing for millions of people who do not fully share in the benefits of a prosperous society; with mass communications, rapid travel, mass production, and automation. These discussions have revealed facts related to change. The information, while significant, is only a fraction of the knowledge needed to understand and adjust to life in the twenty-first century.

THE IMPORTANCE OF AN
EDUCATED SOCIETY

Not too long ago, education was considered the privilege of only the wealthy—the leisure class. The evolution of the American idea of free public education for all, with public schools locally managed, and largely locally financed, has been closely bound to the development of the nation itself. United States educational history reflects the American commitment to the ideal of education for everyone—the conviction that an educated population is essential to an effective democracy, to freedom, and to economic growth.

THE RIGHT TO AN EDUCATION

The national urge to raise the quality of life for all, which—in turn—required providing educational opportunities for all, has produced an addition to the list of basic American rights: the right to an education—or, at least, the right to have an opportunity to acquire an education. Despite a gradually increasing public acceptance of the idea of "full education for every citizen to the limits of his capacity to absorb it," the most casual sampling would reveal thousands of young people who are not accorded this right. From the point of view of the welfare of society—and of the individual as well—this right must be assured.

THE TASK FOR EDUCATION
IN THE TWENTY-FIRST CENTURY

As society becomes increasingly more highly developed and changes occur with ever greater rapidity, not only a person's livelihood, but indeed the very essence of the life he leads—his way of life—will depend upon his education. His ability to discard much that he has learned as it becomes obsolete or irrelevant and to acquire new knowledge—most of it not yet discovered—that will be pertinent to his needs will determine his ability to make the successful transition from life in this decade to a future vastly different in terms of economic and technological achievements.

The development of the nation's schools has been alternately praised and criticized in educational circles, as well as in congressional committees, in industrial conferences, and by the public at large. There is no disagreement, however, that, in its most simple terms, the success of the future will depend to a large degree upon providing more knowledge to more people in less time than is being done today. And this will be a costly enterprise. But perhaps failure to do so would carry an even higher cost.

A NEW ERA IN EDUCATION

This is an era of innovation and change. The methods of gaining new knowledge, transmitting it, and diffusing information and ideas throughout the country must be speeded up. It has become clear that the changes in one area reverberate and indicate new perspectives in others. As an outstanding illustration, the demographic, economic, and social forces fermenting throughout American society are generating significant changes in the nation's educational system. There are new and unprecedented challenges in education, on a national scope, to meet unconventional educational demands—to shift from the traditional school-system emphasis on instruction designed for learning patterns of school-age youth to innovative methods concerned with the learning capabilities of very young children and of adults

Newly discovered phenomena of early learning capacity and the increasing need for modern adults to have opportunities for "refresher" learning experiences to update and upgrade their knowledge and skills raise provocative questions about restricting the delivery of educational services generally to the "school-age" population. Today's circumscribed educational process, viewed by many as a "preparation for life," is not likely to be applicable and acceptable to people living in an age characterized by space exploration, the crumbling of barriers of time and distance, the rising aspirations of all citizens, the proliferation of knowledge, the advances in technology and computerized methods, high productivity, and growing wealth. Modern man will likely regard the continuation of his learning experience as a normal lifetime activity.

TRAINING MANPOWER
IN RELATION TO NEEDS

There is wide recognition that the pressures of new technology combined with a growing number of students put a huge burden on education.[1] Increasingly, business leaders are directing their attention to science and technology as they relate to education and the labor market of the present and future, as indicated in the following statement of concern:

It has been predicted that in 1975 some three-fourths of our labor force will be producing goods and services that have not yet been developed. Unless educators—and other public and private policy makers—demonstrate unusually keen foresight, our future economic and technological achievements could be tarnished by a large and growing reserve of inadequately or inappropriately prepared workers.

If the challenges of the future are to be met, business and education must in fact greatly increase their interaction. Corporate giving doesn't complete business' responsibility to the world of study and schooling.[2]

TABLE 1—School Enrollments, United States, 1962–1975 (Millions)

Educational	1940	1950	1960	1965	1970[a]	1974[a]
Level	29.9	31.5	46.0	55.4	63.0	68.4
Preschool	.7	1.3	2.7	3.1	5.3	6.8
Elementary School	20.6	21.0	29.7	33.3	34.2	34.7
Secondary School	7.1	6.5	9.6	12.8	15.1	16.4
Higher Education	1.5	2.7	4.0	6.2	8.4	10.5

[a] Projected.

EMERGING PATTERNS IN
EDUCATION

As the public school system developed, intensive efforts have been made to provide better educations and equal educational opportunities for

[1] For further discussion of problems and issues concerning education, see James D. Finn and Gabriel D. Ofiesh, "The Emerging Technology of Education," *Educational Implications of Technological Change,* Vol. IV, Appendix: *Technology and the American Economy: The Report of the Commission,* February 1966, p. 34.

[2] Excerpt from a speech by M. A. Wright, President of the U.S. Chamber of Commerce, at Shaw University in Raleigh, North Carolina, on February 13, 1967.

more and more students. Continued interest must now be devoted to assuring that the system will reach out to disadvantaged minority groups which have been largely ignored in the past.

The formal educational system must be adaptable to the changing role and meaning of education. The line of distinction between the formal education program, ending with a diploma, and informal educational activities continued as a lifelong process is becoming faint and fading rapidly. Education acquired prior to graduation can no longer be relied upon as an adequate preparation for a lifetime career. The acceleration of technological change and new scientific discoveries, which make old jobs obsolete and create entirely new kinds of work, has been much discussed as posing requirements for continuing education and skill-renewal. Indeed, it has been suggested that a worker now entering the labor force may expect to be employed in not one, but probably two, and possibly even three or four entirely different kinds of work over his lifetime.

THE IMPACT OF CHANGING
LABOR-FORCE REQUIREMENTS ON THE LOCUS
AND MODUS OF EDUCATION

The probability that many of today's school children will be working in the twenty-first century—on jobs not yet created—challenges the educational system to foster the art of learning and to provide pupils with the kind of broadly based general education they need in order to adapt to changes that will occur in their lifetimes. In other words, the educational system is charged with offering a student a sound basic education as well as opportunities for continuous learning at all levels of education and throughout his lifetime.

New and different kinds of educational services must be developed for a generation which will become increasingly involved in leisure-time and cultural pursuits. The educational system will have to become increasingly involved in the affairs of the community and of the world as it helps each child, woman, and man to adapt to the revolutionary changes in his life. Education will become a vital process of innovation and interaction—for the students, the teachers, the educational institutions, the local communities, and the nation.

PRESENT EDUCATIONAL TRENDS

The educational system, like many other institutions in American society, is in a state of evolution—some might even say revolution. Beginning with the past decade, a whole continuum of new methods for organization and delivery of educational services is being developed—indeed, *has* to be developed—to cope with the ever larger numbers of students and ever growing mass of knowledge.

THE GROWING LEARNING FORCE

The most significant aspects of change in the American educational system over the past decade have been the explosive increase in school enrollments and the continuing rise in educational attainment. The growth in the number of persons engaged in formal learning activities has been phenomenal.[3]

REGULAR SCHOOL ENROLLMENTS: School enrollments—kindergarten through college—increased by 9.4 million from 1960 to 1965, an average increase of nearly two million a year.

As reflected in Table 1, elementary and secondary school enrollments are projected to reach 51 million by 1974. The largest enrollment increases over the past decade have been at the high school level, mainly because children born in the years of very high birth rates immediately following World War II are now progressing through high school. Their impact on elementary schools leveled off as they reached high school age and moved up to swell the enrollment rates for secondary schools. Enrollment in grades nine through twelve nearly tripled in the years 1950–1965, and is expected to reach 16.4 million in 1974. Proportionately smaller increases have been projected for elementary school enrollments because the number of five- and six-year-old children entering the school system is approaching a relatively stable figure.

The largest percentage increase in enrollments in recent yaers has been at the higher education level. Enrollment figures have climbed from 2.7 million in 1950 to 6 million in 1965. By 1974 enrollment may reach 10.5 million.

---

3 In discussions with the author in late 1965 and early 1966, Bertram M. Gross, Professor of Political Science, Syracuse University, first used the term "learning force" to express a broad concept of all of the people involved in some kind of organized group-learning process. He later defined the term "learning force" as embracing "the total number of people developing their capacities through systematic education—that is, where learning is aided by teaching and there are formal, organized efforts to impart knowledge through instruction," and subsequently referred to the term in his article on the State of the Union Message, published in the May/June 1966 issue of *Challenge—The Magazine of Economic Affairs,* Vol. 14, No. 5.

VOCATIONAL, TECHNICAL, AND PROFESSIONAL TRAINING ACTIVITIES OUTSIDE THE FORMAL EDUCATIONAL STRUCTURE: In addition to the growing regular enrollments, there have been dramatic increases in specialized learning activities of a vocational, technical, and professional nature. Although valid statistics have not been compiled on enrollments in correspondence courses or in specialized institutes and commercial schools, reference to city classified directories reveals a large volume and wide variety of such facilities. Recent attempts to determine the extent of participation in such learning activities have produced some rough estimates, which are presented in Table 2.

TABLE 2—Vocational, Technical, and Professional Training Outside the Formal Educational Structure, United States, 1940–1974 (Millions)

Training Institution	1940	1950	1960	1965	1974[a]	1970[a]
	11.8	15.3	18.9	25.0	34.0	48.7
Professional and Technical Training	2.5	3.5	4.0	7.8	9.6	18.1
Company Schools	4.7	6.0	6.7	7.2	12.0	17.5
On-the-Job Training	2.4	2.0	3.4	4.5	6.0	6.0
Correspondence Schools	1.0	1.5	2.0	2.4	2.8	3.2
Armed Forces	1.0	2.0	2.4	2.6	3.0	3.0
All Other	.2	.3	.4	.5	.6	.9

[a] Projected.

OTHER FORMAL EDUCATION ACTIVITIES: The hunger of the American people for education is evident in the great proliferation of formal educational opportunities offered under a variety of sponsorships. Some courses are conducted as commercial enterprises, employing high-pressure advertising and sales techniques to attract customers. Others are provided by institutions (libraries, museums, churches, and charity or other groups) and private instruction of neighborhood or other small groups (for example, Great Books Discussion Groups; literary, poetry, art-appreciation, music, drama, and political and current-events discussion groups; adult leadership training for civilian defense, recreational, or youth work; and first-aid, cooking, home nursing, and other classes conducted by the American Red Cross, Girl Scouts, and other organizations, as well as similar activities offered by industry to employees or members of their families).

Table 3 presents some preliminary estimates based on a study, initiated by Mr. Bertram M. Gross and the author, of adult educational activity and how it is changing in the United States.

TABLE 3—United States Adult Education, 1940–1974 (Millions)

Form	1940	1950	1960	1965	1970[a]	1974[a]
	5.6	6.9	9.6	19.2	24.3	31.1
General	1.5	1.8	3.4	4.5	5.0	6.0
Specialized	2.4	3.0	3.4	4.5	5.5	7.0
Correspondence Courses	1.6	1.9	2.5	2.6	2.9	3.5
All Other	.1	.2	.3	7.6	10.9	14.6

[a] Projected.

RATIO OF LEARNING FORCE TO LABOR FORCE: While the estimates and projections of total educational activity in the United States are still relatively undeveloped, the gross figures on enrollments reflected above are significant. They represent a new area of inquiry into the widely diffused educational function. It must be noted that, because the formal training periods reflected under the various categories vary in duration between two weeks and a two-year or longer period, the number of participants is not equivalent to man-years of training. Indeed, the data limitations suggest further research for more reliable statistics on these largely unidentified —or at least less visible—educational resources and conversion of the participation figures into school-year equivalents.

The estimates do not include any assessment of the very considerable volume of education acquired in learning situations represented by basic training in the home, religious instruction in churches, knowledge and skills gained by children in youth-group activities, unorganized individual learning from television, radio, and other informational media, and self-education, including learning from experience. Even with such an omission, the sum of the learning-force components reach a magnitude approaching 100

TABLE 4—Ratio of United States Education Force to
Labor Force, 1940–1974

Learning Force to Labor Force Ratio (Per cent)	1940	1950	1960	1965	1970[a]	1974[a]
	84.2	82.9	101.9	127.0	141.7	159.4
Learning Force (in Millions)	47.3	53.7	74.5	99.6	121.3	148.2
Labor Force (in Millions)	56.2	64.8	73.1	78.4	85.6	93.0

[a] Projected.

million participants—a startling total, nearly a quarter of a million higher than the number in the total United States labor force! The fact that today the learning force is greater than the labor force, and by 1974 the ratio— even by conservative estimates—will be considerably higher, emphasizes the great dimension of the pending tasks for the educational complex.

THE INCREASING NUMBER
OF TEACHERS

As noted earlier, the rate of increase in the numbers of school-age children is not so rapid now as it was over the last two decades; nevertheless, the absolute numbers of school children are larger, with the corollary result of increasing demands for teachers.

The teaching force, has, of course, increased. This year, more than two million grade and high school teachers and nearly a half-million college and university instructors were teaching the increasing number of students. The shortage of teachers and staff to supplement and support their work probably poses the single greatest obstacle to general improvement in education programs. As reflected in Table 5, the number of regular school classroom teachers and other instructional staff is projected to reach 3.2 million by 1974.

TABLE 5—United States Teaching Force, 1940–1974 (Millions)

Educational Level	1940	1950	1960	1970[a]	1974[a]
	1.0	1.3	2.0	3.0	3.2
Elementary Schools	.6	.7	1.1	1.4	1.4
Secondary Schools	.3	.4	.6	1.1	1.2
Higher Education	.1	.2	.3	.5	.6

[a] Projected.

RISING EDUCATIONAL EXPENDITURES

From time to time, there have been some scattered and unrelated attempts to assess total expenditures for all educational activities. As might be expected, wide variations occur in what has been termed "knowledge industry" expenditures, depending upon the components used in the computations.

In 1958, a figure of $136.4 billion was estimated to cover expenditures for research and development activities, all communication media, and information machines and services, in addition to regular formal educational expenditures.[4] More recently, a $195 billion figure has been used as roughly equivalent to the 1958 estimates, with adjustments for the great expansion in audiovisual materials and educational technology (computers, programmed instruction, and the like) that has occurred.

Although these estimates appear to be extremely high, they may actually be somewhat understated if consideration is given to the increase in total expenditures (both public and private) for formal education, which have been rising steadily by more than 10 per cent a year—a rate greater than the increase in the gross national product (GNP). This year, expenditures for formal education are expected to reach $49 billion, or about 6.5 per cent of the GNP. It has been estimated that they may reach 8 per cent of GNP by 1975.[5]

Spending by all levels of government for education has increased dramatically, from $13 billion in 1956 to $34 billion in 1966; and most of the funds have come consistently from state and local government sources. However, in the last two years the federal share increased from 12 to 16 per cent of the total. Most of the increase in federal funds can be attributed to new support under the Elementary and Secondary Education Act and the Higher Education Act.

Since 1964, federal expenditures for elementary and secondary education have more than doubled, from about 4 per cent to nearly 9 per cent; while the share in higher education rose from 20 per cent to about 22 per cent. However, there has been a shift in the allocation of federal funds; whereas in 1964, 58 per cent of all federal grants for education were made for higher education, the figure dropped to 43 per cent last year, with a resulting increase in support for elementary schools.

For more than a decade, state and local governments have used about 90 per cent of their construction funds to build elementary and secondary schools. From the mid-1950's until about 1962, more than half of the federal government's construction expenditures also went to elementary and secondary schools. Since 1962, however, there have been increasing authorizations for new federal programs for college construction, and last year 93 per cent of federal construction funds went to institutions of higher learning because this is where the great impact of enrollments is, and will be in the future. Because of population trends, elementary and secondary school enrollments will begin to level off, whereas college enrollment will increase dramatically.

---

[4] Fritz Machlup, *The Production and Distribution of Knowledge in the United States* (Princeton, N.J.: Princeton University Press, 1962).

[5] Leonard A. Lecht, *Goals, Priorities and Dollars: The Next Decade* (New York: Free Press, 1966), p. 160.

The importance that Americans place on education is also reflected in private spending. Since 1955, the amount spent has nearly tripled, due mainly to investments in higher education. In 1955, the private sector was investing $1.3 billion in higher education. By 1966, the outlay was about $3.5 billion.

CHANGING METHODS TO MEET NEW DEMANDS

In addition to the millions of youth in compulsory school attendance, millions of adults also attend classes of one sort or another. Thus, acceptance by a most significant segment of the population of the desirability and real need for a continuous, lifelong process of upgrading and expanding

CHART 1—Two-Year Institutions: Enrollments, 1954-1975

Enrollments in two-year institutions have increased steadily from 282,000 in 1954 to 841,400 in 1965, and are expected to reach 1.5 million by 1975. The great majority of students (87.7 percent in 1965) were in public institutions. There were 622 public and private junior colleges in 1965.

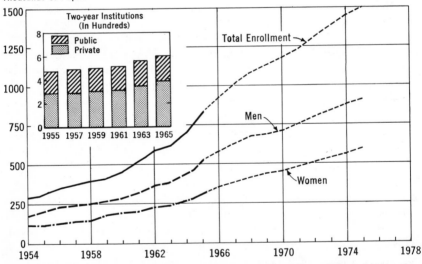

Thousands of Pupils

Source: U.S. Department of Health, Education, and Welfare, Office of Education. *Biennial Survey of Education in the United States, Projections of Educational Statistics to 1975-76*, OE-10030-66; annual *Digest of Educational Statistics*, OE-10024-66. A typical junior college offers the first 2 years of training at the college level and a broad selection of terminal-vocational courses. Academic courses offered by the junior college are transferable for credit to 4-year colleges and universities. Enrollments include full- and part-time resident students taking degree-credit courses. Data are for 50 States and D.C.

knowledge and skills is an educational phenomenon demanding new ways to satisfy the quest for education. The steadily increasing ratio of the learning force to the labor force indicates that educational services are reaching upward, downward, and throughout the whole age-range of our population.

The institutions that are being developed or vastly expanded in number are of many kinds, including junior colleges and vocational and technical schools. During the past decade, junior-college enrollments multiplied two and one-half times—a growth rate nearly twice that of four-year colleges (Chart 1).

Innovations are also being introduced into the classroom, with experiments involving new concepts of learning, course content, and patterns of teaching. As research and development gain a foothold in the traditional conservative school, old notions of how education should be conducted are questioned and revamped. The pressure of the number of students alone forces change: the introduction of more technology into the classroom; innovations in instruction methods and curricula content at all levels, including graduate schools;[6] more research into learning and motivation; and curriculum research—research into what it taught and how it is taught.

EDUCATIONAL GOALS AND ISSUES

With the outlines of change in economic and social institutions everywhere apparent, the rapid pace of events in the world today demands a closer look at the changes occurring, particularly a critical analysis and evaluation of what is happening in education and the direction it is taking. Difficult questions, at present left unexamined or inadequately explored, must be answered. Is the educational system fulfilling the responsibilities that the American people have assigned to it? Is it meeting the requirements of today, and will it meet them in the future? What is the nature of the learning process? How, precisely, does one human being teach another? What functions can a machine perform better than a human instructor? How could schools and classrooms be organized to make it possible for every student to learn at his own pace? These are questions that educators —in co-operation with a host of other specialists—must ask, and for which they must produce reliable answers. Accurate, meaningful educational indicators are a prerequisite for valid answers and for planning effective remedies when needed.

---

[6] For changes in curriculum in recent years, see James B. Conant, *The Comprehensive High School* (New York: McGraw-Hill, 1967).

QUALITATIVE ISSUES

Whatever indicators are developed must take account of the variety of educational goals and the changes in definitions and emphases of these goals. One kind of indicator, for example, would be used to measure the quality of education: Are students' abilities being developed more fully

TABLE 6—Gross National Product Related to Total Expenditures[a] for Education: United States, 1929–1930 to 1965–1966

			Expenditures for Education	
Cal-endar Year	Gross National Product (in Millions)	School Year	Total (in Thousands)	As a Percent of Gross National Product
1	2	3	4	5
1929	$103,095	1929–30	$3,233,601	3.1
1931	75,820	1931–32	2,966,464	3.9
1933	55,601	1933–34	2,294,896	4.1
1935	72,247	1935–36	2,649,914	3.7
1937	90,446	1937–38	3,014,074	3.3
1939	90,494	1939–40	3,199,593	3.5
1941	124,540	1941–42	3,203,548	2.6
1943	191,592	1943–44	3,522,007	1.8
1945	212,010	1945–46	4,167,597	2.0
1947	231,323	1947–48	6,574,379	2.8
1949	256,484	1949–50	8,795,635	3.4
1951	328,404	1951–52	11,312,446	3.4
1953	364,593	1953–54	13,949,876	3.8
1955	397,960	1955–56	16,811,651	4.2
1957	441,134	1957–58	21,119,565	4.8
1959	483,650	1959–60	24,722,464	5.1
1961	520,109	1961–62	29,366,305	5.6
1963	589,238	1963–64	[b]36,600,000	6.2
1965	676,300	1965–66	[b]45,100,000	6.7

[a] Includes expenditures of public and non-public schools at all levels of education (elementary, secondary, and higher education).
[b] Estimated.
Note: Beginning with 1959–1960 school year, includes Alaska and Hawaii.
Sources: U.S., Department of Health, Education, and Welfare, Office of Education, "Biennial Survey of Education in the United States;" "Statistics of State School Systems;" "Financial Statistics of Institutions of Higher Education;" and unpublished data. U.S., Department of Commerce, Office of Business Economics, "Survey of Current Business," August 1965 and April 1966.

today than yesterday? Are adequate attention and funds being concentrated on improving the quality of educational services? Are educational programs developing technical competence to meet work-force requirements—a technical competence founded on a good grounding in basic general principles?

QUANTITATIVE ISSUES

A different kind of indicator would be required to measure the quantity of education: Are more people being educated today than yesterday? Are the numbers of young workers who cannot find jobs being reduced as a wider range of vocational education and job-training opportunities are offered?

EDUCATION AND THE
INDIVIDUAL

The importance of education to the individual has been elevated to one of the highest values in our democratic society. A primary goal of education is to offer each individual an opportunity to develop his abilities to the fullest capacity. Education should help him adapt to a rapidly changing world, to think rationally and creatively, to be independent, and to enjoy a rewarding life. Education should provide him with the skills and knowledge he must have to be a productive member of society; it should elevate his economic status as well as enhance his self-confidence, judgment, creativity, and humanity. Education should contribute to his enjoyment of life and widen the range of choices available to him throughout his life.

EDUCATION AND SOCIETY
(PUBLIC POLICY)

The great basic goals of education are to foster individual fulfillment and to nurture the free, rational, and responsible men and women without whom our kind of society cannot endure. Educated citizens are essential to an effective democracy and a healthy economy. They are politically active, responsible citizens, less subject than others to corruption and less easily influenced by demagoguery. The related problems of poverty and racial injustice are closely linked to the restricted educational opportunities of the disadvantaged. Yet, too often, schooling offered to children in depressed areas is ill-suited to their needs, and public educational programs have not coped adequately with the special educational problems of disadvantaged children.

EDUCATION AND ECONOMIC
PRODUCTIVITY

Educated citizens are productive citizens, whose efforts and abilities and increased demands will add to the nation's economic growth. Economist Theodore Schultz, for example, has estimated that:

> As a source of economic growth, the additional schooling of the labor force would appear to account for about once-fifth of the rise in real national income in the United States.[7]

Education is expected to help break the vicious cycle of poverty, which is often perpetuated from generation to generation. Low educational attainment is a product—and in turn a producer—of poverty, unemployment, and discrimination. Investment in education is expected to pay off in still other gains to the economy: in research and development of new products and in economic efficiencies that result when the labor force has high literacy and higher educational attainment.

DEFINING GOALS

In addition to the broader, basic goals of education mentioned above, there are other—more narrowly defined—goals within the educational system that lead to attainment of the broader aims:

1. to provide equality of educational opportunities to all of the nation's citizens, and
2. to improve the quality of education for all.

To achieve goal number one, action is needed, for example, to:

a. increase the quality of education,
b. provide continuous learning opportunities, and
c. improve the efficiency and economy of the delivery of educational services.

To achieve goal number two, the system will have to:

a. revise and improve curricula,
b. improve the quality of teaching,
c. stimulate research and development, and
d. adopt innovations.

---

[7] Theodore W. Schultz, *The Economic Value of Education* (New York: Columbia University Press, 1963), p. 11.

It can be clearly seen that these goals are complementary, each contributing to the other. Both are concerned with the conservation and development of individuals. And both will produce the benefits that result from strengthening the individual through education: not only will the manpower resources of the nation be improved, but, at the same time, the quality of life for the individual will be enhanced.

EDUCATIONAL INDICATORS

Much discussion, debate, and ferment are going on today about the attainment of national goals. Probably never before in history has there been a period when greater attention was focused on education. Surely there never has been a time when so much money has been spent on education. But much of the discussion, debate, and spending proceeds without basic knowledge of what is happening.

When we survey the voluminous, yet unsuitable, data now available for assessing the products of education, we must conclude that practically none of it measures the output of our educational system in terms that really matter (that is, in terms of what students have learned). Amazement at the revelation of the tremendous lack of suitable indicators is almost overshadowed by the incredible fact that the nation has, year after year, been spending billions of state and local tax dollars on an enterprise without knowing how effective the expenditures are, or even if they are being directed to stated goals. Indicators would provide an insight into changes taking place in education and into existing and potential problems. They would also offer a means of evaluating progress toward defined goals.

It is generally acknowledged that effective plans for achieving educational objectives and the execution of those plans depend upon the availability of continuing, regularly collected, comprehensive information pertinent to the status of education. But what are the data that are pertinent? What information will reflect where we are today, and what must we know to measure the changes that will take place in the future?

PRESENT INDICATORS

Although, as already indicated, there is an urgent need for new indicators, a preliminary examination of those that exist is appropriate.

More than one hundred years ago, the United States Office of Education was directed by the Congress, when it established the Office, to collect "such statistics and facts as shall show the condition and progress" of

American education. Thus, the Office has counted the numbers of pupils, teachers, classrooms, equipment, and other relevant items such as the kinds and numbers of degrees awarded.

In co-operation with the Bureau of the Census, the Office of Education has developed some national historical series showing illiteracy rates of the population, percentage of school-age groups enrolled, retention rates of school population, educational attainment of the population by specific age groups, the median years of school completed by the labor force, the correlation of income and years of school completed, sources of educational revenues, and other quantitative data related to formal education.

But the gaps between what is known and what needs to be known are great.

In addition, there is a critical need to develop new data—through either simple counting procedures, longitudinal studies, or more limited case studies.

But perhaps most important is the need for basic research in education. There are still great gaps in knowledge about learning, motivation, and other aspects of human behavior—the foundations upon which an educational system should be built.

EDUCATIONAL OPPORTUNITY: To some extent, available data are indicators of how well the goal of providing equal educational opportunities to all is being met. At least it is known that 25 million more students are enrolled in formal education today than were in school 25 years ago. The data also enable projections of future needs. In addition, they permit some comparisons among states and regions of educational inputs—pupil-teacher ratios, pupils per classroom, average salaries, and expenditures per pupil.

Much of the support for federal assistance to education grew from the realization that local support varies widely and that when education is inadequate in any one section of the country, the entire nation suffers. Comparisons showing state expenditures per student in 1966-1967—ranging from $335 in Mississippi to $912 in New York—sharply point up the vast disparities and resulting inequities in educational input. Recognition that poor states, though often spending relatively more of their personal income per capita on education, are still not able to provide satisfactory education helped to bring about federal legislation designed to eliminate the disparities in the amount of education offered students in different sections of the nation and from different segments of the population.

QUANTITY OF EDUCATION: Statistics now compiled also are indicators of quantitative output of the educational system. There is, for example, an indicator of the increasing level of educational attainment in the United States, which can be correlated with indicators of variations in the financial support given the schools by different states and regions. In 1960, 30 per cent of the adults in Mississippi were high school graduates, compared with 41 per cent in the entire country.

TABLE 7—Educational Finances (State Rankings)

In 1966–67, the estimated annual current expenditure per pupil in average daily attendance ranged from $912 in New York to $335 in Mississippi, and averaged $569 for the Nation. Per capita expenditures for public schools in 1964–65 ranged from $176 in Alaska to $72 in Arkansas, and averaged $115 for the Nation. Per capita expenditures for education ranged from $247 in Alaska to $98 in Tennessee and averaged $149 for the Nation.

Rank	Average annual current expenditure per pupil in average daily attendance 1966–67		Revenue receipts from Federal funds as per cent of total receipts for elementary and secondary schools, 1963–64[1]		Per capita expenditures			
					For public schools, 1964–65		Direct State and local expenditures for education, 1964–65	
	State	Amount	State	Percent	State	Amount	State	Amount
1.	N.Y. . .	$912	Hawaii	12.0	Alaska	$176	Alaska	$247
2.	Alaska	877	Ark. .	11.1	Nev. . . .	170	Colo. .	221
3.	N.J. . . .	740	N.Mex.	10.5	Calif. .	156	Utah .	219
4.	Hawaii	669	S. Dak.	9.7	Colo. .	154	Wyo. .	205
5.	Wyo...	668	Va. . .	9.5	Utah .	153	Oreg. .	204
6.	Mont. .	665	Miss. .	8.2	Oreg. .	146	Calif. .	203
7.	Conn. .	657	Ariz. .	8.2	Wyo. .	146	Nev. . . .	200
8.	Oreg. .	645	Idaho	8.1	Del. . .	144	Del. . . .	199
9.	Ariz. . .	635	Tenn.	8.1	Mont. .	136	N.Mex.	197
10.	Nev. . .	635	Ala. . .	7.6	N.Y. . .	136	Wash.	189
11.	Minn. .	634	S.C. . .	7.6	N.Mex.	135	Ariz. .	185
12.	Del. . . .	626	Nev. .	7.4	Minn. .	134	Mont. .	182
13.	Calif. .	613	Okla.	7.3	Wash .	133	Minn. .	179
14.	Wis. . .	608	N. Dak.	7.3	Ariz. .	130	Mich. .	178
15.	Md. . . .	603	Ga. . .	7.1	Mich. .	129	Ind. . . .	176
16.	Mass. .	599	Fla. . .	7.1	Iowa .	126	Wis. . . .	175
17.	Pa. . . .	597	Ky. . .	6.6	Wis. . .	125	Iowa . .	175
18.	Mich. .	596	Mont.	6.5	Ind. . .	124	N.Dak.	174
19.	R.I. . . .	596	Colo. .	6.4	Kans. .	120	Kans. .	167
20.	Ill.	591	N.C. .	6.1	N.Dak.	120	N.Y. . .	165
21.	N. Mex.	586	Utah	6.0	N.J. . .	120	S.Dak.	161
22.	Wash.	581	Maine	6.0	Tex. . .	120	Hawaii	158

TABLE 7—Educational Finances (State Rankings) (cont'd)

Rank	Average annual current expenditure per pupil in average daily attendance 1966–67		Revenue receipts from Federal funds as per cent of total receipts for elementary and secondary schools, 1963–64[1]		Per capital expenditures			
					For public schools, 1964–65		Direct State and local expenditures for education, 1964–65	
	State	Amount	State	Percent	State	Percent	State	Percent
23.	Ind. ...	580	N.H. .	6.0	Md. ...	118	Vt. ...	157
24.	Vt.	578	Md. ...	6.0	Conn. .	117	Idaho .	147
25.	Colo. ..	570	R.I. ..	5.7	S. Dak.	117	Tex. ...	146
26.	Iowa ..	567	Nebr.	5.6	Idaho .	111	Md. ...	146
27.	La. ...	567	Kans.	5.4	Nebr. .	108	Nebr. .	144
28.	Va. ...	556	Wyo.	5.2	Ill. ...	106	Okla. .	143
29.	Kans. .	552	Wash.	5.0	Pa. ...	105	Conn. .	140
30.	Okla. .	533	W.Va.	4.9	Mass. .	105	Ill. ...	138
31.	N.H. ...	523	La. ..	4.8	Hawaii	104	N.J. ...	136
32.	S. Dak.	521	Mass.	4.8	Ohio .	101	Fla. ...	128
33.	Mo. ...	506	Tex. .	4.6	Va. ...	101	R.I. ...	128
34.	Utah ..	500	Del. ..	4.4	Vt. ...	99	Pa.	126
35.	N. Dak.	485	Mo. ...	4.3	Fla. ..	99	Ohio .	126
36.	Fla. ...	479	Alaska	4.1	Okla. .	98	Va.	126
37.	Ohio ..	468	Iowa	3.6	R.I. ..	97	La. ...	123
38.	Nebr. .	464	Calif.	3.6	Mo. ..	97	Mass. .	122
39.	Tex. ...	449	Vt. ...	3.5	La. ...	92	Mo. ...	121
40.	Ga. ...	430	Ohio .	3.1	Ga. ...	88	N.H. .	119
41.	Maine .	430	Minn.	3.1	N.C. ...	87	N.C. ...	117
42.	Idaho .	418	Wis. .	3.1	N.H. .	87	Ga. ...	114
43.	N.C. ...	411	Ill. ...	2.8	Maine	83	W.Va.	113
44.	W.Va. .	411	Mich.	2.7	W. Va.	82	Ky. ...	110
45.	Tenn. .	404	Ind. ..	2.7	S.C. ..	80	Maine	108
46.	Ky. ...	400	N.J. ...	2.6	Ala. ..	76	Ala. ..	108
47.	Ark. ...	393	Pa. ..	2.6	Ky. ...	76	Miss. .	105
48.	Ala. ...	390	Conn.[2]	2.5	Tenn. .	74	S.C. ..	103
49.	S.C. ...	373	Oreg.	2.5	Miss. .	73	Ark. ...	99
50.	Miss. ..	335	N.J. ...	2.1	Ark. ..	72	Tenn. .	98
	D.C. ...	693	D.C. .	1.9	D.C. ...	101	D.C. ...	103
	U.S.[3] ..	569	U.S.[3] .	4.2	U.S.[3] .	115	U.S.[3] .	149

Source: U.S. Department of Health, Education, and Welfare, Office of Education; Advanced data, *Fall 1966, Statistics of Public Schools,* (OE-20007-66); *Statistical Summary of State School Systems, 1963-64,* (OE-20006-64), *U.S. Department of Commerce,* Bureau of the Census, *Governmental Finances in 1964-65.* Series G-GF 65-No. 6, *Current Population Reports, Population Estmiates,* Series P-25-No. 301. [1]Includes value of commodities distributed under the school lunch and milk programs. [2]Partially estimated by Office of Education. [3]Includes 50 States and District of Columbia.

TABLE 8—Level of School Completed by Persons 25 Years Old and
Over and 25 to 29 Years Old, by Color; United States, 1940 to 1965

Date, Age, and Color	Per Cent by Level of School Completed			
	Less than 5 years of elementary school	4 years of high school or more	4 or more years of college	Median School Years Completed
1	2	3	4	5
White and Nonwhite 25 years and over:				
March 1965	6.8	49.0	9.4	11.8
March 1964	7.1	48.0	9.1	11.7
March 1962	7.8	46.3	8.9	11.4
March 1959	8.0	42.9	7.9	11.0
March 1957	9.0	40.8	7.5	10.6
October 1952	9.1	38.4	6.9	10.1
April 1950	10.8	33.4	6.0	9.3
April 1947	10.4	32.6	5.4	9.0
April 1940	13.5	24.1	4.6	8.4
25 to 29 years:				
March 1965	2.0	70.3	12.4	12.4
March 1964	2.1	69.2	12.8	12.4
March 1962	2.4	65.9	13.1	12.4
March 1959	3.0	63.3	11.0	12.3
October 1952	3.8	56.7	10.0	12.2
April 1950	4.6	51.7	7.7	12.1
April 1940	5.9	37.8	5.8	10.4
Nonwhite 25 years and over:				
March 1965	18.4	28.6	5.5	9.0
March 1964	18.6	27.5	4.7	8.9
March 1962	22.1	24.8	4.0	8.6
March 1959	23.5	20.0	3.2	8.1
March 1957	26.9	17.8	2.8	7.7
October 1952	30.3	14.7	2.4	7.1
April 1950	31.5	13.2	2.2	6.8
April 1947	31.4	13.2	2.4	6.9
April 1940	41.1	7.5	1.3	5.8
25 to 29 years:				
March 1965	4.8	52.2	8.3	12.1
March 1964	5.3	48.0	7.0	11.8

TABLE 8—Level of School Completed by Persons 25 Years Old and
Over and 25 to 29 Years Old, by Color; United States, 1940 to 1965 (cont'd)

Date, Age, and Color	Per Cent by Level of School Completed			Median School Years Completed
	Less than 5 years of elementary school	4 years of high school or more	4 or more years of college	
1	2	3	4	5
March 1962	6.1	41.6	4.2	11.2
March 1959	7.8	39.1	4.6	10.9
October 1952	15.2	27.8	4.6	9.3
April 1950	15.6	22.9	2.8	8.7
April 1940	26.7	12.1	1.6	7.1

Note: Beginning in 1962, includes Alaska and Hawaii. Statistics for 1962 and subsequent years are not strictly comparable with earlier data.
Source: U.S., Department of Commerce, Bureau of the Census, "Current Population Reports," Series P-20, Nos. 99, 121, and 138; Series P-19, No. 4; and unpublished data.

Also, some already existing indicators show educational output by race; for example, the average years of schooling for the nonwhite population over age 25 in 1965 was 9.0 years, compared with 11.8 years for total population over age 25. Among those aged 25-29, nationwide, some 12.4 per cent of total population had completed four or more years of college, but only 8.3 per cent of nonwhites had done so (Table 8).

QUALITY OF EDUCATION: Although there is a considerable amount of quantitative data, little of it reveals information about the quality of the educational system or its products. Practically none of the data measures output of the system in terms of what students have learned, or inputs in terms of how good the teaching is that is provided for students.

Only very recently have efforts been started to develop and analyze statistics that may furnish some clues as to geographical or racial variations in the quality of the educational output.

The adverse effects of unequal facilities, staff, and services, reinforced by handicaps brought to the school by many minority-group children, are reflected in these recent studies of educational attainment. The effects are clearly apparent in the mental scores of the Armed Forces Qualification Test

(AFQT)—about as close a national indicator of educational strengths and weaknesses as now exists—and in a more limited survey conducted by the Office of Education on equality of educational opportunity.[8]
The AFQT shows that:

> Southern Negroes are behind Southern whites, who are behind whites in all other regions of the country; Southern Negroes are behind Negroes in other parts of the country;
>
> In every State, test performance is significantly higher for whites than for the Negroes;
>
> Negroes who fail the AFQT have, on the average, one more year of schooling than whites who fail the text.[9]

The Office of Education survey showed that Negro students at each grade level tested (grades 1, 3, 6, 9, and 12) scored distinctly lower than white students in the same grades; by the twelfth-grade level, the differences were still greater. Negroes were 10.7 points below white children in nonverbal scores; for example, at the first-grade level, on tests with an average of 50 and a standard deviation of 10, by the twelfth grade, the gap had grown to 11.1 points.[10]

The Office of Education study revealed further that Negroes generally are offered fewer of the facilities assumed to contribute to academic achievement, such as laboratories, libraries, textbooks, and audio-visual aids.[11] However, the results of the survey also implied that differences in family background account for more variations in achievements of white and Negro children than do differences in school facilities.[12] The study which contains much valuable information, emphasizes the need for further inquiry into the problem of equal educational opportunities. To gain insight into the problems raised by the report requires the development of a number of indicators dealing with unequal opportunities for education.

TESTS—USEFULNESS AND LIMITATIONS: Over the years, a considerable amount of testing activity has been undertaken in individual schools in attempts to measure Intelligence Quotient (IQ), attainment

---

[8] Section 402, Civil Rights Act, 1964 (P.L. 88–352), directed the Commissioner of Education to carry out a survey on equality of educational opportunity. The survey was conducted, under contract, for the Commissioner by James S. Coleman, Johns Hopkins University.

[9] Richard de Neufville and Caryl Conner, "How Good Are Our Schools?", *American Education* (October 1966), p. 4.

[10] *ibid.,* p. 6.

[11] *ibid.,* p. 7.

[12] James Coleman, "Equal Schools or Equal Students," *The Public Interest* (July 1966), p. 73.

levels in subject matter, and other student characteristics. However, the test results have not been compiled in any meaningful way or in a way that permits analyses on broad comparative bases. Furthermore, the primary purpose of IQ testing has been to locate an individual child on a scale—not to determine the range of knowledge of a group of children at a given grade or age level.

In addition, there is considerable controversy over the use of IQ tests. Some educators contend that the tests have been misused by teachers who use the test results to limit the opportunities available to a child by placing him in a rigid mold that determines the way he is treated in the school system and hampers him from accomplishing much that he, perhaps, has the ability to do.

Others question exactly what it is that IQ or attainment tests measure. What, for example, is meant by "intelligence"? Would not a test that measures creativity be just as useful? Certainly, today's IQ tests take little account of creativity. But this line of inquiry leads to still a further problem: how to measure creativity.

NEEDED INDICATORS

TO EXTEND EDUCATIONAL OPPORTUNITIES: In spite of the existing multitude of quantitative statistics, additional quantitative as well as qualitative data are needed to measure progress in extending equal educational opportunities. The present series fail to distinguish between rural and urban schools or to show variations among the schools within a community. There is no accurate picture on inputs—in terms of money, students, or resources—for rural schools, or what the output is in levels of student attainment. Similarly, there are no accurate statistics on the input-output of urban slum schools, compared with middle-class-suburban schools. On a national basis, it is not known how man children fail at each grade level and repeat the grade, or how many skip a grade, let alone why.

Data are almost completely lacking on the very important matter of the distribution of dropouts by geographic areas, socioeconomic levels, and degrees of urbanization of their communities. The proportion of dropouts who would have completed high school with adequate financial support or other incentives is not known; nor is there information, on any systematic basis, about what happens to dropouts, although it is clear that many fall into the ranks of the unemployed. An equal lack of information exists about college dropouts (Chart 2).

Accurate national data on school segregation—actual or *de facto*—are not yet available. And a whole new area for research could be devoted to the effects of segregation on the child.

CHART 2—Estimated Retention Rates, Fifth Grade Through College
Graduation: United States, 1957 to 1969.

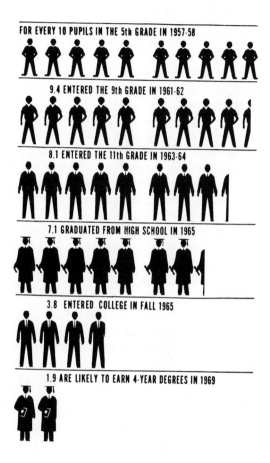

FOR EVERY 10 PUPILS IN THE 5th GRADE IN 1957-58

9.4 ENTERED THE 9th GRADE IN 1961-62

8.1 ENTERED THE 11th GRADE IN 1963-64

7.1 GRADUATED FROM HIGH SCHOOL IN 1965

3.8 ENTERED COLLEGE IN FALL 1965

1.9 ARE LIKELY TO EARN 4-YEAR DEGREES IN 1969

Indicators related to staffing are also needed. No information has been
compiled to show the numbers of teachers and professors who leave the
profession each year, why they leave, or what subsequently happens to
them. How many go to better-paying jobs? Are those who do so among
the most experienced teachers? Is there a pattern of returning to teaching,
say, for women who quit to raise a family? What is the flow of personnel
back and forth among college teaching and business organizations and
government agencies? What are the migration patterns of teachers within
school districts and from lower-paying districts to higher-paying districts?
Although great emphasis is placed on the need for continuing educa-

tion, very little accurate data exists about learning activities outside the usual classroom setting.

Although many people say that learning activities are expanding, almost no data have been collected to back up such a conclusion. And only very rough estimates have been made about the back-and-forth interchange or duplication that exists between the labor force and the learning force. Likewise, little is known about the extent to which employers conduct in-service training or management-improvement courses or provide other opportunities for employees to upgrade their skills and knowledges.

Nor are there any valid measures of the extent of educational activities of social clubs, labor unions, or fraternal organizations. No count has been made of those who engage in self-education with the help of libraries, museums, and cultural facilities, or of those who take advantage of the vast new opportunities through educational television programs.

Without basic quantitative data, it is almost impossible to analyze some of the problems involved in education today. And, clearly, in this age of computers with almost limitless capabilities, it is feasible to begin collecting the data—although that beginning could be on a somewhat limited basis. Perhaps a case-study approach in certain areas would eventually develop into statistical series that could serve as indicators, and any other promising possibilities for developing meaningful indicators should be explored.

TO IMPROVE THE QUALITY OF EDUCATION: When measurement of progress toward the second goal—to improve the quality of education—is attempted, it becomes clear that few significant indicators exist. First, few measures show the output of the system in terms of what students learn, even at the point where formal instruction is given.

A nationwide assessment of educational progress would be of great value not only for allocating public funds to the educational enterprise, but also to the educational community, as well as to educational policy-makers at all levels.

One project concerned with devising testing instruments to assess learning in several subjects is being developed under the leadership of Ralph W. Tyler, Director for the Center for Advanced Study in the Social Sciences. This study, supported by the Carnegie Corporation and the Ford Foundation, represents the first attempt to get nationwide indices of educational output. It is expected to provide greatly needed insights into the strengths and weaknesses of the present educational system.

The problems involved in trying to measure the quality of teaching are as complex as those concerned with measuring student ability. Today there are few, if indeed any, indicators available. Of course, there never has been a nationwide assessment of teaching, and it is doubtful that there ever will be. Although educational statistics reveal that the proportion of public school teachers with substandard certification is higher today than it has been during the last three years, this does not necessarily indicate that the *quality* of teaching has deteriorated. In fact, it is possible that the infusion of "new blood"—Peace Corps veterans, retired persons, and other normally nonteaching, professional workers who were recruited last year to help ease the teacher shortage—could have improved the quality of teaching. It is by no means certain that present accreditation qualifications are necessary for high-quality teaching. Teacher-licensing by state governments affects the entry of persons into the profession. The certification process, clearly, should be looked into, and changes and revisions made, where necessary.

The need for basic research into what constitutes high-quality teaching is urgent. What are the characteristics of a good teacher? How are such characteristics developed? What improvements could be made in recruiting and training teachers? Can measures be developed to show the relative value of in-service training? What would be the effects of new ways to encourage in-training and upgrading of teachers' skills? Can old standards and concepts of professional training be discarded? Could people without teacher training be used effectively in new methods of teaching? Would the injection of a large number of teacher aides or assistants improve the quality of teaching by allowing the instructor to concentrate on important subject matter and individual students?

The development of yardsticks to evaluate the quality of teaching would be important not only for a social inventory—but also as the key to put teaching back into the center of education, particularly higher education. Rewards in terms of salaries, for example, could be more accurately related to measures of the quality of the teaching. Very little is known about the effect of salary levels on high-quality teaching or whether present salary levels attract and retain highly qualified teachers. Likewise, it is not known whether the prestige attached to certain teaching positions is a measurable factor in high-quality teaching.

TO IMPROVE THE ORGANIZATION AND DIRECTION OF THE SYSTEM: Similarly, very few attempts have been made to assess the efficiency and economy of the operation of the formal educational system. The long-term trend toward consolidation of school districts may be cited as an indicator of improved efficiency. Ten years ago there were 55,000 local school districts; today, only 23,500—a reduction of nearly 60 per cent. Last year alone, more than 3,500 school districts were eliminated (Chart 3).

Nevertheless, the impression is widely held that the educational system is slow to adopt new ideas and techniques. How can this impediment to change be overcome?

CHART 3—United States School Districts, 1945-1966

Region	School districts Number	School districts Percentage distribution	Average enrollment per district
United States	26,983	100.0	1,562
North Atlantic	4,006	14.8	2,463
Great Lakes and Plains	14,744	54.6	804
Southeast	1,821	6.8	5,336
West and Southwest	6,412	23.8	1,669

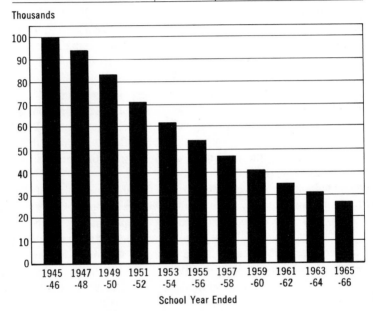

Thousands

School Year Ended

Source: Department of Health, Education, and Welfare, Office of Education, OE-20007-65, Fall 1965 Statistics of Public Schools; and OE-10021-65; Digest of Educational Statistics, 1965 Edition.

TO ASSURE APPROPRIATE EMPHASIS AND FUTURE ORIENTATION OF CONTENT OF THE EDUCATIONAL SYSTEM: Traditionally, the educational system has been both conservative and innovative, transmitting the wisdom of the past and attempting to equip man to cope creatively with an unknown future. Too often, however, emphasis has been on acquiring knowledge of the past. Frequently, there has been neglect for building into the individual a respect for learning in the present, a hope for the future, and a sense of purpose and direction in sharing the problems, challenges, rewards, and responsibilities of society.

In deferring to tradition and continuity, there has—perhaps naturally —too often been resistance to imaginative departures from conventional methods of education. New concepts of what should be taught, as well as *how* and *when* it should be taught have failed to gain wide acceptance.

Clearly, more attention must be given to building a future-oriented educational system. The importance of doing so becomes even more evident if the extension of man's knowledge during this century is contemplated. While it was reasonable, in the eighteenth century, to expect the well-educated man both to have absorbed most of the knowledge from the past and also to keep abreast of new trends, such expectations are not realistic in the twentieth century. In the wake of the information explosion produced by advances in this era, the knowledge problem has become one of collecting, storing, transmitting, and retrieving the multitude of complex facts being produced almost daily.

Since today's youth needs broadly based knowledge and skills to equip him for life in a world vastly more complex than any visionary imagined a generation ago, the educational system is challenged to change methods that, although successful in the past, are no longer enough. What was accepted and fitting in another era may be inadequate for today. Nevertheless, change must be carefully accepted and evaluated. It is necessary to assess the value for the future of present plans for the organization and content of the educational system. Most planning has been confined narrowly to the outlines of on-going institutions, and has not moved into the new dimension of what is possible for the present and necessary for the future —a new conception of where, and how, and when, and to whom educational services will be provided.

TO ASSURE APPLICATION OF EXPERIMENTATION AND INNO-VATION RESULTS TO THE SCHOOL SYSTEM: As the results of research and development efforts become available to help to reorganize the schools and what is taught in them, hard questions must be asked about alternative and better uses of technology in bringing about the comprehensive changes needed in education today. Recent federal legislative support for research and innovation in education reflects growing national concern for improving curricula, methods of teaching, individualized instruction, and experimentation in new patterns for the delivery of services.

It is a truism that the way to excellence in education is through research, which leads to innovation, and then into generally applied practice. But the United States has lagged in applying this principle to education. While financial support for educational research and development has increased in the past few years as a result of federal legislation, the amount is still small when compared with spending by other basic industries. Less than one-half of one per cent of the nation's total outlay for education is spent on research and development, compared with 10 per cent of total outlay in other major industries—nearly twenty times as much is spent on health research and sixty times as much, on defense research.

Not only are the amount and quality of research in education low, but there is relatively little feedback—even from good research—to the local school system. Unpublicized innovations—however successful in experimental application—are far too often not adopted simply because they are unknown. Thus, the results of research in education are too long delayed in application, or lost. It has been estimated that, over-all, there is a thirty-year lag between development of an innovation in education and its widespread adoption. It is fifteen years before 3 per cent of the school districts have made the change. The twenty experimental regional educational laboratories established under federal legislation in 1965 are designed to close this gap by speeding up dissemination of research findings and making research results operative.

It would be fallacious, of course, to assume that all research findings and resulting innovations will be productive. More intensive evaluations are needed of the relative costs and benefits of much high-priced technology, teaching machines, use of television, new teaching methods, and changes in organizational structure before they are widely instituted. Some evaluations may require long-term study, and the results cannot be immediately applied.

LACK OF FEASIBLE INDICATORS—
IMPLICATIONS FOR EDUCATIONAL
RESEARCH

The more readily apparent areas inviting inquiry already noted leave largely unphrased an almost infinite number of questions about education. And as answers for some questions are found, they stimulate still further inquiry. Many separate efforts will be necessary to develop the wide-ranging variety of indicators needed for measuring progress toward the diverse goals in education.

BEHAVIORAL INDICATORS: First, and of great importance, fundamental research into human behavior is needed. Should children with the highest learning abilities be grouped in classes with children of lowest learning abilities? Should children be grouped according to their parents' earning abilities or some other home factors? What are the effects of different groupings on individual children? What are the effects of racial discrimination on learning? What are the reactions of teachers to desegregation policies?

. Can potential dropouts be identified at any early age? What are the characteristics of school dropouts? Answers could point the way for action to reduce the dropout rate. Present data show that although the percentage of students entering college has increased tremendously, the college dropout rate has remained about the same over the past twenty years. Why has the system failed to retain a progressively larger number of students? Outside of a great deal of discussion, relatively little has been done to find valid answers.

LEARNING AND EDUCATION: There is also urgent need for research into the learning process itself. Do we know what really constitutes "intelligence?" How people learn? The factors that motivate them? How knowledge or "learned experience" is retained? What test scores indicate? How to relate early test scores to achievements in later life? Can valid indicators of learning rates be developed? What are the optimum situations for learning by children?

It may be that computers will help to uncover many secrets of learning, may, in fact, offer more promise of learning about learning than any other approach. Studies by Patrick Suppes and Richard C. Atkinson, of the Institute for Mathematical Studies in the Social Sciences at Stanford University, may provide some further answers. They point out that computers keep a minute record of a child's progress so that the point at which learning may falter or stop can be immediately determined.[13]

John Gardner also pointed out that self-teaching machines seem certain to have an impressive impact on the teaching process: "The self-teaching device can individualize instruction in ways that are not now possible— and the student is always an active participant."[14]

Other recent studies have been concerned with the importance of early education.[15] According to Benjamin Bloom, half the growth in intelligence takes place between birth and age 4; a 30 per cent increase, from age 4 to age 8; and only about a 20 per cent gain is made between age 8 and age 17. Such findings suggest that our entire philosophy of education should be

[13] Patrick Suppes, "The Uses of Computers in Education," *Scientific American* (September 1966) p. 9.

[14] John W. Gardner, "National Goals in Education," *Goals for Americans* (New York: American Assembly, Columbia University, 1960), p. 90.

[15] Benjamin Bloom, *Stability and Change in Human Characteristics* (New York: John Wiley, 1964).

re-examined and our present expenditure pattern for education should be reassessed.

Additional experience with Headstart projects, which emphasize the importance of early education and the value of parent involvement, may substantiate some of the research conclusions. Some significant conclusions have already been drawn from Headstart results— the importance of teacher aides and assistants for individual attention to children and the value of follow-through programs in the early school years. Potential effects of the innovative program are far-reaching. Indicators could be developed quite simply to measure changes attributable to Headstart. Longitudinal studies of enrollees in the program could show what happens to them in elementary school, in high school, and beyond. The extent to which local school districts adopt Headstart techniques—parent involvement, use of teacher aides, regular classes for three- and four-year-olds—might also be measured.

EDUCATION AND HUMAN BEHAVIOR: Other interesting questions could be explored by researchers in the educational field. For example: How does the level of a person's education relate to his personal adjustment, happiness, or fulfillment? Are there correlations between various levels of educational attainment and rates of different types of mental illness?

The answers to some questions of this type would depend upon information which could be obtained only from longitudinal studies. And few such studies have been attempted so far, primarily because the price-tag on them is high. However, unless data cover a significant period to permit assessment of results and causative factors, educational policy decisions will be made on the basis of shaky conclusions reached in the light of only fragmented knowledge.

CORRELATION BETWEEN EDUCATIONAL LEVEL AND POLITICAL PARTICIPATION: Another area for inquiry concerns the effects of education on political behavior. Political scientists could examine whether a correlation exists between levels of education and political participation rates. Further study of voting behavior, related to educational level, might produce indicators of how well the educational system is producing politically responsible citizens. Case studies of political leaders could give further insights into the attributes that are associated with leadership ability, and how these characteristics are related to various educational factors.

ECONOMIC INDICATORS: Recently expressed interest by economists in human-resources investment opens up an entirely new area of research. Theodore Schultz, for example, when he became President of the American Economic Association, chose this as the subject of his address.[16] Original

---

[16] Theodore W. Schultz, "Investment in Human Capital," *American Economic Review*, 51: 1–17 (March 1961).

work could develop indicators of progress toward educational goals, stated in terms of the relationships between education and economics.

Further study of the relationship of education to earnings levels would also be helpful. What is the relationship of his educational level to an individual's lifetime earnings? Where does the greatest payback come, in terms of educational input at different levels? Is it at the preschool, elementary school, high school, or graduate school level? (See Table 9.)

An interesting study was made of postcollege careers of June 1958 college graduates—their further studies, work activities, and continuity between studies and work.[17] Longitudinal studies correlating education, experience, and earning levels of diverse occupational groups could furnish valuable insights into whether people use skills they acquire in college, and into a number of other questions.

TABLE 9—Estimated Lifetime Income for Males, by Years of School Completed: United States, 1949, 1956, and 1961

Years of School Completed	1949	1956	1961
1	2	3	4
Income, age 18 to death			
Elementary:			
Total	$113,330	$154,593	$176,008
Less than 8 years	98,222	132,736	151,348
8 years	132,683	180,857	204,530
High school:			
1 to 3 years	152,068	205,277	234,960
4 years	185,279	253,631	272,629
College:			
1 to 3 years	209,282	291,581	333,581
4 years or more	296,377	405,698	452,518
Income, age 25 to 64			
Elementary:			
Total	$91,932	$127,047	$145,519
Less than 8 years	79,654	108,310	124,930
8 years	106,889	148,033	168,810
High school:			
1 to 3 years	121,943	169,501	193,082
4 years	148,649	208,322	224,417
College:			
1 to 3 years	173,166	243,611	273,049
4 years or more	241,427	340,131	360,604

Source: U.S. Department of Commerce, Bureau of the Census, *Statistical Abstract of the United States,* and unpublished data.

---

[17] Bureau of Social Science Research, *Two Years after the College Degree* (Washington, D.C.: U.S. Government Printing Office, for the National Science Foundation, 1963).

Further studies of the payback to employers who upgrade their employees through in-service training and management-improvement courses would reveal information about optimum investment return from training expenditures. Studies to ascertain short-term and long-term manpower needs would provide meaningful guides to education-expenditures allocations. Indicators of trends in occupational requirements could be matched with indicators of educational output. Are schools training people today for the jobs that are now available and for jobs that may be available in the next century? Most likely, the three-year-old child of today will be living in the year 2020. Will his educational experience prepare him for that world?

Education is a long, lead-time operation. A college graduate has normally spent sixteen years in school. Since curricula planning and development require perhaps four years, educators should be developing school curricula today for those who are going to be entering the work force from high school in 1982 or college in 1986. Failure to plan or poor planning for the future by this generation will penalize the next generation.

Provision in the short run of an appropriate mix of skills in the labor force requires not only projection of future manpower requirements but also knowledge of the present mix of skills and how the mix is changing through death or retirement. The schools must fill the gap between the pool of existing manpower, what will exist in the future, and what will be required. To do this, the school system needs information for projecting future requirements to fill demands for trained manpower. And there is little information about the composition by age levels of various groups of skilled and professional workers—for example, physicians, engineers, and teachers. A study by Frederick Harbison and Charles Myers[18] of high-level manpower available and potentially available in individual countries is an example of the inquiries that are needed.

RELEVANT INDICATORS: POWERFUL
FORCES FOR CHANGE
AND MODERNIZATION IN
THE EDUCATIONAL SYSTEM

Looking again at the multiple and diverse goals set for education confirms the importance of developing more than the traditional yardsticks to

---

[18] Frederick Harbison and Charles Myers, *Education, Manpower, and Economic Growth* (New York: McGraw-Hill, 1964).

measure progress. There can be no confidence that decisions *are* the best possible without more data than are now available. The need to educate greater numbers of the population and to open up educational opportunities for those who have not had them in the past also underscores the need to make high-quality educational services available to the entire population.

New measures of educational activities and achievement must be developed and old measures revised to present a composite picture of the status and direction of the American educational system. The urgency of doing so cannot be overstated. The high purpose of American education places this task in a rank of high priority; its accomplishment must proceed without delay. Developing the needed indicators is the joint responsibility of both public and private interests—government, business, educators, labor unions, and civic and community groups.

As noted earlier, some of the data needed for meaningful indicators already exist, but are scattered and fragmented. There are gaps to be filled, new data to be developed. And, most importantly, the data must be presented in an orderly, comprehensive fashion; they must be analyzed and interpreted in a way that will contribute to effective planning and revision of plans for achieving national goals in education.

9

SCIENCE, TECHNOLOGY, AND CHANGE

JOHN McHALE

Change has become our byword and, seemingly, our only constant. Science and technology, as major agencies of change, have not only created a new reality, but permit the coexistence, and possible choice, of many different realities. Man's decisions regarding his dispositions of time, space, and life style are no longer constrained within locally defined and marginal resources. Questions regarding the human condition need no longer be phrased in terms of what we *can* do—but in terms of what we *choose* to do.

The most abrupt and significant change has been the transition from a plurality of remote and relatively autonomous "national" societies to a complexly interdependent world community. It is only within this historical and spatial context that we may even consider the indicators and goals for any locally "great" society. To attempt less would be to succumb to a parochialism whose least fault is unreality, and whose greater tendency is that of a dangerous complacency.

Science and technology are, by their nature, now globally ubiquitous. Their present development is predicated on access to the accumulated knowledge of all men—with the invention of the zero as contemporaneously important as that of the laser. Science knows no borders, nor is it constrained within any preferred local idiom; its laws and methods are, in varying degrees, universally applicable. The more developed a technological system, the more pronounced its trend towards global use: telephones, airlines, and television satellites are inherently world services—minimally requiring the widest global availability for their most efficient operation. The developed industrial nations are thus, in practice, the least autonomous

—the most dependent on global access to knowledge, materials, and markets to sustain their complex industrial systems, and, of necessity rather than choice, the most susceptible to change.

A major aspect of our current difficulty in gauging the full import of scientific and technological change may be due to our "habitual" perspectives. We tend to think of the past in the most immediate terms, of a few human generations, much as we constrain the technological present within the seasonal and diurnal periodicities of an agriculturally based society.

The increased rate, frequency, and penetration of change into so many areas of life are the critical factors in our own period. There is less time for adaptation, both individually and socially, than before, hence more awareness of disruption and uncertainty as associated with change:

1. *Increased frequency:* because of the new relations, and narrowing intervals, between scientific discovery and technological innovation.

2. *Expanded impact and awareness:* through swift transportation and communication, the agencies of change—ideas, artifacts, techniques, images and attitudes—are diffused more rapidly.

3. *Differential rates:* as we go "down" through various industries, for example, aerospace, defense, communications, and air, to surface transport, to housing, we find increased "lags" in utilization of new discoveries and their ancillary techniques.

CHANGING RELATIONS BETWEEN
SCIENCE AND TECHNOLOGY

At first, the material changes wrought in society by new discoveries in science were relatively slow. They gained rapid momentum only when such discovered principles began to be applied to industrial technologies, less than one hundred years ago. Though the social and intellectual bases of society were grossly affected by new "ideas," the full effects of the scientific revolution are not parallel with those of the Industrial Revolution, but occur late in the nineteenth century. The emergence of the scientist as a "professional" is almost coincident with those specific discoveries which form the springboard of modern science—the extension of experimental and measurable ranges into the invisible subsensorial world of atomic, molecular, and "radiation" phenomena. We are still wrestling, in much of present thinking, with the difficulty of orienting ourselves toward this new knowledge—of a world in which many of our major physical transactions and manipulations are now invisible and untouchable.[1] Man can now "see" into the infrared, ultraviolet, and X-ray frequencies, "hear" in the radio frequencies, and may more delicately "feel" through instrumentation than with his most sensitive skin area.

The favorite benchmark for the development of "modern" technology, the Industrial Revolution, occurs somewhat independently of later scientific breakthroughs. Its lineage is much more that of craft-technology tradition, which had pursued its course through specific technological inventions conceived in terms of immediately practical ends. The introduction of the breast harness and stirrup, the proliferation of windmills as prime energy converters, and even Watt's epochal modification of the Newcomen engine predate discovery of the scientific principles of energy dynamics.

The closer interdependence of science and technology is roughly coincident with the two major phases of urgent weaponry requirement. The first, related to World War I, spurred developments in high-strength alloys; energy conversion; air, surface and undersea transport; and radio communciations.

The next phase, during and after World War II, has been called the Second Industrial Revolution, and marked a new relationship between basic scientific research, technical development, and social usage. The major tools, and change agents, of our present period—electronics, automatic control systems, and computers—emerge from this relation, plus the new "software" tools of operations research—decision theory and systems analysis. Within this latter development, the methodologies of physical science are applied to the organization and planning of the research development itself, that is, *organized innovation*. From the fusion of these "tools" and the more direct application of scientific procedures to human affairs comes automation, and, as some have phrased its latest development, *cybernation*.

THE MONITORING AND EVALUATION
OF CHANGE

The role of our intellectual institutions in monitoring and reporting this growth and change has been somewhat aberrant. The early revolt against

---

[1] "Better than 99% of modern technology occurs in the realm of physical phenomena that are sub or ultra to the range of human visibility. . . . We can see the telephone wires but not the conversations taking place therein. We can see the (varieties of) metal parts of airplanes or rockets, but there is nothing to tell us how relatively strong these metals are in comparison to other metals. . . . None of these varieties can be told from the other by the human senses, not even by metallurgists when unaided by instruments. The differences are invisible. World society has throughout its millions of years on earth made its judgments on visible, tangible, sensorially demonstrable criteria"—R. B. Fuller, *Ideas and Integrities* (Englewood Cliffs, N.J.: Prentice-Hall, 1963).

the machine was characteristically spearheaded by the intellectual, who has remained anxiety-ridden by the inherent evils of industrialization, urbanism, and the "modern" way of life. The nineteenth-century middle class subscribed to a more optimistic view, and the working classes more typically sought to improve their lot by direct action which would secure them a more equitable share of the products of their labor—through unions, cooperatives, and the like. Notwithstanding the currently fashionable rush to "the future," the extent to which such earlier bias may still permeate our views of society is still not generally recognized. The recent, and ongoing, revival of "alienation" is probably more reflective of the dilemma of intellectuals, confronted with changes in social and cultural forms which are unaccountable in terms of past traditions, than of attitudes prevalent in the wider society. The intellectuals' acute awareness of the disruptive nature of accelerated change does not usually accommodate the realization that such sustained rates of change may become a new norm—rather than revert to earlier and more stable forms.

Science as an institution, though concerned with the measurement of change—that is, in itself and in its effects on society—is not directed toward the evaluation of such effects: it may tell us how to achieve goals, but not which goals should be sought. Social science, which originated in such social criticism and goal-evaluation, has only gained acceptance as "science" in due ratio to the degree to which it has conformed to the above image.

> While discussion of social change has become increasingly fashionable for social scientists, to discuss the measurement of social progress is distinctly awkward, particularly for sociologists, for we have been firmly schooled in the conviction that progress is not a scientific concept. That is, the argument goes, scientists may observe and perhaps even predict change, but they have no special qualifications for evaluating change by way of approving or disapproving its direction[2]

The issue of scientific neutrality in regard to how science and technology are employed has been under discussion for some time, as their scope, pervasive influence, and long-range implications for society have increased. Developments within science itself have led to greater dependence by "big science" on large-scale government funding. In turn, the new technologies resulting from these developments have made government, industry, and society in general, more dependent upon science. This interdependence is further compounded by the degree to which science is increasingly turned to by government—both for expert guidance in policy-making and planning and for the associated "legitimatizing" function which science now wields as a major institution. Though the latter may not be viewed as such by scientists, it must be admitted as a component feature of the relationship.

One recent commentator has put this whole question succinctly:

> Somehow the R&D explosion spearheaded by the military has permitted the scientific community to live with something near to a personality split; to be a principal agent of change during the work hours in the laboratory and yet not feel committed to the consequences of such change as it enters our daily life. The state of "pureness" of intentions and "non-involvement" in consequences will no longer be possible in a society fully permeated by science. The scientific community gradually becomes aware of this change and is undergoing the painful experience of what seems to many of them, on the face of it, a betrayal of the very principles that made science possible and made it great.[3]

The notion that scientific and technological hazards may require as elaborate an early warning system as guided missiles has only been born as a result of recent emergencies. In such cases as air and water pollution; pesticides, thalidomide, and other drug controls; and increases in radioactivity levels, attention was focused on such problems by individuals, by small groups of scientists, and by journalists and others, usually acting in the capacity of private citizens. In recent years, this has also become more widely the function of special legislative commissions of congressional and senatorial committees; such functions have always been provided for within the governmental apparatus, for example, in the control of food quality and other standards.

Though we are not specifically and separately concerned with the nature of science or the nature of technology, as such, but more with their combined relationship, that is, as science-technology, as determinants of social change, it may be useful to treat certain aspects of each separately in terms of their indicators.

SCIENCE INDICATORS

The major indicators of scientific activity, which are generally available to us, may be classified into three main groups, in terms of:

[2]Eleanor B. Sheldon and Wilbert E. Moore, *Towards the Measurement of Social Change: Implications for Progress* (New York: Russell Sage Foundation, 1966).

[3] Juergen Schmandt, "On the Emergence of a Second-Generation Science Policy in America," *Science and Policy: A Changing Union,* Paper for the Organisation for European Co-operation and Development (OECD), April 1967.

1. Labor force
   a. numbers and types of "scientists and engineers" by field.
   b. distribution of such personnel in various sectors, for example, industry, government, and education.
   c. numbers of scientists and engineers added annually, for example, types and numbers of degrees and certifications awarded.

2. Output
   a. volume of communications, for example, reports, papers, journals, and the like.
   b. numbers of discoveries and inventions—including basic discoveries, as formally "communicated," and applied inventive discoveries, as patented technical devices.

3. Input (expenditures)
   a. distribution of various funds for education, research, and development by source and allocation.
   b. further breakdowns by regional and social sector, for example, state and type of institution or industry.

This accounts for most types of measures compiled by various official and semiofficial agencies. Major sources in the United States are government bureaus, whose annual reports do give a number of indicators of scientific activity, within the above limits, The *Statistical Abstract of the United States* would be a key example. Of initial interest is the amount of space which that publication allocates to science in comparison with other activities: in the 1967 volume, one section and eighteen pages out of thirty-three other sections, totaling 936 pages.[4]

When one turns to the special reports, such as that of the Killian Committee in 1964[5] and others of the National Science Foundation (NSF) and the National Planning Association, the picture is greatly improved. The internal changing structure of the scientific labor force and other significant measures are clearly presented. But these tend to be in wholly *quantitative* terms, with little indication of the type or quality of work being done, other than by "employment" or professional field category. "Years of Experience" is the closest qualitative measure used. We have little indication of what scientists actually "do" in their work—

---

[4] Compare with agriculture (61 pages), banking (40 pages), and manufacturing (46 pages). In terms of attention or importance, as measured by such allocation, science ranks closely with "Public Lands, Parks, and Recreation" (nineteen pages), "Forests" (fifteen pages), or "Outlying Areas under United States Jurisdiction" (fourteen pages). Other sections, of course, do have indicators indirectly related to scientific activity.

[5] *Towards Better Utilization of Scientific and Engineering Talent,* National Academy of Science, 1964.

whether it be teaching, basic research, applied development, or administration. One may usefully quote here from a commentator who has been closely concerned with many facets of scientific activity:

> The usual statistical measures of scientific output fail to take into account the quality factor. For example, studies of scientific productivity indicate that a tiny minority of scientists produce a disproportionate fraction of the scientific publications, numerically speaking, and furthermore, that there is an extraordinarily high correlation between volume of publication by an individual and the significance of his publications, as measured by such things as citations, attributed reputation, etc. If one examines the internal structure of scientific departments, one finds that a small fraction of the professors produce a disproportionate number of the Ph.D.'s and that many of the scientists who later reach eminence have been apprenticed to a tiny number of researchers. Thus, a disproportionate fraction of the activity seems attributable to the apex of the pyramid, even though the base may be necessary to the whole process through providing a selection pool. Failure to really reflect the elite nature of scientific activity is probably one of the greatest weaknesses of many current statistical measures.[6]

Such analyses as are found in the "science of science" share some of the above faults, although they do tell us more about the substance of science. Space does not, unfortunately, allow us to deal adequately with the recent range of this valuable pioneer work. Selected examples and brief comment only will have to suffice.

The work of D. J. de Solla Price [7] is important here, as it endeavors to "turn the tools of science on science itself . . . to measure and generalize, make hypotheses, and derive conclusions." While providing valuable insights on the internal "arrangements" of science, this work is based on gross productivity-output measures, for example, on the numbers of scientists, publications, and institutions, as indirect indicators of the types and quantity of scientific activity; it is also limited to natural science. Another direction might have been to relate the quantitative measures of numbers of scientists, for example, to the key changes in the conceptual framework of science as a more qualitative measure of scientific activity.

As Price says: "It is the brave exception rather than the rule that key breakthroughs are heralded at birth as important work done by important people." One might extend this to suggest that increased scientific activity, as measured simply by an increase in number of scientists in selected

---

[6] Harvey Brooks, Dean, Division of Engineering and Applied Physics, Harvard University (Letter to the author, March 1967).

[7] D. J. de Solla Price, *Science since Babylon* (New Haven: Yale University Press, 1963).

TABLE 1—Federal Fund Distribution: Selected Years
(Millions of Dollars)[a]

Area	1959	1961	1963	1965	1967
Physical Sciences	895	1,757	2,859	3,370	3,649
Life Sciences	420	635	933	1,183	1,427
Psychological Sciences	24	51	72	103	158
Social Sciences	31	45	80	127	222

[a] National Science Foundation, 1966.

sectors, may have not direct relationship to the qualitative advance of science itself. The "bigger" the scientific labor force and the more funds allocated to science, the more likelihood that the over-all pace of scientific discovery will increase, but, as suggested in the comments of Brooks and Price, it is still a relatively small number of scientists who make the breakthroughs and who produce the significant publications. This is where our indicators are presently lacking. We need to know more about what actually goes on in different sciences. More than mere classification of activities, we need some appraisal of *the quality* of actual scientific contributions, which is not conveyed in single-dimension statistics. This will require many types of assessment from different viewpoints, and will be no easy task. But it is of crucial importance as a guide to determining the allocation of funds to science.

Fritz Machlup,[8] dealing with science within the larger conceptual frame of over-all "knowledge-production" in society does give more indication of the relationship of discovery, invention, and "socially new knowledge" to human affairs. But, again, main indicators tend to be constrained within economic and quantitative measures—numbers of patents, personal distribution, and degrees awarded. As Stevan Dedijer, who has made signal contributions in this area, states:

> So far, only a few of the most developed of the 110-odd independent countries in the world have assembled data for even the roughest of the indices required for making research policy decisions. . . . To be useful to the social engineers this quantitative national-policy decision should be translated into measurable concepts defined in terms of actions, men, means, and time. These indices should be related to indices for economic, educational and other policies.[9]

[8] Fritz Machlup, *The Production and Distribution of Knowledge in the United States* (Princeton, N.J.: Princeton University Press, 1962).

[9] Stevan Dedijer, "Measuring the Growth of Science," *Science* (November 1962). Dedijer has also explored in a number of papers the proposition that a nation's research and "information-processing" capacity now constitute more valid and useful indices to over-all development than GNP and other conventional indicators.

TABLE 2—Department of Defense: Research and Development, Tests
and Evaluation: Annual Expenditures (Millions of Dollars)[a]

FY	Total	Missiles	Aircraft	Ships	Astronautics	Ordn.
1968E	7,200	2,388	1,156	288	1,046	314
1967Er	6,700	2,189	1,099	285	937	321
1966r	6,259	1,801	976	283	930	361
1965	6,236	1,901	1,017	249	921	330
1964	7,021	2,352	939	264	1,284	280
1963	6,376	2,241	544	219	946	208
1962	6,319	2,777	624	191	749	227
1961	6,131	3,025	547	209	518	212

[a] Department of Defense, Department of the Treasury (New York: Samson Science Corporation, 1967).

The fiscal indicators of science and research-and-development support do tell us about the over-all finding of the various areas, as related to national goals (see Tables 1, 2, and 3).

As shown by these tables, the prime interest of the government agencies has been in applied science and technology, particularly in relation to defense, aerospace, and atomic energy—though, of course, the figures obviously include basic research.

As may be expected, the physical sciences predominate.

. . . the great bulk of research is directed towards physical sciences, life sciences and engineering. The same is true of fellowship support . . . 73.8 per cent of all government fellowships were awarded to students in these three fields; only 26.2 per cent went to students in the social sciences, education, and other fields.[10]

Over-all allocation of scientific personnel and the funds which encourage specific research-and-development areas underline this. Roughly two-thirds of the most highly trained scientific and technical workers are in space, defense, and associated fields; less than one-third, for example, are engaged in education.

The most recent 1967 report [11] on social research suggests that the federal expenditures in this area are increasing considerably, but concurs with earlier reports on the "difficulty of getting accurate and reliable statistics on agency expenditures for research in the various social science disciplines and on various social problems."

10 *Toward Better Utilization of Scientific and Engineering Talent: A Program for Action,* National Academy of Sciences, 1964.

11 Harold Orleans (ed.), *The Use of Social Research in Federal Domestic Programs,* Staff Study for the Committee on Government Operations, 90th U.S. Congress, 1st Session, April 1967.

The point is made here simply to emphasize the over-all topic of social indicators, with the social sciences as one of the key areas for the compilation of such indicators.

TABLE 3—Science Agencies: Annual Expenditures
(Millions of Dollars)[a]

FY	NASA	AEC	NIH	FAA	NSF
1968E	5,300	2,330	989	827	455
1967Er	5,600	2,270	930	880	395
1966r	5,933	2,403	739	804	368
1965	5,093	2,625	780	795	309
1964	4,171	2,765	910	751	310
1963	2,552	2,758	724	726	206
1962	1,257	2,806	581	698	183

[a] Department of Defense, Department of the Treasury (New York: Samson Science Corporation, 1967).

OTHER SCIENCE INDICATORS

Several points have already been made on this. The question is more one of additional detail, of quality or kind of output. Those indicators already available may be put to augmented use when related more directly to other social accounting areas.

One area which has been least explored is the role of *instrumentation* [12] in science, though the NSF has already compiled materials on this area. The effects of instrumentation advances might be fruitfully extended toward their relation to:

1. the selection and funding of research areas.

2. increases in precision through instrumentation and other non-quantitative developments of scientific output.

3. the allocation and technological displacement of personnel.

4. education and training as affected by instrumentation.

5. direct social effects, that is, of large-scale facilities—*internally,* on the organization of scientific communities and *externally,* on local, regional, and other communities.

---

[12] "The expenditure level for instrumentation development, acquisition, and use is now averaging between 25 and 30 per cent of the total R&D expenditures. The existing inventory of R&D instruments and equipment, measured in original acquisition costs, may be five to seven times the average annual expenditure for new instrumentation," quoted from "Instrumentation and Management of R&D," *Research Development* (August 1966).

One further indicator example might be the continuing report of specific activities, by their practitioners, *in terms of* possible technological effects and social consequences. This is already practiced by many scientists, individually and through their institutions and commissions, but it should be more systematically organized, as an insightful aspect of social accounting, by specifically training personnel and allocating funds for this purpose.[13]

Such trained information scientists may also act as "interpreters" between highly specialized fields, as well as appraisers of the related trends in over-all scientific developments and qualitative analysts of various field contributions for the provision of science indicators.

TECHNOLOGICAL INDICATORS

Within the above discussion, the relation of science to more specifically technological development has been tacitly implied—but the real relationship is far from being one of direct "linear" dependence. The relationship of "intangible" science to usable technology is difficult to assess, in that technologies emerge from a very great number of discrete scientific discoveries *and* technical advances. Discovery in "pure" science is often spurred, for example, by an advance in technical instrumentation—which may, in turn, represent many developmental increments from other scientific and technical fields.

The transistor provides a typical case history, as a basic unit in the development of the computer, electronics, and space communications field. Originally patented in 1930, when the necessary materials for a working device were not available, it was "discovered" by the Bell Telephone Laboratory in 1947. Further development in the early 1950's was due to military need and the provision of massive government-supported research on the required "pure" materials. In this case, though preceded by a number of related theoretical and technical innovations, materials research served as the basis for the development of the practical device.

In lieu of adequate casually related indicators, which we undoubtedly require, one positive viewpoint may be that such relations between basic research and eventual technical advantage do represent permanent "capital" gain for our society. Their minute accountability in terms of traditional cost-profit-loss accounting is not only difficult, but possibly irrelevant.

---

[13] The American Association for the Advancement of Science's Committees on Science and Society and their work with science editors provide a useful paradigm here.

"In order to judge the returns society gets on its investment in R&D, one has to take the entire package, not the choice pieces it contains.[14] The recent "Project Hindsight" opposes the above view. Reviewing selected weapon systems in reverse order, it suggests that science-technology output was more efficient when directed towards well-defined needs, and that undirected basic research was less so—in weapon development.[15] This project is an offshoot of Defense Department program-budgeting and cost-benefit analyses, which develop, in turn, from earlier operations research and systems analysis. These techniques are also part of the basis of "organized innovation" and are of immense value. The general and recent proliferation of the systems mystique is another matter and opens up basic questions regarding concepts of order and "requisite variety" in natural and artificial systems which tend to be glossed over.[16]

Just as the relation between basic and applied scientific research and technological use is difficult to elicit clearly, internal and external indicators of technology itself are considerably intertwined. Most of our measures of technology are based on their economic efficiency—and this may be the best starting point for a discussion which needs to be discursive in nature. We cannot simply put down the "substantive indicators" because much of our present problem is conceptual. We have, in many cases, abundant indicators which we do not recognize as such because they do not conform to our conceptual models of the interaction of technology and society. Recent emergency-pressured attention to various long-standing social consequences of technology are evidence of such lags in conceptuality.

The economic indicators of technological change resemble those cited in the "Science Indicators" section—productivity, work-force distribution, and expenditures. Behind these, there seems to operate a fixed model of relations between input (work, technical devices, and energies) and output (as goods, capital, and more elusive "services"). This fixity is based more on classical economic notions than on technological practice. As Heilbroner states: "We do not have anything approaching a theory of technological

---

[14] R. S. Stone, *Innovation and Research* (Cambridge, Mass.: Arthur D. Little, 1964).

[15] C. W. Sherwin and R. S. Isenson, *Interim Report on "Project Hindsight,"* October 1966. The authors note that their "technique was selective in identifying contributions of recent (post-World War II) science and technology"—therefore admitting prior dependence on earlier "undirected" basic research as providing the basis for such directed research and development.

[16] A key discussion on this point may be found in Stafford Beer, "Below the Twilight Arch—A Mythology of Systems," in D. P. Eckman (ed.), *Systems: Research and Design* (First Systems Symposium; New York: John Wiley & Sons, 1960).

progress and change, still less a unified technological-economic model."[17]

As this area appears particularly threatening to many of the core values of our society, for example, work productivity and the central nature of economic institutions, we seem rather fearful of approaching the task of remodeling our relevant theories.[18] The recent report on "Technology and the American Economy"[19] typifies this reluctance, leaning heavily, for example, on indices of productivity and economic growth, particularly as evidenced in output per man-hour (measured by volume of final output of goods and services produced in a year, divided by the number of man-hours worked in the year). While we cannot adequately review this key report here, and while we may agree with its caution about "the inadequacy of the basis for any sweeping pronouncements about the speed of scientific and technological progress," there are a number of indicators and technological factors which seemingly elude its grasp.

To elicit briefly the weakness in our current techno-economic model, we do need to digress somewhat. One weak aspect relates to the nature of wealth-goods-use value. Preindustrially, the marginal "survival" indicators of land, labor, and artifacts represented wealth, latterly compressed to "capital," functioning as the exchange vehicle for traditional wealth inputs and outputs in the economy. With industrialized mass production, such traditional indicators became obsolete in terms of wealth-goods produced by the machine. For the first time, man could produce utility objects in huge numbers with a precision and use-life greater than any produced previously —in a fraction of the time and with swiftly decreasing investment of human energy. Availability and use became separated from "value" as traditionally set by earlier measures. When manufacturing technologies went over into the invisible ranges of electrical and other radiation energies, this further separated use from intrinsic "wealth" value. For example, the electric light bulb and the telephone are only contact units for access to other systems and have little or no intrinsic value apart from their direct human-use function. Many such products are now typically expendable after a single- or multiple-use cycle, and the materials from which they are made are increasingly "recycled" in a variety of product configurations.

---

[17] R. L. Heilbroner, "The Impact of Technology: The Historic Debate," *Automation and Technological Change*, ed. J. T. Dunlop (Englewood Cliffs, N.J.: Prentice-Hall, 1962).

[18] "It is indeed a source of concern, when the factors (labor, land, and capital) which are explicitly considered in the model account for only 10 per cent of the increase in output per man-hour, the remainder being attributed to an exogenous force (technological innovation) which is little understood, and about which we are able to offer little explanation"—Benton F. Massell, "Capital Formation and Technological Change in U.S. Manufacturing," *Review of Economics and Statistics* (February 1960).

[19] "Technology and the American Economy," Report of the National Commission on Technology, Automation and Economic Progress," 1966, with Appendices I-VI.

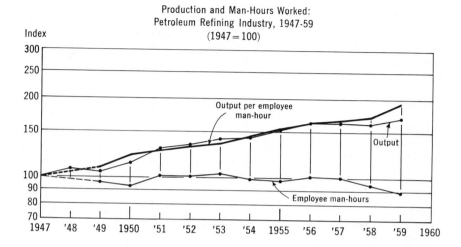

Production and Man-Hours Worked:
Petroleum Refining Industry, 1947-59
(1947 = 100)

Figure   1

Source: U.S. Department of Labor; Manpower Administration; Office of Manpower Policy, Evaluation, and Research; based on data supplied by the Bureau of Labor Statistics.

Note: Man-hours, in advanced technologies' facilities, now bear no direct relation to output. This tends to be masked in over-all measures, as increase of aggregate man-hours *employed* correlates linearly with increased demand and output, as, for example, in the telephone industry. In Crossman's studies of advanced chemical, oil, steel, and electricity plants, man-hours remained nearly constant during varying levels of production. "No short-term relationship between production and employment . . . man-hours worked seemed to depend only on the size of the plant and its complexity and little, if at all, on the current level of production"—E. R. F. W. Crossman, *Automation, Skill, and Manpower Predictions,* Seminar on Manpower Policy and Program, United States Department of Labor, April 1965.

   With the entry of cybernetic control into the industrial process, direct human-labor input in production has even less relevance to economic growth; industrial productivity itself loses its main role as primary societal activity, as society moves farther from marginal survival for most toward possible material abundance for all its members (see Figure 1). In fully automated production, the basic (wealth) resource input is *information*—programming-machine performance. The machines and, increasingly, the material resources forming them and their products are "produced" by other information inputs and recycled and restructured through further information. The only nonexpendable and "value" component in the whole process is man, in his organized and accumulated knowledge and in his

TABLE 4—Increased Industrial Spending for Automation as Percentage of
Over-all Equipment Investment

Business	1963 Actual	1965 Actual	1966 Actual
All business	18%	21%	22%
Manufacturing industries	19	18	20
Other transportation and communications	52	65	67
Electric and gas utilities	7	26	23
Railroads	20	12	12
Mining	14	12	10
Commercial	5	44	66
Airlines[a]	NA	4	3

[a] All airline plants are of recent installation; therefore, less rapid rate of spending is required (New York: Department of Economics, McGraw-Hill, 1966).

Note: In addition, and apart from other non-industry uses, the federal government "uses 2,600 computers, employs 71,000 people in this activity and spends over $2 billion annually to acquire and operate this equipment," Press Release, Office of the President, June 28, 1966.

role as defining the value of the activity by the degree to which it assists or constrains his human functions.

With our obsolete conceptual models of the techno-economic relation, this development has been obscured. Because of "capital" investment in ongoing plants, industry lags in adapting to change, and because of the often inefficient modes in which new equipment and procedures are employed, the measurable growth of automation tends to be obscured—and

TABLE 5—The Knowledge Industry

Area of Operations	Growth since 1930	Current Segment of the Industry (%)
Research and development	fifteenfold	10
Publishing and printing	tenfold	12
Entertainment (broadcasting, movies [including sound movies from telephone laboratories], plays, concerts, phonographs [including stereo], records, and spectator sports)	2.4-fold	6
Information machines (typewriters, copying systems, computers)	fourteenfold	8
Professional services (accounting, architecture, medicine, legal information for businesses)	threefold	9
Communications (as knowledge purveyor)	threefold	7
Education	fourfold	45

Source: W. O. Baker, "Communications Science—Today and Tomorrow," *Science and Society: A Symposium*, Xerox Corporation, 1965.

ENERGY CONVERSION EFFICIENCIES

Steam Locomotive	7%
Automobile engine	10-15%
Reciprocating areo engine	23%
Turbo (at 40,000 feet)	24%
Ram jet (at 1,300 mph)	21%
Gas (general)	30%
Diesel locomotive	35%
Electrical Generating Steam Turbines	40%
Fuel Cells (potential)	80%
Hydro-electric turbines (water wheel)	90%

PERFORMANCE PER ENERGY UNIT INVESTED

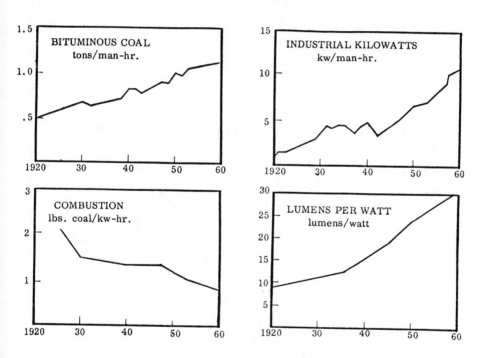

U.S. FIGURES*

* Based on: Chart Series, "Fortune Magazine" (R. B. Fuller)

Figure   2

COMPUTER PERFORMANCE

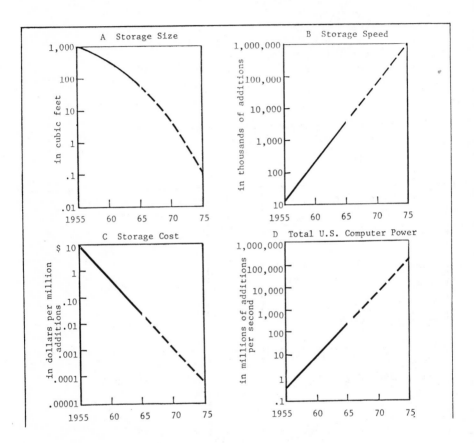

Computer Weight, Volume, Power Costs: In 1953 a computer weighed approximately 5000 lbs., occupied 300-400 cu. ft. and required 40 kw. of power. Today's computer weighs approximately 50 lbs., is a thousand times smaller and uses 265% less power than the 1953 model.

(A) Storage Size: From 1955-65 the storage size of central processing computer unit (cpu) has decreased by a factor of ten. During the next decade, fully integrated circuits may reduce its size by a factor of about 1000.

(B) Storage Speed: From 1955-65 internal speeds have increased by a factor of 200 and by 1975 such speeds are expected to again increase by this amount.

(C) Storage Cost: During the first decade of the computer the cost of performing one million operations decreased from $10.00 to about 5¢. By 1975 it is estimated that this decrease will amount to an additional factor of about 300.

(D) Computer Power: The total installed computer power in the United States during 1955 had a capacity of about one-half million additions per second. By 1965 this capacity increased to 200 million per second and if growth rates are sustained through 1975 the increase in capability will be about 400-fold.

Caption: adapted from W. H. Ware, "Future Computer Technology and Its Impact," D. D. AD 631–941. Office of Technical Services, U. S. Department of Commerce.

Source: P. Armer, "Computer Aspects of Technological Change, Automation and Economic Progress," Rand Corporation, November 1965.

Figure 3

easily deprecated by many traditional analysts. The actual rate of automation growth is one of our key technological indicators. Some growth figures are shown in Table 4.

Other areas in which our present accounting, analysis, and use of technological indicators are inadequate are:

THE KNOWLEDGE INDUSTRY: particularly as explicated in Machlup's work (Table 5). In referring to the above growth, W. O. Baker gives the following analysis:

Accounting now (1965) for about $195 billion of our GNP, and employment of 24 million persons, some third of all non-farm workers . . . (with growth) about a 43% expansion in the last five years . . . rise in real income it 40% from knowledge gain (21% from education of the labor force; 19% from R&D), compared to 14% from capital investment (plant and equipment).

The above growth picture is typically difficult to fit into our present productivity output model, and is one of the indicators of an economy which is now predominately service-oriented rather than production-oriented—leading to a further indicator inadequacy.

THE SERVICE INDUSTRY: Our conceptual model is heavily biased on the visible "agricultural type" of preindustrial accounting, with its

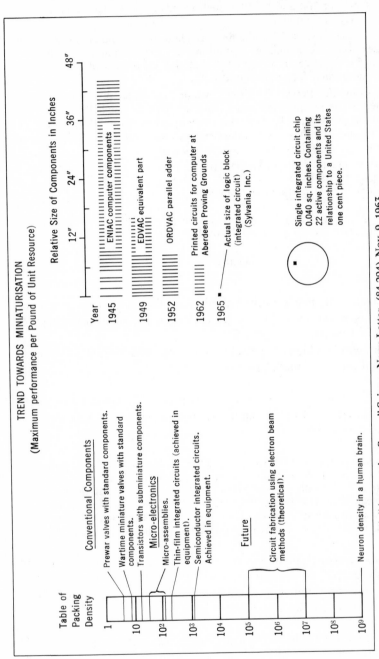

TREND TOWARDS MINIATURISATION
(Maximum performance per Pound of Unit Resource)

Relative Size of Components in Inches

Year		
1945	ENIAC computer components	
1949	EDVAC equivalent part	
1952	ORDVAC parallel adder	
1962	Printed circuits for computer at Aberdeen Proving Grounds	
1965	Actual size of logic block (integrated circuit) (Sylvania, Inc.)	

Single integrated circuit chip 0.040 sq. inches. Containing 22 active components and its relationship to a United States one cent piece.

Table of Packing Density

Conventional Components
— Prewar valves with standard components.
— Wartime miniature valves with standard components.
— Transistors with subminiature components.

Micro-electronics
— Micro-assemblies.
— Thin-film integrated circuits (achieved in equipment).
— Semiconductor integrated circuits. Achieved in equipment.

Future
— Circuit fabrication using electron beam methods (theoretical).

— Neuron density in a human brain.

Sources: (1) "Automation Surge," Science News Letter. (84-294) Nov. 9, 1963.
Sources: (2) "The Exchange," Frank Leary, New York Stock Exchange. Jan. 1965.
Sources: (3) "Miniaturisation ad Infinitum." G. W. A. Dummer. New Scientist (432:500) Feb. 25, 1965.

Figure 4

emphasis on sequentially limited material exchanges of goods. Those major services (such as transportation, communications, and the knowledge industry mentioned above), which pervasively maintain the ongoing society in a less visibly accountable fashion, tend to be less clearly accounted for.

PERFORMANCE PER UNIT OF INVESTED RESOURCE: This area is one which is particularly underrated in traditional techno-economic accounting; yet it is one of the most fundamental and characteristic indicators of technological growth, directly reflected in social use, for example, in the amounts of industrial energies available per capita, in material facilities improving social welfare, and in various services. Typical examples, illustrated in Figures 2, 3, and 4, are: (1) *increases in energy conversion efficiencies;* (2) *performance per unit of materials and energy invested;* and (3) *miniaturization*—the progressive reductions in size, weight, and operating and maintenance energies are most dramatically evident in the microminiaturization of communications and information-processing facilities.

All of the above are trends towards *ephemeralization,* which our customary accounting does not include.

CHANGES IN RESOURCE USE AND ASSOCIATED KEY INDUSTRIES: Cumulative growth rates, as generally shown for our traditional key industries, may not reflect technological growth, but rather sustained and increasing demand. For example, the prime metals industry—steel, copper, aluminum, and the like—may no longer be so central in the techno-economic complex, when we note the increasing growth of the "synthetics" industry (Figure 5). Directly related to the above is the increase in strengths of synthetics and composite materials as against the traditional metals.

Few of the above indicators are accountable within the standard rates of growth—as gauged solely within productivity-output terms. They may be more adequately accounted for within the "input-output" matrix system of W. W. Leontief, which is now coming into wider "indicator" use. One might suggest, however, that, though this model does expand the economic aspect more pragmatically, it may still be too "coarsely" biased, in wholly economic terms, to accommodate certain types of technological factors. Inputs and outputs are as we may conceptually define them. What we need also are models which may enable us to gauge rates of diffusion of change, not only in these sectors more amenable to quantitative measure, but also in others in which scientific and technological change is expressed in *qualitative,* social consequences in society.

MATERIALS REPLACED BY PLASTICS

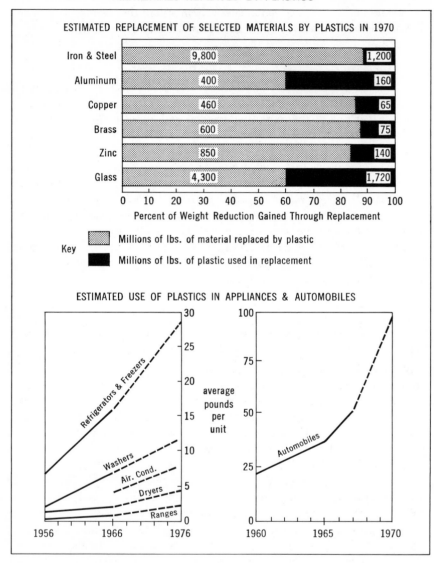

ESTIMATED REPLACEMENT OF SELECTED MATERIALS BY PLASTICS IN 1970

Percent of Weight Reduction Gained Through Replacement

Key
Millions of lbs. of material replaced by plastic
Millions of lbs. of plastic used in replacement

ESTIMATED USE OF PLASTICS IN APPLIANCES & AUTOMOBILES

"Since 1955 the average plastic has dropped in price by about 35%, whereas steel has increased in price by more than 20%. . . . On a weight basis, plastics probably never will be as cheap as steel; but on a volume basis the price difference could all but disappear.

*". . . Tooling costs are lower for plastics than for metals.
Also, complex shapes can be molded in a single operation, and
finishing of parts is virtually eliminated. A metal part often involves the assembly of several components—this means additional
labor cost and a higher price for the finished part."*—"Chemicals
and the Auto Industry," Special Report, *Chemical and Engineering News,* October 22, 1962, p. 17.

Source: (1) *Technology Behind Investment,* (New York: A. D. Little, Inc.) 1965.
(2) "Cost-Price Squeeze Tightens Materials Battle in Major Appliances," *Steel,*
July, 1966.

Figure 5

SOCIAL INDICATORS

MONITORING AND FORECASTING

The presently obvious area for urgently needed indicators of science-
technology development is the rather more negative aspect of monitoring
and forecasting to avoid recent, and ongoing, emergency conditions which
their large-scale use has occasioned. The areas for such indicators go
through many aspects of science-technology and their industrial uses—for
example, from radioactivity levels in relation to uses of atomic energy and
the widespread introduction of new chemical compounds into social uses
about which we have insufficient long-range-effects knowledge (the thalidomide and pesticide controversies), to the more direct effects of environmental deterioration; and from air, water, and land pollution by various
industrial byproducts to the latent consequences of technological change
evidenced in urban congestion.

In many cases, as we have earlier noted, scientists have warned of the
ecological effects of new discoveries, for example, in relation to atomic
energy, and their "accounting" has influenced eventual political policy
decisions.

This is a very large area in which excellent recent work has now been
inaugurated, particularly in various legislative committees of government.[20]
Technological forecasting, which diffuses over into the broader aspect of

---

[20] For example, the United States Congressional Subcommittee on Science,
Research and Development in its 1966 report recommends Technology Assessment
Boards to provide indicators of the undesirable by-products or side-effects of present
and future technologies. From the report of Senator Muskie's Subcommittee on Inter-
governmental Operations, "Technology and Human Environment," has come a
number of more sweeping proposals for comprehensive planning and utilization of
natural resources and technologies.

"futures research," is also being intensely engaged with in many governmental agencies, semigovernmental commissions, and foundation- and university-supported studies.[21]

GENERAL SOCIAL INDICATORS

Within this monitoring and forecasting work, there are many techniques evolved for the delineation of first-, second-, and third-order consequences of technological change—an important characteristic for social indicators. A useful example of this line of attack may be to consider the orders of consequence incident on the development of the internal combustion engine and its use in the automobile. First-order events include road-network-development effects on over-all human mobility, on industry, and the like; second-order might be the more delayed effects on various human institutions—for example, the family, community structure, and the *urbs;* other orders would go on through up until today, including, on the negative side, air pollution, traffic fatalities, and congestion.

The above branching and contingency ordering applied to the broad area of social indicators would eventually take us into every other indicator area in the present range of studies, underlining the pervasive nature of science-technology development as a major change agency.

In general, then, the task of devising social indicators of scientific and technological change involves:

1. Transferring our presently "quantitative" indicators into qualitative contexts and forms—by asking what they mean in terms of some *qualitative* change in human life, in life style, and in the social contents of our major institutions.

2. The use of *surrogate* indicators through which we may interpret given quantitative measures as evidencing a qualitative change in society. For example, measure of life expectancy may be employed, and augmented, to measure improved health, expanded leisure, larger education, and increased social and psychophysical mobility. Or, the number of "safety miles" traveled on various

---

[21] The number of these is now so large that we may mention only a few here: Commission for the Year 2000 (American Academy of Arts and Sciences); Rand Corporation, Systems Development Corporation, and General Electric Tempo groups; and "Program on Technology and Society" (Harvard University). A modest mention may also be pertinent of the World Resources Inventory program, Southern Illinois University, in which the author is engaged. Important work is also being done in this area abroad, the core units being *Futuribles* in Paris, and "Mankind 2000" in London. One of the most comprehensive reports on technological forecasting has recently been completed by Erich Jantsch, of the Directorate for Scientific Affairs of the European OECD, in 1966.

forms of transport may indicate similar accounting of social benefit —as a corrective to the more negative mode of emphasizing travel fatalities.

3. *Access to services:* as income becomes detached from "productivity," in the economic sense discussed above, such access to societal facilities is no longer predicated directly on "earnings" as purchasing power of services but may be more differentially linked to professional-occupational role. For example, we may note the access to communications, information, and transportation services as differentially shared by those in the professions, the academy, government, and business. *Life Services* may make a separate category here, as substituting for those more narrowly defined as "health, education, and welfare" and extended broadly into leisure, recreation, and cultural areas. Life services would connote not only those necessary to the maintenance of life in physical terms but those services which are requisite for its fully participative enjoyment—for over-all well-being—within society.

4. *Choice and constraints:* access to services implies availability and choice. We do not have any compiled indices on the degree and flexibility of *"choice"* or *"alternate life strategies"* open to individuals in our societies. Freedom is not always *"from"* something, but freedom to *choose* various modes and styles of living. A *"choice"* index might well be related to a *"constraints"* index, which would also provide some cross-indication of the limiting societal contingencies—on various forms of social innovation, on discrimination, and the like.

Within the design of such social accounting measures is the problem of basic conceptual model(s) already noted. We need to develop models which will accommodate the various "intangible" and qualitative types of accounting we now require. One possible practical base for the development of more adequate social models may be the human organism itself, described in terms of its life years, its life "spaces," physical and social cycles, and psycho-physical parameters of growth, changing requirements, and needs.[22]

Within the design of social accounting systems are several problems in addition to those of constructing suitable indicators. The first may be for whom such indicators are compiled. Obviously, policy-makers and legislators do require more broadly informative indicators, but we should note that they are presently overwhelmed by factual information already accumulating at an exponential rate. As much of this information is presently undifferentiated, social accounting agencies may also need to encompass the

---

[22] N.B., John Dixon—*Man the Measure: Human Processes and National Policies,* Working Staff Paper, Office of Planning, National Institute of Mental Health (NIMH), 1965—sketches such a model for the disposition of resources in national planning, employing a matrix deriving one ordinate from the human span divided into its various growth cycles, and the other from fiscal inputs of various agencies.

integration and meaningful relation of information within some "human systems" framework such as has already been noted. Not quote so obvious, but perhaps of prior importance, is the task of informing the general public. Present mechanisms for disseminating vital information about the society are far from adequate. A massive amount of such information is freely available, through government publications and other agency services, but its volume and presentation often defeat any attempt to view the full significance of a specific trend or series of policy decisions. The various "news" and communications media do render valuable services in reducing such information to manageable wholes. Within "social accounting," one might consider the development of new modes of communicating social indicators to the society at large, via television, film, the associated use of computer graphics, and the like. This would be facilitated by the establishment of local indicator-information centers linked by computerized systems to various social accounting units.

Of central importance in the development of such "social accounts" is their *comparative presentation in world terms*. We can no longer afford to take an exclusively national view of our major social changes and problems. Though accounting for about one-third of the world's total industrial production, using 32 per cent of minerals and 39 per cent of all oil produced, for only 6 per cent of the world population, we "cannot hope to survive as an island of plenty in a sea of international poverty."[23] To treat the United States, in particular, as a closed system for the purpose of assessing economic and social progress may be not only ineffectual, but grotesquely unreal when present global commitments already strain the sociopolitical and economic fabric.

It is unreal also, even in the general case, when no complexly developed "national" technological system may be treated as a self-sustaining autonomous unit—in technological measures alone, no key industry can now function without access to materials, markets, and facilities directly or indirectly related to the global system.

Social accounting, as constantly reviewed within global indicators, would assist in creating an awareness of the relationship and interdependence of our local and national societies within the context of the larger world community.

The problem of "control" and "funding" introduces other problems regarding the degree of autonomy that such agencies would require for any useful operation. Many social indicators, if widely presented, might conflict with various interest groups and, indeed, with official government policy. The autonomous aspect of social accounts is, therefore, an important one,

---

23 Thomas J. Watson, Jr., Chairman of the Board, IBM Corporation, before the Senate Subcommittee on Manpower and Employment, November 12, 1963.

to ensure the requisite freedom from possible control which may be even logically exercised in terms of the national interest.

This would also bring into discussion *the relation of such accounting to personal privacy.* Present reaction to centralized data-compilations on individual citizens is already of growing concern to many people. "We do not wish to see a composite picture of an individual recorded in a single informational warehouse where the touch of a button would assemble all the governmental information about the person since his birth."[24] This concern is very real and pertinent. Citizen compliance with tax, census, security, travel, and other regulations is mainly one way. Governmental institutions and other agencies have abrogated powers whose checking and control mechanisms are sufficiently unwieldy as to make them immune to scrutiny. Indeed, "need to know" degrees of privacy and protection from interference with private living may be one of the key social indicators which we now require.

The relationship between social indicators and social goals is implied in this extension into the public domain. No set of goals carefully laid out by any chosen group will be of value other than in terms of guidelines for social action by larger group agreement. The prior emphasis on adequate social indicators is necessary for further appraisal of goals. It may then provide the means, through increased awareness and communication of social inadequacies and emergencies, for the attainment of such goals. Social accounting, in itself, could therefore augment and replace many of our presently obsolete modes of expressing and conveying goal orientations and preferred social directions to our legislative assemblies.

> Finding out what we want should become a major object of our attention. . . . There is a vast difference between letting changes occur and choosing the changes we want to bring about by our technological means.[25]

Our current ability to evaluate and determine future goals lags far behind our potential capacity to fulfill any specific goals we may set ourselves. Social accounting, in its widest sense, could provide means for both assessing our directions and framing our goals. The future will be determined not only by what is probable and possible—but by what we, as a society, determine to be necessary, allowable, and ultimately desirable.

---

[24] *The Computer and Invasion of Privacy,* Hearings before the Congressional Subcommittee on Government Operations, July 1966 (Washington, D.C.: U.S. Government Printing Office, 1966), p. 3.

[25] Bertrand de Jouvenel, "Utopia for Practical Purposes," *Daedalus* (Summer 1965).

10

THE MASS MEDIA—
A NEED FOR GREATNESS

ANDRÉ FONTAINE

Taken as a whole and with all their faults, the mass media in the United States, many authorities agree, are the best mankind has seen. Through newspapers, magazines, and broadcasting, more people are given more information than in any other country in history. Through them, each man's recognition that he is involved in all other men's lives, which is one of history's great change-making ideas, has been vastly expanded. As never before and nowhere else, the mass media have done the job given them by James Madison: "A people who mean to be their own governors, must arm themselves with the power knowledge gives." Government regulation of the media is at a minimum—perhaps too much. Financially, they are in robust health. Through them, diverse and unpopular opinions are expressed and spread, less than idealists wish and more than bigots can abide. They have both contributed to and fostered cultural expression and may even have improved the public taste—*may* have.

Most of the numbers that index the health of the mass media are up and climbing. Although big-city mourners regularly lament the death of newspapers, just about as many daily papers are being born in the suburbs as are dying in the cities. The total number has remained nearly constant for twenty years while the number of readers of daily papers has increased faster than the population. Advertising revenue has nearly quadrupled in the same time and now totals nearly $4.5 billion—more than magazines, radio, and television combined. Profits range from 8 to 20 per cent, according to one official of the American Newspaper Publishers Association, as compared with about 6 per cent for the steel industry. A survey of 1965 figures for the New York State Publishers Association showed that news-

246

paper net profits before taxes ranged from $22,000 for the smallest to $1 million for the largest; the average 20,000–25,000-circulation paper yields 17 per cent of income as profit, before taxes. One index of the financial health of newspapers is that it is becoming almost impossible to find a daily paper for sale at a feasible price today.

Magazines, having passed the crisis in the 1950's that took the lives of many, are back in bursting good health. Circulation of magazines was "increasing faster than the growth of the U.S. adult population," according to the Magazine Publishers Association, while advertising revenue for the 1966 was 7 per cent over the previous year.

Broadcasting was equally prosperous. According to the 1967 *Broadcasting Yearbook*, total time sales of both radio and television for 1966 were $2.5 billion, up nearly $200 million from 1965. Some, 6,430 radio and television stations broadcast to nearly 55 million homes with television sets and more than 57 million with radios—all figures up from the previous year. And, the National Association of Broadcasters' annual financial report said that the typical television station had a profit margin of 22.65 per cent and the typical radio station, a margin of 7.65 per cent in 1965. Both were up from 1964.

This is fine, because when the mass media are run by private enterprise it is generally true (with exceptions) that the financially healthiest newspapers, magazines, and broadcasters do the best and most responsible jobs. They can afford to; an editor who has a little leeway in his budget is not under quite so much pressure to print only the sure-fire, and usually less responsible, material—if he is truly an editor and not a money-man.

With all their faults, the media are more responsible today than they were half a century ago. There is less bias in presentation of news, less venality, broader coverage of national and world affairs, more—but not enough—presentation of complex events in a perspective that makes them meaningful to readers and viewers. Even television, which has been the least conscious of its responsibility as an information medium, is showing some signs of recognizing its obligations. Professor William A. Wood, of Columbia University's Graduate School of Journalism,[1] recently estimated that about 30 per cent of television and 20 per cent of radio stations "have reached the point where they do more than give routine attention to news and show real responsibility and quality in news services." And in the list of things they are doing he includes the use of more special-beat reporters by local stations, more regular hours of news programming, more community service during emergencies, more local editorials by broadcasters, and more investigative reporting by stations in half the cities in the country's

---

[1] William A. Wood, "The Sound of Maturity," *Columbia Journalism Review,* Vol. IV, No. 4 (Winter 1966), p. 7.

top fifty markets. Further, both the Ford Foundation and the Carnegie Commission on Educational Television had plans which looked toward building a healthier financial base under educational television. The President's Special Message on Health and Education of February 28, 1967 included elements of each plan and has given some hope that the medium will be able to discharge its obligation to keep Americans informed.

In a speech at the University of Pennsylvania, Dr. Edward M. Glick, director of the American Institute for Political Communication, said:

> Today's press is a far more decent and honorable institution than its predecessors of 100 or even 50 years ago. The media generally— and the larger newspapers and television stations in particular— are doing a much more effective job of disseminating and interpreting the news than was the case at the turn of the century. And the federal government has substantially increased both the scope and quality of its informational output in the past generation.

"All you have to do to see the change," said Wade Nichols,[2] editor of *Good Housekeeping* and one of the most perceptive men in journalism today, "is to go back to the files and compare what was published years ago with what appears today. I think, for example, that all mass media have done an excellent job in handling civil rights issues; 20 years ago all the problems were there, but were generally ignored."

The growing maturity can be seen in individual cases, too. *Look* magazine, under the editorship of the late Daniel Mich, handled more controversial issues, illuminated more social problems, and spotlighted more important trends in United States society than it ever thought of doing twenty years ago. Nichols himself transformed *Redbook* from a frothy, superficial monthly full of boy-meets-girl fiction into a book that dealt soberly and intelligently with some of the realities of life for American young adults—like mixed marriages, the costs of medical care, blockbusting by real estate operators, and lip-service religion. The *Saturday Evening Post,* after a brief flirtation with sensationalism and libel, has steadied down to the kind of responsibility it had under editor Ben Hibbs.

Leading newspapers, too, are responding to the challenge to make their columns more pertinent to their readers' lives. The *Wall Street Journal* regularly prints some of the most trenchant and well-written articles anywhere on subjects which, to the superficial reader, seem far outside its jurisdiction (but actually, of course, are not). Ever since a magnificent series on juvenile crime by Harrison E. Salisbury in the late 1950's, the *New York Times* has carried hundreds of stories that intelligently report and appraise

---

2 In an interview, June 1966.

current problems and issues. Newspapers in a dozen leading cities across the country have recently taken on the job of helping readers who are trapped in the bureaucracy of government and big business, through columns variously called "Action Line," "Watchem," "Quest." They act, in fact, as a kind of ombudsman for their readers.

After the 1964 riots in Watts, the *Los Angeles Times* ran a series which reported not what some study commission found, but what the people of Watts themselves felt and thought about their quandary. A series by Morton Mintz on the pharmaceutical industry, in the *Washington Post*, became first a book, then the spark for a Congressional investigation.

All this is good; it is not great, and it is not even good enough. The rosy generalities mask a number of failures which, though varying in the different media, apply in some measure to all three. These failures must be repaired if the media are to achieve greatness.

PEOPLE SIMPLY DO NOT BELIEVE
MUCH OF WHAT THE MEDIA
TELL THEM

When journalists produce material that their readers reject, they are no longer in the communications business.

Readers do not believe because what they are told contradicts their own experience. Recently the labor editor of *Business Week* opined that, with less than a half-dozen exceptions, there are no labor reporters working for the mass media. Reason: the media ignore labor except when there are strikes, and then their reportage is often antilabor.

This makes no kind of sense. Some 13.5 million Americans are members of unions; most remain members because the union benefits them. They live through the wrestling over individual grievances, the campaigns for bargaining, and elections of union officers; at union meetings they argue out the endorsement of political candidates and their positions on local issues; they are told about—and often support with money—the struggles of other union members locked in a showdown with management, and some of them know the desperate frustration of being trapped in a racket union where venal leaders and employers conspire to exploit them. Yet they read virtually nothing about this whole aspect of their lives in the mass media. Or else what they read, their experience tells them, is distorted.

In the past few years, Congressional hearings have brought out factual information of close concern to millions—the safety of automobiles, the high cost of drugs, deceptions in packaging, and concealed high interest rates for installment buying. Many people knew of these things through their own experience, but the media had ignored them.

Recently, the publisher of a successful Negro newspaper in Baltimore said on a National Educational Television program that the reason he had been able to start and operate his paper profitably was that Baltimore's big newspapers had ignored Negro news. They were far from the only ones in the country which did, even though Negroes make up 10 per cent of United States population.

People are not stupid; obviously they conclude that the media cannot be trusted. If this distortion goes on too long, or occurs in a controversy that is too bitter, their distrust may spread to everything that the newspaper or magazine prints, and they reject it wholly.

But more often they are selective in their disbelief. They may believe what a newspaper prints on its women's pages, or a magazine in its service section, but be quite untouched by either's political reportage.

People disbelieve because they are better educated today. According to Ben H. Bagdikian in the *Columbia Journalism Review* (Winter 1966):

> In 1940 the number of American adults who had gone beyond the eighth grade was 27 million, but in 1964 it was 67 million. . . . The number of white collar, managerial, skilled and professional workers in 1920 was 16 million, in 1965 it was 41 million.

Further, he reported, the sale of books has doubled in the past ten years, and the category with the greatest increase—370 per cent—was in social and economic subjects.

People disbelieve because, under the ceaseless drumfire of advertising and public relations, they are much more sophisticated than media practitioners think. This sophistication enables them to spot a phony message as far as the eye can see, and they-detest being fooled. Thus, to the ancient abjuration that journalists must be unbiased for ethical reasons is added the warning that bias simply does not work. You lose your audience.

Recently the Syracuse, New York, papers ran a shrill, one-sided campaign opposing free state medical aid for the indigent. Many of the stories were written by a reporter named Luther Bliven. After some weeks his paper received—and printed—a one-line letter which said "Please keep Mr. Bliven's editorials off the front page." An informal survey of some 300 residents of all socioeconomic levels in the same city at about the same time revealed that the majority thought that the papers were biased and therefore unreliable. One woman said: "I'm a Republican and they're on my side. But still they ought not to be biased."

Lou Schneider, who writes the "Trade Winds" column for the Bell-McClure Syndicate, criticized editors in the October 15, 1966 issue of *Editor & Publisher* for printing too much good news about business. He wrote:

> Editors own stock and also they do not want to upset local department store management and other advertisers. If the story is not bullish, they simply get another story—140 business editors use the PR Wire publicity stories. No one writes the shady side of the street. . . . Yet readers want knowledgeable news they can depend on. There are 21 million investors in New York Stock Exchange stocks alone and they want straight news about what is happening and what is likely to happen.

When they do not get it, obviously they conclude that the media are not leveling with them.

There is no complete answer to this kind of audience skepticism, simply because no one knows precisely what kind of information people disbelieve or why. The best partial—and too general—answer is found in the old principle of fairness and impartiality. If the people believe a paper or magazine is leveling with them, they accept a good deal of difference of viewpoint without rejecting the entire publication.

The second half of the answer is that editors and writers must know the realities of their readers' concerns, and not let publisher's policy prevent coverage of it.

There is, for example, a general feeling among readers that advertisers determine a medium's policy. Yet scores of editors and writers have said things like: "Never in my 35 years of work has an advertiser influenced anything we have printed." Both are right. The advertiser's influence is subtle and pervasive. Any journalist smart enough to find the right keys on a typewriter quickly learns the taboos, and learns to work within them so surely that he forgets about them. But the readers do not.

If there is an answer, it is probably a lesson that was first learned a quarter-century ago by the *New York Daily News*. A large advertiser objected to something the paper had published and threatened to withdraw its ads. The editor told him to go ahead. The ads were withdrawn, the paper felt the loss, but continued to publish. Within three months, the advertiser asked to come back into the paper and was accepted. The lesson which too many media executives, particularly broadcasters, have not learned is that advertisers need a truly independent publication more than it needs them.

THERE IS NEITHER ENOUGH NOR THE
RIGHT KIND OF INFORMATION
IN THE MEDIA

Information, of course, is simply another word for knowledge, and the increase in the sheer bulk of knowledge is one of the revolutionary changes of our time. It has often been said that the total of human knowledge gained since 1940 equals the amount gained in all the years of human history up to 1940. Some specialized areas have far outstripped others; physicists know, for example, that the quantity of new knowledge in their discipline is doubling every decade. And the social sciences generally are among the leaders in the totals of new learning.

As these areas have grown, they have, of course, become more and more specialized, and researchers in them have come to use language that is more and more esoteric and less and less comprehensible to the layman. A major part of the journalist's job is to serve as a communications bridge between the specialists and the average reader. In recent years he has done more of this in all media than ever before, but measured against the sky-rocketing totals of knowledge his performance has been a roman candle against a Saturn rocket.

It is trite to point out that television is greatly overbalanced in providing entertainment as against information. Kenneth A. Cox, of the Federal Communications Commission, recently gave this reporter some figures on how much. A report by United Research, Inc., he wrote, found that of 476 television stations nearly two-thirds (62 per cent) devoted between 71 and 80 per cent of their time to it. An earlier study (pre-1962), he added, found that 448 network-affiliated stations spent 78 per cent of their time on entertainment as against 6 per cent for news, 2 per cent for education, and 1.4 per cent for discussion. "I believe," he wrote, "that the proportions [for radio] would be roughly comparable."

Despite a few outstanding exceptions like improved half-hours news programs on the network and truly distinguished reporters like Walter Cronkite, Edward P. Morgan, and Eric Sevareid, the quality of information programs is superficial and episodic. The magazine *Broadcasting* reported (July 25, 1966) that the Columbia Broadcasting System (CBS) offered to provide three and a half minutes of world and national news to go into late-night local programs to 192 of its affiliates; only 31 were interested, and the offer was dropped. The *Columbia Journalism Review* (Spring 1966) likewise pointed out that when local stations were given a chance to reject news material on the Vietnam war they did so "in substantial numbers."

Even Columbia Professor Wood's upbeat report on improvements in radio and television news, cited earlier, found increased responsibility in only 20 and 30 per cent of stations—something less than a majority.

Newspapers have fallen short in both quantity and quality. Editors across the country complain that they have not enough space to print all the information they want. Yet experts agree that the average ratio for all newspapers is 65 per cent of their space for advertising and 35 per cent for news; individual editions, of course, often carry a much lower ratio of news— sometimes 15 to 20 per cent.

In the *Columbia Journalism Review* article cited earlier, Ben H. Bagdikian found that while

> newspapers today are physically larger than they used to be, an average of 47 pages in 1964 compared with 28 pages in 1925 . . . there has been no significant increase in non-advertising space. . . . The number of non-advertising pages remained at about 17.

Editors frequently complain about the advertising-news ratio; seldom is it changed. It is set in the business office by the owner or publisher who runs the paper, and the editor is given a layout sheet for each page showing a jagged mountain of ads sloping up to the right and leaving a hole which he may fill with news. The priority clearly shows whether advertising or news is considered the more important.

Mass magazines do it differently. In many, perhaps most, the editor, not the business manager, decides on the number of pages each issue will contain. And the advertising-editorial ratio is dramatically different. In a survey of fifty of the largest national magazines for 1965, for example, well over half the space was devoted to editorial content. In some magazines, including some of the largest, the ratio was as high as 70 per cent editorial. Only sixteen had less than 50 per cent and one less than 40 per cent. The figures are not entirely comparable with newspapers since "editorial" on some magazines included fiction, but the percentage of it in most was small, and more than half had none at all.

Such quantitative measurements, however, tell only part of the story, and probably not the most important part. The real measure of any mass medium is its impact on its audience. Do people believe what they see or read? Does it give them new insights and ideas? Does it help them understand themselves or the realities of their lives and world? Does it give them information that is pertinent to the problems they face and the judgments they must make?

In these areas newspapers—with outstanding exceptions—have largely failed—many not in all areas, but all in some.

Newsweek for November 29, 1965 categorized newspapers as

smug and, of all things, outdated . . . they have fallen behind the times technologically, as employers and, most damningly, in the professional tasks of reporting, writing and editing the news.

Chief cause of this is that the ideas of what readers want and can absorb which editors had forty years ago have been passed down almost unchanged. The ideas then and now were that readers might be reasonably intelligent, but had minuscule amounts of information and that they were primarily interested in crime, disaster, death, sports, comics, scandal, and voyeuristic sex. Through the upheavals of the Great Depression, two wars, and what the late Adlai Stevenson called the five revolutions of the mid-century, this formula has remained virtually unchanged.

The same sort of editorial judgment is perpetuated and disseminated nationwide by the Associated Press and United Press International. Here the stories are written and edited in New York (or state capitals) and punched into computer tapes which are sent over wires to local newsrooms where they are set into type automatically so that the very same wording of the very same stories appears on front pages from Nome to Nashville. It is easy and cheap for an editor to fill his paper with these stories if he wants to, and far too many do. Local angles on national news and local editorial evaluations go out the window unless the editor is strong enough and courageous enough to buck the system and then defend his increased budget expenses to his boss. And in newsrooms, as elsewhere in our organizational society, this kind of courage is rare. But it is essential to greatness.

Today's informed, sophisticated reader demands informed, sophisticated writing and editing. The magazines learned this twenty-five years ago, and the best newspapers are now following their lead—but only a few and only the best. The name of the technique is interpretive, or depth, writing. In it a trained and skillful writer examines a complex situation—juvenile crime, slum housing, water pollution, a seemingly senseless murder—studies the background in the library, talks to experts, interviews people involved, and comes up with what, in his judgment, is the essential truth of the situation. Then he writes his story in a way that gets the reader emotionally involved even as he learns the facts. In writing it, he borrows many of the techniques of fiction writing, and even showmanship, but is bound always, of course, by fact.

This is a difficult, highly skilled, creative kind of writing. It takes time and space, and it cost money, but magazines have built multimillion circulations—and millions for their owners—on it, and the newspapers found in anybody's list of the nation's best ten have done likewise. The *Wall Street Journal* was an early innovator, and its offshoot, *The National Observer*, does it consistently today. After the 1965 blackout in the Northeast, for example, the *Observer* reported what New Yorkers did, thought about, and felt like having Reporter Jane Dowling tell the things that happened to her during the dark hours. Her story was as readable as a whodunit with a touch of poetry.

Speaking at the California Editors Conference recently, Herbert Brucker, editor emeritus of the Hartford *Courant,* said: "Today's news isn't just the gee-whiz event that happened a moment ago. It is also the significant fact or trend that is revealed only when dug out by informed professionals who can write."

This kind of editing and writing is the medicine that the media need. For decades, they have been attacked as presenting too much entertainment and not enough information. But nobody ever attacks a story or play for being too entertaining when it gets the reader emotionally involved, causes him to identify deeply with the problem, and finishes by clarifying for him an essential truth about his condition. And this is precisely what the best interpretive writing in magazines, newspapers, and broadcasting does. The criticism of "too much entertainment" is really the criticism of too much superficial entertainment, which makes no point, carries no message, illuminates no corner of the confused and frightening world we all live in.

Most newspaper editors complain that they have not the time, the staff, nor the money for this kind of writing. They do not have the time because they are still shackled by the old idea that a newspaper must be first with the news—in an age when it is impossible for them to beat radio and television with the story. They do not have the staff partly because they do not train their writers to do the job—or have them trained. And they do not have the money because editorial departments on newspapers are traditionally shortchanged in their budgets. Yet it is the editorial department that produces the most important service a newspaper has to offer, and the one which makes the press the only private industry whose freedom is guaranteed by the Constitution. Without it the paper becomes a shopper's guide —which is a perfectly legitimate publication, but is not a newspaper.

Allen H. Neuharth, general manager of the Gannet Newspapers, told a group of editors on June 21, 1966 that "you can increase your editorial costs by 50 per cent and still not increase the overall production cost of the paper." How low editorial costs are in relation to others is shown by an examination of 1965 figures from Inland Daily Press Association.

On papers of 120,000 circulation and over, editorial costs were half (11 per cent) of the cost of the paper they were printed on (23 per cent of the total cost). This disparity gradually decreased as circulations got smaller; at 22,000-27,000 circulation they were about equal and at circulations under 4,000—a very small daily—the editorial department cost twice as much as the newsprint. The lesson is obvious—more money needs to be spent on editorial departments.

EDITORS NEED MORE POWER WITHIN
THEIR OWN ORGANIZATIONS

It is axiomatic that great publications are the product of great editors, not great business or advertising or circulation men. The *Louisville Courier-Journal* became great as the result of a succession of outstanding editors from Barry Bingham and Mark Ethridge through James Pope to Norman Isaacs. It is the editorial genius of Henry Luce and DeWitt Wallace that has built the magazines of Time, Inc., and the *Reader's Digest* into their preeminence today. These great editors have possessed the ability to win power for themselves in the organizational jungle. But the great are always too rare. A change in the relative power given editors in the media hierarchy would give the necessary scope to men and women who are first-class editors, but who lack the political skills that are needed to climb the organizational ladder.

To do this will not be easy. It must be done by publishers, and publishers are businessmen who deal in dollars and are under vast pressures to show a profit. Further, at meetings of department heads where policy is set, the advertising and circulation managers also talk in dollars and bring in revenue; the editor talks in terms of ideas and other intangibles, brings in no money, but spends plenty. To rise above the pressures of the imbalance requires a transcendent act of will and understanding of values by the publisher which is not only foreign to his training, but beyond the capacity of many.

Some company managements are clever enough to understand this. As part of the Curtis Publishing Company, for example, the *Saturday Evening Post* became such a vital force in America because, as a matter of company policy, its editor was the ultimate boss of the magazine. Ben Hibbs was not only editor, but also vice-president and a member of the board of directors of the company. And he was the final authority on everything that went into the magazine—advertising as well as editorial. *Holiday* quickly grew to preeminence in its field because Ted Patrick had the same authority for his magazine.

But far too few newspaper and magazine editors have this sweeping power. Broadcasting, of course, is just beginning to have editors of any kind. Broadcasting was born out of show business by advertising. It did not have the tradition, as print media did, that the station was an independent entity interposed between the advertiser and the public—an entity called an editor, with opinions, thoughts, and judgments which were imposed on both. This is why broadcasting has been periodically shaken by such upheavals as the recent resignation of Fred W. Friendly, one of the medium's editorial greats, from CBS. It is why broadcasting is far behind print media in the power it gives editors.

If all editors in all media were given the power they need, most would see to it that they got the kind of writing skill the media must have and would give the writers both training and time enough to do the journalistic job that is needed today.

Most would also see to it that young writers are recruited and trained. The media, driven by an annual need of 5,000 new journalists, are just beginning to recruit in the universities; more advanced industries have been doing it for decades. And the media are just beginning to see to it their best writers get advanced training to equip them for specialized reporting and writing. At that, most of such training is financed by foundations, universities, or the writers themselves. In contrast, most progressive industries have been sending their promising young men back to college at their expense for at least a decade.

THERE ARE LARGE GAPS IN THE KNOWLEDGE ANYONE HAS ABOUT THE IMPACT THE MEDIA HAVE ON THEIR AUDIENCES

Solid, reliable research is needed in the following areas, among others.

BROADCASTING

There is little disinterested, reliable research data on total audience, how much time that people spend listening or watching what kind of program, the amount of time devoted to commericals per hour, the effect different kinds of programs, and commercials, have on their audience, and similar questions. Much information of this kind is available from commercial research organizations, but its validity is questionable, especially since the recent congressional hearings concerning the methods. Further, it tries to show how many people are watching a program, but does not measure their reaction. Do they like it? Are they moved by it?

Probably the Federal Communications Commission should provide, and publish periodically, such information both about networks and individual local stations that members of the audience would have reliable yardsticks to judge the stations that they listen to.

PRINT MEDIA

There is no systematic body of knowledge on what techniques of writing, headlining, and graphic presentation are most successful in getting people to read and apprehend the important public issues upon which they must render decisions in the voting booth. Research is both too small in quantity and too superficial in quality.

Recently, Dr. J. B. Haskins, of Newhouse Communications Center, Syracuse University, surveyed existing research on newspapers and found it "primitive." He wrote:

> There is a relatively small body of evidence about newspapers (apart from mechancial innovations) that is methodologically sound, deals with important problems, is understandable and is immediately applicable; however, most newspaper people are either unaware of the existence of that evidence or are unwilling to make changes in traditional procedure.

Among the areas Haskins listed as needing research were:
What can newspapers do to attract and keep high-quality editorial personnel?

What is the best education for journalism? (Should not the federal government give greater support to journalism training as part of its effort to improve training for the public service?)

Since broadcasting has replaced newspapers as the major source of news for the majority of people, how should newspapers redefine their primary function? Should they, as suggested herein, devote their pages to putting the day's news in perspective and building bridges of information between the experts and the public?

What is the role of newspapers in formal public education? Can it be one arm of the process?

To what extent can newspaper publishers and editors define their goals? What are they trying to achieve in audience effects? Can they do it? If they can define their goals, are they the right ones?

ALL MEDIA

There is little sound knowledge of where people get their information. What there is suggests that the media provide a small percentage of that information. A study by Stanford University of where people first heard of the assassination of President John F. Kennedy, found that nearly half (49 per cent) learned it not from radio or television, not from a newspaper, but from another person.

There is little or no research on precisely how sophisticated the media's audience is and on what kind of information it wants. Present categories in which editors present information—national, crime, sex, sports, and the like—may be outdated. Are they? If so, what new categories should replace them as rules of thumb for editors to apportion the contents of their publications and programs?

There is virtually no reliable information on the effects that the media have on the cities they live in. Does a first-class newspaper or broadcaster give its city a better government? more industry and jobs? a healthier cultural climate? better informed and more active citizens? If so, how?

Probably what is needed is government financing for an *independent* agency in a university or foundation which will provide continuous research on the media and publish it regularly. It must *not* be an industry association, *not* a government agency.

THE REALLY DIFFICULT QUESTIONS

If these and other gaps in knowledge are filled, if editors use it and are given the power they need, if writers get the time and training they need, then the media may at last begin to face some of the really difficult questions:

To what extent has newsmen's reportage only of the dramatic distorted their readers' concepts of reality?

It is an ancient rule of journalism that when nothing happens there is no news. If this was ever true, it is no longer. For decades, Negroes lived in slums with rats and garbage and fear, their men jobless, their children uneducated; it went unreported in the mass media until their desperation drove them to violence.

For decades, police, lawyers, and judges have known that there are two kinds of justice in America, one for the rich and one for the poor; was that not news?

In many communities, for decades, real estate brokers, builders, and contractors have had such control of local government that zoning, building, and sanitation codes were either nonexistent or ignored; the situation and its effects were known and unreported by the media.

For decades, our water and air have been quietly and inexorably polluted; where were the reporters?

The answer that the local Establishment which controlled the press was not interested in these matters is too easy; for there are always journalistic Davids who aspire to giant-killing. But these stories take time and perception and digging and thoughtfulness to get, and, with rare exceptions, the media have not made the requisites available.

Can any editor say with certainty that if these and similar situations had been reported, the people's view of their world would not now be different? or that Watts might never have revolted?

To what extent has the media's endless exploitation of violence made violence so prevalent in America?

Last August after Charles Whitman killed fifteen persons in Austin, Texas, Charles Collingwood reported from London that the British were sickened and saddened by their cousins' seemingly incurable addiction to violence. No modern Western nation in the same time span has killed as many of its heads of state while in office as America, according to Professor Carl N. Degler, Vassar historian. Every two minutes some American is killed, or wounded, said Senator Edward Kennedy recently. Has the endless recitation of crime and death on the front pages, the ceaseless depiction on television of the Old West, where violence is shown as a legitimate means to an end, had nothing to do with this?

To what extent have the media contributed to the increase in promiscuity and cheapening of sex?

Thoughtful observers have pointed out that the rush to end the strictures of puritanism and the constant sexual titillation of the media have led people, particularly the young, to engage in sexual relations as fun and games. But sex without the care and concern and responsibility of love is as shallow and unrewarding an escape as alcoholism or narcotics. In encouraging it, how well have the media served the true human values of our society?

To what extent have the media contributed to the popularity of extremism and to the devil theory of international relations?

Any thoughtful review of the McCarthy madness must conclude that if the media did not create McCarthy, they certainly increased his influence. Sober editors wonder, in hindsight, what would have happened to the Senator if they and their colleagues had simply refused to print stories about him. But, in the realities of competition, could they have?

Probably not. But while they reported his demagoguery they could have seen to it their readers also received enough perspective to be able to recognize it for what it was.

McCarthy was a loud and extreme exponent of the devil theory in international affairs—the simplistic idea that everything we do is right, but everything our enemy (currently communism) does is evil. But he was not the only one, either while he was alive or now. Professor Henry Steele Commager, of Amherst, described this well:

> What we have here is a deeply ingrained vanity and arrogance . . . fed by isolation, by school histories, by a filiopietistic sociey which is that we are somehow superior to all other nations, morally and practically, by a thousand editorials, a hundred thousand radio and TV programs which play up the villainy of our enemies— the Russians, the Chinese, the Cubans—and our own morality and nobility.[3]

What editor can say in conscience that he has not contributed to this illusion?

Bernard Kilgore, of the *Wall Street Journal,* has said:

> The newspaper editor of tomorrow will be an egghead . . . the newspaper of the future must become an instrument of educational leadership, an institution of intellectual development—a center of learning.

Speaking May 10, 1966, at the fiftieth anniversary of the Pulitzer Prize awards, James Reston of the *New York Times* said:

> Somewhere there is a line where the old skeptical, combative, publish-and-be-damned tradition of the past . . . may converge with the new intelligence and the new duties and responsibilities of this rising and restless generation. I wish I knew how to find it, for it could help both the newspapers and the nation in their present plight, and it would help us believe again, which, in this age of tricks and techniques, may be our greatest need.

This, then, is the challenge: it is the media's job to illuminate the values of American life, both the false and the true, and to use all their skill and technology to instruct and guide and lead the people into a less anxious and more rewarding way of living. Progressively, as they do this they will answer the need for greatness.

---

[3] In *Current* (January 1964).

11

THE ART OF MEASURING THE ARTS

ALVIN TOFFLER

Since the end of World War II, the United States has witnessed a startling rise in public participation in the arts. The creation of great new cultural centers in cities across the nation is only the most visible sign of this new public interest. Whether gauged by increasing attendance at museums and theaters, by sales of books, by the formation of arts councils (up from 125 in 1964 to approximately 300 in 1966), by the rise of FM radio stations specializing in classical music, or by the creation of the National Foundation on the Arts and Humanities, it is obvious that drastic changes are occurring in our nation's cultural life.

The "culture explosion," until recently a strictly American phenomenon, is, moreover, no longer limited to this country. The arts traditionally have been regarded as being more advanced in Europe than in the United States. Yet there is evidence of rapidly broadening public involvement in the arts in England, France, Sweden, Holland, and other highly industrialized nations as well. So dramatic is this new international wave of interest that France's Minister of Cultural Affairs, André Malraux, in calling for the construction of ninety regional arts centers in his country, declared it to be "the stupefying fact" of the last twenty years.[1] The international character of this phenomenon suggests that, far from being an accident of American history, a "culture explosion" is a predictable part of the transition from an industrial to a postindustrial stage of society.

For anyone interested in the passage to postindustrialism, therefore, this fact, stupefying or not, is too important to ignore. No system of social

---

[1] *New York Times,* December 11, 1966.

accounting could possibly be complete without indicators of the cultural life of the nation. Furthermore, such indicators must cast light on the quality of our cultural life as well as on its size and scope. Just as in the field of medical statistics we need to know not merely what health services are available, but also how good those services are, so, too, in the arts we need to devise objective, even—where possible—quantitative measures of cultural "quality."

This is, of course, a controversial position since the arts are commonly thought to be so subjective and relativistic as to be beyond objective meas-urement, particularly with respect to the issue of quality. The very idea of measuring the arts is abhorrent to many. Quality is popularly regarded not as an aggregate of quantified or quantifiable factors, but rather as a mysterious, metaphysical entity. Nonetheless, an effort not only should, but can, be made to deal with the issue of quality in objective terms. In the paper that follows, I shall sketch the rough requirements for a cultural data system and suggest ways in which the problem of "quality indicators" might be broached.

ART AND SOCIAL CHANGE

Such a system is needed for many reasons. First, we need to achieve more systematic and conscious control over the transition to postindus-trialism. It is essential that as we race into the future, powered by science and technology, we do so with insight into the ways in which people and institutions adjust to change. The empirical study of the arts in contem-porary society can contribute significantly toward this insight. The arts play an important role in integrating individuals into subcultures within the larger society; they provide a running critique of social policy; they act on value systems that accelerate or retard change; and they educate individuals to new role possibilities and styles of life. This is not the place for a treatise on the social functions of the arts,[2] beyond pointing out that these functions are central to an understanding of social change and adaptation.

Unfortunately, despite this relevance, the arts have not yet been sub-jected to systematic empirical analysis in this country. There is an abundant historical and theoretical literature, but little in the way of objective con-temporary data. Indeed, while much criticism has been lavished on "mere head-counting" in the social sciences, in the field of the arts, the reverse

---

[2] For a discussion of the social functions of art, see Alvin Toffler, "The Politics of the Impossible," in Bertram M. Gross (ed.), *The Great Society?* (New York: Basic Books, 1967).

criticism is fair. We have done everything but study them in an objective, empirical fashion. Astonishingly few heads have been counted, and our understanding of social change and adaptation have suffered for it.

I contend, therefore, that a cultural data system is needed, if only to shed light on those processes of change and adaptation that should, in our time, be the central concern of the social sciences.

CULTURAL COST-BENEFITS

There are, however, less theoretical considerations as well. As the arts come to affect larger masses of people, their influence on the style and texture of life deepens. This influence makes itself manifest not merely in such matters as airport design, typography, fashion or interior decoration, but also in the public mood and in the behavior of significant subcultures. The nihilism and pessimism of much Western literature, drama, and art in the past generation cannot be divorced from the rise of such social phenomena as the Provos in Holland and the campus revolt in the United States. The widespread belief among young people that life is absurd has its source in the fictions of Camus and Beckett as well as in the realities of Hiroshima or Watts.

Nor is it only the philosophical content of art that is increasingly influential. The culture boom has brought with it an enormous expansion of what August Heckscher has called the "cultural infrastructure," the organizational machinery of the arts. Institutions devoted to the production or dissemination of cultural goods and services have multiplied. New organizational forms—the arts council and the arts center— have cropped up. Cultural institutions have become more influential in community affairs than ever before. A highly complicated, multibillion-dollar "culture industry has emerged. We need to understand the ideological and organizational impact of decisions being made by those who control and administer this industry.

At the same time, this industry, composed of a great variety of enterprises, ranging from book publishers to art galleries, opera associations, and libraries, is increasingly linked with universities, government agencies, corporations, foundations, and voluntary organizations. This network of ties with the outside world has immeasurably strengthened the culture complex, but it has also made the arts highly sensitive to shocks and upheavals in society at large.

Thus, passage of federal legislation to aid the schools has contributed to revolutionary changes in the publishing branch of the culture industry. Some companies have seen their sales rise by a multiple of five or ten within a single year. A wave of mergers between publishers and electronics manufacturers has been given additional impetus, and publishers have suddenly become aware that technological developments in the field of information retrieval, computer-assisted instruction, and Xerography will deeply affect the future of the book as a cultural artifact.

Other technological developments also hold significance for the arts. The coming widespread use of satellite communication, for example, making it possible for American audiences to watch Japanese, say, or French television broadcasts, cannot but have some impact on cultural tastes. Massive break-throughs in rapid-transit technology will inevitably change the market structure of many cultural institutions. (If New Haven residents can get to Philharmonic Hall at Lincoln Center in thirty minutes, what happens to the New Haven Symphony?) Even decisions about the location of scientific installations affect the arts. The federal decision to build a huge atom accelerator just outside Chicago, for example, implies a great influx of scientific and technical personnel into the area. This will predictably alter the demand for cultural services in the community.

In brief, the arts and the social network interpenetrate at so many points, and in so many new ways, that the ricochet effect of a change in a seemingly distant sector of society now can have serious and perhaps damaging consequences for the future development of painting, music, drama, or dance.

In the past, major technological and social decisions have been made without regard for their potential impact on the arts. Such decisions now being reached in government bureaus, research laboratories, and business offices will affect the nation's cultural life directly and indirectly for decades to come. It is vital that, in making such decisions, we take into account, as one significant entry in the cost-benefit ledger, their likely cultural consequences. This will only become possible, practically speaking, when we succeed in devising a comprehensive cultural data system with built-in quality indicators.

THE POLITICS OF ART

Such a system, however, would be useful not merely as an early warning mechanism alerting us to situations or changes that could prove harmful to the arts; it would also provide a more rational framework for political debate and decision-making. This will be desperately needed before long, because the growth of the culture industry is forcibly pushing new and unfamiliar issues into the political arena.

Take, for example, the question of audience size. Should public policy favor further expansion of the audience for the arts? While the culture public has been noticeably enlarged and democratized in recent years, it is still predominantly middle or upper class in character. Millions of blue-collar workers, Negroes, and poor people remain virtually untouched by the arts. Should this concern policy-makers in an affluent society? Should public funds be used consciously to subsidize lower prices in concert halls and theaters? Should the Department of Labor, in determining, for its own statistical purposes, the minimally decent family budget, allow some amount in it for music lessons or art supplies? Can family life be truly "decent" if there is no allowance for music or art in it? This is an inherently political question. It can be ignored only so long as a society is based on scarcity. It will prove harder to ignore as masses of educated voters begin to engage in the politics of affluence.

There are more technical political questions, too. Increasing sums of public money—state and municipal as well as federal—are flowing into the arts economy. This raises a fundamental question about the extent to which financial support of artistic activities should be integrated with other public programs. For instance, to what degree should support be tied to national, state, or local interests in promoting tourism, industrial development, or, at the State Department level, the objectives of American foreign policy? How much support of the arts should be woven into urban development plans, the war on poverty, or programs of assistance to the aged?

A whole class of questions relates to the machinery of patronage. How much of the money flowing into the arts in the form of patronage or subsidy should be public, and how much private? How much should come from essentially bureaucratic sources such as foundations, corporations, or public agencies, and how much from individuals? (These ratios are, to some degree, adjustable through the manipulation of tax policies.) Similarly, what should the patronage mix be as between the different levels of government? And what new mechanisms can be devised to buffer recipient institutions, such as museums, theaters, or orchestras, from direct political pressures stemming from the support-grant agencies?

Many of the problems concern the aesthetic character or quality of our cultural output. To what degree, for example, should public funds go for the support of innovational or experimental art; to what degree for the support of performances or exhibitions of the best of the past? (This question is similar to that frequently asked in scientific circles about the division of research funds as between pure and applied research.) And yet another critical question has to do with the appropriate balance between amateurism and professionalism in the arts. Should public funds be limited only to support of professionalism, as some of our critics prefer? Or should it be used to encourage amateur activity as well?

These issues may seem unimportant to practical politicians today. Yet they will soon turn out to be inescapably real and highly political, provoking heated conflict in the community, especially among educated, middle-class voters. A good indication of what lies ahead in this regard may be seen in the recent fight over the Metropolitan Opera House in New York. After the opera moved its operations to a new hall at Lincoln Center, an independent committee sprang up to save the old building that had housed the Opera for decades. The opera association opposed these plans. Before the dust had settled, the seemingly simple question of whether New York should or should not tear down the old Metropolitan Opera House turned out to involve not merely the city's cultural community, but the mayor, the governor, the state legislature, the courts, at least two United States senators, philanthropists, an important real estate company, and various ethnic groups and political factions. Even the United Nations had a word to say about it. Similarly complex political struggles over cultural issues can be expected to erupt in cities all over the United States in the years to come and to intrude more and more into the arena of national politics as well. A comprehensive system of data-collection about the arts would lead to more sensible weighing of alternatives and more rational choices among them than is now possible.

THE CULTURE ADMINISTRATORS

Today, most such battles are fought at the level of irresponsible rhetoric. Critics inveigh. Politicians orate. Artists complain. Civic boosters brag. Yet we know so little about the "state of the system," there are so few reliable, empirical facts about the linkage between art and society, that decisions are frequently haphazard and foolish.

This might, of course, be said of many other fields as well. Obviously, the growing demand for better social indicators reflects the inadequacy of data with respect to health, education, and many other important sectors of American life. Yet it is safe to say that in *no* other significant field is the existing data base flimsier.

This is true not simply because of the shortsightedness and lack of imagination of the social sciences, but also because of the bone-deep conviction among many artists and critics that art and data are somehow antagonistic. In the cultural community, it is virtually an article of faith that "numbers"— the word is usually uttered with derision—are irrelevant to art, that quantity and quality bear no relationship to one another. This attitude spills over into a generalized distaste for science, social or otherwise.

Moreover, most arts managers—those charged with the administration of cultural institutions—come to their work from artistic, rather than from business or administrative, backgrounds. Many bring with them the belief that management, itself, is no more than an intuitive art. The result is an unfamiliarity with and disdain for data-collection. This is beginning to change now. As arts institutions grow larger, their staffs become more differentiated and professionalized, and patrons, both public and private, demand more efficiency and accountability. Nevertheless, the resistance of the cultural community helps to explain the paucity of empirical data.

Ironically, such data could prove extremely useful to the organizers and administrators of the culture industry, to trade union officials in the arts, and even, indirectly, to the artist. The availability of comparative data on audience characteristics, on sources of patronage, on programming, and other such matters, could reduce the inefficiency of operation that is still widespread in the field. This, in turn, could help to minimize the diversion of funds for the administrative, as distinct from artistic, functions of cultural institutions. Artists could receive more in payment; more time and attention could be devoted to achieving high quality in output.

To summarize, then, a cultural data system could yield important benefits. First, it could, in a general sense, advance our struggle to contain and channel the accelerating rate of change. Second, more specifically, it could provide the data necessary for decision-makers outside the culture industry to consider the cultural consequences of their actions. Third, it could lay the basis for informed political discussion and decision in matters affecting the arts. Fourth, it could improve administrative efficiency in the arts, thus freeing resources for artistic purposes. And, finally, as we shall see, it might even help to raise the entire level of excellence of our artistic output.

THE CULTURAL DATA SYSTEM

What kind of system would accomplish these ends? No data system can serve all purposes equally well, and in a field as poorly reported on as this one, the initial requirements may seem primitive. The system described below—while it goes far beyond anything now in existence—must be regarded as no more than a starting point.

Implicit in what has been said so far is a restrictive definition of the arts. The terms "culture" or "the arts" have been used more or less narrowly to refer to classical music, opera, dance, theater, the visual arts, and our literary output. This narrow definition will be employed for the remainder of the paper, partly from reasons of convenience, partly because these are, indeed, the fields in which most needs to be done. But it should be made explicit that a cultural data system limited to these alone would be seriously deficient. Information on these subjects must be supplemented by statistical and other data about rock and roll, happenings, jazz, and a wide variety of other phenomena. It must be set in a context provided by compatible data about the output of radio and television, movies, and mass magazines. Moreover, having brought such data together in a single place —an "Arts Section" of the *Statistical Abstract of the United States,* for example—we need to integrate it with the relative wealth of information already available about education, science, research, and communication.

We must begin by developing simple measures of the size of the culture industry: numbers of institutions or establishments, numbers of "consumers" served, detailed data on the characteristics of these consumers, numbers of artists, and the like. We need such information broken down by industry branch—that is, artistic discipline—and by geographical region. We need economic data about the industry, including sales and sources of income. We need data about its output in terms of number of performances, productions, and exhibitions, as well as seating or other physical capacity figures. Above all, we need to classify output in various ways, a subject to which I shall return shortly in the discussion of quality indicators.

We also need to distinguish as clearly as possible between professional and amateur work. (Establishing firm definitions of such terms will be an important and controversial first step in the process of implementing these proposals.) We need to know how the educational establishment feeds the culture industry, in the sense of training both consumers and artist-producers. Moreover, we need data on wages and level of employment in artistic and related occupations, as well as other sources of income that help artists to pay their bills.

This only begins to suggest some of the required information. No effort has been made to be exhaustive.

The tasks of collecting this data and integrating it with existing statistical data in other fields, must, in the end, fall to the Census Bureau. Only the Census Bureau has the skill, experience, and other resources necessary for work on so large a scale. It is too late to introduce these data requirements into the 1970 decennial census, but it is not too early to start work on a special census of the arts for, say, 1972, when the main work connected with the decennial census will be completed. The work of the Census Bureau can be supplemented by that of competent social scientists who can collect data in limited sectors of the field, as Baumol and Bowen have done in their recent work on the professional performing arts.[3] But a comprehen-

---

[3] William J. Baumol and William G. Bowen, *Performing Arts—The Economic Dilemma* (New York: Twentieth Century Fund, 1966).

sive and periodic census of the arts is a precondition for truly rational and imaginative steps to improve the quality of life in the United States.

It need hardly be pointed out that such data must be collected at regular intervals, so that trend lines can be established. Not all such data can come from institutional sources; much will have to be based on sample surveys of the relevant populations and other sources. Only a scattering of the required data is available in useful form today. We are, for example, much weaker in the performing arts than in the field of libraries or museums. We are weakest of all in the amateur sector that cuts all across the board. We are farther along on education and employment than on consumption statistics. We are extremely weak on consumer characteristics and on output-classification. One of the first steps in creating a cultural data system must be to iron out these differences and to make the incoming data compatible from branch to branch of the industry. Then we face the sticky problem of finding the best ways to classify output. This is central to the development of "quality indicators." It can, however, only be decided after we have determined what is meant by "quality indicators."

THE MEASUREMENT OF QUALITY

How does one measure "cultural quality?" This, then, is the next problem, and it is not resolved by laying it at the door of the Census Bureau or any other government agency. The task of defining quality and finding ways to measure it is one in which many artists and social scientists must join, bringing with them a variety of experimental approaches. This work calls for the creation of a number of social science centers devoted to the behavioral analysis of the arts, and the pioneers in it should receive their primary financial backing from imaginative and risk-oriented foundations and universities.

How might such researchers proceed? The method suggested here is not the only way. It is no more than a first attack on the problem. It is of less concern that this method be adopted than that it demonstrate the feasibility of what has been, until now, widely regarded as impossible.

It must be emphasized also that the desire to measure quality does not, by any means, imply a dogmatic approach to the "content" of quality. It does not stem from a univalued aesthetic system. The method proposed here does not assert that abstract painting is always either good or bad, or that the theater of the absurd is necessarily awful. It certainly does not imply that government should legitimate certain schools of art or officially derogate others. That the system could conceivably be used for such purposes is true—but only in the same sense that any technique can be used for evil purposes. What the system *can* do is provide a common language for debate over cultural issues so that proponents of different value systems can, at least, agree on the facts. If it did nothing more, the system could effect a bracing change, a healthy clearing of the cultural air.

If one turns to the writings of artists, critics, and most philosophers on the subject of artistic excellence or, more broadly, cultural "quality," one comes away with a jumble of subjective assertions, conflicting speculations, and semantic tangles. There is no universally—or even widely—accepted definition of the term "quality" with respect to the arts. We must begin, therefore, by constructing a provisional definition, bearing in mind that it should be, when we are finished, a practical definition, one that will prove useful to social policy-makers, either private or public.

In constructing such a definition, we shall start by assuming that quality is not a single, irreducible entity, but a shifting combination of factors. What, then, are these factors? We might begin the task of isolating them by trying to imagine a "high-quality culture."

Imagine a society whose cultural output was (1) copious, (2) richly varied, (3) technically outstanding, and (4) marked by many works of excellence. Imagine further that a significant portion of this output represented (5) contemporary creative work, as distinguished from performances or reproductions of the finest works of the past. Assume that much of this output was also (6) of such high complexity that it required (7) a considerably sophisticated audience. Now imagine that a large and sophisticated audience did exist and, morever, that it was (8) growing in size and that it was (9) highly committed to cultural activities. Imagine there to be (10) a vast amateur movement providing a training ground for both artists and audience. And assume further that the institutions of art, such as museums, theaters, and arts centers, were (11) geographically decentralized, and increasing in number, size, and the efficiency with which they disseminated the work of artists to the public. Suppose that artists in this society were (12) held in high esteem by the public, (1) well remunerated, and that (14) among them were men of undoubted genius. Finally, imagine that the artistic products of this society were (15) consistently applauded in other countries around the globe.

Looking at such a society, might one not draw certain conclusions about its cultural life? Might one not be justified in referring to its high quality?

We might easily argue about the weight to be given to one or another of these factors in forming our judgment. We might wish to add or subtract a factor or two. Nevertheless, it seems to me that even the most unreasonable critics would regard such a society as having a thriving artistic life. Let us, therefore, label this, for our purposes, a "high-quality culture."

QUALITY INDICATORS

Next, let us look more closely at these factors. They are quite varied and comprehensive. Yet all have one thing in common: they are all, to one degree or another, *measurable* phenomena. Some can be measured with relative precision. Others permit of only rough approximations. Yet all can be reduced to quantitative statements. Taking these factors one at a time, let us see how.

(1) We began by describing cultural output in our imaginary society as "copious." When we speak of cultural output we refer to the production of books and classical-music recordings, performances of plays and musicals, operas, ballets, concerts of orchestral or chamber music, art exhibitions, and the like. These are discrete things or events, and are relatively simple to tot up. We can say, for example, that American theaters last year gave X thousand performances. The data requirements described above include numerous measures of quantity of output on which to base a judgment as to whether or not output is "copious."

(2) The next adjective used in describing the imaginary high-quality culture was "richly varied." It is here that the problem of output-classification rears its head. We need to devise classifications of the output of each branch of the culture industry that will reveal, among other things, the degree of variety in that output. If we are referring to theater, for example, we shall want to go beyond the traditional breakdown into "plays" and "musicals"; we shall want to classify each unit of output, whether a performance or a production, into "professional" or "amateur." We shall want to know how many performances, for example, were devoted to seventeenth-, eighteenth-, or nineteenth-century or contemporary drama; how many are tragedies, how many comedies; how many American in origin, how many English, French or other. We might further subdivide into "farce" or "situation comedy," into works of social or political commentary, fantasy, and realism. The finer our system of output-classification, the better we shall be able to gauge variety.

With respect to the visual arts we need to classify output not merely according to whether an exhibition is "special" or "permanent" but according to the school of art represented, whether pre-Raphaelite or pop, cubist, kinetic, or mixed. The same might be said of music. The problem of defining categories will not be simple, but it is by no means impossible. The fact that many works are borderline cases and that skilled judgment may be needed in assigning a work to one or another category or in establishing new categories does not rule out the possibility. The art of classification is already highly developed in museums. There is no reason why it cannot also be developed to the same level in the other arts.

To determine whether the nation's cultural output is diverse or not then becomes a relatively simple matter. It is not necessary to collect data on every single performance or work of art in the country. Rather, it is possible to construct a sampling procedure that would, at regular intervals, check the output of a cross-section of artistic institutions. This is already done in the field of music by the American Society of Composers, Authors, and Publishers, and Broadcast Music, Inc., both of which monitor and log the musical output of radio and television stations in order to enforce royalty payments to their members. The creation of a cross-sectional panel of arts institutions and a system for monitoring the output of both the amateur and professional sector is quite feasible technically. This done, it becomes possible to determine the degree to which cultural output can be regarded as "richly varied."

(3) We next come to the phrase "technically outstanding." By this we mean that the work displays high competence in the purely technical sense. Are the musicians playing the right notes? Are the pirouettes clean? Is the acting skilled? Is the novel filled with clichés and bad transitions? These are matters that can most easily be judged by an artist's peers, and there are broad areas within which a panel of peers would be able to agree. The technical level of our cultural output could, thus, be submitted to carefully assembled panels for technical review. These panels might consist of artists and, perhaps, critics, who would be asked to judge a sampling of output and to render a judgment in quantitative terms. The model for this, too, already exists in the way pianists, for example, are scored in certain artistic competitions. Using such a system, or a modification of it, it becomes possible to measure technical proficiency in quite specific and statistically manipulable terms.

(4) One of the characteristics of this imaginary society is that its cultural output includes many works of excellence. There are no rigid criteria of excellence, certainly none that meet with universal approval. Nonetheless, each years, of the thousands of new novels published, a few survive the critical discussion conducted by both reviewers and readers, and come to stand as works of excellence. The same is true of plays, works of sculpture, musical compositions, and the like. History may later reverse the verdict, but for the time being, they take on a special significance.

Over a period of years, they come to be republished, or reproduced on the stage; they are quoted; they become a standard against which newer works are judged. There are many mechanisms by which the process is formalized—award programs, for example. But the decision as to whether a work is "excellent" or not is, in the end, made by consensus.

This may be a thoroughly inadequate system for judging excellence, but it is the chief method upon which we now rely. Recognizing all its shortcomings, we can nevertheless put it to work in a more systematic fashion in measuring the excellence of cultural output. It is thus possible systematically to monitor a representative sampling of reviews and critical essays, make content analyses of them for all references to individual works of art, and derive from this categorization of these works as "bad," "good," or "excellent."

Since in real life the process of consensus involves more than just professional critics, this categorization can be matched against several other factors. One might be the degree to which audience response concurred with that of the critics, a phenomenon at least roughly measurable in terms of attendance figures, copies of books purchased, and similar statistics. (Popularity, while by no means a determining factor, would thus be given some weight.) Critics and consumers having been given their say, artists, too, must be consulted. Thus, one factor might be the frequency with which other artists cite a work as a creative source or influence.

It is even possible to strengthen the procedure by building in a baseline. This could be done by asking appropriate panels to rank-order a series of artists—say, Bach-Mozart-Brahms-Berlioz-Johann Strauss—in terms of over-all excellence. Having done this, the panels grading current musical output could be asked to relate the categorization derived from content analysis to the Bach-to-Strauss scale.

This naïve procedure can be made as sophisticated as we like. Thus, the term "over-all excellence" implies a unidimensional conception of excellence. It is possible, however, to break this down into component dimensions. One might, for example, devise different lists of rank-ordered artists for such dimensions as "originality" or "structural complexity." These would provide more refined standards against which to measure contemporary output, and might, in fact, be further subdivided.

From such analysis, it becomes possible to classify the individual works in a selected universe as "excellent" or "not excellent." The ratio of excellent works to the total becomes a clue to the frequency with which excellence occurs in the society's total artistic output.

Admittedly, these are groping and highly imperfect methods for dealing with the subtle and difficult problem of excellence, but they represent at least one reasonably objective technique that permits us to take this factor into account in assessing a society's over-all cultural performance. No doubt, other ways can be found, too.

(5) We next spoke of the society's output of contemporary creative work as distinct from presentations of the works of the past. A culture industry that did nothing but disseminate the great works of previous centuries and other nations, no matter how copious, varied, or proficient its output, could be accused of drawing too heavily on its reserves and foreign

credit. We might legitimately expect any society with a "quality" culture to be producing new creative works of its own. (Creative here is not used as a qualitative judgment, but in the purely descriptive sense in which it is commonly used to differentiate between the creative and performing arts.) If output is classified as suggested above, it becomes quite simple to develop contemporary-non-contemporary or native-foreign ratios. Some efforts along this line have already been made with respect to orchestral programming, and indicate what can be done elsewhere. The degree to which a society is producing and disseminating new creative work thus also becomes measurable.

(6) We run into a more difficult problem when we speak of the complexity of the output and the need for sophisticated audience. When we speak of complexity we refer to structural complication of the kind that differentiates *Cantata 140* from *Mary's Little Lamb* or the poems of Gerard Manley Hopkins from those of Edgar Guest. Complexity in certain art forms is objectively determinable. Thus, for example, the complexity of music can probably be measured with mathematical precision by computer. In drama, literature, or the visual arts, it becomes far more difficult. The entire subject of complexity in art demands extended treatment not possible here. Yet at this point, too, a panel of competent critics, asked to rank various works in terms of complexity, could be expected to reach substantial agreement at least on works at both ends of the scale. Even a crude system of categorization would make it possible to measure higher or lower levels of complexity in the works being offered to the public.

(7) Sophistication of audience can be defined in various ways, but the ability to derive pleasure from works of high structural complexity is at least one index. Thus, the development of complexity measures makes possible some assessment of audience sophistication, since it then becomes possible to measure size of audience for works at varying levels of difficulty.

(8) In speaking of our imaginary society, we referred to a growing audience. Given the kind of attendance and consumption statistics suggested above, it becomes simple to determine whether the audience is growing or not, and even to do this by output-classification.

(9) The degree of "commitment" of the audience to artistic activity, whether as active amateurs or as spectators, can be measured, too. Commitment is a subjective matter, but it manifests itself in outward behavior. The decision, for example, to purchase a book or a pair of tickets to a chamber music recital is equally a decision *not* to purchase something else. It represents an allocation of consumer resources, a choice. It is not unfair to suggest that high expenditure, as a percentage of individual income, is a measure of high commitment. To the degree that this is true, we can measure commitment in economic terms. However, the allocation of money is only one

indication of commitment. Another, and perhaps more important, indicator is the commitment of time. Taken together, high expenditure relative to income and high investment of time, suggest high commitment. Given appropriate data about culture consumers, we have ways to measure, at least crudely, degree of commitment.

(10) The size of the amateur movement, and the degree to which it feeds artists and consumers to the professional sector, can be determined by fairly conventional census-type research and can be treated statistically.

(11) The degree of decentralization and the number and size of institutions are similarly determinable by conventional means. The question of efficiency can be approached through comparative economic data. Efficiency obviously cannot be measured in quantitative terms alone. The expenditure of $200,000 to permit 200,000 people to see a bad play at a cost of $1.00 per head is not necessarily more efficient than $200,000 spent to permit 100,000 people see a good play at a cost of $2.00 per head. In few fields are qualitative measures more critical. Yet, through an extension of the techniques described above, it becomes possible to classify institutions according to the quality range within which they customarily operate. It is possible, therefore, to measure economic inputs against output measured in terms of both quantity *and* quality. Moreover, it becomes possible to arrive at estimates of what, at least in economic terms, it ordinarily costs to achieve given levels of quality in each branch of cultural activity.

(12) The degree to which artists are held in esteem by the public is measurable through well-developed techniques for the prestige-ranking of occupations.

(13) The level of remuneration of artists is measurable in simple economic terms, and the implementation of the data-collection system suggested above provides the necessary data. In determining what is "high" or "low" remuneration, comparisons can be made with median income figures for the total society and with the artist-income to median-income ratios of other societies.

(14) The problem of "genius" is, like that of excellence, far more difficult. The appearance of genius is highly unpredictable. Yet there are ways to cope rationally even with this. Despite conflicting theories of art, despite great confusion over aesthetic values, it is possible here, too, to reach wide consensus. Thus, for example, there is today widespread agreement that Frank Lloyd Wright, Charles Chaplin, or Pablo Picasso deserve the label "creative genius." Various attempts have been made in other fields to arrive at objective measures of outstanding individual performance. Thus, scientists have been ranked by the number of publications attributed to them, by the frequency with which their papers are quoted, and the like.[4]

---

[4] Derek J. de Solla Price, *Little Science, Big Science* (New York: Columbia University Press, 1963), chap. ii.

In the arts, it is possible to devise similar measures—a combination, perhaps, of frequency of citation as a source by other artists; awards won, for example, the Nobel Prize; and assessments made by peers and by the public. There is nothing, in principle, that prevents the formulation of a definition of genius based partly on consensus and partly on other objective and measurable data. Once this is done, it becomes theoretically possible to measure its presence or absence.

(15) Finally, in describing our imaginary society, we referred to the applause which its artistic works attract in other countries. This, too, is, an objectively measurable phenomenon. The State Department carefully screens the foreign press, radio, and television. There is no reason why a continuing index of foreign reaction to the arts of the United States could not be devised. In part, this might be based on content analysis of criticism published or broadcast abroad. When an American ballet troupe dances abroad, when an American art exhibit is shown or a novel translated, it is routinely subjected to criticism by both audience and reviewers. Foreign reactions to American art can be gauged by systematically analyzing this response. It can also be measured in terms of prizes or awards won by Americans at major international competitions such as the Venice Biennale, the Tschaikovsky Piano and Violin Festival, and similar events, not to speak of the Nobel Prize. In short, foreign response to American art and artists is also measurable by fairly conventional techniques.

THE SYMBOLS OF QUALITY

Bertram M. Gross writes in "The State of the Nation":

> Some phenomena cannot be directly quantified. We cannot make direct measurements of human satisfactions or of the quantity of certain intangible services. But we can get quantitative measures by using what I call "surrogates." These are indirect indicators that serve as quantitative substitutes for, or representatives of, the phenomena we want to measure.[5]

This, in essence, is what I have proposed here for dealing with the issue of cultural quality.

If it is agreed that "quality" is an aggregate of many factors, and if we can then define these factors in ways that permit measurement, we arrive at a way to measure the "surrogates" or symbols of quality. The question of which factors should go into such a computation is one about which there might—and should—be lively debate. For the factors add up to a definition, and a definition, once widely accepted, takes on a compelling force of its

---

[5] Bertram M. Gross, "The State of the Nation," in Raymond Bauer (ed.), *Social Indicators* (Cambridge, Mass.: The M.I.T. Press, 1966), p. 267.

own. I have tentatively defined "cultural quality" as consisting of fifteen factors. But other factors might be employed instead, and quite a different definition arrived at.

Thus, we might wish to evaluate our cultural output along quite different parameters. We might wish to measure art publications circulated per thousand of the population, or the ratio of hours spent at "live" performances as against those spent in the enjoyment of vicarious or electronically transmitted art. We might want to compare hours spent in active participation in the arts as amateur actors, singers, painters, and the like, with hours spent as spectators at professional events. We might wish to devise some over-all measure of what might be described as the "artistically engaged" population as a percentage of the total population.

The fifteen factors I have suggested here as the surrogates of quality are thus only a few of the many that are possible. I do not offer them as a package. I have used them to illustrate an approach to the problems of measurement, rather than to "sell" any particular definition of "cultural quality."

In fact, not only should there be sharp debate over which factors to be included, but also over the weight given to each factor. Some may wish to place special emphasis on the measures of excellence and genius; others, more socially minded them aesthetically concerned, might wish to weigh heavily such factors as size of audience. This method does not dictate the relative weights of the various factors, but merely provides a well-lighted arena for conflict.

Similarly, there is room for vigorous content over the specification, with respect to each factor, of satisfactory levels of attainment. Thus, it is necessary to specify *how much* diversity adds up to "richly varied," or *how high* one sets the criteria for excellence or genius. The system proposed here, therefore, does not eliminate the need for value judgments to be made; instead, it clarifies the alternatives and takes the discussion of quality down from the lofty level of rhetorical abstraction to that of concrete reality. It becomes a practical tool for policy-making.

Unquestionably, each of these factors is no more than a partial and, no doubt, unreliable indicator of the quality of our cultural life. Yet it can safely be argued that the sum of these measures will be a truer index than any single indicator. I would contend that, even if one or another measure is insufficiently refined, the over-all picture that such a system could give us would be better, more accurate, and far more useful than anything we now have.

The system proposed here suffers from many shortcomings. It is easier, for example, to keep tabs on the output of continuing, established institutions than on the output of ephemeral or *ad hoc* avant garde groupings. Yet such groups may, in the long run, turn out to be extremely important. It relies heavily, though not completely, on data reported by institutions. Yet it is important to find out what is happening in the interstices, so to speak, between institutions. There is a wide variety of informal artistic activities which, in sum, may be highly important and which this system is probably insufficiently discriminating to detect. The system does not, moreover, begin to answer such questions as why one person becomes a concert pianist while another, perhaps equally talented, settles for teaching. It does not probe deeply at all into audience motivation. One might list many other such inadequacies.

Nevertheless, a beginning needs to be made. A cultural data system providing the kind of information suggested above and incorporating quality indicators would, I believe, serve the purposes outlined earlier by providing insight into the processes of social change, by making it possible for decision-makers to weigh the cultural consequences of their behavior, by raising the level of political discussion about the arts, and by improving the efficiency of management in the arts. Moreover, as the pieces of this system come into being, some created by government agencies, others by researchers in universities and elsewhere, one could go much further. Once we have had an opportunity to study the interplay of factors, it should also become possible to predict changes in one by changes in another. This means that we might learn exactly what conditions are necessary to raise or lower each variable. One may not be able to predict the appearance of genius or of some great creative stroke, but, using such a model, it may well become possible to predict the changes in one or another variable that would increase our society's output of cultural excellence. And in this may lie the final justification of the cultural data system idea.

Art is intimately tied to the society, more complexly now, perhaps, than at any time since the rise of industrial society. It is reasonable to study these ties, so that we may better serve whatever values we hold highest. A cultural data system is the basic tool for such a study. The system described here is a rickety, primitive version of the tools that we shall have in the future. But it is a start.

There are several practical steps to be taken to make this "start" real. We need to pull together all the scattered and fragmentary data that now exist, and begin weaving them into an integrated fabric. The Census Bureau needs to begin, even now, preparing for a census of the arts by forming an advisory committee on cultural statistics. The National Foundation on the Arts and Humanities can play a catalytic role by bringing artists and social scientists together in conference— an unprecedented step that should prove stimulating to both groups. Funds, whether from the National Foundation or from the great private foundations, need to be provided for those, like a group at the University of Wisconsin, who are already eager to get on with the work. The National Foundation might also organize a committee on research standards and a clearinghouse for research findings, so that those engaged in the work can best take advantage of each other's discoveries.

But whatever steps are taken first, the important thing is to take them. For the sake of the arts, for the sake of society—and for the sake of those who prefer reason to rhetoric in our discussions of the arts—this system, or some modification of it, should be brought into being. Without it, no broader system of social accounting can claim to be complete.

FOUR

SOCIAL PROBLEMS

12

POVERTY,
INEQUALITY, AND CONFLICT

S. M. MILLER, MARTIN REIN,
PAMELA ROBY, AND BERTRAM M. GROSS

The acceptable term "poverty" has become the way of discussing the more disturbing issue of inequality. "Poverty" has not been fully recognized as the shorthand for a much broader idea because the historic subsistence connotations of the term "poverty" still survive. The result is that we have furious debates which fail to clarify issues. For some, it will come as a shock to learn that their words are the prose of inequality; for others, their statements will surprise them when parsed into nineteenth-century sensibilities about pauperism.

The "discovery" of poverty in the United States did not take place because part of the population lived in worse circumstances than before. Some of those characterized as poor do live in as difficult conditions as the poor of previous generations, but, by and large, that is not the situation of "poverty" today. Some of our contemporary "poor" live on diets or in shelter inadequate for physical survival, but that is far from typical. Nor are most of those characterized as "in poverty," paupers or dependents whose only financial support comes from government.

Nonetheless, worsened conditions, threatened physical survival, and pauperism, singly or together, characterize the historic concern with poverty. In low-income societies, physical survival is often threatened; in nineteenth-century England, pauperism was the focus; in the desperate depression of the 1930's in the United States, a decline in living standards was the issue.

Today, these are not the main issues within the high-income industrial societies. The growing and groping concern with poverty in these societies is a consequence of revelations about inequality. The euphoria of economic growth following World War II overwhelmed doubts about the emphasis on materialism. Economic justice was not an issue, as there was confidence that all in society, especially those at the bottom, were benefiting from expansion. The bigger economic pie was being cut so that the bottommost groups received larger slices.

Gradually, a disturbing recognition upset affluent complacency. The problems of those at the bottom had not been eradicated. The proportion of national income going to the bottommost group has probably not increased in the United States or in most other economies. New forms of division and stratification may be emerging. A man's having a car or a washing machine does not assure that he is a full citizen of society, nor that his children have equal access to decent jobs or education, nor that he lives in decent housing.

Obviously, this kind of "poverty" is different. It is relative deprivation, a comparative position of losing out, that characterizes those who are termed "poor" in the affluent society. The historic term of "poverty," once applied to low-income families in industrializing societies, is found wanting when stretched to the highly industrialized society.

"Poverty," then, has ushered in the issue of inequalities in the affluent society. The ancient term, with its imagery of eliminating starvation and rags, cloaks the new agenda of reducing disparities and inequities. The discussants of poverty are divided on the important questions of which kinds of issues are important and how wide the gap between groups must be before it can be deemed significant.

To be deeply and frontally concerned about relativities is to address oneself to the nature of the divisions and stratifications in society: How large should the divisions be among various groups in society? What are the bases of monetary and status rewards? In what ways can the mechanisms that disburse rewards be changed? In attempting to obtain these changes, how much controversy and agitations to get these changes is desirable or acceptable?

But not all agree on this new agenda; some argue for the desirability of placing the income poverty line at a low level in order to discourage dependency or governmental activity which interfers with market forces. Nonetheless, even proponents of these latter approaches have some concern with relativities. They adjust the income poverty line to changes in the general standard of living, though at a slower rate then those who would more frankly embrace a relative approach.

The social welfare term "poverty" does not incur the disturbance aroused by the political term "inequality." But the ambiguity of our use of "poverty" is preventing the full-scale examination of the issues of inequality: Who gets what? Who does and should benefit from government subsidization? What shape do we wish the income and social profiles of this country to have?

These are difficult questions producing acrimonious debate. Obviously, adherence to the historic view of poverty will lead to a set of indicators which is inadequate for the depiction of the course of inequalities. Futhermore, it is much easier to show progress in social achievement when a fixed income line is employed as a poverty standard; if standards were based upon relativities, we could have the politically embarrassing situation of nonexistent progress. The lack of progress measured by these indicators of inequality would lead many policy officials to argue for a different concept of poverty. Policy critics, however, would advocate the use of these indicators and the augmentation of resources which go to the underclass. *Thus, the conceptualizations of problems can mold policy objectives and constraints.*

This conclusion argues for the importance of having multiple conceptualizations and producers of social indicators. In our view, not all users of indicators have the same needs: indicators can be used for spotting problems and unmet needs, detecting trends and their changes, or assessing policies. Much of the contemporary discussion of indicators is in terms of the policy operators, not the outsiders—the independent, external, critical groups. The needs of official agencies for social indicators of poverty may be different, for example, from those of civil rights groups. Our concern in this essay is to look at the poverty and inequality issues more from the perspectives of nongovernmental groups than from those of official agencies.[1]

In studying social indicators, two perspectives are possible: one moves from the problem to needed indicators; the other, the assessment of current policies, moves from programs to indicators. Because of space limitations, we are viewing poverty in terms of the problems rather than the programs. Both perspectives are needed.

POVERTY—AN INCOME OR SOCIAL CONDITION?

Much of the current discussion of poverty is posed in terms of an income line: How many families and individuals are living below this line, adjusted for family size and other conditions? At what rate is this number being reduced? The availability of these figures and the historic view of

---

[1] We will not discuss the inequalities which affect other than low-income groups, for example, youth, women, and minority groups.

poverty in terms of pauperism lead to the emphasis on the income figures. But income is only *one* of the dimensions of poverty and inequality today.

In the last third of this century, we need new approaches to the quality of life in every country. We suggest that *a minimum approach by government in any society with significant inequalities must provide for rising minimum levels not only of incomes, assets, and basic services, but also of self-respect and opportunities for social mobility and participation in many forms of decision-making.*

The approach which we suggest broadens the economic perspective from a narrow concern with "income." The starting point is Titmuss' conceptualization of income as the "command over resources over time."[2] This moves us to a growing concern with assets as disguised income and as the source of future income (pensions) and with services as an increasingly important ingredient of a standard of life. But even this expanded perspective fails to measure all the concerns that we have today in dealing with poverty and inequality. The concern is also with the individual's political role, the opportunities for his children, and his self-respect. This broadened view of "the command over resources" requires us to range beyond the economic. Many of the hesitations about "the war on poverty" in the United States have occurred because it has been viewed through an exceedingly narrow income lens. Poverty is not only a condition of economic insufficiency; it is also social and political exclusion.[3]

The general position which we espouse in this paper is that income alone is an inadequate indicator of level of living. Movement along the varied dimensions of well-being is not always synchronized—advance or loss along one dimension does not necessarily means that similar movement occurs on the other dimensions. For example, although the current income of two families may be the same, the level of living of one may be vastly below that of the other because of the families' different housing conditions.

We frequently refer in the following analysis to the poorest of the poor, for we suspect that their conditions are more difficult than that of the rest of the poor and that their interests, by and large, are neglected in current discussions of poverty programs.

---

2 Richard M. Titmuss, *Income Distribution and Social Change* (London: G. Allen and Unwin, 1962) and *Essays on the Welfare State* (New Haven, Conn.: Yale University Press, 1958). See also Bertram Gross (ed.), *Action under Planning* (New York: McGraw-Hill, 1966), chap. vii. This approach has been expanded by Bertram Gross and S. M. Miller in an unpublished paper.

3 See S. M. Miller and Frank Riessman, "The New Income," *Social Class and Social Policy* (New York: Basic Books, forthcoming). Also, S. M. Miller and Pamela Roby, "Class, Status, and Power Revisited," a paper presented to the American Sociological Association, San Francisco, August 1967.

We shall discuss, then, six dimensions of well-being—income, assets, basic services, education and social mobility, political position, and status and self-respect. The longest discussion concerns income because there is a complicated literature of immediate policy significance in this area. But we do not mean to minimize thereby the other neglected dimensions of well-being.

INCOMES

Most discussions of poverty center about the income line or level which differentiates the poor from the non-poor. How to define that line is obviously important, but two other aspects are also important. These are the stability and the source of income. Because the source of individuals' incomes affects their social honor, it will be discussed under the section on status.

LEVEL

There are three basic approaches to defining an adequate level of income. The first defines poverty thresholds in relation to a cost-of-living budget estimate. This is the "poverty line" approach which marks current policy. The second defines the adequacy level in relation to mean or median family income for the United States. The third views poverty in terms of the share of total national income going to the bottom 10, 20, or 30 per cent of the population.

BUDGET-ORIENTED APPROACHES

Obviously, the line which separates the poor from the nonpoor or the poorer from the poor is not clear-cut. A fundamental issue is delineating the cutoff point between the poor and the others is whether poverty is to be considered as barest survival or as inadequacy in terms of prevailing standards. A second issue that veers into the technical is how many gradations and modifications should be made for varying conditions (family size and composition, regional cost differences, and the like) which affect the assessment of need.

Within the budget-oriented approaches, wide variations exist in the placement of the poverty line. Obviously, the aim is to provide an "adequate" level of income; immediately, the issue then becomes "adequate for what?" An income level that permits a family to "survive" is one thing; an income level that brings families closer to prevailing standards is quite another; and an income level that provides a stimulus for social mobility, a great concern of the war on poverty, is probably still another. Where the line is drawn will deeply affect the number and characteristics of those who are defined as "poor." And it will as deeply affect the assessment of failure or success in poverty-reduction efforts.

We believe that poverty lines based upon budget-oriented approaches will continue to be inadequate because of the deep political implications which each upward adjustment involves. Although a budget-based poverty line may be rapidly falling farther behind the rising standard of living enjoyed by the rest of the population, it will not be adjusted upward until that change appears politically feasible. For this reason, we believe that, in the United States, it is more appropriate to use the comparative approach to poverty (for instance, to define families as suffering from income poverty if they are below one-half of the nation's median income) or to view poverty in terms of the income share going to units in the lower end of the income distribution.[4] In this way, the criteria delineating the poor would automatically be shifted upward with the general society's rising level of living and would be more independent of political issues.

COMPARATIVE INCOME

What is the scope and character of poverty when we move from budget-oriented approaches to a comparative approach? In this procedure, median or mean family income for the United States is taken as the standard; the poverty line is 50 per cent of the standard, and the line for the poorest of the poor could be 33 to 25 per cent of the standard.[5] This approach openly embraces the notion that a poverty condition is a relative phenomenon—the poor are those who have fallen behind the grades and standards of the society as a whole, as Galbraith stated.[6]

---

[4] Of course, the comparative or income share approaches would be inadequate in countries in which a large proportion of the population is living at or beneath a minimum subsistence level.

[5] The median is the point which breaks a distribution in half: 50 per cent of the population is above the point, 50 per cent below. The mean is the conventional average; all incomes are totaled and then divided by the number of incomes. The mean 1962 family income was $8,151; the median family income was $5,747.

[6] John K. Galbraith, The Affluent Society (Boston: Houghton Mifflin, 1958).

TABLE 1—Percentage of U. S. Families Classified as Poor by
Relative and Absolute Standards, 1947–1960

Year	Median Income (1959) dollars)	Percentage of Families with Income		
		Less than one-half the median†	Less than $3,000 (1959 prices)	Less than $2,000 (1959 prices)
1947	3,957	19.0	33.9	19.1
1948	3,868	19.4	34.7	19.8
1949	3,807	20.1	35.9	21.3
1950	4,036	20.0	33.0	19.8
1951	4,164	19.0	30.9	17.9
1952	4,277	19.0	29.3	17.8
1953	4,627	19.9	27.1	16.8
1954	4,530	20.7	28.7	18.1
1955	4,817	19.9	25.9	16.0
1956	5,129	19.5	23.6	14.2
1957	5,148	20.0	23.5	14.2
1958	5,143	19.9	23.8	14.1
1959	5,417	19.9	22.7	13.4
1960	5,547	20.2	22.1	13.2

†Estimated by interpolation.
Source: Victor R. Fuchs, "Toward a Theory of Poverty," in Task Force on Economic Growth and Opportunity, The Concept of Poverty (Washington, D.C.: Chamber of Commerce of the United States, 1965).

Using the standard of 50 per cent of median family income, the poverty line was $2,774 in 1960.[7] Twenty per cent of the nation's families in 1960 were living below this level, that is, they were "in poverty." This contrasts with Orshansky's figure, which showed 24 per cent of 1960 households in poverty, and converges with the Council of Economic Advisors' approach, which found that 20 per cent of the country's families had incomes below $3,000 (1962 prices) in 1960.[8]

The trend data are particularly striking: *the median income standard shows that the percentage of poor has not declined since 1947.* Between

[7] Victor R. Fuchs, "Toward a Theory of Poverty," in Task Force on Economic Growth and Opportunity, The Concept of Poverty (Washington, D.C.: Chamber of Commerce of the United States, 1965), p. 75.

[8] In 1965, 19 per cent of all households (families and unrelated individuals) were poor, according to the Social Security Administration's poverty-income standard. See The Annual Report of the Council of Economic Advisors (Washington, D.C.: U.S. Government Printing Office, 1967), p. p. 40.

1947 and 1960, as shown in Table 1, although families with incomes less than $3,000 (1959 prices) declined from 33.9 per cent to 20.2 per cent, families with incomes less than one-half the median increased from 19 per cent to 20.2 per cent.

POVERTY AS INCOME SHARE

A third way of looking at the income component of poverty is in terms of the share of total national income that goes to the bottom 10, 20, or 30 per cent. In this approach, poverty is simply regarded as inequality. It is the income fate of a specific group at the bottom of society that is the issue. Obviously, from this perspective, we cannot have trends in the numbers and percentages of poor. The question instead will be: How well is the bottom group doing? (Some critics of poverty efforts have not always understood that talking about poverty as income share prevents talking about trends in the extent of poverty).

Data on the size distribution of income are available, but not in great detail. The discouraging report, as shown in Table 2, is that the percentage

TABLE 2—Distribution of Total Money Income Received by Each Fifth and the Top 5 Per cent of Families and Unrelated Individuals, 1947 to 1962

Year	Total	Census (Total Money Income)					
		Lowest fifth	Second fifth	Middle fifth	Fourth fifth	Highest fifth	Top 5 per cent
1962	100.0	3.3	10.5	17.3	24.6	44.2	17.3
1961	100.0	3.3	10.0	17.0	24.5	45.2	18.2
1960	100.0	3.4	10.3	17.4	24.4	44.5	17.9
1959	100.0	3.4	10.4	17.6	24.3	44.3	17.6
1958	100.0	3.5	10.7	17.8	24.6	43.4	16.9
1957	100.0	3.5	10.8	18.0	24.7	43.1	16.8
1956	100.0	3.4	10.6	17.5	24.5	44.0	17.5
1955	100.0	3.3	10.6	17.4	24.6	44.2	18.0
1954	100.0	3.1	10.2	17.5	24.7	44.5	17.7
1953	100.0	3.2	10.8	17.5	24.6	43.9	17.6
1952	100.0	3.5	10.7	17.2	24.0	44.6	18.9
1951	100.0	3.5	11.2	17.5	24.3	43.6	17.6
1950	100.0	3.2	10.4	17.2	24.1	45.1	18.2
1949	100.0	3.3	10.5	17.1	24.1	45.0	17.9
1948	100.0	3.6	10.7	17.1	23.9	44.8	18.1
1947	100.0	3.6	10.6	16.7	23.5	45.6	18.8

Source: Herman P. Miller, *Income Distribution in the United States* (A 1960 Census Monograph; Washington, D.C.: U.S. Government Printing Office, for the United States Bureau of the Census, 1966), p. 21.

of total money income going to the bottom 20 per cent of families and unrelated individuals has hovered between 3 and 4 per cent since 1947. Total money income going to the lowest quintile declined from 3.6 per cent in 1947 and 1948 to 3.3 per cent in 1961 and 1962. Over the years from 1950 to 1960, the share fluctuated from 3.1 per cent to 3.5 per cent, but never attained the 3.6 per cent of 1947 and 1948.[9] Great progress has not been made in increasing the share of the bottom 20 per cent, despite the decline in the share of the top 5 per cent. Indeed, the earlier focusing on the revolution in which all Americans were partaking of economic expansion.[10]

Which families are most likely to be in the bottom levels of the nation's income distribution? The University of Michigan Survey Research Center's Reports on Consumer Finances show that, in 1964, 42 per cent of the South, as compared with 24 or 25 per cent of other regions, had aggregate family incomes falling within the nation's bottom three income deciles. Of the aged (persons aged 65 and over), 28 per cent fell within the lowest deciles and two-thirds within the lowest three deciles of the nation's income distribution. Twenty-four per cent of nonwhite as compared with 9 per cent of white families had incomes falling within the bottom decile, and 58 per cent of nonwhite families in contrast to 27 per cent of white families fell within the bottom 30 per cent of the nation's income distribution.[11]

The data on income shares should be much more detailed so that it would be possible to compare what is happening to various groups (aged, employed, minority groups, and the like) of the poor within cities of varying size, in regions, and in urban-rural areas. We especially need information on the income shares of Negroes by place of residence, age, and employment status, for it is clear that the problem of Negroes is not only

---

[9] The slight decline in the percentage of income held by the bottom quintile may be accounted for by the changing composition of households. A much greater percentage of aged poor live alone now then ten years ago. This change increases the percentage of low-income households. The shares received by the middle and fourth quintiles rose between 1947 and 1962 while the percentage of total money income held by the highest quintile declined—Herman P. Miller, *Income Distribution in the United States* (A 1960 Census Monograph; Washington, D.C.: U.S. Government Printing Office, for the United States Bureau of the Census, 1966), p. 21.

[10] A technical aside: Economic statisticians, despite their inventiveness, have failed to innovate new measures of income inequality. The Gini coefficient, the most popular tool for estimating inequality in income distribution, is not sensitive to the question of which points in the distribution suffer most from inequality. New measures of inequality are needed for the more complicated concerns of today. One example is top-bottom ratios which compare the share of the top income group—for instance, the upper tenth—with the share of the bottom group. For a useful approach, see Harry T. Oshima, "The International Comparison of Size Distribution of Family Incomes, with Special Reference to Asia," *Review of Economics and Statistics*, 44 (1962). Bruce Russett has done some interesting work in probing different approaches to inequality measurement.

[11] Survey Research Center, University of Michigan, *1965 Survey of Consumer Finances* (Ann Arbor: University of Michigan Press, 1966), Tables 1-5, p. 19.

achieving a better level of living but also reducing the gap between them and the rest of society. As American society turns more squarely to the issues of inequality, better and more detailed information on income shares will be needed.

PERSPECTIVES ON INCOME LINES

Is there one best way of measuring the extent of and trends in poverty? Can these various approaches be reduced to one? We doubt it. In part, this is because different interest groups prefer various ways of thinking about poverty. Those concerned with economic growth in the context of price stability would move toward definitions of poverty along a compressed budget approach; civil rights groups would focus on the income share going to Negroes. Behind these different orientations and stresses is the uncertainty about what poverty means in the affluent society.

In our view, budget-oriented approaches are inadequate. The better ones, like Orshansky's, sneak in relative issues under the guise of absolute standards. Since our outlook is to avoid ambiguity, and since we believe that, over the long run, forthright discussion of issues best meets the needs of the underclass, we advocate clear-cut presentation of poverty data in terms of inequality.[12]

The inequality emphasis leads to concern with the bottom 20 per cent generally and the bottom 10 per cent particularly. It may be difficult to be concerned about the plight of persons within the bottom 20 per cent of the United States when their incomes would make them well off in many other societies. While we should not blind ourselves to the magnitude and severity of poverty in other nations, we should not thereby minimize the extent of the poverty problem in our midst.

STABILITY OF INCOME

Variations in income can be viewed in two ways: variation within a year and variations between years. The assured and stable income within a year of white-collar persons is becoming the principal income-differentiating dimension between them and blue-collar workers, who frequently earn higher incomes. The confidence that income is assured for all of the year is an important amenity apart from the level of income. White-collar workers' obtaining of income in predictable weekly or monthly amounts helps them to make decisions governing their activity.

---

[12] Note that a political theory is involved in the choice of ambiguity or clarity in depicting the extent of a problem. Our orientation, it should be noted, goes against the stance of most "successful" politicians.

To what extent the poor's income is stable over the year is unclear. Louis Ferman's notion of an "irregular economy" of the poor would suggest that even within the low level of income of the poor there are sizable gyrations in income levels. While some of the poor, like those on welfare, have a somewhat assured but low income, many have an uncertain and unpredictable income, dependent on economic circumstances and their wits. Data on the within-a-year income stream of various groups of the poor would be useful.

The variation of income over the years is obviously more important than the within-year changes.[13] Are the poor, no matter what income approach is used, the same group from year to year except for a relative few who escape? Or is the composition of poverty constantly changing with some falling and some more climbing out? Or do many of those who escape one year move up only as far as the near-poor level and then fall back into poverty? Is there a pullout-fallback syndrome with families moving back and forth across the poverty line, never much above or below?

Data gathered by the Survey Research Center (see Table 3) reveal considerable mobility between the bottom third and the other two-thirds. Of the spending unit heads aged fifty-five to sixty-four who had incomes in the bottom third in 1928, 51 per cent were in the bottom, 30 per cent in the middle, and 18 per cent in the top third in 1960. Obviously, there is much more income mobility than is implicit in most discussions of the poverty population. The question remains, however: "Who moved?" Did families at the bottom of the lowest third experience the same amount of mobility as those at the top of the third? Is there a low-income group who do not experience much improvement, while the rest of the poor in any year is made up of families who are temporarily in poverty?

There is great need for a longitudinal study of family income employing a cohort (the same group) that is studied over time with an over-sampling of the poor and near-poor. An important item in the study would be delineation of the factors in shifts in income. For example, to what extent has a family moved across the poverty line because of a demographic shift (for instance, a child marrying at the age of eighteen and leaving the family) which may not reflect great changes in family well-being? Or is movement out of poverty due to additional wage-earners, to income gains of the main wage-earner, or to improved transfer payments? Cohort analysis is probably the most important instrument for measuring family income and the other dimensions of well-being discussed below.

---

[13] Otis Dudley Duncan has redirected our attention to this problem. It is possible to conceptualize income poverty in terms of a lifetime rather than a year. In this perspective, the poor would be those families whose lifetime income is below a lifetime poverty-income line.

TABLE 3—Positions of Spending Unit Heads in Income Distributions of
Earlier Years: 1928–1960 (Expressed as Percentages)

	Group Aged 55 to 64 in Early 1961				Group Aged 45 to 54 in Early 1961				Group Aged 35 to 44 in Early 1961			
	1955 Position				1955 Position				1955 Position			
1960 Position	Bot- tom Third	Mid- dle Third	Top Third	Total	Bot- tom Third	Mid- dle Third	Top Third	Total	Bot- tom Third	Mid- dle Third	Top Third	Total
Bottom Third	69	27	6	100	69	24	9	100	63	27	12	100
Middle Third	30	51	18	100	27	51	21	100	27	48	24	100
Top Third	0	24	75	100	3	27	69	100	12	24	63	100
Total	100	100	100		100	100	100		100	100	100	

	1947 Position				1947 Position				1947 Position			
1960 Position	Bot- tom Third	Mid- dle Third	Top Third	Total	Bot- tom Third	Mid- dle Third	Top Third	Total	Bot- tom Third	Mid- dle Third	Top Third	Total
Bottom Third	57	30	15	100	60	21	20	100	45	30	24	100
Middle Third	33	42	24	100	30	48	24	100	27	39	33	100
Top Third	9	27	63	100	9	30	57	100	27	30	45	100
Total	100	100	100		100	100	100		100	100	100	

	1940 Position				1940 Position			
1960 Position	Bot- tom Third	Mid- dle Third	Top Third	Total	Bot- tom Third	Mid- dle Third	Top Third	Total
Bottom Third	54	30	18	100	51	27	21	100
Middle Third	33	39	24	100	30	42	27	100
Top Third	12	33	62	100	15	33	54	100
Total	100	100	100		100	100	100	

	1928 Position			
1960 Position	Bot- tom Third	Mid- dle Third	Top Third	Total
Bottom Third	51	27	21	100
Middle Third	30	39	30	100
Top Third	18	33	51	100
Total	100	100	100	

[2] Source: Calculated from 1961 *Survey of Consumer Finances, op. cit.,* p. 76, Table 5–3.

The policy implications of income mobility are very important. Should attention be concentrated on the potentially mobile to give them a secure hold on the nonpoor rungs of the income ladder or on those immobile at the bottom of the ladder? If the poor are not a stable group, are those present policies concerned with breaking "the culture of poverty" well-aimed?

Our own discussions below inadequately mirror the issue of shifting and permanent groups in poverty. The problem of minimum levels in various areas of well-being is enormously complicated by the existence of large numbers who are temporarily below the poverty level.

ASSETS

Current income is an inadequate indicator of the economic position of a family. First, it does not provide an adequate basis for comparing poor and nonpoor groups, since some of the income of the nonpoor is received in ways (for example, capital gains) purposely designated to appear as nonincome in order to reduce taxation. Second, current income inadequately reflects the future command over resources. Savings and pension accumulations are important in the future picture. Further, they affect present satisfactions by providing confidence about the future. Third, past expenditures affect present well-being, as in the case of household furnishings. Fourth, income does not always adequately reflect the character of housing. Fifth, the aged with low incomes (and others temporarily with low income) may have nonpoverty levels of living because of the use of their accumulated assets.

Consequently, we have included a variety of items under the close appellation of assets. (We do not discuss capital gains since they are included in discussions of income level.) For symmetry as much as for substance, we have included housing under assets, thereby treating rental units as though they, too, were owner-occupied. Other assets are consumers' durables, savings, and insurance.

HOUSING

There are two ways of thinking about housing goals. One is in terms of relativities. How close to "average" levels should the existence of the poor be? For example, should the housing space available to the poor have a minimum level of half of the dwelling space per unit of the nonpoor? A second approach is in terms of presumably scientifically derivable standards of need and subsistence. Clearly, this is what is implied in the budget analyses of food needs. In housing, there is a minimal public health standard of density per room. This standard is regarded as scientific rather than cultural or political.[14] The Bureau of the Census in 1960 used certain visible

---

[14] In general, we support the use of relativities rather than absolute standards. Fixed standards have the political value of being "beyond politics," thus producing feasibility, but we doubt that, over a term of years, standards can move up rapidly to keep pace with an economy that is swiftly expanding. In general, our aim is to have forthright discussions of inequalities rather than improvements through subterfuge. We do not have confidence in subterfuge as an enduring political device.

defects to classify housing as "deteriorating" or "dilapidated."[15] It also gathered data on water supply, toilet and bathing facilities, sources of water, and sewage disposal.

By Census criteria, 16 per cent of all housing units were classified as either deteriorating or dilapidated in 1960. Units with incomes under $2,000 are nearly two and a half times as likely to be living in such substandard dwelling places as persons in the total population.[16]

Unfortunately, any assessment of changes over time must be very rough because of the change in the Census definition of substandard housing.[17] Oscar Ornati, comparing trends in the percentage of income groups living in any type of substandard housing, estimates that the lowest income group had the least proportionate improvement in housing between 1950 and 1960.[18] On the other hand, it should be noted that 74 per cent of homeowners with incomes under $3,000 lived in sound housing in 1959,[19] and 4 per cent had houses valued at $25,000 or more in 1964.[20]

When we move beyond standards of sheer adequacy to broader criteria of space, facilities, and housing style, the differences between the poor and non-poor become more marked. On the financial side, 30 per cent of the houses owned by nonfarm families with under $3,000 incomes were valued at under $5,000, as compared with only 9 per cent of those owned by all

---

[15] See *U.S. Census of Housing, 1960,* Vol. A: *Metropolitan Housing,* Final Report, HC (2)-1, p. lxii.
"Deteriorating housing needs more repair than would be provided in the course of regular maintenance. Such housing has one or more defects of an intermediate nature that must be corrected if the unit is to continue to provide safe and adequate shelter.
"Dilapidated housing does not provide safe and adequate shelter and in its present condition endangers the health, safety, or well-being of the occupants. Such housing has one or more critical defects; or has a combination of intermediate defects in sufficient number or extent to require considerable repair or rebuilding; or is of inadequate original construction. The defects are either so critical or so widespread that the structure should be extensively repaired, rebuilt, or torn down." It is doubtful if these concepts are adequate for the post-World War II period.

[16] Thirty-nine per cent of those with incomes under $2,000, as compared with 20 per cent of the $3,000-$3,999 income category, lived in substandard units.

[17] Deteriorated housing with plumbing was classified as substandard in 1960 but not in 1950.

[18] Oscar Ornati, *Poverty Amid Affluence* (New York: Twentieth Century Fund, 1966), p. 179.

[19] Sixty-one per cent of families and individuals with under $3,000 incomes living in rented units had "sound" housing in 1959, *U.S. Census of Housing, op. cit.,* pp. 1-6, Table A-4.

[20] University of Michigan, Survey Research Center, *1964 Survey of Consumer Finances* (Ann Arbor: University of Michigan Press, 1965), p. 88.

nonfarm homeowning families in 1963.[21] Fifty-four per cent of the families in the lowest, as compared with only 14 per cent of families in the highest, income quintile did not own their own home.[22]

The poor put a higher percentage of their income into housing.[23] More importantly, do the poor get less for their housing dollar? The data are lacking here. The unavailability of insurance in poor housing areas indicates that low-income families attain little security for their housing dollar. The poor are also less able to maintain or enhance their housing investment.[24] The unavailability of loan funds for low-income persons as well as the low income itself make financing of expensive repairs or additions very difficult.

The subsidy system is believed to even out the differences between the poor and nonpoor. But a full view of subsidies which includes foregone taxes as well as direct transfers, reveals that the nonpoor benefit more from federal housing activity than the poor! If the loss in taxes resulting from the deductibility of interest payments on mortgages is compared with direct housing subsidies to the poor, the former is two and a half times the latter: the nonpoor have federal housing benefits of $2.9 billion, the poor, of $820 million.[25] (The indirect benefits to the nonpoor of Federal Housing Administration (FHA) government insurance, which lowers interest charges, are not included in these calculations.)

The poorest benefit very little from federal housing expenditures. They are usually ineligible for public housing because they have very low incomes, present housekeeping problems, or live in areas where public housing is very scarce.[26] In an analysis of four New York City housing projects, Ornati found that, on the average, the median educational attainment of household heads was higher in housing projects than in adjoining tracts. Nearly half of the families occupying public housing in 1963 were not poor.[27] The rent subsidy program provided for in 1965 legislation, as

21 University of Michigan, Survey Research Center, *1963 Survey of Consumer Finances* (Ann Arbor: University of Michigan Press, 1964), p. 88.

22 University of Michigan, Survey Research Center, *1965 Survey of Consumer Finances* (Ann Arbor: University of Michigan Press, 1966), p. 117.

23 *1964 Survey of Consumer Finances, op. cit.,* p. 31. In 1964, nonfarm rent-paying families with less than $3,000 incomes paid a median monthly rent of $45 as compared with $65 paid by those with $3,000-$4,900 incomes.

24 *Ibid.,* p. 35. Only 18 per cent of non-farm families with under $3,000 incomes, as compared with 34 per cent of the total non-farm population, had housing addition and repair expenditures of over $49 in 1964.

25 Alvin L. Schorr. "National Community and Housing Policy," *Social Service Review,* (1965), p. 434.

26 Alvin L. Schorr, "Housing" (Manuscript, August 1965), p. 6. Almost 60 per cent of substandard housing is in rural areas.

27 David Caplovitz, *The Poor Pay More* (New York: Free Press, 1963).

Schorr has pointed out, is also directed primarily toward those at the high end of the low-income scale.

CONSUMERS' DURABLES

Consumers' durables are today an important component of the level of living. Current income inadequately indicates the command over resources of this kind. We believe that enormous variations exist in the possession of durables among low-income families, but information is very spotty. Interpretations of the meaning of possessions have added to the confusion.[28]

One of the problems in ascertaining whether working-class families were becoming "middle class" was the assumption that to own certain things indicated a zeal for the middle-class value system. Aside from the imputation of a peculiar status concern in purchases, this reasoning suffered from the inadequate realization that better-off families were moving much beyond working-class families in consumers' purchases—when workers' families were buying toasters, middle-class families were moving on to bun-warmers and the like.

Similarly, one is easily surprised at the variety and cost of household appliances available to the poor. For example, in New York City, 95 per cent of low-income families have television sets. By contrast, the nonpoor have had significant gains. They use planes to visit distant relatives, while video-tape machines automatically record the television programs missed when away from home.

Comparisons should take into consideration the lower quality of furnishings of the poor. For example, many of the washing machines of low-income families are old, hand-operated washers in need of major repairs, as is obvious on the porches of homes in the hollows of Appalachia. Also, the poor pay more, so that expenditure is an inadequate indicator of value.

What standard of consumers' durables should be used for the poverty line? One is in terms of minimal needs which home economists and other specialists could define: What is the supply of durables that every family should have? In essence, many durables are no longer in the luxury class. For example, a refrigerator might be considered as part of a basic durables minimum. In some areas of the country, a car might be. Home furnishings of beds, chairs, tables, and some pictures might be another. Constructing a minimum durables standard would require attention to the average durable levels of nonpoor families and some estimate of what is a reasonable gap

---

[28] S. M. Miller and Frank Riessman, "Are Workers Middle Class?", *Dissent* (1962).

in terms of service and esthetics. Presumably, the policy that flows from this approach is to insure that each family has the ingredients of the minimum durables standards. Welfare departments have constructed such budgets, though at very low levels. Families have no choice in what kind of items they would like to have.

A different approach would maximize choice among the low-income. The dollar value of the durables of the nonpoor would be the basis of a standard of durables for the poor. The latter would have funds available to them up to perhaps one-half of the value of the nonpoor's durables and could spend the available amounts on whatever durables they pleased.

These two approaches illustrate that the nature of indicators—in this case physical or monetary quantities—may affect the character of policy.

SAVINGS

Liquid assets are not only an important protector against emergencies; they also can break the fall into poverty. For want of savings, any emergency drains a low-income family. Debt ensues; the family may have to move and change employment. Savings not only provide some psychological security; they are an important instrument in maintaining or improving economic conditions.

Savings are obviously concentrated: 25 per cent of spending units in the highest income quintile (top fifth), as compared with less than 9 per cent in the bottom three quintiles, had liquid assets totaling over $5,000 in 1960.[29] The form of asset-holding is important, for it affects the possibility of assets increasing in value or yielding income: 62 per cent of families with incomes of $15,000 and over had stockholdings valued at $1,000 or more; 3 per cent of families with under $3,000 income held stock above this level. (Most of these families were over 65.)[30]

From the point of view of inequality, it is important to pay attention to savings and other forms of assets. If income alone is considered, then the differences between the poor and nonpoor appear narrower than they are. For example, the asset level of the nonpoor aged not only puts them in a higher income bracket than the aged poor, but provides a stream of income over the future. (Many assets are forms of deferred income.)

What should be the goal in the area of liquid assets? The minimum level of liquid assets should be twice the weekly income. Achievement of this goal is difficult, since the poor might well utilize savings for current needs, so that a long-run asset-building program would become a current income program.

[29] *1960 Survey of Consumer Finances, op. cit.,* p. 79.
[30] *1964 Survey of Consumer Finances, op. cit.,* p. 96.

INSURANCE

The average American who lives to the age of 65 can expect to live for another fifteen years. A tenth or more of the current income of many individuals is devoted to providing security for their later years. Thus, the command over future resources is a major concern of Americans today. It affects not only the calculation of current income but the satisfactions and security derived from earnings. Because of space limitations, we address ourselves only to the issue of insuring against income losses because of age, ignoring unemployment and other insurances.

The present methods of protecting against old age serve to worsen inequalities: the concentration of income among the aged is greater than it is among younger age groups or for the nation as a whole. In 1960 the upper 20 per cent of families headed by a person over 64 received 52 per cent of that group's aggregate income, as compared with 42 per cent received by the upper fifth of the nation as a whole and 37 per cent of the age group 25 to 34.[31] Less than 0.5 per cent of families with incomes under $3,000 in 1964, as compared with 2 per cent of all families, had savings in the form of retirement funds or old-age pensions.[32]

As Margaret Gordon has pointed out, although Congress in recent years has tended to adjust upward Old Age Survivors, Disability and Health Insurance benefits proportionately with increases in the consumer price index, the question may be raised whether a special cost-of-living index for the aged should be constructed. This procedure might make a marked difference because of pronounced increases in the cost of certain items, such as medical care, which figure prominently in the budgets of elderly people.[33]

The system of transfer through public assistance only partially reduces the inequalities of private savings and returns and the distribution of social security and private pension benefits.[34] With the extension of life and the

---

[31] Herman Miller, *op. cit.*, p. 75.

[32] *1964 Survey of Consumer Finances, op. cit.*, p. 114. At each income level, persons who contribute to private pension funds save more in a given year than those who do not contribute, and tend to devote the same fraction of their income to life insurance—Margaret S. Gordon, *The Economics of Welfare Policies* (New York: Columbia University Press, 1963), p. 50.

[33] Margaret S. Gordon, *op. cit.*, p. 55.

[34] No one who lives out the fifteen years of past-65 expectancy has paid into social security as much as he receives from it. The payment from social security is based more on the symbolism of contribution than on actual contribution. Musgrave found that, in 1954, effective social insurance tax rates were regressive over the income distribution as a whole and fairly uniform for tax brackets under $5,000—Gordon, *op. cit.*, p. 25.

concern about the future, deferred income in the form of pensions should be an important consideration in today's assessment of economic well-being. In regarding pension accumulations as an important aspect of one's standard of living before 65, a difficult question emerges. The public welfare system will provide aid to the aged with low incomes; in 1965, 2.1 million aged persons (over 64) received public assistance in the form of Old Age Assistance.[35] Can we consider different levels of pension accumulations today as important when welfare will be available for those who are poor in their old age? One response to this is that welfare is stigmatizing. Another is that welfare payments are low, so that while an income "floor" is available, it does not provide much security and confidence about the future. Depending on public authorities to provide a small amount of money to keep one going is quite different from having a guaranteed future. In reality, even this low welfare floor is only a grating: 22 per cent of the aged still fall beneath the poverty line.[36]

BASIC SERVICES

Income and assets are important components of the command over resources, but they do not include the increasingly important area of services. These services include education and training, health, neighborhood amenities, protection, social services, and transportation. In the high-income society, services compose a high and increasing proportion of expenditures and furnish important segments of total satisfaction and well-being.

The connection between family income and basic services is close but incomplete. A fairly well-to-do rural family can have inadequate immediate health care because no health center is nearby, while an urban low-income family may have access to an excellent medical teaching center. Or, two families with the same low level of income can be in very different environments—one in an overcrowded area with few recreational facilities, poor sanitation and garbage control, inadequate police protection, and little transportation; the other, in a high-density area which has outstanding services. This example illustrates the contention that in Sweden the poor are less worse off than in the United States because their low incomes are *not* associated with poor basic services.

---

[35] *Social Security Bulletin* (February 1967), pp. 1, 44.

[36] Mollie Orshansky, "More about the Poor in 1964," *Social Security Bulletin*, (May 1966), p. 5.

Below, we discuss five issues in conceptualizing and measuring basic services. First, basic services are usually associated with the public sector, but this is not inevitable. The growth of fringe benefits in private employment means that many basic services are provided through employment. In the United States, many hospital insurance plans and health services are provided by private employers; over-all, fringe benefits comprise about 20 per cent of the wage bill, a smaller share than in many other countries. While the history of the growth of basic services for the poor has, to a large extent, meant the enlargement of the public sector, this may not be intrinsic to the development of the services. Indeed, in England, conservative groups like the Institute of Economic Affairs are strongly insisting that more and better basic services can be provided through increased reliance on the market.[37] The sharp distinction between public and private sectors may be increasingly unuseful.

Second, are basic services to be considered as amenities or investments? As amenities, services directly increase the consumption of individuals. They are not means to the attainment of other resources; they are themselves important components of the level of living. As investments, however, they are ways of improving the capacity of individuals to gain access to resources through the private market: for example, better health services and better transportation to jobs increase the individual's or the family's capacity to earn.

The trend of liberal thought is to transmute goals into means. What is desirable as a goal is not defended on that basis but on the contention that it is instrumental to the achievement of other goals. Rationality—the effectiveness of a program to achieve another program—supplants desirability— a program is desired of itself. We strongly doubt that many of the things we characterize as investments in human resources, for example, health programs, are really effective methods to increase earning capacity.[38] Consequently, we prefer to look at basic services as amenities rather than as investments in human resources development.

A third problem discussed earlier in connection with income is the question of what the goals are in the area of basic services. Is the objective a minimum or adequate level? Or is the objective a question of relative distribution between those at the bottom and other groups in society? In the second case, it is a question of distribution of resources; in the first, it

---

[37] On the other hand, the recommendations of the Institute of Economic Affairs and similar groups largely ignore the issue of reductions in inequalities.

[38] Martin Rein and S. M. Miller, "Poverty, Policy, and Choice," in Leonard Goodman (ed.), *Economic Progress and Social Welfare* (New York: Columbia University Press, 1966). A version of this article appears in *Trans-Action* (October 1967).

is a question of standards. Adequacy is the major criterion in an essential thing like health services, but as general conditions improve in a society, questions of relative distribution assume greater importance.

Fourth, a particularly sensitive problem is the connection between services and well-being. Do services actually contribute to improved circumstances of life or is their usefulness overstated? For example, some evidence suggests that personal health services (as contrasted with public health measures) do not have a high impact upon physical well-being. Similar questions have been raised about the effectiveness of case-work services and psychotherapy.

Since we measure most services by their costs and quantities, we do not have an estimate of their yield, especially to people of different income levels, as the services may yield more to one group than to another. This differential yield could be a product of differences in quality. What purports to be the same basic service, for example, school education, can be widely varying in quality.

Fifth is the issue of the availability versus the utilization of services. To some analysts, the issue is services available to a particular population. If the group does not use it, for whatever reason, that is their own prerogative; we cannot then condemn the service organization for the resultant inequitable distribution of its resources to the nonpoor. The contrasting notion is that the issue is actual delivery of the services. Availability of service is not sufficient; direct efforts are needed to cope with the obstacles which result in low utilization by the poor. The problem of utilization is especially acute with the isolated groups and the poorest of the poor.

We deal below with these basic services: health, neighborhood amenities, transportation, and legal and social services. The field of education will be discussed in the following section with our analysis of social mobility.

HEALTH

The poor of all ages consult doctors, dentists, and medical specialists less frequently than do the nonpoor.[39] The rate of visits to physicians'

---

[39] 4.6 physician consultations were made per year by persons with family income under $2,000 as compared with 5.7 by those with family income over $7,000; youth under fifteen in families with under $2,000 made 3.0 visits as compared with 5.7 made per year by youth in families with income over $7,000. *Over three times as many dental visits* were made per year by persons with incomes over $7,000 as by those with family income under $2,000—U.S., Department of Health, Education, and Welfare, "Health Status and Family Income: United States," *Vital and Health Statistics: Data from the National Health Survey,* Series 10, No. 9 (May 1964); and Charlotte Muller, "Income and the Receipt of Medical Care," *American Journal of Public Health,* 55 (April 1965), p. 514.

offices, as compared with telephone or hospital clinic visits, also declines with income. Short-stay hospital utilization, in terms of rates of discharges, age for age, is somewhat less for low-income than high-income persons.[40] Utilization of immunization and pediatric services has also been found to be inversely related to income.[41]

Do the poor use health services less because they are healthier? The answer is probably no. Charlotte Muller succinctly summarizes the findings: "Identifying the low-income group is tantamount to identifying a high probability of medical needs as shown by various indexes of prevalence and severity of disability illness."[42]

While low-income persons (under $2,000 family income) made less than a third as many dental visits per year as high-income persons (family incomes tover $7,000), nearly four times as many low-income as high-income persons required extractions when they made dental visits.[43] Although persons with low family incomes had lower rates of hospitalization, they required more days of care when they were hospitalized.[44] Restricted activity days as well as bed-disability days are over twice as frequent in the lowest as in the highest income group.[45] The lowest income class also has the highest rates of heart diseases, diabetes mellitus, arthritis, and diseases of female genital organs.[46]

The pattern of mortality rates is similar to that of illnesses. In major United States cities, higher infant mortality rates generally prevail in nonwhite areas. Nationally, the gap between death rates for white and nonwhite infants is increasing.[47] Fetal loss varies with instability of income, measured by husband's unemployment history.[48]

---

[40] U.S., Department of Health, Education, and Welfare, *op. cit.*

[41] Oscar Ornati, *op. cit.,* p. 75.

[42] Muller, *op. cit.,* p. 517.

[43] Muller, *ibid.,* p. 514.

[44] U.S., Department of Health, Education, and Welfare, *op. cit.,* p. 15.

[45] These contrasts are found even after the higher proportion of aged among the lowest income group are allowed for—U.S., National Health Survey, *Health Statistics,* Series B-7, B-8, B-10, Washington, D.C., 1960.

[46] Ornati, *op. cit.,* p. 75.

[47] In 1964, the nonwhite infant death rate was 41.1 per 100,000, a level not recorded for white infants since 1941—*Trans-Action,* Vol. 4, No. 5 (April 1967), p. 4. The maternal mortality rate among Mississippi Negroes is 15.3 per 10,000 live births, more than six times the national average for whites of 2.5—Elinor Langer, "Who Makes Our Health Policy?", *Physicians' Forum* (June 1967).

[48] Ronald Freedman, Lolagene C. Coombs, and Judith Friedman, "Social Correlates of Fetal Mortality," *The Milbank Memorial Fund Quarterly,* Vol. 44 (1966), p. 337. The data are from intensive interviews obtained by the Detroit Area Study of the University of Michigan.

The relationship between infrequent health care, poor health, and low income is more intricate than an analysis based solely upon these data would indicate.[49] Income is only one aspect of poverty. The complexity of the interrelationships among the dimensions of poverty and health is demonstrated by Hauser and Kitagawa's recent analysis of mortality in the United States. Both education and income vary inversely with mortality; but, although education differentials in mortality are larger than income differentials for women, the opposite is true for men.[50]

Education is more highly correlated with the frequency of visits to physicians than is income.[51] Persons who lack health education are frequently unable to identify and care for minor symptoms in time to prevent major medical problems. Lack of experience with professionals also causes the poor to hesitate to seek their help before an ailment is severe. Others who have experienced difficulty in communicating their needs or have felt stigmatized and out-of-place within professional surroundings will delay their return as long as possible. In some areas of the country, great strides appear to have been made in health services for the poor, but most regions need enormous improvements.[52]

---

[49] Charles Kadushin takes exception with the findings summarized above. He concludes: "The fact is that the lower classes are not more likely than the middle class to have a disease or condition but they do react more violently to it and are more concerned about it. Nonetheless, neither sociologists nor public health researchers have for the most part taken proper note of the split between getting sick and reacting to it," "Social Class and the Experience of Ill Health," *Sociological Inquiry*, 34 (Winter 1964) and in "Health and Social Class," *New Society*, December 24, 1964, p. 10. Aaron Antonovsky challenges Kadushin's analysis in a soon-to-be-published paper.

[50] Evelyn M. Kitagawa and Philip M. Hauser, "Education and Income Differentials in Mortality: United States, 1960," University of Chicago Population Center (Manuscript, 1967). The mortality index for men, age 25 to 64, with less than five years of schooling was 49 per cent higher than for men with some college; it was 86 per cent higher for men with less than $2,000 family income than for men with over $10,000 income. For women the rate was 98 per cent higher for those with less than five years of education than for college alumnae, and 41 per cent higher for those with less than $2,000 family income than for those with over $10,000. Because the Census definition of income, which was used in the analysis, does not take into account savings and other forms of capital or the income decline which generally occurs prior to death, the authors judge education to be a better indicator of Social-Economic State (SES) than income for the purposes of their study.

[51] Ornati, *op. cit.*, p. 74.

[52] Gouverneur Ambulatory Care Unit of Beth Israel Hospital in New York's Lower East Side and other agencies in the largest United States cities now employ professionals as well as nonprofessionals who speak many dialects of Chinese as well as Spanish.

What criteria are to be used to judge the quality of services?[53] Patient-satisfaction? Recovery rates? Professional evaluations? Each has its pitfalls. The difficulties involved in developing these indicators are amplified by questions of professional authority. Nonetheless, a few assessments have been made of professional care. A study of expectant mothers in metropolitan Boston showed that the percentage judged to have received satisfactory medical care rose steadily with income.[54]

But poor treatment is not confined to the poor, nor excellent care to the well-to-do. Sliding scales mean that higher dollar figures for medical expenditures do not necessarily reflect better care. Good health care is frequently distributed on the basis of neither medical nor financial need, but on the basis of the medical interest of the patient's case or the patient's ability to manipulate the system.

Obviously, income affects the ability of a family to obtain medical services for which it must pay, and to purchase hospital and surgical insurance which will cover a portion of potential medical expenses.[55] Muller reports, however, that for every dollar spent by consumers or financed by their premiums and the payments of employers, or by insurance carriers on their behalf, or by philanthropies, another 25 cents is spent out of the public

---

[53] A formal test of the major criteria is developed in Bertram Gross, "What Are Your Organization's Objectives?", *Human Relations* (August 1965).

[54] Muller, *op. cit.*, p. 517. See also J. Ehrlich, M. A. Morehead, and R. E. Trussell, *The Quantity, Quality, and Costs of Medical and Hospital Care Secured by a Sample of Teamster Families in the New York Area* (New York: School of Public Health and Administrative Medicine, Columbia University, 1962) and M. A. Morehead, et al., *A Study of the Quality of Hospital Care Secured by a Sample of Teamster Family Members in New York City* (New York: School of Public Health and Administrative Medicine, Columbia University, 1964). These studies document how frequently the care received by members of a union through traditional sources proved inadequate. The relationships between quality of care and hospital and physician characteristics are analyzed. The proportion of consumption and income going to medical care is relatively high in the lowest income group (9.3 per cent), declining to 6.3 per cent at $4,000, staying close to this proportion as income continues to rise. High proportionate expenditure in low-income groups is only partly due to age (67 was the average age of heads of families with under $1,000 incomes). The average per capita family medical expenditure is $100 for families with below $3,000 income and $248 for families with income over $15,000—Muller, *op. cit.*, p. 519. Between 1953 and 1958 the mean gross family expenditure for personal health services increased considerably more among low-income rather than high-income families. Families with under $2,000 income experienced a 27 per cent increase; those with $2,000-$3,499, a 49 per cent increase; and those with $7,500 and over, a 16 per cent increase—Olin Anderson, Patricia Collette, and J. J. Feldman, *Changes in Family Medical Care Expenditures and Voluntary Health Service: A Five Year Resurvey* (London: Oxford University Press, 1963), p. 17.

[55] While many doctors donate outstanding services to low-income patients or use sliding scales, the share of industrial and philanthropic services in private spending is small—4½ per cent out of $23.8 billion private expenditures for medical service (Muller, *op. cit.*, p. 512).

treasury.[56] Much of this public spending is channeled to the poor, but, as Alvin Schorr has pointed out, the neediest do not necessarily receive their share of the benefits of public programs.

What are the goals in health? The goals can be specified in terms of services—the distribution and utilization of services—and in terms of mortality and morbidity. Are health and longevity areas in which our society no longer finds class differences acceptable? We have the odd feeling that American society implicitly argues for equality of outcome in health and longevity—and for inequality in the distribution of services!

To reduce the disparities among the rich and poor may require more than rectifying the distribution of services. In mental retardation, where there are pronounced differences in incidence, the mother's conditions of life during the prenatal period are undoubtedly more important than medical services. Health is not only a reflection of health services.

The adequacy of health services is a general problem in our society. Despite enormous expenditures, the United States has fallen behind many other nations in crucial indicators of health. The plight of the poor is directing attention to the general medical situation, with the possibility of improved health services for all.

NEIGHBORHOOD AMENITIES

Neighborhood amenities refer to such important influences on the character of a habitat as sanitation control; police and fire protection; recreational facilities; libraries, parks, and playgrounds; and the condition of streets and roads. What we are attempting to convey by neighborhood amenities are conditions which are usually collectively provided for a neighborhood through public expenditures of one kind or another.

A common observation in many large cities is to note the differences in the sanitation pick-up for low-income and better-off neighborhoods. In low-income neighborhoods, especially those which are not politically important or are opposed to the party in power, sanitation pickup is sporadic, infrequent, and very inadequate. The areas that complain the most and are strongly organized are most likely to get satisfactory garbage control. As a result, the poorest are likely to have inadequate sanitation and garbage control.

A common complaint in many low-income areas is inadequate police protection. This complaint is coupled with grievances about police brutality.

---

[56] Alvin Schorr, *Children,* 11, 4: 129 (July-August, 1964). This point is made by Brian Abel-Smith in his seminal essay, "Whose Welfare State?," in Norman MacKenzie (ed.), *Conviction* (London: MacGibbon & Kee, 1959).

Arguments about excessive police force do not mean that police *aid* is not desired.[57]

The Senate Ribicoff Hearing's data show that the citizens of Harlem and Watts are concerned about the inadequate availability of police as well as the excessive use of force by police. Data cross the country on the degree of police availability and activity in low-income areas are hard to obtain. Due to the high incidence of crime in these areas, there is a general impression that there is inadequate police protection in these areas. Of course, the underlying issue is the extent to which having more police would drastically reduce this rate. The kinds and quality of police services are the important issues.[58] The objectives of police services are still being debated, and important new programs have been recommended.

Similarly, the data on the availability of fire protection in low-income areas are very spotty. We know that insurance companies are reluctant to insure in these areas. It would be useful to try to develop some index of police and fire protection which would mirror changes over time in the degree of availability of such facilities.

An adequate measure of recreational facilities is difficult to construct. This is partly because transportation to distant recreational facilities is differentially distributed. Patricia Sexton found:

> There are more parks and recreation areas in the upper-income areas of Detroit than in the lower-income areas. The smallest amount of park space per 10,000 people is found in the oldest part of the city . . . where the lowest-income groups live. In one large section of this area (130,000 population), there are only 2.6 acres of recreation area per 10,000 people—as compared with 30 acres in the highest-income area.

Children in these areas also tend to be much less mobile than children in upper-income areas. Poorer children (because their parents usually do not have cars or the money for travel or summer camps or even for local bus transportation) are virtually imprisoned in the crowded areas where they live. When recreation facilities in these areas are not adequate, it is

---

[57] *New York Times,* September 4, 1967, Section 1, p. 1. Data from a survey conducted by the J. F. Kraft public opinion organization in Harlem and released by Senator Ribicoff suggest that residents are more concerned about police protection than police brutality. The persons interviewed wanted more instead of fewer police in neighborhoods.

[58] In a random sample of 10,000 householders during the summer of 1965, the National Opinion Research Center found that almost 14 per cent of the Negroes interviewed, as compared with only 3 per cent of the whites, responded that police respectfulness "toward people like yourself was not so good"—Philip H. Ennis, "Crime Victims and the Police," *Trans-Action,* 4, 7 (June 1967), p. 42.

very difficult for lower-income children to go elsewhere to find them.[59] Limited evidence on use of national parks seems to suggest that the national parks are more likely to be used by middle-income rather than lowest-income people. On the other hand, some ethnic groups which have a history of outdoor use, like the Puerto Ricans, are probably more likely than other groups to use park facilities.

Museums and libraries seem to be disproportionately used by the non-poor, although trend data are exceedingly sparse. These facilities, which are expensive, tend to be concentrated in their uses among a limited segment of a population. This, it could be argued, is the result of low-income ideas about museums rather than of questions of effective delivery. However, efforts to try to decentralize such facilities and make them interesting and attractive to the poor might be effective, at least some believe. Thomas Hoving, Metropolitan Museum director, argues otherwise—art museums lose what they have to offer in the way of relief from the routine world when they are set up in store fronts. Therefore, his efforts are oriented toward bringing the poor to the central museum.

It would be useful to develop cultural indices which would reveal the use of facilities such as museums and libraries. These indices could indicate the degree of success of concerted policies to deepen the use of these facilities by poor and low-educated groups. The use of museums and libraries by socialist-oriented workers in Poland and other European nations suggests that some gain could be made.[60]

PUBLIC TRANSPORTATION

Public transportation is of more importance to the poor than the non-poor. Today, job opportunities are multiplying in the suburbs, out of reach of the poor in the center-city. Low-income persons cannot afford costly long-distance commuting by car and generally lack other transportation alternatives.[61] On the other hand, they cannot afford, or are not permitted

---

[59] Patricia Sexton, *Education and Income* (New York: Viking Press, 1961), pp. 143-144.

[60] See Feleks Gross, *The Polish Worker: A Study of a Social Stratum* (New York: Roy, 1945). César Grâna notes that when the school children of polyglot New York do visit a museum, they find themselves "the guests of a mansion conceived, not only as a monument to 'values,' but as a re-enactment of the patrician past"—César Grâna, "The Private Lives of Public Museums," *Trans-Action*, 4, 5 (1965), pp. 23-24.

[61] Dorothy K. Newman, "The Decentralization of Jobs," *Monthly Labor Review* (May 1967). It would cost a worker in Harlem $40 a month to commute by public transportation to work in an aircraft plant in Farmingdale, Long Island; in a parts plant in Yonkers, Westchester; or in a basic chemical plant on Staten Island.

because of racial discrimination, to live near the new factories, hospitals, commercial buildings, schools, and stores in the periphery of the city. A minimum level of access to transportation is important.

LEGAL SERVICES

Our society prides itself that all are equal before the law. In practice, the bright-minded and better-educated are better treated by judicial officials and have easier access to better legal services than do the poor. In the case of the law, the goal obviously is that the low-income citizen should be as well treated as the better-off. But this would mean an equal distribution of legal services—a far cry from our present situation.[62]

Jerome Carlin, after studying lawyer's ethics in New York City, described the present state of legal services for the poor:

> The best trained, most technically skilled, and ethically most responsible lawyers are reserved to the upper reaches of business and society. This leaves the least competent, least well-trained, and least ethical lawyers to the smaller business concerns and lower-income individuals. As a result, the most helpless clients who most need protection are least likely to get it.
>
> The uneven character of legal services, moreover, leads to a highly selective development of the law itself. Those areas that reflect the interest of large corporations and wealthy individuals are most likely to be elaborated; law dealing with the poor and other disadvantaged groups, particularly in the consumer, landlord-tenant, welfare, and domestic relations areas remains largely neglected and underdeveloped.
>
> Whatever efforts have been made by leaders of the profession to cope with these problems have been largely ineffective. Lack of leadership is particularly evident in the failure of the organized bar to seek and to support new forms of legal representation that might help in extending legal services to a larger segment of the population.[63]

A series of decisions like the cases of *Gideon* v. *Wainwright* and *Brotherhood of Railroad Trainmen* v. *Virginia* and the surprising success

---

[62] In New York City, fewer than 5 per cent of the lawyers report that the median income of their clients is under $5,000 a year, although half of the total families and unrelated individuals in New York City have incomes under this amount. Conversely, 70 per cent of the lawyers in New York City report that the median income of their clients is in excess of $10,000, though fewer than 10 per cent of New York's families and unrelated individuals receive incomes that high—U.S., Department of Health, Education, and Welfare, *Extension of Legal Services to the Poor.*

[63] Jerome E. Carlin, *Lawyers' Ethics: A Survey of the New York City Bar* (New York: Russell Sage Foundation, 1966), p. 177.

of the Office of Economic Opportunity (OEO) in promoting legal services to the poor have reduced the disparities between the legal conditions facing the poor, and the services available to them, and the situations of the non-poor.[64] But a gap continues; how wide it is, is uncertain, and it would be useful—and not impossible—to construct and maintain indices of legal treatment and services.[65]

SOCIAL MOBILITY AND EDUCATION

The poverty programs of the Economic Opportunity Act of 1964 were largely youth programs; the intent was to break the connection between the situation of low-income parents and the prospects of their children. These were programs aimed at increasing the rate of intergenerational social mobility of low-income youth.[66] More generally, questions of equality and social justice involve issues of social mobility. Life chances are defined largely as questions of opportunity for an individual to rise occupationally in his lifetime or for his children to move into the better situations of the society, thus surpassing the economic level of his parents.

Education is increasingly the route to social mobility in our credential-oriented society. For this reason, we discuss it in this section rather than in the preceding section on basic services. While education has many dimensions other than its contribution to occupational advance, this dimension is the major attraction of education at this point. Educational sophistication is also protection against bureaucratic manipulation. It is an aid in learning how to get services. And, for Negroes in particular, it is a barrier to offhand humiliating treatment, especially by police.

Why treat social mobility independently? Does not improvement in family income *automatically* result in improvement in social mobility chances? The data as shown in Figure 1 do not support this conclusion: the education of a family, in most situations, is more important than the income of the family in affecting how far the youth goes in school. Furthermore, two families of the same income obviously fare quite differently in other respects if the offspring of one have a much better chance of higher education and resulting better job prospects than the other. To some extent,

---

[64] See Jerome E. Carlin and Jan Howard, "Legal Representation and Class Justice," *UCLA Law Review,* 12 (January 1965), p. 432.

[65] 372 U.S. 335 (1963) and 377 U.S. I (1964).

[66] A contrasting approach toward improving social conditions tends to be family-oriented, more concerned with the aged than youth. These two approaches are discussed in S. M. Miller, "Poverty," in *Proceedings,* Sixth World Congress of Sociology, 1967.

then, social mobility is a dimension of well-being deserving of separate attention. It is one of most crucial indicators of a socially democratic society.

EDUCATION

We deal first with data on education, then with the social mobility data. In education, we can look at various types of indicators. One level of indicators is the expenditures data—how much is spent on children of different income levels? The Syracuse University study of school expenditures, by Alan Campbell, Jesse Burkhead, Seymour Sachs, and associates, shows that in 1962, in thirty-five of the largest metropolitan areas, expenditures in central cities—where there are many children of low-income families—was $145 per pupil less than in their contiguous suburbs—where there are few children of low-income families.[67] One of the most disturbing findings in the investigation is that state funds go relatively more to the suburbs than to the cities; in state aid, suburban schools receive forty dollars more per pupil than city schools. Even more disconcerting, the gap between cities and suburbs is growing: the 1962 difference did not exist in 1958, for then the two areas were spending the same amount.

The importance of school expenditures is indicated by the finding that the proportion of National Merit finalists is related to a locality's support for education.[68]

When differences in the quality of the product—the return per dollar of expenditures—are considered, the gap is probably even larger than the gross education figures indicate. It is likely that there are fewer and poorer services rendered per dollar in low-income schools than in higher-income schools.

Data for the city of Detroit in the late 1950's show that for children in families in the below $7,000 income category, 18 per cent of the total teaching time is by "Emergency Substitutes in Regular Positions," as compared with 5.5 per cent for the children in families with above $7,000 family incomes.[69] According to Project Talent findings, teacher experience is highly correlated with student achievement.

---

[67] The report is summarized in the *Carnegie Quarterly*, 14 (Fall 1966). The Coleman Report on education has some contradictory evidence, but it is highly debatable. The data reported in Morgan et al., *Income and Welfare in the United States, op. cit.*, tends to support the general notion of differences in per capita educational expenditures between high- and low-income communities.

[68] Robert C. Nichols, "The Financial Status of National Merit Finalists," *Science*, 149 (September 1965), p. 1071.

[69] Patricia C. Sexton, *op. cit.*, p. 120.

Figure 1—Percentage of Youth, Age 16–20, Who Are Enrolled in or
Attended College, by Father's Education and Family Income, 1960

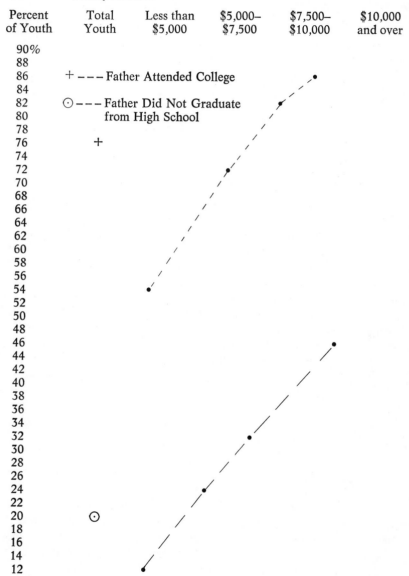

Family Income:

Percent of Youth	Total Youth	Less than $5,000	$5,000– $7,500	$7,500– $10,000	$10,000 and over

Source: Pamela Roby, "The Economic Prospects of High School Dropouts, Graduates, and College Graduates," Youth Development Center, Syracuse University, 1965
(mimeographed). Adapted from U.S., Bureau of the Census, *Current Population
Reports*, P-20, No. 110 (July 24, 1961), Table 10, p. 15.

TABLE 4—Percentage of Male High School Graduates Who Entered College Within One Year After Completing High School, by Aptitude Percentile and Family Income.[a]

Family Income	Aptitude Level, Percentile				
	0–49.9	50–74.9	75–89.9	90–97.9	98–100
Less than $3,000	19.6	48.2	75.4	87.9	100.0
$3,000–$5,999	27.3	52.5	73.3	86.7	96.1
$6,000–$8,999	31.9	59.7	80.6	88.6	95.2
$9,000–$11,999	40.2	66.8	83.9	92.5	95.9
$12,000 plus	49.7	79.7	90.1	96.7	98.5

[a] Calculated from Hearings before Subcommittee on Education, Committee on Education and Labor, House of Representatives, 88th Congress, 1st and 2nd Sessions.

Table 4 indicates that adequate college financial aid is probably available—to the top 2 per cent of the nation's youth. For even those who fall within two to ten percentage points from the top in ability, family income is an important determinant of who shall go to college.

Median educational attainment levels of the low-income and Negroes are growing. But here, particularly, the absolute level is probably not as important as the relative level. For if the low-income children increase their median levels while the children of the higher-income change theirs even more, the former may not be much advantaged in terms of job prospects. In interpreting median data, it is important to recognize that more years of high school have much less importance than the jump to a high school diploma. Although the over-all difference in educational attainment is narrowing, *the difference between the percentage of whites and nonwhites with high school diplomas or college educations has remained the same over the past decade.*

Goals of education for the low-income are much more significantly stated in terms of what percentage should be high school or college *graduates* than in terms of median years of education.

Despite the staggering amount of educational statistics, gaps still exist. Needed are statistics for localities on the distribution and quality of educational statistics. Units smaller than a city are needed. On the product side, data are needed on the achievement of students. It is important to link expenditures to attainments for specific localities—a need not met in the important national testing program which Ralph Tyler has been urging and the organizations of school officials have been resisting. Studies of charts of students from their entrance into school through maturity would be particularly useful; the objective would be to discern the influences of school characteristics on their achievements.

MOBILITY

The social mobility rates that we are concerned about are intergenerational. We ignore in this discussion intragenerational mobility—the changes in occupations of an individual over his lifetime—or stratum mobility—the changes in income and other benefits of an occupation compared to other occupations. These are both important processes, to which not enough attention has been paid in current discussions of mobility. Nor do we discuss geographic mobility, which is frequently, though not necessarily, involved in the patterning of social mobility. And we ignore all the difficulties intrinsic to mobility studies.[70]

Surprisingly, the United States has lagged behind many other nations in conducting a national study which was mainly addressed to issues of social mobility. In 1962, this lack was remedied in the very useful investigation by the Bureau of the Census which was stimulated by, and conducted in close co-operation with, the sociologists Otis Dudley Duncan and Peter Blau. We will use this study. It would be rewarding to conduct such a study every five years to see changes in the rates and patterns of social mobility in the United States.

Children of families at the bottom of the occupational hierarchy had much less chance of moving into upper-level jobs than children born in families at these levels. A son of a Negro manual worker has less than a quarter of the chance of a white-collar non-Negro son to get into a white-collar job. The chance of the white manual worker's son is slightly more than half that of the latter.[71]

The degree of stability of upper-level families is an indication of the openness of society (as well as of economic change and growth). Here, we find downward mobility from the nonmanual into the manual classes to be 22 per cent in the United States, 42 per cent in Great Britain, 37 per cent in Denmark, and 44 per cent in Canada.[72]

The Negro data are disturbing. The Negro mobility rate from lower manual occupations is about half (51 per cent) that of the white from these same occupations. More disturbing is the finding that among Negro sons of white-collar fathers, 72.4 per cent went into manual occupations, as compared with 23.4 per cent of non-Negro sons. This rate of downward mobility

---

[70] S. M. Miller, "Comparative Social Mobility," *Current Sociology*, IX-1 (1960), chap. i.

[71] Otis Dudley Duncan, Survey Research Center, University of Michigan, unpublished tabulations.

[72] The foreign data are from S. M. Miller, "Comparative Social Mobility," *op. cit.:* they are for earlier years than the U.S.A. figures. But the earlier U.S.A. data suggest that there is a significant gap in downward fluidity between the U.S.A. and a number of other nations.

is spectacular, even when we allow for the likelihood that, for some, the movement may be into manual occupations that pay as well or better than marginal middle-class occupations.[73]

The Negro data indicate the inadequacies of utilizing national figures. Data for regions of the country would probably show that the South has a much lower rate of social mobility than other parts of the country.

What is the target in social mobility? Obviously, income, the occupational and social contacts of families, the know-how, and the educational support all combine to make it difficult to reduce sharply competitive advantages. But substantial reduction of differences is possible. Specific targets over a ten- and twenty-year period are probably desirable to reduce social mobility differentials. The improvement of the education of those at the bottom, the reduction of the emphasis on educational credentials as intrinsic to occupational entrance, and the more effective reliance on upgrading and training on the job are among the ways that social mobility patterns can become political questions.

Cutting the link betwen parent's position and child's is one of the core goals of a fluid society. (One can argue the position that the goal is only to break the link for those at the bottom, not those in already more advantaged positions.) Careful collection and analysis of data of this kind are essential to keeping the issue under public scrutiny.

POLITICAL POSITION

The improvement of economic position does not always bring with it advances in political position. Indeed, many analysts argue that it is the inconsistency between rising economic power and stunted political power that is most likely to make a group revolutionary or militant. A major part of Max Weber's implicit critique of Marx's theory of class is to stress the possible disjunctures between economic and social and political positions.

Historically, the movement towards political advance of the bottommost groups has been a striving for citizenship rights of suffrage. The nineteenth century in Europe can be seen as a long-drawn-out struggle for the extension of voting rights to the disenfranchised. The fight was largely won by World War I in most countries that employ the term "democratic." The formal, legal right to vote is no longer an issue in most countries. The actual use and importance of that right is the more important question today, with

---

[73] The statements in this paragraph are based on special, unpublished tabulations by Otis Dudley Duncan. We are grateful to him for his willingness to let us publish them before his own material appears.

the disturbing exception of Negroes in the American South, who still suffer from concerted efforts to limit their voting.

As Scammon's data show,[74] the frequency of voting decreases the lower the income. Some would argue, as one may infer from Berelson,[75] that it is desirable to have a low voting rate among the low-income and low-educated because they are likely to be ill-informed, antidemocratic voters. But the general sentiment would be that democracy is defined, in part, as the integration of the low-income into the political process.

What should be the target for the voting of the low-income? No group has 100 per cent voting rates. To move to the level of the higher-income group ($10,000 and over), the rate is 84.9 per cent, in contrast to the 49.6 per cent rate in families below $2,000 and the 57.6 per cent rate in the $2,000–$2,999 range. The largest jump in rates is between the $3,000–$4,999 and the $5,000–$7,999 rate, where the change is from the 62.7 to the 72.4 per cent level.[76] This latter figure might well serve as the goal for voting rights among the low-income.[77]

To achieve this level would require not only eliminating the *de facto* resistances to Negro voting, but also reducing the varied requirements that limit voting—for example, residence requirements, English-language literacy, and loss of voting rights because of imprisonment.[78] Increasing the ease of voting may also be necessary—more polling places, longer polling hours, and elimination of registration, so that only one visit is needed in order to vote. A third barrier to voting is, of course, a lack of interest in voting and the political process—whether due to apathy or to a feeling that the issues and candidates are not important or do not involve a significant choice.

The implicit notion here is that low voting rates among the low-income should not be regarded as only a defect of the nonvoters but as a criticism of the political process.

Voting is but one level of the issue of political rights. Another is that of the importance of the vote. This leads to the question which underlies the agitation about reapportionment: Are voters in different areas securing

---

[74] Richard M. Scammon, "Electoral Participation," *Social Goals and Indicators for American Society*, Vol. I, THE ANNALS, Vol. 371 (May 1967), Table 4, p. 63.

[75] Bernard Berelson, Paul F. Lazarsfeld, and W. N. McPhee, *Voting* (Chicago: University of Chicago Press, 1954).

[76] Scammon, *op. cit.*, p. 63.

[77] Here, as elsewhere in this paper, we are not discussing the inequalities which affect other than the low-income. In the case of youth, the obvious point is the issue of the lowering of the voting age to eighteen.

[78] David Caplovitz and other students of Harlem voting patterns contend that when adjustments are made for noneligibles, the voting rate in this locality is as high as in high-income neighborhoods. If this is so, increasing the ease of voting is not important. On the other hand, some data show that a lower proportion of registered low-income than high-income persons actually do vote.

equal representation in a legislative body, whether it be Congress, a state assembly, or a city council? At another, more subtle level, the question is: Do the representatives of the low-income groups have as much sensitivity to their constituents' interests and wishes as do the representatives of higher-income groups? Indicators of this type are difficult, but not impossible, and are best developed and maintained by nongovernmental groups. The simplest form is the American Federation of Labor–Congress of Industrial Organizations (AFL–CIO) report on the voting records on key labor issues of congressmen and senators. The main issues (and positions) for low-income individuals could be delineated,[79] and representatives from low-income districts could be rated on how they stood on these issues; this could be done by civil rights and poverty groups. If similar measures were maintained for higher-income groups, it would be possible to see if there are large differences in the sensitivity of representatives of different socioeconomic groups.[80] It would seem a "natural" for civil rights groups and poverty groups like the Citizens' Crusade against Poverty to maintain such indices.

"Sensitivity of representatives" perhaps begs the issue because the question frequently is: Are the legislative decisions of deep significance to low-income voters? If the issues are marginal in importance, then the sensitivity of the representatives is not central. The radical critics raise the question whether the overlap of the two main parties buries crucial issues of redistribution, since the effort is to appeal to a mythical voter of the center. From the point of view of the low-income, to what extent are the issues that come before legislative bodies of central importance? Are their glaring needs untouched? This analysis could be done both absolutely and relatively (the total number of issues relevant to the low-income and the ratio of these issues to the number relevant to the nonpoor). Obviously, a mode of analysis along these lines is exceedingly difficult and could best be pursued outside the government.

---

[79] What the needed response is on a particular issue from the point of view of a particular income or socioeconomic grouping is not undebatable. But there would be a high degree of agreement on most issues, whether by a panel of experts thinking in terms of a particular group or by a sample of the group itself. At least, this is a testable proposition.

[80] Since most voting districts are not homogeneous (and the larger, the greater the heterogeneity), a representative would have to be rated in terms of his sensitivity to a particular group, rather than to the district as a whole. As less direct way of measuring sensitivity is the MacRae method of seeing to what extent a district is a potential swing district. The higher the potential, the greater the sensitivity of the representatives. Are low-income districts more likely than high-income districts to favor one candidate or party so overwhelmingly that a representative feels little pressure for responding to his constitutents' needs and feelings?

Indeed, except for voting rates, it is likely that most appraisals of performance in the political realm can only be carried through by independent groups. This is the result not only of the strong repercussions of these views and the likelihood of manipulation of results for partisan purposes, but, more importantly, of the fact that competing indicators and interpretations are inevitable and desirable. Different groups and interests would want quite different sets of information and would interpret them in very contrasting ways.

Our analysis so far has been at the level of voting and representation. But a good deal of what is important in terms of political position and process is not in the development of policy but in its administration. The militant attacks on "the welfare state" are, in part, sparked by concerns about administrative injustices and inhumanity. A modern view of political process and power must analyze the relationships of individuals to bureaucracies. The proliferation of governmental agencies means that a good deal of what affects the life of the poor emanates from bureaucracies and bureaucrats. Important decisions are made administratively as well as legislatively. The way in which agency officials treat the low-income may be more important than the law which the officials purport to administer.

First, the *quality of treatment* is one important aspect of bureaucratic functioning. The issue of decency in behavior of officials towards citizen-clients has been raised most sharply recently in the realm of public welfare, where there have been charges of invasion of privacy (checking of homes in "midnight raids," to see if there is evasion of the "no man in the home rule"), the utilization of welfare as a means of social control, and generally humiliating treatment of clients by welfare officials.[81] How to set up indicators of quality of treatment is not clear; perhaps it is easiest to do this if treatment is governed by rights and rules.

Where aid (money and services) is provided to the poor, the latter's claim to this aid is frequently ambiguous. Do they have rights as citizens to these services or are they dependents who lose the privilege of rights because of their dependent status? Increasingly, the issue is raised (see, for example, the report of the 1966 Advisory Committee on Public Welfare) that the provisioning of cash and services becomes a right for individuals. If an individual is refused aid, he should be able to appeal—if necessary, to an adjudicating body that is independent of the agency. If he is poorly treated, he could protest and demand to have the official punished. The example of police review boards leaps to mind.

Second, it would be possible to work up indicators of *rights* and *grievances*. To what extent do programs in aid of the poor have statements of

---

[81] Charles A. Reich, "Individual Rights and Social Welfare: The Emerging Legal Issues," *The Yale Law Journal,* 74 (1965).

rights that are meaningful and effective? Does an agency have a grievance procedure which meets the criteria of effectiveness (the history of union experiences with grievance procedures would probably offer many ways of evaluating procedures): Who uses it, on what issues, with what results? Indicators of rights and grievances could be developed by governmental agencies, but would undoubtedly be limited; outside groups would be more effective in formulating more comprehensive indicators.

Third, in a "pluralistic society," the interests of individuals are represented by organizations and associations. To what extent is the pluralism of American society democratic? Do the low-income have effective representative organizations? Do other groups? How involved are the low-income in the discussions of their groups? What changes are taking place?

Several studies show that membership in voluntary associations increases with status and that membership in associations increases interest in presidential elections.[82] Gradations within the low-income strata are important. In a study of New York City poor, David Caplovitz found that "for the sample as a whole, and within each racial group, the more solvent families more often belong to the voluntary associations." This suggests that the relationship between voluntary-association membership, voting, and social class found in the general population "occurs within the lower class as well; the less the financial stability of the low income family, the less its participation in the life of the broader community."[83]

Quality of treatment, rights and grievance, and representation are important and inadequately supplied today by bureaucracies. But a new demand has emerged which is insufficiently represented in indicators of these types. This fourth issue has been dramatically phrased in that ambiguous phrase of "maximum feasible participation," the right to share in the decision-making of administrative agencies. Since so many important decisions are made outside the realm of the legislature, administrative law-making and allocations become increasingly important. While the demand for participation has had many different sides to it—many initially supported it because it would reduce the psychological feeling of powerlessness—in this context, participation is clearly a political act of involvement in important decisions which are nonlegislative. OEO is experimenting with indicators of grass-roots involvement in local community action programs, and, hopefully, these indicators may be adaptable to broader use, as participation issues are much wider than poverty programs.

---

[82] Charles R. Wright and Herbert H. Hyman, "Voluntary Association Memberships of American Adults: Evidence from National Sample Surveys," *American Sociological Review*, 23 (1958).

[83] David Caplovitz, *op. cit.*, pp. 133–134.

The new politics will increasingly involve the relationships of citizens to the welfare state's apparatus. While the participation issue has just begun to be raised in terms of the poor, it will increasingly be raised for other groups in society. The issues of the welfare state are most acute for the poor, but affect other citizens as well. It may be that the call for political participation in decision-making on a wider scale is not a call for reduction of inequalities, as better-off citizens also have limited participation. But their losses from inadequate sharing in decision-making may be less important to them than to the poor, who are so deeply affected by bureaucratic practices. Refinements of measures of "participation" are needed.

A fifth issue is that of the psychological feeling of powerlessness.[84] The poor feel less able to control their destinies than do other groups in society. "The government," "they," and "city hall" loom large, threatening and immovable to many of the poor. Changes in the feeling of powerlessness would not only affect willingness to try to vote, to make changes and share in decision-making, but they may also have importance in their own right as constituting an important state of well-being. Indicators of changes in feelings of powerlessness could be constructed on the basis of the studies of alienation and anomie (indeed, they have been involved in some evaluations of poverty programs). Public opinion surveys could provide relevant data on the indicators. It may turn out that feelings of "powerlessness" are segmented politically. Some institutions may appear to be more permeable than others, and indicators of particular institutions may be necessary.

As with all subjective indicators, the danger of manipulation is important: policies may successfully aim at making people feel more politically powerful even though their political potency has not grown. Here again, it would be important for nongovernmental groups to gauge independently the realistic significance of changed feelings of powerlessness. (And the converse may occur: increased political control without decreased feelings of powerlessness.)

We have talked about power in the political realm, whether at the federal, state, local, or bureaucratic-organizational level. As Dahrendorf has asserted, "class is about power."[85] The conflict about authority is the

---

[84] Melvin Seeman, "On the Meaning of Alienation," *American Sociological Review*, 24 (1959), pp. 783–791. Seeman identifies five alternative meanings of alienation: powerlessness, meaninglessness, normlessness, isolation, and self-estrangement. Blauner demonstrates that because the conditions of work and existence in various industrial environments are quite different, the industry in which the man works is fateful in furthering or abating each of the five dimensions of alienation examined by Seeman—Robert Blauner, *Alienation and Freedom: The Factory Worker and His Industry* (Chicago: University of Chicago Press, 1964).

[85] Ralf Dahrendorf, "Recent Changes in the Class Structure of European Societies," *Daedalus*, 93 (Winter 1964).

universal issue of which the Marxist concern with property is a special though important case.[86] We have not addressed power and authority relationships in the workplace, a sixth dimension of power.

The jobs of the poor are less frequently rationalized than the jobs of the better-off;[87] they are less frequently organized into unions; low-skilled workers are more easily replaceable than high-skilled workers, so that employers can be more forceful with the former. Or so it would seem. Indicators of workplace independence and participation would be useful to develop, for the nature of job authority is an important part of well-being, even if we do not fully recognize it as such today.[88]

We suspect that the discussions of democracy in the political process will be supplemented in the next years by the reopening of questions about authority at work, although not necessarily in the old forms of socialist ownership or of shibboleths of worker participation.

STATUS AND SATISFACTION

Why is status important? As we have pointed out earlier, a gain in income that is stigmatized diminishes the satisfactions of the income-recipients. Further, it may be that a major issue of the poor today is their social exclusion, rather than their income level. Being included in society—which means being accorded respect and accepted in social and political relations with others—is increasingly an important part of the issue of inequality.[89]

Status refers to the views that others hold of an individual. This view affects the way in which individuals are treated—with approval or with disapprobation, with respect or dishonor. The "two nations" of Disraeli and Harrington, the have's and the have-not's, are divided not only by income and hope, but by respect as well. The immediate view is that the gulf between the have's and have-not's has been reduced, but a more accurate view is probably that more individuals are now have's and are accept-

---

86 Ralf Dahrendorf, *Class and Class Conflict in Industrial Society* (Stanford, Calif.: Stanford University Press, 1959).

87 Blauner has reported the wide variations of responsibility and freedom among blue-collar jobs. He has reopened a number of important issues—Robert Blauner, *op. cit.*

88 S. M. Miller and Ira Harrison, "Types of Dropouts—The Unemployables," in Arthur Hartak and William Gomberg (eds.), *Blue Collar World* (Englewood Cliffs, N.J.: Prentice-Hall, 1964).

89 We do not discuss mass and other styles of culture in this paper. But issues of culture will probably re-emerge as important; they have done so very forcefully with regard to Negro culture and history.

able. What about those left behind in the general advance of society? Are they less likely now to be viewed as subhuman, undeserving of attention? There probably has been a growth of humanity, but there still is a sizable difference in the ways in which the low-income and others are regarded.

The United States no longer has a legal basis for dishonor in the form of laws requiring discrimination against minority groups. But the practices of discrimination frequently exist—on the job, in housing, in public facilities, and in education. Data for overt discrimination are difficult to collect. Crucial activities and localities could be studied, however, to see changes in discrimination patterns and frequency. National cross-sections of minority-group members could be studied over time (preferably as a panel) to see whether they have had changing experiences with discrimination. In the case of discrimination, the goal is clear-cut: the total elimination of discrimination on the basis of race, religion, ethnic extraction, and income.

Discrimination is the most striking case of status barriers. But it is not the main dimension today. The more important dimensions surround the prestige of various groupings in society and the nature of the interactions among groups. Data are lacking on the ways in which low-income groups are rated by others. The most common data available are those on occupational prestige; they uniformly show that the occupations held by the low-income are at the bottom. In 1947 and 1963, janitors, bartenders, share-croppers, garbage-collectors, street-sweepers, and shoeshiners were ranked among the bottom ten in prestige of ninety occupations in nationwide samples.

But what is the goal in reduction of prestige differences? We do not anticipate complete equality here, but some reduction in the range of differences. Unfortunately, we have not been able to find data dealing with compression or expansion of the occupational-prestige range within a nation. Setting specific goals would require more knowledge of trends. The greater difficulty is that the policies to follow are not clear.[90]

Studies of communities have revealed the stratification and exclusions which occur.[91] These studies report the fact of different ratings, but not the span of the differences in ratings. It would seem not too difficult to develop measures of the differences among groups, whether stratified by income, occupation, or more complex sets of measurements. The use of these meas-

---

[90] Robert W. Hodge, Paul M. Siegel, and Peter H. Rossi, "Occupational Prestige in the United States: 1925–1963," in Reinhard Bendix and S. M. Lipset (eds.), *Class Status and Power* (New York: Free Press, 1966), Table 1, p. 325.

[91] Cf. Robert S. Lynd and Helen M. Lynd, *Middletown: A Study in Contemporary American Culture* (New York: Harcourt, Brace, 1929); W. Lloyd Warner, "The Yankee City Series," and *American Life: Dream and Reality* (Chicago: University of Chicago Press, 1953); and Arthur Vidich and Joseph Bensman, *Small Town in Mass Society* (Princeton, N.J.: Princeton University Press, 1958).

ures over time would inform our guesses as to whether the gulfs among strata are increasing or decreasing.

One simple measure does already exist, but its interpretation is subject to considerable controversy. This indicator is the degree and kind of interaction which exists among individuals and families of different economic standing. (In many community studies, especially those influenced by Warner, position in the community is defined by reputàtion, an assessment which is influenced by the patterns of interaction among families of a community. The measure that we seek would require arraying individuals on an indicator such as income and then studying the differences in interaction patterns.) The evidence is unmistakable—low rates of cross-class, nonjob interaction.

The target here is unclear. Should the goal be random sorting of interaction so that individuals of high income (or education) are as likely to associate with individuals of low income as with their income peers? Should the goal be that ethnic-group members associate no more frequently with fellow ethnics than with nonethnics? Many would argue for ethnic solidarity—at least for political purposes—among deprived groups like Negroes. While we lack clarity about goals for a society that, in rhetoric at least, is pictured as socially democratic, information over time on these patterns would still be useful in depicting the extent to which gulfs among groups are being narrowed.

Interestingly, it is in this area of contact, social distance, and social honor that we have the greatest difficulty in specifying targets. For in this sensitive area, the cloudy, ambiguous slogans of American values and goals provide little direction. A more systematic collection of the kinds of information suggested here may force re-examination of broad tenets and specific behaviors which are poorly articulated or understood.

The basis for and the way in which one receives income affect the satisfactions derived from income. In American society, income that is not obtained directly or indirectly from work or education (for example, scholarships) is likely to be demeaned. Some 15 per cent of adult units with under $1,000 income received payments in the form of public welfare, accompanied by demeaning means tests.

Transfer payments to upper, unlike lower, income groups generally have the seal of social acceptance. Social security, government payments to farmers, and indirect subsidies in the form of tax deductions, allowances, and exemptions are generally accepted forms of government transfers. Fifty-five per cent of total 1963 government payments to farmers went to the top 11 per cent of all farmers, those with farm sales of $20,000 and over.[92]

[92] Theodore Schultz, "Public Approaches to Minimize Poverty," in Leo Fishman (ed.), *Poverty Amid Affluence* (New Haven, Conn.: Yale University Press, 1966).

Many of the discussions of the reform of the welfare system are concerned with the importance of removing the stigma associated with receiving income in this way. The concern is largely, though not exclusively, with the degradation of the means-test ceremonials. In effect, then, we are in the midst of a *politicalization of status* where the distribution of stigma through the distribution of income and service is being challenged. Stigma is now a political issue; the demand is for mechanisms, like the negative income tax, welfare rights, or family allowances, which reduce the possibilities of families' having low status because of the way that they procure income. (In part, too, as we shall discuss shortly, the effort is to change the recipients' views of themselves by removing the stigmatizing procedures.) While it would be difficult to construct, an index of income stigma would be a useful indicator in measuring poverty movement.[93]

Our discussion of status has been of external views of the poor. But a very important area is the way that the poor look upon themselves. A significant aspect of satisfactory life is the degree of acceptance of self, the agreeability of self-image, the satisfactions with life. In addition to statistical data of actual inequalities, indicators are needed of individuals' perceptions of inequalities in each dimension of well-being: incomes, assets, basic services, social mobility and education, political position, and status. In England, Runciman has demonstrated the extent to which attitudes toward social inequalities have failed to correspond with the facts of inequality, whether economic, social, or political.[94] These are difficult issues to discuss in the context of policies without being reminded of *1984*; but the dangers of their manipulation should not prevent us from first exploring some issues, even if, on civil libertarian, democratic grounds, we later decide that we do not wish to pursue study and action along these lines.

In contrast to the "good savage, healthy and free" view of the poor, most measures show that they enjoy life less than do other groups. As one would expect in an industrial, instrumentally oriented society, the available data are largely about job satisfaction and morale. Here, the results are almost all in the same direction: the higher the job level, the greater the degree of job satisfaction: for example, only 16 percent of unskilled auto workers as compared with over 90 per cent of mathematicians and urban university professors reported that they would try to get into a similar type of work if they could start over again.[95]

According to the findings of Bradburn and Caplovitz' study on happiness, job dissatisfaction is an instance of relative deprivation. Men in a

---

[93] This measure may run the danger of perpetuating stigmatizing practices.

[94] W. G. Runciman, *Relative Deprivation and Social Justice: A Study of Attitudes to Social Inequality in Twentieth-Century England* (Berkeley and Los Angeles: University of California Press, 1966).

[95] Harold Wilensky, "Varieties of Work Experience," in Henry Borow (ed.), *Man in a World of Work* (Boston: Houghton Mifflin, 1964), p. 137.

low socioeconomic position in prosperous communities were found more dissatisfied with their jobs than similar men in depressed communities.[96]

Studies of mental health show the higher rate of severe illness among the lowest socioeconomic groups. For example, in the most famous survey,[97] class V, the bottom group, had a schizophrenic rate of 895 per 100,000 while class 1-II had a rate of 111. Unfortunately, as in most studies, this investigation is marred by the possibility of underenumerating of illness in the upper-income groups. More complex assessments of mental health show that the bottommost class is characterized by more emotional instability than higher-placed groups.[98]

As a goal, the reduction of mental illness, especially severe mental illness, among lower socioeconomic groups would be important, as well as reducing the rates as rapidly as they are reduced among the higher groups.

The importance of dignity, satisfaction, self-respect, and self-image is evidenced in Negroes' calling for institutional settings, especially in schools, which foster the development of positive self-images. While, in part, this demand is clearly political in terms of power, at another level it is a psychologically based demand, insisting that the development among Negroes of positive attitudes toward themselves is a responsibility of society. While one can argue about the best way to do this—whether "black power" and separate institutions are the only instruments—the intent of the goal—positive self-image—is one which many would accept as a societal obligation. *The differential distribution of positive feelings about one's self is perhaps the essence of inequality.*

Recently, studies have been aimed at studying the elusive issue of happiness.[99] These studies, which provide a base for the development of

---

[96] Norman M. Bradburn and David Caplovitz, *Reports on Happiness: A Pilot Study of Behavior Related to Mental Health* (Chicago: Aldine, 1965).

[97] August B. Hollingshead and Frederic Redlich, *Social Class and Mental Illness* (New York: John Wiley and Sons, 1958), p. 232.

[98] Srole and his associates surveyed midtown Manhattan by interviewing a cross-section of residents of their homes. Persons classified as "well" rose steadily from 9.7 per cent in the lowest socioeconomic category (F) to 24.4 per cent in the highest (A): those classified as "impaired" declined from 33.7 to 16.4 per cent in the second highest category and then rose slightly to 17.5 per cent in the highest SES. The term "incapacitated" was applied to category F, 3.3 per cent of category B, and 1.9 per cent of category A. Studies of this kind are subject to the criticism that similar symptoms may not have the same implications and intensity in groups differentially placed in society. See L. Srole, T. S. Langner, S. T. Michael, M. K. Opler, and T. A. C. Rennie, *Mental Health in the Metropolis* (New York: McGraw-Hill, 1962).

[99] Cf. Norman M. Bradburn and David Caplovitz *op. cit.;* G. Gurin, J. Veroff, and S. Feld, *Americans View Their Mental Health* (New York: Basic Books, 1960); L. Srole, T. S. Langner, S. T. Michael, M. K. Opler, and T. A. C. Rennie, *op. cit.;* Derek L. Phillips, "Social Participation and Happiness," *American Journal of Sociology,* 72, 5 (March 1967).

time-series investigations of the nation's psychological well-being, indicate that positive and negative feelings vary independently of each other. Again, the interrelationships among education and income are complex. Education and happiness are positively related for those who earn less than $7,000 a year, but negatively related among wealthier people.[100]

The Bradburn-Caplovitz study of happiness in four medium-size communities demonstrates the importance of many items which are not included in the definition of an "adequate level of income." Going for a ride in a car as well as eating in a restaurant several times a week and participating in or watching games or sports activities are related to positive feelings. The degree of a community's economic depression is reflected in the happiness of lower, but not higher, socioeconomic groups. Economic privation through loss of job, low income, or increased vulnerability to economic stress with increasing age were found to affect the feelings of individuals most greatly.[101]

In dealing with status and self-respect, we are in the most troublesome realms, where manipulation and invasion of privacy are grave threats. But the ultimate tests of inequality are not only in income alone; societies with fairly similar income profiles can have enormous differences in the distribution of other values. The dangers should not obscure the recognition of what the ultimate objectives are, nor should the seeming neutrality of the material elements of well-being lead us into taking easy measurements which eliminate study of the new demands that are being made of the affluent society. For example, in the kibbutz, it has been reported that the differential of greatest importance in affecting people's treatment by others and view of themselves is length of stay in the kibbutz.[102] "Stratification" was pronounced, despite the equality ni the distribution of income.

CONCLUSION

A specific timetable of inequality-reduction is needed. Without clear-cut targets we cannot assess our progress. In income we, would urge that we set as a goal the reduction of the number of families below a family poverty line to 5 per cent by 1975. (The line should move in relation to prices and general economic advance.) We could seek to expand the share of income going to the bottom 20 per cent by 2 per cent to 3 per cent in the next ten years. In other discussions, specific targets should be set up. The

---

[100] Bradburn and Caplovitz, *op. cit.*, p. 11.

[101] *ibid.*, pp. 46, 63.

[102] Eva Rosenfeld, "Social Stratification in a Classless Society," *American Sociological Review*, 16 (December 1951).

absence of concrete targets hinders the building up of interest groups and the intense counterplay of competing strategies.

In emphasizing the importance of inequality and of its varied forms, we are not implicitly arguing the case that there should not be any important distinctions among individuals. Rather, we believe that a number of inequalities are much greater than many realize and that they are hard to defend on the basis even of an economically rational allocation of benefits. We are also critical of them on the basis of our view of what is a desirable society.[103]

We believe that greater awareness of the extent of inequalities, an awareness which would be deepened by the presentation of the kinds of indicators suggested here, would make possible more useful discussions of inequality: How many differences and what kind are we really willing to live with?

It could be argued that unconscious inequality is preferable to conscious inequality, that if society is unaware of the degree of inequality and of the processes leading to it, society is less damaging to disadvantaged individuals than if there were a sorting out of the disadvantaged. This is a danger, eloquently expressed by Michael Young in *The Rise of the Meritocracy.*

But we do find it hard to accept the notion that *at this time* unawareness of inequalities is more kind to the disadvantaged than public discussion of these inequalities.

> Considered only in terms of opportunity and power, class [that is, inequality] appears as a unilateral possession of privileges, a greater accumulation of benefits and powers in one sector of society than another. But class is clearly more than this. It is a universal loss. There is one human need it violates in all members of society, oppressors and oppressed alike; the need of men for each other. It is in its aspects as a pure human *division*, rather than an economic or political disparity, which is most often ignored and yet which wholly describes class.[104]

One does not have to embrace the idea of complete equality to feel that reductions in inequality are desirable.[105]

---

103 For interesting discussions of inequality, see W. G. Runciman, *op. cit.;* Bertram de Jouvenel, *The Ethics of Redistribution* (Cambridge, England: Cambridge University Press, 1952); Lee Rainwater, "Towards A Society of Average Men," unpublished; and Robin Blackburn, "Inequality and Exploitation," *New Left Review,* No. 42 (March–April 1967).

104 Perry Anderson, "Sweden: A Study in Social Democracy," *New Left Review* (May 1961).

105 See S. M. Miller and Martin Rein, "Poverty, Inequality, and Policy," in Howard Becker (ed.), *Social Problems* (New York: John Wiley & Sons, 1966).

The fact that many of the poor in the United States would be well off in low-income societies suggests that more is involved in "poverty" than just low levels of the physical conditions of life. The issues of relative deprivation appear to be more important. In that perspective, we must increasingly turn to the indicators of inequality as well as of "poverty," which implies a scientific standard of subsistence. The second half of the twentieth century requires more sensitive instruments than the nineteenth century.

Poverty is "income-insufficiency," but it is more than that in the affluent society. To be able to discuss poverty and inequality requires an understanding of the changing dynamics and desirable products of the society. As in many other cases—for example, the indictment of education because of its inadequate development of low-income youngsters has probably improved education for all—the situation of the poor is forcing social scientists and actionists to understand better the society in which the disturbing questions of humanity still haunt the economic cornucopia. *The issues of distribution—who should get what—inevitably lead to questioning the character of the "what."*

Social indicators will not tell us what choices to make between growth and inequality-reduction, between spending money on health services or education, between price increases or expansion, and the like. But they can prevent us from ignoring the fact that we are making choices. Effective measurements will improve our ability to comprehend which kinds of programs are likely to be useful for a particular purpose. But we believe that the hopes for compelling evaluations and knowledge are at least premature. Rather, we look to new knowledge brought out by social indicators to direct us, freshly and more acutely, to the issues of choice that are frequently ignored in a political rhetoric and a social science which lag behind the subtleties of late twentieth-century life. Social indicators can arouse groups, outside the government as well as within, to delineate what "progress" is and how well it is being achieved and distributed. In these assessments, low consensus will emerge. The ensuing debates would be around the central issues of a just society. Social indicators would then contribute to useful conflict rather than to evasive complacency.

13

EMPLOYMENT AND THE "NEW ECONOMICS"

LEON H. KEYSERLING

There is always a driving temptation to look at the problem of employment and unemployment from some "new" perspective, or at least with
some "new" accent. This search for the "new" leads to much discussion of
issues such as these: whether the jobs can be so tailored as to "bring out the
best" in the infinitely variegated human beings who hold these jobs; whether
each individual should be put first in the kind of job which he thinks he might
like most, or which in the judgment of someone else might contribute most
to his personal development; whether we should not start trying to shape
an economic system in which everyone should be entirely free to work or
not to work, as work is customarily defined, on the ground that many
people may reach higher peaks of personal cultivation if they are provided
with good incomes without pressures being imposed upon them to earn
their livings in a full-employment environment.

This compulsion to find something "new" should not be regarded as
an unalloyed evil. It may always yield some fruitful results, and have some
value even as an intellectual pastime. But neither as a practical endeavor
nor as a pastime should this search for the "new" be excessively honored.
What is "new" should always yield to what is needed, whether old or new.

The top social priority, in terms of human needs, is easy to identify.
Massive unemployment, whether attributable to the general economic environment or to the personal characteristics of the victims or to some combination of the two, is still by far our most important and unsolved
economic and social burden. This is particularly true because the massive
unemployment which now exists is intimately associated with poverty,

330

human deterioration, personal bitterness and resentment, and social restiveness or rebellion, whether translated into pernicious or potentially constructive individual or group action.

Whether or not it is better for a person who is highly cultivated to hold a job at pay or to be free instead to write poetry or paint pictures (even if he cannot do this well enough for others to pay him for the results), the Negroes in Watts and Harlem and elsewhere, and most of the unemployed, whether black or white or younger or older or male or female, do not have this kind of cultivation. The real alternative for them, in the near future, is between jobs—not the best possible job, but some decent job at once—and further deterioration and despair.

Under these conditions, we believe that the top priority for the foreseeable future is to restore and maintain a full-employment environment (with compensation adequate to assure for all workers at least a minimum-adequacy standard of living) for all those who are employable, or who can be made employable through additional training and education. We believe that the creation of jobs toward this end should accent those jobs which yield the goods and services most needed by the nation and the people at large, an entirely clear and measurable objective, and that the unemployed should be enabled to flow into these jobs. This strikes me as preferable on all scores to any effort, more dubious and imponderable in results, to match the new jobs to the workers instead of the workers to the jobs. As we shall show, for profoundly social reasons, we are not yet ready to disassociate work from the content of the output, nor view the job just in terms of the occupant. Production *for* consumption still requires primary attention; at the same time, primary focus upon a sustained full-employment environment would offer to the worker more effective choices among jobs than any alternative course.

Our views are fortified by primary concern about the evolution of national economic and social policies at the level of the federal government, because prime remedial measures are mainly within the ambit of federal action. These federal policies should confine themselves mostly, though not entirely, to a few massive programs dealing with the economic environment and structure. Federal action should be very wary of participation in the personal processing or "uplifting" of scores of millions of displaced and downtrodden individuals. The recent obstacles confronting the so-called war on poverty are a prime illustration of what happens when this mistaken course is excessively pursued—pursued partly in the unavowed desire to get by on the cheap without spending a lot of money, and pursued partly in the unavowed desire to blame the individual excessively for deficiencies which reside primarily in the nationwide environment and in basic national economic and social problems.

DEFINITION OF FULL EMPLOYMENT

We define the desirable full-employment goal as a sustained condition where only about 2 per cent of the civilian labor force is unemployed full-time, as officially and conventionally measured. During World War II, unemployment was reduced, at best, to close to one per cent. Unfortunately, economists have not yet recognized how much this genuinely full-employment environment contributed to living standards and personal development and aspirations, and what a driving force toward economic and social progress this new experience during World War II has been since then.

In addition, account should be taken of the full-time equivalent of part-time unemployment: broadly speaking, 100,000 people placed involuntarily on a half-time week should be counted as the equivalent of 50,000 people unemployed full-time, because even part-time unemployment adds to their uncertainties and resentment and plunges most of them into poverty (if they were not there even when fully employed, due to deficient pay). Part-time unemployment also diminishes *pro tanto* the national output, a consideration to which we shall refer further. Widespread part-time unemployment also leads to careless and inefficient utilization of those employed, which is bad both for society and for the individual, particularly the types of individuals who are most likely to be selected for part-time unemployment.

There is also what we call concealed unemployment, in that lack of adequate job opportunity leads millions to withdraw from active search for work, and, upon such withdrawal, they do not enter into the official count of the unemployed. Taking into account these three types of unemployment, the true level of unemployment should be held to about 3 per cent of a civilian labor force of the size which would exist in a full-employment environment.

RELATIONSHIP BETWEEN FULL
EMPLOYMENT AND OPTIMUM
ECONOMIC GROWTH

During the past few years, we have had what some regard as a high or optimum rate of economic growth, and yet we have not come close to restoration of full employment. This has led many who should know better to argue that economic growth, in itself, does not solve the unemployment problem. But there is no merit in this argument. What really happened during these recent years was that the rate of economic growth required to restore full employment was underestimated, and, correspondingly, the policies undertaken to restore full employment were far too limited in size and scope.)

Careful analysis leads to the conclusion that optimum economic growth and sustained full employment are both correlative and concomitant. The rate of productivity advance is favorably conditioned by full employment, and people at work manifestly produce more goods and services than people not at work. It follows that there is no way to define an optimum rate of economic growth except to regard it as that rate which results from full utilization of all our productive resources, including the labor force. Indeed, all experience has shown that the national policies required for optimum economic growth are practically identical with the national policies required for sustained full employment, not only in an economic sense narrowly conceived, but also in psychological and political terms. Conversely, it is also true that the disequilibrium within the economy which militates against economic growth is the same as that which militates against full employment.

Those who have failed to recognize this have argued that full employment makes use of marginal workers who, on the average, are less efficient than those who remain employed even when unemployment is high. This is a truism; but it might be inferred from this truism that our economy would be most efficient if it employed only the 50 million most efficient workers. Output *per worker* might conceivably be higher under that condition, but *total* output would be far lower than with full employment. It is noteworthy that no economist who resorts to the fallacious argument just referred to would fail to insist that full employment is essential during a full-scale war, when full production and optimum economic growth are essential.

THE DEFICIENT RECORD DURING
RECENT YEARS

Although the "new economics" since 1961 has made some gains, it has failed dismally to restore full employment, or anything approximating it. In 1953, despite the ending of the Korean war at the start of that year, full-time unemployment, as officially measured, was only 2.9 per cent. In consequence of recession, full-time unemployment rose to 5.6 per cent in 1954. Within two years, it was reduced to 4.2 per cent in 1956. In 1958, in consequence of the recession of 1957–1958, full-time unemployment rose to 6.8 per cent, and stood at 6.7 per cent in 1961 in consequence of the 1960–1961 recession.

In the five years from 1961 to 1966, full-time unemployment was brought down only to 3.9 per cent in 1966, which in some ways was a less satisfactory record than bringing it down to 4.2 per cent within two years after the recession which terminated in 1954. In early 1967, there were few so optimistic as to forecast that full-time unemployment would average less than 4 per cent during 1967 as a whole.

This leads to the conclusion that the ardent propagandists of the "new economics," instead of bragging repeatedly that "unemployment is not at the lowest level in eight (or eleven or thirteen) years," should awaken to the fact that taking five years to bring unemployment down to a level about twice as high as it ought to be, or a full third higher than it ought to be, even if one accepts 3 per cent unemployment as consistent with full employment, is hardly anything to brag about. And, today, a full-time employment rate in the neighborhood of 4 per cent mean a true level of unemployment of 5.5 to 6 per cent.

This is only part of the picture. A full-time unemployment rate of close to 4 per cent means, as of the time of this writing, a full-time unemployment rate of 7.5 per cent among Negroes, more than 10 per cent among young people, aged 16–21, out of school and in need of work, about 25 per cent among young Negro females out of school and in need of work, and up to 40 per cent in some critical areas of some cities. This is intolerable, and it is even more intolerable that we are now witnessing increased unemployment among these groups.

The same comments, in substance, apply to economic growth. The economic growth rate during the most recent years would have been adequate if it had commenced from a full-employment base. But it has been entirely inadequate as a road toward *restoration* of full employment. Moreover, the economic growth rate began to shrink very seriously around the middle of 1965, and is now running, and is commonly forecast to continue to run for some time to come, at an average annual rate of less than 3 per cent. The adverse impact of this upon public revenues and needed public programs was again demonstrated in the fiscal 1968 federal budget, proposed in January 1967.

As a matter of fact, while the economic upturn following the recession of 1960–1961 has been much longer than those following the recessions of 1949, 1953–1954, and 1957–1958, the fundamental economic disequilibrium which led to recessions after earlier upturns has not been dealt with effectively by the "new economics." There was nothing remarkable in the fact that a huge shot-in-the-arm, in the form of the massive tax reductions of 1964, prolonged for a time the economic upturn. Even that amount of money thrown into the streets would have done that. This shot-in-the-arm, as will be shown, represented a fundamentally erroneous diagnosis both in economic and social terms. Since the middle of 1965, the consequences of this have become increasingly apparent, both in economic and social terms. And the end is not yet.

OBJECTIONS TO FULL EMPLOYMENT

The objections to full employment, entirely meretricious in my view, are manifold, persistent, and prestigious. In *The Affluent Society,* written in 1958, Professor Galbraith urged "abandonment of our national commitment to full employment," although full-time unemployment in that year as a whole reached the monstrous level of almost 7 per cent (with true unemployment of about 10 per cent)—and although three years later the New Frontiersmen (of whom he was one) made their central purpose the cutting of full-time unemployment to below 4 per cent. Professor Galbraith argued that full employment was unnecessary because the more rapid expansion of production and the more rapid economic growth which would result from full employment was no longer needed; that high employment would disturb "social balance" by being "inflationary"; and that a humane system of unemployment benefits was an adequate substitute for employment.

Dr. Robert Theobald has gone considerably further, urging that we should concentrate upon achieving what he has very recently called "full unemployment." He urges this on the social grounds that we have become so rich and productive an economy that what we need most is the fuller development of the individual personally, and that "full unemployment" will contribute most toward this end, by enabling the individual to concentrate upon personal development. Dr. Theobald insists also that technology and automation are advancing so rapidly that massive unemployment far beyond that suffered during the Great Depression is entirely unavoidable in any event, and that we should not only resign ourselves to this circumstance but actually encourage its advent.

Even in economic terms narrowly conceived, it is charitable to call these arguments nothing worse than preposterous. There has been a distinctly noticeable trend toward accelerating productivity gains over the decades. But even projecting these trends liberally for a decade or longer ahead, a United States economic growth rate averaging annually in the neighborhood of 5 per cent would be sufficient to absorb those productivity gains, and to provide full employment for a growing labor force. Considering that we achieved an average annual economic growth rate of about 9 per cent during World War II, with so many millions of our young people in the Armed Forces and therefore not in the productive process, and despite the inefficiencies and dislocations of total war, there is nothing exceedingly difficult about maintaining, during the years ahead, the growth rate of 5 per cent which we have actually bettered during 1962–1966. And as we have already succeeded in reducing full-time unemployment from almost 7 per cent in 1958 to slightly less than 4 per cent in early 1967, why cannot we reduce it much farther if we really try? Why should we accept Dr. Theobald's fantastic estimate that unemployment must rise to 80 per cent or higher by ten years from now?

The President's Council of Economic Advisers (CEA), which in early 1961 set an *interim* target of reducing full-time unemployment to 4 per cent, is now in 1967 insisting that the current 4 per cent full-time unemployment rate borders upon "overemployment," that this has "inflationary" portents, and that consequently we should deliberately adopt national economic policies to hold down the rate of economic growth to about 4 per cent during the years immediately ahead. The recently proposed tax increase is a step in that direction. This entire approach is dangerously wrong.

A 4 per cent growth rate would not hold unemployment constant, as the CEA insists it would; instead, it would lead to large increases in unemployment in due course. There has never been a time since the end of World War I when reasonably full resource use has been sustained for a significant number of years without an average annual growth rate of 4.5 to 5 per cent. Looking to the future, the Secretary of Labor has told us recently that productivity in the private economy has been advancing at about 3.5 per cent a year during the last six years. In view of technological trends, this rate of advance will not be reduced in the years ahead, unless productivity growth is artificially inhibited by excessively idle resources of plant and manpower. The labor force in the years ahead will continue to grow 1.5 per cent a year or better, unless more concealed unemployment (nonparticipation in the labor force) results from scarcity of job opportunity. Joining the productivity and labor-force factors, it is entirely clear that we must grow at least 5 per cent a year to absorb the annual increments in productivity and in the civilian labor force, even *after* reasonable full resource use is restored by cutting existing unemployment by more than one-third, and preferably in half. To *achieve* this restoration even by early 1969, we need to grow about 6 per cent annually until then (and 5 per cent thereafter).

THE "INFLATIONARY" ARGUMENT

Of course, the argument is advanced by many of the high priests of academic economics (which might be rechristened "nonobservational economics" that an economic growth rate in excess of 4 per cent would be "inflationary." That is an old argument indeed. But the CEA, in contributing to the general tendency to exaggerate this prospect, ignores both empirical observation and its own pronouncements during recent years. There is no persuasive evidence, either overseas or in the United States, that an optimum economic growth rate, short of the hyperpressures of a full-scale war mobilization, is more inflationary than a seriously deficient growth rate. During 1953–1960, the average annual United States economic growth rate in real terms was only 2.4 per cent, and was punctuated by three recessions. Yet we witnessed the "paradox" of very substantial inflation during parts of this period, even during the recession of 1957–1958. During 1960–1965, the average annual real rate of economic growth was approximately doubled. Yet we enjoyed relative price stability, and CEA itself took legitimate pride in the combination of higher economic growth and more price stability.

To be sure, price increases have been excessive from mid-1965 forward. But even if we look at the whole period 1960 to date, it provides rather conclusive evidence that a high rate of economic growth averages annually less inflation than stagnation and recession—short of a deep depression. A large part of the reason for this is that, in a largely administered price system, the effort is made to compensate for an inadequate volume of business by lifting prices to obtain excessive per-unit returns. My own belief is that awareness of the economic slowdown, and some fears of a recession later on, constitute a main explanation of the most serious of the price increases during the past year, in the desire to "get while the getting is good." Another explanation of the most recent inflation is selective shortages, as in farm products and medical facilities and personnel, due to long devotion to scarcity economics and long aversion to the economics of full-employment abundance.

Assuming for the moment that we were not entirely correct in the immediately foregoing argument, the idea of "trading off" optimum growth and full employment for a slightly slower rate of price increase is pure nonsense. Price stability in itself is no virtue, as indicated by the fact that the Great Depression came upon us after seven years of remarkable price stability, except for *falling* farm prices. More important than the absolute trends in prices are the *relative* trends in prices and incomes throughout the structure. It is maladjustments in these *relationships* that work against both economic equilibrium and social justice.

Even if one were to accept the non-demonstrable thesis that a full-time unemployment rate of 2 per cent, rather than 4 per cent, and a more satisfactory economic growth rate, would exert somewhat more pressure upon prices, it is utterly unconscionable that we should ask millions of unemployed and their families to be the insurers of the affluent against somewhat higher prices on their third cars, extra steak dinners, and additional fur coats. If the economy were now really in danger from the type of inflation which results from excessive aggregate demand (which we deny), then we should have the courage and decency (through properly selective tax increases and other measures) to repress the scores of billions of dollars of demand for the superfluous or the secondary, instead of conducting the war against inflation by saddling the burden of this war upon the unemployed and upon the great priorities of our national needs.

FULL EMPLOYMENT, ECONOMIC
GROWTH, AND NATIONAL NEEDS

Even putting aside the meretricious argument that the unemployed in Watts and Harlem and elsewhere, black and white, young and older, male and female, might be helped more by "full unemployment" with guaranteed incomes than by full employment, there is this controlling fact: we have not yet reached a state in the industrial arts, even in the United States, where the speculative individual benefits to be derived from high unemployment can compete with the nonspeculative benefits to be derived from the optimum economic growth which sustained full employment would yield.

Let us look at the facts. We still have about 32 million people living in poverty. We still have another 28 million people living above poverty, as currently defined, but nonetheless living in deprivation, with incomes far below the minimum requirements for an adequacy standard in the American context. Regardless of *why* these 60 million people are where they are, it is inescapably true that none of these people can be lifted to an adequate standard of living without an increase in the goods and services flowing to them. This is true, whether increasing that flow depends upon changing the poor and deprived, or changing the economic and social treatment they receive. And why stop with the poor and deprived? Even an urban multiple-person family with an income of $10,000, which would place it very far above the median United States multi-person family income, feels legitimately that it is hard-pressed to enjoy the goods and services and niceties which are regarded as essential by college professors with incomes several times that amount who do not feel that they have too much, and who write books about our "private opulence" as a nation. More than three-quarters of our senior citizens, close to 20 million in number, still live in abject poverty, as do more than 40 per cent of our farm families.

Beyond this, due to neglect of the public sector, our cities are falling into decay; our transportation systems are obsolete; our airs and waters are filled with poison; about 40 per cent of our people, despite Medicare, cannot obtain satisfactory medical services at costs within their means; a majority of our public schools are in shambles and our teachers underpaid;

and hundreds of thousands of young people each year cannot pursue education to the limits of their abilities and inclinations because they lack the means to do so. Far from the United States being surfeited or saturated as a whole with material things, it will take a decade or longer, even with the *full* use of our resources and a much more socially minded distribution of the product, to abolish evils which stand as a glaring indictment of our society and a growing menace to every American. To meet all of these needs, *without* programs of redistribution so severe as to entail gross domestic conflict, if not so severe as to be entirely unattainable, will require the full use of our burgeoning productive resources.

A few further qualifications may help to drive home this point. Due to the inadequate rate of economic growth from 1953 through 1966, we forfeited more than 700 billion dollars worth of production of goods and services—gross national product (GNP), measured in 1965 dollars—and suffered 35 million man-years of unnecessary and unmerited unemployment. This led to untold human suffering in the private sector. It simultaneously deprived governments at all levels of more than 200 billion dollars in public revenues at existing tax rates, with consequent and progressive neglect of the great priorities of our public needs.

A full-employment economic growth rate averaging about 5 per cent during the decade ahead would yield an aggregate of about 500 billion dollars *more* in total national production over the ten-year period, or an average of about 50 billion *more* per year, than would be yielded by the 4 per cent growth rate (accompanied by excessive unemployment), to which the Council of Economic Advisers now appears to be wedded. Considering that only about 13 billion dollars a year of resource use, properly allocated, would be needed annually to lift 32 million Americans out of the poverty cellar, we can see immediately the immense potentials of sustained full employment and optimum economic growth. All this is especially relevant today, when our national economic programs are short-changing so dangerously the programs more relevant to a war against poverty and against the tremendous deficiencies in the public sector, and when our international efforts are thereby brought into such a proximate clash with our domestic needs.

AGGREGATE APPROACH TO
FULL EMPLOYMENT

The aggregate approach to restoration of full employment insists that increases in total spending or demand, if large enough, will eliminate unemployment in excess of "frictional" or minimum unemployment. These increases in total spending may be achieved by fiscal policies, counting both their direct and indirect or "multiplier" effects. These fiscal policies may take the form of larger public outlays, without corresponding increases in taxation. They may take the form of tax reduction to induce more private spending, without corresponding reduction in public spending.

In addition, increases in total spending may be promoted in the private sector by correcting maladjustments in the distribution of income which cause saving to rise faster than it is actually utilized for production and employment purposes; idle manpower and plant are manifestations of such excess saving. At other times, the distribution maladjustments might cause spending to rise faster than the growth in production capabilities—result, classic inflation (not to be confused with the recent manifestations of inflation, discussed earlier). The needed corrections in the private sector may be achieved through voluntary adjustments in prices, wages, profits, and investments, which would bring into better balance our ability to produce and our efforts to consume. Adjustments in the private sector may also result from public policies which impose private obligations, such as minimum-wage legislation, various aspects of the Social Security program, federal price-wage guidelines, and some regulatory programs.

In very large measure, the aggregate approach to full employment expresses an inescapable and even palpable truth. Not a single unemployed person can get a job anywhere (except by taking it away from somebody else), unless there is additional spending to employ this person, even if there is a current job opening waiting to be filled. This means more aggregate spending. And since this additional spending adds to our total production of goods and services, there is a clear and direct correlation between the reduction of unemployment and the rate of economic growth. The foregoing is true even if the unemployed are unemployed because of personal deficiencies, and failure to recognize this explains some of the arid and confusing controversy between the aggregate school and the structural school.

FLAWS IN THE AGGREGATE
APPROACH, AS APPLIED
BY THE "NEW ECONOMICS"

In the main, the "new economics" has adopted the aggregate approach to full employment, but has done so far too timidly; the measures adopted have simply not been powerful enough to reduce unemployment to acceptable levels. And the swingover in 1967 from a stimulative fiscal policy to a restraining fiscal policy, despite a serious shrinkage in the rate of economic growth and increasing weaknesses in many important sectors of the economy, has represented a return to primary concern with the immediate condition of the federal budget rather than primary concern with the state of the national economy. This strange swingover negates the inflated claims made on behalf of the "new economics," that it had brought about a great "consensus" in favor of making the federal budget subservient to national needs, and in favor of concentrating upon removing the deficits in the national economy rather than the deficit in the federal budget.

Second, the aggregate approach, as applied by the "new economics," has neglected the core meaning of the new technology and automation: a dollar of additional spending for one purpose will not help the job situation as much as a dollar of additional spending for another purpose. There are some industries where the rate of output per man-hour will continue to rise faster than any likely increase in demand for the products of these industries, no matter how much money consumers have jingling in their pockets. For example, using an index of 100 to represent the ratio of employment to production in the base period 1947–1949, this ratio by 1966 had fallen to 38.8 in agriculture; 52.9 in all manufacturing; 62.6 in iron and steel; 54.0 in electrical machinery and equipment; 54.3 in motor vehicles and other transportation equipment; and 43.4 in railroads. And these trends, in the main, will persist.

We therefore need to redirect an increasing portion of total demand toward those goods and services where the increases in real national needs from year to year are so great that expansion of output to meet these needs in full will outrun the rate of advance in technology and productivity, and thus contribute millions of additional jobs. This will also provide a job-product mix including a much higher proportion of semiskilled and relatively unskilled jobs; this is what large portions of the unemployed need at once. It is futile to train people for job patterns of the past, which we could not repeat if we would, and should not repeat if we could.

For, even apart from technological considerations, and although almost any kind of employment is better than unemployment, employment cannot be the sole criterion. We do not want leaf-raking or pyramid-building. We cannot be satisfied with a million more jobs resulting from construction of luxurious hotels on the beaches and from production of superfluous gadgets by the hundreds of millions, if this substitutes for the additional jobs which would result from creation of effective demand and markets for the things we need most as a nation and a people. This consideration unites the goal of full employment with the goals for meeting the other priorities of our national needs, especially the abolition of poverty.

Third, the "new economics," in striving to increase aggregate demand by increasing purchasing power without regard to the distribution of this purchasing power, has almost inexplicably ignored the whole problem of economic balance or equilibrium. We have had repeated empirical proof that the deficient economic performance since 1953 has resulted more from the maldistribution of purchasing power than from a deficiency in the aggregate. Each of the recessions during the Eisenhower Administration occurred when incomes and other funds available for private investment in the means of production grew so much more rapidly than funds available for private consumer spending and public spending combined that the increase in our ability to produce far outran the consumption of combined private spending and public outlays.

This situation was very apparent again in 1964. Yet the massive tax reductions allocated an entirely undue portion of the increased purchasing power to corporate investors and to high-income people who save much larger portions of their after-tax incomes for investment purposes than those lower down in the income structure. The results were entirely foreseeable: this fiscal policy, combined with a monetary policy which also has been perverse in its income consequences, and with price-wage guidelines which were highly biased toward profits at the expense of wages, exacerbated an inordinate investment boom. During the past few years, private investment in production of durable equipment has increased several times as fast as public consumption and public outlays combined, the latter being sacrificed to the misplaced tax reduction. By 1966, the Council of Economic Advisers was endeavoring, albeit with weak measures, to redress the consequences of its own defaults in analysis and foresight by advocating with success the suspension of the investment tax credit (later restored). I cannot say that the timing of this action was bad, because this tax concession was wrongly directed *ab initio*.

However, in 1967, with the economic growth rate having already declined greatly, with the imbalances in the economy becoming more pronounced, and with many informed people fearing that we were moving toward still another recession, the Council urged a 6 per cent tax *increase* across the board. This was a wrong measure, made further defective because such a tax increase would not compensate nearly enough for the regressive nature of the tax cuts of 1964 and the tax concessions of 1962 and 1965.

Fourth, and most important of all, even if the basic economic policies of the "new economics" had dealt properly with the problem of economic equilibrium (which they did *not*), these policies were fatally defective because they took absolutely no account of ultimate values and national needs. Insofar as the policy succeeded temporarily in accelerating economic growth and reducing unemployment, it did so by augmenting the production of the goods and services the nation needed least, on terms which involved further repression of public outlays directed towards goods and services which the nation needs most. Even *if* a million unemployed could be put to work by filling job vacancies in luxury-hotels, perfumery-manufacturing plants, sports palaces, gardening, television-color-set production, and so on an *ad infinitum*, should we not instead put them to work replacing the slum ghettos, serving as lower-grade technicians in hospitals, cleaning up the Potomac, building mass-transport systems, and moving forward more vigorously all along the front of the Great Society? Even if, to avoid "inflation," this required (by some tax increases of a highly *progressive* nature) *cutbacks* in some of the demand for goods and services of tinsel value, should we not still do it?

STRUCTURAL APPROACH TO FULL EMPLOYMENT

The structural approach to full employment, as usually defined, explains unemployment largely in terms of the "unfitness" of the unemployed, and urges the training and retraining programs which would enable them to fill job openings which (it is claimed) already exist, or which (it is claimed) would automatically result from better-prepared seekers for jobs.

While there can be no doubt that we need even better programs of training and retraining than we now have, we must reject most emphatically the proposition that the main reason for excessive unemployment resides in the personal characteristics of the unemployed. This fallacy rests upon failure to distinguish between the reasons why too many are unemployed, and the reason why particular people are *selected* for unemployment when there are not enough jobs to go around.

If the current level of full-time unemployment were to rise from about 4 per cent of the civilian labor force to 8 per cent, due to insufficient spending to hold unemployment steady, the additional unemployment would be manily among the "vulnerables." These would be the older workers; the young people seeking to enter the labor force for the first time; the semiskilled and relatively unskilled; the nonwhites rather than the whites, and the women rather than the men, insofar as discrimination against nonwhites and women remained, or because discrimination during the past century and longer has prevented nonwhites and women on the average from having the degree of training and education which others have. But to say that this would be the *reason* why they became unemployed would be like saying that, if half of the people in a lifeboat died from exposure because they were not as strong as the others in the boat, the cause was the condition of their health rather than the shipwreck. Conversely, the reduction of unemployment to only about one per cent of the civilian labor force during World War II provided jobs for those who had just previously been called "unfit," and also for millions who customarily did not enter the labor force at all.

RELEVANT ASPECTS OF THE
POVERTY PROGRAM

Just as there has been too much stress upon the characteristics of the individual and too little attention to over-all economic and social default in dealing with unemployment, the same trouble has occurred with a vengeance in our treatment, to date, of the poverty problem. The relevance of this to the unemployment problem has received far too little attention.

The aspect of the current "war against poverty" which centers in the program of the Office of Economic Opportunity under the Economic Opportunity Act of 1964 is of tremendous significance. This program reflects the dedication of the President and the Congress to this war. It has already helped to reveal the nature and scope of the poverty problem, and in a short time has made measurable gains against some aspects of this problem. Yet the major aspects of a full-scale war against poverty cannot be found within the confines of the Economic Opportunity Act. Nor are these aspects supported adequately by other national policies and programs.

The main reason why the war against poverty has not accomplished more to date is because those who first developed the outlines of this program failed to appreciate the extent to which effective attacks upon unemployment and poverty are inseparably intertwined. This is obscured by stressing the wide numerical disparity between the 32 million poor and a full-time unemployment rate of not far from 4 per cent, or only about 3 million people, comprising, with their dependents, perhaps fewer than 9 million people, in that many of the unemployed are unattached individuals.

In the first place, the true level of unemployment (contrasted with the full-time unemployment rate of about 4 per cent) is somewhere between 5.5 and 6 per cent, or the equivalent of about 3¾–4¼ million full-time jobs. Translating these breadwinners into their family equivalents, this comes to about 11¼–13 million people.

In the second place, the *same people* are not unemployed throughout the year. In a year when the full-time unemployment rate averages 4 per cent, perhaps 12 per cent of the labor force is unemployed for periods averaging about three months within the year. The consequent loss of income drags the majority of them below the poverty-income ceiling for the year as a whole, if they were not there already, even when fully employed, because of the substandard wages.

Even allowing for the fact that not all of the unemployed and their families are poor, it appears that about 40 per cent of all the poverty in the United States is directly attributable to full-time unemployment or part-time unemployment, and that another 20 per cent of the population are poor because of substandard wages paid to their breadwinners when employed (which, in itself, is an aspect of an unsatisfactory employment environment). This accounts for about *60 per cent* of all the United States poor.

Moreover, the policies and programs designed to assure sustained full employment would necessarily include enlarging greatly the purchasing power of the other 40 per cent of the United States poor who cannot or should not be employed, through adequate welfare payments or guaranteed incomes. This 40 per cent includes almost all of the 25 per cent or so of the poor who are in consumer units headed by senior citizens (granted that some of these senior citizens should be accorded employment opportunity). It includes also the about 13 per cent of the United States poor who are in consumer units headed by women who cannot or should not work (almost 32 per cent of the United States poor are in consumer units headed by women, but much more than half of these women have or should have job opportunities). The remaining 2 per cent are in various categories. Thus, a full-blown employment program would encompass, in one way or another, measures addressed to practically all of the poor, and not just to those in the "employable" population.

The consequence of the prevalent view is not to recognize how predominant a part of the treatment of the poverty problem depends upon full employment policies, and income assistance policies for those who cannot or should not be gainfully employed. Such policies are not generated by personal processing of the poor. Indeed, without prompt development and application of such policies, the war against poverty already has generated tragic resentment and reaction, by lifting expectancies much more rapidly than they are being fulfilled.

There is, of course, an appealing note in the concentration of the Office of Economic Opportunity's program upon the young. Insofar as this approach is based upon recognition that millions of the young have become warped and twisted by the poverty environment in which they have lived, it deserves vigorous support. But insofar as this approach relates to improvement of their general education, it may be proper to ask whether we should not concentrate also upon improving our general educational systems and changing the environment in which these young people live so that they will not drop out of school even if their classrooms are pleasant and their teachers good. Insofar as this approach is based upon the training of the young in a vocational sense, the earlier-stated proposition applies—that we need to know better what to train them for and that in a full-employment environment most of them would be drawn into jobs and trained on the job.

And insofar as concentration upon the young carries any implication that it is too late to do much about their elders, this misinterprets the whole nature of the economic and social problem confronting us all. If we are addressing ourselves to the more than 16 million poor children in the United States, rather than to the relatively few who may be involved for a short period of time in special youth programs, we should all ask these pertinent questions: Can we really rescue the young, without rescuing their parents? Can we really rescue their parents, without profound alterations in the whole environment in which they live—especially the employment environment and the housing environment?

The deficiencies on almost all vital fronts which we have sought to depict do not arise from our failure as a nation or a people to articulate in *qualitative* terms the full scope of what we ought to do. For example, hardly any item in a full catalogue of our needs is omited from the President's 1967 State of the Union Message. Indeed, the general public is coming to believe that we are covering the waterfront, or even attempting more than our resources permit.

But we are not filling qualitative aspirations with adequate quantitative content, and thus we are doing far too little, even while so many think that we are attempting far too much. We are not sufficiently identifying priorities in their order of importance, which is a *sine qua non* for an effective war against poverty, unemployment, and other domestic evils, no less than when we were engaged in a successful full-scale war against external enemies. We are allowing emphasis upon individual, community, and group responsibilities, appropriate in their place, to substitute for the needed federal role in developing an over-all program and bringing to it an adequate amount of federal support. We have a multiplicity of *plans,* but no unifying *plan.*

We are now being told that we need time to digest the plethora of programs which has resulted just because priorities have not emerged. We are frightened by administrative difficulties arising out of the medley, and we are thus ignoring that, while we should be attempting fewer programs, these should be on a tremendously larger scale and with much more rationalization. Perhaps as the most serious consequence of all this, we are becoming frozen in the dogma of "what we cannot afford," instead of being made free by realization of our actual potentials.

There have been suggestions for additional enterprises or agencies at the federal level, such as a Council of Social Advisers. But we think that we could make more progress if we commenced to utilize the Employment Act of 1946, in accord with its original mandate, as a prime instrument for planning under freedom. Only thus can we overcome the defects in economic analysis and the shortcomings in social programs which are not separable.

The Reports of the President and of the Council of Economic Advisers under the Employment Act should specify long-range goals, running five and perhaps ten years ahead, for sustained maximum employment, production, and purchasing power. These goals should be divided into components identifying what portions of our total output should serve the great priorities of our national needs. There should be specific goals for the total liquidation of United States poverty. There should be incorporated the concept of a specific adequate standard of living for all Americans, assured in the main by the commitment to sustained full employment and supplemented by measures to guarantee this adequate standard of living to all those who cannot earn it through gainful employment.

Every economic and related social policy and program conducted by the federal government, or involving federal legislation, should be geared (1) to the above goals and (2) to an unqualified commitment, by the federal government itself, to make up the difference between the full achievement of the goals and those portions of them which can elsewhere be achieved. The federal budget, national monetary policies, social security and housing and farm policies, and all other national policies and programs importantly affecting the development and treatment of our economic resources, including our human resources, should be included in the Reports under the Employment Act.

INDICATIVE MODEL: A "FREEDOM BUDGET" FOR ALL AMERICANS

An indicative model as to what should be contained in the Economic Reports of the President is set forth in A "Freedom Budget" for All Americans, published by the A. Philip Randolph Institute in October 1966, and now evoking wide and increasing interest throughout the nation. The title imports complementing the crusade for civil rights and liberties with a crusade for what Franklin Delano Roosevelt called 'freedom from want," not only for Negroes but for all Americans, and not only with respect to private incomes but also with respect to public services and the entire living environment.[1]

---

[1] Copies of this pamphlet may be obtanied from the A. Philip Randolph Institute, 217 West 125 Street, New York, New York, or from Leon H. Keyserling, 1001 Connecticut Avenue, N.W., Washington, D.C.

The "Freedom Budget" finds that, even if our economic growth record during the years ahead is only moderately good, rather than as high as it ought to be in view of our responsibilities and capabilities, our total national production (GNP) during the ten years 1966–1975 inclusive, *measured in 1964 dollars,* should average annually in the neighborhood of 230–240 billion dollars higher than it was in 1965. Through this "economic growth dividend," during the ten-year period 1966–1975 inclusive, we should enjoy about 2.3–2.4 trillion dollars of GNP in excess of what it would be if our GNP during these ten years remained constant at the 1965 level.

The "Freedom Budget" combines these moderate estimates of our rapidly advancing total-production capabilities with estimates of what portions of the "economic growth dividend" should be allocated toward meeting the great priorities of our domestic needs. These priorities include, among others, attainment of the following goals by the end of 1975: virtual liquidation of poverty in the United States; rehousing the fifth of our people who live in urban and rural slums; renewal of our decaying cities and obsolescent mass transportation systems; conservation and improvement of our natural resources, including extraction of poison from our air and waters; provision of adequate medical care, at costs within their means, for the entire population; and opening up educational opportunity for all, at costs within their means, up to the limits of their ambitions and capabilities.

The two main operating weapons recommended in the "Freedom Budget" are: (1) restoration and maintenance of full employment for all able and willing to work, including those needing training and education toward this end, with federally supported guaranteed employment for all those unable to obtain employment at a living-adequacy standard of pay elsewhere. This federally supported employment would concentrate upon serving the great national priorities in the public sector, of a type not made available in sufficient quantity and quality in the private sector even under conditions of high prosperity; and (2) the gradual substitution of a universal federally supported guaranteed annual income for the medley of inadequate and conflicting programs now bearing upon income aid for consumer units which, even in a full-employment environment, should not look to gainful employment for their support.

The "Freedom Budget" estimates that all of these national priority programs, requiring new combinations of private and public efforts at all levels, would absorb at most only one-quarter of the "economic growth dividend" of about 2.3–2.4 trillion dollars during the ten-year period 1966–1975 inclusive. This would leave at least three-fourths of this "economic growth dividend" to add to the incomes and enjoyments of those who are

TABLE—"Freedom Budget" Goals for the Federal Budget in 1964 Dollars[a]

Federal Outlays	Calendar 1965 (Actual)		Fiscal 1968 (Actual)[b]		Calendar 1970 (Goals)		Calendar 1975 (Goals)	
	Total ($Billions)	$ Per Capita	Total ($Billions)	$ Per Capita	Total ($Billions)	$ Per Capita	Total ($Billions)	$ Per Capita
Total[c]	98.7	507.27	121.1	600.99	135.0	645.93	155.0	685.84
National Defense, Space Technology, All International	61.0	313.51	76.8	380.93	77.5	370.82	87.5	387.17
All Domestic Programs	37.7	193.76	44.3	220.06	57.5	275.12	67.5	298.67
Economic Opportunity Program	0.6	3.08	1.7	8.28	3.0	14.36	4.0	17.70
Housing and Community Development	0.1	0.51	0.9	4.55	3.4	16.03	3.8	16.81
Agriculture and Natural Resources	6.8	34.95	6.0	29.78	10.5	50.24	12.0	53.10
Education	2.1	10.79	2.5	12.53	7.0	33.49	9.5	42.04
Health Services and Research	2.1	10.76	4.3	21.22	4.8	22.97	7.0	30.97
Public Assistance; Labor, Manpower, and Other Welfare Services	3.8	19.53	4.2	20.81	6.6	31.58	7.5	33.18

[a] The "Freedom Budget" was developed in 1964 dollars. To convert the table and all previously cited "Freedom Budget" dollar items into the price levels used by the President for his fiscal 1968 Budget, all such items would need to be lifted about 11.5 per cent. To illustrate, this conversion would lift the "All Federal Outlays" line in the table to 110 billion dollars for calendar 1965, 135 billion for fiscal 1968, 150.5 billion for calendar 1970, and 173 billion for calendar 1975.

[b] As originally proposed by the President in January 1967 (but expressed in 1964 dollars).

[c] The goal totals include large federal contributions to increase old-age insurance benefits.

already comfortable, affluent, or even wealthy, and for all other national purposes.

The "Freedom Budget" does not propose that the ratio of total federal outlays to GNP increase during this ten-year period as a whole, although this ratio should increase during the next year or two. But the "Freedom Budget" does stress the inescapable role of the federal budget as the most important and powerful single instrument for identifying and helping to fulfill our great national priorities. Thus, while allowing for increases in defense, space, and international outlays in accord with current and foreseeable trends, the "Freedom Budget" proposes that federal outlays for these domestic priorities should be at least 5 billion dollars higher during the year ahead than are now contemplated, and that, during the ten-year period 1966–1975 inclusive, these domestic priority outlays in the federal budget should average annually about 18.5 billion dollars higher than during 1965, or total about 185 billion dollars higher during the ten-year period 1966–1975 inclusive, than if they remained constant during these ten years at their 1965 levels. These proposed increases would come to only about *one-thirteenth* of the "economic growth dividend" of 2.3–2.4 trillion dollars, certainly a very moderate share of that "dividend" to be devoted to the great priorities which are now so honored in words and so neglected in deeds. Including also generous and expanding allowances for national defense, space technology, and all international outlays, in accord with the composite judgment of the best-informed experts, total federal outlays as proposed in the "Freedom Budget" would average annually about 35.5 billion dollars higher, and over the ten years 1966–1975 aggregate about 355 billion dollars higher, than if the federal budget remained stationary during these ten years at its 1965 size. This 355 billion dollars would be only about *one-seventh* of the "economic growth dividend," which is a considerably smaller share of that "dividend" than the share of GNP preempted by the federal budget during recent years.

The table sets forth the "Freedom Budget" proposals with respect to the federal budget.

Even at existing rates of federal taxation, the "economic growth dividend" would yield increased federal revenues far in excess of the proposed increases in federal outlays. This imports that the proposals in the "Freedom Budget" would not be inflationary, because they would absorb so small a portion of our growth potential and would not add to the federal deficit over the years.

But even if the priority programs set forth in the "Freedom Budget" were to threaten to impose excessive pressures and inflationary strains upon the United States economy, and excessive federal deficits, the appropriate remedy in that event would be to cut back on what we need least, not on what we need most. Especially in view of the massive tax reductions of 1964, there is room and to spare for massive tax increases, levied on progressive principles to restrain relatively nonessential investment and consumption, in the unlikely event that this proved necessary to translate into reality a war against want in the broad sense that the "Freedom Budget" defines such a war.

It is to be hoped that the "Freedom Budget" will help to arouse the American people and their government to the pursuit of one increasing purpose in our economic and social life, pointed toward lifting our performance in accord with our natural and institutional endowments. The cry of what we "cannot afford is erecting a dichotomy between our international and domestic efforts, turning those who support the former against what we should be doing at home, and turning many of those victimized by what we are not doing at home into an uninformed opposition to what we may need to do overseas. Nothing could be more dangerous in a democracy, and the quicker we reconcile our search for peace and freedom for the individual everywhere with our quest for tranquility and freedom from want at home, the better off we shall all be.

14

DISCRIMINATION AGAINST NEGROES

OTIS DUDLEY DUNCAN

There is something to be said for phrasing policy goals (as distinguished from program objectives) in deliberately vague terms. No one can say for sure what is meant by health, welfare, or security, but it is agreed that our affluent society enjoys a greater measure of these desiderata than could have been imagined a century ago; yet it falls short of what we now want. Goals are conditioned by what is known, or at least suspected, to be feasible. Social ideals gain and lose content with the progress of knowledge and the accumulation of experience. Today we recognize as forms of inequality, or manifestations of discrimination, social patterns that were accepted only a few years ago—not because they were then deemed just, but simply because they were still unidentified.

As we bring knowledge to bear upon the achievement of "freedom from discrimination," we shall inevitably alter the very concept of discrimination. Indeed, it may not be premature to forecast a decline in the usefulness of the concept for deliberations on our society's future. Already the operative meaning of this goal is shifting from an emphasis on the mere elimination of various sanctioned and routinized discriminatory practices. What we really want is freedom from the *results* of discrimination. But since we can only measure—or, actually, infer—some of these results, our goal might better be stated in positive but open-ended terms: freedom *of* full participation. Remediable limitations on full participation will then appear as undesirable, whether or not one could convincingly attribute them to discrimination in some fairly definite sense of the word. Fullness of participation might come to mean the opportunity to share completely the responsibilities, risks, and hazards of citizenship, as well as the rewards of achievement and acceptance.

FUNCTIONS OF INDICATORS

In one sense, the measures of welfare and participation needed to ascertain the status and changes of status of a minority presumed to be subject to discrimination are no different from the measures required for the population as a whole—save, of course, that they must be available specifically for the minority as such. We already have much knowledge about the properties and uses of statistical indicators which we are not applying fully to the diagnosis of discrimination or to the measurement of progress (or lack of progress) in removing discrimination. Many of the statistics issued for the total population are also available for the "nonwhite" segment. However, "nonwhites" are not a single minority, but rather a congeries of minorities—Negroes, several distinct groups of Oriental extraction, and Indian-Americans—with very different kinds of social positions and life chances. If the subsequent discussion must rely heavily on contrasts between white and "nonwhite," let it be understood that the latter is merely a more or less unsatisfactory substitute for Negro-American. The possibility of a parallel discussion for other so-called racial categories, not to mention national-cultural or religious minorities, is severely limited by the lack of comparable data.

There is a sense, however, in which the mere availability of parallel series of indicators for the several minority groups (including the "majority," which is simply the largest of the minorities) would not be sufficient to reveal the incidence and effects of discrimination. Limitations on fullness

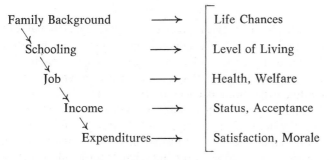

Figure   1—The Socioeconomic Life Cycle: Schematic Representation.

of participation may indeed be suspected from the mere existence of a majority-minority differential, as when it is observed that the median income of families with a nonwhite head was, in 1965, 55 per cent of that of families with a white head. What we need to know are the *components* of this differential: What is the relative importance of lack of equal pay for equal work, the lack of access to equal employment opportunity given equal qualifications, the lack of equal qualifications due to unequal access to training, and so on? Without condoning any of these kinds of inequality, a pragmatic strategy will concentrate first or most heavily on those forms that are most amenable to manipulation by policy and that offer the greatest payoff through a cumulation of direct and indirect effects.

We need, therefore, not only to have comprehensive series of indicators (even though this is the minimum requirement) but also methods, models, and materials suited to disentangle the causal relationships among indicators. The measurement of discrimination itself presupposes analysis of such relationships, for the empirical evidence of discrimination consists, we suppose, in the demonstration of inequality on one measure, after the contributions to that inequality made by variables other than discrimination have been evaluated. Residential segregation, for example, may be taken to measure the extent of discrimination in the housing market only after allowance is made for differences in ability to pay for housing.[1] That the latter, in turn, may reflect some other form of discrimination is a separable problem, and the separation had best be made, if we seek understanding and not mere documentation of our lack of progress in achieving full participation.

TWO TYPES OF HANDICAP

We are already able to suggest a conceptual paradigm, though not yet an operational model, of the "socioeconomic life cycle," which will serve to illustrate the necessity of considering relationships among indicators. The scheme in Figure 1 assumes that in the career of an individual or cohort of individuals the circumstances of the family of orientation—its size, structure, socioeconomic status, stability, and so on—provide a set of "initial conditions" whose effects are transmitted through subsequent stages of attainment and achievement. In focusing on the education-occupation-income-consumption nexus, we are stressing what Moore and Sheldon term the "distributive" variables.[2] These are surely relevant in many compli-

---

[1] Karl E. Taeuber, "Residential Segregation," *Scientific American,* 213 (August 1965), pp. 12–19.

[2] Wilbert E. Moore and Eleanor Bernert Sheldon, "Monitoring Social Change: A Conceptual and Programmatic Statement," *Proceedings of the Social Statistics Section, 1965* (Washington, D.C.: American Statistical Association, 1966), pp. 144–149.

cated ways to the outcomes rather ambiguously designated by terms like "life chances" and "welfare" at the right of the diagram. Other determinants might better be treated in terms of a "sociopolitical life cycle," referring to participation in and actions taken by voluntary and religious organizations, unions, social movements, and political structures and processes proper. Such a complication of our conceptual framework is beyond the scope of a discussion which has already raised issues too complex for more than an overly simplified exposition. As a first, though admittedly unsatisfactory, approximation, the sociopolitical context may be taken as a configuration of "exogenous" influences on the socioeconomic processes to be considered here.

A respectable beginning has been made in uncovering some of the mechanisms of the socioeconomic life cycle, or selected aspects of it, as they operate in the general population of this country. Informative data from longitudinal and retrospective studies on representative samples permit something more than impressionistic estimates of how and how much the advantages or handicaps at one stage are transmitted to the succeeding ones.[3] Such evidence, however, does not exist for earlier time periods in a

What we can say with some confidence about the Negro-American in particular is that he is subject to more than his share of the kinds of handicaps that result in lower than average outcomes of the socioeconomic cycle for anyone, white or Negro. Thus, readily available statistics reviewed in accessible sources[4] indicate that Negroes, in disproportionate numbers, (1) experience unstable family situations and depend on meager family resources; (2) attain less than average amounts of education; (3) are employed in lower-level jobs; (4) secure low incomes; (5) have an inefficient pattern of expenditures; and (6) in consequence, are characterized by inferior life chances, low levels of living and welfare, and impaired satisform that allows reliable inference of trends. And it does not exist (save in the most rudimentary form for "nonwhites") for the minorities whose life-cycle patterns are presumed to deviate widely from the American norm.

---

3 Peter M. Blau and Otis Dudley Duncan, *The American Occupational Structure* (New York: John Wiley and Sons, in press); Bruce K. Eckland, "Academic Ability, Higher Education, and Occupational Mobility," *American Sociological Review*, 30 (October 1965), pp. 735–746; William H. Sewell and J. Michael Armer, "Neighborhood Context and College Plans," *American Sociological Review*, 31 (April 1966), pp. 159–168.

4 Rashi Fein, "An Economic and Social Profile of the Negro Amercian," *Dædalus, Proceedings of the American Academy of Arts and Sciences*, 94 (Fall 1965), pp. 815–846; U.S., Department of Health, Education, and Welfare, *White-Nonwhite Differentials in Health, Education, and Welfare*, reprinted from *Indicators* (February–October, 1965); U.S., Department of Labor, *The Negroes in the United States: Their Economic and Social Situation, Bureau of Labor Statistics Bulletin*, No. 1511 (Washington, D.C.: U.S. Government Printing Office, 1966).

factions. In the chain of causation which the diagram seeks to suggest, each of these handicaps operates to set up the handicaps at later stages: schooling is terminated early partly because family support is inadequate; job opportunities are inferior partly because educational preparation is not good; low income is partly due to poor job opportunities; expenditures are inefficient and insufficient partly because of low income; Negroes get less out of life partly because of cumulative inadequacies at each stage of the life cycle.

These handicaps, to reiterate, are not peculiar to the incumbents of a particular minority status. They are shared by others whose start in life or subsequent misfortune puts them at a disadvantage. It is only when we superimpose upon these "general handicaps" the collection of "specific handicaps" of racial status that the plight of the Negro begins to be fully revealed: (1) Unstable and inadequate family backgrounds of Negroes are not merely the consequence of "poverty"; they are in part due to segregation. (2) Comparing white and Negro children similar in background, the latter are likely to get less schooling. The same number of years of schooling means less education for the Negro, owing to separate and unequal education. (3) With the same educational preparation, job discrimination by employers and unions handicaps the Negro in the labor market. (4) For the same work—or, at any rate, at the same occupational level—the Negro gets less pay and less job security. (5) At the same income level, limitations on credit and lack of access to some parts of the market render the Negro's dollar less effective in buying power. (6) At the same positions on scales of educational and occupational achievement and at similar levels of living and welfare, the Negro's social status suffers in the estimate of the general population—even when he "has it made" he has not.

Although these conclusions can be stated with some confidence, we actually do not yet have many adequate analyses of the respective roles of general handicaps and minority-specific handicaps in quantitative terms. There are only a few painstaking studies which come to grips with the problem of estimating the "cost of being Negro";[5] and, to repeat, such estimates are, by and large, not yet possible for minorities other than Negroes or for different periods of time. The issue is not one of academic nicety, for any program designed to move the society toward fullness of participation will be built on assumptions as to the relative proportions of general and specific handicaps and their relative responsiveness to various methods of inducing change.

---

[5] Paul M. Siegel, "On the Cost of Being a Negro," *Sociological Inquiry*, 35 (Winter 1965), pp. 41–57.

STATISTICAL RESOURCES

An evaluation of gaps in our information can proceed either from a comparison between what we do know and what we should know, or from an identification of discrepancies between what we do know and what we could know, assuming merely a concerted application of presently available techniques. The latter, more modest, criterion is accepted here, since the goals of social measurement, like the goals of society itself, expand as our capabilities are augmented.[6]

Information, of a sort, on the condition of one minority was built into the very foundations of our statistical system with the provision of the Constitution (Article I, Section 2) for apportionment of representation among the States "according to their respective numbers, which shall be determined by adding to the whole number of free persons, including those bound to service for a term of years, and excluding Indians not taxed, three-fifths of all other persons." In addition to the count of "all other persons," the First Census provided a classification of the free population by color.

Statistics by race or color have been collected at every subsequent census, though it is curious to note the apparent changes in the purpose and associated practices of this statistical work. In his report of May 1862 to the Senate, the Superintendent of the 1860 Census described the "progress and decline of African slavery in our country." Taking note of the higher rate of increase of the slave than of the free colored population, he ventured to forecast that "if large numbers of slaves shall be hereafter emancipated, so many will be transferred from a faster to a slower rate of increase."

---

[6] This section and subsequent discussion are based on a comprehensive review of existing and potential time series of social statistics that shed light on the status of the Negro population: Otis Dudley Duncan, "Social Mobility of the American Negro: Prospects for a Program of Studies," unpublished discussion paper drafted for the Public Affairs Programs of the Ford Foundation, 4 June 1964. The memorandum included an "Inventory of Data Needs and Resources" in each of the following categories: school attendance and educational attainment; employment, occupation, industry, and union membership; income, possessions, health, consumer expenditures, and welfare and social security; housing; family composition and illegitimacy; political participation; crime, delinquency, and the administration of justice; social acceptance, morale, aspiration, and cultural assimilation; basic demography. The inventory is partially updated by the items listed in footnotes 4, 14, 22, 24, and 26, and by recent publications of the United States Bureau of the Census, *1960 Census of Population*, Supplementary Reports, PC (S1)-46, "Subject Guide to 1960 Census Data for the Negro Population" (April 7, 1964); *Current Population Reports*, Series P-20, No. 142, "Negro Population: March 1964" (October 11, 1965); *ibid.*, No. 155, "Negro Population: March 1965" (September 27, 1966). See also the discussion of "statistics of opportunity" in Otis Dudley Duncan, "The 1970 Census: Challenge and Opportunity," *1966 Proceedings of the Social Statistics Section* (Washington, D.C.: American Statistical Association, 1966), pp. 2–6.

A concern with race mixture presumably occasioned in 1850 the intro-duction of the subcategory, "mulatto," which continued in use through 1910 despite the admitted uncertainty of the classification. Popular anthro-pology was given free rein in the Census of 1890, where the term "black" refers to persons "having three-fourths or more black blood," other persons with any proportion of "black blood" being classified as "mulattoes," "quadroons," or "octoroons."

The monumental report of the Census Bureau, *Negro Population, 1790–1915,* issued in 1918, undertook to document the "progress of the Negro race." Symptomatic of that progress, one is led to suppose, was the circumstance that "the tabulations for this report were made by a corps of Negro clerks working under the efficient direction of three men of their own race." Its successor of 1935, *Negroes in the United States, 1920–1932,* likewise was based on the work of "a corps of Negro clerks." The scope of these two reports has not been matched in any more recent official compila-tions. The 1935 report, for example, includes sections on Negro religious bodies and retail establishments, as well as occupations and strictly demo-graphic topics.

While the Censuses of 1940, 1950, and 1960 include voluminous tabu-lations for white and "nonwhite" persons, the recording of the "progress of the Negro race" is no longer a featured subject of textual discussion. The recently revived attention to statistics on Negroes (rather than "non-whites") evidently is a response, rather, to the current interest in civil rights and racial equality. For some time, the Bureau of the Census has been careful to emphasize that "the concept of race . . . is derived from that which is commonly accepted by the general public. It does not, therefore, reflect clear-cut definitions of biological stock."

Table 1 assembles data illustrative of the kinds of annual time series that are available in regular statistical reports. While vital statistics and some kinds of administrative information (like the series on executions) are available for several decades, much of our present capability rests upon the expansion of the work of the Bureau of the Census into the area of monthly and annual sample surveys, following World War II. The illustra-tions are not meant to represent the full scope of the current statistical series, and do not include at all the many valuable items of information that become available decennially or on a one-time basis. They do, how-ever, provide instructive samples of the tasks that would challenge an enterprise devoted to assembling the raw information for productive delib-erations on means and ends in the struggle for full participation. In fact, several of the series are shown because they exemplify some of the more serious difficulties of analysis and interpretation, and, thus, the kinds of qualifications that would have to accompany their inclusion in an official or unofficial Social Report on Freedom from Discrimination.

TABLE 1—Illustrative Time Series of Annual Data (Averages for Three-Year Periods) for the Nonwhite (N) and White (W) Population of the United States: 1948–1965

Series					Period		
		1948–50	1951–53	1954–56	1957–59	1960–62	1963–65
School Enrollment, Per Cent of Males Age 14–17	N	70.7	75.5	83.1	86.2	88.8	92.4[a]
	W	84.5	87.2	89.6	91.7	92.9	94.6[a]
Per Cent High School Graduates, Male Labor Force	N	(NA)[c]	15.1[b]	(NA)	21.7[b]	27.3[b]	32.3[a]
	W	(NA)	42.1[b]	(NA)	49.4[b]	53.5[b]	56.8[a]
Per Cent of Male Workers with Year-round Full-Time Jobs	N	50.2[b]	53.0	55.6[a]	51.3	51.8	55.2[a]
	W	66.8[b]	69.9	68.8[a]	66.0	65.3	67.2[a]
Per Cent of Employed Persons in White-collar Jobs	N	9.6[a]	9.7[b]	12.2[a]	14.0[a]	16.4	18.6
	W	39.7[a]	39.8[b]	42.2[a]	45.6[a]	46.8	47.2
Median Income of Families (Dollars)	N	1,762	2,277	2,529	2,797	3,251	3,758
	W	3,329	4,122	4,646	5,370	6,018	6,859
Infant Deaths per 1,000 Live Births	N	46.1	45.5	42.6	44.4	41.8	41.3[a]
	W	28.5	25.4	23.6	23.4	22.5	21.9[a]
Deaths from Tuberculosis per 100,000 Population	N	71.5	42.2	21.9	16.2	12.3	10.4[a]
	W	21.0	13.0	7.7	6.0	4.6	3.8[a]
Homicides per 100,000 Population	N	29.1	26.1	23.6	22.0	21.5	22.4[a]
	W	2.8	2.5	2.3	2.4	2.6	2.7[a]
Suicides per 100,000 Population	N	4.2	3.9	3.9	4.3	4.6	4.8[a]
	W	12.2	10.9	10.9	11.1	11.4	11.8[a]
Per Cent of Married Women with Husband Absent	N	(NA)	16.0	19.6	20.3	19.8	21.0
	W	(NA)	4.6[a]	5.0	4.2	4.3	4.4
Subfamilies per 100 Families	N	12.1	10.1[a]	10.4	9.2	7.4	6.4
	W	6.1	4.4[a]	4.2	3.4	2.8	2.4
Births per 1,000 Women Age 15–44	N	135	144	156	162	152	143[a]
	W	103	110	114	116	111	102[a]
Per Cent of Live Births Illegitimate	N	17.1	18.6	20.2	21.2	22.3	24.0[a]
	W	1.8	1.6	1.9	2.1	2.5	3.2[a]
Per Cent of Aged Population Receiving OASDI Benefits	N	9.3	18.3	28.4	41.0	53.0	65.0
	W	17.3	30.0	43.8	59.4	69.6	77.0
Prisoners Executed under Civil Authority, Annual Number	N	65	42	40	31	25	5
	W	42	41	34	23	23	9

[a] Based on data for only two years.
[b] Data for only one year.
[c] NA: Not available.
Source: Various federal publications; Old-Age and Survivors Disability Insurance Program (OASDI) figures from unpublished calculations of the Office of Research and Statistics, Social Security Administration.

STATISTICAL HAZARDS

The first obstacle—let us face it honestly—is that figures usually do not mean what they appear to mean. This is not to endorse the popular estimate that places statistics in a category of veracity somewhat lower than "damned lies." Rather, it is to emphasize that no isolated item of information, quantitative or verbal, is self-explanatory. It can only take on a reliable meaning or guide an intelligent decision when placed in a context. Statisticians, contrary to popular assumption, are not fond of quoting single figures as measures of progress or predicament—that is a fine art most assiduously cultivated by nonstatisticians in election years.

Among the elementary cautions in interpreting time series, like the examples in Table 1, are these: (1) Large relative gains come easier from a starting point near the floor than from one approaching a ceiling. Thus, white-collar employment for nonwhites doubled during the one and one-half decades covered by Table 1, and could easily double again in a subsequent period of equal length, but school enrollment at ages fourteen to seventeen could increase by no more than 50 per cent after 1949, having already reached seven-tenths of its ceiling value by then. (2) Absolute differences often give an opposite impression from that conveyed by relative differences. At the beginning of the period covered in the table, the nonwhite illegitimacy ratio was 9.5 times as large as the white; at the end, 7.5 times. In terms of the nonwhite-white difference in percentages, however, the change was from 15.3 to 20.8. (3) The quantities in a time series often require one or more kinds of rudimentary standardization before any interpretation can be ventured. Comparisons of tuberculosis death rates should take into account differences in age composition. Changes in dollar income should be measured against changes in the value of the dollar. Figures on executions must be related to the number exposed to risk—the respective population sizes or, better, numbers convicted of capital offenses. Where the statistical agency or analyst does not provide such adjustments, the sophisticated reader should at least make rough mental allowances for their probable effect. Thus, it is clear that Negroes have been disproportionately subject to capital punishment, given the recent approximate equality of the absolute numbers of executions of whites and nonwhites as against the fact that nonwhites are about one-ninth of the population.

Other hazards may be less evident, but nonetheless real. The illegitimacy ratio is based in part on estimates, and the estimating technique and probable range of error have not been adequately evaluated. After 1959, the birth series are no longer "corrected for underregistration." This introduces a discontinuity into the series and raises some question about the validity of the corrections for earlier years. Figures on school attendance may give rise to misleading impressions if no allowance is made for differences in age-grade relationships. The entry of "suicide" as the cause of death on the death certificate is often a matter of judgment or conjecture on the part of the physician, and no one knows (for example) how many automobile accident fatalities, recorded in another category of violent deaths, occurred to drivers in a suicidal frame of mind. A number of the series in Table 1 are based on samples, and the figures for nonwhites are subject to relatively high sampling errors, even after taking three-year averages.

If the foregoing kinds of qualifications may be regarded as "technical" difficulties in the interpretation of time series, there are still more difficult issues that arise even in the case of series whose statistical properties are wholly satisfactory. These pertain to the causal interrelations and the social "meaning" of the changes.

One writer has argued that we should eschew comparisons of rates of change, as well as measures of change in either absolute or relative differences. He proposes instead of these conventional indicators of convergence or divergence a "time-lag statistic: how many years earlier did the white American . . . attain the particular level (say, of health, education, income) that the Negro . . . has reached only today."[7] Changes in the length of this period, which we may wish to term the "Fein gap," after its inventor, are taken to be indicative of whether the Negro is catching up or falling behind. These will often tell a different story than will the other measures of discrepancy. Indeed, if there is anything to the theory of the "privilege of backwardness," the mere failure of the Fein gap to diminish over the years, even though both white and Negro indicators are in the direction of improvment, suggests a degree of exclusion from the fruits of social progress.

Obviously, there are both technical and conceptual limitations on the analysis of Fein gaps. For one thing, many series are not long enough or frequent enough for them to be ascertained reliably. The very concept is applicable, moreover, only to series that have a cumulative, evolutionary, or progressive character. They are well suited, in theory, to measures of health, education, and income, but less so to indicators of family structure and function, for example, although the latter are suspected to have strong bearing on opportunities and participation.

Even where calculation of the Fein gap lends meaning to data on "the progress of the Negro race," we only have a better description of the predicament, but not an explanation of it, not to mention a directive for appropriate meliorative action. Large values of this statistic or unfavorable changes in it may signalize a social problem, but do little to pinpoint its causes or to suggest its remedies.

---

[7] Fein, *op. cit.*, pp. 817–819.

This is an important distinction. Hence, we should like to emphasize it with a figure of speech, at the risk of introducing misleading connotations. A particular series may be either "symptomatic" or "diagnostic," or sometimes both. The treatment it may seem to call for can be directed toward symptoms or causes, or both. Interpretation and action, if they are not to be misconceived or misdirected, presuppose analysis. For illustration, the series on percentage of aged persons receiving OASDI benefits (Table 1) serves, symptomatically, to sum up aspects of the history of labor-force participation and employment of the cohorts qualifying for benefits on the basis of age:

> In the early days of the social security program, the exclusion of farm labor, domestic service, and certain other types of work from the system meant that relatively fewer Negroes than white persons could share in the protection offered. . . . The 1950, 1954, and 1956 amendments removed most of the restrictions from coverage. These liberalizations, as well as the accelerated movement of the Negro from farm work into city jobs, mean that more and more Negroes have a stake in the old-age, survivors, and disability insurance program.[8]

The quotation suggests the lines of analysis that would have to be explored to explain the color differential, its year-by-year changes, and the fact that the Fein gap for this series has varied between about 3 and 4.5 years over the period 1946–1965. The series is a composite result of heterogeneous causes, the disentangling of which invites a substantial research effort.

Such an effort is indeed required if we should try to devise a program to shorten the Fein gap or if we should seek to estimate whether existing programs or those contemplated for other reasons will have this effect. The series as it stands has little "diagnostic" value, but is of considerable "symptomatic" interest.

To be sure, programs to treat symptoms are no more to be disdained than is the analogous procedure in medical practice, provided the practitioner is clear about what he is doing. The symptomatic data suggest that current income-maintenance programs for the immediate future will require provisions to compensate for the differential coverage of OASDI, even as we work to contrive manpower policies and social insurance schemes that ultimately will remove the causes of the discrepancy.

Other examples of primarily "symptomatic" series will be found in Table 1. When the Fein gap in suicide rates has been reduced to zero, we will know that the Negro-American has attained his full share of the kinds

---

[8] Mollie Orshansky, "The Aged Negro and His Income," *Social Security Bulletin*, 27 (February 1964), p. 9.

of troubles afflicting other Americans, and "freedom from discrimination" will probably be a dead issue.

INTERPRETATIONS AND MODELS

This argument implies that no elaboration or refinement of the function of "social bookkeeping"—essential as improvements therein surely are—will ultimately satisfy the need for statistical intelligence as a basis for policy-formulation and program-evaluation. Policies and programs involve a means-ends calculus predicated upon dependable knowledge of cause-and-effect relationships. We are familiar with this pattern of connections between knowledge and action in the strictly economic sphere, as when monetary, fiscal, and tax measures are calculated in the light of theories and measurements predicting their effects on employment and prices. It hardly needs to be argued that present theory and measurement practices are not adequate for such calculation in the realm of social opportunities. Even if we had a "Council of Social Advisors" to complement the work of the Council of Economic Advisors, it is not wholly clear what their charge should be.

Yet the present state of the art would permit much more to be done with a modest expansion of our allocation of resources to the problem. We have empirical relationships between education, employment, occupational status, family structure, and income, for example, or can readily develop same from statistics on hand or in the files of data-collection agencies. Analysis of past changes or projections of future changes should be able to suggest how much of the gap in income is due to the gap in education, how much to less-than-full employment, and how much to inequality of compensation at equivalent occupational levels and for equivalent periods of work. Well-known and rudimentary statistical techniques of cross-tabulation, covariance and regression analysis, direct and indirect standardization, and the like can be brought into play so that the statistical information implicit in our present data-collection systems is made to yield something closer to a realistic "estimate of the situation" than can be had from a mere congeries of "facts."

Sometimes even a simple rearrangement of data lying at hand will yield unexpected insights. One gets a rather different perspective on comparative occupation trends, for example, when the data are arranged so as to highlight changes over time for identical cohorts, defined by year of birth and subdivided by amount of formal education. Reversal of the previous trend of white-nonwhite convergence in occupation distributions of young college graduates during the 1950's, for example, suggests a restoration of

some of the barriers that had been temporarily breached during and immediately after World War II.[9]

The tendency of these remarks, therefore, is to register dissatisfaction
with any plan that stops with periodic compilation and display of "indicators" of the extent or degree of discrimination, and still more dissatisfaction with any proposal to produce a single "index" of the status of a
minority group.

The National Commission on Technology, Automation, and Economic
Progress, in its recently issued report,[10] has seized upon a remark of
Myrdal: "We should . . . have liked to present in our study a general index,
year by year or at least decade by decade, as a quantitative expression of
the movement of the entire system we are studying: the status of the Negro
in America."[11] Neither the Commission nor others who have been intrigued
by the notion of a "general index" studied closely enough Myrdal's further
remarks, in which he virtually retracted his advice to engage in the construction of "a general index of Negro status" in favor of a more penetrating prescription: "Ideally, the scientific solution of the Negro problem
should . . . be given in the form of an interconnected series of quantitative
equations, describing the movement of the actual system under various
influences. . . . [T]his complete, quantitative and truly scientific solution . . .
remains as the scientific ideal steering our endeavors."[12] The Commission
may have improved upon this formulation—though we doubt it—in asking
for "a system of social accounts," the specifications for which are barely
adumbrated in the Commission's report.

SOCIAL SCIENCE: A THIRD FORCE

It gives one pause, moreover, to encounter the Commission's recommendation that the task of developing a "system of social accounts" be
taken over by the Council of Economic Advisers. The Commission cor-
rectly assumed that most of the sources for this enterprise would consist of
time series organized for continuous and regular production by federal
statistical agencies. Casual acquaintance with the capabilities of these agen-

9 Nathan Hare, "Recent Trends in the Occupational Mobility of Negroes, 1930–
1960: An Intracohort Analysis," *Social Forces,* 44 (December 1965), pp. 166–173. See
also Dorothy S. Brady, *Age and the Income Distribution,* Social Security Administration Research Report No. 8 (Washington, D.C.: U.S. Government Printing Office,
1965).

10 *Technology and the American Economy,* Vol. 1 (Washington, D.C.: U.S. Government Printing Office, 1966), p. 98.

11 Gunnar Myrdal, *An American Dilemma* (New York: Harper, 1944), p. 1068.

12 ibid., p. 1069.

cies does, indeed, suggest that they are ill-suited to assume responsibility for an "accounting system." It does not follow that the only alternative is to assign it to an official policy-making body. Although the interaction of policy-formulation and policy-defense with scientific analysis is still inadequately understood, I believe careful scrutiny of social research conducted intramurally (within the federal establishment) will reveal too many instances where the two functions have been confounded to an undesirable degree. An "official theory" to the effect that school dropout is a major source of various social pathologies is too easily converted into statistical procedures which virtually preclude an independent assessment of the merits of this theory and of its cogency as an intellectual cornerstone of current programs.[13] (The reader may be familiar with other examples, such as those stemming from official and unexamined assumptions about the "inheritance of poverty.")

We would propose as an alternative at least worth discussion that the continuing task of assessing movement toward freedom from discrimination be accepted by a privately organized enterprise which might, to be sure, come to enjoy a paragovernmental status in view of its inescapable reliance on federal statistical resources and its requirement for continuous liaison with the relevant agencies. It would be mandatory, however, for such a unit to be independent of the administrative apparatus and of any commitment to the specific programs of the party currently in office. It would require substantial resources to undertake continuing inquiries on matters too "sensitive" for direct federal surveillance[14] and to command the continuing participation of some of the best minds in the social sciences. Among other things, such a body would be free to criticize the actions of government (and especially the assumptions underlying them) and to assess in a nonpartisan mood the government's progress as well as that of civil society in moving toward fullness of participation.

Perhaps this is what the aforementioned National Commission had in mind in suggesting that "some national body of distinguished private citizens . . . be concerned with 'monitoring' social change, forecasting possible social trends, and suggesting policy alternatives to deal with them."[15] That a minority of the Commission itself took exception to this recommendation may suggest that the initiative needs to be taken in the private sector.

---

[13] Beverly Duncan, "Early Work Experience of Graduates and Dropouts," *Demography*, 4, no. 1, 1967.

[14] For example, the studies undertaken by the National Opinion Research Center and by Louis Harris and Associates; see Paul B. Sheatsley, "White Attitudes toward the Negro," *Dædalus, Proceedings of the American Academy of Arts and Sciences,* 95 (Winter 1966), pp. 217–238; William Brink and Louis Harris, *The Negro Revolution in America* (New York: Simon and Schuster, 1964).

[15] *Technology and the American Economy, op. cit.,* p. 106.

TARGETS AND TRENDS

Developments of the last decade reflect the recrudescence of an interest in measuring social trends which had been dormant since the early
1930's. Perhaps it was the preoccupation with the exigencies of the Depression that precluded an adequate follow-up to the beginning made with
Recent Social Trends[16] and the short-lived annual series on social changes
issued by the *American Journal of Sociology*.[17] The revival was presaged
by the monumental efforts devoted to *Historical Statistics* and the continua-
tions and revisions thereof.[18] Within the last decade we have seen much
activity in compiling, presenting, and discussing "trends" and "indicators,"
both on the part of government agencies and in academic circles.[19]

Perhaps this is the time—while applauding and encouraging such
activity—to undertake a re-examination and appraisal of the philosophy
and methods of trend-analysis. Karl Popper has given us a start on the former with his profound aphorism: *Trends are not laws.*[20] The movements of
a time series do not represent a trajectory whose history reveals its own law
of motion so that the *terminus ad quem* is in principle predictable from the
record of the past. We might well abandon the ballistic imagery, including
reference to targets, if it is going to betray us into the expectation that
trend-analysis will by itself provide a means of knowing what is going to
occur and how soon.

Trends are merely the raw material of social analysis, and improvements in their measurement only accentuate the challenge to grapple with
fundamental issues of social causation. As a purely empirical proposition,
it may well be, as Ogburn claimed,[21] that extrapolating a trend is likely to
yield a smaller forecasting error than assuming that next year will be the
same as last year. Yet this rule provides no basis for anticipating reversals

---

16 President's Research Committee on Social Trends, *Recent Social Trends in the
United States* (New York: McGraw-Hill, 1933).

17 Vols. 34–40, 47 (1929–1935, 1942), edited by William F. Ogburn.

18 U.S., Bureau of the Census, *Historical Statistics of the United States, 1789–1945*
(Washington, D.C.: U.S. Government Printing Office, 1949); *Historical Statistics of
the United States: Colonial Times to 1957* (Washington, D.C.: U.S. Government
Printing Office, 1960); *Historical Statistics of the United States: Colonial Times to
1957: Continuation to 1962 and Revisions* (Washington, D.C.: U.S. Government
Printing Office, 1965).

19 U.S., Department of Health, Education, and Welfare, *HEW Trends* (annual)
and *HEW Indicators* (monthly); Raymond A. Bauer (ed.), *Social Indicators* (Cambridge, Mass.: M.I.T. Press, 1966).

20 Karl R. Popper, *The Poverty of Historicism* (Boston: Beacon Press, 1957), pp.
115 ff.

21 "Social Trends," in *William F. Ogburn on Culture and Social Change*, ed. by
O. D. Duncan (Chicago: University of Chicago Press, 1964).

or changes in trends and little basis enough even for understanding past alterations of their directions.

Of course, we now take "target" to refer, not to the level that a trend will seek out of its own accord, but to the magnitude that we hope we can cause it to attain. Save, perhaps, for some restricted areas of the economic realm, procedures for specifying targets in this sense are far to primitive to be dignified by referring to them as "methods." Even where we have contrived massive social experiments in response to major problems, the opportunity has seldom been seized to analyze them by techniques simulating (as closely as can be) those suited to making inferences from experiments. Two decades after the fact, who can say on any scientific basis what the social effects of the "G.I. Bill of Rights" have been? If we cannot assess the efficacy of past expedients, dare we project the impact of current ones?

Lacking method, we hope for wisdom—a small hope, perhaps, but not a negligible one. A beginning of wisdom can be found in a simply stated principle: some things are easier to change than others (a thinly disguised paraphrase of the hypothesis of cultural lag).

The principle explains, among other things, why it is possible to find all kinds of evidence of "progress" in the time series portraying the status of the Negro minority, but at the same time to "prove"—resorting to figures in lieu of "damned lies"—that we are standing still or falling behind in removing discrimination. Not all forms and consequences of discrimination will disappear all at once,[22] and this is why the "general index" of Negro status will remain a statistical fantasy.

Let us summarize some net impressions, not as scientific conclusions but as propositions whose disconfirmation would put us ahead of where we are now in understanding our predicament.

(1) There are two areas of bedrock resistance to "the progress of the Negro race": residential segregation and the weakness of Negro family structure. The appraisal of the former is, broadly speaking, hardly controversial. We are making scarcely any gain in reducing apartheid in housing.[23] Yet even the militant edge of the civil rights movement has come to define this as a strategic focus only in recent months. Social analysts have been preoccupied up to now with the arduous task of measuring the trend,

---

[22] G. Franklin Edwards, "Community and Class Realities: The Ordeal of Change," *Dædalus*, 95 (Winter 1966), pp. 1–23.

[23] The definitive work which conveys this distressing intelligence (Karl E. Taeuber and Alma F. Taeuber, *Negroes in Cities* [Chicago: Aldine, 1965]) provides a base line for the needed program of measuring segregation patterns at least quinquennially. Unfortunately, the rate of change of the segregation index used by the Taeubers is so slow, owing to the inertia of segregation patterns, that more frequent measurement would be merely redundant. For this purpose among others, however, a mid-decade census is badly needed.

or lack of trend, in segregation indexes. They will next turn, we may hope, to the ever more difficult problem of testing our suspicions concerning its profound importance as an obstacle to change in contexts not manifestly linked to housing patterns.

The diagnosis of the situation in Negro family life, by contrast, is controversial indeed (as witness the reception of the "Moynihan Report"). Yet there cannot be much argument with the facts: the illegitimacy ratio does not go down; the prevalence of rearing in broken families does not decrease; the proportion of families headed by females does not decline; the undoubling of households, represented by reduction in the ratio of subfamilies to families (Table 1), probably reflects improved economic conditions and some increase in the supply of housing, but may actually indicate a loosening of the bonds of the extended family. Whatever the inadequacies of the educational system, we now know that the school is presented at the beginning of the first grade with children whose family experience has not prepared them intellectually for competition with the majority.[24]

(2) The record on strictly socioeconomic measures can only be described as mixed. Averages of educational attainment, occupational status, and income disclose a rising trend for nonwhites as for whites. One can discount or exaggerate the trends by manipulating ratios, absolute differences, and Fein gaps. Closer study of the underlying statistical distributions only compounds the confusion. In the movement toward near-universal literacy, the white and nonwhite series converge; analyzing the proportions continuing from high school graduation on to college graduation reveals a widening of the gap. The obstacle to our understanding here, as I have tried to suggest already, is not a lack of "indicators," but a failure to conceptualize adequately the interrelations of contingencies in the socioeconomic life cycle and to produce quantitative estimates of the relative importance of various sources of change.

(3) Measures of life chances and welfare again offer the opportunity to discern contradictory tendencies. The trends suggest that we are applying (if too slowly) our knowledge of how to reduce death rates from infectious disease and the proportions of living in housing classified as "substanard" by current administrative definitions. While reasons can always be found to be dissatisfied with rates of progress, we could even risk some projections of trajectories to their "targets" in some of the magnitudes subsumed under these categories. To focus attention on them unduly would be to engage in self-congratulation while avoiding the more treacherous areas of analysis and decision.

---

24 U.S., Office of Education, *Equality of Educational Opportunity* (Washington, D.C.: U.S. Government Printing Office, 1966), especially pp. 221–222.

INTERRELATIONSHIPS

Here, as in earlier parts of the discussion, we must emphasize the basic obstacle impeding a responsible attempt to designate "targets": It is not a lack of sufficient "indicators" (though we could do with many more regular and reliable time series), but a lack of knowledge of causal connections among indicator variables. To illustrate how grave this weakness really is, let us summarize the *best* example we have been able to find dealing with time changes in an indicator in relation to antecedent variables in the socio-economic life cycle. It hardly amounts to the "interconnected series of quantitative equations" that Myrdal called for, but it does suggest that our present analytical capabilities have outrun the supply of data suited to multiple-variable analysis.

The example pertains to educational attainment, indexed by number of years of formal schooling completed. We are well aware of the importance popularly and officially attributed to raising the level of schooling in the Negro population.[25] Family background has been implicated in the "tangle of pathology" that holds back Negro educational achievement: "The effect of broken families on the performance of Negro youth has not been extensively measured, but studies that have been made show an unmistakable influence." [26]

The regression statistics summarized in Table 2 pertain to a causal model in which educational attainment of whites and nonwhites depends on four family-background characteristics: the educational attainment of the head of the family in which the individual grew up; the occupational level of the family head; the classification of the family as intact (grew up with both parents) or broken (grew up in a family with one or both parents missing); and the number of children in the family (respondent's number of siblings). The data permit white-nonwhite comparisons of the estimated effects of these influences on schooling for three age groups: 47-61, 37-46, and 27-36. The age progression in data ascertained retrospectively in 1962 for all three groups provides a tolerable approximation to time-series observations on successive cohorts completing their educational careers.[27]

---

[25] Wilbur J. Cohen, "Social Policy for the Nineteen Seventies," *Health, Education, and Welfare Indicators* (May 1966).

[26] U.S., Department of Labor, *The Negro Family: The Case for National Action* (Washington, D.C.: U.S. Government Printing Office, 1965), p. 36.

[27] Beverly Duncan, *Family Factors and School Dropout: 1920–1960,* Co-operative Research Project No. 2258, United States Office of Education (Ann Arbor: University of Michigan, 1965). This source provides a more elaborate analysis for more detailed age intervals. See also Beverly Duncan, "Education and Social Background," *American Journal of Sociology,* 72 (January 1967), pp. 363–372.

In several respects, there is a rather stable pattern of relationships evident in these data spanning approximately one-third of a century of educational experience. For all three cohorts of both whites and nonwhites, it was an advantage to grow up in an intact family whose head had achieved high levels of schooling and occupational status, and a disadvantage to grow up with a large number of siblings. There is a fairly clear indication, as well, of the relative importance of the four variables that here represent "family background" (see especially the lower panel of Table 2). Education and occupation of family head account for larger parts of the variation in schooling than do intact family and number of siblings. For whites, head's occupation has been slightly more important than head's education, while the reverse has held for nonwhites. Apart from the rather anomalous coefficient for number of siblings in the youngest group of nonwhites, size of family has been a more important factor than rearing in an intact family.

Because of the rather high sampling variability in the data for nonwhites, caution must be exercised in inferring time changes in the relationship of schooling to background factors. It may be significant, however, that the effect of intact family diminished for whites (comparing the oldest and youngest cohorts) while it increased for nonwhites. The white-nonwhite contrast that is apparently most reliable pertains to occupation of family head. As one can see from the raw-score coefficients, this factor has a similar influence on schooling in both groups. However, the variability of occupation levels is less among nonwhite family heads; hence the contribution of this variable to educational outcome is of lesser relative importance among nonwhites than among whites when the coefficients are expressed in standard form. For this reason primarily, the coefficient of determination (square of the multiple correlation) is consistently smaller for nonwhites than for whites. The background factors here measured account for less of the variation in schooling for nonwhites than they do for whites.

To summarize the over-all effect of family background in producing white-nonwhite differences in schooling, Table 3 presents estimates derived from the regression equations. Comparing the oldest and youngest cohorts, there is a decrease from 3.5 to 2.0 in the mean difference, by color, in number of school years completed. Despite some inconsistency between the alternative estimates of background effects, it appears that both components of this difference have likewise diminished, that is, the difference between whites and nonwhites due to the measured background variables has decreased, while the residual difference, attributed to "color" *per se* in the regression model, has decreased as well. For the oldest cohort, the difference due to "color" was rather unambiguously larger than the dif-

TABLE 2—Regression of Number of School Years Completed on Family-
Background Variables, by Color, for Selected Age Groups of
U.S. Native Males: March 1962

Color and Age in 1962	Independent Variables					Coefficient of Determination
	Color	Education of Family Head	Occupation of Family Head[a]	Intact Family	Number of Siblings	
	Partial Regression Coefficients, Raw Form					
Total						
27 to 36	0.843	0.197	0.040	0.744	−0.199	.277
37 to 46	1.956	0.196	0.042	0.659	−0.222	.312
47 to 61	2.061	0.229	0.047	1.116	−0.213	.325
White						
27 to 36	. . .	0.192	0.040	0.671	−0.225	.267
37 to 46	. . .	0.195	0.041	0.626	−0.223	.281
47 to 61	. . .	0.217	0.047	1.203	−0.222	.283
Nonwhite						
27 to 36	. . .	0.220	0.034	0.763	−0.043	.136
37 to 46	. . .	0.199	0.055	0.718	−0.246	.137
47 to 61	. . .	0.329	0.051	0.435	−0.168	.167
	Partial Regression Coefficients, Standard Form					
Total						
27 to 36	0.078	0.218	0.259	0.083	−0.178	.277
37 to 46	0.164	0.215	0.252	0.071	−0.185	.312
47 to 61	0.165	0.238	0.251	0.113	−0.169	.325
White						
27 to 36	. . .	0.215	0.267	0.073	−0.198	.267
37 to 46	. . .	0.224	0.270	0.069	−0.195	.281
47 to 61	. . .	0.234	0.270	0.122	−0.184	.283
Nonwhite						
27 to 36	. . .	0.245	0.157	0.105	−0.044	.136
37 to 46	. . .	0.185	0.167	0.083	−0.191	.137
47 to 61	. . .	0.314	0.155	0.052	−0.129	.167

[a] Occupations scored on Duncan's socioeconomic index, which has a range of 0 to 96 and a standard deviation of about 24 points in the United States male population aged 25–64 in 1962.

ference due to background; this was no longer true for the youngest cohort. The reason we cannot be completely confident of such a conclusion is simply that the background variables do not have the same weights in the two populations; hence a hypothetical calculation in which they are equalized with respect to background cannot yield a unique result. The conclusion just stated would suggest, however, a slight relaxation of "discrimination," if the residual difference due to "color" is taken to measure discrimination.

One further conclusion can be quite firmly stated. Only a small part of the improvement in educational attainment for both whites and non-whites can be attributed to improvements in background factors. For whites, the increase in educational attainment, from the oldest to the youngest cohort, amounted to 1.8 school years, of which 0.6 year can be explained by the advantage with respect to background variables enjoyed

TABLE 3—Mean Number of Years of School Completed, by Color, for Selected Age Groups, with Alternative Estimates of the Effect of Background Derived from Regressions in Table 2, for United States Native Males: March 1962

Item	Age Group		
	27 to 36	37 to 46	47 to 61
White Mean School Years	11.9	11.2	10.1
Nonwhite Mean School Years	9.9	8.1	6.6
Gross Difference	2.0	3.1	3.5
Difference Due to Background[a]			
Set A	1.2	1.1	1.4
Set B	1.2	0.9	1.5
Set C	0.9	1.4	1.6
Residual Difference Due to "Color"[a]			
Set A	0.8	2.0	2.1
Set B	0.8	1.2	2.0
Set C	1.1	1.7	1.9

[a] Set A: Effect of color estimated as coefficient for color in regression for total population.
    Set B: Effect of color estimated by using regression for whites with mean background composition of nonwhites.
    Set C: Effect of color estimated by using regression for nonwhites with mean background composition of whites.

by the younger men. For nonwhites, the over-all increase was 3.3 years, while an increase of only 0.6 or 0.8 year (depending on the basis of the calculation) can be attributed to improved circumstances of the family of origin. Of the various handicaps or advantages that a family may confer upon its children, the most important as a determinant of educational attainment is simply year of birth! The youngest cohort of nonwhites almost matches the oldest cohort of whites, so that the combination of background handicaps and those specifically due to "color" is about comparable in effect to the passage of two or three decades of time. The residual color effect alone amounts to no more than the amount of change occurring in a decade. (The reader may note that this example shows how multiple-variable studies can provide a breakdown of the Fein gap into its components of general and minority-specific handicaps.)

CAVEAT

All this is relevant to our general goal of freedom from discrimination, however, only on the assumption that educational advance will provide a major part of the solution to the larger problem. There is room for doubt.

For the foreseeable future, closing of the educational gap will mean increasing proportions of Negroes completing high school and attaining some college education short of graduation. But it is at this level of educational attainment that the dissimilarity of occupational levels between whites and Negroes is most pronounced.

In 1960, the occupation distributions of men 25-34 years old were such that a minimum of 35.4 per cent of the nonwhites would have to be shifted from one major occupation group to another in order for whites and nonwhites to have the same distribution. There was pronounced variation in the amount of net mobility thus required to produce equalization within grouping defined by education attainment. Siegel[28] gives the following figures:

Schooling	White-Nonwhite Index of Dissimilarity
None	18.6 per cent
Elementary, 1–4	19.9
Elementary, 5–7	26.1
Elementary, 8	27.0
High School, 1–3	28.2
High School, 4	33.4
College, 1–3	34.4
College, 4+	18.6

It is not, therefore, the high school "dropout" who feels the greatest force of occupational discrimination, but the high school graduate or the man who completes some college work short of graduation. To be sure, the

---

[28] Siegel, op. cit., Table 1. The picture would be even less favorable if we had statistics for Negroes rather than for the misleading composite of all "nonwhites." As Lorimer and Jones point out, "nonwhite" is a "heterogeneous classification used by the census to simplify its tabulations at the cost of providing confused information," Frank Lorimer and Dorothy S. Jones, "The Demographic Characteristics of the Negro Population in the United States," *Journal of Negro Education,* 22 (Summer 1953), p. 250.

college graduate may have to render his professional or technical services in a segregated setting; but he is not prevented to the same degree as the college "dropout" or high school graduate from achieving the occupational level for which his training purportedly prepared him. At the other end of the scale, poorly educated Negroes do not suffer as much *relative* deprivation as those who attain the minimum standard of elementary schooling. Some years ago, we had occasion to comment on this circumstance:

> It is at the boundary between high school and college educational attainment that the occupational inequality is the greatest. One wonders if we do not have here a good part of the explanation for the recent rise in effective agitation by Negroes for equal rights and opportunities. With goodly numbers of Negroes in the younger cohorts attaining sufficient education to understand their personal situation in social terms, and with the personal situation being one of a rather hard "ceiling" on both educational attainment and occupational mobility, it is hardly surprising that organized and intelligent forms of protest are increasingly in evidence. The coming upsurge in numbers of young adults—those who, among other things, are reaching the age that qualifies them to vote—applies to the Negro as well as the white. As compared with, say, the 1930's, when the proportion of adults in the youngest adult age groups was equally high, the cohorts reaching these ages in the 1960's will include much larger proportions who have finished high school and who live in urban areas affording intense personal contacts as well as access to a wide range of mass media of communication. One can only hope that the unrest so easily generated in such a population can lead to constructive organization rather than being dissipated only by costly and unproductive forms of rebellion.[29]

Leaving aside the observation that conjectures no more than five years old begin to betray their age, there continues to be validity in the point that educational progress may only mean "that Negroes are just beginning to be exposed to a whole new area of segregation." [30] The inference is weak, to be sure, for the very reason we have been stressing—lack of trend data on interrelationships among components of the socioeconomic life cycle. The development of adequate models and information systems to reveal these interrelationships is prerequisite to specification of the "targets" toward which we would bend the trends.

---

[29] Otis Dudley Duncan, "Population Trends, Mobility and Social Change," presented to the Seminar on Dimensions of American Society, sponsored by the American Association of Colleges for Teacher Education, Committee on Studies, 4–8 October 1961 (ms., p. 58).

[30] Siegel, *op. cit.*, p. 46. Cf. Hare, *op. cit.*, p. 172.

15

SOCIAL BREAKDOWN

NATHAN GOLDMAN

The breakdown of society has been the concern of philosophers, theologians, psychiatrists, psychologists, poets and novelists, and social scientists ever since Adam ate the forbidden fruit and learned the difference between right and wrong.[1] Very early in the history of mankind there appeared, thus, a breach in the control exercised by the social norms over the members of the society. Since then, social breakdown has been blamed on the Devil, climatic changes, man's instinctual make-up, the economic system, alcohol, the loss of charismatic leadership, the completion of the immanent cycle of life and death of society, contamination of the purity of blood of a racial group, cultural lag, and so on. In every period of history, the disorganization, if not the end, of society has been lamented.

According to reports from a large variety of sources, American society is in a serious state of moral and social disintegration. Drug addiction, alcoholism, prostitution, gambling, divorce, venereal disease, illegitimacy, poverty, homosexuality, crime, riots, racial discrimination, and many other morally abhorrent conditions are said to be at all-time highs. Our solid middle-class citizens, the backbone of Western civilization, are described as reveling in alcohol, infidelity, abortions, gambling, and the like, in hundreds of Peyton Places over the country. Youth vociferously and flagrantly reject the mores of their ancestors, flaunting their use of marijuana and LSD, sexual freedom and birth control, miniskirts and pornography. We are fed daily movies or television programs glamorizing violence, prostitution, crime, and adultery.

We are repeatedly reminded that one out of every four marriages this year will end in divorce, and that in the United States about one out of five

---

[1] It may be of some significance that the second recorded act of man and the first recorded act of woman were deviations from the established conduct norm.

marriages is preceded by conception. It is predicted that one person in twelve in American society will spend some time in a mental hospital before he dies. It is lamented that 60 per cent of college students are using dangerous drugs. We are told authoritatively that there are about five million alcoholics in the United States. Statistics are adduced to show that suicides are increasing, ranking now as fourth among the causes of death among Americans between the years of 18 and 45. We are informed that about one out of every 16 live births is illegitimate, and over 40 per cent of these children are born to mothers between the ages of 15 and 19.

These forms of behavior, which deviate from the accepted norms of our Judaeo-Christian culture, are proclaimed as indicators of the disorganized state of the society. They are enunciated as proof that Western society is rapidly breaking down, that it is in a state of crisis and even on its way to extinction. To the social scientist, these reports provide a serious challenge. He raises questions about the definitions of the phenomena in question, the reliability of the statistics used, and the interpretation of the data. In fact, as will be shown later, it is possible that some of these accepted indicators of disorganization may be conventionally structured ways of meeting problems created by strains in the social system, and thus are forms of *organization* rather than disorganization.

There is a considerable sociological literature in the area of social breakdown, appearing under the various titles of social disorganization, social problems, or deviant behavior. However, in discussing the concept of social disorganization or of deviant behavior, each author generally refers to a more or less conventional list of social problems. These social problems are considered as undesirable social situations, and as indicators of the state of the society. They are regarded "either as symptomatic of imminent disorganization or as direct manifestations of an existing state of disorganization."[2] Generally designated as such indicators are problems of crime and delinquency, problems of the family such as divorce and desertion, alcoholism, drug addiction, prostitution, mental disorder, suicide, illegitimacy, and the like. Depending on the orientation of the author, other unpleasant or undesirable situations, such as women in industry, migration, totalitarianism, the violation of social liberties, overpopulation, unemployment, corruption in public office, poverty, popular culture, and the like may be classed as social problems and as indicators of the sorry state of our society.

Our concern in this chapter will be with some of these problems which have been customarily used as indicators of social breakdown or disorganization. We shall examine the sources of, and the reliability of, infor-

---

[2] John F. Cuber, William F. Kenkel, and Robert A. Harper, *Problems of American Society* (New York: Holt, Rinehart & Winston, 1964), p. 33.

mation on family breakdown, alcohol and drug addiction, personal breakdown, and sexual deviation, and the validity of the use of these social problems as indicators of the state or condition of the society. In our selection of these specific social problems for discussion, we are not necessarily implying that these are the most significant problems for the society, but that they are the ones most commonly used. Other forms of societally defined offensive behavior such as gambling, incest, child-beating, abortion, begging, and the whole gamut of fraudulent activities in business and in public office might also have been considered.

An attempt will be made to reformulate the problem of societal breakdown by a shift in the focus of attention from the problem behavior of groups or individuals to the structural characteristics of the social system itself. Suggestions for the development of new indicators of the state of the society will be attempted.

FAMILY BREAKDOWN

Disorganization of the family is considered by most critics of the contemporary scene as the basic and most crucial problem of American society. Divorce, desertion, and separation are generally viewed as serious breaks in the institution of the family, the "backbone" of Western civilization. Breakdown of the family carries with it a loss of its institutionalized function of child-socialization and its role in the development of the affectional and empathic aspects of personality. A variety of behavioral and personality aberrations have been credited to deficiencies in the functioning of the family.

DIVORCE

The popular conception of a burgeoning divorce rate is only partly borne out by available statistics. The rate of divorces granted in a calendar year per 1,000 married females 15 years of age and over increased steadily from 8.0 in 1920, to a peak of 17.9 in 1946. It decreased from that point until 1955 when it leveled off at 9.3 per 1,000 married females, and has remained fairly stable since[3] (see Table 1). Moreover, the ratio of divorces to marriages performed annually has remained fairly constant from 1950 to 1960 (Table 1). Since about 1952, there has been a ratio of about 250 divorces granted annually to every 1,000 marriages performed in the same year.

---

[3] U.S., Department of Health, Education, and Welfare, *Trends* (Washington, D.C.: U.S. Government Printing Office, 1965), p. S-5.

TABLE 1—Family Disorganization

Date	Divorces Granted per 1,000 Marriages Performed (a)	Divorces Granted per 1,000 Married Females (b)	Divorces per 1,000 Ever-Married Females (c)		
			Total	White	Nonwhite
1940	165	8.8	22.0	22.0	22.0
1945	300	14.4	(1947) 27.0	26.0	31.0
1950	230	10.3	30.0	30.0	35.0
1952	254	10.1	28.0	27.0	35.0
1954	254	9.5	28.0	27.0	39.0
1956	241	9.4	30.0	29.0	40.0
1958	253	8.9	29.0	28.0	35.0
1960	258	9.2	33.0	30.0	54.0
1961	261	9.6	35.0	33.0	48.0
1962	250	9.4	33.0	31.0	50.0
1963	—	—	35.0	33.0	55.0
1964	—	—	38.0	36.0	51.0

(a) U.S., Department of Health, Education, and Welfare, *Trends* (Washington, D.C.: U.S. Government Printing Office, 1965), Table S-4.

(b) *Statistical Abstract of the United States, 1965*, p. 62.

(c) Adapted from: U.S., Department of Labor, Office of Policy Planning and Research, *The Negro Family* (Washington, D. C.: U.S. Government Printing Office, 1964), p. 77.

It has been suggested on the basis of these data that one of every four marriages is doomed to failure. This is a gross misinterpretation of the data, in the nature of a "conceptual lie." The divorce rate, to be meaningful, should be computed not on the basis of currently contracted marriages, but on the total of ever-existing marriages, a much larger number. Table 1 (c) indicates that the rate of divorces granted per 1,000 ever-married women fluctuated around 30.0 during the 1950's and then rose slowly to 38.0 in 1964. Negro marriages seem, however, to be breaking down at a greater rate than white marriages.

> Divorces have increased of late for both whites and nonwhites, but at a much greater rate for the latter. In 1940 both groups had a divorce rate of 2.2 per cent. By 1964 the white rate had risen to 3.6 per cent, but the nonwhite had reached 5.1 per cent—40 per cent greater than the formerly equal white rate.[4]

Thus, there seems to be some justification for the claim of an increase in divorce, but not to the extent that one of every four marriages is doomed.

---

[4] U.S., Department of Labor, Office of Policy Planning and Research, *The Negro Family* (Washington, D.C.: U.S. Government Printing Office Office, 1964), p. 12.

The effect of divorce on the family is somewhat mitigated by the fact that most divorced persons remarry shortly after the divorce. "At every age level, even through the seventies, marriage rates for the divorced are higher than for the rest of the population. In fact, about 94 per cent of divorced women over thirty eventually remarry."[5] Moreover, the high divorce rate is partially offset by the lowered death rate so that "the average married couple . . . actually lives together longer than did their grandparents."[6]

SEPARATION

The extent of family breakdown in American society is not fully reflected in divorce statistics. Divorce occurs, usually, after the family is disorganized, merely giving final legal status to an already disrupted marriage. Desertions and separations would seem to be better indicators of family breakdown. Accurate data on desertion are not available on a national level, but data on separations (including desertion) may be found in the Census Bureau reports. Since 1950, these Census Bureau reports have indicated that approximately 2 per cent of white women, and 14 per cent of the nonwhite, mostly Negro women, are separated from their husbands. Although the rate of separation for nonwhite women is about seven times that of the rate of white women, both rates have increased only slightly during the past decade.

The number of children living in families with fathers absent might be more useful as an indicator of family breakdown than divorce or separation. Moynihan shows a 50 per cent increase from 1940 to 1963 in the number of children receiving assistance under the Aid to Families with Dependent Children (AFDC) program, both white and nonwhite, whose fathers were absent from the family for reasons other than death or incapacity of some sort. In 1963, two-thirds of the approximately three million children on AFDC came from such father-absent families, as against less than one-third of the 835,000 children in 1950. This increase may be considered, at least in part, a reflection of the increase in separation and desertion of the father from the home.

The effects of this high rate of separation and desertion are most keenly felt in the Negro family, from which is drawn a disproportionately high number of AFDC children. Moynihan reports that 14 per cent of Negro children are receiving such aid, as against 2 per cent of white children. Moreover, 56 per cent of the nation's nonwhite children receive

---

[5] Russell R. Dynes, Alfred C. Clarke, Simon Dinitz, and Iwao Ishino, *Social Problems* (New York: Oxford University Press, 1964), p. 115.

[6] *ibid.*, p. 116.

AFDC assistance at some time in their childhood, while only 8 per cent of the white children are so aided.[7]

ILLEGITIMACY

The illegitimacy rate for the nation has increased by approximately 70 per cent since 1940. The increase was steady but slow, from a ratio of 37.9 illegitimate births per 1,000 live births in 1940, to 63.3 in 1963 (Table 2). Contrary to popular belief

> the teen-age illegitimate mother is the *one* age group that has not increased its *rate* of illegitimate births in the recent years. Over a period of almost a generation, since 1938, the trend is ever more striking: in 1938, the rate for teen-agers was higher than that for any age group except those 20–24 years old. Now, the rate for this younger group is lower than for any group under 35.[8]

The Negro illegitimacy rate was about ten times that of the white rate until about 1960, when it dropped to eight times the white rate. Although the amount of illegitimacy has increased in both groups, the rate of increase for Negroes seems to be slowing down somewhat, relative to that for whites, after 1950 from that in the previous period. In the decade after 1940, the white rate dropped by 1 per cent while the Negro rate increased by 67 per cent; in the decade after 1950, the white rate increased by 30 per cent while the nonwhite rate increased by only 25 per cent. The apparent overall increase in rates may not reflect a genuine rise, however. Some of it might be due to improved record-keeping, and to greater use of public facilities for the delivery of illegitimate children where they then become officially registered. The differential between white and Negro illegitimacy rates may be, in part, accounted for by the greater ability, based on greater economic resources, of the white unmarried mother to conceal her pregnancy. She could purchase the services of an abortionist, or move to a city (or even to Puerto Rico or Europe) where she is unknown, to have her child. Also, there is a greater tendency among Negroes than among whites to accept the illegitimate child as a member of an extended family group where it may then be registered by the census-takers.

---

[7] U.S., Department of Labor, Office of Policy Planning and Research, *The Negro Family, op. cit.,* p. 12.

[8] William J. Goode, "Family Disorganization," in *Contemporary Social Problems,* ed. Robert K. Merton and Robert A. Nisbet (New York: Harcourt, Brace, & World, 1966), p. 490.

TABLE 2—Family Breakdown

Date	Per Cent Women Separated from Husbands (a)		Per Cent Families Headed by Women (b)		Illegitimate Births per 1,000 Live Births (c)		
	White	Nonwhite	White	Nonwhite	Total	White	Nonwhite
1940	—	—	—	—	37.9	19.5	168.3
1945	—	—	—	—	42.9	23.6	179.3
1950	2.0	13.9	8.4	19.1	39.8	17.5	179.6
1952	1.8	12.4	9.2	17.9	39.1	16.3	198.5
1954	1.9	12.7	8.3	19.2	44.0	18.2	198.5
1956	1.9	14.2	8.8	20.5	46.5	19.0	204.0
1958	1.9	16.0	8.6	22.4	49.6	20.9	212.3
1960	1.9	13.8	8.7	22.4	52.7	22.9	215.8
1961	2.2	14.3	8.9	21.6	56.3	25.3	223.4
1962	2.0	14.9	8.6	23.2	58.8	27.5	229.9
1963	1.9	14.6	—	—	63.3	30.7	235.9
1964	2.2	14.8	—	—	—	—	—

(a) From: *The Negro Family, op. cit.*, p. 58.
(b) *ibid.*, p. 61.
(c) *ibid.*, p. 59.

THE NEGRO FAMILY

Special attention has been given recently to the Negro family. From the available data, it may be said that although the Negro still exceeds whites in rates of divorce, in the proportion of families with female head (See Table 2), separation from husbands, and illegitimacy, the gap between the two groups in family stability appears to be narrowing. It is expected that as the Negro becomes better integrated into the economic and social system of American society, this gap will narrow further.

SOURCES OF DATA

National statistics of family breakdown are found in the population reports of the Bureau of the Census, and in the reports of the Vital Statistics Division of the Department of Health, Education, and Welfare. The Census Bureau reports, obtained from the national decennial survey, provide information on marital status (single, married, divorced, widowed), and whether the married person is living with his spouse, based on a sample (25 per cent in 1960) of the total. In cases where one partner is declared absent, distinction is made between those temporarily absent from the home and those from whom the spouse is separated. The latter may

include those legally separated, those waiting for divorce, and those temporarily or permanently estranged because of marital discord. There is no
indication of the specific nature of the separation, nor the length of time
it has been in effect.

The Census Bureau statistics on family breakdown suffer from a
number of defects. The information might be obtained from housekeepers,
neighbors, or others in the household in the absence of the respondent.
There may be different reports by each spouse about the state of the marriage. Some persons may misrepresent their marital status: unwed mothers
may represent themselves as either divorced, separated, or widowed, and
childless divorced persons may prefer to be known as single. A comparison
between persons reporting themselves as divorced on the 1950 census and
on a current population survey showed only a 70 per cent agreement.[9]
865,000 women and 1,342,000 men were listed in 1958 as "separated"
from their mates.[10] Such a discrepancy in numbers raises some doubt about
the reliability of these data, especially since it has been reported that three-
fourths of the divorced men remarry, as against two-thirds of divorced
women.[11]

The Vital Statistics Division of the Public Health Service publishes
data obtained directly from twenty states forming a Division Registration
Area. Each state registrar or bureau of vital statistics forwards divorce and
annulment data from local sources to the Public Health Service. Thus, in
the Vital Statistics Reports we have an official tabulation of divorces and
annulments granted, a much more reliable, although not necessarily more
valid, measure of family dissolution than that provided in the Census
reports. However, the Vital Statistics Reports suffer from the fact that they
represent a limited sample of the nation. The Divorce Registration Area, in
1962, was composed of about twenty states largely in the rural South and
Midwest. The Northeast, populous New York, New Jersey, Illinois, and
California, among others, are not included.

These Vital Statistics Reports data are presented in a variety of ways:
divorces granted per 1,000 population, divorces granted per 1,000 marriage
ceremonies per year, divorces granted annually per 1,000 married women
aged 15 years and over, and divorces per 1,000 ever-married women. The

---

9 Alexander Broel-Plateris, "Associations Between Marriage Disruption, Permis-
siveness of Divorce Laws, and Selected Social Variables," in *Contributions to Urban
Sociology*, ed. Ernest W. Burgess and Donald J. Bogue (Chicago: University of Chicago
Press, 1964), p. 515.

10 U.S., Department of Commerce, Bureau of the Census, "Population Characteristics, Marital Status, and Family Status: March 1958," *Current Population Reports*
(November 1958), Table 1.

11 Clifford Kirkpatrick, *The Family* (New York: Ronald Press, 1963), p. 592.

ratio of divorces to population will be affected by population fluctuations and the age of the population. The crude rate of divorces to marriages performed will be affected also by the age of the population. Moreover, as a measure of family breakdown, the crude divorce rate is complicated by the fact that there is a varying time lapse between actual separation and the awarding of the divorce decree. The erroneous impression would be established that a specific proportion of marriages performed in one year will end in divorce. The ratio of divorces in a given year to *existing* or *ever-existing* marriages provides a more satisfactory picture of the state of family breakdown. It provides, however, information only on the proportion of marriages which end in divorce in a given year, with no indication of the length of time the marriages had been in effect.

Thomas C. Monahan suggests that, to measure the strength or weakness of the marriage relationship, the crude rate of divorces per 1,000 married couples be replaced with a duration-specific rate. This would provide the ratio of divorces in marriages of a specified duration to the total number of marriages of the same duration. Thus, we would have a measure of the durability of the marital bond. Such a measure would not be affected by sharp yearly fluctuations in marriages or divorces, or population characteristics, and would provide a trustworthy reflection of the divorce pattern in the nation.[12] Data on the duration of marriage to time of divorce decree, not separation, were available in the United States only until 1932. Thus, we have currently no adequate statistics on family breakdown in the form of separation, and only partially adequate statistics on divorce.

Data on illegitimate births to white and nonwhite women are received by the National Center for Health Statistics from thirty-four states and the District of Columbia. The United States is grouped into nine geographic divisions in which the rate of illegitimate births obtained from reporting states is applied to all states in that division. In each reporting state, figures since 1956 are based on a 50 per cent sample of births. In cases of illegitimate births reported as second or higher births for the mother, it cannot be determined from the data whether previous deliveries occurred out of wedlock. Thus, we have no indication of the frequency, per unwed mother, of illegitimate births. The degree of error in these illegitimacy reports is presumed high and unknown. No corrections are made for misstatements about legitimacy status or failure to register. They are further limited in that the reports are not received from such populous states as New York, Massachusetts, and California.

---

[12] Thomas C. Monahan, "When Married Couples Part: Statistical Trends and Relationships in Divorce," *American Sociological Review, 27* (1962), p. 625.

RECOMMENDATIONS

It would seem highly desirable to expand the collection area for statistics of family breakdown. The limited Divorce Registration Area should be replaced by one more nearly reflecting the population characteristics of the country as a whole, and additional separation information should be obtained. This sample should include representative proportions of urban as well as rural areas, industrial, commercial, residential, and the like. The pattern established by the Children's Bureau in selecting a representative sample of Juvenile Courts for registration of juvenile delinquency cases might well be followed. Information on separations could be obtained from a variety of sources. Courts or public welfare agencies could supply records of suits for nonsupport of families. Social case-work agencies, especially public welfare, have information regarding a variety of family problems in the community. It might be feasible for the local Family or Children's Court to collect such data for forwarding to the state registrar along with divorce and annulment records. To insure standardization and reliability of reporting, it would probably be necessary for a federal agency such as the Public Health Service to organize and to subsidize the collection of these data.

Some definitions of currently loosely used terms would have to be developed, so as to distinguish various forms of separation: What are the criteria for desertion? What about the kind of separation which is broken by the occasional return of the husband? Census questions regarding separation would need to be expanded to include more accurate data on kind and length of separation.

ADDICTIONS

DRUNKENNESS AND ALCOHOLISM

The use of alcohol has always been widespread in American society.[13] It is deeply ingrained in American tradition, stemming from early American colonists and the culture patterns brought by various immigrants from the Old World. Recent studies show that between 60 per cent and 70 per cent of the adult population in the United States drink some form of alcoholic beverage (See Table 3). Straus points out that to this figure should be

---

[13] See Raymond G. McCarthy and Edgar M. Douglass, *Alcohol and Social Responsibility* (New York: Thomas Y. Crowell and Yale Plan Clinic, 1949), chap. 1: "The Historical Background of Drinking."

added an estimated 8 to 10 million young people who were found, in studies of drinking in high school and college, to drink on some occasions. He suggests that "from 80 to 90 million Americans above the age of 15 can be considered as users of alcoholic beverages."[14]

TABLE 3—Alcohol Use

Date	Estimated Alcohol Users (% Adult Population)	Drinkers In Millions		Alcoholics In Millions	Addicted Drinkers In Millions
1945 (a)	67	1940 (d)	40	2.4	0.6
1946 (a)	67	1947 (e)	50	3.0	0.75
1949 (a)	58	1948 (d)	65	4.0	1.0
1950 (a)	60	1955 (f)	70	5.0	1.0
1951 (a)	59	1963 (g)	70	5.0	1.0
1952 (a)	60				
1956 (a)	60				
1958 (b)	60				
1963 (c)	71				
1964 (c)	63				

(a) Jessie Bernard, *Social Problems at Midcentury* (New York: Dryden Press, 1957), pp. 244–245.

(b) Walter Reckless, *The Crime Problem* (New York: Appleton-Century-Crofts, 1967), p. 190.

(c) Robert Straus, "Alcohol" in *Contemporary Social Problems*, ed. Robert K. Merton and Robert A. Nisbet (New York: Harcourt, Brace, 1966), p. 250.

(d) Edwin M. Lemert, *Social Pathology* (New York: McGraw-Hill, 1951), p. 342.

(e) Walter C. Reckless, *The Crime Problem* (New York: Appleton-Century-Crofts, 1967), p. 191.

(f) Jessie Bernard, *Social Problems at Midcentury* (New York: Dryden Press, 1957), p. 268, note 15.

(g) Russell R. Dynes, Alfred C. Clarke, Simon Dinitz and Iawao Ishino, *Social Problems* (New York: Oxford University Press, 1964), p. 530.

Although the estimated number of adult drinkers of alcoholic beverages has increased from about 40 million in 1940 to about 70 million in 1962, the pattern of drinking seems to have shifted from distilled spirits to the consumption of beer and wine. In the 100 years between 1840 and 1950, the proportion of alcohol consumed in the form of distilled spirits dropped from about 90 per cent to about 40 per cent, while the proportion of alcohol in the form of beer rose from 6 per cent to 49 per cent and wine, from 4 per cent to 11 per cent. During this period the adult per capita con-

---

[14] Robert Straus, "Alcohol," in *Contemporary Social Problems*, ed. Robert K. Merton and Robert A. Nisbet, *op. cit.*, p. 250.

sumption of distilled spirits dropped from 4.17 to 1.72 gallons, while that for beer rose from 2.70 to 23.21 gallons and wine from 0.46 to 1.27 gallons. However, the over-all consumption of absolute alcohol remained constant during this 100-year period, 2.07 gallons per capita in 1850 compared with 2.04 gallons in 1950.[15] More Americans seem to be drinking more fermented and less distilled beverages, and at an earlier age than formerly.

It is estimated that about 6 per cent of the nation's drinkers become problem drinkers or alcoholics. These are currently said to number between four and five million persons (see Table 3). Of these, about 1½ per cent, or about one million persons, are said to be engaged in persistent, pathological, uncontrollable drinking, with deterioration of psychological and social functioning.[16] Such chronic addicted alcoholics represent 15 per cent of first admissions to state and county mental hospitals. In 1962 there were 23,500 resident patients in state, county, and federal institutions for conditions associated with the excessive use of alcohol.[17] Although facilities in psychiatric hospitals, general hospitals with psychiatric facilities, and alcoholism clinics have expanded markedly during the past decade, the bulk of the population of chronic addicted alcoholics remains untreated.

The excessive use of alcohol is often related to another social problem, that of crime. Offenses usually involving alcohol—drunkenness, disorderly conduct, vagrancy, drunken driving, and violation of liquor laws—have constituted, since 1956, between 55 per cent and 60 per cent of the total arrests recorded by the Federal Bureau of Investigation (FBI) on a national basis. Walter C. Reckless estimates that, in 1965, 65 per cent of all cases coming before municipal, police, and justice-of-the-peace courts were charged with drunkenness.[18]

Citing several studies, Reckless indicates that a very high proportion of adult offenders have been found to have been under the influence of alcohol at the time of commission of the offense. In a Columbus, Ohio, study of felony arrests in 1951–1953, over 60 per cent were found to be under the influence of alcohol (more than 0.5 per cent alcohol in urine) at the time of arrest. "These included over 80 per cent of the people arrested for concealed weapons, cuttings and shootings, over 60 per cent of those arrested for robbery, burglary, larceny, forgery, and auto theft, and 45 per cent of those arrested for rape." Also, alcohol was found by Marvin E. Wolfgang, in a study of Philadelphia Police Department Homicide Squad files, to be present in the victim, the offender, or both, in over 60 per cent

---

[15] *ibid.,* p. 248.

[16] *ibid.,* p. 260.

[17] U.S., Department of Health, Education, and Welfare, *Trends, op. cit.,* p. 12.

[18] Walter C. Reckless, *The Crime Problem* (New York: Appleton-Century-Crofts, 1967), p. 194.

of the cases.[19] Thus, alcohol, in addition to being an important problem for the society, is a significant contributor to another serious problem, that of crime.

Although it may be considered a social problem of serious dimensions, the true extent of the misuse of alcohol as a community problem remains unknown. Many cases of alcoholism, especially among women, do not come to the attention of public agencies where records may be kept. The economically secure alcoholic may be treated in a private clinic or hospital, the female "pantry drinker" may be known only to her family, and neither may ever be known to the police or the public mental hospital. The business executive in a large corporation may be protected from prying outsiders by management, and workers protected by the union steward.[20] Some may live in an economically marginal state without coming into conflict with the law or otherwise being identified. Moreover, in most states, police concern is limited to *public* intoxication, and the excessive drinker or the compulsive drinker who confines his drinking to private clubs or to his home will not become a police statistic.

Distinction is not made in official records between the alcoholic and the inebriate. Arrests for public intoxication include many persons who are not either addicted or nonaddicted alcoholics, and alcoholics may be convicted of offenses other than drunkenness. The statistics of arrest for drunkenness are further complicated by the fact that different communities use different charges for the man or woman who is found in public in an intoxicated condition. Thus, arrest statistics are of little use in estimating the amount of alcoholism in the community.

However, since we are concerned with the general problem of societal breakdown, it may be appropriate to include intoxication and associated offenses, although not always involving alcoholics, with the data on alcoholism as a community problem. The drunk on the street represents a level of conduct which may be harmful to the best interests of the society. Unlike the compulsive drinker, the drunk represents a conscious and voluntary involvement in excessive drinking. It represents, in many instances, a socially sanctioned excessive use of alcohol. As such, it may be considered a significant social problem.

We have little information about alcoholism, either problem drinkers or compulsive addicted drinkers, among our two largest nonwhite minority groups, the Negro and the American Indian. It is popularly believed, and to some extent reflected in crime statistics, that there is considerable excessive use of alcohol in these two groups. It would be essential for the

---

19 *ibid.*, p. 197.
20 Howard S. Becker, *Outsiders* (New York: Free Press, 1963), p. 169.

establishment, by legislation or otherwise, of programs to improve the social plight of these two minority groups to know the extent of alcoholism among them.

To obtain an adequate index of alcoholism as a social problem, it would be necessary, first of all, to achieve agreement on a definition of alcoholism. This should enable us to distinguish between statistics of the incidence of drinking, of drunkenness, and chronic alcoholism, which are frequently confused in professional literature and in the public press. Since alcoholism is considered more and more as an illness, the medical profession might be called on to organize such a definition for official use. Statistical information might be obtained from both public and private agencies, and from those general hospitals now admitting alcoholics for treatment. Public and private agencies for the study of alcoholism and the treatment of the alcoholic have multiplied in the past two decades. Public and private case-work agencies have become concerned with the alcoholic. National and local councils and information centers on problems of alcoholism exist in various parts of the country. Moreover, in recent years, private industry and labor unions have become concerned with the alcoholic in their ranks. Insurance companies have data on alcoholism in their records. A central registry in each state could collect and process information from all of these sources. In New York State this information could be drawn from the newly established Division on Alcoholism in the State Department of Mental Health.

DRUG USE

Addiction to the use of narcotic drugs is generally considered a serious social problem in the United States, especially as it occurs among minority groups in our metropolitan areas. This concern is enhanced by indications that the use of some dangerous drugs, although non-narcotic and nonaddictive, is spreading into middle-class and upper-middle-class neighborhoods. The press carries frequent sensational reports of the widespread use by high school and by college students of marijuana, barbiturates, amphetamines and LSD. However, the actual number of narcotics addicts and the actual extent of use of dangerous but nonaddictive drugs is essentially unknown. We have some data, on a national and local level, of arrests, conviction, and commitment of persons accused of illegally selling or possessing narcotics or other dangerous drugs. We also have some data on addicts who apply for hospital treatment. However, as a measure of the extent of the problem of drug use these data are far from complete or adequate. Unless they become involved in crime to support the drug habit, many addicts can avoid public identification. Middle-class addicts and professional persons who have access to drugs rarely fall into the hands of the police.

The Bureau of Narcotics of the United States Treasury Department has published an annual count of addicts in the United States since 1953. Reports are collected from law-enforcement officials across the nation, and are presented annually in "Traffic in Opium and Other Dangerous Drugs." A list of "active" addicts is compiled from addict-identification cards submitted by local law-enforcement officials on addicts who "come to their attention." The names of newly reported addicts are added to the list, giving a count of new addicts and recidivists. However, if the name of a listed addict is not repeated in a five-year period, he is dropped from the list on the assumption that he is either dead or no longer a user of drugs.

In addition to the Bureau of Narcotics data, statistics on nonfederal narcotics arrests are reported in the *Uniform Crime Reports* of the Federal Bureau of Investigation. However, these narcotics-arrest data, obtained from police over the nation, do not cover the period prior to 1930, and are adequate only since about 1960. They do not reliably distinguish between sellers and users, and do not contain information on addicts other than those specifically arrested on narcotics charges. The Bureau of the Census includes in its annual report on prison populations the number of prisoners incarcerated on narcotics charges. One may find, also, information on local conditions in state and city reports on apprehended violators of the narcotics laws.

The Bureau of Narcotics estimates that there are between 45,000 and 60,000 drug addicts, a ratio of about 1 person in 4,000, in the United States. It was reported to the United Nations Commission on Narcotic Drugs that on December 31, 1960, there were 44,906 addicts in the United States.[21] The current situation represents, according to the Bureau of Narcotics, a tremendous *decrease* in the number of addicts since the passage of the Harrison Act in 1914. At that time, it was estimated that there were about 200,000 persons, or one person in 400, addicted to opiates, which could be easily and legally obtained. The number of drug addicts is reported to have dropped sharply to about 20,000 in 1946, rising again to about 60,000 in the 1950's, and again decreasing in the 1960's to a point where one in 4,000 is estimated to be addicted.[22]

However, in the Price Daniel Senate subcommittee hearings and in the Hale Boggs House subcommittee hearings, it was found in 1955 that the total of the estimates by California, New York, Illinois, and Ohio state

---

[21] Alfred R. Lindesmith, *The Addict and the Law* (Bloomington: Indiana University Press, 1965), p. 100.

[22] U.S., Treasury Department, Bureau of Narcotics, *Narcotics Addiction* (Washington, D.C.: U:S. Government Printing Office, 1964), p. 5.

authorities, for these four states alone, was 65,000 addicts. Clausen points out that while the Bureau of Narcotics reported 7,412 narcotics addicts in Califrornia in 1962, the State of California listed 13,620 known addicts and users within the state. He estimates, from fragments of data, between 50,000 and 100,000 persons addicted to opiates in the United States. This figure does not include users of marijuana or other nonaddicting but dangerous drugs.[23]

Narcotics addiction has been to a large extent a problem of our large metropolitan centers. It is estimated by the Bureau of Narcotics that 48 per cent of the nation's narcotics addicts are in New York State, largely in New York City. Moreover, in New York, it is largely a problem of the Negro and Puerto Rican minorities. A recent report of the Bureau of Narcotics indicates, however, a decrease in the number of addicts among Negroes and an increase in the number of white addicts. Although Negro addicts still outnumber other groups, the number of Negroes among newly reported addicts has been declining annually during the past ten years. "In 1956, Negroes accounted for 56.8 per cent of all new addicts. In 1965 . . . the Negro portion has dropped to 40.2 per cent." The number of new Negro addicts added dropped from 5,395 in 1956 to 2,419 in 1965.[24] There is an unverified impression among community workers that many former drug addicts have turned to the more easily obtained and less expensive alcohol for their "kicks."

Drug addicts who can financially support their habit may never come to official attention so as to become included in the official statistics. Those who have legal access to drugs, such as doctors, dentists, nurses, and pharmacists may avoid detection, or, if detected, be privately punished by their respective professional organizations without publicity. "Doctors addicted to narcotics are punished lightly when they come to the attention of law enforcement authorities. A doctor found stealing from hospital narcotics supplies, is, ordinarily, simply asked to leave the hospital; he is not turned over to the police." [25] Winick refers to a study in 1942, which showed that of 457 consecutive admissions for Meperidine (Demerol) addiction to the United States Public Health Service Hospital at Lexington, about one-third were physicians and osteopaths. It was estimated by the United States Commissioner of Narcotics in 1957 that about 1 in 100 physicians were addicted to the use of opiates. This rate of addiction is considerably greater than the estimated rate of 1 in 3,000 in the general

23 John A. Clausen, "Drug Addiction," in *Contemporary Social Problems,* ed. Robert K. Merton and Robert A. Nisbet, *op. cit.,* pp. 204–205.

24 *New York Times,* March 30, 1967.

25 Howard S. Becker, *op. cit.,* p. 169.

population.[26] It is highly probable that some physician drug addicts, as well as nurses, dentists, and pharmacists, evaded detection by law-enforcement agencies.

The spreading use of marijuana, barbiturates, LSD, and amphetamines, classified as dangerous but nonaddictive drugs, among middle-class high school and college youth has caused much alarm among the citizens of the United States. Dr. Henry B. Bruyn, health director at the University of California at Berkeley, is quoted in an Associated Press report as saying that one out of every four students at Berkeley smokes marijuana. He estimated also that as many as 60 per cent of students in some eastern urban universities smoked marijuana.[27] Henry Giordano, United States Narcotics Commissioner, testified before a House Appropriations subcommittee that there was an increase in arrests for the illegal use of marijuana from 7,000 in 1964 to more than 15,000 in 1966.[28] Such drug use seems to be spreading among middle-class high school and college youth. Twenty-two youths, mostly from middle-class and upper-middle-class families, were arraigned in Queens County (New York) on charges of selling or possessing marijuana, LSD, barbiturates, amphetamines and hashish.[29] Clausen makes reference to the increasing occasional use of dangerous but nonaddicting drugs. "Increasingly, persons arrested for drug offenses are found to be using a variety of so-called dangerous drugs . . . such as amphetamines ('benzedrine') or hallucinogens on an occasional or 'spree' basis." He reminds us, however, that we have little data on the extent of such occasional use "beyond impressions from arrest data, reports in the public press, and pronouncements of advocates of free drug use or their opponents."[30]

In terms of the extent of the problem of drug addiction, it might be considered of less significance as an indicator of social disorganization than are other social problems. "Compared with mental illness, juvenile delinquency and other problems . . . it occurs infrequently and in more delimited population groups. For these groups it is a grave problem." [31] However, the crime which accompanies drug addiction and the unemployment and the social degradation of the addict add to the seriousness of the problem. Also, the seeming spread of nonnarcotic drug use, if it is, in fact, true, should be a matter of grave concern. This situation might be considered as an indicator of an as yet undiagnosed deep malaise in the social system.

---

[26] Charles Winick, "Physical Narcotic Addicts," *Social Problems,* 9 (1961), p. 175.
[27] *Syracuse Herald-Journal,* March 29, 1967.
[28] *New York Times,* March 18, 1967.
[29] *ibid.,* March 30, 1967.
[30] John A. Clausen, *Drug Addiction, op. cit.,* p. 195.
[31] *ibid.,* p. 235.

We must, however, develop ways of collecting adequate data on the nature, extent, and distribution of the problem.

Lindesmith emphasizes the unsatisfactory nature of available data on drug addiction for index purposes. Because of variations in enforcement policies, in detection, and in registration techniques, these figures cannot be considered as a constant proportion of drug addicts in the community. To assess the extent of the problem of drug addiction, we need to know the number of *addicts* known to the police for violation of the narcotics laws, the number of addicts known for violation of other laws, the number of addicts known only to various community agencies, the number of addicts securing legal drugs from doctors and pharmacists, and the number of institutionalized users. We need information, which we do not at present have, on the occasional user and on the patterns of spread in the community. Distinction should be made, in police and institution reports, between nonusers arrested or incarcerated for sale of narcotics, and addicts who were also sellers. With these data, we may be able to estimate, more reliably than at present, parameters of the problem of drug addiction.

It would be desirable to separate the criminal-law-enforcement from the rehabilitative functions. It might be well to reserve the latter for some agency involved in public health work, leaving the police function of tracking down sources of illicit narcotics to the Bureau of Narcotics of the Treasury Department.

PERSONAL BREAKDOWN

MENTAL DISORDER

The Department of Health, Education, and Welfare publishes annual reports on mental disorder in the United States in *Patients in Mental Hospitals and Data on Patients of Outpatient Psychiatric Clinics.* The former includes patients in private hospitals and institutions, as well as federal, state, and county institutions. The latter includes general hospitals with psychiatric services and also outpatient psychiatric clinics.

It is estimated that there were about 565,500 patients residing in mental hospitals at the end of the fiscal year 1964.[32] The rate for 1964 was 298.7 patients per 100,000 civilian population, a drop from a rate of 310.6 in 1963. In fact, the rate has been dropping steadily from a high of 409.0 in 1945. New admissions to mental hospitals, however, have been increasing steadily, but length of stay has been decreasing (see Table 4).

---

[32] Department of Health, Education, and Welfare, *Trends, op. cit.,* p. S-29.

TABLE 4—Personal Breakdown

Date	Mental Hospital Admissions per 100,000 Population (a)	Resident in Mental Hospital per 100,000 Population (b)	Suicides per 100,000 Population (c)
1940	1.4	363.7	—
1945	1.9	409.0	—
1950	2.0	384.9	11.4
1952	2.0	389.0	—
1954	2.1	391.3	—
1956	2.3	377.9	(1955) 10.2
1958	2.3	360.8	—
1960	2.3	343.2	10.6
1961	2.4	332.5	10.4
1962	2.6	321.8	10.9
1963	2.6	310.6	11.0
1964	—	298.7	—

(a) U. S., Department of Health, Education, and Welfare, *Trends, op. cit.*, Table S-29.

(b) *ibid.*, Table S-28.

(c) *Statistical Abstract of the United States, 1965, op. cit.*, p. 59.

One group, the aged, seems to be increasing in admissions to mental hospitals. This is probably not an indication of increasing mental breakdown in our older citizens, but rather a reflection of the increase in life span.[33]

Interpetation of these data is complicated by the changing public attitude toward mental disorder. The increase in admissions to mental hospitals may reflect a greater acceptance of mental disorder as a disease, especially when it can be treated in the psychiatric ward of a general hospital. However, Goldhamer and Marshall, in their study of first admissions to Massachusetts and New York institutions during the periods 1840–1885 and 1917–1940, find that "there has been no long-term increase during the last century in the incidence of psychosis of early and middle life."[34] It is probable that, with the lessening of the stigma attached to mental illness, and the public awareness of new techniques and facilities for handling psychiatric cases, there has been an increase in the readiness to use psychiatric facilities.

[33] John A. Clausen, "Mental Disorders," in *Contemporary Social Problems*, ed. Robert K. Merton and Robert A. Nisbet, *op. cit.*, p. 37.

[34] Herbert Goldhamer and Andrew Marshall, *Psychosis and Civilization* (New York: Free Press, 1953), p. 92.

These mental hospital statistics, however, are not accurate indicators of the state of mental health of the nation. It is estimated that an additional 379,000 nonhospitalized patients are treated annually in mental hygiene clinics, and from 365,000 to 451,000 are seen annually by private psychiatrists.[35] Many others, probably less disturbed, are seen by ministers, social workers, physicians, and clinical psychologists. These additional data, however, are not available.

To have reliable data on the extent of mental disorder in our society we need to consider those sources of information which are not now tapped by Department of Health, Education, and Welfare reports. In states where psychologists and social workers are licensed, such data might be made available through a central agency. Since public welfare agencies are associated either with a local, county, or state government, data could be collected through a state department of public welfare. Many private agencies are associated with a local Community Chest which might be used as an information-collecting agency. An area-sampling procedure would, of course, have to be worked out to get a representative sample of the nation. Also, care should be taken to include private as well as public agencies, hospitals and clinics, to avoid a distorted social-class representation in the data.

SUICIDE

Suicide is considered the ultimate breakdown of the person, and related to social breakdown. Suicide is considered by some "primarily a social phenomenon, and the majority of persons who commit suicide reflect the disorganization of the society."[36] In 1960 there were 19,540 suicides in the United States, a rate of 10.8 per 100,000 persons. This rate has remained fairly constant over a number of years.[37] Although ranked eleventh in the causes of death in the 1950's, suicide now ranks fourth in the causes of death among Americans aged 18–45, probably because of the elimination, by improved medical practice, of other causes of death.[38]

The principal source of national data on suicides consists in the Vital Statistics collected by the Public Health Service of the Department of Health, Education, and Welfare. These are based on a 10 per cent sample of death certificates filed with state vital statistics offices by local physicians

---

[35] Russell R. Dynes, *et al, Social Problems, op. cit.*, p. 406 .

[36] Mabel A. Elliott and Francis E. Merrill, *Social Disorganization* (New York: Harper, 1961), p. 315.

[37] Russell R. Dynes *et al., Social Problems, op. cit.*, p. 503.

[38] U.S., Department of Health, Education, and Welfare, *Trends, op. cit.*, p. 4.

and hospital authorities, which are forwarded to the Public Health Service National Center for Health Statistics in Washington.

The reliability of statistics on suicide is generally questioned. Zilboorg goes so far as to say that the data on suicide deserves little, if any, credence.[39] Suicides are concealed by relatives and physicians, and many cases of suicide may pass for accidental death, especially "one-car" accidents. A person unsuccessfully attempting suicide might die of an effect related to the attempt, and not be recorded a suicide. Suicide might be achieved by a negative act, by deliberately not protecting oneself against fatal injury.

Although there seems to be no increase in suicide rates during the past decade, this cannot be said with certainty because it seems almost impossible to obtain reliable statistics of suicide. If the social stigma attached to suicide were lessened, there might be less concealment. It might be possible to change the form of the death certificate so that doctors would report not only the cause but also the circumstances of death. A good deal of information on suicides has been collected by life insurance companies in the United States. The use of such records to supplement or correct government records might provide a more reliable index of suicides in the country than the Vital Statistics reports.

SEXUAL DEVIATION

PROSTITUTION

Prostitution is generally considered a concomitant of moral degeneracy and disorganization of a community. However, it is less a matter of public concern now than in the period 1910–1940.[40] This decreased concern is probably a function of increased sexual freedom for women in the United States and the decreased visibility of the prostitute. According to Clinard, prostitution accounts for less than 10 per cent of the total nonmarital sexual outlets for males.[41]

There is no way of ascertaining the number of women who support themselves by selling sexual favors either on a full-time or part-time basis. Police arrests are notoriously unreliable in this area, especially since newer

---

[39] Jack P. Gibbs, "Suicide," in *Contemporary Social Problems*, ed. Robert K. Merton and Robert A. Nisbet, *op. cit.*, p. 286.

[40] Kingsley Davis, "Sexual Behavior," in *Contemporary Social Problems*, ed. Robert K. Merton and Robert A. Nisbet, *op. cit.*, p. 348, note 49.

[41] Marshall Clinard, *Sociology of Deviant Behavior* (New York: Holt, Rinehart & Winston, 1963), p. 250.

types of prostitute—the call girl, for one—are not exposed to public contact with police. Clinard, in 1963, estimated that there were about 275,000 women in America who live by prostitution alone.[42] Even if there were some adequate way of counting full-time professional prostitutes, since they constitute such a small proportion of women engaged in illicit sex relations either for money or for other favors, the figures would be meaningless as a measure of breakdown of sexual norms in American society.

HOMOSEXUALITY

Homosexual behavior is considered abhorrent in American society and is generally punished as a crime. It is generally seen as a threat to the institution of the family and the virility of our society. However, the amount and kind of harm done to the society is debatable. English and European literature provides many instances of socially, artistically, and economically productive persons who in their private lives prefer as partners persons of their own sex.

We have no official statistics on homosexuality. Lemert estimates between three and four million homosexuals in the United States.[43] Thus, this form of proscribed sexual behavior, considered by most as more degenerate than prostitution, far exceeds the estimated number of prostitutes. Kinsey found that although 37 per cent of his white male sample had at some time or another participated in homosexual behavior, only about 4 per cent had been exclusively homosexual.[44] One of the problems posed by such studies consists in the lack of agreement on the definition of homosexuality and the lack of an adequate classification of its various forms. These would need to be developed before reliable measurement of the extent of this form of sexual deviation can be attempted.

Beyond these estimates of prostitution and of homosexuality, we have no measures of the amount of sexual pathology in our society. How, and whether or not, they contribute to the "breakdown" of our society is problematic. Police information on homosexuality is limited to arrests of those homosexuals who have a high degree of public visibility. These are either transvestites, or those apprehended in "crimes against nature" such as sodomy and fellatio. We have no basis even for speculation about the extent to which homosexuality is prevalent among middle-class men and women who are conventional in all other areas of conduct. Some information might be obtained from the Mattachine Society, a national organi-

---

42 *ibid.*, p. 250.

43 Edwin M. Lemert, *Social Pathology* (New York: McGraw-Hill, 1953), p. 237.

44 Kingsley Davis, "Social Behavior," *op. cit.*, p. 343.

zation of homosexuals with headquarters in Los Angeles, dedicated to protecting the political and social rights and welfare of the homosexual. However, because of their position as pleaders for a special cause, their estimates of the extent of homosexuality will need careful evaluation.

INADEQUACY OF CURRENT
INDICATORS

Thus, when existing data on societal breakdown are examined critically, it is difficult to indicate the extent of a problem or to say that it is more or less than in some previous period. Some of these problems generally considered serious, such as drug addiction and alcoholism, when examined in the light of historical reports, journalistic accounts, and some official statistics, seem actually to be decreasing. Within the limits of the inadequate data which we have, it might be said that illegitimacy, family separation, and mental hospital admission of the aged seem to be increasing. However, the question is raised whether these statistical increases are "real" or concomitants of increased public concern or better record-keeping.

The lack of data, coupled with the unclear and varying definitions of the indicators of social breakdown which we have considered, and the differential reporting at various levels, make it most difficult to assess the amount of social breakdown in our society. Moreover, there is overlapping between various measures of disorganization—a prostitute may be an alcoholic and have an illegitimate child—so that a count of deviants and of instances of deviation would not necessarily coincide. Some are frequently found together, such as prostitution and female drug addiction, alcoholism and family disorganization, or suicide and mental disorder. On the other hand, a single instance of social breakdown, such as desertion, alcoholism, or suicide, may directly or indirectly affect the lives of a number of people.

A serious handicap in the translation of social-problems data into indicators of the social state of the nation lies in the fact that we have no common units of measurement. Is an increase in the rate of automobile thefts to be considered as "serious" as an increase in the rate of family desertion? Is an increase in the rate of illegitimate children less seriously damaging than a similar increase in the rate of drug addiction? Currently, judgment of the gravity of a situation is based on one's individual value system rather than on some objectively determined measure of harm or damage. Furthermore, the lack of a common unit of measurement makes it impossible to combine various indicators into a general index of social breakdown.

The interpretation of these statistics as indicators of social disorganization is further complicated by the fact that the greater the concern of the community about a given problem, and the more the public has been sensitized to the problem, and the better the public and private facilities for handling the problem, the greater will be the number of instances brought to official attention and thus recorded. The greater the confidence of the public in treatment facilities for the mentally disordered, the drug addict, the alcoholic, and the delinquent, the greater will be the public's use of these facilities, and the more instances will come to light. The Children's Bureau urges that, because of differences in state laws, differences in facilities for handling the problem, and limitations in the collection and processing of data, juvenile court statistics be used cautiously. These data may be taken to indicate, however, "how frequently one important community resource, the juvenile court, is utilized for dealing with such cases."[45] The degree of use will depend on the confidence which the lay and professional publics have in the institutions for dealing with a particular problem.

The use of these data as indicators of social breakdown is hampered by the fact of the intimate relationship between the various indicators. Alcoholism and family breakdown, illegitimacy and prostitution, or drug addiction and mental disease frequently occur together in one person. These intercorrelations undoubtedly serve to exaggerate the picture of societal breakdown.

However, even though we could accept these data as reliable, we would then be faced by the question of their meaning with respect to societal breakdown. What is the significance of desertion, or of drug addiction, or of homosexuality, for societal functioning? How can these be integrated into a perspective for viewing the state of our society? It is proposed that we look at the problem of social deviation or social problems as a reaction of members of the society to strains in the social system to which they belong.

DEVIATION AS REACTION TO STRAIN

The effectiveness of any organization, whether it be a society, a club, a factory, or a library, depends on the extent to which the members carry out activities or functions necessary to keep the enterprise going in a direction determined by the nature of the enterprise itself. A factory will have

---

[45] U.S., Department of Health, Education, and Welfare, Children's Bureau, *Juvenile Court Statistics,* Statistical Series No. 79 (Washington, D.C.: U.S. Government Printing Office, 1963), p. iii.

different functional requirements from a family, or a boys' gang, or an academic class. These functions are carried out in the form of tasks which are allocated to different functionaries of the organization. A series of related tasks would constitute a role which is generally given a label, such as mother, lathe-operator, library-cataloguer, car salesman, or lecturer. A combination of roles may be designated a status, such as head of household, skilled machinist, college professor, businessman, or librarian.

Societal disorganization may be seen as a situation in which the functional requirements for maintenance of the society are not being met. The disturbance in the pattern of social relations follows when members of the group are unable or are not allowed to participate fully in the social system, to carry out the roles conventionally expected of them as members of the organization. They may be assigned tasks and roles not consistent with their age, sex, education, or status as a citizen in a democracy. They may be prevented from assuming or exercising role functions conventionally expected of them in the social, political, or economic system in which they find themselves. They may be unable to accept the conventional roles for reasons of personal pathology. At the extreme, they may find themselves in a social situation in which they have *no* roles, where they have no part to play in the maintenance of the system. They are in a situation in which they are not needed, yet one from which they cannot extricate themselves.

Such persons without roles, or with limited roles, become problems *for* the society and, when they exist in large numbers, may become organized into what may be called a culture: of poverty, of deprivation, of homosexuality, of delinquency, of alcoholism, and the like. Such groups, relegated to a position of subordinate or limited role participation, themselves become sources of strain in the society. They have little reason for maintaining the allegiance to societal norms which is normally fostered and reinforced by interaction with other individuals and groups in the course of playing a series of related roles. Thus, not being involved in an interdependent pattern of role expectations they find it possible to engage in behavior in violation of the conventional normative system of the society. In the past two generations, the poor and the Negro have been subjected to a shrinking or narrowing of roles in American society, to the point that they are now more or less roleless persons. The roles conventionally ascribed to the poor and to the poor Negro have been either dropped or assigned to automated devices. More recently, the limited roles assigned the Negro and the poor, as a result of expanded perspectives provided by World War II, by education, and by the expansion of mass communications, have been perceived as inconsistent with the status of American citizen. The result has been a greater feeling of relative deprivation and an increased demand for rights and opportunities available to their fellow citizens yet always beyond their own grasp. Frustrations which were formerly resignedly accepted now arouse aggressive action.

The conditions of social disorganization discussed previously in this paper indicate the inability of certain persons to carry out roles defined as necessary or desirable in our society. The deserter has mishandled and discarded the roles of father and spouse which have been ascribed to the mature male by hallowed tradition in Western society. The homosexual eschews the male role with its associated tasks involving heterosexual aggressiveness, predatory behavior, a paternal role, and the like, expected of him in Western society by reason of birth as a biological male. The alcoholic evades the practice of various roles expected of him on the basis of age, education, marital status, and citizenship. Although the role played by the prostitute may be seen as having a function in modern industrial society, it is not the role conventionally ascribed to, or expected of, the female in the Judaeo-Christian tradition.

Such deviations from conventional role expectations have utility as indicators of areas of strain in our society. Widespread relinquishing of role responsibility in a given sector of society—an age group, a minority group, a socioeconomic group—may indicate the nature and locus of societal strain. High rates of crime, family desertion, drunkenness, sexual promiscuity, unemployment, and the like may serve as warnings to the society that its various institutions are not meeting the needs of its members, or of a significantly large number of its members. People are unable to perform the social, economic, political, parental, sexual, and other roles expected of them because of various social and psychological impedimenta in their way. The resultant group or individual behavior deviations may serve to highlight situations of institutional or structural strain in the society.

Some forms of deviant behavior of individuals or groups may serve to reduce strain in the social system by providing outlets for aggressions aroused by societal frustrations. Deviant behavior may be accepted as alternate roles, which then may become incorporated into the system. If these alternate roles, however, are not accepted or if they become intolerable in the light of new knowledge or new norms, the cathartic effect is lost and even greater strain may be aroused. Consideration of the deviant roles in a society as strain-reducing mechanisms and as alternatives to conventional roles would aid in identifying areas of societal strain.

The inability of the individual or of groups of individuals to carry out roles conventionally expected of them is generally considered by the society as undesirable, and as a situation about which something should be done. Such deviations from the norm are considered as harmful or dysfunctional to the social system, impeding predictability of behavior on which co-operative action is so dependent. In spite of such disapproval, however, these conditions persist and, in some cases, even flourish and expand. There appears to be, in our society, a high degree of inability to organize our forces to act positively in the removal or alleviation of the situation deemed so undesirable. This inability to achieve consensus, to mobilize energies to eradicate, or at least to control, situations which have been designated problems for the society is *the* crucial problem *of* the society.

With respect to some problem behaviors, we find ourselves currently in a state of unstable equilibrium.[46] One such problem is prostitution, which the society condemns, yet at the same time tolerates. We glamorize it in our literature and on the stage. It might be said that in the area of sexual behavior our society is in a state of relative disorganization. We cannot achieve consensus—either to sanction premarital sexual relations, adultery, and prostitution, or completely and effectively to condemn them. We condemn and punish the drunk and the drug addict; yet at the same time we consider them as "sick." We define the psychotic as sick, yet confine him involuntarily to prisonlike institutions which in only rare instances bear any resemblance to a medical institution.[47]

These are instances of the confusion, the lack of consensus, in our society about situations defined as social—and undesirable—problems. The social disorganization inheres, not only in these problems or in the situations which bring them about, but in the inability of the society to achieve consensus and to organize effectively into an active agent to do something about these situations. Mental disorder, crime, drug addiction, family breakdown, and the like are problems *for* the society. The problem *of* society is the inability to achieve consensus, to mobilize resources, to organize for effective action in situations which it has defined as those harmful to its existence. In some cases, the society is unable to organize because of lack of consensus. In other cases, although the society desires to do so, it cannot engage in effective action because of lack of knowledge about the problem and techniques for its solution. In either case, mobilization of resources is impossible, and a situation agreed on as undesirable continues to create strains for the society.

There may be agreement in a society about the need for doing something about a social problem, but action is blocked by disagreement on the methods to be used. Because of the interrelatedness of societal institutions, it is almost impossible to intervene in one area of social life without affecting one or more others. The proposed solution to a problem might involve techniques which would be seen as producing undesired changes for some

---

[46] Edwin M. Lemert, *Social Pathology, op. cit.,* pp. 60–61.

[47] See the incisive analysis of mental hospital incarceration by Thomas Szasz, in *The Myth of Mental Illness* (New York: Harper, 1961).

groups in another area of social life. Giving the Negro equal job opportunities in the South would put him in a competitive position for jobs with poor whites, who might then be relegated to an inferior socioeconomic position with respect to the Negro. This would be, in the ideology of the Southerner, an intolerable situation—worse than the accusation of the violation of humanitarian principles.

One of the consequences of the lack of consensus with respect to the definition of deviant behavior as a social problem and the lack of ability to organize effectively for action has been the exploitation of the deviant group by others. This has resulted in the limited participation of the deviant group in the social system, resulting in an alienation of the group, and a removal from public view. Thus, communication is minimized, and myths, about both the dominant and minority groups, spring up, increasing the social distance between them. It is easy, then, to discriminate the deviant from others and act selectively toward him. By limiting his socialization, in terms of schooling, job training, and the like, he is further prevented from participating in the social system, and kept in a subordinate position. Thus, an ever-widening gap between his role expectations and those open to him is faced by the deviant person. Unless he somehow disturbs the complacency or the conscience of the influential members of the society, the deviant may be used and tolerated rather than be considered as a problem for the society.

Strain, problems, and some degree of disorganization are the price we must pay for living in a dynamic, progressive society. Change, technological and social, is rapid and frequent, bringing with it shifts in roles, and even the disorganization or elimination of roles. Problems for the society arise which are either denied legitimacy or denied because we do not know what to do with them. A completely organized society would have all aspects of conduct under control, with no allowance for deviation. Such a society would be impervious to change, and would be stricken with the formalism of "mechanism supreme" which "becomes an evil when it suppresses individuality and stupefies or misdirects the energies of human nature."[48] Our task is to allow for and stimulate change, yet to minimize the resultant strains in the social system, and to involve the participation of all or most members of the society in social roles appropriate to their status as citizens.

A major goal of the authors of this volume is to develop a series of indicators which will enable us to identify and locate situations of strain which interfere with the ideal functioning of our society as defined in the social, political, economic, and moral philosophies of our time. We could

---

[48] Charles Horton Cooley, *Social Organization* (New York: Charles Scribner's Sons, 1924), p. 342.

then allocate social and economic resources for the elimination or alleviation of these undesirable conditions or situations. We have, to be sure, made some attempts to rectify some of the conditions designated as problems for the society, but they have too often been piecemeal, poorly organized, and not oriented toward the root of the problem, and have fallen fallow. Our task in devising indicators of the social state of the nation thus appears to have two dimensions: the identification and location of social problems, and the identification and analysis of those processes within the society which stand in the way of efforts to remove these avowedly undesirable conditions. We have attempted, with limited success, the former; the latter remains as yet largely unconsidered. Society has pointed the finger at *them*—the alcoholic, the deserter, the drug addict, the homosexual—but has failed to consider its own role in the perpetuation of these problems, either directly or by inaction. Some indicator of the discrepancy between the societal attitude toward its problems and the extent and sincerity of its efforts to remove or alleviate them would contribute much to the understanding of the degree of consensus about the values upon which American democracy is founded.

It cannot be emphasized too strongly that the social problems which we have been discussing—divorce, desertion, alcoholism, drug addiction—are *indicators* of social breakdown, are overt signs of strains in the society, and are not the strains themselves. In fact, they may be considered as forms of organization, rather than disorganization, of the social system. They represent more or less conventional and structured ways of meeting strains, many of which, as described above, result from restrictions, confusion, and inadequacy in role performance. Any program of amelioration or social betterment *must* be directed at the processes or situations of which divorce, illegitimacy, and the like are indicators. Efforts at "controlling" divorce, drug addiction, or alcoholism, without getting at the strains of which these are indicators, will not only be ineffective but may be positively harmful. Resources which might be more effectively used would be channelled into punitive or other control measures and away from an attack on the societal strains responsible for the disorganized social roles, and the apathy and prejudice of the public which allows problem behavior to continue in a state of unstable equilibrium.

We have been hampered in our attempts to analyze the disorganization of social relations in our society by a lack of reliable data on the locus and extent of various forms of problem behavior, by a lack of clearly stated and commonly accepted definitions of social problems, and by a distraction of attention from the strains of our society to the indicators of these strains. In our attack on situations defined in our moral and ethical codes as undesirable, we have been impeded by disagreement on the nature of the problem and on what might or should be done about it. These are situations which must be rectified before we can expect any sort of valid evaluation of the social state of the country.

To accomplish this task would require a large-scale organized attack on the problems indicated above. Such an endeavor would require financial support, expertise in a variety of disciplines, and access to information beyond the scope of any private group or organization. It is suggested, therefore, that there be established a department or bureau of social statistics in the federal government. Such a department or bureau must not be identified with an agency operating in one of the problem areas. It should not be one which has a vested interest in maximizing or minimizing the problems to be analyzed. It should be a data-collecting and analyzing bureau whose budget is not tied to its effectiveness in ameliorating a specific problem situation. Also, because of the personal nature of much of the information to be gathered, it should be able to guarantee the privacy of the respondents.

Such an agency could be patterned after the Census Bureau, which has the required skills and equipment for the collection of information on a national level and a tradition of privacy in the handling of data. The operating staff, composed largely of social scientists, some with a strong demographic leaning, would be charged with the responsibility of devising definitions and classification schemes, the organization of data-collecting methods, and the collection, interpretation, and dissemination of information on the social state of the nation. An especially crucial assignment would be to develop indicators of the extent to which the society is able, or willing, to organize its resources around the task of reducing social strains to which it is subject—or, conversely, indicators of its tolerance of situations defined by its members as intolerable or undesirable. Only with such data will we be able to direct our energies intelligently toward the solution of social strains, to build a society in which the possibility of role participation in the social, economic, and political systems would be available to all members of the society.

16

NATIONAL GOALS AND INDICATORS FOR THE REDUCTION OF CRIME AND DELINQUENCY

DANIEL GLASER

The goal of reducing crime and delinquency is inherently elusive, for when this goal is approached it usually is so redefined as to make it more distant. As the great French sociologist Emile Durkheim pointed out in the nineteenth century, societies will always have crime, for they must always recognize some border between acceptable and intolerable behavior; even in "a society of saints, a perfect cloister of exemplary individuals," acts that we today call crimes might be unknown, but acts that we would regard as minor faults would be considered gross violations of their behavior standards.[1] Apart from shifting definitions, there is much fluctuation in the thoroughness and precision of counting that which is called crime. Thus, we usually are uncertain as to whether changes in crime rates represent changes in a population's behavior, changes in the definition of

[1] Emile Durkheim, *The Rules of Sociological Method* (New York: Free Press, 1950), pp. 65–73. For impressive data on the historic universality of crime, but its probable decline in recent decades, see Elwin H. Powell, "Crime as a Function of Anomie," *Journal of Criminal Law, Criminology and Police Science*, Vol. 57 (1966), pp. 161–171. On delinquency rates, one of the best statements is Albert K. Cohen and James F. Short, Jr., "Juvenile Delinquency," in R. E. Merton and R. A. Nisbet (eds.), *Contemporary Social Problems* (2nd ed; New York: Harcourt, Brace and World, 1966), pp. 846–897. An elegant synopsis of Durkheim's argument will be found in Leon Radzinowicz, *Ideology and Crime* (New York: Columbia University Press, 1966), pp. 71–74.

crime, or changes in the extent to which criminal behavior is reported and recorded. Nevertheless, some general formulation of crime and delinquency reduction goals is possible, and considerable precision can be achieved in estimating progress towards these goals. A first step to this is an analysis of the major variations in offenses.

TYPES OF CRIME AND DELINQUENCY

All crime consists of violation of criminal law. This law includes: (1) statutes—what laymen call "the laws"—in which legislative bodies authorize other government agencies to impose penalties on persons who commit specified acts; (2) court decisions, as well as commentaries by legal scholars, on the meaning of these statutes; and (3) generally unwritten and changing customs of law-enforcement personnel and of judicial officials, in their compliance with the criminal statutes, decisions and commentaries.[2] This law is further modified by individual or situational deviations of practice. The latter create strains ultimately leading either to action to suppress deviant practices, or to alteration of one of the above-enumerated components of law to legalize what was formerly deviant.

Delinquency consists of crimes committed by persons who are not considered subject to criminal laws because of their young age. It also consists of a variety of behavior commonly regarded as conducive to criminality, such as persistently disobeying parents or teachers (incorrigibility) or running away from home. The age differentiating delinquency from crime varies from one state to the next, but it is most often the eighteenth birthday. After this birthday, one may disobey parents or run away from home with impunity from the law. However, almost all states specify some age range (for example, fourteen to eighteen) in which the courts can exercise discretion in determining whether an act is delinquency or crime; if offenses by a person in this age range are serious or persistent, they may be dealt with as crimes, which means that he may be sent to a prison for adult criminals instead of to a training school for juvenile delinquents.

That which the law calls "crime" has been changing throughout recorded history, always differs somewhat from one legal jurisdiction to the next, and everywhere is extremely diverse. Nevertheless, it almost always includes four broad categories, as follows:

---

[2] Cf., Victor Sudnow, "Normal Crimes," *Social Problems,* Vol. 12 (1965), pp. 255–276.

(1)   PREDATORY CRIMES are what we most often think of as "crime": acts which have a definite and intended victim. The victim either has property taken away—by stealth, force, threat, or deceit—or is physically or sexually assaulted. This is the most readily counted type of crime, because the victim usually reports it. Property crimes are the most frequent, but assaultive crimes usually are regarded as the crimes of greatest public concern.

(2)   ILLEGAL SERVICE CRIMES do not have a very definite victim; instead, they involve a relationship between a criminal and his customer. The services declared illegal at various times and places have included provision of alcoholic beverages, narcotics, gambling, prostitution, government favors, usurious loans, and many other things for which a demand arises which legitimate businesses are not permitted to fill. Illegal service crimes generally are believed to be much more extensive than predatory crimes in the amount of money and the number of persons they involve. However, because both parties to such crimes—the criminal and the customer—share an interest in not reporting the offense, they are relatively seldom prosecuted and are not counted readily.

(3)   PUBLIC DISORDER CRIMES also lack a specific victim in most cases; they consist of acts dealt with as crimes only when performed before an audience that is offended or is believed likely to be offended. If done with no audience or a tolerant audience, these acts are not regarded as crimes. The statutes label these offenses "disorderly conduct," "drunkenness," "indecent exposure," "vagrancy," and other terms, all of which are imprecisely defined and may often overlap. More arrests are made for public disorder crimes than for predatory or illegal service offenses, although the public disorder offenses generally are considered much less damaging to society than these other categories of crime.

(4)   CRIMES OF NEGLIGENCE usually involve an unintended victim. Automobile-driving infractions are the most common crimes in this category. Sometimes the unintended victim is one which the law infers is potential, rather than actual, as in the crimes of speeding or "reckless driving," when these offenders are prosecuted even when no accident occurs.

While these four categories do not quite exhaust all crimes distinguished by law, they encompass those involved in over 99 per cent of police activity in most countries where treason or disloyal thought is not the basis for an appreciable amount of police action.

An additional category, "status crime," also describes some offenses in some countries at particular times in history, such as periods when it was a crime to be of a particular religion or national descent. Our courts have ruled that there can be no status crimes in the United States, although, unofficially, status affects the administration of the law everywhere.[3] As we have seen, the status of childhood may make a person a delinquent when he commits certain acts, although he would not be a delinquent if he did the same acts after his eighteenth birthday. It is alleged that, in some circumstances, the status of being a narcotics addict, a chronic alcoholic, a minority-group member, or merly a very poor person suffices to make the agents of the law define one as criminal. However, if this status has this effect, it usually is only after a criminal offense has been alleged. The status differential in the application of criminal statutes is part of the informal and unofficial component of the law which makes completely precise definitions and accurate counts difficult.

Each of the four types of crime enumerated above poses different problems in the specification of goals and indicators, and will be dealt with separately. All are complicated by the tendency for the crimes to be differentially defined in practice according to the statuses of both the offender and his victim, customer, or audience.

PREDATORY OFFENSES

It has become popular among social scientists in recent years to suggest, as Becker expresses it, that "deviance is *not* a quality of the act a person commits, but rather a consequence of the application by others of rules and sanctions to an 'offender.' "[4] However, exponents of this

---

[3] The most explicit United States Supreme Court decision on this, declaring drug addiction a disease and not an offense, was *Robinson* v. *California*, No. 55 (October term, 1961), published June 25, 1962. This is already having far-reaching effects in lower court decisions on narcotics and drunkenness arrests, and in supporting other decisions on the illegality of ex-criminal registration laws.

[4] Cf. Howard S. Becker, *Outsiders* (New York: Free Press, 1963), p. 9. For similar statements see John Kitsuse, "Societal Reaction to Deviance: Problems of Theory and Method," *Social Problems*, Vol. 9 (1962), pp. 247–256, Kai T. Erikson, "Notes on the Sociology of Deviance," *Social Problems*, Vol. 9 (1962), pp. 307–314. For a summary of questions such a conception raises, in addition to those addressed by proponents of this conception, see: Jack P. Gibbs, "Conceptions of Deviant Behavior: The Old and the New." *Pacific Sociological Review*, Vol. 9 (1966), pp. 9–14. Recent more sophisticated discussions on crime as a perpetual consequence of conflict in society, and of the societal benefits from such conflict, also do not differentiate types of crime. They fail to consider the possibility that those types of predation that are quite universally regarded as crime (for example, intrasociety murder, robbery, and fraud) are usually dysfunctional to the society, although one might be able to specify the types of exceptional conditions when they are functional. See: Richard Quinney, "A Conception of Man and Society for Criminology," *Sociological Quarterly*, Vol. 6 (1965), pp. 119–127; Austin T. Turk, "Conflict and Criminology," *American Sociological Review*, Vol. 31 (1966), pp. 338–352.

approach, who propose that we primarily study the process by which acts are labeled criminal if we are to understand criminal behavior, find illustrations chiefly among illegal service or public disorder offenses. Variation in the public definition of most predatory crimes is not appreciable, especially outside of so-called "white-collar crimes." The categories of predatory crimes most commonly distinguished in the law—for example, murder, robbery, burglary, theft, fraud, and rape—have almost everywhere and always been employed to denote essentially the same types of behavior as criminal. In almost all societies, they comprise the majority of acts for which severe negative sanctions are imposed.

For almost every category of predatory crime, unlike some of the illegal service and public disorder crimes, there has never been appreciable disagreement with the view that a national goal should be reduction of the behavior called criminal, rather than a change in the definition of the offense. There is evidence, both from historical reports on the cases dealt with by early criminal courts, and from the statistical scaling of societies by culture traits, that government agencies concerned with reducing predatory crime arise because of the anarchy which otherwise results from feuding between criminals and their victims. The objective statistical comparison of forty-eight socities by Freeman and Winch indicates that unless a society develops agencies to settle private grievances provoked by predatory offenses, it generally does not—and probably cannot—maintain full-time teachers, preachers, bureaucracies or other essentials of technological development and cultural complexity.[5]

The major problem in measuring progress towards the goal of reducing predatory crimes is that the range of predation defined as crime seems to increase as society becomes more complicated. However, this increase is not in the broad rubrics into which predatory crimes have always been divided, but in the subdivisions of some traditional clusterings. The primary division in predatory crimes is that between crimes against persons and crimes against property. New kinds of offense are mainly in the latter division. Each poses different problems in identifying trends and assessing indicators.

OFFENSES AGAINST PERSONS

Homicide, of course, is considered the most serious crime against persons. For this reason it probably has been the most completely reported

---

[5] Linton C. Freeman and Robert F. Winch, "Societal Complexity: An Empirical Test of a Typology of Societies," *American Journal of Sociology*, Vol. 62 (1957), pp. 461–466.

and recorded. Indeed, we have two independently collected federal tabulations of its frequency: that compiled from physicians' death certificates by the Office of Vital Statistics, and that compiled by the Federal Bureau of Investigation (FBI) from reports on crimes known to the police. A comparison of the trends, according to these two sources, may be a useful starting point for a discussion of the state of American crime statistics.

No statistics collected on a national basis from voluntary reporting by autonomous local agencies is likely to be absolutely complete. However, reports on the causes of death have been filed with state agencies by physicians since colonial days because of their implications for legal inheritance. National statistics have been compiled from them in the United States since the end of the nineteenth century, following models begun much earlier in European countries. Crime statistics have been collected on a national basis in the United States only since 1930, when the FBI began to tabulate them under a Uniform Crime Reports program sponsored by the International Association of Chiefs of Police. However, for many years only a minority of the more than 50,000 United States police forces submitted these reports to the FBI, and only in the 1960's has the reporting increased to cover over 90 per cent of the United States population. The convergence of police and death certificate homicide rates since the reorganization of FBI tabulation systems in 1958 is one of several types of evidence of the FBI's current attainment of a highly comprehensive coverage of crimes known to the police.

Table 1 indicates that over the past thirty years the rate of homicide has diminished almost by half, despite our disturbance in 1966 by highly publicized offenses, such as the cold-blooded murder of nurses in Chicago, a boy's deliberate killing of everyone he found in a beauty parlor in Arizona, and the random assassinations by a deranged sniper in the University of Texas tower. The slight upward trends within this over-all decline shown in Table 1 are in large part accounted for by shifts in the age composition of the population (21-24 is the model age range for homicide, the range which post-World War II babies now are entering). It has been suggested that part of the decline in the murder rate may be due to the improvement in emergency medical treatment, so that what once might have been murder ends up today as assault, since the victim recovers. This is not demonstrated by the fact that during this period in which the homicide rate halved, the felonious assault rate doubled, for the assault rate has always been so many times greater than the homicide rate that it would not not be greatly affected by changes of some homicides to assaults. However, the shift in relative rates of assault and homicide provides an interesting basis for inference regarding the meaning of changes in crime rates for all offenses other than homicide.

Assault may include anything from a spat between spouses, street corner fisticuffs, or a barroom brawl, to an attack with a knife or gun. Whether it is reported to the police at all, whether they make an arrest or not, and whether it is officially called a felony (a crime for which over a year of imprisonment may be imposed) or a misdemeanor (a crime with maximum penalty not over one year of confinement) depends on numerous variables. These include the community's tolerance for violence, the provocation which started the conflict, the statuses of the participants, the audience for the conflict, the injury which results, the formality of police-community relationships, the size of the police force in relation to the size and density of the population, the skills and interests of lawyers for the defense and prosecution, and many other factors. Clearly, trends in aggravated assaults tabulated by the police could reflect shifts in frequencies for these variables affecting the reporting and definition of assaults, quite independently of any trends in the frequency of physical conflict among people. Indeed, there are several reasons for believing that the doubling in the last thirty years in the assault rate reported by the police may be due only to an increase in the proportion of assaults that are tabulated by the police: assaultive behavior may actually have been diminishing in frequency during this period when official assault rates were increasing.

There is considerable evidence that the tendency to settle differences by violence varies inversely with various indices of social status, particularly with education.[6] The school is distinctly concerned with instilling norms and skills for verbal rather than physical resolution of controversy. It is especially successful in this when schooling extends through high school and beyond—an educational level achieved by a majority of the population only in the current decade. Related to this increase in education is the expansion of white-collar and of other nonmanual occupations, where violence is eschewed. These trends in recent decades should have been conducive to a reduction in the frequency of assault. However, such trends occur in combination with a rapid shift of the least educated and least skilled population from rural to urban residence, where there is less tolerance of assult than that which prevails in the rural areas, and more recourse to the police when assault occurs. This rural-urban migration and the greater police involvement in coping with assault when it occurs in cities may account entirely for the increase in assault rates indicated in Table 1: that is, the increase may represent primarily an increase in police tabulation of assaultive offenses previously less regularly reported and recorded.

Table 2 indicates that crimes of violence are much more frequent in relation to population in the South Atlantic states than elsewhere, and

---

[6] See world-wide data on "working-class authoritarianism" in Seymour Lipset, *Political Man*, (Garden City, N.Y.: Doubleday, 1960), chap. 4.

TABLE 1—Major Crimes in the United States, 1933–1965:
Rates per 100,000 Population

Year	Deaths Ascribed to Homicide[a]	Crimes Reported by the Police[b]						Auto Theft
		Murder and Non-negligent Man-slaughter	Rape[c]	Aggravated Assault	Burglary	Larceny[d]	
1933	9.6	7.1	5.9	50.7	378.9	756.9	320.2
1934	9.5	6.7	6.4	49.4	334.8	771.0	287.3
1935	8.3	6.0	7.2	45.8	310.1	650.0	211.6
1936	8.0	6.2	7.9	46.1	274.5	631.5	188.3
1937	7.6	6.1	8.5	45.3	287.6	688.8	190.4
1938	6.8	5.3	8.3	44.4	289.2	725.1	166.5
1939	6.4	5.4	8.8	46.4	299.6	770.5	158.0
1940	6.2	5.4	8.9	45.8	298.3	793.2	174.7
1941	6.0	5.5	9.2	48.4	284.7	809.6	188.5
1942	5.8	5.5	10.1	52.1	252.5	776.0	167.7
1943	5.0	4.8	10.7	49.7	257.8	710.7	187.7
1944	4.9	4.7	10.3	44.9	219.3	549.3	156.8
1945	5.6	5.1	10.9	48.4	240.4	557.6	179.2
1946	6.3	6.5	11.9	56.5	273.8	621.8	176.7
1947	6.0	6.1	13.0	59.8	269.8	609.6	138.6
1948	5.9	6.0	12.3	62.6	275.3	633.7	128.3
1949	5.4	5.6	12.5	64.6	320.6	702.1	120.5
1950	5.3	5.1	11.3	60.4	290.4	656.5	118.3
1951	4.9	4.8	10.9	56.0	278.8	680.9	130.6
1952	5.2	5.0	11.1	62.7	303.5	718.0	143.4
1953	4.8	4.7	12.0	67.9	343.2	757.4	151.6
1954	4.8	4.6	12.1	69.3	376.4	813.3	145.6
1955	4.5	4.8	13.3	69.0	361.7	819.2	151.0
1956	4.6	4.8	14.1	70.3	383.2	949.9	174.1
1957	4.5	4.8	14.7	73.8	434.0	1038.4	197.8
1958	4.5	4.7	8.4	65.3	393.4	226.1	162.4
1959	4.6	4.8	8.3	67.3	358.9	227.0	162.3
1960	4.7	5.1	8.7	72.6	457.9	264.8	179.2
1961	4.7	4.7	8.8	72.7	466.0	272.3	178.3
1962	4.9	4.5	8.8	75.1	480.4	290.5	192.9
1963	4.9	4.5	8.7	78.4	517.6	324.3	211.6
1964	5.1	4.8	10.7	96.6	580.4	368.2	242.0
1965		5.1	11.6	106.6	605.3	393.3	251.0

[a] Based on physicians' death certificates, as compiled in the United States Office of Vital Statistics yearly publications. Rates are based on the total United States population.

[c] Rates priod to 1944 are based on urban reports only. The population based is always that indicated in *Uniform Crime Reports* for the reporting areas.

[c] Rape reports from 1958 on are for forcible rape only, excluding statutory rape.

[d] Larceny reports from 1958 on are limited to thefts of money or goods valued at $50 or more.

about five times as frequent there as in the New England states. This pattern exists despite the facts that there is less urbanization and that there are fewer fulltime police officers in relation to population in Southern states than in New England, hence presumably less complete police coverage of assaults. Apparently, the Southern states are characterized more than other states by a cultural tradition in which violence is expected in reaction to rebuff or disagreement.[7]

TABLE 2—Major Crimes in the United States:
by Region, Rates per 100,000 Population[a]

Region	Deaths As- scribed to Homi- cide	Murder and Non- negligent Man- slaughter	Forci- ble Rape	Aggra- vated Assault	Burglary	All Major Offenses
Total U.S.	5.1	5.1	11.6	106.6	605.3	1,434.3
New England	1.7	2.1	5.0	43.6	520.2	1,255.2
Middle Atlantic	4.0	4.0	9.6	97.4	514.6	1,367.4
East North Central	3.2	4.0	12.9	93.7	529.3	1,339.3
West North Central	3.0	3.1	9.3	61.0	509.5	1,102.2
South Atlantic	9.1	8.4	11.5	165.8	588.1	1,389.2
East South Central	9.1	8.4	9.1	108.0	445.0	1,000.0
West South Central	8.0	7.0	10.9	123.9	571.4	1,257.2
Mountain	4.5	3.9	13.2	84.0	642.5	1,529.6
Pacific	4.1	4.3	18.5	122.9	1,078.5	2,365.6

a Homicide rates are from U.S., Public Health Service, National Office of Vital Statistics,*Vital Statistics of the U.S.: Annual Report of 1964*, Vol. II. *Mortality* (Washington, D.C.: U.S. Government Printing Office, 1966), Part A, Table 1–44, p. 1–39; other offense data are from *Uniform Crime Reports, 1965* (Washington, D.C.: Federal Bureau of Investigation, 1966), Table 2.

This Southern subculture of violence seems to have an important bearing on the fact that, in the United States as a whole, more Negroes are arrested for homicide and for assault than are whites, although whites are nine times as numerous as Negroes. While the high rates for Negroes reflect

---

[7] M. E. Wolfgang and F. Ferracuti, *The Subculture of Violence* (London: Tavistock, 1967).

their lower economic status, and perhaps a greater readiness of the police to arrest them, that the racial difference is also a function of the geographic subcultures was demonstrated brilliantly by the sociologists Pettigrew and Spier.[8] They were able to predict Negro homicide rates all over the country impressively well by the homicide rate of whites in the state of origin of Negroes. Apparently, it is the Southern tradition of readier use of violence, shared by both races there, which the Negroes have carried elsewhere in their recent rapid migrations. The problem of Negro homicide and assault rates, then, is primarily one of the racial apartheid of our cities, especially in the North, which slows down the rate of cultural change by segregating Negro bearers of this more Southern tradition.

A second type of segregation associated with violence is the segregation of age groups from one another. As Eisenstadt has shown in a comparison of societies in different stages of technological development and urbanization, an increase in the proportion of a person's daily life spent with persons of his own age level is one consequence of technological change.[9] The increased extent to which recreation is pursued away from the home, the decrease in contacts among neighbors, the decrease of three-generation households, the increased employment of married women—all these things place children and youth more than ever "on their own." These conditions foster the growth and pervasiveness of distinctive youth cultures, with values and customs differing from those of the adult world. To some extent the youth social world provides anticipatory socialization for adult roles. However, groups are especially prone to promote deviant values when dominated by youth who are reacting to failure in school and in work. The segregation of out-of-school and out-of-work youth in a world of their own may be the most critical type of segregation problem we face in trying to diminish crime.

Rape is a predatory crime in which the suffering inflicted upon the victim by the offender includes, in addition to the agony from the offense itself, intense feelings of shame in having been victimized. Therefore, an interest in not reporting the rape often is shared by the rapist and his victim. Accordingly, the actual number of rapes committed may be several times the figure of approximately one per year per 10,000 people indicated by the FBI's tabulations in Table 1. For example, a tactfully administered inquiry, guaranteeing anonymity, revealed that of 291 female students at a midwest university, 10.9 per cent in the previous academic year suffered "forceful attempts at intercourse," and 6.2 per cent suffered "aggressively forceful attempts at sex intercourse in the course of which menacing threats

---

[8] Thomas F. Pettigrew and Rosalind B. Spier, "The Ecological Structure of Negro Homicide," *American Journal of Sociology,* Vol. 67 (1962), pp. 621–629.

[9] S. A. Eisenstadt, *From Generation to Generation,* (New York: Free Press, 1956).

or coercive infliction of physical pain were employed."[10] Yet none of these episodes was reported to authorities. If the offenses reported are always a small fraction of those occurring, then Table 1's figures on an increase in the total number may readily represent an increase in the proportion reported to the police, rather than an actual increase in the frequency of rape. An increase in the proportion reported might be expected as a consequence of many other recent trends: urbanization, the consequent anonymity of people in their communities, the growing tolerance for frank discussion regarding sex, and the adoption by newspapers of a policy of not identifying rape victims.

CRIMES AGAINST PROPERTY

In sharp contrast to the decline in homicide, and more pronounced than trends in other types of crime against persons, has been the apparent increase in crimes against property. This increase reflects basic changes in societal conditions, the changes which Adam Smith and Emile Durkheim called "the division of labor," and which we today refer to as "development" or "modernization," in comparing other societies with our own. Indeed, one index of development is the proportion of property crimes to total crimes in official statistics. It is also a good index of urbanization. The shift from a subsistence to an exchange economy, the accompanying differentiation of occupations, the growth of production and consumption values, the progressively greater variety of consumer goods widely available, the change from a rural to an urban way of life in all sectors of our sprawling metropolitan regions—all of these things increase the disparity between economic means and consumption aspirations for some segments of our society, as well as the opportunities for theft and fraud.

As a result of the growing affluence of our society, one basic difficulty in assessing trends in crimes against property is that of standards for determining which offenses are too minor to merit tabulation. Strictly speaking, taking someone else's money is theft, regardless of whether the amount taken is one cent or one million dollars. As a practical matter, of course, the smaller thefts generally are not counted. "Petty" theft (or "petty larceny") is a misdemeanor, and generally it is defined by statute as a theft of less than $50 in money or goods; when larger sums are taken it is "grand theft" (or "larceny"), a felony. This cutoff point, however, does not change systematically with inflation. It is possible that a major part of the reported

---

[10] C. Kirkpatrick and E. Kanin, "Male Sex Aggression on a University Campus," *American Sociological Review*, Vol. 22 (1957), pp. 52–58.

increase in felonious theft and burglary—two offenses which contribute over two-thirds of the FBI's totals for "Index" crimes—comes from an increase in the value of goods available, and from new pressures for reporting thefts to the police. This is indicated in the following observations by Biderman:

> Economic developments that multiply the number of valuables worth more than $50 that thieves can steal will . . . boost the crime rate, given the same propensities for theft among the population. In recent years, there have been two such economic developments: affluence and inflation. . . . Since the distribution of the value of objects involved in reported thefts is roughly pyramidal— there are about three times as many petty larcencies reported as there are indexed larcenies—one would expect inflation to be reflected exponentially in the rise in the Crime Index. The proportion of index larcenies to all larcenies has stayed just about constant, however, which suggests the possibility that more small thefts are being reported and thefts of valuable objects are becoming relatively less frequent.
>
> An unknown but decided influence on the Crime Index comes from another feature of affluence. . . . More of the population . . . come to need and to be able to afford insurance against theft. . . . While there has been a steady rise in the number of ordinary burglarly and theft premiums written, the bulk of such protection is now incorporated in . . . "multiple-line" coverages. . . . (These) increased twenty-four-fold between 1955 and 1964. When a theft occurs to an insured homeowner, he is . . . likely to conform to the reporting requirements for establishing an insurance claim. The rise of the crime rate attributable to this factor is a useful indicator for measuring the burden of work placed on the police but not for indicating how much lawbreaking is occurring in the United States.
>
> The proliferation of insured property plays a role in the single social development most responsible for increases in the Crime Index—that is, the ubiquitous automobile.
>
> The central fact about the automobile is the sheer rise in the distribution among the population of a consequential, stealable item of property. . . . Another special feature of the automobile, however, is that the legal controls pertaining to it . . . make the car theft . . . less subject to errors of underreporting than any other category of crime against property. . . . The system of almost universal and unique registration of automobiles and the legal responsibility of the owner for use . . . of the automobile registered to him . . . lead victims to report auto theft promptly, whether or not the car is insured. . . . Car thefts account for about one-sixth of all indexed crimes.[11]

---

[11] Albert D. Biderman, "Social Indicators and Goals," in Raymond A. Bauer (ed.), *Social Indicators* (Cambridge, Mass.: Massachusetts Institute of Technology Press, 1966), pp. 118–121.

It is noteworthy that the ratio of automobiles stolen to automobiles registered in the United States has remained at a constant 1 to 155 for several years. In addition to the increase in automobiles, a major factor in the increase of auto theft in the early 1960's was simply that the products of the post-World War II baby boom reached the auto-stealing age in this period, for the median age of arrest for auto theft is sixteen.

FRAUD AND "WHITE-COLLAR" CRIMES

The FBI's Index of Crimes, based on offenses known to the police, does not include figures for various types of fraud, such as forgery, confidence games, and embezzlement. However, their arrest data, which are less complete, support an estimate that well over 100,000 arrests are made annually for these offenses. These crimes differ from most other property offenses, first, in being committed by somewhat older persons; their median age at arrest is over thirty, as against a median of eighteen for arrestees for other types of felony. Secondly, although sometimes committed by "teams," they are more often committed alone than are other felonies. Thirdly, and related to this, is that, unlike the more common property crimes, they usually appear to be committed by persons generally conceiving of themselves as respectable and conventional citizens, who do not need collaboration for social and subcultural support in crime.

Forgery arrests are predominantly of petty offenders, so called "naïve forgers," who generally are alcoholics seeking to continue a drinking spree, rather than systematic forgers for profit. A high check-forging rate is the price we pay for ready check-cashing; it is a relatively rare offense in countries where checks cannot be cashed promptly except at a bank where one is known personally. The main social cost of most forgery is not the money procured illegally, but the cost of the long term of confinement that the state imposes on petty forgers, at the urging of victimized merchants. Large-scale professional check-forging and confidence-game teams are a more serious but much less frequent problem.

Most other types of fraud and embezzlement, like misrepresentation in selling, cheating on expense accounts or income tax reports, deliberately erroneous billing, and juggling of accounts to cover depletions from funds, probably are not usually reported to the police. Some of the reasons for this nonreporting also account for the fact that most shop-lifting and most pilfering of supplies by employees is not reported to the police. In the first place, these crimes—if discovered at all—generally are not discovered promptly, and when the crimes are discovered, the perpetrator often cannot be determined precisely. Secondly, the victim usually is a corporation, a government agency, or the general public, rather than a specific individual who can be the complainant in court. Smigel and others have shown that people have much less negative evaluations of cheating directed against corporations than of cheating directed against persons.[12]

A third reason for nonreporting of "white-collar" crime is a tendency for the victims to be much more indulgent about these types of offense than they would be about more traditional categories of crime against person or property. Businesses regard these losses as part of their overhead, and regardless of the letter of the law, prevailing morality often regards such crimes as transactions in which the victim must fend for himself. Indeed, white-collar crimes seem to be viewed as violations of specialized occupational norms, expressed in organizational rules and regulations, rather than as challenges to the basic societal values which are enforced through the criminal law. This shift from concern with values to concern with norms was a trend which Durkheim observed, and which he predicted would continue with the increasing division of labor in society. It represents what he called a shift from the mechanical solidarity of society, based on uniform feelings about morality in behavior, to organic solidarity, based on interdependence of behavior. This shift is accompanied, as he predicted, by a greater growth in "restitutive" (contract and regulatory) law then in "repressive" (criminal) law.[13]

"White-collar offenders" may include both corporations and their individual officials, each prosecuted separately, as in antitrust and consumer-fraud cases. Legal action may include not only the filing of criminal charges, but also civil suits for redress and for punitive damages. In addition, many white-collar offenses may be punished by the actions of government regulatory agencies, such as the Federal Communications Commission, rather than by the courts, although appeal to the courts is always possible. Indeed, in many offenses, such as failure of government employees to report a conflict of interest in their activities, congressional or legislative investigating committees have a quasi-judicial function. To assess the dimensions of these crimes, one obviously must analyze records of the regulatory and investigative agencies, in addition to studying court reports. However, a major problem in assessment will always be the shifting and nebulous border line between what is considered criminal and what is accepted as legitimate. In view of the large monetary gains from these offenses, of which only a few are prosecuted as crimes, it probably will always be possible to make a case for the refrain: "The law locks up the

---

[12] Erwin Smigel, "Public Attitudes Toward Stealing as Related to the Size of the Victim Organization," *American Sociological Review,* Vol. 21 (1956), pp. 320–327.

[13] E. Durkheim, *The Division of Labor* (New York: Free Press, 1947).

hapless felon who steals the goose from off the common, but lets the happy felon loose who steals the common from the goose."

ASSESSMENT OF THE PREDATORY
CRIME PROBLEM

The major method of assessing the crime problem in the United States has been through the *Uniform Crime Reports* of the FBI. A 1958 reorganization of these reports introduced an Index of Crime, based on crimes known to the police for seven major types of predatory offense: murder and nonnegligent manslaughter, forcible rape, robbery, aggravated assault, burglary, larceny of $50 or over, and auto theft. This was a considerable improvement over previous national crime ratings by total crimes known to the police, because the latter included all minor offenses. However, all seven offenses used in this Index are given equal weight, so that a theft of $50 counts as much as a murder in the total Index. Professors Thorsten Sellin and Marvin Wolfgang have developed a highly sophisticated weighting system for construction of a delinquency or crime index from many types of offense. This weights each type of offense on the basis of its scaling by public opinion regarding its relative seriousness. Their system now is being adopted in several major cities and is being studied in a number of foreign countries.[14]

All of the above types of index have two major limitations from the standpoint of developing public policy on the basis of crime indicators. The first is that they still exclude those crimes not regularly reported to the police, for which other types of possible indicators will be suggested. The second, and most important, deficiency of the indexes (from the standpoint of assessing problems and progress in crime control) is that the indexes are a fusion of data on disparate types of crime, for which distinctly different kinds of information are needed in prevention or control efforts.

The President's Commission on Law Enforcement and the Administration of Justice undertook in 1966 one correction for the underreporting of crime which results when crime data are based on offenses known to the police. A representative sample of the general population of the United States was asked a series of questions on the extent to which they have been victims of crimes in the past year. They also were asked whether they reported the offenses to the police, and, if so, with what consequences. While these data may also be imperfect, their deficiencies are different from those of police reports on crime. If such a poll were repeated at regular

---

[14] Thorsten Sellin and Marvin E. Wolfgang, *The Measurement of Delinquency* (New York: John Wiley & Sons, 1964).

intervals in a standardized fashion, powerful data on the prevalence and reporting of crime could be procured by comparing the poll findings with the police statistics.

A major limitation of this type of opinion poll is the fact that corporations and government agencies may be the victims of the largest amount of property crime in the United States, and they will not be included in a sample of private persons. Much of the crime that these organizations suffer —such as shoplifting, pilfering by employees, falsified expense records, embezzled accounts, graft, and "kickbacks"—is not noted when the offenses occur. They may never be known precisely, although their volume can be estimated by careful analysis of inventories and accounts, and by periodic spotchecks. The volume of crimes against such organizations, apart from those offenses which they report to the police, can only be estimated by well-planned surveys of samples of corporations, government agencies, and other organizations, and only if these surveys are directed by specialists in accounting and in industrial security.

In summary, our knowledge of the prevalence of predatory crime nationally would be greatly enhanced by the publication of a series of separate periodic reports on different categories of crime. Each report would deal with a type or types of crime posing distinctive measurement problems, would present the best estimates from currently available indicators, would assess the accuracy of these estimates, and would analyze the estimated rates in terms of the geographic, temporal, and other correlates of the offenses covered. For example, these reports might include the following:

(1)   A REPORT ON HOMICIDE. This would present separately rates based on physicians' death certificates and those based on reports by the police, would discuss whatever discrepancies might be found between these two rates, and would analyze the data in terms of region, attributes of the victims, arrests, outcome of prosecution, and other aspects of homicide that are of criminological and public policy interest.

(2)   A REPORT ON OFFENSES AGAINST PROPERTY. This could be a single report, or a series of separate reports on the types of property offenses posing unique measurement and control problems. In any case, for each of these offenses, data would be presented on crimes known to the police and on the property crimes of which, in periodic polls, a representative sample of the national population reported themselves to be the victim. These two data sources might suffice for reports on burglary and on robbery, but for reports on theft and on fraud additional data sources could include observational spot-checks and analysis of stock records and financial accounts in a sample of corporations and other organizations.

Much theft by customers or by employees is only recorded in the files of private police organizations. From all of these types of data sources, one should seek information on the value of currency and of property taken and on the type and number of items of property taken, apart from estimates of the number of separate offenses. Again, the reports could analyze and interpret the discrepancies between the findings from these different data sources, as well as the trends and correlates of the data on separate offenses, to provide a basis for conclusions on the problems these crimes pose.

(3)   A REPORT ON ASSAULT. As with the offenses against property, the main sources for this report would be crimes reported to the police and crimes reported by a survey of victims. However, instead of assessing crimes in terms of dollars or items taken, they would be classified by such aspects as the severity of physical injury, the circumstances or apparent provocation, the weapons employed, the personal attributes of offender and victim, the social relationship between them, and so forth. The poll's indication of the correlations between these factors and nonreporting to the police, and the ecology of nonreporting, would be of special interest.

A number of additional reports could readily be proposed for predatory crimes not discussed above, each of which would supply unique types of data. The crime of robbery warrants a unique report because it consists of the taking of someone's property by force or threat of force; therefore, it can be classified from both the aspects suggested for offenses against property and for those proposed for assault. The appreciable unreported volume of rape and attempted rape might be estimated by the responses obtained in confidential interviews with representative samples of women. Data from fire departments and insurance companies would supplement police data on arson. The relevance of these unique indicators for specific crimes highlights the deficiencies in our knowledge on crime trends which result if we employ only indicators from a single source for all types of crime.

The reports suggested in the preceding paragraphs would all be tremendously enhanced in practical value if they included the most precise statements possible on the risk of being a victim of each major type of crime. These figures could show variations in risk according to the potential victim's age, sex, location, hour, season, occupation, type of stealable property, and other variables. Some calculations of this sort already are made by insurance firms and by police forces, but they would be of greatest public benefit if collected in a standardized and comprehensive fashion. The citizen's concern with the crime problem, after all, is not what the number of crimes is, but how dangerous crime is for him. In connection with this, the public opinion polls proposed earlier could inquire about public fear of being a victim of crime, to determine the relationship of such fear to actual risk, so that the public might be advised as to the extent to which their fears are unrealistically great or small. For some offenses, notably hostile or sexual assaults, a relevant factor in the risk is the victim's provocative behavior. If risk and fear data were collected before and after experiments with various police practices, judicial policies, public education campaigns, or other crime prevention measures, the effectiveness of these measures could be assessed much more scientifically than is now possible.[15]

ILLEGAL SERVICES

It is highly probable that transactions in illegal gambling, prostitution, narcotics sales, and untaxed whiskey in the United States involve billions of dollars annually, and provide employment for tens of thousands of people. Two problems arise in the measurement and control of these offenses that are quite different from problems posed by predatory crimes. The primary difficulty is that illegal service endeavors persist because they satisfy customers, and satisfied customers do not complain to the police, thus drastically limiting the possibility of official knowledge on the frequency of these crimes.

The second problem is quite opposite in origin, but similar in effects. These businesses, like those which are legal, attract most trade when their location and their offerings are widely known. In some cases they are also most profitable if their investment in physical plant, equipment, and personnel is appreciable. Therefore, those who sell illegal services are often strongly motivated to render their investment secure by corrupting the police, even paying in advance to assure that they are not closed down excessively. Where such circumstances prevail, police have an interest in hiding whatever knowledge of these illegal service operations they do obtain.

In view of these two measurement problems, precise estimation of the extent of illegal service crimes probably is impossible. Trends in their frequency, however, can be inferred from a variety of crude indicators. One clue to the prevalence of illegal gambling on horse races is the sale of racing-tip newspapers in areas where legal horse betting does not exist, or is out of season. A quick index of the bookmaking business can be obtained

---

[15] For a fuller discussion of issues dealt with in this paragraph see Stanton Wheeler, "Criminal Statistics: A Reformulation of the Problem," *Proceedings of the American Statistical Association 1965 Meeting*, to appear in *Journal of Criminology, Criminal Law and Police Science*.

by counting the number of restaurant customers reading the racing news with their 10 A.M. coffee during weekdays in the winter in northern cities. A measure of the prevalence of prostitution is provided by having investigators check the readiness with which cab-drivers or bellhops will lead them to prostitutes. The price of narcotics is an inverse index of their availability. However, the arrest rate for any of these offenses is not an index of its prevalence, but an index of police activity; indeed, the arrest rate may be independent of the actual crime rate or may even be inversely correlated with the crime rate.

Perhaps the main problem in measuring national control of illegal service crimes is the ambivalence of our goals. We condone public gambling at some locations, such as public horse-race tracks or the state of Nevada, but not elsewhere, although we permit private gambling almost everywhere. We once outlawed sale of alcoholic beverages, then we legalized them, but we still attempt to curb the consumption of some substances, such as marijuana, which are not clearly more harmful than alcohol. We tolerate much promiscuity, but prohibit prostitution, and, indeed, we effectively regulate only the style and location of public solicitation, not the actual exchange of sexual favors for other values, goods, or services. What seems to be involved in all of this is our oscillation between absolutism in endeavoring to suppress private vices, and pragmatism in tolerating vices which are so prevalent that we cannot readily suppress them.[16] We are confronted with some social costs and some social gains in any public policy on these matters, and every policy is a compromise which everyone eventually finds somewhat unsatisfactory.

The dilemmas indicated here reflect a few general principles. One is that any effort to prohibit by law the sale of goods or services that are in wide demand creates a highly attractive opportunity for persons who have no scruples about violating the law. A second principle is that the police and other public officials, as representatives of the general public, will frequently be reluctant to carry out rigorously any laws directed against practices that much of the public condones. A third principle is that competition among illegal businessmen is not likely to be regulated by legitimate agencies, but by acts of violence arranged by these businessmen, so that illegal service businesses are likely to have links with predatory criminals. A fourth principle is that one cannot apprehend most offenders whose crime is the provision of services to private vices.

---

[16] This is, essentially, Max Weber's distinction between *Wert*rationality (absolutism) and *Zweck*rationality (substantive rationality or pragmatism). In general, societal complexity seems to promote the latter and render the former infrequent and impractical. Max Weber, *The Theory of Social and Economic Organization* (New York: Oxford University Press, 1947), pp. 115–116.

The four principles listed above all are cited as arguments for the legalization of services to common vices, no matter how personally harmful these vices may be for those who pursue them to excess. However, two counterarguments contend that education against these vices is strengthened when the vices are declared illegal. The first argument is that such laws have an educational influence because they formally assert the state's disapproval. The second argument is that if laws against services for vices can be enforced sufficiently to make these illegal practices less readily visible than they otherwise would be, the vices become less enticing to the uninitiated population than they would be if freely available. Thus, it is argued that even though drinking was widespread under prohibition, it became even more extensive after repeal because bars and liquor stores became conspicuous in almost every business area, whereas speakeasies had been more hidden and inaccessible.

Systems for control over services to private vices seem to be evolving which strike a balance between complete permissiveness and complete suppression, to minimize the social damage both from these vices, and from efforts to suppress them. In most European countries, and increasingly in the United States, local gambling on distant sporting events, as well as lotteries and games of chance, are legalized, but limits are placed on the size of bets or on advance knowledge of the odds, to discourage professional or excessive gambling. Also, much of the profit and control in these enterprises is restricted to government agencies, to private charities, or, minimally, to persons presumed free of association with predatory criminals. While liquor is freely sold, we also have increasingly severe and certain penalties for liquor sales to intoxicated persons and for drunken driving.

In Western Europe, narcotics are available to addicts legally from physicians, but in only the least harmful forms and dosages and in conjunction with some effort at therapy. In the United States the administration of methadone or other narcotic substitutes by physicians, in conjunction with therapeutic programs, is a new and perhaps ultimately more effective method of minimizing the social costs of this vice. By contrast, our suppression programs made narcotics addiction in the United States uniquely associated with predatory crime pursued to pay the high cost of illegal drugs.[17]

Prostitution appears to have been rendered less attractive to women than formerly, especially in organized houses. Probably the main reason

---

[17] A highly comprehensive and concise summary of the problems involved in measuring the dimensions of the narcotics problem in the United States is provided in Hans W. Mattick's review article "Narcotics and the Law," *University of Chicago Law Review*, Vol. 33 (1966), pp. 603-614.

for this is that women increasingly have access to more rewarding legitimate occupations. Likewise important has been the development of somewhat more similar standards of sexual conduct for both sexes, instead of an extreme double standard.

Concomitant with the foregoing are trends of increased professionalization in the police, and of increased middleclass participation in politics, both of which reduce the prospects for corruption in police activity against illegal services. All of these trends in both the market and the responses to such services merit assessment, in conjunction with any effort to estimate trends in the dimensions of illegal service crimes.

PUBLIC DISORDER AND

NEGLIGENCE OFFENSES

Some behavior, and even some physical conditions of the human body, such as drunkenness or nudity, are legitimate in private and violations of criminal law in public. Some other behavior, such as homosexuality and adultery, are defined by statutes as criminal in any situation, although they actually are rarely prosecuted as crimes. Indeed, there is a movement to define homosexuality as criminal only if force is used to compel others to engage in it, if adults are involved in it with minors, or if it is pursued in public. (These now are the only conditions under which homosexual acts are criminal in Illinois.) Noisiness and profanity also are offenses when judges rule that they are inappropriate in time or place, as in domestic arguments or festivities which disturb the sleep of the neighbors. Even wandering across the countryside as a vagrant or loitering in public places can be criminal.

These offenses differ from those discussed in the preceding sections, for they involve neither a deliberate preying on victims nor a seeking of customers; their common feature is only that they become annoying to a complainant, whose rights to immunity from such annoyance are upheld by law. Either they interfere with the complainant's legitimate activities, or they offend his standards of taste on the appearance of public places.

Coping with these offenses has become a major component of police activity. In 1965 there were over two million arrests for drunkenness or disorderly conduct reported to the FBI, over twice the number of arrests on felony charges. These—as well as vagrancy—are rather omnibus charges, which, in practice, are sometimes used for any or all of the specific behaviors or conditions described in the preceding paragraph. Public disorder offenses increasingly promote a convergence of function in police and social work agencies. Domestic discord or personal distress are the most common basis for police calls in many communities.

As families scatter and close-knit communities or neighborhoods diminish, the functioning of police officers as counselors and friends increases. They share these roles with the clergy, as well as with public welfare and mental health agencies.[18] Indeed, there is an increasingly hazy border line between criminal and mental health problems. Referral to mental health agencies rather than to criminal prosecution is becoming the preferred government measure for control of nonpredatory offenses, such as drunkenness and narcotics usage, as well as for the control of some predatory crimes, especially sex offenses. This trend increases the extent to which police processing is a matter of informal referral to nonjudicial agencies, especially with those crimes considered less serious, so that records of police knowledge and police action in such crimes is especially incomplete.

Negligence offenses, which involve primarily the careless driving of automobiles, at first appear to be a totally different type of problem than the other crimes discussed in this chapter. These offenses are, in part, a function of highway and vehicle engineering and of safety education. Of course, with crimes of negligence—as with many other crimes—reported rates are a direct function, and actual rates probably are an inverse function, of the frequency of police patrol. Furthermore, speeders and other reckless drivers resemble disorderly conduct offenders in being thoughtless about the peace and comfort of others rather than deliberately predatory or exploitative. Also noteworthy here is the claim that intoxication is a factor in about half the auto fatalities in the United States.

It is quite clear that we only confound an assessment of the crime problem in this country if public disorder and negligence offenses are considered jointly with predatory and illegal service crimes, as though they were all parts of a single problem. While the same police and court systems may, to some extent, handle all these diverse matters, the types of behavior the crimes involve differ greatly in motivation and in etiology, as well as in the quality and consistency of the public response they evoke.

EFFECTIVENESS OF CRIMINAL
CORRECTION AGENCIES

Two aspects of crime control are *prevention,* or assuring that no crime develops in persons currently noncriminal, and *correction,* or changing criminals into law-abiding citizens. Both are reflected by the statistics on

---

[18] Elaine and Ian M. Cumming, and Laura Edell, "Policeman as Philosopher, Guide and Friend," *Social Problems,* Vol. 12 (1965), pp. 276–286.

reported crimes, discussed thus far. However, much additional information is obtainable when individuals are identified as delinquent or criminal, since we can then study their personal attributes, as well as the effectiveness of correctional policies. The latter is especially important because, as pointed out by Wilkins, the goal of criminal correction is more manageable than that of crime prevention.[19] This statement implies that we are likely to gain more crime control per dollar by effectively keeping people from committing a second or subsequent known offense than by concentrating on prevention of their first crime, for in correction we concentrate our efforts on a few people of high crime potential, while in prevention we spread our energies over the whole population. At any rate, recidivism prevention is the specific task of correction, while crime prevention is a goal served by almost all social institutions—the family, the school, and the church, for example—in conjunction with their primary goals.

Two major problems now impede assessment of the effectiveness of correction endeavors. The first is the practice of compiling correctional statistics on a cross-sectional basis (offenders dealt with on a given date or in a given period) instead of on a longitudinal basis (the rate at which offenders avoid or revert to crime in a given period following correctional efforts with them). The second problem is that when longitudinal statistics are compiled, they are derived from the files of only one or two of the several independently administered correctional agencies in an area. Because each agency's performance largely determines the cases received by the other agencies, it is difficult to assess the effectiveness of these agencies separately unless one has information on the criminality which follows releases from each of them.

Correction actually begins not with the courts, but with the police, who exercise much more discretion in determining what happens to an offender than most people realize. For example, on the average, only about half the juveniles arrested by the police are referred to the courts, but this proportion varies from almost zero to almost 100 per cent in different jurisdictions.[20] Obviously, variation in police practice greatly determines the input of the courts.

---

[19] Leslie T. Wilkins, "Crime, Corrections and Costs," *United Nations International Review of Criminal Policy*, No. 25 (1967).

[20] Examination of *Uniform Crime Reports* data for individual police agencies indicate that release rates vary from less than 5 to more than 95 per cent. Averages by type of city are presented in "Police Distribution of Juvenile Offenders Taken Into Custody," *Crime in the United States: Uniform Crime Reports 1965* (Washington, D.C.: Federal Bureau of Investigation, 1966, Table 13). Research into the community and organizational sources of this variation is currently being conducted under the direction of David J. Bordua. See David J. Bordua, "Deviant Behavior and Social Control: Recent Trends," THE ANNALS of the American Academy of Political and Social Science, Vol. 369 (January 1967); Robert E. Ford, "Variations in Juvenile Release Ratios among Police Departments" (Mimeographed paper available through Sociology Department, University of Illinois, Urbana).

Judges vary greatly in the percentage of criminal cases in which they suspended sentence, grant probation, or sentence to an institution, even in areas with similar crime rates—indeed, even when there are several judges within a single court. Therefore, the effectiveness of either probation or prison in two different jurisdictions cannot be evaluated by comparison of subsequent crime rates unless one is certain that the offenders receiving these dispositions are similar in the two jurisdictions.

Where probation is used extensively, both the probation officers and the prisons generally deal with more crime-prone offenders than they handle where probation is granted only to the small fraction who are the best risks and the remainder are sent to prison. Therefore, an area low in probation use should have lower failure rates in both probation and prison than the areas of high probation use. Yet if probation is more effective than prison, the high-probation-use areas should have greater over-all correctional effectiveness than the low ones. This can be illustrated by hypothetical figures approximating data actually obtained separately for probation and for prison in scattered effectiveness studies. If Area A with 1,000 felons in a given period granted probation to only 100 and sent 900 to prison, subsequent felony conviction might be incurred by only 10 per cent of its probationers and 30 per cent of its prisoners, for a total of 280 recidivists. If Area B, also with 1,000 felons, granted probation to 700 and sent 300 to prison it might find subsequent felony convictions for 20 per cent of its probationers and 40 per cent of its prisoners, but these would comprise only 260 recidivists, less than the total in Area A. Thus, Area B, with higher failure rates on both probation and parole, would actually have more effective crime control from its correctional program than Area A (and, incidentally, at much less cost, since probation costs only about one-tenth the cost of imprisonment).

In addition, it should be noted that the effectiveness of parole boards depends on the population received by correctional institutions. In turn, parole-board release policies determine both the type of inmate left in institutions and the kind of offenders with whom parole-supervision officers must work, thus affecting evaluation of these correction agencies. This, of course, limits efforts to compare the effectiveness of prisons or of parole supervision in different areas.

It is clear that assessment of correctional effectiveness requires longitudinal data on the cases dealt with by all of the correctional agencies in a given area. Ideally, the samples studied for assessment purposes should be a cross section of all persons arrested during a specified period some years in the past—perhaps ten or fifteen years. Rates of subsequent felony convictions can then be compared for similar types of offender subjected to different police, court, probation, prison, or parole policies. For the goal of crime control, the objective should be analysis of long-run criminal records to indicate the statistically optimum judicial and correctional policy for each reliably distinguishable type of offender.

When we first proposed essentially the foregoing, over a decade ago,[21] we labeled such data "Criminal Career Statistics," and discussed it in the next few years with various federal crime statistics personnel in the FBI, the Administrative Office of United States Courts, and the United States Bureau of Prisons. What could become a major breakthrough in the provision of statistical summaries of past experience with alternative judicial and correctional decisions then began, for the FBI initiated routine accumulation of longitudinal data on the criminal careers of federal offenders. However, this has been utilized only for the new "Careers in Crime," "Profiles," and "Follow-up" sections of the *Uniform Crime Reports,* which are completely irrelevant to estimation of the effects of judicial and correctional decisions. Indeed, we are advised:

> "Careers in Crime" was never intended to measure the success or failure of correctional programs since all persons entered into the system, until a legitimate follow-up period could be established, were, of course, failures.[22]

Because probation and suspended sentences are alternatives to imprisonment, it is important to note that when the FBI followed the criminal record of all federal probationers in two areas for five years beyond their discharge from probation, they found that more than four-fifths received no further convictions for either felonies or misdemeanors.[23] Such a low recidivism rate has never been found for a cross-section of prisoners. To test judicial policies, the FBI would have to compare criminal records in a long follow-up period for representative samples of three categories of

---

[21] Daniel Glaser, "Testing Correctional Decisions," *Journal of Criminology. Criminal Law and Police Science,* Vol. 45 (1955), pp. 679–684; Glaser, "Institution Statistics," *Proceedings, American Correctional Association* (1956), pp. 279–283, republished as "Administrative Use of Institutional Statistics," *Journal of the National Probation and Parole Association,* Vol. 3 (1957), pp. 288–291; Glaser, "Released Offender Statistics: A Proposal for a National Program," *American Journal of Correction,* Vol. 19 (1957), pp. 15–17, 25; Glaser, *The Effectiveness of a Prison and Parole System* (Indianapolis: Bobbs-Merrill, 1964), pp. 31–35.

[22] Letter of February 1, 1967, from Jerome J. Daunt, Inspector, Uniform Crime Reporting Section, Federal Bureau of Investigation, to Bertram M. Gross, commenting on a first draft of this article.

[23] Ralph W. England, "A Study of Post-Probation Recidivism among 500 Federal Offenders," *Federal Probation,* Vol. 19 (1955), pp. 10–16; Morris G. Caldwell, "Preview of a New Type of Probation Study Made in Alabama," *Federal Probation,* Vol. 15 (June 1951), pp. 3–11; Ralph W. England, "What is Responsible for Satisfactory Probation and Post-Probation Outcome," *Journal of Criminal Law, Criminology and Police Science,* Vol. 47 (1957), pp. 667–676.

offender adjudicated in a prior period: those released by suspended sentence, those placed on probation, and those sentenced to prison. Preferably, the cases thus compared should be matched on all other variables on which information is submitted to the FBI: age, offense, prior criminal record, and race. To test parole-board policies, the FBI would have to compare the recidivism rates of dischargees, conditional releasees, and parolees, preferably matched by duration of imprisonment prior to release, and well as by the variables indicated for testing judicial policies.

The ideal testing procedure, with correctional as with medical measures, is controlled experimentation. Random assignment of a given type of offender to alternative correctional programs greatly increases the prospect that differences in the subsequent criminality of offenders in the different programs is due to the effect of these programs rather than to differences in the types of offender selected for each program. However, the prevailing views of some measures as more lenient or more risky than others has prevented much deliberate experimentation. Therefore, for knowledge on the relative effectiveness of correctional alternatives we have to rely mainly on statistically identifying the consequences of the considerable variation in use of these alternatives which occurs routinely in the independent decisions of the many legislating, policing, adjudicating, paroling, and correction-administering agencies in our country.

In conclusion, one should ask why longitudinal statistics are so seldom compiled, and why, when they are compiled by police agencies, it is in a manner irrelevant to evaluating correctional effectiveness. The answer to both questions, I believe, lies in the division of responsibilities for dealing with offenders among so many completely autonomous agencies. All the agencies which successively handle an offender—police, courts, confinement institutions, parole boards, and parole supervisors—if concerned with research at all, tend to be concerned mainly with research to aid the budgeting of their own operations. They evaluate effectiveness in terms of the little evidence available while they process the offender, and have little interest in finding out what happens to cases after they are transferred to the next agency. Indeed, it is where probation, institutions, the parole board, and parole supervision are administered as one integrated unit, with a single head responsible for the effectiveness of all (as in the Wisconsin Division of Correction or the California Youth Authority), that evaluative statistics on correctional effectiveness have been most adequately compiled. If decisions of the police and the courts could also be studied by such integrated agencies, even more significant evaluative statistics would be possible. The isolation of the police, the judiciary, and corrections from each other has been the major source of inefficiency and frustration in the work of each of these agencies in the United States. This isolation can only be diminished when they truly collaborate in measuring the effectiveness of the total government attack on crime in any jurisdiction, instead of each preoccupying itself only with counting and recording its own volume of activity.

CONCLUSION

It should be evident from the foregoing that formulation of crime-reduction goals and assessment of progress towards achieving them is over-whelmingly confounded if one encompasses all types of offense in single generalizations on "crime." Some analytic distinctions have been suggested to permit the separate consideration of those groups of offenses which share highly unique measurement and goal-formulation problems. Finally, it was pointed out that assessment of the effectiveness of police, court, and correctional agency programs requires crime statistics different from those gathered to estimate the prevalence of crime. Above all, it is clear that the crime-reducing effects of any one of these agencies cannot adequately be assessed separately, since the impact of each agency is greatly affected by that of the agencies from which it receives its offenders, or to which it sends them.

To envision the absolute elimination of crime as a national goal seems unrealistic, in view of society's continuously shifting definitions of crime. Nevertheless, to strive for an end to those predatory offenses that are relatively unambiguous and have always been designated criminal is not unrealistic: progress can be made toward such goals—for example, the elimination of murder—even if their achievement is never complete. As Bertram Gross points out, standards of order, honesty, loyalty, and justice are universal.[24] However, each of these values subsumes a wide range of behavior in which distinctions of the substantial, the trivial, and the segment of uncertainty between these extremes vary and shift tremendously. For example, difficulties in measuring trends in "white-collar" crimes stem from the fact that the definition of honesty, particularly in contractual relationships, involves much that is a matter of prevailing custom and unwritten understandings in particular industries or businesses, rather than a matter of discrete moral and legal distinctions of the acceptable from the unacceptable. Nevertheless, for those predatory offenses that the law defines somewhat unambiguously—murder, check-forgery, bank robbery, and many others—we can with some realism formulate goals of crime reduction and measure progress towards their achievement.

---

[24] Bertram M. Gross, "Social Systems Accounting," in Bauer, op. cit., pp. 247–249.

In all crimes, but especially in those consisting of illegal service to private vices, of public disorder, or of negligence, the most practical national goal is to minimize the net social damage from both the measures of crime control and the behavior toward which these measures are directed. When actions to control service to a vice lead to more social damage than the vice itself produces—for example, when they lead to extensive corruption of law enforcement or they promote a large amount of predatory crime in efforts to satisfy the vice—then methods of regulation or control should be sought that are less costly to society, even if this means tolerating more of the vice. This, of course, was the choice we took in repealing the Eighteenth Amendment to the United States Constitution, and analogous choices have been suggested in the regulation of gambling and of drug use. Similarly, we may frequently have to decide when our values make the controls needed to reduce public disorder or negligence more objectionable than the order or safety they might achieve.

Diverse types of research were suggested to improve our estimates of progress in the achievement of crime-control goals. These suggestions included: (1) periodic opinion polling of representative samples of the population on the extent to which they have been victims of predatory crime; (2) systematic observations or investigations, at regular intervals, on various indices, of the consequences of measures taken to control them; (3) long-term follow-ups to determine the rates of return to crime by similar offenders subjected to different types of correctional action. As the Kinsey reports and many "admitted delinquency" studies have shown, valuable estimates of the prevalence of some types of criminal and delinquent behavior and their correlates, can also be obtained with impressive validity by well-administered interviews or questionnaires asking people for anonymous admissions of the extent to which they have engaged in such behavior.[25] All of these measures would help fill various gaps indicated in current sources of national data on crime, but these sources—police reports to the FBI, physician's reports on the causes of death forwarded to the Bureau of Vital Statistics, and juvenile court reports to the United States Children's Bureau—would still be the major data sources.

All of these data are only likely to be collected, co-ordinated, and fully interpreted in terms of national and local crime problems, if a national research agency is created for this purpose. What appears to be needed is a federal office or bureau for criminological research, comparable in its research and dissemination activities to such diverse existing agencies as the Bureau of Labor Statistics, the Children's Bureau, the Department of

---

[25] John P. Clark and Larry L. Tifft, "Polygraph and Interview Validation of Self-Reported Deviant Behavior," *American Sociological Review*, Vol. 31 (1966), pp. 516–523.

Agriculture, and the Council of Economic Advisors. The optimum administrative status and placement of such an agency within the federal government probably is as a separate office or bureau within the Department of Justice. It would have to use the FBI criminal-record data, and ultimately other information on criminal careers from the files of judicial and correctional agencies, in addition to gathering survey information itself or contracting for such research. It should work with all agencies concerned with the policing, adjudication, correction, or prevention of crime and delinquency, yet not be dominated by any one of them. To assure this breadth of perspective it would be most desirable that such an agency operate under an advisory board representing all the major academic professional and public service groups highly concerned with the control of crime, in addition to the representatives of all concerned types of government agency on the national, state, and local level.

17

HEALTH AND WELL-BEING

PHILIP R. LEE

In his message to the Congress on "Advancing the Nation's Health" in 1965, President Johnson states that the health goal of the nation is "good health for every citizen to the limits of this country's capacity to provide it."

Health is both a generalized and a very relative concept which has been defined in a variety of ways. To some, it has meant merely freedom from physical disease or pain. To others, it has meant a sense of well-being as well as an absence of disease. In recent years, the concept has been broadened to include social well-being.

Definitions of health and disease differ markedly from one cultural setting to another and, often, from one period in history to another. Health, whether mental, physical, or social, is socially defined. Unless people label a condition as one of disease or abnormality, it is not a health problem in their society. In the past, some diseases, such as malaria or hookworm, have been so widespread as to be considered a normal condition.

The relationship between income, social class, and the utilization of health services points up clearly the relativity of definitions of health. When income is more than adequate for basic needs, one's list of desirables, or even of necessities, can include many values several steps removed from mere survival. One can insist on treatment for physical discomfort, can take measures to provide for future health and prolongation of life, and can afford to think of annual medical examinations as routine. On the other hand, when income is uncertain and not always enough to provide food and shelter, health is likely to be defined as the ability to keep working. Treatment is postponed until acute symptoms or disability preclude work. Often, the wage earner gets medical care which other members of the family do without because their symptoms are not recognized as illness.

434

Beyond their effects on definition of health and disease, the hardships of poverty seem to nudge health and medical care downward in the hierarchy of values. When a household operates with a minimum of material necessities, first aspirations are often for a better place to live, for more and better household equipment or furnishings—even for some luxuries. Health comes farther down the list.

The importance of the environment in relation to health and disease has long been recognized. The definition of disease by May[1] as "that alteration of living cells or tissues that jeopardizes survival in their environment" is one which clearly states the relationship.

It has become evident, as definitions have broadened and attitudes have changed, that concern for problems of health and disease cannot be divorced from such factors as economic status, housing, nutrition, education, social class and custom, sanitation, geography, transportation, recreation, crime and delinquency, employment, racial background, and a host of others. Gradually, we are learning that countless elements are pertinent in health status: genetic, endocrine, and neurophysiologic as well as psychosocial, cultural, and economic. We are seeking answers to a myriad of intriguing questions—about normal and abnormal growth and development, emotional ability or inability to cope with stress, and the balances which allow an individual to function adequately.

In recent years the accumulation of improved data and their widespread dissemination contributed significantly to the passage by the Eightyninth Congress of major federal programs to pay for or to support the development of health and medical services for the aged and the poor. These developments mark a public recognition of the relationship of poverty and disease so well described by Winslow,[2] and a reflection of a growing trend toward equality of opportunity.

In the multidiscipline approach to health problems, we may discover that some of the answers will best be found in quarters other than the medical profession. It may be that improved housing will have a greater effect on total health than will the development of community health services. Or perhaps a family allowance for children might serve the purpose better than the development of an array of services to meet the needs of children. Only further study and evaluation can provide the enlightened solutions. Thus, we are forced to develop new techniques for evaluation and measurement of the factors in question, to provide us with the comprehensive information needed for the establishment of national health goals and for action toward their attainment.

---

1 Jacques M. May, *Studies in Disease Ecology* (New York: Hafner, 1961), p. xv.

2 C. E. A. Winslow, *The Cost of Sickness and the Price of Health* (Geneva: World Health Organization, 1951), p. 106.

This chapter will be concerned particularly with a discussion of currently available techniques for measurement and the scope of the material which is produced through such techniques. It will discuss some of the ways in which national goals are established, as well as stating the nature of these goals as we seek them now.

MEASURING HEALTH STATUS

In the past, quantitative evaluation of the population's health status was based on measurement of the negative aspects of health—for example, the death rate and the array of vital statistics which have long been collected by states and the federal government. Such measurements were not only valuable in their time; they were reliable and accurate in terms of what they measured, and they still remain a fundamental source of essential information. However, they no longer yield enough information on which to establish goals and to determine policy.[3] Increasing attention is being focused on chronic disease and disability.[4]

In 1956, dissatisfaction with traditional measures of health and disease led to the establishment of the National Health Survey, with its far more comprehensive methods of measurement. There are two principal types of survey: in one, the information is collected by means of interviews (Health Interview Survey) and in the other, by means of direct physical examination (Health Examination Survey).

The interview survey began in 1957 and has been in continuous operation since that time. The data from these surveys measure the social and economic impact of illness, how it affects people's lives, what action they take to prevent or treat illness, and what the results have been. The Health Examination Survey, also based on a national sample, collects diagnostic and physiological data by means of detailed clinical examinations with objective measurements and tests.

Although surveys of people are important, it is also necessary to collect information about and from the providers of service. This includes, for example, information about the services which hospitals and other institutions perform, the nature of the facilities, the nature of the patients treated, the cost of care, and related data.

The National Center for Health Statistics is the best source of data not only on mortality and morbidity but on general medical care statistics

---

[3] Forrest E. Linder, "The Health of the American People," *Scientific American,* Vol. 214, No. 6 (June 1966), pp. 21–29.

[4] Monroe Lerner and Odin W. Anderson, *Health Progress in the United States: 1900–1960* (Chicago: University of Chicago Press, 1963), p. 354.

as well. During the fiscal year 1967, data will be collected on utilization of hospitals, nursing homes, and home-care services.

A number of other departments and agencies collect relevant information. The Social Security Administration has collected data on health and medical care costs by object of expenditure for many years. Data-collection will be expanded as a result of the Medicare program. The divisions of the Social and Rehabilitation Service collect data on needs and services. Data on medical care prices are collected by the Bureau of Labor Statistics. The American Medical Association, the American Hospital Association, the Association of American Medical Colleges, and a number of other private organizations and institutions gather and analyze valuable data on manpower, facilities, services, costs, prices, and other factors.

There is an urgent need to improve the limited capability of state health departments in health and medical care statistics. Statistical offices are facing greatly expanding responsibilities for evaluation and planning of public health and medical care programs.

MORTALITY

Mortality declined rapidly between 1900 and 1950. The influenza epidemic of 1918–1919 caused a sharp, but temporary, rise in an otherwise generally declining rate. The "crude" or actual death rate declined from 17.2 per 1,000 population in 1900 to a low of 9.2 per 1,000 in 1954. The death rate since that time has fluctuated between 9.6 and 9.3. It was 9.4 in 1965 and was estimated to be 9.5 in 1966. When these "crude" mortality rates are age-adjusted the resulting rate of decline is even greater, although the 1965 figure remains slightly above the figure for 1954.

The largest relative declines in mortality have occurred during childhood, although there have been significant declines at all ages in this century. The mortality rate was lower for females at the turn of the century and since then has declined more rapidly than the male rate.

Mortality from communicable diseases has shown a striking decline in the United States since 1900. For example, influenza and pneumonia declined from 202.2 deaths (per 100.000) in 1900 to 37.3 in 1960. The rate for tuberculosis dropped from 194.4 to 6.1 during this same period. Equally impressive falls have occurred in the death rate for a number of other communicable diseases.

A similar pattern has not occurred for the chronic diseases. The age-adjusted death rate for heart disease rose from 167.3 deaths per 100,000 population in 1900 to 286.2 in 1960, an increase of 71 per cent. The death rate from cancer, the nation's second leading cause of death, continues to rise. In 1937, the year the National Cancer Institute was created, there were 144,774 cancer deaths in the United States, a crude death rate of 112.4 per 100,000 population. It is estimated that in 1967, 30 years later, 305,000 deaths will bring the rate up to 153 per 100,000. The most striking increase in cancer incidence and mortality has been that for cancer of the lung. Today, the death rate from lung cancer is about eight times what it was thirty years ago.

Accidents remain a major cause of death, just as they have been for the past sixty years. The importance of traffic accidents as a cause of death has increased, while home and industrial accidents have declined, relatively, in importance.

These data give only a very incomplete picture of the health status of the population. Life is not synonymous with health. We have succeeded in prolonging the lives of many without relieving them of the burden of illness and disability.

In addition, there is some dissatisfaction with present methods for deriving death rates for specific diseases. The dissatisfaction has led a number of investigators to seek refinements in the system of compiling rates on the basis of the underlying and contributing causes of death. With the adoption of the revised International Classification of Diseases in 1968, it is hoped that the United States mortality tabulations will include each year a detailed analysis of the combination of conditions associated with death.

Maternal and infant mortality rates have come to be recognized as two of the most sensitive indicators of health status. Impressive reductions in both have occurred in the United States, and virtually all other countries of the world, during this century.

Maternal mortality began to decline in this country about 1930. Since then, it has dropped from 67.3 (for each 10,000 live births) to 3 in 1965. This decline has continued.

Infant mortality, in contrast, showed little decline after 1955, until 1966. In 1955 it was 26.4 per 1,000 live births. In 1965 it was 24.7. In 1966 the estimated rate was 23.4. Infant mortality varies as much as 50 per cent from one state to another. It is twice as high for the nonwhite as for the white infant.

The over-all mortality rate in the United States has been consistently higher for nonwhites than for whites. Maternal and infant mortality rates are perhaps the most sensitive indicators of the gap in health status between whites and nonwhites. Despite dramatic improvements for both population groups during this century, the differentials in infant mortality appear to be changing very little.

The high infant mortality for nonwhites is associated with the relative absence of medical care, lower educational levels, poor housing, overcrowding, and low family income. These, in turn, show marked variation from one region of the country to another (Table 1).

In addition to higher maternal and infant mortality, the nonwhite population suffers more from tuberculosis, influenza, pneumonia, measles, dysentery, hypertension, and many other diseases than does the white population.

All of these differentials reflect a complex set of interrelated problems of racial discrimination, poverty or wealth, educational levels, housing, stress from social, cultural, physical, psychological, and biological influences, motivation, and the availability and quality of medical care. They cannot be corrected until the relationships of all of these factors are identified, understood, and dealt with.

MORBIDITY AND DISABILITY

There are a number of measures—mortality, morbidity, and activity-limitation—that help to measure the impact of specific diseases.

On the basis of National Health Survey interviews, it is estimated that, during the period July 1, 1963—June 30, 1964, Americans suffered 390 million acute illnesses—series enough to require medical attention or at least cause limitation of the patient's normal activities. Some 200 million of these illnesses were respiratory. There were more than 55 million cases of nonrespiratory illness, about the same number of accidents, and some 20 million illnesses related to the digestive system. Collectively, these acute conditions accounted for well over half of the bed-disability days that year as well as of the time lost from work.

Although acute illness and injury loom large in the statistics, chronic conditions often have a greater impact on the individual, his family, and society. Of the population surveyed in 1962-1963, some 80 million suffered from one or more chronic conditions. Of these 80 million: 58 million were not restricted in their activities; 12 million could engage in major activities only to a limited extent; 6 million, although able to do their basic work, were limited in other activities; and 4 million were so disabled that they could not work, keep house, or go to school.

The total amount of illness can be measured in a number of different ways. One of the most useful is the amount of disability a population suffers during a given period of time. The most comprehensive measure of disability is in terms of the number of days of restricted activity.

During the year July 1962–June 1963, the civilian noninstitutionalized population of the United States experienced an estimated 3 billion days of restricted activity due to illness or injury. The 3 billion days included more than a billion days of confinement in bed, 415 million days lost from work, and more than 200 million days lost from school.

TABLE 1—Range of Values for Selected Indices for Nonwhites in
Census Divisions and United States Median for Whites

Item	Nonwhite		White
	In Poorest Division[a]	In Best Division[a]	U. S.
Infant mortality per 1,000 live births (1962)	46.9 (ESC)	30.7 (P)	22.3
Median school years completed (1960)	6.7 (ESC)	10.3 (P)	10.9
Per cent college graduates, of males 25–29 (1960)	3.6 (ESC)	9.8 (P)	15.6
Per cent housing sound with all plumbing (1960)	23.1 (ESC)	70.9 (P)	79.7
Per cent housing with more than 1 person per room (1960)	46.0 (M)	18.2 (NE)	9.8
Family income (1963)	$2,520 (S)	$5,417 (W)	$6,548
Per cent families with income under $3,000 (1963)	58.4 (S)	19.8 (W)	15.9

[a] "ESC" stands for the East South Central division; "P" for Pacific; "NE" for New England; "M" for Mountain; "S" for South; and "W" for West.

Source: Rashi Fein, "An Economic and Social Profile of the Negro American," *Daedalus* (Fall 1965). Issued as Vol. 94, No. 4, of the *Proceedings of the American Academy of Arts and Sciences,* p. 838.

There are significant variations in disability days related to age and place of residence, as well as family income. To some extent, these factors work, and more than 200 million days lost from school. illness.[5]

MEASURING THE EFFECTS OF SPECIFIC ILLNESSES

The most important cause of death in the United States is cardio-vascular disease. And not only does it kill, but it exacts a heavy toll in illness and disability.

More than 54 per cent of all deaths in the United States are due to cardiovascular disease—almost one million deaths in 1965. More than a fourth—251,229 of these deaths—occurred in people who had not yet reached the age of 65.

Coronary artery disease—mainly heart attacks—continued to be the most important single cause of death in 1965, with a toll of 559,293. Strokes were second with 201,057 deaths.

---

[5] U. S., National Center for Health Statistics, *Medical Care, Health Status, and Family Income,* Series 10, No. 9 (Washington, D.C.: Department of Health, Education, and Welfare, May 1964), p. 70.

The Health Examination Survey of the National Center for Health Statistics has revealed that 14.6 million Americans between the ages of eighteen and seventy-nine suffer from clearly identifiable heart disease of various forms including hypertension, congenital defects, and rheumatic heart disease. The importance of cardiovascular disease as a cause of distress among the American people must not be underemphasized. It is the chronic condition most frequently reported as causing limitation of activity, and for persons who were completely unable to carry on their major activity—working, keeping house, or going to school—heart disease, arthritis and rheumatism, and visual impairments were the leading causes of such limitations.[6]

AN INDEX OF HEALTH

The desirability of a general index of health has long been evident. When the emphasis was primarily on the prolongation of life, mortality was an adequate measure of the health status of the population. There are now a number of other measures of health status, particularly morbidity and disability. In his recent, thorough review of this problem, Sullivan conceded:

> If the level of health of the United States population is to be measured by an index more sensitive and more comprehensive than mortality indexes, a measurable concept of morbidity seems essential. The approach outlined here defines "morbidity" in terms of the total impact of illness upon the population and leads to measures of the volume of disability during a year. Then measures can, if desired, be combined with measures of mortality to obtain a single index reflecting both mortality and morbidity.[7]

The measures currently available, mortality, morbidity, and disability, do not provide an index of positive health and well-being. A number of individuals and groups have struggled with this problem without reaching any satisfactory conclusions. It is hoped that these efforts will continue, that definitions will be precise, and that evaluations will be critical.

---

[6] U.S., Department of Health, Education, and Welfare, *Trends* (Washington, D.C.: Department of Health, Education, and Welfare, 1965), Part I, p. S–15.

[7] D. F. Sullivan, *Conceptual Problems in Developing an Index of Health,* U.S., National Center for Health Statistics, Series 2, No. 17 (Washington, D.C.: Department of Health, Education, and Welfare, 1966), p. 18.

MEASURING THE COSTS OF ILLNESS

In recent years a number of studies have been made relating to the costs of illness and the benefits of various types of disease-control programs.[8]

An excellent framework for calculating the economic costs of illness, disability, and death has recently been provided.[9] In this detailed analysis, methods are presented for calculating the annual direct costs of illness, including health expenditures, by diagnosis and object of expenditure; the annual indirect cost of illness, including earnings and other productivity losses due to illness, disability and death; and the total economic cost of mortality, with an examination of the estimated cost or value of an individual's future earnings.

The increasing importance of the chronic diseases is evident, not only in the mortality statistics (Figure 1) and the measures of disability (Figure 2), but also in terms of the economic cost of illness.

The total amount of annual economic cost—the sum of the direct expenditures for medical care and indirect costs of illness, disability, and death—was estimated to be $58 billion in 1963.

Diseases of the circulatory system, collectively, are the most expensive American national illness in terms of loss of productivity. However, when the morbidity and mortality factors are combined and indirect costs calculated, mental illness emerges as the most important single problem.

The figures, however, cannot tell the whole study. Alcoholism is a disease which contributes to morbidity and mortality from a number of diseases; it is a direct cause of much illness, absenteeism, and lowered productivity. Yet the diagnosis is often overlooked or not made because of the social consequences.

It is estimated that the United States has 5 million alcoholics and an economic loss through alcoholism amounting to at least $2 billion a year. Yet, these figures do not include the effect of alcohol consumption on the 50,000 fatalities in auto accidents every year. Some estimate that 50 per cent of fatal auto accidents are associated with alcohol, often involving a chronic alcoholic.

Here again is the interaction of psychological, physical, environmental, and cultural factors. An alcoholic is sick—physically, emotionally, and

[8] U.S., Department of Health, Education, and Welfare, *Program Analysis: Disease Control Programs, 1966* (Washington, D.C.: Department of Health, Education, and Welfare, 1966), No. 1–5.

[9] Dorothy P. Rice, *Estimating the Cost of Illness*, U.S., Department of Health, Education, and Welfare, "Health Economics Series," No. 6 (Washington, D.C.: Department of Health, Education, and Welfare, May 1966).

TRENDS IN SELECTED CAUSES OF DEATH
United States,1900-66

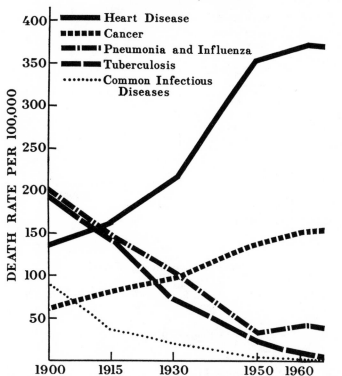

Source: National Cancer Institute, United States Public Health Service.

Figure 1

socially—as the consequences of such varied circumstances as stress, emotional infirmity, social pressures, and his own biochemistry. In turn, he is a thorn in society's side, when he loses his job, neglects his children, or, most specifically, when he drives his car. Adequate and sensitive indicators do not yet exist to measure these important elements.

MEASURING RELATED FACTORS

More than thirty years ago, Sydenstricker[10] discussed in detail the relation of geographic environment, urban and rural environment, eco-

---

[10] Edgar Sydenstricker, *Health and Environment* (New York: McGraw-Hill, 1933), p. 217.

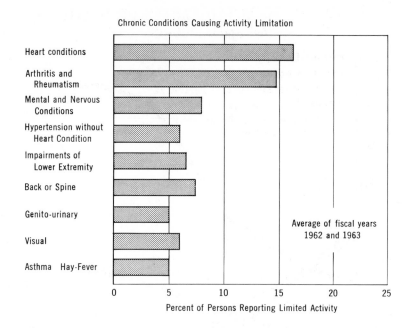

Source: United States Public Health Service, *Vital and Health Statistics,* Series 10, No. 17.

Figure   2

nomic status, social environment, and occupational environment to mortality. The relationship of poverty to disease has long been recognized. Although it is difficult to define these precise relations, more and more information is available to shed light on some of them.

For example, a study on "levels of living," by Cowhig and Beale,[11] adopted the premise that to meet the minimum standards a household should have a dwelling unit in sound condition, hot water piped inside the structure, a telephone, and an automobile.

The investigators found that in the rural farm population, only 49 per cent of the white households had all four factors, and the figure for the nonwhite households was only 4 per cent. Family income was also directly related to levels of living. Nonwhite families at every income level had significantly lower percentages living in premises that met minimum standards (Table 2).

---

[11] James D. Cowhig and Calvin L. Beale, "Levels of Living among Whites and Non-whites," *Health, Education, and Welfare Indicators* (February–October 1965), p. 56.

TABLE 2—Level of Living for White and Nonwhite Households
in the United States, 1960

Item	Percentage Living in Premises Meeting Minimum Standards	
	White	Nonwhite
Residence		
Urban	76	36
Rural nonfarm	63	5
Rural farm	49	4
Family Income (1959)		
Under $1,000	35	2
$1,000–1,999	38	6
$2,000–2,999	38	17
$3,000–3,999	46	23
$4,000–4,999	59	32
$5,000–6,999	73	41
$7,000–9,999	84	60
$10,000 and over	91	68

Source: James D. Cowhig, *Urban and Rural Levels of Living, 1960,* Agricultural Economic Report No. 79 (Washington, D.C.: United States Department of Agriculture, July 1965), Tables 1 and 2.

While the automobile's importance in relation to health and disease may be debatable, an unsound dwelling unit is clearly a health hazard. The lack of hot running water can be the same. And the presence or absence of a telephone can make a life-or-death difference in an emergency.

The association of poor housing with other factors has been studied in a number of cities. In one city, an area dominated by poor housing had twice the number of ambulance runs and fire calls, four times the number of visiting nurse calls, and fourteen times the number of people receiving welfare payments as a middle-income area in the same city. In another city, the poor housing area produced 36 per cent of the city's juvenile delinquents and 76 per cent of the city's tuberculosis cases, even though it represented less than 25 per cent of the city's total population.

Education is unquestionably one of the major factors in relation to health and disease. Studies show that the uneducated are likely to have lower income, bigger families, and more illness; they are deprived of the health-enhancing advantages of proper nutrition, housing, recreation, and medical care. Yet thousands of children are filtered out of the school system before they receive even basic minimums of educational requirements.

For every ten pupils in the fifth grade in 1957–1958, only 1.9 were expected to earn four-year college degrees in 1969.[12]

Nutrition is an obvious factor in health, and this can be demonstrated most clearly in an examination of the diet of the Negro population. In the South, the customary high-carbohydrate, low-protein diet is somewhat improved by the accessibility of fresh fruits and vegetables from home gardens in season. However, when Southern Negroes move to the North, they lack this added benefit and exist largely on starchy foods and fats. The problem has been clearly described by Mayer:

> Careful perusal of the records available in large cities, as well as the collection of impressions of experienced physicians, dietitians, and health administrators, leaves little doubt that our Negro slums represent the greatest concentration of anemias, growth failures, dermatitis of doubtful orgin, accidents of pregnancy, and other signs associated with malnutrition. A number of cases of acute malnutrition are seen every year among the Negro patients of our general hospitals, including, occasionally, such fullblown syndromes as kwashiorkor.[13]

Still another significant related factor is the distribution of health manpower, strikingly uneven from state to state. The national average ratio is 142 physicians per 100,000 population—but this figure, like the general mortality rates, conceals more than it reveals. New York State has 211 physicians per 100,000 population; Mississippi has only 74; Alaska, 66. The same is true for dentists, with a national average ratio of 52 per 100,000 population—but with a rate of 79 in New York and only 22 in South Carolina. The distribution of professional nurses is in the same pattern. The national average is 298 per 100,000 population, but Massachusetts has 502 and Arkansas, only 120.

A striking example of uneven manpower distribution is in Watts, Los Angeles County, California, the low-income and largely Negro community which was torn by racial rioting in August of 1965. A study of the two districts involved—the southeastern district and the southern district—showed ratios of 38 physicians per 100,000 population in the southeastern district and 45 physicians per 100,000 in the southern district, as compared to the country-wide ratio of 127 per 100,000.[14] In these two districts, there were 15.1 dentists per 100,000 population, as compared to the state-

---

12 "Statistic of the Month," *American Education*, Vol. 1, No. 7 (July–August 1965), back cover.

13 Jean Mayer, "The Nutritional Status of American Negroes," *Nutrition Review*, Vol. 23, No. 6 (June 1965), p. 161.

14 Milton I. Roemer, "Health Resources and Services in the Watts Area of Los Angeles," *California's Health* (February-March, 1966), pp. 123–143.

wide ratio of 67 per 100,000. The districts have eight hospitals with a total capacity of 454 beds—only two of them accredited by the Joint Commission. There is one public health nurse for each 5,230 people, though the desirable ratio for such an area is one for each 2,000.

The health level in Watts is correspondingly low. This pattern applies specifically in mental health; for example, while the rate of admissions of psychotic patients to state mental hospitals from Los Angeles County as a whole was 92 per 100,000 population in 1964, it was 163 from the southern district and 145 from the southeastern district of Watts.

There are an increasing number of environmental hazards—air pollution, water pollution, noise, crowding, automobiles, radiation, and odors—that may pose obvious or subtle threats to health. Some of these are immediate (traffic accidents) while others require twenty years or more to produce overt disease (lung cancer due to radiation hazard in uranium mines). Some can be measured precisely, and their effects can be predicted. For others, we are just beginning to appreciate their possible significance. Measurement of these physical, chemical, and psychological hazards will become increasingly important in the future.

THE DETERMINATION OF

HEALTH GOALS

There is an abundance of evidence of the new national determination that good health is the birthright of every American. There is growing recognition that national goals in health are involved in a multiplicity of political, social, economic, medical, scientific, and other forces. It is clearly recognized, also, that the economic toll of illness is an intolerable burden on the American society, and that this society can no longer afford to neglect the disease and disability which afflict so many of its members.

The setting of specific goals in the health field is a complex process. Measures that have been adequate in the past to assess needs, to help set priorities, and to evaluate progress are not adequate for the future. We are concerned with indices, but we must be equally concerned with the quality of services and the manner in which they are provided, even though the indices do not change. To measure quality, some agreement must be reached on what is meant by the quality of medical care. Although a number of measures exist, it is likely that no single or comprehensive criterion can, or will, be developed.

Quality has many ingredients. It must include not only technical or scientific criteria, but the social indices that are really measures of the values we hold as critical to our society. If we believe that people must have human dignity, if we believe that people have the right to be treated with respect, the measure of the health of our society may very well be reflected in whether or not we give appointments to a patient, whether we treat him in such a way that he understands what we are doing, and whether he can participate in the determination of how services will be provided. Thus, we have other kinds of social goals, and indices of these, which must be part of any over-all design and strategy of program development and evaluation.

Although over-all objectives can be defined in relation to health as a right, it is necessary to define them more precisely. For example, Dr. William H. Stewart, the Surgeon General of the United States Public Health Service, has proposed that our objectives should be:[15]

(1)   Every person who is ill, from whatever cause, should have a place to go; he should know where it is; he should have the assurance that it will give him the skilled and compassionate care he needs, when he needs it.

(2)   The disease which can be prevented should, in fact, be prevented—for all the people. Those which can be controlled, and those which can be treated, should be treated.

(3)   Those in our society who are, effectively, beyond the present reach of medical assistance—the senile, the mentally retarded, and the mentally ill who can only be institutionalized—should be treated in accordance with the most humanitarian standards. We must develop the resources and summon the dedication to preserve and to foster the dignity of the individual throughout his life.

(4)   The people of the United States should live with the confidence that their environment is free of significant menaces to their health and safety.

(5)   Health careers should be characterized by excellence in educational preparation, efficiency in use of skills, and opportunity for unlimited advancement to higher levels of service.

(6)   A sense of permanence and stability should permeate the climate of biomedical science. Our national commitment to scientific advance should remain firm. But we should also encourage maximum flexibility on the part of scientists and institutions; stability at the cost of rigidity would be fatal to progress.

(7)   The United States must carry its knowledge and skills to people around the world who need what we know and must help other nations to develop their own resources for health, on a scale hitherto unapproached.

---

[15] William H. Stewart (personal communication).

Significant improvement in the health of the people or achievement of specific health objectives cannot be achieved by the fragmented efforts of separate health professions, institutions, and agencies working alone. A unified effort is mandatory. In addition to specific health program objectives, it is essential that our society strive to achieve the following objectives which will contribute significantly to health goals:

(a)   economic conditions which eliminate, to the maximum extent, poverty and its attendant health hazards;

(b)   legal and social systems which stress social justice and equality of opportunity, in fact as well as in theory;

(c)   education for all citizens, based on their capacity to absorb it; and

(d)   public information and communications that permit citizens an informed choice and provide adequate and unbiased health information.

One of the most difficult and poorly developed areas in health is the measurement of program effectiveness. In many areas, specific measurements cannot be relied upon to tell the whole story. For example, it may be perfectly possible to reduce alcohol consumption with a demonstrable reduction in the incidence of cirrhosis of the liver. However, if, at the same time, psychosomatic symptoms go up, the indices which we have used may not reflect an improvement in health but only a shift in symptomatology. The critical problem is that the indices must be so measured that we do not delude ourselves that we are improving health when we may be only exchanging one disease or set of symptoms for another.

In recent months, efforts have been made to analyze specific programs on a cost-effectiveness basis. In measuring the effectiveness of health programs, "cost-benefit analysis," and the "planning, programming, budgeting system" represent newly applied tools, long used in industry and the Department of Defense. These methods are simply the logical extensions of the application of reason to the solution of complex problems. Given limited resources, and limited or no opportunity for enlarging the resources, sound decision requires careful identification of the targets. In this new concept of the right of each individual to good health, proper targets must be visualized and priorities assigned in terms of overcoming the greatest deprivation of health and health services—whether this is due to lack of facilities, of personnel, or of economic or social access to existing services.

THE ACHIEVEMENT OF GOALS
AND OBJECTIVES

If access to the means of good health is, indeed, a right, government must be involved in defending, preserving, and extending the right to all people. During the past thirty years, the federal government has been increasingly involved in a number of areas, directly related to health, that are designed to extend this right.

These include:

(1)   programs designed to advance research in the cause, prevention, and treatment of disease;

(2)   programs to meet the manpower, facility, and other resource requirements of the health care system;

(3)   programs designed to stimulate local, regional, and state initiative and improve the effectiveness of federal-state and local efforts;

(4)   programs to remove the financial barriers to health care;

(5)   programs to improve the quality and availability of health care; and

(6)   programs designed to protect the consumer and to reduce the hazards in, and improve the quality of, our environment.

The translation of specific objectives to immediate action programs could be illustrated by a number of examples. To reduce or remove financial barriers and improve the quality and availability of health care, a number of programs provided or supported by local, state, and federal government have been necessary: Medicare, Medicaid, crippled children's services, maternal and child health services, hospital and health-facility construction (Hill-Burton), Veterans and Public Health Service medical care programs, neighborhood health centers and services, maternal and infant care projects, comprehensive services for children and youth in low-income areas, and migrant-health services. These programs have helped, but much remains to be done. The multiplicity of programs which have developed in response to the felt need of the time have imposed a responsibility on the federal government for effective coordination. This responsibility is just beginning to be met.

The future success of public and private efforts to achieve national goals rests on the availability of knowledge and resources and their effective deployment. Dollars are crucial. In order to have the dollars to command the other resources, continued economic growth in the future is essential.

It is also essential that the rise in medical care costs be within reason, or many will be deprived of the benefits of such services. The costs of medical care, particularly hospital care and physicians' services, are rising more rapidly than at any time in the past thirty years.[16]

In projecting the costs of health and medical care into the next decade, assuming a maintenance of the status quo in terms of cost and quality, Lecht predicted that total spending would rise to $39 billion by 1975.[17] This compares with the $34 billion level of 1963. We would then be spending $5 billion more a year without increasing per capita costs.

Costs will rise, but so will income. It has been predicted that a reasonable estimate of gross national product in 1975 will be between $900 billion and $1,090 billion. It is likely that disposable personal income will rise from $469 billion in 1965 to $777 billion in 1975. Private medical care costs, which aggregated $28.1 billion, or 6 per cent of disposable personal income in 1965, may well rise to $46.6 billion in 1975.

With rising income, a greater share may go for medical care. A modest rise to 6.6 per cent would make $51.3 billion available for medical care.[18]

In addition to private expenditures for medical care, it is clear that public expenditures will rise as well. Research, manpower development and training, the construction of facilities, payment for medical services, and other federally supported programs have shown a rapid increase in the past ten years. A significant share represents the shift from local or state expenditures to a federal expenditure (for example, Medicare). Should the public programs only maintain their present 25 per cent share of the total expenditure it is likely that they would increase to more than $15 billion by 1975. It is expected, however, that a greater per cent of the costs will be borne by public funds.

In projecting the cost of "aspiration standards" in 1975, Lecht estimated a total expenditure of $85 billion. This would be equivalent to more than doubling the per capita expenditures for health and medical care by 1975. This is not a likely possibility, but the greater availability of private and public funds should make possible the achievement of significant improvements over today's standards. We should expect market progress, particularly in the areas of maternal and child health, improved health services for the poor, the disadvantaged, and the chronically ill, as well as improved and expanded programs of health manpower development, bio-

---

16 U.S., Department of Health, Education, and Welfare, *A Report to the President on Medical Care Prices* (Washington, D.C.: United States Government Printing Office, February 1967), p. 38.

17 Leonard A. Lecht, *Goals, Priorities and Dollars: The Next Decade* (New York: Free Press, 1966), p. 365.

18 Jules Backman, "Economic Aspects of Medical Care in the Next Decade," Presented to the National Pharmaceutical Council Symposium, Washington, D.C., December 1, 1966.

medical research, health services, research and development, and the construction of facilities.

The annual expenditure for health and medical care in the United States now exceeds $43 billion, or about 6 per cent of the gross national product. The American people cannot afford to spend this huge sum unless it is used wisely, compassionately, and effectively. But if this end can be achieved—if the birthright of physical, mental, and social well-being can truly be claimed by every man, woman, and child—not a penny will be wasted.

FIVE

ENVIRONMENTS

18

THE NATURAL ENVIRONMENT

JOSEPH L. FISHER

It is surely a truism that economic development and social welfare are closely linked with the management of the natural environment and the production of raw materials. The central economic problem over the ages has been that of wresting a living from the natural environment of land, water, and minerals. In most of the world, certainly among the two billion or more people living at low material levels in the less developed countries, this central problem continues in its classic form, with the Malthusian ghost of too many people always lurking nearby. But in the United States the resources problem has taken a new turn.

In the United States the problem of the sheer amount of raw materials, while still very important for economic growth and even for elementary well-being of the 15 per cent of the population in the poverty classification, has receded from its number-one position on the national agenda for natural resources. Now and for the future, the qualitative problem calls for concerted attention. More and more people are concerned with water pollution, air pollution, pesticides and radioactive fallout, solid wastes, the preservation of areas for outdoor recreation and for open space, the design and arrangement of both the urban and rural landscape, noise, the use of the radio spectrum, and other qualitative elements or attributes of the natural environment. Feature writers for the magazines and legislators alike are directing our attention to the aesthetic, social, and even ethical aspects of man's use of the natural environment. National leaders in and out of government are telling the American public that an ecological as well as an economic approach to the problems of the natural environment will be necessary if that environment is to contribute the food and fiber, the minerals and water, and the other materials necessary for a high level of living and also is to be preserved, maintained, and otherwise managed so as to

455

support indefinitely into the future the basis for good living for a growing population. Living in harmony with nature has become a matter of conscious attention and national policy, just as much as getting a living from nature.

Much has been said and written recently about the deterioration of the natural environment: our streams and lakes, it is alleged, have become more polluted; the air over our cities has become more smoggy; our roadsides and rural landscape have become more littered; farm land and ponds are being damaged by pesticides; our central city areas have degenerated into slums; our suburbs are vast extensions of monotony; and radioactive fallout threatens everyone. To what extent is all of this true? What indicators, however loose and indirect, can be utilized in tracing the trends of how the condition of our natural environment is changing? To what extent is it necessary to view these changes in terms of stipulated goals of environmental quality, and what are some of these goals?

RESOURCE QUANTITY INDICATORS

Economic indicators are available which tell something about the quantitative side of the resources picture. These include statistics of production and consumption of food products, forest products, energy commodities, metals, water, and so on through a long list. Costs of production and prices of these items are also available. Whether or not a particular raw material, or category of raw materials, is becoming scarcer or more plentiful is indicated by such measures as production or consumption per capita over a period of years, by cost or price trends adjusted for changes in costs and prices generally, by rates of production or consumption expressed in terms of available supplies or reserves, and by output per input of labor, land, or some other basic factor.[1] Tested by these indicators, which are quantitative in nature, one can say generally that raw materials and resource products in the United States over the past century have not been becoming scarcer. Per capita production and consumption have been increasing; real costs have not been rising in any general sense; production efficiency has been going up; and the resource base itself does not seem less adequate now than it did decades ago, having in mind new discoveries, technological advances, and substitutions. Broadly speaking, improved

---

[1] See Harold J. Barnett and Chandler Morse, *Scarcity and Growth: The Economics of Natural Resource Availability* (Baltimore: Johns Hopkins Press, 1963), and Joseph L. Fisher and Neal Potter, *World Prospects for Natural Resources: Some Projections of Demand and Indicators of Supply to the Year 2000* (Washington, D.C.: Resources for the Future, 1964).

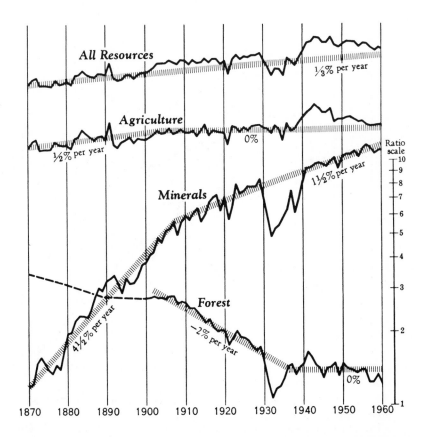

Figure   1—U.S. Resource Sectors: Per Capita Consumption, 1870–1960.

Source: Joseph L. Fisher and Neal Potter, *World Prospects for Natural Resources* (Washington, D.C.: Resources for the Future, 1964).

technology has more than offset tendencies for resources to become scarcer in a physical sense. Figures 1, 2, and 3 summarize these quantitative trends over a long historical period.

Looking to the future, one may say with some confidence that social welfare in this country will be upheld for at least several decades ahead, so far as the quantities of resource products are concerned. But this comforting outlook requires several assumptions: (1) a continuation of research and development leading to technological innovation in the numerous resource sectors, (2) a continued capacity to import supplies of oil, iron ore, and many metals from abroad where they can be produced more

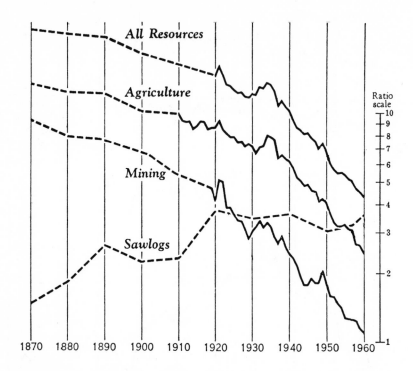

Figure   2—U.S. Resource Sectors: Employment/Output, 1870–1960.[a]
Source: Fisher and Potter, *op. cit.* (see Figure 1).
[a] The dashed lines indicate periods for which the data are available less frequently than on an annual basis.

cheaply, (3) an intensification of conservation programs and better management and use of resources, and (4) improved policies, both governmental and private, across the board. Also, of course, it will be necessary to avoid major and devastating war and to avoid protracted or frequent depressions. But granting all this, which seems reasonable in the light of recent trends, it should be possible to support a population 50 million larger by 1980 and 150 million larger by 2000—if it should grow that rapidly—living at ever higher levels so far as the natural resource base of the country is concerned. Of course, there will be difficulties here and there with particular raw materials—enough fresh water in certain arid parts of the country or enough clean water in certain eastern river basins, or enough of this, that, or the other metal—but the general picture is favorable. For example, if we should begin to run low or, more accurately, to run into

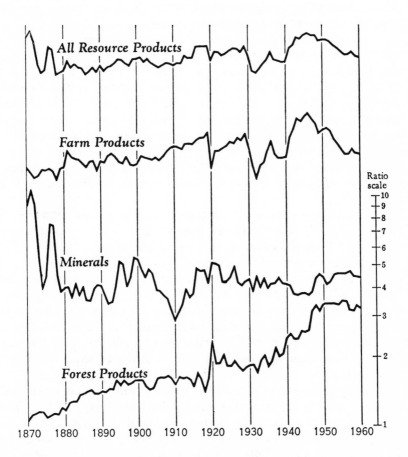

Figure 3—U.S. Resource Sectors: Deflated Prices, 1870–1960.
Source: Fisher and Potter, *op. cit.* (see Figure 1).

increasing relative costs of conventional underground liquid oil in this country, then it should be possible to turn increasingly to imports from the Middle East and elsewhere, to the devleopment of oil shale which exists in very large amounts in the Colorado Plateau, to higher degrees of recovery from existing oil fields, and even to coal as a source of additional liquid fuel. Furthermore, nuclear power will be coming on fast and can substitute for certain uses of petroleum, while coal reserves remain plentiful for a long time to come.

Looking far beyond the end of the century, demographic and economic projections tend to become either exercises in prophecy or sterile and mechanical extrapolations of recent trends, based mainly on assumptions of birth rates and productivity increases. In any case, the future time span relevant for most current decisions about resource development and use does not extend that far ahead, even though the effects of some of these decisions do have a bearing on what things will be like beyond the year 2000. But very long-range indicators for raw materials and environmental conditions become less and less reliable as the time ahead considered lengthens, primarily because one cannot see very clearly, and hence does not take into account, the numerous human, social, and institutional reactions that will probably occur to alter the picture. Effective, widespread population-limitation is one possibility; another is the full-scale application of known techniques of agricultural production in the less developed countries.

Also, it has to be pointed out that this optimistic view of the next few decades applies only to the United States and, probably, the other economically more developed countries such as Canada, Europe, the Soviet Union, Japan, and Australia and New Zealand. For most of the rest of the world, no such rosy picture can be drawn; for two-thirds of mankind the ghost of Malthus still rides, and they will be hard-pressed to make even modest gains in per capita food consumption. Rising per capita use of energy from coal, oil, gas, and hydropower and good prospects in the future for nuclear power provide hope that more and cheaper fertilizers, irrigation water, farm mechanization, and transport will set food production decisively on an upward path.

Although the rest of this chapter will deal with environmental quality, it should never be forgotten that social welfare rests very largely on people having enough food and other resource materials to support an adequate rate of economic growth and provide for health and well-being. Social goals and indicators include the more conventional economic and material goals and indicators, but they must go beyond these into other dimensions. For the natural environment, this further dimension has to do with the maintenance and further improvement of the quality of that environment.

INDICATORS OF ENVIRONMENTAL QUALITY: GENERAL REMARKS

Goals and indicators with respect to the quality of the natural environment are difficult to conceive and more difficult to work with. Surprisingly little of a rigorous and analytical character has been done.[2] In the first place, qualitative matters are highly subjective; opinions frequently differ sharply as to what makes up higher quality. Second, the major elements of the natural environment such as land, water, and air are expected to yield a variety of uses and satisfactions, leading frequently to conflicts among different users. Compromises and trade-offs have to be found among them: for example, the sport fisherman wants very pure and uncontaminated water while the industrialist wants to use water as a means of diluting and carrying away waste materials. Third, it is not easy to determine from the human or social point of view exactly where to measure environmental quality—for example, should it be the quality of the water in the glass as it is raised to a person's lips? Fourth, quality questions involve interpersonal, intertemporal, and interregional comparisons which bedevil efforts to find general indicators and goals that will hold steady over time. Fifth, the services desired from resource materials and the natural environment frequently are jointly produced: for example, a dam and reservoir augment water supplies which can be used for hydroelectricity, municipal and industrial uses, irrigation agriculture, navigation, flood control and watershed production, recreation, and the flushing away of effluents. The problem of allocating the various elements of the cost of building the dam among the several services of uses is difficult to solve in a rational and equitable manner.

Despite all difficulties, Americans want to know how things are going with their natural environment: Is water or air pollution getting worse or not? Is the countryside becoming more messy or not? Is the air over our cities becoming more foul or not? These are legitimate and important questions; indicators of the trends must be found which will relate specified environmental conditions to social welfare.

No single over-all indicator of natural environmental quality is in sight. The incidence of various diseases, length of life, days lost from work on account of illness, and the like, although of obvious importance, are not satisfactory indicators of environmental conditions because they are affected by many other things. On the qualitative side, there appears to be no equivalent, in general, to per capita production or consumption of raw materials on the quantitative side. And use of gross quantitative indicators for qualitative purposes is highly debatable. Gross national product, for example, includes not only what might be called positive elements such as expendi-

---

[2] For example, the monthly *Health, Education, and Welfare Indicators* put out by the United States Department of Health, Education, and Welfare carries only two relevant charts and tables: one showing bond sales for municipal water, sewer, and sewage-treatment facilities construction and the other showing the net interest cost of the bonds.

tures for food, housing, and machinery, but also negative or defensive elements such as rather large expenditures for those activities which serve only to eliminate the mess and discomfort created in the course of production and consumption. A not insignificant amount of gross national product is of the wheel-spinning variety: it merely helps to keep us from falling back in our level of living.

One test can be applied to any proposal to protect or improve environmental quality, and that is to compare estimates of the resulting social benefits with social costs. The greater the net social benefits, however measured, the more desirable the particular project. Many difficulties arise in making such benefit and cost estimates. Among them are what items of benefit and cost to include in the estimates; what rate or rates of discount to apply to benefits and costs which will accrue at different times in the future; what cost and price levels to assume for the future; what to do about those particular benefits and costs which it is decided cannot properly be estimated in monetary terms; and how to allocate the joint costs of a project among separate identifiable uses or users. In addition, all of the usual difficulties associated with making use of index numbers to trace trends over time will be present in dealing with environmental quality variables. But enough for now on the difficulties of the job; indicators of environmental conditions must be found. The more rational they are the better, but, in any case, some kind of indicators will be used.

WATER-QUALITY INDICATORS
AND THEIR DIFFICULTIES

Our longest experience among the various major categories of pollution and environmental damage has probably been with water pollution. Water is a deceptive commodity; it appears to be more or less the same everywhere, but actually it varies over wide ranges with respect to many characteristics. What is suitable water for certain industrial purposes such as cooling would be quite unacceptable as drinking water. And acceptable drinking water may contain far too many impurities to be used as process water in certain industrial operations in which exceedingly high-quality water is absolutely necessary. In this kind of situation, one can hardly expect to find uniform and simple standards or uniform and simple indicators of conditions.

The recently passed Water Pollution Control Act requires each state to establish, by July 1, 1967, water-quality standards for its streams and lakes acceptable to the federal authorities; otherwise the federal govern-

TABLE 1—Indicators of Water Quality Appropriate for Particular Uses

Quality Indicators / Uses	Amount of Flow	Dissolved Oxygen	Inorganics	Coliform	Turbidity	Temperature	Solid Wastes	Others
Agriculture	V*		V			V		
Industry	V	V	V		V	V		
Municipal	V	V	V	V	V	V	V	
Flood control	V						V	
Navigation	V		V				V	
Hydropower	V							
Watershed protection	V						V	
Fish and wildlife	V	V	V		V	V	V	
Scenic amenity	V	V			V	V	V	
Sewage dilution and transport	V	V	V		V	V		
Recreation Swimming								
Boating	V	V	V	V	V	V	V	
Fishing								

* V simply means that the quality characteristic is important for the particular use; absence means it is unimportant.

ment will promulgate standards. Apparently, the state standards in most cases are being worked out in terms of objective measurements of certain physical characteristics of water in the streams: biochemical oxygen demand (BOD), which measures the pollution in the water by the amount of dissolved oxygen required to decompose it; the coliform count, which is a generalized measure of bacterial content of the water; turbidity, which expresses the amount of suspended soil and other sediments in the water; inorganic mineral content; temperature; and perhaps others. Each of these is an indicator of the condition of water in a particular part of a stream, and records can be kept to trace changes over time. Such physical indicators are chiefly helpful for-in-the-stream uses such as recreation (swimming, boating, and fishing) and for scenic amenity. They are less helpful as indicators of consumption uses for domestic or industrial purposes and hardly at all helpful for electric power, flood control, and navigation. Table 1 sets out the situation schematically.

Under each quality characteristic should be inserted the best indicators available. Some of the indicators would be unambiguous and quite reliable; others would be more general and less reliable. Variations over appropriate intervals of time would have to be noted; in some cases, daily or even hourly, in other cases, monthly or seasonal. Certain of the quality characteristics would be unimportant for certain uses, at least within wide limits; thus, for navigation, the amount of flow is the essential thing, while the others are of little or no importance. For fish, on the other hand, virtually all of the quality indicators are of considerable significance.

Interrelations among the quality characteristics and uses are numerous, complex, subtle, and frequently not well understood—thereby necessitating careful and knowledgeable uses of most of the indicators. For example, coal mine drainage pollutes streams with acid, an inorganic material. This causes a reduction in oxygen-using bacteria. This, in turn, slows down the decomposition of organic substances, reduces the demand for dissolved oxygen in the stream, and checks growth of algae. As a result, the stream is less turbid and looks beautifully clear, but actually is contaminated with more organic material as well as with the acid. Furthermore, fish life may be impossible. Some kinds of pollution are associated in a positive way—that is, the more of one, the more of the other—while others are associated negatively. The range over which a particular characteristic varies is frequently significant. At higher temperatures, organics in the water are degraded more rapidly and use up dissolved oxygen more rapidly, whereas at lower temperatures these processes are slowed. But at still lower temperatures all significance may be lost because the water is too cold for recreational use anyway.

The schematic table shows that the amount of flow is important for all uses, and that all quality characteristics are important for municipal (including household) uses and recreation uses. For other uses some quality characteristics are significant, and for still others not. The straightforward physical indicators on which water-quality regulations are customarily based are more helpful in connection with in-stream uses like recreation than for away-from-the-stream uses like municipal and industrial. This is because the latter require much smaller amounts of water, especially if the water is recycled, as such water can often be purified sufficiently by treatment, thereby making treatment of the whole stream quite unnecessary. Technical apparatus as well as natural processes can intervene between the stream and the user, or between different users, so that one has to know the point to which the quality indicator applies.

Physical indicators of water quality may not tell much about individual or social welfare, largely because they do not embrace considerations of cost and benefit in either the economic or the social senses. In the case of the Delaware estuary, an account of which follows, an effort is being made to estimate the costs and benefits associated with the attainment of alternative levels of water quality and to establish a process of analysis, discussion, and decision which involves all interested parties.

THE DELAWARE ESTUARY CASE

The approach being taken now to water-quality standards in the Delaware River estuary from Trenton, New Jersey, to the Bay is instructive.[3] Some five different "objective sets" have been postulated as alternative goals. The highest set would permit large increases in water-contact recreation in the estuary and also make special provision for high-level dissolved oxygen content during the spring and fall migration periods of shad and other anadromous fish. The other sets grade off to set number 5 which would do no more than maintain 1964 conditions in the estuary and prevent any further deterioration of water quality. The following table for objective set number 3, which is intermediate among the sets, sketches water-quality goals for different reaches of the river below Trenton in terms of variety of objective qualitative measures.

The next step was to estimate the costs of alternative programs for achieving each of the identified objective sets. The costs, of course, diminished through the successive five sets as the standards were lowered. For each set, the least cost combination of measures was sought. Of great importance was the cost-sensitivity of various measures for achieving the stipulated dissolved oxygen content of the water at particular times of the year and in particular reaches of the river. The difference in cost between maintaining three parts per million of dissolved oxygen in the summer time in critical reaches, called for in objective set 3, and four parts per million, as in objective set 2, proved to be considerable.

Against an organized display of costs there were arrayed the estimated benefits that would be associated with each of the objective sets. Admittedly, dollar estimates of benefits are hazardous, but without such estimates comparisons with costs become clumsy and highly impressionistic. It is interesting to note that the Delaware Estuary Comprehensive Study found very little basis for assigning benefits to muncipal and industrial water users. Well-known and effective treatment measures apparently are a cheaper way of attaining aceptable standards for such purposes without any necessity for much more massive and expensive efforts, such as low-flow augmentation, to clean up the water in the river. In fact, some industries reported that higher levels of dissolved oxygen content at their intake points would lead to increased costs because of greater corrosion.

The major part of the benefits would be for recreational improvement, including swimming, boating, and sport fishing. Scenic amenity, which is of major current interest, would be preserved so long as there was enough

---

[3] The following paragraphs on the Delaware estuary experience are based on a draft of a chapter being prepared for publication in a book on water-quality management by my colleagues in Resources for the Future, Allen V. Kneese and Blair T. Bower.

TABLE 2—Water Quality Goals for Objective Set III

Location groupings by section: Trenton (≈1–3), Bristol (≈4), Torresdale (≈5–7), Philadelphia / Camden (≈8–16), Chester (≈17–19), Wilmington (≈20–22), New Castle (≈23–26), Liston Point (≈27–30).

Quality[a,b] — Section	1	2	3	4	5	6	7	8	9	10	11	12	13	14	15	16	17	18	19	20	21	22	23	24	25	26	27	28	29	30
Dissolved Oxygen[c]	5.5					5.5		3.0												3.0		4.5				4.5		6.5		6.5
Chlorides[d]													50			250														
Coliforms (#/100 ml.)	5000[f]					5000[f]																		5000[f]						5000[f]
Coliforms 5/30–9/15		4000[e]			4000[e]																				4000[e]			4000[e]		
Turbidity (Tu)	Natural Levels + 30					Natural Levels + 30														Natural Levels + 30										Natural Levels + 30
Turbidity 5/30–9/15	Natural Levels							Natural Levels + 30												Natural Level										Natural Level
pH[g] (pH Units)	6.5–8.5							6.5–8.5																				6.5–8.5		
pH[g] 5/30–9/15	7.0–8.5							7.0–8.5																6.5–6.5			7.0–8.5			
Alkalinity[g]	20–50					20–50		20–120																						20–120
Hardness[h]	95					95		150								150														
Temperature[g] (°F)	Present Levels																										Present Levels			
Phenols[h]	.001					.001		.005								.005		.01												.01
Syndets[h]	1.0																													1.0
Oil & Grease	Negligible																									Negligible				
Floating Debris	Negligible																									Negligible				
Toxic Substances	Negligible																									Negligible				

[a] rg/l unless specified.   [b] Not less stringent than present levels.   [c] Summer average.   [d] Maximum 15-day mean.   [e] Maximum level.   [f] Monthly geometric mean.   [g] Desirable range.   [h] Monthly mean geometric mean.

Source: Delaware Estuary Comprehensive Study, Preliminary Report and Findings, U.S., Department of the Interior, Federal Water Pollution Control Association, Philadelphia, July 1966.

dissolved oxygen in the water to prevent septic conditions and foul odors. In addition, of course, floating material and trash would have to be screened out, and it would be desirable to hold down the amount of sediment that might be suspended in the water. A reasonably sophisticated effort to estimate the recreational benefits, based on user-days and recreation expenditures, when combined with minor amounts of other kinds of benefits, resulted in total estimated benefits for objective set 3 somewhat exceeding total estimated costs. For objective sets 1 and 2, calling for higher levels of water quality, the estimated costs were generally greater than the estimated benefits.

The purpose of monetary comparisons of benefits and costs was not to single out one of the objective sets with its appropriate collection of treatment and other measures to recommend; rather, it was to illuminate the whole subject and to put before the public and the legislative decision-makers a systematically organized display of information about costs and benefits of various alternatives on the basis of which a rational and generally acceptable choice could be made. In the case of the Delaware estuary, this was done, and there was a public hearing on the whole subject in which various groups and individuals expressed their preferences among the alternatives presented. According to participants in the hearing, the level of discussion and analysis was extremely high and led to the encouraging conclusion that this kind of process for analyzing water-quality problems in a specific estuary was an effective means for helping the public to understand the situation and arrive at the "best" course of action. If this particular decision-making process on the Delaware had a shortcoming, it was that the full range of measures for dealing with pollution was not taken into account. Low-flow augmentation and conventional treatment were considered thoroughly; dredging, diversion of waste from critical reaches, and mechanical reoxygenation of the estuary were given less attention, although the last one, on a preliminary look, appears to be the cheapest of all measures for increasing the dissolved oxygen content of the water.

BRIEF CONSIDERATION OF
AIR POLLUTION INDICATORS

In many respects air pollution poses the same kind of problems as water pollution. There are a number of different pollutants, including particulate matter (soot, ash, grime, and the like), carbon monoxide, sulphur compounds, and radioactive isotopes, among others. Air has various uses: for breathing, in industry, for the operation of internal combustion engines, as a transport medium for planes, as visual amenity, for recreation (flying kites and gliders), and generally as a means for diluting and transporting waste materials discharged into the atmosphere. Like water, air is a fluid, but it moves more freely and unpredictably than water, which always flows downhill. At least until recently, air has been regarded as a free good in the economist's sense: no one has had to pay for it; everyone has been able to consume all he wished; and very few regulations have been placed upon its use or the kinds of materials discharged into it. Pittsburgh and a few other cities, however, have long been concerned with dirty air: as early as 1913, an extensive study of smoke damage was done in Pittsburgh, which still provides the basis for national estimates of such damage.

In the last few years, air as a resource or feature of the natural environment seems to have crossed a kind of threshold. Rather suddenly, it has become widely apparent that the resource air has to be studied, conserved, and managed like other resources. In most of the metropolitan areas of the country, large numbers of people now realize that free and uncontrolled use of air can result in the imposition of costs, hardships, and unpleasantness on the population generally. In a few dramatic cases, air pollution has led to widespread and severe respiratory disorder and even to some deaths. More typically, air pollution causes damages, such as eye discomfort, soiling of fabrics, injury to crops, impairment of scenery, and breakdowns in machinery. Total annual damages and costs have been estimated, crudely, to run to some ten billion dollars.

A consideration of indicators for air quality runs along lines similar to the consideration of water-quality indicators. One might draw up a schematic table showing the various uses of air in the rows and the various quality indicators in the columns. There would be similarly complex and subtle interrelations among various indicators and uses, as in the water-quality case. Some headway is being made with developing and recording indicators of the physical condition of the air at critical points: sulphur compounds near smokestacks of coal-burning electricity-generating stations, carbon monoxide in cities with heavy automobile traffic, radioactive monitoring stations at strategic locations, plus more generalized indicators of amount of particulate matter in the atmosphere. The latter actually has been measured in a few places for a long time.

As in the water case, physical indicators of air pollution tend to fall quite far short of indicating effects on individuals and communities, although they do offer a first approximation. To move from the physical indicators to something more closely approaching social indicators requires the introduction of cost and benefit estimates of measures to achieve stipulated goals or standards of air quality. Ideally, the aim should be to arrive at estimates of net benefits associated with the achievement of selected levels of quality, with social-cost and social-benefit considerations included along with the monetary or economic ones. Thus far, with one or two exceptions, this kind of analysis has not been applied in any systematic way to air quality in any of our metropolitan areas where the problems are most acute. The difficulties in making estimates of net benefit would be formidable and would run along lines similar to those mentioned for water pollution. It would make sense for several airsheds over metropolitan areas to be selected for which net benefit estimates for air-quality programs could be worked out. One might conceive of minimum standards of air quality set by law or local ordinance in terms of specified physical characteristics, with cost and benefit governing the selection of standards and treatment or with regulation measures which would exceed the minimum standards, to reflect more closely what the people affected might want. The people in the air shed involved would have to find appropriate and democratic ways for reaching decisions about levels of air quality that would be both desirable and practical from the economic and political viewpoints. Trade-offs between different kinds of air pollution would have to be considered, since air absolutely pure in every respect lies beyond practical reach. As in the case of the Delaware estuary already described, the information-gathering, discussion, and decision process becomes of central importance not only to the installation of air-quality control systems, but also to the establishment of goals and standards. It is through processes of this sort that communities can move from the basic physical indicators to a consideration of social consequences and possibilities.

Other forms of environmental pollution also exist and cause damages. Solid-waste disposal, for example, is a major challenge in virtually all cities. Old newspapers, packages, bottles, cans, and the like pile up very rapidly in every household, office building, and industrial plant. These have to be deposed of by burning, reclaiming the valuable materials, using for land fill, and so on. Another form of environmental disturbance is noise from airplanes, trucks, and automobiles; certain industrial and machine processes; and even people, when they are brought together in large numbers. The advent of subsonic and, soon, supersonic jet planes adds a dramatic, if not traumatic, case in point.

CONCLUDING OBSERVATIONS

Not only are there numerous interrelations among water-quality characteristics and indicators, and also for those of air quality, but there are exceedingly intricate and interesting interrelations of environmental quality across the board. For example, coal-burning electricity-generating plants may discharge fly ash, sulphur compounds, and the like from the smoke-stacks directly into the air above cities, thereby polluting the air; or much of the particulate matter can be filtered or washed out before discharge into the air, along with some of the sulphur compounds, and carried by water into nearby streams and lakes, thereby polluting the water; or the sooty material can be extracted before it is discharged into the air and then dried and hauled away for burning or dumping, thereby again contributing to air pollution or, conceivably, to pollution of the landscape. Considerations like these lead one to wish to examine the possibilities for approaching environmental quality on the basis of metropolitan areas or larger regions which embrace the various forms of environmental pollution in some comprehensive way. The term "environmental problem shed" has been used. For a given problem shed, the various physical indicators could be worked out, as they apply to water, air, solid wastes, and the like, and an effort could be made to go beyond this to a consideration of costs and benefits of various groups of measures aimed to achieve specified standards of environmental quality across the board. New laws, institutions, and modes of administration and regulation would probably be necessary in any such approach, and these would have to be thought through and experimented with on a limited basis before any general application would be warranted.

In conclusion, several summary points can be made. First, environmental-quality indicators now being used are almost entirely indicators of physical condition, and are not as directly relevant or meaningful for social welfare as one would like, or as most people seem to think. (Even these are not available on any comprehensive basis.) Second, probably the basic indicator for social welfare would be one dealing with net social benefits (benefits minus costs or losses in some sense) that would result from selected interrelated measures to achieve acceptable levels of water or air quality. Perhaps a second-best objective would be the minimizing of social costs of the selected measures in cases where estimates of benefit seem to be impossible. Third, the processes by which decisions relating to environmental quality standards and programs are reached need to be given careful attention because certain important social benefits and costs cannot be measured satisfactorily in engineering or economic terms, and, furthermore, typically there will be alternatives from which choices have to be made. Fourth, absolute goals for environmental quality are less important than directions and rates of change for which statistical indicators are necessary. Fifth, although the qualitative aspects of the natural environment seem more closely related to social welfare, one should not lose sight of the basic importance of quantities of resource products and services for the good life in a great society. Even within the problem of water quality, for example, the sheer amount of water or flow is a principal means for diluting effluents and carrying them away. Finally, much research and development will be needed, not only on environmental pollution, but on creating and improving the indicators of the trends in such pollution and its effect on people. This is a task for social statisticians working with medical scientists, industrial, agricultural, and sanitary engineers, economists, sociologists, administrators, and others.

19

URBAN ENVIRONMENT: NEW YORK CITY

BARRY GOTTEHRER

*If children were run down in our streets, something would
be done. All over the world things are becoming more intolerable but we are tolerating them. Unless someone comes up with
some jolly good solutions, the problems facing cities may become more lethal than the bomb.*[1]

BARBARA WARD

In New York, a city of eight million people and region of twice that number, 1966 will be remembered, as the year that people finally stopped
tolerating the intolerable and a city government attempted to come up with
some jolly good solutions.

The success or failure of these efforts to modernize municipal government and to make life truly livable in one city has meaning that extends far
beyond New York City's five boroughs and far beyond the geographical
borders of the 1,100 different governments that constitute metropolitan
New York.

The experiment in New York City is of immense interest and far-
reaching significance to urbanists the world over—for there is at stake
nothing less than the governability of the urban center of our future.

---

[1] Delivered in a speech at a New York City Planning Commission Symposium,
October 1964.

472

If New York City, with its vast problems and vast resources, can be governed effectively and meaningfully for all its citizens, then what city cannot be tamed?[2]

Yet if New York City cannot be governed effectively and meaningfully for all its citizens, then what chance do the world's other urban centers have in their struggle to survive into the twenty-first century?

This article will deal with the attempts of New York City and its government to cope with its massive problems in the past, to experiment in new directions in the present, and to develop meaningful social indicators and goals for the future.

THE PAST: GOVERNMENT BY CRISIS

In late summer of 1964, more than a dozen of New York City's prominent business and civic leaders gathered for a private luncheon to discuss a matter of grave importance to all New Yorkers—the future of the city and what they, as members of the power elite of varying political persuasions, could do to save it.

At the end of two hours, they had reached some rather disquieting conclusions. Though they agreed, to a man, that New York was truly a city in a crisis of worsening social and physical dimensions, there was little they would do jointly or publicly to halt its decline.

Though unstated, their reasons were obvious. As part of the business and civic establishment of a one-party city, whose voters showed little inclination for change,[3] New York City's elite found it more expedient to remain silent.[4]

What these business and civic leaders chose to accept with no more than silent disapproval was a city administration that preferred prolonged negotiation to decisive action, one that responded more to political expediencies than to social indicators of the real needs of its eight million citizens, and, finally, one that did little visibly to refute the popular theory

---

[2] New York City today is a city of sharp contrasts—it is the richest city in the world; yet nearly one-fifth of its people live in poverty. Its welfare roll of 600,000 people is larger than the total population of five different states.

[3] The Democratic party had controlled City Hall for the previous twenty years, and the incumbent three-term Mayor, Robert F. Wagner, Jr., was, in mid-1964, believed to be unusually popular with the voters.

[4] Not too long after this unpublicized gathering, Edward J. Logue, the outspoken administrator of the Boston Redevelopment Agency, summed up his impressions of New York's power elite: "In no city, with the possible exception of Calcutta, have the business leaders and establishment talked more and done less than they have in New York."

that New York City was truly ungovernable and that it was doing the best job possible under the circumstances.

Even his most outspoken critics did not question Mayor Robert F. Wagner's integrity and sincerity, his love for the city and its people, or his accomplishments—notably in the construction of housing and schools.[5] What they did question, however—increasingly as crisis began to pile upon crisis during the final years of his third term—was the soundness of Mayor Wagner's theory of government.

"When in doubt, don't" was the advice which Mayor Wagner had received from his father, the late Senator from New York, and, as one of his critics pointed out, he "didn't" during his twelve years as Mayor. In essence, rather than create controversy and risk being wrong publicly by acting boldly, the Mayor would consider each issue at great length, invariably assigning a special citizens' committee to study the problem until it had been dropped from the headlines, concluding that, given time, another crisis would always come along to supplant the current one in the public's mind. Among pressing crises assigned to special committees were the 1964 racial disturbances, the growing narcotics problem, the city's dire fiscal crisis, and the loss of industry.[6]

There are some people who still believe that Wagner's way was the only practical way to govern a city with so vast a complexity of pressure groups and single-issue citizens. To others, however, it became increasingly clear as the crises in all our cities deepened that the Wagner method was not working. By avoiding hasty or bold action, Wagner clearly avoided making a number of errors of commission. But, at the same time, as problems worsened in one area after another, his administration became increasingly guilty of errors of omission.

The city's Title 1 urban renewal program exploded in scandal when the administration chose not to act until too late. The television film industry left the city when the administration chose not to act. Parks and hospitals declined when the administration chose not to act at all. And the government itself became increasingly ungovernable when the adminis-

---

[5] Despite impressive construction figures, the gap between housing supply and need continued to widen during Wagner's tenure.

[6] According to the Citizens' Budget Commission's annual report of 1966 (page 14): "In April 1964, the New York City Planning Commission engaged Arthur D. Little, Inc. to do a study of the feasibility of making a fresh start on industrial development in New York City . . . had it not been for a public statement by CBS Executive Director John M. Leavens, on Feb. 23, 1965, who raised the question of why the report had not been made public by the city at all. Once made public, the report did provoke a great deal of discussion but no part of city government showed any inclination toward doing anything about it. As a consequence, problems of economic redevelopment that cried out for some sort of solution remained unsolved and the hoped for impact of the Little report was deadened by bureaucratic inertia."

tration chose not to act. There is no way of determining what would have happened in each of these cases if the administration had acted decisively, but it is clear what happened when the administration chose not to.

By the early 1960's, it had become fashionable to conclude that New York City truly was an ungovernable mess. One of the better-written examples was Barbara Carter's article in *The Reporter Magazine* which, in 1964, two years after the city's last charter revision, concluded pessimistically:

> The wheels of power may spin somewhat more freely at the top but the antique structure of most of the bureaucratic agencies below seems as obdurate and unsusceptible to change as ever under the new charter. Obviously the *New York Times* was far too hopeful when it announced that "All New Yorkers from Hunter Island to Tottenville will soon be living under a government adequate to their modern needs." That was back on November 4, 1936, when the now discarded charter was approved. The prediction still seems off by light years.[7]

This conclusion was not surprising. It is hard to imagine a government anywhere where social indicators and social goals played so insignificant a role in the decision-making process.

Perhaps the most glaring example of haphazard decision-making and bureaucratic inefficiency was the history of the city administration in developing a master plan which would set forth long-range plans and goals for the city. The lack of communication between the City Planning Commission and City Hall dated back to the days of Mayor Fiorello LaGuardia, who set up the commission in 1938, charged it with producing a master plan, and then promptly ignored its suggestions. Twenty-eight years later, though a vast majority of other major cities had long-range development plans or were in the final stages of preparing them, New York City still had a Planning Commission, but it did not have its first master plan.

In view of this history, it is not difficult to understand why much of the city's physical development has been disorderly and unsound, based less on social goals and indicators of any relevance than on the politics and pressures of the moment.

For example, long-range planning and social goals might indicate that a public housing project might best be placed near a middle-income area in Queens, but pressure from the middle-income residents and the area's councilmen and borough president would invariably force it to be built elsewhere.

---

[7] Barbara Carter, "New York City—Can It Be Governed?," *The Reporter Magazine,* January 30, 1964, p. 45.

The vast majority of urban renewal and poverty funds were distributed throughout the city politically, rather than being concentrated in the areas of greatest need. Yet even when the administration decided to rely on varying forms of social data, it seems to have miscalculated badly. For example, in poverty areas based on 1960 Census figures, the city failed to include East New York as one of the areas of greatest need.

By early 1966, shortly before racial and poverty disturbances in this small section of Brooklyn nearly triggered city-wide riots, it became clear that the 1960 figures and data were totally useless in documenting the extreme poverty and deprivation of East New York, which did not receive a single dollar in poverty funds until the summer of 1966. Yet East New York's failure to receive desperately needed poverty funds could not be blamed in full on improperly used data. The fact remained that this small community, with an unorganized citizenry and fragmented political leadership, had not supplied sufficient pressure on City Hall. Central Harlem, on the other hand, with Representative Adam Powell heading the House Education and Labor Committee, with an extremely vocal and politically astute citizenry, and with Dr. Kenneth Clark's brilliant portrait of poverty, "Youth in the Ghetto," had not remained silent. By the end of 1965, Central Harlem had already received more than ten million dollars in city and federal poverty funds.

Governmental failure to develop meaningful indicators—and the proper application of those already available—was apparent in many areas. Crime statistics were reported only partially (unlike Chicago), thereby presenting a more comforting portrait of New York's crime problem but an inaccurate one.

Despite the increasing flow of manufacturing jobs from the city since 1955, city officials did little to determine the precise reasons for which corporations were leaving until nearly ten years later.

In several instances (funds for building demolition, sewage improvements, and neighborhood facilities), New York City did not receive available federal aid simply because its officials did not take advantage of their availability.

And, during the days of the mounting water crisis, the city's Water Commissioner, whose chief experience had come as an official of an electricians' union, declared publicly that, based on previous rainfall patterns and indicators, New York City could not possibly run out of water under any circumstances. He could not seem to comprehend that the water crisis, already the worst in the city's history, had made all previous indicators meaningless.

Yet the most critical problems facing New York City were centered primarily in two areas—the city's dire fiscal affairs and the structure of the government itself.

During the twelve years of Mayor Wagner's administration, the annual expense budget—that is, the one dealing with day-to-day operating expenses, as opposed to the capital budget which concerns outlays for public works—soared from $1.5 billion for the 1953–1954 fiscal year to $3.9 billion for the 1965–1966 fiscal year, an increase of 160 per cent. Traditionally, the daily expenditures contained in the expense budget have been covered by income from taxes and other sources (notably federal and state aid). Only the capital budget is traditionally financed by borrowing. Thus, when the Mayor announced, in the spring of 1965, that the city would have to borrow $255 million to meet a $500 million increase in outlays in his 1965–1966 expense budget, even those people resigned to skyrocketing city expenditures were shocked.

City Comptroller Abraham Beame, a Democrat who had been handpicked to run with the Mayor in 1961, called the proposal "fiscally unsound," and declared that the plan to borrow now, and hopefully repay later, was an attack on the credit and fiscal standing of the city, and a deviation from the traditional financial practices of New York and most other cities. And Mark E. Richardson, Executive Vice-President of the New York Chamber of Commerce, said: "This reflects absolutely miserable planning. New York is in a fiscal crisis."

According to most of the fiscal experts, New York City's fiscal crisis had not been inevitable. A great many people, both Democrats and Republicans, firmly believed that the crisis was precipitated by the financial policies of the incumbent administration. As early as 1958, business leaders began to express concern over what they termed the city administration's lack of fiscal planning. The size of the expense budget and the number of municipal employees had continued to soar even though the city's population had decreased slightly. One after another, fiscal experts began to call for immediate changes in the city's financial policies and the establishment of long-range fiscal planning. Despite the growing concern, the administration continued to practice "crisis financing," relying on the crazy-quilt addition of one tax after another to meet each financial emergency.

By the spring of 1962, the city's fiscal future had become so troubled that the Citizens' Budget Commission called for an immediate broad-scale review of municipal expenditures and revenues. In October 1963, the Mayor finally gave his approval to the setting up of the Temporary Commission on City Finances, a group of fiscal experts who were to study the problem and attempt to set the city on firm financial footing once again.

But the administration did little to adopt the desperately needed fiscal economies. In fact, by overestimating anticipated tax revenues, City Hall intensified the problem. In fiscal 1963–1964 alone, the administration overestimated its yield from four different sources—the sales tax, the general business tax, the financial business tax, and the tax on sales of city property—by nearly $70 million. By 1964, it had become apparent to almost everyone that there were not many more areas that could be profitably taxed. At that point, the city was collecting $2.321 billion in local revenues, $1.219 billion in real estate taxes, $460 million in sales and various user taxes, $208 million in a regressive gross-receipts tax, and $433 million from other sources. The city sales tax, which had been increased from 3 to 4 per cent in 1963–1964, was a dismal failure, and did not produce anywhere near the anticipated revenue. And the adoption of a state-wide sales tax in 1965 further complicated the city's financial problems.

Yet not even the Mayor's most outspoken fiscal critics were prepared for his budget message of 1965–1966. To obtain the $255 million that was needed to close the gap between the record spending program he projected and revenues then available, the mayor planned to increase the real estate tax. However, even though businessmen opposed the increase and predicted that it would further stimulate the already critical exodus of manufacturing concerns from the city, it was not the tax itself that outraged Comptroller Beame and nearly every other fiscal expert in the city. In order to increase the real estate taxes, New York City first had to obtain an amendment to the state constitution—a complicated process involving the passage of the amendment by two successive legislatures and approval by the voters of a referendum. The Mayor, therefore, could not hope to get the full authorization before January 1, 1967. In the meantime, he proposed to borrow $255 million he needed to balance his budget. The loan would then be paid off from the real estate taxes collected after the amendment has been passed.

Never had the critics of the administration's fiscal program been provided with such ammunition. If the Mayor had planned ahead and practiced long-range fiscal procedures, they said, he would have been able to anticipate the 1965–1966 deficit, which many of them had predicted, and could have sought the real estate taxing power two years before. By not doing this, he had not only placed the 1965–1966 budget on very unstable ground but had left himself—or his successor—with an even bigger fiscal problem for 1966–1967.

A *New York Times* editorial excoriated the Mayor for his actions:

> The city would borrow at the rate of $250 million a year until the voters of New York State approved in referendum a constitutional amendment relaxing the city's property tax restrictions. If they turned down the proposal, the city would be in deep, deep trouble. So while Mr. Wagner pictures this as a budget reflecting "responsive" government, what it really is is irresponsible government.

After all the lip-service paid to long-range fiscal planning to avoid perennial crisis, it is simply incredible that City Hall could so badly foresee the future that it did not, a year or two ago, lay the groundwork for the orderly financing of budgetary increases that are as certain as night following day. Because of past overreliance on borrowing, debt service is $595 million—up $81 million over this year. It constitutes 14 per cent of the entire budget. Yet to avoid an unpleasant tax, the Mayor would now add millions of dollars to interest charges by borrowing even more heavily and for current expenses. This is not a sound budget. "Balanced" only by wishful thinking, on the iffy hope that the voters will pull the city out of a hole a year and a half hence, it is a glaring example of political makeshift.[8]

Yet, if the city's fiscal affairs were in serious disorder, the governmental structure, consisting of more than fifty different departments and agencies and more than a hundred special committees, was totally chaotic —virtually impossible for one man to administer and virtually impossible for the average citizen to comprehend, with increasing waste and duplication and little attempt at coordinated planning.

Ever since 1938, when the last charter attempt was made to consolidate city agencies, the proliferation of municipal agencies had been astounding. Excluding the mass of committees, some permanent, many long forgotten, a staggering list of new departments had been created.[9]

In study after study, the need for municipal reform and reorganization was made abundantly clear. As early as 1953, the Temporary State Commission to Study the Organizational Structure of the Government of the City of New York reported:

---

[8] Mayor Wagner, in his last year in office, was able to get the state legislature to approve the amendment once. However, in 1966, when Mayor Lindsay tried to get the Democratic-controlled legislature to approve it the necessary second time and put it on the ballot, the legislature rejected it. In effect, then, Mayor Wagner borrowed funds in anticipation of a tax that New York never received.

[9] Division of Veterans Affairs (1944); Youth Board (1947); Division of Radio Broadcasting (1948); Office of Civil Defense (1950); Department of Traffic (1950); Board of Hospitals (1950); Air Pollution Control Dept. (1952); Air Pollution Control Board (1952); Interdepartmental Health Council (1952); Department of Personnel (1954); Department of Labor (1954); Community Mental Health Board (1954); Department of Commerce & Public Events (1954); Committee on Intergroup Relations (1955); Board of Ethics (1959); Department of Real Estate (1959); Emergency Control Board (1961); Housing & Redevelopment Board (1961); Office of Coordinator of Narcotics Control (1961); Youth Counsel Bureau (1961); Landmarks Preservation Commission (1962); Department of Relocation (1962); Rent & Rehabilitation Commission (1962); Commission on Human Rights (1962); Department of Public Events (1962); Department of Commerce & Industrial Development (1962); Council Against Poverty (1964); Anti-Poverty Operations Board (1964); Economic Opportunity Committee (1964).

As social and economic units, the great metropolitan centers of the country have outgrown the organization of their governments. Governmental structures designed for a different day and a different set of problems have proved inadequate to meet the demands of a population that has multiplied rapidly and spread far beyond the borders of the original cities. Constitutional and other legal structures imposed in a predominantly rural era restrict the ability of cities to respond effectively to new conditions. Administrative machinery designed to serve a relatively small community has been patched and repaired and expanded piecemeal to perform many new services for a population that expects a great deal in the way of welfare and service activities. Consequently, throughout the country, the large cities have been in varying states of crisis and in varying stages of response to the crisis.[10]

Yet, like most past reports calling for drastic changes in the city's municipal structure, this one was given a prominent place on the bookshelves of most city officials, but brought little positive or concrete reform. As governmental experts Professors Wallace Sayre and Herbert Kaufman concluded:

The gaps between the proposals and the changes actually made provide much of the grist for the next administrative survey and its new packages of recommendations. Administrative reorganization and management improvement efforts thus tend to become a continuous activity within the city's governmental and political system.[11]

Thus, while foundation after foundation and special committee after special committee pondered the city's burgeoning bureaucracy and made recommendations that gathered dust for the most part, New York's administrative structure became more cumbersome and more impractical. It is impossible to comprehend the city's Rube Goldberg structure without specific examples.[12]

(1) Three separate city agencies had jurisdiction over the paving of city streets. The Department of Highways paved the thoroughfares of the city except those on bridges across navigable streams and those which are

---

[10] Report of the Temporary State Commission to Study the Organizational Structure of the Government of the City of New York, 1953, p. 28.

[11] Wallace S. Sayre and Herbert Kaufman, *Governing New York City: Politics in the Metropolis* (New York: Russell Sage Foundation, 1960), p. 734.

[12] Herbert Hoover pointed out a similar situation in 1925 when he reported on the federal government's custodianship of the nation's bears. Mr. Hoover learned and reported that brown bears were under the jurisdiction of the Department of Agriculture, grizzly bears under the Treasury Department, and polar bears under Hoover's own Department of Commerce.

either in the parks or denominated "parkways." The Department of Public Works had the responsibility for paving streets over bridges. And the Department of Parks was charged with paving and maintaining parkways and streets through parks. All three maintained engineering and labor forces of their own to perform these functions.

(2) The Department of Water Supply, Gas, and Electricity was charged with making studies of use, present and future needs, and reserve requirements of the water supply system, and prepared studies of population growth projections to determine future needs. So, however, did the Board of Water Supply, which used different statistical bases and, consequently, produced widely different answers to the same questions about future water needs.

(3) Approximately thirty job training, career development, and placement programs were administered by a galaxy of city agencies—ranging from the Department of Welfare to the Port Authority.

(4) The Department of Health operated well-baby clinics; the Department of Hospitals operated sick-baby clinics; the Bureau of School Health of the Department of Health maintained school clinics. Thus, one child might be treated at any one of these agencies; yet at no place was there a single, unified record of his medical history.

(5) Four different agencies operated slum rehabilitation programs with city and federal money; yet there was no over-all policy or co-ordination among them.

(6) Routine chest X-rays were taken by the Department of Health in the neighborhoods and by the Department of Hospitals within clinics. Immunizations, routine examinations for working papers, and summer jobs were handled in the Health Department but not in Department of Hospitals facilities. This meant that a patient identified with a Department of Hospitals facility for on-going care had to go to a Department of Health facility in another building for the other services.

(7) Eight separate city agencies shared partial responsibility for the winter emergency housing repair program. Responsibility for rehabilitation and repair of buildings was dispersed among six different agencies.

(8) Public assistance recipients were entitled to complete dentistry, which was provided at only one place in each borough. Their children, however, could go to the Department of Health facilities, which provided care up to the age of fourteen. The Department of Hospitals facilities only pulled teeth. For example, at the Morrisania Dental Clinic in the Bronx, the facility was split each day between the Department of Hospitals and Health personnel, but there was no co-ordination because the two departments could not agree on technique. The same two departments maintained their own computer systems, which did not relate to each other. They also

had nursing and social service divisions that rarely communicated with each other. Additionally, each had a bureau for tuberculosis control, conducted its own chest X-ray programs, and maintained individual inspection teams for proprietary nursing homes and hospitals.

(9) Information about real property and buildings in the city was collected by every one of six different agencies, yet was not systematically exchanged.[13]

As impossible as it was for the Mayor to administer this management nightmare rationally, it had become equally impossible for the citizen who needed help the most to be able to work his way through the maze to find it.

As was pointed out by a 1966 study group, headed by Mitchell Sviridoff:

> The social service structure in the city is a labyrinth. Even if a client succeeds in finding his way through the maze, he does not always find a sympathetic response. One civic organization characterized the problem this way: People can get help if they know exactly what they need; where to get it; can spare the time, money and energy to travel a long way to the source; can afford to wait their turn once they get there; to not mind the occasional indifference or hostility of a receptionist; and shed anxiety and distrust when they finally get to see the man or woman in charge. The problem is that those who are most in need of service are likely to be the least resourceful, with the result that the better equipped get most and the neediest least.[14]

This was New York City of 1965—a government increasingly estranged from its citizenry, a government strangling in its own bureaucracy, a government on the verge of fiscal bankruptcy, a government left to drift by the business establishment, and, perhaps most significant, a government moving aimlessly without meaningful goals and ignoring even those social indicators available to it.

Though it was still possible that New York might not be ungovernable, it was apparent to nearly everyone that New York City of 1965 was being governed neither effectively nor meaningfully. A special City Club of New York report concluded:

> City government need not act only in response to pressure. . . .
> The city is facing the worst crisis of its life. It is facing a crisis of worsening problems that do not respond to the politics of drift and get by. . . . We need tangible evidence of the ability of the city's

---

[13] Examples of waste contained in the Mayor's Task Force on Reorganization of New York City Government, December 1966, pp. 12–16.

[14] *Developing New York City's Human Resources,* Vol. 1, June 1966, p. 29.

leadership, public and private, to achieve the essential goals. Hope deferred maketh the heart sick. But action can mobilize the city's greatest resource—the aspirations of its people.[15]

THE PRESENT: GOVERNMENT
BY EXPERIMENT

Not long after John Lindsay took office as Mayor of New York in January of 1966, two of his aides, both newcomers to municipal government, were trying to track down everyone on the City Hall payroll of the previous administration. It was, to say the least, a unique experience.

Some people occupying space in City Hall did not appear on the Mayor's payroll. Others appeared on his payroll but were working out of various departments. And there were even a few on his payroll whom no one had seen for months.

Each door that they opened seemed to produce another example of unusual management practices. Finally, one of the assistants, an expert in corporate management, shook his head in disbelief.

"You know," he said, "if I owned this business, I'd sell it immediately."

It was a funny line, but it did not take them long to discover how funny it really was—in early 1966 it would have been extremely difficult to find anyone willing to take the City of New York for nothing.

Without doubt, the biggest difference between the city government of 1965 and the city government of 1966 was reflected in the totally different attitudes and personalities of the two men who ran them.

Mayor Wagner was like a baseball batter who likes to wait out every pitch, looking for a walk, swinging only when necessary, dependable but not colorful, and consistent but too cautious to break up a ball game. Lindsay, on the other hand, was a free swinger, going for anything close to the plate, looking for the big hit, colorful and able to break up a ball game, and inconsistent but dramatic even when he struck out.

"It is better to make 100 bold and imaginative decisions and chance being wrong five times, than to play it safe and make no decisions at all," Lindsay said. "If New York City is to be governed properly, its government should be intolerant of waste, impatient with delay and capable of fast, decisive action in carrying out its policies and programs."

---

[15] *Goals for New York: A Challenge to Greatness in the Life of Our City,* City Club of New York, 1965.

With these words, despite the advice of many people to take his time before trying to change the city, Lindsay plunged into what has to be the most action-filled government year in New York since LaGuardia took over a bankrupt administration and drove it back to health.[16]

Unlike his predecessor, Lindsay quickly demonstrated his belief that government should be visible, and visibly, day after day, he began to battle to change the city. Though his batting average was not as high as he or many of the people who voted for him would have liked, it was still remarkably impressive. In the short space of one year, he took on most of the New York establishment—ranging from Mike Quill and the Transit Authority (he won a moral victory, but it cost the city money) to the Police Department (he won and is bringing streamlined methods to the department, but he lost his Civilian Review Board) and from the establishment (he has drawn business and corporate leaders into civic participation to a greater degree than ever before) to the ghetto (he has been unable to change the basic conditions of the ghetto, but is one of the most popular mayors in ghetto history).

Unlike Wagner, he has made errors of commission (critics point to his handling of the transit strike and his haste in establishing tow-away regulations on which he had to back down a few days later), but, more significant, he has already brought sorely needed reform and the first sign of order to a city of chaos—in finances, in program budgeting, in the establishment of long-range planning, in governmental reorganization, in attracting top urbanists from all over the country, many of them Democrats, and in the recognition, accumulation, and use of social indicators in laying out meaningful social goals for the future in a host of other areas.[17]

It was in his struggle to bring fiscal reform to New York City that Lindsay set the tone for the first year of his administration. Immediately rejecting the previous administration's "borrow now, pay later" plan, Lindsay quickly instituted a job freeze and other economies (none of which equaled his campaign promises, however), put through a sweeping tax

---

[16] "LaGuardia used to read the comics to the kiddies," Lindsay often has said, "and I read tragedies to the adults."

[17] Among the nationally recognized experts whom Lindsay has attracted to New York are Police Commissioner Howard Leary, Philadelphia; Corporation Counsel J. Lee Rankin, former Solicitor General of the United States; Human Resources Administrator Mitchell Sviridoff, New Haven; Budget Director Frederick Hayes, Washington, D.C.; Welfare Commissioner Mitchell Ginsberg, Columbia University; Corrections Commissioner George McGrath, former Correction Commissioner of Massachusetts; Air Pollution Commissioner Austin Heller, United States Public Health Service; Housing Administrator Jason Nathan, Federal Urban Renewal Administration; Housing Authority Chairman Walter Washington, head of Public Housing in District of Columbia; and Recreation and Cultural Affairs Administrator August Heckscher, former head of the Twentieth Century Fund.

program featuring a stock transfer tax and a personal income tax that included commuters for the first time, raised subway and bus fares 5 cents to 20 cents (breaking another campaign promise), and managed to bridge a huge $500 million deficit. In one year of a new administration, New York's expense budget was on a pay-as-you-go basis once again.

Lindsay's fiscal achievements and reform did not come easily—he had to fight publicly with Governor Nelson Rockefeller who was facing an election campaign, and he did not make many friends by increasing transit fares—but it was a fight that fiscal and management experts believe had to be made regardless of the costs.

"A year old administration has grappled bravely, sometimes frustratedly with finances and services," wrote Harold Riegelman of the Citizens Budget Commission. "Its efforts have been sincere, in the right direction and fruitful to a remarkable degree considering the dimensions of the accumulated trouble." [18]

Despite a lowering of the city's credit rating from good to better medium grade[19] and an estimated budget gap in excess of $300 million in 1967–1968, the Wagner-appointed Temporary Commission on City Finances and the First National City Bank are convinced that New York City has finally turned the fiscal and economic corner.

The Temporary Commission on City Finances concluded in its final report:

> Does this dilemma, still severe despite progress against it, mean that New York is ungovernable and in permanent decline? The answer is no. We feel instead that New York is now beginning to achieve some fiscal improvement. The magnitude and urgency of the situation are widely recognized. The Mayor advocates economy, greater revenue and the elimination of current expense borrowing. Some new revenues have been authorized. The groundwork has been laid, too, for better personal practices, improved transportation coordination, larger intergovernmental aid, and more effective municipal management. The administration can move forward from these hopeful beginnings during the next three years.[20]

---

[18] New York: A New Course, Citizens Budget Commission Annual Report 1966, p. 3.

[19] Even in lowering the city's credit rating, thereby raising the interest that New York must pay on its bonds, Standard & Poors commented: "Mayor Lindsay has made considerable progress in the fiscal area and the city's continuing ability to meet debt requirement is, of course, not questioned. Despite these unmistakable points of strength, New York is the leading example of the blight that has centered on major cities. This has produced staggering fiscal problems. The problems will not soon be resolved."

[20] Temporary Commission on City Finances, Final Report, August 1966, p. 3.

TABLE 1—Sources of City Revenues: Expense Budget, City of New York, 1965–1966 to 1967–1968
(in Millions of Dollars)

Item	1965–1966		1966–1967			1967–1968
	Authorized	Adjusted[a]	Proposed By City	Authorized By Legislature and Council	Estimated By Commission	Estimated By Commission
Real Estate Tax	$1,408	$1,408	$1,573	$1,573	$1,573	$1,670
General Fund:						
Sales Tax	396	389	370	380	377	390
Business and Financial Taxes[b]	211	214	292	280	268	290
Income and Earnings Taxes	—	—	385	160	144	150
Stock Transfer Tax	80	90[c]	150	170[c]	160[c]	140
Water Charges	54	50	83	83	83	100
Commercial Occupancy Tax	71	72	73	73	73	75
Cigarette Tax	40	33	33	38	35	35
Other General Fund Revenues[d]	223	222	225	242	242	251
	$1,075	$1,070	$1,611	$1,426	$1,382	$1,431
Less: Revenue Anticipation Notes	56	45	56	45	45	45
	$1,019	$1,025	$1,555	$1,381	$1,337	$1,386
Grants and Aid:						
State Per Capita Aid[d]	$ 98	$ 99	$ 99	$ 99	$ 99	$ 99
State Functional Grants[d]	700	710	782	805	805	880
Federal Aid (Some via State)	264	347	508	508	508	565
	$1,062	$1,156	$1,389	$1,412	$1,412	$1,544
Miscellaneous Revenues	$ 74	$ 75	$ 98	$ 143	$ 143	$ 100
Total Revenues	$3,563	$3,664	$4,615	$4,509	$4,465	$4,700
Deficit	312	301	0	45	35	400
Total Expenditures	$3,875	$3,965	$4,615	$4,554	$4,500	$5,100

a Estimated by the Commission from *tentative* end-of-year figures.

b Gross Receipts and Financial Taxes, 1965–1966. Business Income and Related Taxes, 1966–1967 and 1967–1968. Some collections for both 1966–1967 and 1967–1968, included here in those years, will actually occur in the first fifteen days of the subsequent fiscal year since the final collection date for each year has been shifted to July 15.

c Stock transfer tax revenues of $20 million, actually received by the City from the State in 1965–1966, were not taken up in the general fund until 1966–1967. Hence, this $20 million is here excluded from 1965–1966 but included in 1966–1967.

d Per capita aid is included in the General Fund in City accounting but is shown here under Grants and Aid. In addition to State assistance shown under Grants and Aid, the State makes other payments to the City from shared taxes and for special purposes, mostly taken up in the General Fund. The figures for Total State Assistance, including these payments for the years shown in the table, are: $943 authorized and $967 adjusted for 1965–1966; $1,098 proposed, $1,186 authorized, and $1,176 estimated for 1966–1967; $1,186 estimated for 1967–1968.

And in its report, the First National City Bank also liked what it saw:

The problem of assuring a healthy future for New York City is not a simple one. However, the city already has the resources to solve its problems and at the same time to set a proud example to cities throughout the nation in tackling the multitude of difficulties besetting them. New York City contains within itself the seeds of its own redemption. What is needed now is an effective marshalling of these resources in a unified report to overcome the problems affecting the city.[21]

Listed as "very encouraging signs" in this economic survey were Mayor Lindsay's "positive attitude toward business"; a strengthened program to facilitate the growth of businesses in the city; the "concern of the City Planning Commission with the future needs and requirements of the business community"; and the involvement of prominent business leaders in an Economic Development Council and a New York Public Development Corporation.

Yet it was in the sweeping governmental reorganization—and the initiation of program budgeting that is integrated with it—that Lindsay has changed the face of New York's government the most. He has done away with more than a hundred special committees and proposed the reorganization of more than fifty departments and agencies into ten administrations, each under an administrator who reports directly to the Mayor. The Police and Fire Departments report directly to the Mayor and are not in an administration. The ten administrations are: Corrections, Economic Development, Environmental Protection, Financial Management, General Services, Health Services, Housing and Development, Human Resources, Recreation and Cultural Affairs, and Transportation.

Though he was able to put some of these changes into effect by executive order, Mayor Lindsay was forced to go before the Democratic-controlled City Council seeking approval for the vast majority of the reorganization. By spring 1967, the City Council still had not acted on the reorganization package. The Mayor told the Council:

We cannot obtain the maximum production from every dollar we spend with an old line, traditionally bureaucratic government administration any more than the Ford Motor Company can remain one of the top three by operating out of its original backyard garage. Reorganization will reduce or end duplication of services. Reorganization will enable us to share more facilities. Reorganization will centralize rational policy-making. Reorganization will

---

[21] *Metropolis New York: An Economic Survey,* First National City Bank, November 1966, pp. 20, 21.

TABLE 2—Sources of City Revenues: Expense Budget as Adopted,
City of New York, 1954–1955 to 1966–1967
(in Millions of Dollars)

Fiscal Year	Expense Budget[a]	Real Estate Tax Levy	General Fund	State Aid	Federal Aid	Supplemental Revenues
1954–1955	$1,596	$ 746	$ 527	$196	$ 69	$ 58
1955–1956	1,736	808	558	220	76	74
1956–1957	1,854	858	601	259	74	61
1957–1958	1,934	875	648	268	81	62
1958–1959	1,992	932	621	303	88	46
1959–1960	2,175	978	730	318	99	49
1960–1961	2,345	1,027	796	373	99	51
1961–1962	2,542	1,069	879	399	142	54
1962–1963	2,785	1,133	955	486	152	59
1963–1964	3,083	1,219	1,124	502	178	60
1964–1965	3,355	1,312	1,232	548	199	64
1965–1966	3,875	1,408	1,173	708	264	323[b]
1966–1967	4,554	1,573	1,525	876	508	72

[a] Totals of revenues may not add exactly to Expense Budget, due to rounding.
[b] Includes proceeds of then pending legislation to permit issuance of $256 million in 5-year serial bonds.
Source: Annual Reports of the Committee on Finance of the New York City Council . . . with respect to the Budget Tax Levy and Tax Rates for the Fiscal Year.

give the Mayor a more clear-cut, responsive executive arm through which to communicate instructions and control performance. Most important, reorganization will give city government a greater sensitivity and fluidity in fulfilling the need of its citizens. It will break down, in human and professional terms, the present municipal monolith.[22]

Though critics of the reorganization (virtually every major civic group supported all or part of it) claimed that it would merely add another, high-salaried layer of bureaucracy to city government, support for the programs came from some surprising places.

"New York City's reorganization plan seems like a step in the right direction," commented former Vice-President Hubert Humphrey. "The trouble with most cities has been that their administration is so hopelessly outdated that they have been unable to key in with many federal programs just because of poor coordination."

In his 1967 State of the Union Message, President Johnson said:

---

[22] Mayor Lindsay's speech before New York City Council, January 26, 1967.

Each state and county and city needs to examine its capacity for government in today's world. . . . Some will need to reorganize and reshape their methods of reorganization and reshape their methods of administration. . . . Change is the law of life. Those who look only to the past or the present are certain to miss the future.

And, in 1966, when he signed Executive Order 11297 instructing the Department of Housing and Urban Development to create special groups to meet with local officials on urban problems, the President said:

With this order, we have taken a step forward in the federal government. But the Mayors and city officials . . . are on the front line in the city itself where the battle against blight, ignorance, disease and poverty must be waged and won.

Thus I urge city and state governments to follow our example and improve the lines of communication and coordination. In this way, we can work together with unity of purpose to bring the good life to people in every American City.[23]

The most immediate—and probably the most lasting—changes of the reorganization come in the areas of human resources and housing. In a city in which every fourth family earns less than $4,000 a year and in which previous poverty and job training programs have lacked the necessary co-ordination to make a meaningful dent in the problem, the Human Resources Administration, which proposes to bring all the programs under one roof and interrelate them, offers new hope that New York's deprived might finally be able to break out of the ghetto.

In the report *Developing New York City Human Resources*, Mitchell Sviridoff speaks more specifically:

If a head of a family has completed training courses, there must be follow-up to help him find a job. If family problems jeopardize his performance, social services must be brought into play to relieve the pressure. If one of his children needs day care, it must be provided. A school-age child must get the kind of education that fits his talents and prepares him for a career of opportunity. These services are funded and operated by many different agencies. The father's training course may be federally financed; the job may be located through the State Employment Service and in co-operation with employer and labor groups; the social services may be city-sponsored; day care may be provided through voluntary agencies

---

[23] Two federal acts that recently included strong wording requiring streamlined municipal governments as a prerequisite for receiving funds are the Demonstration Cities and the Economic Opportunities Acts, which should bring New York under its reorganization more than $120 million next year.

or through community action under the antipoverty program; guidance counselling and education are, of course, the job of the public school system. The problem is to pull all these services together in terms of a set of clear over-all objectives.[24]

Additionally, in a city in which some 500,000 New York families cannot find suitable housing and in which 800,000 dwelling units (nearly one-third of the city inventory) are located in deteriorating areas, the reorganization is expected to provide several new directions in the housing area, to speed up construction, and to put the city in a position where it can qualify for increased federal funds. The most noticeable change: rather than spread the projects throughout the city, it plans an all-out effort to rehabilitate the city's three major slum ghettos—Harlem, South Bronx, and Central Brooklyn.

Running throughout the entire reorganization is Mayor Lindsay's decision to integrate the capital and expense budgeting processes and to bring program planning and budgeting, introduced in the Department of Defense by Secretary Robert S. McNamara, to New York as a means of establishing indicators and determining goals for the future. New York City's traditional system of expense budgeting—like that of most other cities—can tell you certain things—for example, how much the city is spending for how many employees, supplies, and equipment in each department. Yet what it fails to show are the facts that are most valuable to those charged with making policy, developing programs, and trying to measure performance—namely, what programs the money will buy, could buy, or should buy.

The primary aim of a program-planning-budget system is to guarantee a more efficient and more effective use of the city's financial resources. This is achieved by defining various governmental activities in terms of program objectives and then evaluating the alternative ways to reach these objectives with the emphasis on providing the most service per dollar expended.

Under the traditional system of municipal budgeting, the Sanitation Commissioner would present the Mayor with a budget request calling for, let us say, 200 new trucks, 3 new incinerators, and 1,000 additional men to operate them. He would be able to present certain supporting data, but, in the end, there is really no broad standard or indicator to measure his request. Too often, the final evaluation might be the result of a table-pounding session between the Commissioner and Budget Director about whether he really needed 200 new trucks.

Under program-planning-budgeting, the Commissioner will present his request in a totally different manner. He can start by saying that one of his department's long-range objectives is the removal of waste. With 200 new

[24] Mitchell Sviridoff, *Developing New York City Human Resources,* Vol. 1 (New York: Institute of Public Administration, 1966), p. 8.

trucks, 3 new incinerators, and 1,000 more men, he can point out, he will be able to keep x amount of city streets x per cent cleaner than they are at present. No longer will the city administration be asked to buy 200 yellow sanitation trucks; instead the question now will be the amount of waste disposal that the money would buy. With a tight budget and effective program budgeting, the city administration no longer will have to make a choice between 200 new sanitation trucks or 300 new police cars. The police cars could be evaluated in terms of increased number of miles that would be patroled and a projected decrease in the crime rate in the area to be patroled. Therefore, this fundamental resource allocation, under program budgeting, will be viewed as a choice between a measurable degree of increased waste disposal and a degree of decreased incidents

For the first time, New York City and its officials should be able to make valued judgments—based on indicators and long-range goals—on budget allocations rather than bending to neighborhood pressures. Mayor Lindsay explained:

> When I say we must establish a capability in city government for orderly program planning, I do not mean we can anticipate every crisis—or that having anticipated a crisis, we can invariably prevent it. But I do mean that we can, if we have the appropriate administrative machinery, acquire the necessary information to make decisions on such matters as:
> "Is it more important to treat narcotic addicts in Harlem or to build day-care centers in East Jamaica?"
> "Should we use prime portions of the Staten Island shoreline for recreation or for commercial purposes?"
> "Should we commit capital funds to building another East Side subway or pledge them to reconstruction of the West Side Highway?"
> Similar issues are presented to the Mayor daily. With clear lines of authority and communication, and more direct administrative control, it will be possible to demand of our city agencies realistic long-range estimates which will enable us to find answers to these and other critical questions. A current question is:
> "If we embark on, or continue a particular program, how much will it cost us to maintain the same level of service two or three or four years from now? Where will we find the money to do it?
> The ability to determine that answer, regularly and accurately, is invaluable to the future of New York's government and the well-being of the city it governs.[25]

In this age in which all of our country's cities look once again to New York for solutions, these experiments to govern not by computer, but by human decision and human reason, based on sound indicators and data, are a key to the future development of the city of man.

---

[25] Speech by Mayor Lindsay before City Council, January 26, 1967.

THE FUTURE: GOVERNMENT
BY REASON

American government should be wise and frugal, which shall restrain men from injuring one another, which shall leave them otherwise free to regulate their own pursuits of industry and improvement, and shall not take from the mouth of labor the bread it has earned. This is the sum of good government, and this is necessary to close the circle of our felicities.

THOMAS JEFFERSON

To a great many people, the future of the modern city, the direction it will take into the twenty-first century, will be considerably determined by the success or failure of the present years of experimentation in New York.

What does the immediate future hold for New York City?

Fiscal experts agree that the city must receive substantially increased federal and state aid.

It is for this reason that the City of New York has opened its own office in Washington.

It is for this reason that Mayor Lindsay and the mayors of several of our country's other major cities have been meeting to discuss and set urban priorities so that they can lobby as an unprecedented urban bloc for additional federal funds.

And it is for this reason that Mayor Lindsay and several other mayors, most of them Democrats, have joined together to press for a federal tax-sharing program.

Additionally, particularly in transportation and air and water pollution and conservation, the city administration already is moving toward developing greater regional ties to seek regional solutions.

Of high priority in New York this year is the State Constitutional Convention. For the city administration, the key issues will revolve around attempts to seek increased home rule powers, particularly in the area of taxation and possibly in the area of education. Though the Mayor of New York must answer for the actions of the city's school system, he has little control over the budget and, what is more important, he does not get his fourth appointment to the seven-member Board of Education until the spring of his fourth and last year in office. In other words, a first-term Mayor must answer for the inadequacies of the educational system (as Mayor Lindsay has during the recent integration troubles in East Harlem and Brooklyn), yet in no way can he change these policies, as offensive as they may be to him.

Also in the future will be a renewed attempt to establish a chain of Neighborhood Mayors' Offices throughout the City, thereby bringing services directly to the people and trying to involve people in their government once again. The proposal, twice rejected by the Democratic City Council because it does not want a Republican Mayor supplying services in the neighborhoods, as needed and as welcome as they may be, will not be dropped. One Neighborhood City Hall, established in East New York with private contributions after the racial disturbances last summer, has already demonstrated its value to the community and will serve as a pilot model for others if the City Council continues to withhold city money for the program. As the Mayor pointed out:

> If the people were getting what they need in services through political clubs and the Councilmanic system, there would be no need for this program. But there is a great need here and I am committed to see it operate on a citywide basis.

Commitment alone, however, will not be enough to save our cities. Even if Mayor Lindsay is able to change the fiscal and structural face of New York significantly, thereby making it possible to govern meaningfully, there is no guarantee that he can attract the sorely needed middle management experts and bright young people to make sure that his programs are carried through at all levels of government. Additionally, even with the government regrouped into ten administrations, there will always remain the problem of making each of the administrators work together with the others for the common good rather than work to protect and enhance his own special interest.

One possible solution is the use of task forces set up independently of the city government and free of the bureaucracy, but with good access to City Hall itself. These task forces—made up of specialists and special interest people who would work for a task force but not for the city full-time—would not only bridge the gap between the administrations, but would also provide a continuing stream of alternatives for the man at the top.

Yet even here it would be up to the Mayor himself to decide whether he would actually utilize the task forces in decision-making or merely use them to buy time and public opinion. During the first fifteen months of his administration, Mayor Lindsay relied heavily on the findings of several task forces—notably those recommending reorganization of government and the poverty and housing programs.

In addition, Lindsay has centered in the office of the Deputy Mayor–City Administrator the collection and co-ordination of meaningful social indicators and their use in evaluating and determining governmental action.

The City Administrator's office has been working closely with research groups at several of the city's universities, developing meaningful data in several areas—notably in health, education, library, and sanitation services.

Here, too, however, the problem lies not so much in the collection and evaluation of the data as in its being put to a meaningful use, and not merely occupying space on someone's bookshelf.

Actually, it all depends on the man at the top—the man who ultimately must make the decisions. If he finds it easier or more expedient to govern by crisis rather than by reason, the collection of all the social indicators in the world, no matter how meaningful they may be, will be little more than busy-work. If, however, he chooses to govern by reason, there is no limit to the role that meaningful indicators can play in the decision-making process.

Can government by reason succeed in a city so vast, so complex, and so troubled as New York? No one can know for 'sure after only one year of a new administration. Mistakes have been made, and others will be made. But, to a great many people, these mistakes are clearly the price of urban progress, a progress that will one day enable a Mayor of New York to deliver a candid annual message on the "State of the City," or the "State of the Metropolis," substituting honest appraisals of its present and future needs for the traditional recital of accomplishments.

How far is New York away from preparing a true State of the City Message, one in which physical and social plans and goals are outlined and the minuses are presented as candidly as the pluses?

The answer, hopefully, is that such a possibility is not far away. Though there is presently a scarcity of reliable indicators, it is anticipated that program budgeting and independent research will produce the sorely needed data.

It will then be up to the man at the top to make his choice. And, in a visible government, ruled by reason, the choice would seem obvious.

20

URBAN ENVIRONMENT: GENERAL

DANIEL P. MOYNIHAN

A characteristic theme of American politics at this time, and an emerging element of American sensibility, is that of "urban crisis." Shorn of a tendency to overdo, much of this comes down to a common-sense concern with the immediate social and physical environment on the part of a society that has been perhaps overmuch involved with questions of cosmic import—and cosmic inscrutability. This tendency is likely to become more, not less pronounced: the current military involvement in Asia is demonstrating to the nation clearly enough that there are limits to its desire to manage the world, just as there are limits to the world's desire to be managed. Peace is likely to bring a very considerable inward turning, and this is more than likely to be defined in terms of an "attack" (there is no avoiding an excess of aggressiveness in American life) on the problems of cities. Current expositions of the subject, for example, the hearings conducted by Senator Abraham Ribicoff's Subcommittee on Executive Reorganization of the United States Senate Committee on Government Operations, as well as President Johnson's plans for a model cities program, provide the rudiments of a postwar planning program. The proposals will be there when, as may be the case, the national government is, of a sudden, looking about for something else to do. Moreover, in a nation that increasingly senses the immense burdens imposed by the racial barriers and hostilities of the present, concern for "urban affairs" is certain to emerge as the most acceptable code word for "Negro" problems —and the white attitudes that give rise to so many of them.

In the familiar pattern, this poses both an opportunity and a problem for the social sciences. Irving Louis Horowitz has put it thus: "The problem of social policy becomes acute precisely to the degree to which social science becomes exact." The demonstrated feasibility of putting social science information and theory to work on social problems imposes a new and special set of strains both on policy-makers and on those who would advise them. To a degree that has not, perhaps, existed since the age of theological certitude, it becomes possible to be "right" or "wrong," and difficult—even impossible—to avoid scrutiny in just these terms. There is no turning back: we have bit this bullet, and had best get on with the slaughter of a good many of those cherished notions which are certain to perish in the first data runs. It will be easy enough to demonstrate what does not work: the job of social science must be to provide some plausible suggestions as to what will work.

THREE GENERAL PROPOSITIONS

Three general propositions may be made. First of all, it is essential that all concerned with the development of a system of urban social indicators be prepared in advance to find themselves accused of having betrayed some of those very causes with which they have been most allied. Concern about urban affairs derives directly from concern about urban problems: it involves the statement by certain persons that certain things are not as they ought to be, and must be changed for the better. Such attitudes are almost always minority views, at least in the beginning. As a group, however, American social scientists are peculiarly prone to sharing and prone to creating such concerns. They are problem-prone and reform-minded, and inevitably come to be seen as allies by those about whose problems they are most concerned. These latter, becoming accustomed to having social scientists on their side, easily come to assume that social science will be. This does not always happen, a fact not easily forgiven. Knowledge is power, and in contemporary society social scientists are often in the position of handing power about in an almost absent-minded way. Professional ethics, at least as ideally defined, can lead them to hand out the very best arguments to those whom they would consider the very worst contenders. This is a dilemma not yet well understood, and certainly not resolved. For the moment, the most that can be done is to be forewarned.[1]

The second proposition is that the way in which urban indicators are developed is likely to have considerable influence on the level of government—and of abstraction—at which the problems are dealt with. Specifically, if urban indicators remain for the most part "national" statistics, a powerful built-in tendency to seek "national" solutions will emerge.

---

[1] See Daniel P. Moynihan, "Education of the Urban Poor," Address to the Harvard Club and the M.I.T. Alumni Center of New York City, March 1, 1967, mimeographed.

This is no small matter. The economic policies of the federal government over the past two generations—beginning with the New Deal—have been brilliantly successful. But they have concentrated attention on data at the continental, even the global level—"aggregatics" in Bertram Gross's allusive term—to the exclusion, or at very least the neglect, of specific circumstances. Thus, the United States has, quite possibly, the best employment data in the world, but there is no city in the nation that knows what its unemployment rate is. And while the economy of the nation booms, sizzles, and soars, it has somehow become a practice for city workers to riot every summer; after which disturbances, enquiries determine that quite astonishing numbers of them were without work. An impressive number of contradictions have somehow slipped through the interstices of the macro-policy net. We are the richest nation on earth, with some of the worst slums; the most educated, with some of the most marginal school children; and the most mobile, with some of the most rigid caste confinements. One likely source of these contradictions is the reluctance, even the refusal, of many public organizations to report, much less to insist on, the relationship between their activities and concerns with other problems. This must be presumed to be part of the explanation behind Scott Greer's statement that "at a cost of more than three billion dollars, the Urban Renewal Agency has succeeded in materially reducing the supply of low cost housing in American cities." Insisting that one thing has nothing to do with another is likely to have the effect of intensifying rather than moderating the unavoidable interactions.

A third general consideration may be termed a matter of temperament. It has to do with the fact that urban social indicators are almost certainly going to be developed by professors and government executives who will be far more concerned with what is bad about cities than with what is good about them. These men will judge good and bad in terms of their own rather special values acquired in the course of family, religious, educational, and occupational experiences that, by and large, are quite different from those of the urban masses whose condition they will seek to measure. The idea of social indicators, and of an urban subset, is pre-eminently a product of the American intellectual world, although, of course, with a whole European tradition behind it. But the particular quality of the American intellectual—quite distinct from his European counterpart—has been the tendency to view cities with alarm, fear, and distaste, a history which Morton and Lucia White have summed up as "one of adverse metaphysical speculation and bad dreams about urban life, of aesthetic and moral recoil from the American city's ugliness, commercialism, and crime."[2] Surely

---

[2] Morton and Lucia White, *The Intellectual versus the City* (Cambridge, Mass.: Harvard University Press and M.I.T. Press, 1962), p. 75.

some measure of the present concern with ugliness, commercialism, and crime is simply an inversion of the earlier views: precisely the same judgment about cities is handed down, with only a gloss of compassion and concern that things might somehow be made otherwise. The view that when one is tired of London one is tired of life is not one that has met much favor on American campuses—nor yet the proposition put to Hennessy by Dooley that while the country might be where the good things in life come from, it is the city that they go *to*. Neither the great Tory nor the Chicago saloonkeeper spoke with the accents of liberal academia: the one too confident, the other too clever for that special world.

The task, then, is to make the most of the special kinds of sensibility that will be brought to bear on cities by this group, including one of its most attractive qualities, the awareness that tastes differ and a willingness to allow, even to encourage, them to do so. A further, almost a defining characteristic of American academics of the present age is the realization that everything has to do with everything else. American professors may be obscure, but they are hardly simple-minded. Their judgment as to what facts are relevant to the urban condition is likely to approach that condition itself in complexity and detail.

FOUR GUIDELINES

With these considerations in mind, it becomes possible to lay down four general guidelines for a system of urban social indicators, not so much as rules than as principles. It is contended merely that, to the extent information is organized along these principles, it is more likely than not to be useful and to be used.

FIRST, *URBAN SOCIAL INDICATORS*
SHOULD BE IN THE REALM
OF DISAGGREGATION AND
CORRELATION

To the greatest possible extent the data should be organized in terms of the Standard Metropolitan Statistical Areas (SMSA's) as defined by the Bureau of Census (there are now 227 SMSA's) and by census tract levels where this is highly significant, as in the case of poverty neighborhoods. Data should be organized in terms of political jurisdictions as well, so that they may be used by government organizations and by political candidates and parties. Moreover, if the relations between different phenomena are to be perceived and responded to in the workaday world of municipal affairs, it is necessary for the indicators to report such relations in the form of correlations and similar mathematical analyses, rather than to await the random initiatives of individual scholars. The relationships of functions such as unemployment to welfare dependency, to use but one example, are matters of fundamental interest to city government, but are rarely known, and even less often commented upon. Social indicators can bring these relations into the open, as it were, making them at once more visible and less threatening.

It will be obvious that some forms of urban indicators, such as air pollution or noise levels, are necessarily defined in terms of specific localities, and will automatically be reported in such terms. Similarly, there are apt to be many topics about which local data would be desirable, but for which survey costs would be greater than the likely return. The point in every instance is simply to collect as much specifically local data as resources permit.

SECOND, *INASMUCH AS URBAN SOCIAL INDICATORS CANNOT BE APOLITICAL, THEY MUST BE PAN-POLITICAL*

The very existence of such indicators is a political fact, responding to the desire of a small body of opinion that there should be greater awareness of urban problems—in order that there should be more effective political action in dealing with them. Such information cannot be neutral. The choice of what is to be included, the manner of presenting it and the interrelations that are sought out will reflect profound political attitudes and interests. They must, therefore, cater to as wide as possible a spectrum of political interests. Ideally, the volume of urban social indicators, should they become a reality, will be found on the desks of the head speech writers for all the mayoralty candidates in all the cities that are covered. What applies to the central cities should be equally the case for the surrounding suburbs: the distinction between city and suburb is merely a way of describing one aspect of the urban situation. The greatest danger of the enterprise is that the indicators will be shaped primarily in terms of the political attitudes and social programs of liberal Democrats, for the simple reason that most of the men conceiving the effort and carrying it forward will be of that persuasion. A deliberate effort should be made to include subjects of interest to other parties and more conservative points of view.

Crime is an important instance. It is, and for several generations has been, one of the most important political issues in the nation. There is probably no other issue that is so specifically identified by the public as an "urban" issue and an "urban" problem. It is also a racial problem. For that reason and for a combination of others, liberal academics have tended to ignore or skirt the issue, hoping, perhaps, that it would go away or in some way escape the attention of the public. Nothing of the sort has happened: crime in the streets has become, if anything, a more explosive issue as time has passed. Thus, in his special message proposing the Safe Streets and Crime Control Act of 1967, President Johnson reported that in a recent survey of two of our largest cities: "43 per cent of those interviewed stayed off the streets at night." A survey conducted for the Commission on Law Enforcement and the Administration of Justice showed that crime, after race relations, is clearly thought to be the most important domestic problem.[3] This is the kind of information that can be collected in the present and which can be built into a time series from which important political arguments and deductions can be derived.

Similarly, the racial component of crime must be lived with. The President's Commission on Crime in the District of Columbia has reported that Negro males committed 76 per cent of all serious offenses in the District in the years 1961–1965, and that Negro males and females together accounted for 86 per cent. This represents a rising proportion. In the decade 1950–1960, Negro males committed only 69 per cent of such offenses, while the male-female combination was only 77 per cent. These figures clearly correspond to the impressions of the white community, including the congressional community in the District, and these impressions will not recede simply because such information is not included in a series of urban indicators. If anything, the opposite might be the case: fears are often exaggerated, and will tend to persist for some time after the reality changes. Properly compiled urban crime statistics would probably show stable crime rates in terms of age groups, and will surely pick up declining crime rates well in advance of the popular perception. (Note the wide attention given to the recent announcement by the Bureau of Narcotics that the incidence of Negro drug addiction appears to be declining while that of whites is rising.) At a less heated level of concern is the Republican party's interest in increasing the opportunities of low-income Americans to own their own homes, as recently announced by Congressman Gerald R. Ford and Senator Charles H. Percy. This is a matter easily enough measured, and ought to be included in the housing data on American cities. As times passes, it may abet the Republican cause, or injure it, but in any event the indicators will be relevant to the political world which inspired them.

---

[3] *The Challenge of Crime in a Free Society,* Report by the President's Commission on Law Enforcement and Administration of Justice, February 1967, p. 51.

THIRD, *URBAN SOCIAL INDICATORS SHOULD BE CONCERNED WITH THE FUTURE AS WELL AS WITH THE PRESENT*

For some reason, government (and, to a lesser degree, business), although they collect and calculate a considerable range of "facts" about the future, are nonetheless curiously hesitant about making them public in any very assertive way. This is surely a mistake. Most public policy proceeds from assumptions as to what the future will be like, and these assumptions can often be significantly influenced by perfectly "knowable" information. In areas such as labor-force composition and school enrollment, this can be done with considerable accuracy, and can be used to much greater purpose than has been the case. As an example, current projections of the white and nonwhite population of the United States, when calculated in percentage terms, suggest that the school integration problem will be considerably greater than one might assume from the proposition that "Negroes make up about one-tenth of the population." The nonwhite proportion of the population between ages five and nine over the coming years is projected as follows:

TABLE 1—Projections of Nonwhite Proportion of United States
Population, 1970–1985

Year	High Fertility Projection (%)	Low Fertility Projection (%)
1970	15.8	15.8
1975	16.3	15.9
1980	16.7	15.9
1985	17.2	16.1

Source: Derived from *Current Population Reports: Population Estimates,* Series P-25, No. 345, July 29, 1966, "Projections of the White and Non-White Population of the United States, by Age and Sex, to 1985."

This would suggest, for example, that, in the very near future, upwards of one child in five entering public schools, nationally, will be nonwhite. Obviously, these proportions are much greater in certain central city areas, but, here again, it is possible to forecast with acceptable degrees of probable accuracy.

FOURTH, *URBAN INDICATORS* *SHOULD SEEK TO PROVIDE* *COMPARISONS BETWEEN LOCAL* *DATA, AVERAGE NATIONAL DATA,* *AND DATA CORRESPONDING TO* *"BEST PRACTICE" IN VARIOUS FIELDS*

The Council of Economic Advisors' well-established practice of including in their Annual Report an analysis of the "gap" between the actual and the potential gross national product provides an excellent instance of the power of this type of analysis to create pressures for more effective social and economic policies.[4] A quite startling instance of wide disparities in performance will be found in the Selective Service rejection rates. Thus, in 1965, 48 per cent of the young men called up in South Carolina failed the mental examination, as contrasted with a failure rate of 5 per cent in Iowa. A wide difference in rejection rates exists between whites and nonwhites, and very probably between social class and neighborhood, if the data were available at this level of disaggregation. In 1965, for example, the disqualification rate for white draftees of 14.7 per cent contrasts sharply with a mental disqualification rate for Negroes of 59.6 per cent. With effort, it is likely that a considerable range of national test performance of this kind could be disaggregated to local areas, perhaps health and school districts, with possibly important consequences in terms of local judgments as to the adequacy of community services. In North Carolina, for example, the high rate of Selective Service mental-test rejections has become an issue of considerable concern.

Those things being said, it remains only to assert Bertram Gross's formulation: The object of social indicators should be to report "the condition of man in the metropolitan area" and to do so in three categories: (1) people as individuals, (2) families, and (3) institutions.[5]

INDIVIDUALS

NUMBERS, DISTRIBUTION, AND DENSITY

The threshold data of any system of urban social indicators should be the direct census counts of individuals by age, sex, race, and any other

---

[4] See *Economic Report of the President,* January 1967, "The Annual Report of the Council of Economic Advisors," Chart 1, p. 43.

[5] Bertram M. Gross, "The City of Man: A Social Systems Reckoning," *Man's Environment: The Next 50 Years* (Bloomington: University of Indiana Press, 1967).

general categories that may emerge as relevant. This type of information will become increasingly more current and more accurate, but some effort should be made to indicate where the data is presently limited or not accurate. Thus the male-female ratio among nonwhites suggests not only that the information-gathering process is imperfect, but, much more important, that this is so because of a social problem of considerable dimensions.

TABLE 2—Ratio of Males per 100 Females in the Population
by Color, July 1, 1963

Age	Males per 100 Females	
	White	Nonwhite
Under 5	104.4	100.4
5–9 years	103.9	100.0
10–14 years	104.0	100.0
15–19 years	103.2	99.5
20–24 years	101.2	95.1
25–29 years	100.1	89.1
30–34 years	99.2	86.6
35–39 years	97.5	86.8
40–44 years	96.2	89.9
45–49 years	96.5	90.6

Source: *Current Population Reports,* Series P-25, No. 276, Table 1 (total population, including armed forces abroad).

The distribution of urban population in terms of race and income level is an indispensable set of urban data. Segregation indices, as outlined by Otis Dudley Duncan and Beverly Duncan,[6] should be compiled for every SMSA in the nation, and changes over time should be carefully recorded. Studies such as James Coleman's *Equality of Educational Opportunity* strongly suggest that the stratification of white neighborhoods into homogeneous social and economic groups will have the same impact on those in the lower white strata as does race segregation on lower-status Negroes. This would argue in favor of much more extensive efforts to learn how this kind of "one-class" white neighborhood is developing, particularly in low-density suburbanized areas.

Techniques of computer mapping are advancing rapidly, and are readily adaptable to this type of use. They are similarly available to chart

---

[6] See: Otis Dudley Duncan and Beverly Duncan, "A Methodological Analysis of Segregation Indexes," *American Sociological Review* 20 (April 1955), pp. 210–217; and Karl Taeuber and A. F. Taeuber, *Negroes in Cities* (Chicago: University of Chicago Press, 1965).

population densities, with perhaps special reference to changes over time and changes during the 24-hour work-day cycle. Since automobiles are an indispensable and an increasingly inseparable adjunct to individuals, some measure of density in this respect ought certainly to be included.

MOVEMENT

Americans continue to be an immensely mobile, almost a nomadic people, and as Doxiades observes, in the manner of nomads everywhere, lavish considerably more affection on their means of transportation than on their temporary abodes. It is clear that this movement responds to the differing levels of economic opportunity in different cities. Movement from the countryside is not likely to be of great significance in the future. Half of the counties in the United States lost population in the 1950's, while the current drop in farm employment suggests that a bottom of sorts is soon to be reached. Hence, most future migration will be from city to city. Because this particularly affects Southern Negroes and, more generally, all low-income groups, it would seem past time that cities began to have some measure of in- and out-migration between SMSA's. Such information would be of particular importance should there develop some effort to provide settling-in services for low-income migrants.

Similarly, a good deal more could be usefully known about movement within metropolitan areas, both the outflow to the suburbs and the reverse flow, or so one hears, of middle-aged couples whose children have established households of their own.

EMPLOYMENT AND INCOME

There is no single area where disaggregation is more urgently needed than that of employment. Given dependable data on employment and income, it is more than likely that cities and metropolitan areas will be able to respond to opportunities and negotiate hazards with a measure of effectiveness far beyond the contemporary level of campaign promises by mayoralty candidates and ad hoc gatherings of concerned corporation executives. Disaggregation must go beyond the labor market area, to the point where something is learned about employment conditions in the deepest slums. A pioneering effort in this direction has been made by the United States Department of Labor in a study of unemployment in the worst slums of twenty major cities, made public in March 1967. The surveys found that "the nonwhite (principally Negro) unemployment rate is about (or more than) three times the white unemployment rate in 8 of these areas, two times as high in 6 or more, half again as high in 2 others."[7] A "subemployment" rate was calculated that ranged as high as 47.4 per cent in San Antonio. But, just as important, it was found that these rates, while high, concerned small numbers of persons, and the study concluded that "the problem is clearly of manageable proportions." Thus does information reveal both the existence of a social problem and the fact that it is of a size that it can be faced.

Categories of labor-force data of greatest concern to economic and social planning are well known; again it is the disaggregation that is of the essence. Special note might, however, be taken of the increasing significance in female labor-force participation rates. (In the District of Columbia, nonwhite female labor-force participation reaches as high as 66 per cent.) Similarly, great attention is paid to the prospects for increases or decreases in the overall number of jobs in different occupational categories —that is, manufacturing employment will rise or decline by this per cent of that number. Too little attention is paid to the distribution of job openings that will occur though replacement needs. This source of new job opportunities for individuals is very large indeed, and is often quite at variance with the unemployment elements in the labor force. Similarly, much more close attention needs to be paid to the differentials in income between men and women, between the races, and among men and women of different races. The closing of the white-nonwhite income gap for females is, for example, in dramatic contrast to the persisting gaps for males.

The distribution of job opportunities between low-skill and high-skill occupations has been a traditional concern of economists. Increasingly, city officials are likely also to be concerned with the *location* of such openings. Thus, there appears to be a powerful long-term trend for new business or new industries to locate outside central cities. In the period 1954–1965, for example, over 80 per cent of the value of new industrial construction in the Boston, Los Angeles, San Francisco, and Washington, D.C., Standard Metropolitan Statistical Areas was located outside the central city. Wendell D. MacDonald, Regional Director of the Bureau of Labor Statistics in the Boston Area, states flatly that this trend is "intensifying the employment problems of the poor, especially Negroes."

---

[7] U.S., Department of Labor, "A Sharper Look at Unemployment in U.S. Cities and Slums," a Summary Report submitted to the President by the Secretary of Labor, March 1967, p. 1.

ANTISOCIAL BEHAVIOR

Crime data have probably been the weakest areas of social indicators in recent decades—here as in so many other areas it has not been ignorance that has hurt so much as "knowing all those things that aren't so." The work of the President's Commission provides an important baseline from which it should be possible to move on to a reasonably dependable system of measuring the extent and nature of antisocial behavior.

A much neglected area of police encounters with citizens is that of traffic-law enforcement. The persistent view that somehow a person arrested for a traffic offense has not "really" been arrested suggests that American citizens are getting used to being arrested: a proposition that Orwell has had something to say about. The incidence of arrest by armed police on the highways is a cause for national concern. Surely there are better ways to regulate a transportation system. In any event, nothing is likely to be done in this area until the true incidence of such events is clearly recorded.

HEALTH

Although the disaggregation of health indices would seem to be a rather straightforward affair, there are yet a number of puzzles to be solved. It is possible that careful area studies will show differences of considerable importance that will relate to social and economic issues such as air pollution, slum housing, industrial diseases, and the like. One potentially important source of localized information would be the medical rejection rate for Selective Service examinations, which could be charted by census tract if the effort were only made. Contrary to general impressions, these rejection rates show an inverse relationship between performance on the mental and the medical examination. Areas with high mental failure rates have low medical failure rates, and vice versa. This is also true, although less strikingly so, of whites and Negroes. This difference has not been explained and, of course, conflicts with what is generally thought to be the case. Mental-test rejection rates are a measure of community success or failure in education, because the test is perfectly uniform and the rates of failure widely divergent. For this reason, mental-test rejection rates have a potential as an indicator of the greatest importance.

PARTICIPATION RATES

Participation rates are likely to become the most popular form of urban social indicators. It is here that citizens are most likely to find some measure of their own performance in terms which relate to the populace at large. Because the range of such indices is very considerable, it is, perhaps,

TABLE 3—Percent of New Private Nonresidential Building Outside the Central Cities of Standard Metropolitan Statistical Areas (SMSA's), 1954–1965[a]

Type of New Nonresidential Building	United States	Percent of Valuation of Permits Authorized for New Nonresidential Building									
		Atlanta	Boston	Chicago	Detroit	Indianapolis	Los Angeles	New York	Philadelphia	San Francisco	Washington, D. C.
All types[b]	49	42.5	68.0	63	71.1	44.2	62	44.0	67.3	63.1	64.3
Business	46	40.5	69.6	61	72.5	49.5	63	43.6	69.3	63.6	62.1
Industrial	63	65.9	82.0	73	74.9	60.8	86	75.3	75.5	83.6	83.7
Stores and other mercantile buildings	53	39.5	74.2	67	77.4	51.8	66	70.6	72.1	72.4	88.6
Office buildings	27	21.0	51.2	39	58.3	20.8	41	18.2	51.1	37.2	47.0
Gasoline and service stations	53	60.1	82.0	59	65.0	56.3	62	64.7	72.6	73.0	80.8
Community	45	47.6	67.1	66	70.2	40.1	63	37.8	67.6	64.1	63.8
Educational	50	56.9	71.8	69	79.4	45.8	59	33.5	72.3	73.1	57.4
Hospital and institutional	36	32.2	41.0	58	61.6	10.0	70	31.7	43.0	52.5	61.4
Religious	54	58.9	85.6	68	74.1	58.7	70	61.1	80.4	64.8	75.2
Amusement	48	29.6	64.2	75	43.0	51.9	50	32.6	71.8	55.0	94.1

[a] Excludes data for 1959, for which comparable information is not available.

[b] Includes types not shown separately and excludes major additions and alterations for which type of building is not shown.

Source: Unpublished data of the Bureau of the Census, tabulated at the request of the Bureau of Labor Statistics. Based on a sample of over 3,000 permit-issuing places. Prepared in: U.S., Dept. of Labor, Bureau of Labor Statistics, Division of Economic Studies.

not likely that more than a few basic matters can be dealt with at the outset. These should pertain to involvement in basic social institutions: how many persons are in school, at what age group, in which neighborhoods, related in what ways to family income and other correlates; how many persons vote, again in terms of age, sex, race, and neighborhood; how many persons pay taxes of different kinds; how many trade union members are there; and what other organizations have large memberships in the area.

Clearly, it would be of considerable value if objections to public agencies' gathering information on religious affiliation and the actual attendance of religious services could be overcome. At the very least, a system of urban social indicators should include, in addition to public institutions, those private, religious-affiliated institutions that provide the equivalent of public services, and should indicate the relative importance of such private services. Parochial schools, in particular, ought to be thought of as integral elements in the education system and listed as such. Measures such as *de facto* race segregation in schools ought to be applied to private as well as public schools.

Before long it ought to be possible to construct indices on the more organized forms of participation in community affairs, such as the sources of financial contributions to community activities. Harvey M. Sapolsky, for example, has shown that, contrary to what might be the general impression, the per capita level of United Fund contributions in the Chicago area tends to be considerably higher in the working-class communities than in middle-class communities nearby. As James Q. Wilson noted when looking at a similar listing on another occasion, Gary and East Chicago have steel mills and, for citizens, Negroes and Poles, while Skokie and Hammond have shopkeepers and professionals for citizens.

Similarly, a special effort should be made to learn more about the use of cultural facilities such as museums and attendance at theatrical and

TABLE 4—Per Capita United Fund Contributions in the Chicago Area[a]

Community	Contribution per Capita
Skokie	$0.80
Hammond	1.21
Des Plaines	1.66
Oak Ridge/River Forest	3.83
East Chicago	4.27
Chicago	4.50
Gary	4.70

[a] Mr. Harvey M. Sapolsky kindly made this information available to me, based on data reported in a publication of United Community Funds and Councils of America, Inc. (some figures rounded).

musical performances in the manner that Baumol and Bowen have recently explored in their book, *The Performing Arts*.[8] Baumol and Bowen have shown that the arts audience is drawn from an extremely narrow segment of the American population. This group is one which is well educated, whose incomes are high, who are predominantly in the professions, and who are in their late youth or early middle age. Obviously, these findings have important implications for those who make policy relating to the arts.

THE FAMILY

Expectations perhaps to the contrary, the family remains the basic social unit of American society. For reasons that run deep in the national character, it is a subject that is not easily submitted to public discussion or made an avowed objective of public policy. On the other hand, a considerable range of data relating to family concerns is now more or less routinely collected by the Census Bureau, and, disaggregated to SMSA or neighborhood units, would provide important kinds of information. Family size and structure, income, housing, age distribution, and similar information constitute the base of any information system in this field. Particular attention should be paid to measures of fertility levels, such as adjusted birth rates and total fertility rates, which provide essential information about future social needs and developments, and which will often reveal social problems that are concealed in more familiar social and economic data. Information on illegitimacy trends and infant mortality rates are apt to be similarly revealing, and of direct utility in the allocation, for example, of family-planning services.

A need that is not at present met, however, is that of relating the larger movements of the economy to family welfare. The relationship is direct and obvious, but somehow ignored. Moreover, in certain circumstances it may turn out to be not nearly so obvious as might have been supposed. In any event, there is probably no better way to insist upon the interrelationship of things, as well as to demonstrate the degree to which so many social problems have economic origins, as to insist upon and demonstrate these relationships in a system of urban social indicators.

For example, a striking correlation can be shown to exist between the unemployment rate for nonwhite males aged twenty and over and the per cent of nonwhite married women separated from their husbands. Working back from the separation rate recorded each March, there is, for example, a correlation of .81 at four months.

---

[8] See William J. Baumol and William G. Bowen, *The Performing Arts: The Economic Dilemma* (New York: Twentieth Century Fund, 1966).

TABLE 5—Quarterly Unemployment Rates for Nonwhite Males
Aged 20 and Over
(Not Seasonally Adjusted)

Year	First Quarter	Second Quarter	Third Quarter	Fourth Quarter
1950	12.7	8.1	7.4	5.6
1951	6.4	3.0	3.4	3.5
1952	5.5	3.5	4.5	3.3
1953	4.6	4.3	2.7	4.0
1954	10.1	8.9	8.5	8.6
1955	10.9	7.7	6.4	5.9
1956	8.0	6.5	6.4	5.8
1957	8.3	7.0	6.7	8.3
1958	14.4	13.5	12.1	11.0
1959	13.9	9.1	9.5	9.3
1960	11.7	8.8	8.5	9.5
1961	14.0	11.6	11.1	10.1
1962	12.3	10.4	9.3	8.2
1963	11.9	8.9	7.8	8.0
1964	10.1	7.3	6.8	6.4
1965	8.7			
Centered Average for Three Consecutive Quarters				
1950		9.4	7.0	6.5
1951	5.0	4.3	3.3	4.1
1952	4.2	4.5	3.8	4.1
1953	4.1	3.9	3.7	5.6
1954	7.7	9.2	8.7	9.3
1955	9.1	8.3	6.7	6.8
1956	6.8	7.0	6.2	6.8
1957	7.0	7.3	7.3	9.8
1958	12.1	13.3	12.2	12.3
1959	11.3	10.8	9.3	10.2
1960	9.9	9.7	8.9	10.7
1961	11.7	12.2	10.9	11.2
1962	10.9	10.7	9.3	9.8
1963	9.7	9.5	8.2	8.6
1964	8.5	8.1	6.8	7.3

TABLE 6—Actual Values, Trend Values, and Deviation from Trend

Year	Percent of Nonwhite Married Women Separated from Their Husbands (March Data)			Unemployment Rate for Nonwhite Males Aged 20 and Over (9-Month Average Centered in Previous November)		
	Actual	Trend	Deviation	Actual	Trend	Deviation
1950	13.9	12.3	+1.6			
1951	12.1	12.6	−0.5	6.5	5.3	+1.2
1952	12.4	12.8	−0.4	4.1	5.7	+1.6
1953	10.6	13.0	−2.4	4.1	6.2	−2.1
1954	12.7	13.3	−0.6	5.6	6.7	−1.1
1955	15.1	13.5	+1.6	9.3	7.1	+2.2
1956	14.2	13.7	+0.5	6.8	7.6	−0.8
1957	13.1	14.0	−0.9	6.8	8.1	−1.3
1958	16.0	14.2	+1.8	9.8	8.5	+1.3
1959	17.6	14.4	+3.2	12.3	9.0	+3.3
1960	13.8	14.7	−0.9	10.2	9.5	+0.7
1961	14.3	14.9	−0.6	10.7	9.9	+0.8
1962	14.9	15.1	−0.2	11.2	10.4	+0.8
1963	14.6	15.3	−0.7	9.8	10.9	−1.1
1964	14.8	15.6	−0.8	8.6	11.3	−2.7
1965	15.3	15.8	−0.5	7.3	11.8	−4.5

Source: Bureau of Labor Statistics.

These very high correlations are for the period 1953–1964, a time of relative peace in the world, but also of intermittent high unemployment, especially for nonwhite males. It is interesting to note from Charts 2 and 3, that, with the onset of the 1960's, the strong presumed influence of employment on family structures appears to give out, so that the separation rate begins to rise even when the unemployment rate is falling. The exact implications from such data would be difficult to assess, certainly in the short run, but it is a trend that persons concerned with employment and

TABLE 7—Correlation Coefficients for Various Time Lags

Time Interval from Unemployment Rate to Separation Rate	Correlation Coefficient[a]
Number of Months	%
1	.73
4	.81
7	.76
10	.66
13	.49 (not significant at 5 per cent level)

[a] Correlation Coefficient calculated for the years 1953 through 1964.

Chart   1—Percent of Nonwhite Married Women Separated from Their Husbands and Unemployment Rate for Nonwhite Males 20 and Over

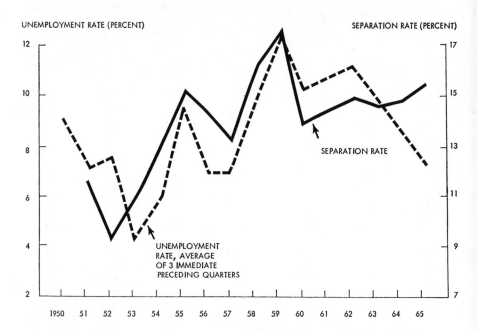

Chart   2—Percent of Nonwhite Married Women Separated from Their Husbands and Unemployment Rate for Nonwhite Males 20 and Over: Deviations from Linear Trend

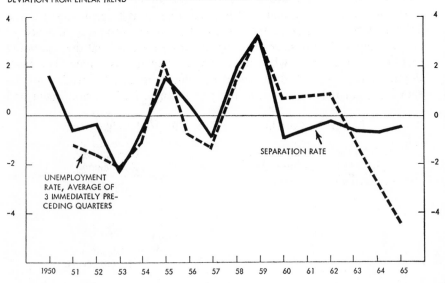

Chart 3—Correlation Between Percent of Nonwhite Married Women
Separated from Their Husbands (Deviations from 1958–1964 Trend)
an Unemployment Rate of Nonwhite Males Aged 20+
(Deviations from Trend), for Various Time Lags

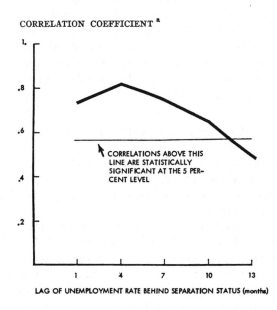

CORRELATION COEFFICIENT [a]

LAG OF UNEMPLOYMENT RATE BEHIND SEPARATION STATUS (months)

[a] Correlation Coefficient calculated for the years 1953 through 1964.

family welfare would want to keep careful track of. An almost exactly
similar phenomenon appears in the relationship between the nonwhite
unemployment rate and the number of *new* Aid to Families of Dependent
Children (AFDC) cases during this period.

An index of family welfare that is not widely available for the nation,
and not at all for different communities, is the incidence rate for children
supported by the AFDC program. In June 1965, some 46 children in 1,000
were receiving AFDC support. In 1963, a life-time incidence rate was estimated at 159 per 1,000, with nonwhite children having a recipient-rate
incidence approximately six times greater than whites. Given more recent
trends, this would suggest that approximately one white child in ten and
six nonwhite children in ten live in a family supported by AFDC payments
at one time or another during their youth. If these rates could be reduced

to area rates, it is likely that important social information would result.[9]

A recent study by the research division of the Teamsters Joint Council No. 16 of New York City has suggested an interesting approach to relating social and economic data. The study showed that, in 1956, the number of persons in New York City receiving welfare assistance amounted to 8.9 per cent of the nongovernment work force. Ten years later in 1966 this proportion had risen to 17.9 per cent.[10] It is probable also that much information can be gained from special studies such as the "diagnostic surveys" of welfare and medical needs of persons in depressed neighborhoods that are now being sponsored by the Urban Renewal Administration, although it is not clear how well "one-time" studies of this kind would fit in with an ongoing statistical series.

POVERTY NEIGHBORHOODS

From the point of view of urban social indicators, one of the most immediate benefits of the federal government's "war on poverty" are the studies of the "poverty areas" in American cities being carried out by the Bureau of the Census. For the first time, it is possible not only to assess the condition of families in given neighborhoods but to gain some sense of the changing levels of well-being in the neighborhood itself. The ever-present problem of in- and out-migration makes it hazardous to assert that changes in a neighborhood are necessarily changes that occur to the same collection of individuals, but, from the point of view of city government, it is often just as important, and sometimes even more so, to know in which direction a neighborhood is moving.

A recent Census study of Negro families in Cleveland illustrates quite strikingly the interest that such information can have, in this case lending support to the hypothesis that, in recent years, urban Negro communities have shown a tendency to divide between an increasingly prosperous and mobile "middle-class" group and—in relative and even absolute terms—a lower-class group living under steadily deteriorating conditions. The Census study describes nine poverty neighborhoods in Cleveland (of which three have only negligible numbers of Negroes). In 1960, 91 per cent of Cleveland's Negro population, some 228,322 persons, lived in these poverty neighborhoods, while another 22,496, or 9 per cent of the Negro population, lived elsewhere in the city. In the course of the next five years, the

---

[9] See Robert H. Mugge, "Demographic Analysis and Public Assistance," Paper prepared for presentation at the Annual Meeting of the Population Association of America, New York City, April 30, 1966, mimeographed.

[10] See press release by the International Brotherhood of Teamsters Joint Council No. 16, New York City, February 11, 1967.

Negro proportion of the population of Cleveland increased from 29 per cent to 34 per cent, and the actual number grew by 25,458. The proportion of the Negro population outside the poverty areas, however, grew to 15 per cent of the total Negro population, amounting now to 41,451 persons.

During this period, the proportion of Negro families living in poverty remained about the same: it was 26.1 per cent in 1959 and 25.4 per cent in 1964. However, the experience of Negro families living outside the poverty area was one of steady improvement, while the conditions of life in the poverty areas grew *worse*.

Among Negro families living outside the poverty area, the incidence of poverty dropped from 17.9 per cent to 9.8 per cent. Median family income rose $1,107 to a total of $7,285 in 1964. The number of female-headed families dropped from 13.9 per cent in 1959, to 9.1 per cent in 1964. The male unemployment rate dropped from 10 per cent in 1960 to 8 per cent in 1965, while the labor-force participation rate rose from 77.6 per cent to 82.2 per cent. This latter contrasts with a 1965 national labor force participation rate of 75.2 per cent (Negro) or 77.6 per cent (over-all).

By contrast, life in the Negro slums was getting worse. The incidence of poverty *rose* from 26.9 per cent to 28.5 per cent. Median family income (1959–1964) increased only $132 to a level of $5,085. The proportion of female-headed families (1959–1964) rose from 20 per cent to 25 per cent. The male unemployment rate (1960–1965) dropped from 13 per cent to 11 per cent, but so also did male labor-force participation, which *declined* from 78.6 per cent to 73.1 per cent.

These over-all rates for the poverty areas conceal even sharper deteriorations in some neighborhoods. Thus, in the Hough section, median family income (1959–1964) declined $766 to $3,966, while in nearby West Central it declined to $2,984. This decline was associated with a significant rise in female-headed families between 1959 and 1964, from 22.5 per cent to 32.1 per cent in Hough, and from 32.6 per cent to 35.1 per cent in West Central. In Hough, three-quarters of female-headed families were living below the poverty line in 1964, and the proportion was not far different elsewhere in the poverty areas. Perhaps significantly, the proportion of families with female heads living below the poverty line outside the poverty areas declined (1959–1964) from 53.5 per cent to 25 per cent, which may suggest that a different type of female-headed household is involved. In an area such as West Central, the male unemployment rate rose to 20.4 per cent in 1965, and the labor-force participation rate dropped to 58.7 per cent. In Hough, the number of children living in poverty increased by one-third.

Whether or not the rioting that occurred in these neighborhoods in 1965 could have been predicted, it will surely be seen that these were areas in which the fabric of social life was deteriorating rapidly and in which increasing numbers of persons were living in conditions of extreme deprivation.

INSTITUTIONS

Corresponding to the data about individuals and families that is now more or less routinely collected, there needs also to be developed a range of information that might be termed "institutional demography." Cities are organized around institutions, some public, some private, some not quite one or the other. The number, variety, and perhaps also the vigor of these institutions do much to establish the "character" and quality of an urban environment. Washington is one kind of city, Pittsburgh another, and the differences are readily to be grasped from the great differences in the types of institutions that characterize the two cities.

Public service organizations constitute a familiar category of urban institution, and will be the most readily described. At the same time, considerable art will be required to give some sense of order and hierarchy to the "1400 Governments" that link and overlap to provide the public services of most metropolitan areas. An especially difficult but important task is that of providing some measure of levels of taxation and public expenditure between the different jurisdictions, over time within jurisdictions, and also of intergovernment transfer payments. In a study of thirty-six SMSA's, Alan K. Campbell and Philip Meranto have, with great force, shown the differences in the revenue structures of central cities in contrast to the surrounding suburbs and the consequences for educational expenditure:

> The cost and number of noneducational governmental services tend to increase with the size and density of a district and to consume a larger proportion of the budget in major cities where many services are provided for nonresidents as well as for residents. It is reasonable to suggest that this "municipal overburden" is supported at the expense of the education function.
>
> The figures . . . show that the central cities were supporting these expenditure levels by taxes that were $23.29 per capita higher than in areas outside the cities. In contrast, the cities received about $5.00 per capita less in total inter-governmental aid and, most importantly, $12.31 less per capita in education aid than did suburban areas, where income was higher. In other words, not only are central cities pressed to support a large array of services by a relatively shrinking tax base, but they tax themselves more heavily to do so and they receive less inter-governmental aid than the more wealthy communities in their metropolitan area.[11]

---

[11] Alan K. Campbell and Philip Meranto, "The Metropolitan Education Dilemma: Matching Resources to Needs," *Urban Affairs Quarterly,* Vol. II, No. 1 (September 1966), p. 57.

Whether difficulties of this kind are to be overcome or not is a question to which few would venture an answer, but it is reasonable to suppose that this will not be done until the facts of the disparities involved are clearly and repeatedly set forth in a readily available and authoritative manner.

    Business enterprises have been and for the time being continue to be the characteristic economic institution of cities. Their number, size, location, growth, or decline are fundamental urban facts, and not nearly so accessible as might be supposed. It is likely that this subject will be particularly plagued by the problem of presenting information in sufficient detail to be of interest to students, while retaining some comprehensibility for general users, as, for example, in distinguishing between locally owned and managed enterprises and those that are branches of larger concerns. As a general rule, it would seem wise to respond to the more general interest, at least in the early stage of any program development.

    Information media are enterprises of distinct importance and are likely to be of considerable interest to urbanists. The number of newspaper and radio and television stations in an area, and of their audiences, are essential data.

    Educational institutions if not yet the dominant institutions of the contemporary American city are well on the way to becoming so. In many cities, it is likely that the "education force" has come to outnumber the "work force," and in any event the direct and growing relevance of education to economic activity is now generally acknowledged. Here again, differences in school enrollment and educational institutions vary significantly among the major urban areas. Moreover, the significance of the "learning industry" increasingly lies as much in the amount and kind of employment it provides and generates, as in its more immediate "educational product." Thus, Charles Abrams recently commented that "the loss of a university is much more serious [to a city] than the loss of several industrial institutions," adding that while industries and business are a part of the necessary economic superstructure of a city, universities are part of the very foundation.[12]

    Associational groupings refers to the great variety of voluntary organizations that characterize any urban setting. The varying patterns of membership in political parties, churches and synagogues, trade unions, fraternal associations, and the like as much as any single factor help to define the distinctive as well as the shared qualities of American cities. Much more could usefully be recorded about their membership. In particular, it is devoutly to be wished that the absurd but reigning fears that prevent the Census Bureau from gathering information on religious affiliation will give way before the great and legitimate interest in this subject on the part of

---

[12] See *New York Times,* February 21, 1967.

the general public no less than specialists—not to mention religious leaders and activists.

Along with the more formal arrangements of institutions, there are patterns of urban life that shape the quality and define the nature of the experience in such ways that they, too, are institutions: organized patterns of behavior. These are the elements that go to make up what might be called the "urban ecology." They are many, diffuse, and often impossible to measure—what is to be said about the ambiance of San Francisco, or the dread sameness of Jersey City? On the other hand, many of these qualities are quantifiable—and are quantified. Air pollution levels, noise levels, and crime levels are all reportable and immensely significant, the more so if followed over time. Moreover, as noted by the recent report by the President's Commission on Law Enforcement and Administration of Justice, there are wide and intriguing variations in rates for different offenses:

> Los Angeles is 1st for rape and 4th for aggravated assualt but 20th for murder, with a murder rate less than half that of St. Louis. Chicago has the highest rate for robbery but a relatively low rate for burglary. New York is 5th in larcenies $50 and over, but 54th for larcenies under $50. The risk of auto theft is about 50 per cent greater in Boston than anywhere else in the country, but in Boston the likelihood of other kinds of theft is about the average for cities over 250,000.[13]

It may be hoped that the report of the Crime Commission will have some effect on the quality of crime statistics in the nation's cities, most especially that the practice of recording crime "consumption," that is the incidence of crime victims in the population, will be continued.

Almost a subject to itself in the area of urban ecologies is the matter of densities. The urban condition is at once defined by densities and at certain points spoiled by them: densities of population (66,000 persons per square mile in Central Harlem) and automobiles, land uses in terms of streets, housing, parks, industry, and concentrations of race and social class. Very possibly, in the end we shall come to see that it is not the recorded levels of such measures that determine the quality of urban life so much as our choices as to what it is we shall measure and how widely the meaning of those measures is diffused to the people, who are the city.

Referring once again to Dr. Johnson: to ask what one would care to know about the city is to ask what one needs to know about life. One may begin anywhere, and there is no ending. But given the present range of

---

[13] *The Challenge of Crime in a Free Society,* a Report by the President's Commission on Law Enforcement and Administration of Justice (Washington, D.C.: U.S. Government Printing Office, 1967), p. 29.

perceived problems faced by American cities, it is reasonable to concentrate attention on the twin problems of density and poverty, in all their ramifications of congestion, revenue crises, pollution, racial tension, personal disorganization, lagging education, failing public services, and so through the spectrum of issues that at present conceal from us the great human triumphs that are embedded in much of American urban life, and the even greater achievements that could yet come to pass.

INDEX

521